Honor
&
Respect

A name pronounced is the recognition

of the individual to whom it belongs.

He who can pronounce my name aright,

he can call me,

and is entitled to my love and service.

Henry David Thoreau 1817–1862

A Week on the Concord and Merrimack Rivers 1849

Honor & Respect

The Official Guide to Names, Titles, and Forms of Address

Robert Hickey

Foreword by Pamela Eyring

The Protocol School of Washington®

COLUMBIA, SOUTH CAROLINA

Published by The Protocol School of Washington®
Post Office Box 676, Columbia, South Carolina 29202
www.psow.com

This publication is designed to provide accurate and widely
accepted information on the subject matter covered. It is sold
with the understanding that the author and publisher are not
engaged in rendering legal advice or other professional services.
If legal advice or other services are required, the services of a
competent professional should be sought.

First edition published 2008
Published in the United States of America
Printed by Yangjisa Co., Ltd., Seoul, Korea

Copy editors: Joanne Laurence, E.J. Decker
Consulting editor: Hilda Regier
Publishing advisors: Dan Wallace, Ivey Pittle Wallace
Educational alliance partner:

>The Etiquette and Leadership Institute
Watkinsville, Georgia 30677
www.etiquetteleadership.com

ISBN: 978-0-615-19806-4

10 9 8 7 6 5 4 3 2 1

To

Dorothea Johnson

Founder

The Protocol School of Washington

Contents

Author's Note

"... from the very start the dictionary's creators were involved in a debate. ... Would it show something more like an open air menagerie pulsing with ever changing life, admitting even the newest words and meanings? Was the dictionary to be prescriptive, showing how language should be used, or descriptive, reflecting how it actually is used?"

"Connections"
Edward Rothstein
New York Times
Monday, November 26, 2007

Honor & Respect is a record of how officials are directly addressed in English at the beginning of the millennium. It is not an arbiter of what is correct: It is a resource bringing together the most formal forms of address.

Included are both well-known forms and forms appearing for the first time. In both cases I have conferred with the current office holders, their colleagues, and their staffs to confirm today's practices.

To those who use a form of address I have not included, I don't suggest other forms are incorrect: It would be impossible to include all correct forms. However, having looked at so many forms while working on this book, I suggest the forms presented here as being both refined and widely welcomed by the office holders.

This book is compiled from a U.S. point of view. While Americans are familiar with royal titles and personal rank, they rarely have the background to know how to address a sultan, knight, or member of a privy council. Rather than explain each tradition, which is beyond the scope of this book, I only describe the form of address. U.S. readers are encouraged to explore these traditions: They offer rich insight into other cultures.

I intentionally excluded offices that no longer exist, but it is likely I have forgotten some and jettisoned others before their time. I welcome your input, comments, and suggestions to *editor@psow.com* for inclusion in future editions.

Robert Hickey

Foreword

The Protocol School of Washington® enjoys a lively back and forth communication with its 2,100 plus graduates in the United States and 42 other countries. These highly-accomplished, working professionals include corporate, diplomatic, military, and government protocol officers and corporate etiquette consultants and trainers. We encourage these ambassadors to the world to keep in touch with any questions they have as they plan and orchestrate some of the most sensitive VIP visits, ceremonies, meetings and special events happening today.

The greatest number of questions we receive from our graduates relate to the topics you'll find comprehensively covered in this book – names, titles, and forms of address. These topics are complicated but must be mastered by professionals planning high-level events. All officials and event participants appreciate receiving the honors of their rank and the courtesies of their office. When distinguished visitors see their names presented in the proper way, they feel they are personally and warmly welcomed.

My colleague, Robert Hickey, is uniquely positioned to author this important and comprehensive reference work. Robert has been a key trainer with The Protocol School of Washington since its inception twenty years ago. He is an internationally-recognized expert in understanding and properly using titles and forms of address. Robert's commitment to the fine art and science of facilitating events for people of different cultures is simply unparalleled.

As you use this book, I welcome you to become our ally in the promotion of contemporary, universally accepted protocol and etiquette in our communities and around the world. You'll find the answers to virtually everything that relates to names, titles and forms of address. Like other educational offerings of The Protocol School of Washington, this critical knowledge will help fuel your success in our rapidly-changing global marketplace. Enjoy!

Pamela Eyring
Owner & Director
Protocol School of Washington

With Gratitude

Maria del Carmen Aguirre, Attaché, Embassy of Mexico, Washington, DC

Jeane Anderson, Sarah Baack, and Sarah Putlock, The Protocol School of Washington®, Columbia, South Carolina

Diane Brown; Major, USAF, Retired; Former Deputy Chief of Protocol, Office of the Secretary of Defense, Washington, DC

Pamela Eyring, Director of The Protocol School of Washington® and former Chief of Protocol, Wright-Patterson Air Force Base, Dayton, Ohio

Tina M. Farrenkopf, JD, Associate Director, National Tribal Justice Resource Center, Boulder, Colorado

Dorothea Johnson, founder and former Director, The Protocol School of Washington®, Dorothea Johnson Productions, Falmouth, Maine

Wendy Jones, Senior Manager, Customer Relations and Protocol, the Boeing Company, Washington, DC

Nicole L. Krakora, Director, Special Events and Protocol, Smithsonian Institution, Washington, DC

Daisy Kiley, Protocol Officer, 2d Marine Division, Camp Lejeune, North Carolina

Patrice H. Kunesh, Assistant Professor of Law, the University of South Dakota School of Law, Vermillion, South Dakota

tom kunesh, Secretary, Tennessee Commission of Indian Affairs

Debra M. Lassiter, Cindy H. Haygood, and April B. McLean, The Etiquette & Leadership Institute, Watkinsville, Georgia

Wilvia Medina, Director, the Medina Institute, Baltimore, Maryland

Cynthia Rambo, Chief, 9AF/USCENTAF Protocol, Shaw Air Force Base, South Carolina

John H. Remer, Jr., corporate etiquette and international protocol consultant, St. Andrews, New Brunswick, Canada

Kerry S. Rice, Lieutenant Colonel, USAF, Retired; former Chief of Protocol, USAF Academy, Colorado; Headquarters Pacific Air Forces, Hawaii; and Headquarters United States Air Forces in Europe, Germany

Kathleen D. Ryan, CGMP, President, KDRyan, Inc., Protocol Consulting, Alexandria, Virginia; Lieutenant Colonel, USAF, Retired; and former Chief of Protocol, United States Air Force, Washington, DC

Michel Thomas, Director, and Anne-France Ballarò, Public Relation Manager, MEPE: Monaco Etiquette & Protocol Expertise, Principality of Monaco

Acknowledgments

Andrea Acosta, etiquette and protocol consultant, San José, Costa Rica

Kateri Aguilar, Office of the Governor of the Conchiti Tribe, Conchiti, New Mexico

Felice Alexrod, Senior Vice President, Protocol, Lehman Brothers, New York, New York

Husain Mohamed Al Mahmood, First Secretary, Embassy of the Kingdom of Bahrain, Washington, DC

Dastur Dr. Kersey Antia, Zoroastrian Association, Chicago, Illinois

Iman M. Asfour, United States Department of State, Kingdom of Saudi Arabia

Boureima Balima, Embassy of Burkina Faso, Washington, DC

Pamela Bangart, Chief of Protocol, Executive Council Office, Government of Yukon, Whitehorse, Yukon, Canada

John T. Banks, Associate Director, Communication, General Conference World Headquarters, Seventh-day Adventist Church, Silver Spring, Maryland

The Honorable Gary Bass, Chief Judge, Tulalip Tribal Court, Tulalip, Washington

Annette Bastaja, Official Secretary and Chief of Staff to the Governor of Queensland, Brisbane, Queensland, Australia

David Beamish, Lord Speaker's Office, House of Parliament, London, England

Joyce Bear, Manager, Cultural Preservation, Muscogee (Creek) Nation, Okmulgee, Oklahoma

Sheikh Mohammed Belal, Embassy of People's Republic of Bangladesh, Washington DC

William L. Bell, Political and Economic Assistant, American Embassy, Conakry, Guinea

Christopher Berry, Privy Council Office, London, England

Retha Blakely, international protocol and business etiquette consultant, Austin, Texas

Denise Board, executive assistant to the Chief Executive, Saint Peter Port, Bailiwick of Guernsey

GPCAPT Anne Borzycki, RAAF, Russell Offices, Canberra ACT, Australia

Juliet Bunch, Web Editor, Information Office, Royal Embassy of Saudi Arabia, Washington, DC

Cecelia Campana, Assistant to the Ambassador, Embassy of Peru, Washington, DC

Eva Cernikova, Embassy of the Czech Republic, Washington, DC

Cathy Cheeseman, executive assistant to the Commissioner of the Yukon, Whitehorse, Yukon, Canada

Metropolitan Christopher, the Serbian Orthodox Church of the United States of America and Canada, St. Sava Monastery, Libertyville, Illinois

Emin Cohodarevic, Attaché, Embassy of Bosnia and Herzegovina, Washington DC

Daryl Crawford, Executive Director, Inter-Tribal Council of Nevada, Sparks, Nevada

Jacqueline Curran, Public Relations Officer, Office of the Houses of the Oireachtas, Dublin, Ireland

Barbara Dailey, Consulate of the Commonwealth of Dominca, New York, New York

Sybil Davis, CHE, Lead Professor, Hospitality Education Department,
Greenville Technical College, Greenville, South Carolina

Laura DeBuys, the Salvation Army Headquarters, New York, New York

Sergeant Major François Desfossés, i/c Dress and Deportment, Protocol and Ceremonies
for the National Capital Region, Royal Canadian Mounted Police

Michale De La Haye, Greffier of the States (Clerk of the States Assembly),
Saint Helier, Bailiwick of Jersey

Christine DeLeon, Office of the Ambassador, Embassy of the Republic of Lebanon,
Washington, DC

Dudley Delie, Second Secretary, Embassy of the Republic of Namibia, Washington, DC

April Derr, Office of Governor Mark Sanford, Executive Assistant to the Governor
and Deputy Chief of Staff, Columbia, South Carolina

Ruthann Devine, certified etiquette and protocol consultant, Greenville,
South Carolina

Chavdar Borislavov Dimov, Counselor, Deputy Chief of Mission,
Embassy of the Republic of Bulgaria, Washington, DC

Elenna Dionisio, Senior Protocol Officer, Department of the Premier and Cabinet
of Western Australia, Perth, Western Australia, Australia

Prapan Disyatat, First Secretary, Embassy of Thailand, Washington, DC

Hanne Dollerup, Office of the Ambassador, Royal Danish Embassy, Washington, DC

Commander Karen Downes, USNR, certified etiquette and protocol consultant, Bedford,
New Hampshire

Igor Dukoski, Second Secretary, Embassy of the Republic of Macedonia,
Washington, DC

Szilvia Dudás, Assistant to the Deputy Chief of Mission,
Embassy of the Republic of Hungary, Washington, DC

Fatuma Dulae, Embassy of the Republic of Djibouti, Washington, DC

Lawrence Dunham, Assistant Chief of Protocol, Retired, U.S. Department of State

David Early, Senior Communications Officer, Department of Communications,
United States Conference of Catholic Bishops, Washington, DC

Gervais Edmond Bindzi Edzimbi, First Secretary, Embassy of the Republic of Cameroon,
Washington, DC

Riham El-Hawary, CPBS, Director, Persona International, Cairo, Egypt

Jo Elkington, Wing Commander, Deputy Director Communication and
Reputation Management, Air Force Headquarters, Canberra ACT, Australia

Bernard Eloko, Counselor, Embassy of the Republic of the Congo, Washington, DC

The Honourable Pat Farmer, MP, Parliamentary Secretary for the Minister of Education,
Science, and Training, Spokesperson for Western Sidney, Parliament House,
Canberra ACT, Australia

Zoltan Feher, JD, Press Counselor, Chief Creative Officer, Embassy of Hungary, Washington, DC

Lisa Fields, Court Administrator, Cherokee Nation Supreme Court, Tahlequah, Oklahoma

Maria Guchupin, Office of the Governor of the Jemez Tribe, Jemez, New Mexico

Michel Gallant, Manager, Protocol and Secretariat Services, Supreme Court of Canada, Ottawa, Ontario, Canada

Claudio Gantes, Counselor, Political Department, Congressional Affairs, Embassy of Chile, Washington, DC

Sofia Garcia, Embassy of Portugal, Washington, DC

Rachel Gatewood, Acting Parliamentary Adviser to the Speaker, Legislative Assembly, Parliament of Victoria, Melbourne, Victoria, Australia

Nikkie Gazenbeek, Protocol Officer, Protocol and Special Events Branch, Department of Premier and Cabinet of Victoria, Melbourne, Victoria, Australia

Bill Glanz, Assistant Press Secretary, International Association of Fire Fighters, AFL-CIO, Washington, DC

Chour Thong Goh, First Secretary, Embassy of the Republic of Singapore, Washington, DC

Angela Gore, Embassy of New Zealand, Washington, DC

Jan Goss, certified etiquette and protocol consultant, Austin, Texas

Maxene Grabe, Judicial Assistant and Tribal Court Clerk, Confederated Tribes of Coos, Lower Umpqua & Siuslaw Indians, Coos Bay, Oregon

Lori Graves, public relations, Saginaw-Chippewa Tribe, Mt. Pleasant, Michigan

Deirdre Grimes, Legislative Assembly of Ontario, Toronto, Ontario, Canada

Sigrídur Gunnarsdóttir, Attaché, Protocol Department, Ministry for Foreign Affairs, Republic of Iceland, Reykjavik

Carolyn Gwathmey, United States Marshals Service, Arlington, Virginia

Malgorzata Hacus-Safianik, Second Secretary, Chief of Protocol, Embassy of the Republic of Poland, Washington, DC

Christine Hargove, Embassy of the Republic of Austria, Washington, DC

Maria Harrison, Manager Protocol Unit, Government of South Australia, Adelaide, South Australia, Australia

Cáit Hayes, Inter Parliamentary Unit, Houses of the Oireachtas, Dublin, Ireland

Denise Healy, Communications Manager, Federal Magistrates Court of Australia, Melbourne, Victoria, Australia

Alice Hecht, Chief of Protocol, Executive Office of the Secretary-General, United Nations, New York, New York

Kairn Heinzl, Austrian Press and Information Office, Embassy of Republic of Austria, Washington, DC

Lindsay N. Henderson, Consular Chief, American Embassy, Tbilisi, Georgia

Juan Henriquez, Embassy of the Republic of South Africa, Washington, DC

SrA Perri E. Hiott, Protocol Specialist, Shaw Air Force Base, South Carolina, SC

Major John Hodgson, The Salvation Army Headquarters, New York, New York

Nicole M. Homer, Judicial Law Clerk, Ho-Chunk Nation Trial Courts,
    Black River Falls, Wisconsin

Ron Horan, Director, Defence Newspapers, Department of Defence
    of the Commonwealth of Australia, Canberra ACT, Australia

Cinda Hughes, Legislative Associate, Cultural Preservation, National Congress of
    American Indians, Washington DC

Japan Information and Culture Center of the Embassy of Japan, Washington, DC

Don Jessee, Public Affairs Office, The Church of Jesus Christ of Latter-day Saints,
    Salt Lake City, Utah

Gary Jones, Manager, Committees on Publication, the First Church of Christ, Scientist,
    Boston, Massachusetts

Sandra Julian, Secretary to the Minister of Foreign Affairs of Trinidad and Tobago,
    Port of Spain, Trinidad and Tobago

Doreen I. Kagarama, First Secretary, Embassy of the Republic of Rwanda,
    Washington, DC

Sam Katz, Detectives Endowment Association, Inc., New York, New York

Jill Kelly, Personal Assistant to the Honourable A. M. Gleeson, AC,
    Chief Justice of Australia, Canberra, Australia

Matthew J. Keller, Advisor, Embassy of the Principality of Liechtenstein,
    Washington, DC

Moazzam Ahmad Khan, Counselor, Embassy of the Islamic Republic of Pakistan,
    Washington, DC

His Excellency Mikhail Khvostov, Ambassador Extraordinary and Plenipotentiary
    of the Republic of Belarus, Washington, DC

Kristina Krantcheva, corporate etiquette and international protocol consultant,
    CM Consulting, Sofia, Bulgaria

Petar Kraytchev, Congressional Liaison Officer, Embassy of the Republic of Bulgaria,
    Washington, DC

Simone Kreutzer, Consul for Press and Cultural Affairs, Consulate-General of the
    Kingdom of the Netherlands, Washington, DC

Suimonkul A. Kutbidinov, Protocol Assistant, Embassy of the United States of America
    to the Kyrgyz Republic, Bishkek, Kyrgyzstan

Andrea Lagos, Press Attaché, Embassy of Chile, Washington, DC

Caitlin Lally, National Governors Association, Washington, DC

Debi LaMantia, Public Relations Manager, Interparliamentary and Public Relations
    Branch, Legislative Assembly of Ontario, Toronto, Ontario, Canada

Jan A. Larsen, Counselor, Embassy of Norway, Washington, DC

Lana Laurino, Deputy Director Command Protocol,
NORAD USNORTHCOM Headquarters, Peterson AFB, Colorado

Suzanne S. Leno, Protocol Assistant, American Embassy, Conakry, Guinea

Carole Leonhardt, etiquette and protocol consultant, Portland, Oregon

Herb LeRoy, Private Secretary to the Lieutenant Governor of British Columbia,
Victoria, British Columbia, Canada

The Honorable Jennie Lillard, Mekko, Kialegee Tribal Town, Wetumka, Oklahoma

Leslie Logan, Public Relations Office, St. Regis Mohawk Tribe, Akwesasne, New York

Penijamini R. Tuikubulau Lomaloma, First Secretary and Charge d'Affairs ad Interim,
Embassy of the Republic of the Fiji Islands, Washington, DC

Sergio Lopez, Press and Public Diplomacy Office, Delegation of the European
Commission, Washington, DC

Lawna Macleod, Executive Assistant to the Commissioner of the Yukon,
Whitehorse, Yukon, Canada

Virginia Madison, Chief of Protocol, Cayman Islands Government,
Grand Cayman, Cayman Islands

Raegan Mager, Administrative Assistant Office of the Commissioner
of the Northwest Territories, Yellowknife, Northwest Territories, Canada

Noelani Manoa, First Secretary, Permanent Mission of the Independent State of Samoa
to the United Nations, New York, New York

Father John Matusiak, Orothodox Church in America, Syosset, New York

Reta E. Muasau, Command Protocol Officer, NORAD USNORTHCOM Headquarters,
Peterson AFB, Colorado Springs, Colorado

Margaret McDonald, Private Secretary to the Speaker,
Parliament of New South Wales, Sydney, New South Wales, Australia

Brigid McGlynn, Private Secretary to Mr. Kieran Coughlan, Clerk of the Dáil,
Houses of the Oireachtas, Dublin, Ireland

Jane McIntosh, the State Ceremonial and Corporate Events Directorate,
State Ceremonial and Canadian Symbols, Department of Canadian Heritage,
Ottawa, Ontario, Canada

Lieutenant Mark F. McKinnon, MS, PA-C, USPHS, Executive Assistant, ASPR,
Office of the Assistant Secretary for Preparedness and Response, Office of the
Secretary, Department of Health and Human Services, Washington, DC

Glenda Milrod, Research and Correspondence Coordinator,
Office of the Lieutenant Governor of Ontario, Toronto, Ontario, Canada

Marolyn Miner, General Secretary's Office, Church of the Nazarene, Kansas City,
Missouri

Michelle Moffat, Chief of Staff, Office of the Honourable Bob Baldwin, MP,
Federal Member for Paterson, Parliamentary Secretary to the Minister
for Industry Tourism and Resources, Canberra ACT, Australia

Elaine Montoya, Office the Governor of the Isleta Tribe, Isleta Isleta, New Mexico

Carlos A. Morales, Minister Counselor, Embassy of Colombia, Washington, DC

Tim Moroney, Historical Projects Officer, Queensland Parliamentary Service, Parliament House, Queensland, Australia

Dr. Uma Mysorekar, President, The Hindu Temple Society of North America, Flushing, New York

Kerri Neuendorf, Executive Assistant Office of the Director-General Department of the Premier and Cabinet, Brisbane, Queensland, Australia

Andrea Nicandri, Manager of Visits and Protocol for Defence, Embassy of the Commonwealth of Australia, Washington, DC

Art O'Leary Office of the Director of Committees, Information and Communications, the Houses of the Oireachtas, Dublin, Ireland

Inga Ozola, Assistant to the Ambassador, Embassy of Latvia, Washington, DC

Hilary Penfold, QC, Secretary, Department of Parliamentary Services, Parliament House, Commonwealth of Australia, Canberra ACT, Australia

Treva Penny, Office Administrator, Nez Perce Tribal Executive Committee, Lapwai, Idaho

Makota Corina Phori, First Secretary, Embassy of the Kingdom of Lesotho, Washington, DC

Lynn Pigeon, Protocol Coordinator, International and Interparliamentary Affairs, Parliament, Ottawa, Ontario

Ülle-Marika Põldma, Director of the Protocol Department of the State Chancellery, Tallinn, Estonia

Laura Poynton, Executive Officer, State Protocol Office, Hobart, Tasmania, Australia

Enri Prieto, First Secretary, Consulate of the Republic of Peru, Denver, Colorado

Matthew Purvis, House of Lords Information Office, House of Parliament, London, England

RAAF Inquiries, Royal Australian Air Force, Russell Offices Department of Defence, Canberra ACT, Australia

Tania Valerie Raguz, First Secretary, Embassy of the the Republic of Croatia, Washington, DC

Syed Meesam Razvi, United Nations Representative, Imam Al-Khoei Benevolent Foundation, Imam Al-Khoei Islamic Center, Jamaica, New York

Judith Richards, Embassy of Jamaica, Washington, DC

Bret G. Rider, U.S. Department of State, United Arab Emirates

Judit Rigó, Embassy of the Republic of Hungary, Washington, DC

Sergeant Pierre Rioux, International Visits & Protocol Section, Royal Canadian Mounted Police

CMSgt Darryl Robinson, Operations Coordinator, USDAO, Amman, Jordan

Judith Anne Rolle, Third Secretary and Charge d'Affairs ad Interim, Embassy of the Commonwealth of Dominica, Washington, DC

Rebecca Root, Court Administrator, Court of Indian Offenses Ute Mountain Ute, Towaoc, Oklahoma

Irma A. Rosa, Counselor, Political Affairs Section, Embassy of Honduras, Washington, DC

Hajjatul Islam Sheikh Fadhel Al-Sahlani, Imam Al-Khoel Islamic Center, New York

Meg Sakka, certified etiquette and protocol consultant, Amman, Jordan

Dawadash Sambuu, Second Secretary, Embassy of Mongolia, Washington, DC

Rhea Santos, Office of the Ambassador, Embassy of the State of Kuwait, Washington, DC

Carmen Scherkenbach, Protocol Office of the Embassy of the Federal Republic of Germany, Washington, DC

Tony Sclafani, Public Information Office, New York City Fire Department, New York, New York

Florencio Joel Alberto Sele, Minister-Counselor, Embassy of the Republic of Mozambique, Washington, DC

Penny Sexton, Clerk of Court, Court of Indian Offenses for the Miami Tribe, Miami, Oklahoma

Sue Shaffer, Chairwoman, Cow Creek Band of Umpqua Indians Community Council, Roseburg, Oregon

Imam Mohammad Shamsi Ali, Deputy Director, the Islamic Cultural Center of New York, New York

Melvin R. Sheldon, Chairman, Tulalip Board of Directors, Tulalip Reservation, Marysville, Washington

Pavel Shidlovsky, Counselor, Embassy of the Republic of Belarus, Washington, DC

Lynda Shurko, Serials Library Technician, Alberta Legislature Library, Edmonton, Alberta, Canada

Beatrice Siboni, Embassy of the Grand Duchy of Luxembourg, Washington, DC

Ousmane Sidibé, Translator, American Embassy, Conakry, Guinea

Tania Silva M, Embassy of the Republic of Nicaragua, Washington, DC

Roger M. C. Sims, FSA, Librarian Archivist, Manx National Heritage, Manx Museum, Kingswood Grove, Douglas, Isle of Man

Giani Amarjit Singh, Guru Gobind Singh Sikh Center, Plainview, New York, New York

Kathy Smith, Senior Associate, Communications, the First Church of Christ, Scientist, Boston, Boston, Massachusetts

Ken Smith, Director-General, Department of the Premier and Cabinet, Brisbane, Queensland, Australia

Nikki Stephanopoulos, Press Officer, News and Information and Public Affairs, Greek Orthodox Archdiocese of America, New York, New York

Rabbi Elliot Stevens, Central Conference of American Rabbis, New York, New York

Gunilla Stone, Social Secretary, Embassy of Sweden, Washington, DC

Sandra Sulzer, Embassy of Austria, Washington, DC

Keith Surface, Office of Public Relations,
   The General Council of the Assemblies of God, Springfield, Missouri

Philip Swan, Privy Council Office, London, England

Francis R. Szabo, U.S. Department of State, Republic of Tajikistan

Suhaimi Tajuddin, Embassy of Malaysia, Washington DC

Kate Thompson, Executive Assistant to the Minister for Immigration and Citizenship,
   Commonwealth of Australia, Canberra ACT, Australia

Captain Robert W. Thompson, USN, Retired, Arlington, Virginia

Aissatou Traore, Information Officer, Embassy Of Mali, Washington, DC

Monica Trubiano, Cultural Department, Embassy of Guatemala, Washington, DC

Julia Ver Ploeg, certified etiquette consultant, Nottingham, New Hampshire

Mariel Vilcha, Office of the Ambassador, Embassy of the Dominican Republic,
   Washington, DC

Bärbel Vollmann, Federal Ministry of Education and Research, Bonn, Germany

Channoch Vong, Third Secretary, Royal Embassy of Cambodia, Washington, DC

Kim Wheeler, Library Assistant, Supreme Court of Queensland Library,
   Brisbane, Queensland, Australia

Lynn Williams, certified etiquette and protocol consultant, Columbia, South Carolina

Fred Wilson, National Sheriff's Association, Alexandria, Virginia

Kristiina Zeroual, Assistant to the Ambassador, Embassy of Finland, Washington DC

Jeffrey G. Zoubek, U.S. Department of State, Bishkek, Kyrgyz Republic

PART I
Terms, Style & Use

1 Terms & Definitions

Abbot, Abbess

Abbot is the masculine title for the head of a monastery or abbey.

Abbot is also used in Christian Orthodox churches, with the related title *archimandrite* specifically denoting an unmarried head of a monastery.

An *abbess* or *mother superior* is a nun who is the head of a convent.

See also *Prior*.

Acronym

An *acronym* is a string of initial letters forming a shorthand version of a longer name. *Acronyms* are frequently pronounced as if they were a word: NATO for *North Atlantic Treaty Organization*.

See also *Initialisms* and *Post-nominal Abbreviation*.

Administrator

Administrator is sometimes a title for a head of government as in Akrotiri, an overseas territory of the United Kingdom, or the Cocos Islands, a territory of Australia.

Aide-de-Camp

An *aide-de-camp* is a personal assistant, or official of his or her own considerable rank, who accompanies a higher-ranking official on official business. *Honorary*

AIR – AST

aide-de-camp may be the title of distinction for a person who will participate in, or preside at, ceremonies. Examples of *aides-de-camp* include:

- A mid-level army or air force military officer assigned to serve a *general*.
- A military officer assigned to a royal household to serve the *monarch*.
- A military officer assigned to the *governor-general*, or a *lieutenant governor* of a province.

Air Attaché
An air attaché, usually a high-ranking air force officer, is an expert on air force issues at a diplomatic mission.

Alderman
Alderman is a position on a city or county council or board. Equivalent titles would be *councilman* or *councilwoman*. *Alderman* is used after the name in an introduction or on a business envelope for identification, but not formally as an honorific. It is sometimes used as an honorific or in place of the name in conversation.

Ambassador
Ambassador is a diplomatic rank, honorific, position, and the highest official *envoy* or *diplomatic agent* accredited to a foreign government as the official resident representative of his own government. *Ambassadors, high commissioners*, and *nuncios* are of equal status. Sometimes an *ambassador* is the head of a permanent *diplomatic mission* of one country to another. Other times an *ambassador* will be a special emissary to an organization or institution, or have other duties. There are several types of ambassadors:

- *Ambassador:* a person with the rank of ambassador.
- *Ambassador at large:* an ambassador whose duty addresses a specific issue rather than a country.
- *Ambassador designate:* a person designated by a chief of state who has not yet been confirmed and who has not taken the oath of office.
- *Ambassador extraordinary:* a representative of a chief of state to another chief of state before presentation of his or her credentials.
- *Ambassador extraordinary and plenipotentiary:* a representative of a chief of state who has been recognized by a receiving chief of state.

Ameer, Amir, Amira
See *Emir*.

Apostolic Delegate, Nuncio, Prefect, Vicar
Apostolic delegate is the title of a diplomatic representative of the *Holy See*.

Papal nuncio and *apostolic nuncio* are titles for a diplomatic representative of the *Holy See* with the rank of *ambassador*.

An *apostolic prefect* oversees an *apostolic prefecture*, an area designated by the *Holy See* to be governed less directly from Rome and more directly by a local based *apostolic prefect*. Address the officeholder by his hierarchical rank and identify as the *apostolic prefect*.

Apostolic vicar is a rank held by a bishop who oversees a *vicariate apostolic*, an area designated by the *Holy See* where missionary work is in progress and which is a precursor to a *diocese*. Address the officeholder by his hierarchical rank and identify as the *apostolic vicar*.

See also *Nuncio*.

Archbishop

An *archbishop* is a prestigious office, title, and honorific for a *bishop* who oversees a prestigious *diocese* called an *archdiocese*.

See also *Bishop*.

Archimandrite

An *archimandrite* is an unmarried Christian Orthodox *priest* who is a member of a monastic order and the head of an abbey of *monks*.

Architect, Architetto, Arquitecto

In some languages *architect* is used as an honorific in the way *doctor* is used in English.

For example, *architetto* and *architetta*, masculine and feminine Italian honorifics for an *architect*, are used before the name. The formula is the same as for the use of the honorifics *doctor* or *mister*:

- Introduction: *(architetto or architetta) (full name)*
- Introduction, one person to another: *(architetto or architetta) (family name)*
- Conversation: *(architetto or architetta) (family name)*
- Conversation, less formal: *(architetto or architetta)*

Sometimes the *'degree'* is combined with an equivalent of Mr./Mrs./Miss to create a compound honorific as in Spanish: *Señor arquitecto (name)* or *Señora arquitecta (name)*.

In English conversation with a foreign architect it is correct to use the customary English honorifics Mr./Mrs./Miss/Ms. and identify the individual as an architect after his or her name.

Archpriest

Archpriest is a title held by a high priest in a Christian Orthodox church.

An *archpriest* in the Roman Catholic Church is a priest who is the highest *priest* among other *priests*, and who may be an assistant to a *bishop*.

The title is used after the name in an introduction or on an envelope for identification but not as an honorific.

Astronomer Royal

The *Astronomer Royal* and the *Astronomer Royal of Scotland* are honorary positions in the royal household of the United Kingdom. Holders of the offices are addressed by their personal title, if any, and identified after their name by the post held.

ATT – BAR

Attaché

Attaché is a position at a diplomatic mission often held by a civilian or military technical expert. The position is included after the name in an introduction or on a business envelope for identification but not as an honorific.

Attorney, Advocate, Avvocato

Attorney is not traditionally used as an honorific in address in the United States, but sometimes attorneys will informally answer their phone *Attorney (surname)* for clear identification, or will be identified in the third person as *Attorney (surname)*.

In some languages *attorney* or *lawyer* is used as an honorific in the way *doctor* is used in English. For example, languages that use *attorney* as an honorific include Bulgarian *advocate* or Italian *avvocato*.

In English conversation with a foreign lawyer it is correct to use one of the customary English honorific for lawyers: *Mr./Ms./Mrs./Miss*.

See also *Esquire*.

Attorney General

An *Attorney General* is a chief law officer and manager of legal matters in a state.

On a national level the *Attorney General* usually has the rank of *minister* or *secretary* and is a member of a head of government's cabinet. In foreign governments equivalent titles are *minister of justice* or *secretary of justice*.

Auditor General

An *auditor general* is a chief accounting officer and manager of income and expenditures in a state.

Autocephalous Church

An *autocephalous church* is a hierarchical church whose highest official does not report to a higher-ranking official. For example, in a Christian Orthodox church the head of an autocephalous church holds the title of *patriarch* or *pope* and is addressed as *Holiness* or *Beatitude*. An *archbishop, metropolitan bishop,* and *bishop* who reports to a higher ranking official is usually addressed as *Eminence, Most Reverend.* or *Right Reverend.*

Autonomous Community, Autonomous City

An *autonomous community* is a geographic area and an administrative division in a nation, *e.g.*, the Kingdom of Spain. Spain's 50 provinces are grouped into 17 *autonomous communities* and two *autonomous cities* including Andalusia (Andalucia), Aragon, Asturias, Baleares, Ceuta, Canarias, Cantabria, Castilla-La Mancha, Castilla y Leon, Cataluna, Comunidad Valenciana, Extremadura, Galicia, La Rioja, Madrid, Melilla, Murcia, Navarra, and Pais Vasco. Each *autonomous community* has its own parliament and regional government.

In an introduction the *autonomous community* would be included for specificity: *Member of the (autonomous community) Parliament in the Kingdom of Spain, (honorific) (surname)*.

ATT – BAR

Ayatollah

Ayatollah (*sign of God* in Arabic) is a title and honorific of a Shiite Muslim cleric. Unlike western clergy who often have administrative duties, an *ayatollah* will have earned his title by being a recognized scholar of Islamic theology, law, science, and philosophy. An *ayatollah* ranks above an *imam* and below a *grand ayatollah*.

B

Bailiff

Bailiff is a title held by a judicial officer who keeps order in the courtroom and guards prisoners or jurors during deliberation.

    Bailiff is also a high civil officer in *bailiwicks* such as the *Bailiwick of Jersey* or the *Bailiwick of Guernsey*, crown dependencies of the United Kingdom. For example, the *bailiff of Jersey* is appointed by the monarch and serves as president of the legislature and in the Royal Court.

    Bailiff is used after the name in an introduction or on an envelope for identification, but not as an honorific: Mr. *(full name)*, *Bailiff of (jurisdiction)*.

Bailiwick

A *bailiwick* is a territorial and administrative division under the jurisdiction of a *bailiff*. The usage survives in British Crown dependencies such as Jersey and Guernsey.

Baptismal Name

A *baptismal name* is most often a synonym for a *given name* or *first name*. It is literally the name given to a Christian child at baptism.

Baron, Baroness

Baron is the British form of a title for a nobleman of hereditary ranking below *viscount*.

    A *baroness* is a woman who holds the title in her own right, or *baroness* can be a *courtesy title* given to the wife or widow of a *baron*. The husband of a *baroness* is addressed as Mr. *(name)*, unless he has a title of his own.

    Sometimes a *baroness* (*e.g.*, in Germany and Austria) is an unmarried daughter of a *baron*. In other languages the equivalent titles are:

- French: *baron* and *baroness*
- Italian: *barone* and *baronessa*
- Spanish: *baron* and *baronesa*
- Austrian German: *baron* and *baronin*
- German: *barón/freiherr* and *baronin/freifrau*
- Swedish: *baron* and *baronessa*

See also *Lord, Lady*.

BAR – CAL

Baronet
Baronet is the hereditary British title held by commoners for a *knighthood* called a *baronetcy*. A *baronet* ranks above a *knight* (except for a *Knight of the Garter*) but below a *baron*.

Barrister
A *barrister* is a legal professional similar to an *attorney at law* or *lawyer* who works in concert with a *solicitor*. A *barrister* represents clients in higher courts, arguing cases in front of a judge and jury. A *solicitor* prepares legal documents, advises clients, and represents them in lower courts. *Barrister* is most frequently used in Commonwealth nations.

Bishop
Bishop is an office, title, and honorific with different precedence and duties in different religious communities.

A *bishop* in the Roman Catholic, Episcopal, and Christian Orthodox churches is a high-ranking cleric with spiritual and administrative authority over numerous *priests* and churches in a city or large area. The area a *bishop* oversees is called a *diocese* or *bishopric*.

A *metropolitan bishop* is an *archbishop* who oversees a number of *dioceses*.

A *suffragan bishop* is an assistant to a higher-ranking *bishop*.

A *titular bishop* is a *bishop* who does not have the obligation to oversee a *diocese*, and holds title to a *titular see*. Because he has the title but not the day-to-day responsibilities, a *titular bishop* might take on special projects for the church or devote himself to prayer.

Bishop in the Church of Jesus Christ of Latter-day Saints is the title of a lay minister and volunteer leader of a congregation called a *ward*.

Presiding bishop is the title of the head of the entire Episcopal Church with both spiritual and administrative responsibilities.

A *Methodist bishop* is an administrative superintendent in the United Methodist Church and is elected by the clergy to appoint clergy for local churches and perform ordinations.

See also *Archbishop*.

Bookends, Bookending
Bookending is the practice of using a formal form of address to begin and end a conversation, but using something less formal in the middle. For example, if in conversation with a *queen*, one would begin and end with *Your Majesty*, but use *Ma'am* in between.

Brother
A *brother* is a member of a religious order who takes vows and provides non-sacramental service. This contrasts with *priests* who are ordained members of orders. *Brothers* are more likely to work in education, health care, or social work. Orders of brothers include the Marist Brothers (Society of Mary) and the Christian Brothers.

BAR – CAL

Brother is frequently used as an honorific and in place of a name in conversation by members of a church: *Brother (name)* or *Brother.*

C

Cabinet, Cabinet Minister

A *cabinet* is a group of senior officials who advise a head of government. Members of cabinets hold offices such as *minister of (portfolio)*, *secretary of (portfolio)*, *Attorney General*, and *treasurer* and are generically called *cabinet ministers* or *cabinet secretaries*. *Executive council* and *council of ministers* are synonyms for *cabinet*. In countries that address high officials with courtesy titles, members of the *cabinet* are addressed with courtesy titles such as *the Honorable* or *Your Excellency*.

For example, in a parliamentary government the *cabinet*, formed by the *prime minister*, who is the first among equals, and the other *ministers of (portfolio)*, form a government.

Calling Cards

A *calling card* is a card printed with a person's contact information. In the diplomatic arena it is a diplomat's formal business card. It can also be a personal card with the person's name, telephone number, and address.

The *calling* in the card's name refers to its use when making an unannounced visit to an acquaintance's residence at times established for visitors to be welcome. If the individual sought by the caller is not at home (or if the *diplomat* is not at his or her *post*), a *calling card* is left as a record of the visit.

Cards left can be folded or inscribed.

Folding the upper left-hand corner indicates a visit.

- Upper right-hand corner: *congratulations*
- Lower left-hand corner: *leaving of the area by the individual named on the card*
- Lower right-hand corner: *condolence*

Brief messages are written in pencil if the card was delivered in person. Messages are written in ink if the card is mailed or sent by messenger. The following initials on the card would be written on the lower left-hand corner.

- **n.b.** (*notez bien*): *note well*
- **p.c.** (*pour condoléance*): *condolence*
- **p.f.** (*pour féliciter*): *thanks*
- **p.f.n.a.** (*pour faire nouvel an*): *happy new year*
- **p.m.** (*pour memoire*): *to remind*
- **p.p.** (*pour présenter*): *congratulations*
- **p.p.c.** (*pour prendre congé*): *to take leave*
- **p.r.** (*pour remercier*): *farewell*

CAL – CHA

Calls, Calling

Calls and *calling* refer to the practice of a diplomat visiting his or her contacts at a new post.

Canon

A *canon* is a *priest*, an official, or member of a *chapter* at a cathedral.

Canton

A *canton* is a small geographic area and administrative division. *Canton* most directly translates as *region* or *state*. For example, the Swiss Confederation is composed of 26 *cantons*: Aargau, Appenzell Ausser-Rhoden, Appenzell Inner-Rhoden, Basel-Landschaft, Basel-Stadt, Bern, Fribourg, Geneve, Glarus, Graubunden, Jura, Luzern, Neuchatel, Nidwalden, Obwalden, Sankt Gallen, Schaffhausen, Schwyz, Solothurn, Thurgau, Ticino, Uri, Valais, Vaud, Zug, and Zurich.

Use of a *canton* in an introduction could be: *Member of the Swiss Confederation's Federal Assembly from (canton), (honorific) (surname).*

Other countries with *cantons* include Belgium, Bosnia and Herzegovina, Costa Rica, Ecuador, France, and Luxembourg.

Cantor

Cantor is the title and an honorific for an official at a *synagogue* who sings prayers, or leads the musical parts of a Jewish liturgical service.

Captain Regent

Captain regent is the title of the two *co-chiefs of state* in San Marino. A *captain regent* is addressed as a member of the Great and General Council (parliament), and is identified after his or her name as *Captain Regent of the Republic San Marino.*

Cardinal

Cardinal is a rank, title, and honorific for a very high official in the Roman Catholic Church. *Cardinals* are appointed by the *pope* and are members of the College of Cardinals, the body that elects the *pope*. There are three ranks of *cardinal*:

- *Cardinal bishops* are *bishops* of *sees* (a post or church) near Rome.
- *Cardinal priests* are *bishops* outside of the vicinity of Rome. Of the 32 *archbishops* in the United States only some are *cardinals*. Elevating an *archbishop* or *bishop* to the rank of *cardinal* is at the discretion of the *pope*.
- *Cardinal deacons* are *bishops* who hold positions in the *curia* (the papal government) in Rome.

Career Diplomat

A *career diplomat* is a professional member of a state's diplomatic corps, rather than a person who becomes a *diplomat* by political appointment.

Chair

The *chair* is the person who is in charge of a meeting, or who is occupying the chair's place. For example, in the U.S. House of Representatives the *speaker* or the *acting speaker* could at various times be the *chair*.

Chamberlain

A *chamberlain* is an official of an administration of a noble chief of state.

In Norway the *lord chamberlain* is the manager of a royal household.

In the United Kingdom the *lord chamberlain* is the senior, but part-time and largely ceremonial, office in the royal household. He attends to the *monarch* at coronations, and oversees the conduct and general business of the royal household as a whole.

The *great lord chamberlain* is a special honorary post in the United Kingdom responsible for royal affairs in the houses of parliament. It is a hereditary title vested in the families of the Marquessate of Cholmondeley, the Earldom of Ancaster, and the Marquessate of Lincolnshire.

The *Lord Chamberlain's Office* in the United Kingdom, which is directed by a *comptroller* — not the *lord chamberlain* — organizes ceremonies, state visits, protocol, honors and insignia, household appointments and warrants, royal transportation, investitures, garden parties, the opening of Parliament, and royal weddings and funerals.

A *chamberlain* is addressed by his or her personal title and identified by *office* after the name.

Chan

Chan, a gender-neutral Japanese diminutive honorific, is used in conversation as a suffix to the family name when addressing children or very close friends: *(family name)-chan*.

Chancellery

A *chancellery* is the rank, office, or office building of a *chancellor* or the department headed by a *chancellor*. Chancellery is also used as a synonym for chancery.

Chancellor

Chancellor is the title and honorific for a very high official.

In academia, a *chancellor* is the head of a university, *e.g.*, Vanderbilt University, or head of a statewide system where individual campuses each have a *president*, *e.g.*, at the University of Alabama. In some cases a *chancellor* will be a ceremonial position and there will be a non-ceremonial *vice-chancellor*, *e.g.*, at the College of William and Mary.

In U.S. government there are just a few *chancellors*. In Delaware and Tennessee, a *chancellor* or *vice-chancellor* is a *judge* in certain courts with jurisdiction in equity cases called *Courts of Chancery* or *Chancery Courts*.

CHA – COM

In foreign governments a *chancellor* may be:

- The head of government: *Chancellor of the Federal Republic of Germany.*
- The head of an executive department such as justice, *e.g., Chancellor of Justice* in Finland, or finance, *e.g., Chancellor of the Exchequer* in the United Kingdom.
- The head an assembly: *Lord Chancellor* in the House of Lords in the Parliament of the United Kingdom.
- A member of the United Kingdom's cabinet: *The Chancellor of the Duchy of Lancaster.*
- In a Christian Orthodox church, a *chancellor* conducts administrative work for the patriarch in the Great Chancellery.

Chancery
A *chancery* is the business office or office building of a diplomatic mission, embassy, or religious order.

Chaplain
Chaplain is a title and honorific for a member of the clergy who conducts religious services for an institution, organization, assembly, or a unit of an armed service.

Chargé d'affaires
Chargé d'affaires is a title and office held by a *diplomat* sent to handle the affairs of his or her government in place of an accredited ambassador. It is a synonym for a *chief of mission*.

A *chargé d'affaires ad interim* (*chargé d'affaires, a.i.*) is a *diplomat* who is temporarily *chief of mission* during the absence of an *ambassador*.

A *chargé d'affaires* is addressed as *Mr./Mrs./Ms. (name)* and identified as a *chargé d'affaires* after the name in an introduction or on a business envelope for identification.

Chief Magistrate
See *Magistrate*.

Chief Minister
Chief minister is sometimes an office and honorific for a high official. For example, in Australia both Norfolk Island and Northern Territory have as their head of government a *chief minister*.

Chief of Mission, COM
Chief of mission is the highest position at an overseas mission or embassy of the United States. A *chief of mission* can have the rank of *ambassador* or *minister*, or the title *chargé d'affaires*.

Chief of State, Head of State
A *chief of state* or *head of state* is the highest official and the most prominent public and formal representative of a country. It is neither a title nor an honorific.

In many republics a *president* is both the *chief of state* and *head of government*. In an absolute monarchy the *monarch* is both the *chief of state* and *head of government*.

CHA – COM

COUNTRY	FORM OF GOVERNMENT	CHIEF OF STATE & HEAD OF GOVERNMENT
Benin	Republic	**President**
Mexico	Republic	**President**
United States	Republic	**President**
Brunei Darussalam	Sultanate	**Sultan**
Saudi Arabia	Monarchy	**King**

In parliamentary governments, the *chief of state* and *head of government* are separate offices. In these instances the *chief of state* typically takes on many ceremonial functions.

COUNTRY	FORM OF GOVERNMENT	CHIEF OF STATE	HEAD OF GOVERNMENT
Albania	Parliamentary republic	**President**	Prime minister
Japan	Constitutional monarchy	**Emperor**	Prime minister
Sweden	Constitutional monarchy	**King**	Prime minister
United Kingdom	Constitutional monarchy	**Queen**	Prime minister
Brunei	Constitutional sultanate	**Sultan**	Prime minister
Qatar	Constitutional emirate	**Emir**	Prime minister
Luxembourg	Constitutional monarchy	**Grand Duke**	Prime minister

Chiefs of state have other titles including:

COUNTRY	FORM OF GOVERNMENT	CHIEF OF STATE	HEAD OF GOVERNMENT
Holy See/Vatican	Ecclesiastical	**Pope**	Secretary of state
Monaco	Principality	**Prince**	Minister of state
San Marino	Republic	**Co-chiefs of State**	Secretary of state

See also *Head of Government.*

Christian Name

Christian name is a synonym for a *given name* or *first name*. It is the name given to a Christian child at baptism.

Collectivity

In the French Republic *collectivity, overseas collectivity, departmental collectivity,* and *territorial collectivity* are administrative divisions with independent local governments.

Collectivity is part of the name of French overseas territories such as the *Overseas Collectivity of Saint Martin* and *Territorial Collectivity of Mayotte.*

Colors

Colors refers to flags or flag raising ceremonies. Ceremonies at different times of day include *morning colors* and *evening colors.*

Commercial Attaché

A *commercial attaché* or *commercial officer* is a *foreign service officer* at a diplomatic mission representing and promoting the commercial or business interests of his or her country.

COM – CON

Commissioner

Commissioner is a title, office, and honorific for an executive who is the head of a council, board, commission, agency, or authority.

A *commissioner*, appointed by the *Governor-in-Council of Canada* (the *Governor-general of Canada* acting under the advice of the federal cabinet), is the representative of the Canadian government to a territory. The *Commissioner of the Northwest Territories*, *Commissioner of Nunavit*, and *Commissioner of the Yukon* are the chief executive officers in their Canadian territories.

In the European Commission, offices that are the equivalent of *minister* or *secretary of (portfolio)* in the cabinet of the European Union's president are *commissioners of (portfolio)*.

Commissioner is often used as an honorific for officeholders and in place of the name in conversation.

See also *High Commissioner*.

Commoner

In an imperial, royal, or noble state, an individual is a *commoner*, a *peer*, or the *sovereign chief of state*.

Commonwealth

A *commonwealth* is a group or association of self-governing countries, states, nations, or peoples united by a common purpose. The *Commonwealth of Australia*, a nation, and the *Commonwealth of Virginia*, a state within a nation, incorporate *commonwealth* into their names.

Commonwealth of Nations

The *Commonwealth of Nations* is an association of nations that includes the *Commonwealth realms* and more than 35 other states. Members of the *Commonwealth of Nations* which are not *Commonwealth realms* include: Bangladesh, Botswana, Brunei Darussalam, Cyprus, Ghana, India, Nigeria, Singapore, South Africa, and many others.

Commonwealth Realm

A *Commonwealth realm* is any one of the nations within the Commonwealth of Nations whose *chief of state* is the same *monarch* as that of the United Kingdom. *Commonwealth realms* include: Antigua and Barbuda, Australia, the Bahamas, Barbados, Belize, Canada, Grenada, Jamaica, New Zealand, Papua New Guinea, St. Kitts and Nevis, St. Lucia, St. Vincent and the Grenadines, Solomon Islands, Tuvalu, and the United Kingdom of Great Britain and Northern Ireland.

Commune

A *commune* is a small geographic area and low-level administrative division, usually a city, town, or village. For example, the Principality of Liechtenstein is composed of 11 *communes*: Balzers, Eschen, Gamprin, Mauren, Planken, Ruggell, Schaan, Schellenberg, Triesen, Triesenberg, and Vaduz.

COM – CON

In an introduction the *commune* would be included for specificity: *Member of the Principality of Liechtenstein's Parliament from (commune), (honorific) (surname)*.

Other countries with *communes* include Chile, France, Belgium, and Luxembourg.

Companion

A *companion* is a level of an award of honor.

Some orders of *knighthood*, e.g., the Most Honourable Order of Bath, have a rank of membership lower than *knight* called *companion*. The *companion* member uses a post-nominal abbreviation of the order after his or her name, but is not addressed as *sir, dame*, or *lady* as a *knight* in the order would be.

Another example of *companion* as an award of honor is the Order of Australia, in which companion is the highest of the four honors below *knight* or *dame*.

See also *Knight*.

Company-Grade Officer

A *company-grade officer* or *company officer* is a commissioned officer assigned to a company as its leader, having the rank of second lieutenant, first lieutenant, or captain in the U.S. Army, Air Force, or Marine Corps. In the U.S. Navy an officer of the equivalent rank is a *junior officer*.

Confederation

A *confederation* is a form of government in which semi-autonomous communities create a central government. Related to a *federation, confederation* implies a looser union in which the central government is weaker than in a *federation*.

For example, the *Confederate States of America* were organized to ensure states' rights over federal power. And although Switzerland is named officially the *Swiss Confederation*, its government is more similar in structure and action to a *federal republic* than a *federation*.

See also *Federation*.

Congress of Vienna, 1815

The *Congress of Vienna*, an 1815 convention of European leaders in Vienna, Austria, dealt with the political and social issues after Napoleon's defeat at Waterloo. It reseated royal houses that had been expelled, redrew Europe's borders, removed many of the vestiges of the Holy Roman Empire, and condemned Europe's participation in the slave trade. Although many of the decrees did not endure, they represented an attempt by Austria, France, Great Britain, Prussia, and Russia to deal with Europe as an organic whole. Regions affected by the convention's agreements included Belgium, the Cape of Good Hope, Denmark, Finland, the German States, the Italian states, Luxembourg, Malta, Mauritius, Netherlands, Poland, Portugal, Spain, Sweden, Switzerland, Tobago, Trinidad, and Turkey.

CON – COU

A longer lasting accomplishment of the Council was the adoption of previously unwritten rules of diplomacy. It established:

- The classes of the heads of diplomatic missions.
- The determining of precedence within these classes by the date of presentation of a diplomat's credentials.
- The system for signing treaties in alphabetical order by the country's name in French.
- The distinction between great powers and powers with limited interests. Great powers exchanged *ambassadors*. Powers of limited interest were lesser states (such as the United States at that time) whose envoys only held the rank of *minister*.

See also *Vienna Convention on Diplomatic Relations, 1961*.

Congressman, Congresswoman

Congressman and *congresswoman* describe members of the U.S. Congress which includes the *members* of the House of Representatives and *senators* of the Senate.

Traditionally *congressman* and *congresswoman* are not titles, honorifics, ranks, or offices. However, sometimes members of the House of Representatives use the terms as honorifics for clarity. They might, for example, have their phone answered *"Congressman (name)'s office"* rather than *"Mr./Ms. (name)'s office,"* or the *member's* staff might use *"the Congressman"* when referring to the member. Some representatives are identified as *Congressman (name)* on the banner of their web site. While *Congressman (name)* may not be a traditional honorific in direct address, it may be preferred by a *member* of the House of Representatives, so follow the preference of the bearer.

Consort

A *consort* is the husband or wife of a *monarch* or other noble person.

A *prince consort* is a husband of a *reigning queen* who is not a *king*. A *reigning king's* wife is often crowned a *queen*. A *reigning queen's* husband is not made a *king* but most often a *prince*, since *king* would outrank the *queen*.

Consul

A *consul* is an office held by a high ranking *diplomat* who heads a *consulate*, an office of a foreign power in charge of interactions with individuals and businesses. A consul's responsibilities include issuing passports and visas, and offering commercial and personal assistance to citizens. *Consuls* are entitled to some but not all diplomatic privileges and immunities.

A *vice-consul* reports to a consul.

A *consul general* is a consul of the first rank who heads a consulate general, a larger consular office where consuls and vice-consuls may also be assigned.

A *consular agent* or an *honorary consul* is a person who performs limited consular functions in a foreign city where there is no *mission*.

All these offices — *consul, general consul, vice-consul,* and the others — are

CON – COU

used after the name in an introduction or on a business envelope for identification, but not as honorifics.

Consulate

A *consulate* is a diplomatic office headed by a *consul*, which issues passports and visas, and offers commercial and personal assistance to citizens.

See also *Diplomatic Mission*.

Co-Prince

A *co-prince* is a *co-chief of state* in the Principality of Andorra. One *co-prince* is the *president of France*; the other is the *bishop of Urgell*. Both are represented in Andorra by a *prefect*.

Councilman, Councilor, Councillor, Councilwoman

Councilmen and *councilwomen* are *members* of a city or county council. The position can be either elected or appointed. *Councilor* or *councillor* are terms used in Great Britain, Canada, Australia, South Africa, and other parts of the Commonwealth, and sometimes in the United States, since they are gender neutral.

Councilman and *councilwoman* are used after the name in an introduction or on a business envelope for identification, but not traditionally as honorifics in the United States. However, the staff of *members* of a council use the terms as honorifics for clarity, as when answering the phone "*Councilman (surname)'s office*" rather than "*Mr./Ms. (surname)'s office*" or when referring to the member as the *Councilman*. While *Councilman (surname)* may not be traditional, it is sometimes used, so follow the preference of the bearer.

In Commonwealth countries *Cr.* is used as an honorific for a *councillor*.

Counselor, Counsellor

Counselor is a mid-rank position at a diplomatic mission. *Counselor* is a diplomatic title accorded to a head of a section in the embassy, such as *counselor for defense research*, *finance counselor*, or *political counselor*. A *counselor* is lower than a *minister*. A *minister-counselor* is ranked between counselor and minister.

A *minister-counselor* is a diplomat who holds a high position at an embassy. A *minister-counselor* is frequently the *deputy chief of mission*, the second highest office. In the United States a *minister-counselor* is sometimes addressed with the courtesy title *the Honorable* however, internationally *Your Excellency* is often reserved for the rank of minister and above. Check for preference of the bearer.

Both *counselor* and *minister-counselor* are used after the name in an introduction or on an official envelope for identification, but neither is an honorific.

Counsellor is the British spelling.

Count, Countess

Count is a title and honorific for a nobleman of hereditary rank in European countries. A *county* is the territory under the jurisdiction of a *count*.

A *countess* is a noblewoman who holds the title in her own right or is the wife

COU – CZA

or widow of a *count*. In Britain, *countess* is the title for a woman who holds the title in her own right, or is the wife of an *earl*. The husband of a *countess* is not addressed with a courtesy title: He is addressed as *Mr. (name)*, unless he has a title of his own.

In other languages the equivalent titles are:

* French: *comte* and *comtesse*
* German: *graf* and *gräfin*
* Italian: *conte* and *contessa*
* Spanish: *conde* and *condesa*
* Swedish: *greve* and *grevinna*

Country

A *country* is a geographic area.

See also *State* and *Nation*.

Country Desk

A *country desk* is an office in a *state department* focusing on current issues in and with a foreign country.

Country Team

A *country team* is an *ambassador*'s cabinet of advisers. It includes both *diplomats* assigned to the mission and other professionals (military, agricultural, aid, information, and cultural) working at the embassy.

County

A *county* is a territorial and administrative division. Traditionally it is the domain of a *count*.

In the United States a *county* is a subdivision of a *state*.

In many countries a *county* is the largest territorial division, and is the equivalent of a *state* or *province*. Albania, Estonia, Hungary, Ireland, Latvia, Liberia, Norway, and Romania are all divided into *counties*.

For example, the Republic of Croatia is divided into 20 *counties*. In an introduction the *county* would be included for specificity: *Member of the Republic of Croatia's Assembly from (county), (honorific) (surname)*.

Court of Cassation

A *court of cassation* is the highest appeals court of a nation. The title is used in the judiciary of France and in countries established in the French tradition. It is the equivalent of the *U.S. Supreme Court*.

Courtesy Lord

A *courtesy lord* is a British term describing the granting of the honorific *lord* as a courtesy to a man who will one day inherit the title meriting the honorific. Examples of *courtesy lords* include the eldest sons of *dukes*, *marquesses*, and *earls*.

Courtesy Title

A *courtesy title* is a title given by custom or courtesy rather than by right, due to

16

holding title to an office. For example:

- Any faculty member at a university might be addressed as *Professor (name)* in conversation as a *courtesy*, whether his or her rank is *professor, associate professor, assistant professor,* or *instructor.*
- *The Honorable* is a *courtesy title* used before a full name when addressing current and former holders of elected office.
- *The Reverend* is a *courtesy title* used before a full name when addressing clergy of many ranks and denominations.
- In the British peerage a *courtesy title* is a noble form of address that may be used by the son or wife of a nobleman. For example, a *peer* of the rank of *duke* may also hold other lesser, titles. If so, his eldest son may use one of his father's lesser titles during his father's lifetime as a *courtesy*. The wife of a *duke* may be addressed as a *duchess* as a *courtesy* even though she does not hold the title in her own right.
- The heir of a French noble title may be addressed with the title by friends and acquaintances *as a courtesy*, although the nobility of France was abolished.

When trying to ascertain the correct *courtesy title* (*excellency, honorable, etc.*) to use with an international official, is it important to check the preference of the bearer and the traditions of a country. There are more than 200 governmental entities in the world, each with its own laws and traditions. While there are similarities, each government has it own hierarchy and preferred forms of address.

Cr.
Cr. is an abbreviation used in Commonwealth countries for *councillor*, or member of a council. For example: Cr. *(name) is currently serving his second term on the Council of Redlands.*

Crown Prince, Crown Princess
See *Prince*.

Curate
A *curate* is a priest who is an assistant to a rector or pastor of a parish. *Curate* is used after a priest's name for identification.

Custodian of the Two Holy Mosques
The two holiest cities in Islam, Mecca and Medina, are both located in Saudi Arabia. The king of Saudi Arabia is addressed with the courtesy title *the Custodian of the Two Holy Mosques.*

Czar, Czarina
The *czar*, also spelled *tsar* or *tzar*, was the masculine title and honorific of the monarch of Russia, and the *emperor* of a much larger area from Poland to Siberia.

Czarina, also spelled *tsarina* or *tzarina*, the feminine form, was used by a woman who held the title in her own right or was the wife of the monarch.

DAM – DEP

Dame

Dame is an honorific used before the name of a female *knight*.
See also *Sir*.

Dastur

Dastur is a title and honorific for a Zoroastrian high priest.

Dato, Datuk

Dato and *datuk* are variant spellings of a lifetime chivalrous title and honorific granted by the government of Malaysia to outstanding individuals. Titled persons use post-nominal abbreviations to denote their decorations, similar to British *knights*. In writing these titled persons are addressed with the courtesy title *the Honorable*.

DCM

See *Deputy Chief of Mission*.

Deacon, Deaconess

Deacon and *deaconess* are the masculine and feminine forms of a title and honorific for a cleric just below the rank of *priest* in the Episcopal, Christian Orthodox, and Roman Catholic churches.

Deacon in many Protestant Christian churches is the title for a lay person who assists in religious, administrative, and pastoral affairs.

Deacon in the Church of Jesus Christ of Latter-day Saints is a title for a young man who assists at religious services and church activities.

Dean, Doyen

A *dean* is a senior member of a group.

Dean in academia is a title and honorific for an administrator of a faculty, college, or division of a university.

A *dean* in the Roman Catholic Church is a *priest* who supervises several *parishes* within a *diocese*. In the ecclesiastical hierarchy of the Roman Catholic Church there is a *dean* of the College of Cardinals.

A *dean* in the Church of England and Episcopal Church is a head of a chapter of *priests* who serve at a cathedral or collegiate church. At a cathedral the governing body is a *chapter of canons*, and a *dean* will serve as its head.

A *diplomat* who has served the longest at a post is known as the *dean* or *doyen of a diplomatic corps*. For example, in Washington, D.C., the foreign *ambassador* who has represented his or her country the longest in the United States is known as the *dean of the Washington diplomatic corps*. Seniority depends on the date of arrival in the capital coupled with the official presentation of credentials. The

DAM – DEP

duties of this *dean* are chiefly ceremonial in nature. The *dean* of the diplomatic corps is addressed as an *ambassador*, and identified as *dean* after his or her name when that fact is pertinent.

Deemster

Deemster is a title for a *judge* in a high court. In the High Court of Justice on the Isle of Man there are officers with the title of *first deemster, second deemster*, and *deputy deemster*. A *deemster* is addressed with the courtesy title *the Honourable*, with the title of the office following his or her name for identification.

Delegate

A *delegate* is an official representative to or member of an official body.

In the U.S. House of Representatives non-voting members from territories and the District of Columbia hold the office of *delegate*.

In the Commonwealth of Virginia, a *delegate* is an office and sometimes an honorific for the officeholder in the House of Delegates.

Department

A *department* is the major territorial subdivision of a country and is comparable to a *state* or *province*. For example, the Republic of Columbia is divided into 32 *departments*.

In an introduction, department would be included for specificity: *Member of the Republic of Columbia's House of Representatives from (department), (honorific) (surname)*.

Other countries divided into *departments* include Argentina, Benin, Bolivia, Guatemala, Honduras, Nicaragua, Paraguay, and Uruguay.

Dependency

A *dependency* is a region that belongs to another country but is neither fully a part of that country nor an independent state. For example, *Territory of New Caledonia and Dependencies* is a *dependency* of France, and Bouvet Island is a *dependency* of Norway.

Deputy

Deputy is a designation for second in command to a higher office; *e.g., deputy prime minister* is second in command to a *prime minister*.

Although the higher officeholder is addressed as *Mr./Madame (office)*, *Mr./Madame Deputy (office)* is rarely used. Address as *Mr./Ms./Dr./etc. (name)* and identify as *deputy-(office)*. *Deputy-(name of office)* is used as an honorific in conversation and in a letter's salutation.

Deputy is also a title and honorific for a member of a legislature. Such members addressed as *Deputy (name)* or *Mr./Madame/Mrs. Deputy (name)*. A *deputy* serves in a national legislature called a *house of deputies* or a *chamber of deputies*, and even in elected bodies whose name does not include *deputy*.

* In Italy, the bicameral parliament is made up of two houses: the Senate whose members are *senators*, and a Chamber of Deputies whose members are *deputies*.

DEP – DUK

- In Kyrgyzstan, members of the parliament are *deputies* in the Supreme Council of Kyrgyzstan.

Deputy Chief of Mission, DCM

A *deputy chief of mission* is an office of the second in command at an *embassy* who becomes the *charge d'affaires* in the *ambassador's* absence. *Deputy chief of mission* is mainly used in the United States and in U.S. diplomatic circles. Address a *deputy chief of mission* as Mr./Ms. *(name)* or by his or her *diplomatic rank*, and identify by *office* in writing or in a formal introduction.

Detective

Detective is an office and honorific for a member of a police department who investigates crimes.

Detectives have stepped ranks of seniority such as *detective first grade* and *detective second grade*, but all are addressed as *Detective (name)* in direct address.

Detective is not used socially: Address as Mr./Ms. *(name)*.

Diplomat

A *diplomat* is a member of the *diplomatic corps*. *Diplomatic ranks* afforded address as *His/Her Excellency* include *ambassador* and *minister*. Other ranks of diplomats include *minister-counselor, counselor, secretary (first, second, and third)*, *attaché*, and *assistant attaché*. A member of the *diplomatic corps* represents his or her country and works along side of the *consular corps*, which protects and handles the affairs of nationals in the host country.

Diplomatic Agent

A *diplomatic agent* is any person who carries out diplomatic activities of his or her government in the country to which he/she is accredited.

Diplomatic Corps

Diplomatic corps includes *diplomats* and staff at *diplomatic missions*.

Diplomatic Immunity

Diplomatic immunity is a reciprocal exemption from liability granted by one country to the diplomatic representatives (*diplomats*) of another country.

Diplomatic Mission

A *diplomatic mission* is a group of people sent by one nation to represent their homeland's interests in another nation.

An *embassy* is a permanent diplomatic mission headed by an *ambassador*.

A *consulate* is a diplomatic office headed by a *consul*, which issues passports and visas, and offers commercial and personal assistance to citizens.

A country with an *embassy* in the capital may have *consulates* in several cities to serve economic interests. An *embassy* may include a *consulate*, but while the operation of an *embassy* implies diplomatic relations between the countries, a *consulate* does not.

DEP – DUK

Docteur, Doctor, Doktor, *etc.*
In English the professional degree and title *doctor* is used as an honorific:
- Introduction: *Doctor (full name)*
- Introduction, one person to another: *Doctor (surname)*
- Conversation: *Doctor (surname)*
- Conversation, less formal: *Doctor*

In many languages the honorific *doctor* is combined with an equivalent of *Mr.*, *Mrs.*, or *Miss* to create a double honorific: *Monsieur le docteur (name)* in French, or *Senhor doutor (name)* or *Senhora doutora (name)* in Portuguese.

DOD
DOD is shorthand for *Department of Defense.*

Dom
Dom is an honorific (used in the Dominican Friars or the Benedictines) for a member. Ordained members are addressed formally as *the Reverend Dom (name)*, *(post nominal of his order)* and less formally and in speaking as *Dom (name)*. Lay members are addressed as *Dom (name)*.

Doyen
See *Dean.*

Dual Accreditation
A *diplomat* who is simultaneously accredited to two nations has *dual accreditation*. For example, the *Ambassador of Canada to the People's Republic of China*, who maintains residence in Beijing, might have *dual accreditation* and also be Canada's *non-resident ambassador* to the *Democratic People's Republic of Korea*.

Duke, Duchess
Duke is a title and honorific for a nobleman of highest hereditary rank in various European countries. The domain of a *duke* is a *duchy*.

A *duchess* is a woman who holds the title in her own right, or is the wife or widow of a *duke* and receives the title as a *courtesy title*. The husband of a *duchess* is not given a courtesy title and is addressed as *Mr. (name)*, unless he has his own title. In other languages the equivalent titles are:
- French: *duc* and *duchesse*
- Italian: *duca* and *ducessa*
- Portuguese and Spanish: *duque* and *duquesa*
- German: *herzog* and *herzogin*
- Swedish: *hertig* and *hertsoginya*

In the *grand duchy* such as the Grand Duchy of Luxembourg, the *chief of state* is a *grand duke*.

In Belgium, the heir to the throne is styled *Duke of Brabant*.

In the United Kingdom a *royal duke*, who is a *duke* who is a member of the *royal family*, is addressed as *Your Royal Highness*.

DV – ENG

DV
DV is an acronym for *distinguished visitor*.

Earl, Countess
Earl is a British title and honorific for a nobleman of hereditary rank. The domain of an *earl* is an *earldom. Count* and *county* are the equivalent terms used elsewhere in Europe.

An *earl* ranks below a *marquess* and above a *viscount*.

A *countess* is a woman who holds the title in her own right, or is the wife or widow of an *earl* who receives the title as a *courtesy*.

See also *Lord, Lady*.

Earl Marshal
The *Earl Marshal* is a very high honorary royal post in the United Kingdom with duties at state ceremonies such as coronations and the opening of Parliament. It is a hereditary office vested in the *Dukedom of Norfolk*. The *Earl Marshal* is addressed by his personal title and identified by *office*.

Economist
In some languages, *economist* is used as an honorific in the way *doctor* is used in English. It often appears as *Econ. (name)* with foreign officials.

Elder
Elder is a position in many religious communities held by clergy or senior lay members who provide stewardship in spiritual and/or administrative matters.

Among the Seventh-day Adventists, *elder* is an honorific for clergy.

In the Jehovah's Witnesses, *elder* is both a title and honorific for lay leaders.

In the Church of Jesus Christ of Latter-day Saints, *elder* is the honorific for members of quorums, such as the Quorum of the Seventy, and missionaries.

In many Protestant denominations an *elder* is a senior lay position at a church. As such *elder* is used after the name in an introduction or on an official envelope for identification, but not as an honorific.

An *elder* is also a member of an elected assembly such as the House of Elders in Afghanistan.

Elector
Elector describes a person who is eligible to vote in an election.

Embassy
An *embassy* is a permanent *diplomatic mission* headed by an *ambassador*.
See also *Diplomatic Mission*.

Emeritus
Emeritus is an adjective used in a title to describe a retired professional in relation to his or her former position, *e.g.*, a professor emeritus. It is used in documents where it is necessary to clarify the professional status and in introductions, but not in any form of direct address.

Emir, Emirate
Emir (also spelled *ameer* or *amir*) is an English term for a high Arab nobleman. The word *emir* is taken from *emirate*, mimicking the relationship between the words *king* and *kingdom*. However, *emir* is not actually a title or office in all the *emirates*. In Qatar they do use the term *emir* for their noble chief of state, but in Kuwait the preferred title of the noble chief of state is *prince*. In *emirates* of the United Arab Republic the noble chief of state is a *ruler*.

Emissary
An *emissary* is any person sent on a mission to represent the interests of a person or state.

Emperor, Empress
Emperor is the title for the imperial *chief of state* of an *empire*. *Emperors* rank above *kings*. Today, the only remaining imperial throne is that of the *Emperor of Japan*.
Empress is the title for a woman who holds the title in her own right, or is the wife of an *emperor* and receives the *courtesies* of an *empress*.

Engineer, Engenheiro, Ingeniero, Inziner, *etc.*
In some languages, *engineer* is used as an honorific in the way *doctor* is used in English. It often appears as *Eng. (name)* with foreign officials.
The formula is the same as for the honorifics *doctor* and *mister*:
- Introduction: *(Engineer) (full name)*
- Introduction, one person to another: *(Engineer) (surname)*
- Conversation: *(Engineer) (surname)*
- Conversation, less formal: *(Engineer)*

Sometimes the *'degree'* is combined with an equivalent of *Mr.*, *Mrs.*, or *Miss* to create a compound honorific:
- Spanish: *señor ingeniero* and *señora ingeniera*
- Magyar (Hungarian): *mérnök úr* and *mérnök né*

ENV – FED

In English conversation with a foreign engineer it is correct to use the customary English honorifics for engineers: *Mr.*, *Mrs.*, *and Miss.*

Envoy
An *envoy* can be any senior diplomat.

Ervad
Ervad is a title and honorific for a Zoroastrian priest.

Escort Card
An *escort card*, *seating card*, *take-in card*, or *table card* is a card received by a guest at a dinner event on which is written the name of another guest. At larger events it will also contain the number of the table at which these guests are seated.

The card is typically presented inside a small envelope with the name of the guest on the outside front. The addressee is to find the other guest and escort that guest from the pre-dinner reception to dinner, where they will be seated together.

At events where guests are not asked to escort other prescribed guests to dinner, the term is used for a card with only the number of the table at which the guest will be seated.

See also *YASA*.

Esquire
Esquire is a post-nominal courtesy title.

In the United States *esquire*, frequently abbreviated *Esq.*, is used in place of any other honorific with attorneys, lawyers, and justices of the peace.

In the United Kingdom *esquire* is a title for sons of nobles who have no other title, and for many offices including: commissioners and officers in certain courts, lawyers, justices of the peace, members of the royal household or anyone granted the title by the monarch, royal academicians, sheriffs, and other senior officers.

Examples: *(Full name)*, *Esq.*
            (Initials) *(surname)*, *Esq.*

Etiquette
Etiquette is a code of conventions, proprieties, or accepted behavior within a community. While *etiquette* is widely understood and described, it is unofficial, unwritten, and changes over time.

Excellency
Excellency is a *courtesy title* and form of direct address for high officials

It is frequently used when addressing a high-ranking foreign official such as a *president*, *prime minister*, *cabinet minister*, *ambassador*, *governor-general*, or *governor*, and other officials. *Excellency* is also to address a Roman Catholic *nuncio*, and certain U.S. state officials, *e.g.*, the governor of Massachusetts.

His/Her Excellency precedes the officeholder's full name on envelopes, and the officeholder may be addressed in conversation as *Your Excellency* in place of his or her name or *sir* or *madam*.

American *ambassadors*, addressed by U.S. citizens as *the Honorable*, are sometimes addressed as *Your Excellency* by foreign officials since in the diplomatic arena accredited diplomats are addressed as *Your Excellency*.

Executive Branch

The *executive* is the *branch* of government that executes the laws of the state.

In the government of the United States the *executive branch* includes the *President, cabinet,* and the *executive departments*. In the government of the Commonwealth of Australia the *executive branch* includes the *governor-general, prime minister, ministers of (portfolio),* and *executive departments*.

The *executive branch* is one of the three branches of governments along with the *legislature* and the *judiciary*.

Family Name

The *family name*, or *surname*, is the part of a person's name that indicates the family to which he or she belongs.

In many cultures the *family name* is at the end of a complete name and is also called a *last name*. And while the *family name* is often the father's *family name*, there are many exceptions:

- In Spanish, a person frequently uses a *family name* derived from both parents' names.
- In Iceland most people use only their *given name* and *patronymic name*, but some include a *family name* between the two.
- In Russia most people use a *patronymic name* as a *middle name* between their given and family names.
- Traditionally, Tibetans, Javanese, Burmese, and many royal families do not use *family names* at all.

Father, Mother

Father is an honorific used by *priests* in the Roman Catholic and Episcopal churches. *Mother* is an honorific for women priests in the Episcopal Church.

See also *Fr.* and *Prior*.

Federal Executive Council

The *Federal Executive Council* is composed of current and former *ministers* and *parliamentary secretaries* in the Commonwealth of Australia. Similar to the *privy councils* in Canada and the United Kingdom, members in the *Federal Executive*

FED – FSO

Council are addressed with the courtesy title *the Honourable* for life.

Federation

A *federation* is a form of government in which partially self-governing *states* create a strong central federal government. Many *federations* describe themselves as *federal republics*. Examples include:

- Federal Democratic Republic of Ethiopia
- Federal Republic of Germany
- Federative Republic of Brazil
- United Mexican States
- United States of America

Other *federations* are *constitutional monarchies*, such as Canada and the Commonwealth of Australia.

See also *Confederation*.

Field Grade

Field grade or *field officer* describes a commissioned military officer who outranks a *company officer* but is lower in rank than a *general officer*. In the U.S. Army this would include officers ranking above a *captain* and below a *brigadier general:* the ranks of *major, lieutenant colonel*, and *colonel*.

Firefighter, Fireman, Firewoman

A *firefighter* is a member of a fire brigade or department. *Firefighters* can be either career or volunteer.

Commissioner, deputy commissioner, assistant commissioner, associate commissioner, chief fire marshal, chief of (portfolio), chief, deputy chief, vice-chief, assistant chief, division chief, and *battalion chief* are ranks and honorifics used by administrators in firefighting organizations. Use the *full title*, e.g., *deputy chief*, as an honorific in writing or a formal introduction, and the *basic title*, e.g., *chief*, in conversation. Many former officials use their ranked honorific for life, but such use is at the preference of the bearer.

Lower administrative offices such as *director* are not used as honorifics. Address officeholders as Mr./Ms. *(name)* and identify by *office*.

Captain, lieutenant, and *sergeant* are paramilitary ranks and honorifics used by *firefighters*. Use the rank as an honorific in direct address. The highest former officials use their ranked honorific for life, but such use is at the preference of the bearer.

Firefighter is the title for the basic position in a fire department. It can be used as an honorific, but usually the person is addressed as Mr./Ms. *(name)* and identified as a *firefighter*.

Other firefighting positions include *engineer, driver*, and *lineman*. Address them as Mr./Ms. *(name)* and identify by *office*.

First Name

A *first name* is usually a synonym for a *given name:* the name that appears first in a complete name. It is most often combined with a *surname* or *family name* and other names to form a complete *name string*.

FED – FSO

Called a *first name* because it appears first in many cultures, not all cultures place the *given name* first. For example, the *given name* appears last in Korean names.

Flag Officer
A *flag officer* is a naval officer whose rank entitles him or her to fly a personal flag when in command. Flag officers include stepped ranks of *admiral* and *commodore*. *Flag officer* is the equivalent of *general officer*, the term used by land and air armed services for a *field marshal* or any of the stepped ranks of *general*.

Foreign Service Officer
A *foreign service officer* is a career member of a state's *diplomatic corps*, as opposed to a person who becomes a *diplomat* by political appointment.

Forename
A *forename* is a synonym for a *given name* or *first name*.

Forms of Address
Forms of address include terms used in direct communication with a holder of a position in a hierarchy.

This contrasts with descriptive terms used to identify officeholders in the third person: If the *President of the United States* is *James Buchanan*, while he might be referred to as *President Buchanan* in the media, he is directly addressed as *Mr. President*.

Forms of address include:
- The name in an address on an official envelope
- The name in a letter's salutation
- The name in an address on a social envelope
- The name on an invitation's inside envelope
- The name on a place card
- The name in a formal and complete introduction
- The name in an introduction of one person to another
- The name by which you address someone in a conversation

Fr.
Fr., an abbreviation for the Latin *frater*, meaning *brother*, is used as an honorific for *priests* or *friars*. For example:
Friar: Fr. *(full name)*, OP
Father: Fr. *(full name)*, SJ

Friar
Friar is a title and honorific for a member of a religious order such as the Dominican Friars in the Roman Catholic Church.

F.S.O.
F.S.O. is an abbreviation for a *Foreign Service Officer*, an American *career diplomat*.

GEN – GRA

General Officer
A *general officer* is a land or air military officer of high rank such as a *field marshal* or one of the stepped ranks of *general*. It is the equivalent of *flag officer* or an officer of flag rank, terms used by the navy for *commodore* and the stepped ranks of *admiral*.

General Superior
See *Superior General*.

Giani
Giani, meaning a spiritual person, is an office and honorific for someone learned in Sikh doctrine who leads congregational prayers.

Given Name
In European and other cultures a *given name* is a *personal name*. It is used with the *family name* or *surname* to form a complete name string. When it appears first, it is called a *first name*. When there are two *given names*, the second *given name* is called a *middle name*. In contrast, in Chinese, Korean, and Hungarian the *family name* appears first and the *given name* appears last.

Government Leader
Government leader is a title and position of the head of government. In Canada, the *Government Leader/Premier of Territorial Government* is the head of a territorial government.

See also *Leader of Government*.

Governor, Lieutenant Governor
Governor is a title and honorific for a high official in a government.

In the United States, *governor* is the title and honorific for the highest elected official in a state, directing the *executive branch* of government.

A *governor* may also be a *vice-royal representative* of a sovereign *chief of state*. In British Overseas Territories *governor* is the title and honorific for the representative of the *chief of state*, the monarch of the United Kingdom. *Governor* is also the title of the British monarch's representative to each of Australia's states and the representative of the monarch of the Netherlands to Aruba.

In American Samoa the *governor* is the *head of government* appointed by the *chief of state*, the president of the United States.

A *lieutenant governor* is second in rank to a *governor* or *governor-general*. In the United States, a *lieutenant governor* is the second highest elected state office. In the United Kingdom, a *lieutenant-governor* is the British monarch's vice-royal, ceremonial representative to a province or dependency, *e.g.*, Isle of Man or

Guernsey. In these instances Mr. *Lieutenant Governor* could be used in conversation, but normally a *lieutenant governor* is addressed as *Mr./Ms./Dr./etc. (surname)* rather than the cumbersome *Lieutenant Governor (surname)*.

Governor is the title frequently given to the head of a nation's central bank or reserve bank. Such a *governor* is a member of a *board of governors*, but is not addressed with the honorific *governor* as is a *governor of a state*. A *board of governors* is made up of members, not *governors*. *Governor of the (central bank of country)*, *chairman of the board of governors*, *member of a board of governors*, or *governor for (area of responsibility)* are used after the name for identification in an introduction or in writing an address on an official envelope, but not as an honorific. Use the honorifics *Mr./Mrs./Ms./Miss*.

Governorate

A *governorate* is an administrative division or subdivision of a country under the jurisdiction of a *governor*. For example, Bahrain is divided into five *governorates*: Asamah, Janubiyah, Muharraq, Shamaliyah, and Wasat.

In an introduction the *governorate* would be included for specificity: *Governor of (governorate) in the Kingdom of Bahrain, Governor (surname)*.

Countries with *governorates* include Egypt, Iraq, Jordan, Lebanon, Kuwait, Oman, Tunisia, and Yemen.

Governor-General

A *governor general* or *governor-general* (hyphenated in some countries) is a *viceroyal* representative of a non-resident sovereign *chief of state*. In Australia, Canada, New Zealand, Jamaica, and other members of the Commonwealth, a *governor general* is the nominal *chief of state* appointed by the monarch on the advice of the country's *prime minister*.

Graded Titles, Graded Ranks

Graded titles are *titles* which indicate stepped seniority within a *basic rank*.

For example, in the military the *basic rank* of *general* includes four *graded ranks*: *general*, *lieutenant general*, *major general*, and *brigadier general*.

	GRADED RANK	BASIC RANK	STARS
Highest general	General	General	four-star
	Lieutenant General	General	three-star
	Major General	General	two-star
Lowest general	Brigadier General	General	one-star

In academia, the *basic rank* of *professor* may include *graded ranks* such as *professor*, *associate professor*, and *assistant professor*.

In both the armed services and academia use the *basic rank* in verbal address and conversation and the *graded rank* in writing and formal introductions.

On a social envelope, use the complete *graded rank/rating*. On the invitation's inside envelope, as in conversation, use the *basic rank/rating*.

GRA – HEA

Grand Ayatollah

Grand ayatollah (meaning *great sign of God* in Arabic) is a title and honorific of a Shiite Muslim cleric. A *grand ayatollah* will be a renowned and influential scholar of Islamic theology, law, science, and philosophy, and the holder of a high office such as head of the Shiite seminary. *Grand ayatollah* ranks above *ayatollah* and *imam*.

Grand Duke, Grand Duchess, Grand Duchy

Grand duke is the masculine title of a royal *chief of state* in a *grand duchy*. The title is not used as an honorific: The royal person is addressed as *Your Royal Highness*.

Grand duchess is the title for a woman who holds the title in her own right, or is the wife of a *grand duke* and receives the *courtesies* of a *grand duchess*.

Grand Mufti

Grand mufti is a title for a very high Sunni Muslim cleric. A *grand mufti* serves a specific country, e.g., the *Grand Mufti of Syria* or the *Grand Mufti of Saudi Arabia*.

A *grand mufti* is addressed in correspondence as *His Eminence* and in conversation as *Your Eminence*.

Grandee

A *grandee* is a member of the nobility, or a *peer*, in Spain.

Granthi

A *granthi* is a Sikh ceremonial leader who arranges daily religious services, reads from the scriptures, maintains the gurdwara premises, and teaches and advises community members.

Guru

A *guru* in Hindu and Buddhist traditions is a personal spiritual teacher or holy man who is held in very high esteem. Generally *guru* is neither an official position nor an honorific, but as a form of respectful address it is sometimes combined with a given or family name:

> Guru (given name)
> Guru (surname)

Guru was a title for the founding prophets of the Sikhs: The *Ten Gurus of Sikhism*. But *guru* is no longer an office or title used with contemporary Sikhs.

Head of Government

A *head of government* is the highest office in a country's government.
In many governments the *head of government* is also *chief of state*.

COUNTRY	FORM OF GOVERNMENT	CHIEF OF STATE & HEAD OF GOVERNMENT
United States	Republic	**President**
Brunei Darussalam	Sultanate	**Sultan**
Saudi Arabia	Monarchy	**King**

In parliamentary governments the *chief of state* may hold various titles, but the *head of government* is usually a *prime minister*.

COUNTRY	FORM OF GOVERNMENT	CHIEF OF STATE	HEAD OF GOVERNMENT
Albania	Parliamentary republic	President	**Prime minister**
Japan	Constitutional monarchy	Emperor	**Prime minister**
Sweden	Constitutional monarchy	King	**Prime minister**
United Kingdom	Constitutional monarchy	Queen	**Prime minister**
Brunei	Constitutional sultanate	Sultan	**Prime minister**
Qatar	Constitutional emirate	Amir	**Prime minister**
Luxembourg	Constitutional monarchy	Grand Duke	**Prime minister**

However, the *head of government* can have many titles.

COUNTRY	FORM OF GOVERNMENT	CHIEF OF STATE	HEAD OF GOVERNMENT
Albania	Parliamentary republic	President	**Prime minister**
Germany	Federal republic	President	**Chancellor**
China	People's republic	President	**Premier**
Holy See/Vatican	Ecclesiastical	Pope	**Secretary of state**
Guernsey	British crown dependency	Queen	**Chief minister**
Monaco	Principality	Prince	**Minister of state**
Liechtenstein	Constitutional monarchy	Prince	**Head of government**

See also *Chief of State*.

Head of Mission

The *head of mission* is the person sent by one *chief of state* to represent his or her country's national interests to another *chief of state*.

Head of State

See *Chief of State*.

HEI – HON

Heir Apparent

Heir apparent is the descriptive term for, or the position held by, the first in line to inherit a royal crown or noble title. The *crown prince* or *crown princess* in a kingdom, grand duchy, emirate, or principality is an *heir apparent*.

Hereditary Peer

A *hereditary peer* is a person whose noble title is inherited, and as the holder of a noble title the person is a *peer* and member of the *peerage*. This contrasts with a *life peer* who is made a peer for his or her lifetime and whose title lapses at death.

Hereditary Prince, Hereditary Princess

See *Prince*.

Hierarchy

A *hierarchy* is a system that ranks one person or thing above another. *Hierarchical titles* are titles within an organized body.

Almost every organization has a *hierarchy*, but the term *hierarchical title* is frequently associated with ecclesiastical officials in successive *ranks* or *orders* within a church.

High Commissioner

A *high commissioner* is a high-ranking appointed official with the rank of *ambassador*. *High commissioners*, *ambassadors*, and *nuncios* are of equal status. Within a commonwealth of nations, a *high commissioner* rather than an *ambassador* is sent by one member nation to another as the highest diplomatic representative. For example:

- As members of the United Kingdom, Canada and Australia exchange *high commissioners* rather than *ambassadors*.
- A *high commissioner* is the highest representative of the French president to New Caledonia, a territorial collectivity of France.

A *high commission* is a *diplomatic mission* of one commonwealth country in another. For example, Canada has a *high commission* in Canberra, Australia, rather than an *embassy*. At the United Nations, *high commissioners* head *commissions* on various topics such as human rights or refugees.

High Steward

High steward is an honorary or ceremonial office in British academia. *High Steward of (university)* could be used as a very formal salutation, but otherwise it is used for identification after the name, not as an honorific.

Highness

Highness is a title and form of address for a noble person with the rank of *prince* or *princess* in a kingdom, a chief-of-state *prince* in Qatar and Kuwait, the chief-of-state *rulers* of the emirates that form the United Arab Emirates, and certain heirs apparent. It is used with the possessive pronouns *your, their, his* and *her*. Abbreviated forms of *highness* include:

H.H.	*His/Her Highness*
T.H.	*Their Highnesses*

His Honor, Her Honor, Your Honor

His/Her Honor is a diminutive version of *the Honorable*, the *courtesy title* used when addressing certain high officeholders, especially judges and mayors.

In the United States *Your Honor* is used in direct conversation with judges and mayors in place of their names. In writing they are addressed as *the Honorable (full name)* and identified by *office*.

In Commonwealth nations, *His/Her Honour* is a courtesy title used in writing and conversation. Example: Patricia Kennett, Chief Judge of Queensland, Australia, is introduced as *Her Honour Chief Judge Patricia Kennett*.

Holy Father

Holy Father is a form of address used in conversation with the *pope* of the Roman Catholic Church. *Most Holy Father* is used in the salutation of a letter.

See also *Pope*.

Holy See

The *Holy See* is another name for the *State of the Vatican City*. A *see* is the domain of a *bishop*.

Honorable

The Honorable is a *courtesy title* used with persons of high rank.

In any written form or in a formal introduction *the Honorable* is always used before a full name: *The Honorable (full name), member of the House of Representatives from Maine*, or *the Honorable (full name), senator from New York*.

It is also used while speaking to refer in the third person to an official who would be addressed as *the Honorable*: *"The honorable member retired after a distinguished career in the House of Representatives"* or *"... according to the honorable senator from New York."*

In the United States, elected officials and those appointed by the President of the United States are addressed with the courtesy title *the Honorable* while in office and after completion of service. In other countries the title is typically used only with current governmental officeholders and its continued use is frequently limited to only the very highest, most decorated officials.

Other related *courtesy titles* include: *the Right Honorable* and *the Most Honorable*.

Honorific

An *honorific*, or *honorific prefix*, is a grammatical form in spoken or written address used as a sign of respect. Some authors apply *honorific* only to ordinary terms such as *Mr.*, *Mrs.*, *Ms.*, and *Miss* and call all more specific terms — *Dr.*, *professor*, *chief*, and *commissioner* — *courtesy titles*.

IMA – KNI

Imam

Imam is an Arabic title and honorific for an Islamic religious leader. Among the Shiite Muslims *imam* is a high title for a recognized religious leader, scholar, and teacher. Among the Sunni Muslims an *imam* is a prayer leader at a mosque.

Imperial Majesty

Imperial majesty is a title and form of address for an *emperor* or *empress*. It is used with the possessive pronouns such as *your*, *his*, and *her*. Abbreviated forms of *imperial majesty* include:

H.I.M.   *His/her imperial majesty*
T.I.M.   *Their imperial majesties*

Initialisms

Initialisms, or *post-nominal abbreviations*, are strings of letters that appear after a person's name denoting decorations, honors, and affiliations. *Initialisms* are written without periods, with a comma separating two or more sets of *initialisms*. An *initialism* is not pronounced as a word or recited as letters: The honor it stands for is fully spoken. There are dozens to hundreds of *initialisms* per country, and more than 190 countries, so there are too many *initialisms* to list. But the meaning of each is now easy to find on the internet. Examples include:

- (Full name), AO   *AO = Officer of the Order of Australia*
- (Full name), CPA   *CPA = Certified Public Accountant*
- (Full name), MD   *MD = Doctor of Medicine*
- Mr. (full name), MP   *MP = Member of Parliament, Canada*
- The Hon. (full name), PC   *PC = Member of the Privy Council, Canada*
- (Full name), PhD   *PhD = Doctor of Philosophy*
- The Reverend (full name), SJ   *SJ = Member, Society of Jesus (the Jesuits)*

Interest Section

An *interest section* is an office responsible for handling the national and diplomatic affairs of **country A,** which is housed in the *embassy* of **country B** located in **country C**, when **country A** and **country C** do not have diplomatic relations.

Internuncio

An *internuncio* is an ecclesiastical *envoy*. See also *Nuncio*.

Interpreter

An *interpreter* is a person who translates conversation orally and simultaneously from one language into another language. See also *Translator*.

J

Judge, Justice

Judge is an office, title, and honorific for a person who hears cases in a court of law. *Justice* is a title and honorific for a *judge* of an appellate court.

A *chief justice* is the head judge in a national supreme court. In lower courts the highest-ranking *judge* is most often called a *chief judge*.

Junior Officer

A *junior officer* is a *commissioned officer* assigned to a unit of a larger force as its leader. For example, in the U.S. Navy a *junior officer* has the rank of *second lieutenant* or *first lieutenant*. In the U.S. Army, Air Force, or Marine Corps a *junior officer* is a *captain* or *lieutenant*.

Justice of the Peace

A *justice of the peace* is an elected or appointed local official who can witness documents, perform marriages, and enforce local laws. The official is lower than a *judge* of a high court and is sometimes equivalent to a *magistrate*.

Justices of the peace, who use the post-nominal abbreviation JP, are not generally required to have a formal legal education in order to qualify for the office.

K

King, Queen

King is the masculine title of a royal *chief of state*. The area ruled by a *king* is a *kingdom*. The title is not used as an honorific: The royal person is addressed as *Your Majesty*.

Queen is the title for a woman who holds the title in her own right, or is the wife of a *king* and receives the *courtesies* of a *queen*.

King Consort

See *Consort*.

Knight

Knight is, except in rare instances, a non-hereditary title conferred by a sovereign *chief of state* in recognition of personal merit or service to the country.

KUN – LOR

There are different levels of *knighthood*, *e.g.*, *knight grand cross*, *knight commander*, or *knight grand commander*, but each is addressed as a *knight*: His or her exact level of honor is specified by the post-nominal abbreviation.

There are sometimes lower honors within the *order of knighthood* such as *companion*, *lieutenant*, or *member*. These individuals are not addressed as *knights*, but do use the post nominals of their honor.

Knighthood is still granted in some royal states including Denmark and the Netherlands. In Great Britain the knight is styled as *sir* or *lady/dame*.

Related terms include:

- French: *chevalier*
- German: *ritter*
- Italian: *cavaliere*
- Portuguese: *cavaleiro*
- Spanish: *caballero*

See also *Companion*.

Kun

Kun, a Japanese honorific, is used in conversation as a suffix to the *family name*. It is used when addressing someone of a lower or junior status; by men when addressing other men of the same or equal status; and by teachers, parents, and relatives when addressing boys: *(Surname)-kun*.

Lady Mayoress

Lady Mayoress is a traditional though unofficial title used when addressing the wife of a *lord mayor* of a city. No corresponding title is given to the husband of a *lord mayor*.

Last Name

A *family name* placed at the end of a name is called a *last name*.

Lawyer

See *Attorney* and *Esquire*.

Leader of Government

Leader of Government is a title for the head of the majority party of a house of Parliament.

For example, in Canada the *Leader of Government* in the Senate is the leader of the majority party and is a member of the *prime minister's* cabinet. There is also a *Leader of Government* in the House of Commons, more commonly called the *Government Leader*. The officeholder is addressed as a member of the assembly and identified by *office*.

Leader of Government Business

Leader of Government Business is the title of the Cayman Islands' *head of government* (equivalent to a *prime minister*). The *Leader of Government Business* is addressed as *the Honourable* and identified by *office*.

Leader of the Opposition

Leader of the Opposition is a title for the head of the minority party of a house of parliament.

For example, in Australia the *Leader of the Opposition* in the Senate is the leader of the minority party and a member of the *prime minister's cabinet*. There is also a *Leader of the Opposition* in the Australian House of Commons.

Legate

A *legate* is a representative sent on a mission. Neither an office nor title, the term is most often used with a cleric who is a *diplomatic representative* of the *pope*.

Legation

A *legation* is a diplomatic mission in a foreign country of lower rank than an *embassy*. It is headed by a *diplomat* of lower rank than an *ambassador*, such as a *minister*.

Lieutenant

A *lieutenant* is a junior to mid-level officer in an organization.

Lieutenant Governor

See *Governor*.

Life Peer

A *life peer* is a person given a noble title for use during his or her lifetime. A *life peer's* title lapses upon his or her death, unlike a *hereditary peer's* title, which is inherited. In the United Kingdom, a *life peer* is a member of the House of Lords and (usually) has the rank of *baron*.

Lord and Lady

Lord and *lady* are honorifics for certain nobles, high officials, and *bishops* in the Anglican Church.

In British practice, the title held by a nobleman may be a *place name*, a *family name*, a *surname of place name*, or other combination of names. In many instances nobles are addressed in speaking as: *Lord/Lady (the first name after the title)*, which can be either a place name or family name. For example:

THE TITLE HELD	ADDRESS
The Marquess of Bath (*Bath is a place name*)	Lord Bath
The Countess of Wessex (*Wessex is a place name*)	Lady Wessex
The Earl Suffolk and Berkshire (*place name*) *and* (*place name*)	Lord Suffolk
The Viscount Allenby of Migiddo (*family name*) *of* (*place name*)	Lord Allenby
The Baroness Amos (*Amos is a family name*)	Lady Amos
A Bishop of the Church of England	My Lord

LOR – MAR

Lord Mayor
Lord mayor is the title of the *mayor* of a larger city or of a special district within a city. The United Kingdom, Australia, Canada, Denmark, and Germany all have cities traditionally headed by *lord mayors*.

Lord Steward
The *Lord Steward* is a high office in the royal household of the United Kingdom. At state visits, banquets, and other important ceremonial occasions he presents guests to the monarch and his or her visitors. The *Lord Steward* is always a *peer* and is addressed by his personal title and identified by *office*.

Ma'am
Ma'am may be used in place of a name when addressing a woman. Most often used by a lower-ranking person addressing a higher-ranking person, it indicates deference.

Madam
Madam is used as a formal honorific (the equivalent of *Mr.*), most frequently when addressing a woman holding a high office. It is combined with the title held: *madam president* or *madam secretary*.

    Madam can also be used in direct address with a private citizen in place of her name, but such use is dramatic and done for emphasis.

Madame, Mademoiselle
Madame and *mademoiselle*, French honorifics, are the equivalents of *Mrs.* and *Miss*.

Magistrate
A *magistrate* is the judge of a Magistrate Court. In the United States, *magistrate* is an office held by a *judge* and the term is not used as an honorific. In Commonwealth nations *magistrate* is both an office and an honorific.

Mahatma
Mahatma is a Hindi honorific showing high respect for a person of great holiness and spirituality.

Maiden Name
When a woman changes her *family name* to that of her husband upon marriage, her former *family name* is called her *maiden name*.

LOR – MAR

Majesty

Majesty is a title and form of address used to address a *king* or *queen*. It is used with the possessive pronouns such as *your*, *his*, and *her*. Abbreviated forms of *majesty* include:

H.M.	*His/Her Majesty*
T.M.	*Their Majesties*

Marquess, Marchioness

Marquess is the British spelling for *marquis*, a noble title and honorific for the hereditary rank below *duke* and above *earl*. The domain of a *marquess* is a *marquessate*.

A *marchioness* is a noblewoman who holds the title in her own right or is the wife or widow of a *marquess*. The husband of a *marchioness* is not addressed with a *courtesy title* but as Mr. *(name)* unless he has his own title.

In other languages equivalent titles are:

- French: *marquis* and *marquise*
- German: *markgraf* and *markgräfin*
- Italian: *marchese* and *marchesa*
- Spanish: *marqués* and *marquesa*

See also *Lord, Lady*.

Marshal

A *marshal* is an official who carries out the policies and procedures of an organization.

When used as a title for a law enforcement official, *marshal* is equivalent to *constable* or *sheriff*. In the U.S. Marshals Service, an agency of the Department of Justice, *marshals* are responsible for the transport of prisoners and security for the U.S. district courts, and they also issue and enforce certain civil actions and processes.

A *fire marshal* is a high official who advises governments on fire codes, public safety, and fire administration. *Fire marshals* are identified as the *fire marshal of (jurisdiction)* but are addressed as Mr./Ms. *(name)* if they hold no other office, or as *Chief/Commissioner/etc. (name)* if they hold such a title in a firefighting organization.

At an event, a *marshal* or *grand marshal* is the highest ceremonial official.

A *marshal*, a traditional officer of the Royal Household of the Kingdom of Denmark, has the complete title of *marshal of the court*. In the United Kingdom, the *Marshal of the Diplomatic Corps* is a part of the *Lord Chamberlain's Office* and is a link between the monarch and the heads of foreign diplomatic missions.

Marshal is the title for the presiding officials in the upper and lower houses of the national assembly of Poland.

In the Australian Air Force *air marshals* are high-ranking officers: 011, *marshal of the Air Force*; 010, *air chief-marshal*; 09, *air marshal*; 08, *air vice-marshal*.

See also *Earl Marshal*.

MAS – MON

Master

Master is a traditional honorific for a boy who is not old enough to be addressed as *Mr.* It is used most frequently in an address on an envelope. Use of *master* outside conservative circles is considered old fashioned.

In the United Kingdom a *master* is also the head of a college, such as a constituent college of a university. For example, a *master* heads Pembroke College of Oxford University. *Dear Master of (college)* is used as a salutation, but otherwise the office is used for identification after the name, not as an honorific.

Master of the Horse

The *Master of the Horse* is an honorary post in the United Kingdom ceremonially responsible for the royal carriages and horses. The *Master of the Horse* is addressed by his personal title and identified by *office*.

Master of the Queen's Music

The *Master of the Queen's Music*, an honorary post in the United Kingdom, is the musical equivalent of *poet laureate*. The *Master of the Queen's Music* is addressed by his or her personal title and identified after the name by *office*.

Matronymic Names

A *matronymic name* incorporates the *given name* of a person's mother. A *matronymic name* is used by custom to emphasize ties to the mother or end ties with the father, or by personal preference.

The matronymic naming formula is applied as follows in Iceland:

- The complete name of Reynis, son of Anna Ericdottir, would be:

  (Son's given name) + (mother's given name + son) = Reynis Annason.

- The complete name of Anna, daughter of Anna Ericson, would be:

  (Daughter's given name) + (mother's given name + dottir) = Anna Annadottir.

See also *Patronymic Names*.

Mayor

Mayor is the title and honorific for the holder of the highest office in a city.

Mekko, Micco

Mekko and *micco* are variant spellings of the title and honorific of a high rank in certain Native American tribes. Both spellings translate as *king*. *Mekko* is the more frequent spelling among the Creek Tribes; *Micco* is more typical among the Seminole. The domain of a *mekko* or *micco* is a *tribal town*.

Metropolitan

Metropolitan is a title and honorific of a Christian Orthodox *bishop* for the churches in a city or *diocese*.

In the Roman Catholic Church *metropolitan bishop* is the title for an *archbishop* who oversees a number of *dioceses*. The title is used after the name in an introduction or on an official envelope for identification, but the officeholder is addressed as a *bishop*. See also *Bishop*.

MAS – MON

Middle Name
When a person has two *given names*, the second *given name* is called a *middle name*.

Military Attaché
A *military attaché*, usually a high-ranking officer, is an expert on military issues at a *diplomatic mission*.

Minister, Minister-Counselor, Chief Minister
A *minister* is a high-ranking government official or a diplomat.

In a parliamentary system the *cabinet* formed by the *prime minister* and the *ministers* forms the *government*. A *minister of (portfolio)* in a government's *council of ministers* or *cabinet* is in charge of a *ministry*, a government department. A *portfolio* is an area of a *minister's* responsibility such as foreign affairs or agriculture. Such ministers are frequently addressed as *Mr./Madame Prime Minister* or *Mr./Madame Minister*.

In diplomacy a *minister* or *minister-counselor* is a senior advisor to an *ambassador*, and is frequently the *deputy chief of mission*: the second highest officer. At a legation a *minister* would be the chief of the diplomatic mission, but few legations still exist.

Chief minister can also be the title of high elected office. In Monserrat, the leader of the majority party in the Legislative Council is the *head of government* and has the title of *chief minister*.

Mission
A *mission* is a generic term for an embassy or an official delegation of diplomats, civilians, and military personnel to a foreign country which functions under the supervision of an *ambassador*.

Monarch, Monarchy
A *monarchy* is a form of government with a single person as the sovereign *chief of state*. In a *constitutional monarchy* the role of the monarch may be ceremonial. An *absolute monarch* is *chief of state* and *head of government*.

A *monarch* reigns over a realm. Most *monarchs* inherit the office and hold it for life. Upon his or her death succession is to a predetermined *heir apparent*.

Monarchs can hold a variety of offices and use different titles including:

- Emperor/empress
- King/queen
- Sultan
- Grand duke/grand duchess
- Prince/princess

The *pope* is a *monarch* of an *ecclesiastical government*, elected by the College of Cardinals.

The *co-princes* of Andorra are *appointed monarchs*: One *co-prince is* appointed by the president of France, and the other *co-prince* (the Bishop of Urgell) is appointed by the Catholic Church.

MON – NON

Monk

A *monk* is a person who dedicates his life to prayer and contemplation, usually taking vows and leading an ascetic life in a monastery. A *monk* may be a *novice*, *brother*, or *priest*. The term is not used as an honorific.

Monsignor

Monsignor is an honorific for a priest in the Roman Catholic Church who has been appointed an honorary member of the pontifical family by the *pope*. When the designee is a *priest*, *monsignor* replaces *father* as the honorific: *Monsignor (full name)*. When the designee is a *bishop*, the form of address is: *Monsignor Bishop (full name)*.

Mother

See *Father* and *Prior*.

Mother Superior

See *Abbot*.

MP

MP is a post-nominal abbreviation for *Member of Parliament*, widely used by current members of a parliament. The initials MP appear after a member's name as in *(honorific) (full name)*, MP, or *the Honourable (full name)*, MP.

In bicameral parliaments, it is most often used in the lower house, *e.g.*, Canada's House of Commons.

MPP

MPP is a post-nominal abbreviation for *Member of the Provincial Parliament*, used by members of the Canadian provincial legislature in Ontario. It appears after the member's name in a complete form of address: *(Honorific) (full name)*, MPP.

Ms.

Ms. is an honorific for a woman that does not specify marital status. It is frequently used in the business arena regardless of what the woman chooses to call herself in her private life.

In professional environments outside the United States Ms. is not ubiquitous: *Mrs. (woman's name)* and *Miss (name)* are common. In many countries *Mrs. (woman's name)* is used by working women without any implication of their marital status.

Mufti

Mufti is the title for an attorney who interprets Islamic law.

See also *Grand Mufti*.

MON – NON

Mullah, Mulla, Molla, Mollah

Mullah, mulla, molla, and *mollah* are variant spellings for a Farsi title and honorific of an Islamic teacher. A *mullah* is addressed as *Mullah (given name)*. A higher-ranking mullah is addressed as *Akhun (given name)*.

Nation

Nation refers to a *people* who share common customs, traditions, origins, history, and sometimes a language.

    See also *Country* and *State*.

n.b.

The abbreviation *n.b.* stands for *notez bien*: note well.

    The *n.b.* is written on the lower left-hand corner of a *calling card* to direct attention to a message written elsewhere on the card.

    See also *Calling Card*.

NCO

See *Non-Commissioned Officer*.

Nobles, Nobility

Nobles belong to a hereditary class with high social and political status. A member of a country's *nobility* holds a *noble title* of stepped rank such as *duke* or *duchess*, or *earl* or *countess*.

    Today the prevalence of *nobility* varies greatly from country to country.

- In countries where there are reigning monarchs, *e.g.,* Great Britain or Spain, the structure and forms of address used with nobility are intact.
- In Norway there is a reigning monarch, but *nobility* was abolished in 1821 with the plan that existing *noble titles* would continue until the line died out. Today just three *noble lines* continue.
- In France *nobility* was dissolved in 1789 as being incompatible with the equality of all citizens before the law. Thus in France (and in many other republics) *noble titles* continue as hereditary marks of honor with social status, but do not officially exist. The *aristocratic seat* may have been abolished but the forms of address relating to the *noble title* are sometimes used at the preference of the bearer.

Non-Commissioned Officer, Non-Commissioned Members

A *non-commissioned officer, non-commissioned member, noncom,* or *NCO* is an enlisted member of an armed force.

NOT – PAR

Notary

A *notary*, or *notary public*, is an office whose holder is empowered to witness signatures, certify a document's validity, and take depositions.

Notary or *notary public* is used after the name in an introduction or on an official envelope for identification, but not as an honorific. In an introduction the fact that the person is a notary would be included for specificity: *I would like to introduce the notary who will witness our signatures today, Ms. (surname)*.

Nun

A *nun* is a woman who has taken vows and lives in a convent, abbey, cloister, priory, or monastery. The term *nun* is sometimes used to specify a cloistered person, while *sister* is used to specify a person dedicated to teaching or ministering to the sick, homeless, or needy. Both are addressed as *Sister (name)*.

Nunciature

A *nunciature* is the office of a *nuncio*, a diplomatic representative of the *Holy See*.

Nuncio

A *nuncio* is a diplomatic representative of the *Holy See*, an *ambassador* of the *pope*. A *nuncio* is a *bishop* or *archbishop* and is addressed with *courtesies* of his rank and identified after his name as a *nuncio*. *Nuncios, high commissioners*, and *ambassadors* are of equal status.

An *internuncio* is a diplomatic representative, or envoy, of the *pope* of a rank just below *nuncio*, equivalent to *minister*.

Oblast

An *oblast* is a geographic area and administrative division which most directly translates as *province*. For example, the Russian Federation is composed of 48 *oblasts* including Kaliningrad, Leningrad, Moscow, Novgorod, and Volgograd.

In an introduction the *oblast* would be included for specificity: *Member of the Russian Federation's Federal Assembly from (oblast), Mr./Ms. (surname)*.

Other countries with *oblasts* include Bulgaria, Kyrgyzstan, and Ukraine.

Okrug

An *okrug* is a geographic area and administrative division which most directly translates as *county* or *district*. For example, the Russian Federation is composed of seven *okrugs* including Aga Buryat, Chukotka, Khanty-Mansi, Koryak, Nenets, Ust-Orda Buryat, and Yamalo-Nenets.

In an introduction the *okrug* would be included for specificity: *Member of the Russian Federation's Federal Assembly from (okrug), Mr./Ms. (surname)*.

Other countries with *okrugs* include Bulgaria and Serbia.

Ombudsman
An *ombudsman* is an office with the responsibility to receive complaints for an organization from those outside the organization. Not an honorific, the term is used after the name for identification.

P

Pandit, Pundit
Pandit or *pundit* is a Hindu honorific for a learned person or *priest*. It precedes the name, *Pandit (name)*, or can be used in place of the name in conversation as in *Good morning, Pandit.*

Papal Nuncio
A *papal nuncio* or *apostolic nuncio* is a diplomatic representative of the *Holy See* with the rank of *ambassador*. See also *Nuncio.*

Paramount Ruler
Paramount ruler is the most frequent translation of *Yang DiPertuan Agung*, the elected Malaysian royal *chief of state*. It also translates as *He who is made Supreme Lord, and Supreme Head.* In English the office is often less specifically referred to as *king.*

Parish
A *parish* is a geographic area and administrative division of some Christian churches. Use of a *parish* in an introduction could be: *The Reverend (full name), pastor of (name of parish) in (city).*

A *parish* is also a geographic area and administrative division of a government. Barbados is divided into 11 *parishes* and one city. Other countries similarly divided into *parishes* include Andorra, Antigua and Barbuda, Dominica, Grenada, and Montserrat. The state of Louisiana is divided into 64 *parishes*.

In an introduction the *parish* would be included for specificity: *Member of Barbados Parliament from (parish), Mr./Ms. (surname).*

Parliament
A *parliament* is an elected legislative body. A country that has a *parliament* is said to have a *parliamentary form of government.*

Parliaments can be unicameral or bicameral, and can have elected or appointed members. *Parliament* is rarely the name of a legislative body: In the United Kingdom *Parliament* is the institution created by the combination of the House of Lords and the House of Commons, as in the United States *Congress* is the institution created by the combination of the Senate and the House of Representatives.

PAR – PF

Legislative bodies that call themselves a *parliament* often employ the *parliamentary system* in which the *head of government* (usually a *prime minister*) is elected by and responsible to *parliament*.

See also MP and *Westminster System*.

Parliamentary Secretary

A *parliamentary secretary* is an assistant to a *minister for (portfolio)* in a *cabinet*. The office is equivalent to an *assistant-minister* or *deputy-minister* in the executive department. *Parliamentary secretaries* are chosen from members of parliament.

Passport

A *passport* is an official document issued to a person by his or her government certifying citizenship and requesting foreign governments to grant the individual safe passage, lawful aid, and protection while under that government's jurisdiction.

Patriarch

A *patriarch* is the highest *bishop* of a Christian Orthodox church, such as the Armenian, Coptic, Greek, Syrian, or Russian Orthodox Churches.

The *patriarch's* title includes the city of his seat, *e.g.*, the Ecumenical Patriarch of Constantinople. His authority is over a domain called a *see*, as in the *See of Constantinople*. Other *sees* include Antioch, Alexandria, Moscow, and Jerusalem.

Both *Your Holiness* and *Your Beatitude* are used to address patriarchs. The titles are roughly equivalent, and which is preferred is a matter of tradition and translation. For example, in Slavonic, the liturgical language of the Eastern Orthodox Church, the *Patriarch of Moscow* is addressed as *blazhenstvo*. *Blazhenstvo* translates *blessed*, which might have implied the use of *Your Beatitude*, but in English *Your Holiness* is traditional address for this patriarch.

Patronymic Names

A *patronymic name* identifies the given name of a person's father. A *patronymic name* is not a *family name*. A *patronymic name* is a capsule description: Reynis Armannson and Anna Armanndottir are the son and daughter of Armann.

In the *patronymic* tradition the complete name of Reynis, son of Armann Ericson, would be:

- *(Son's given name)* + *(father's given name + son)* = *Reynis Armannson*

The complete name of Anna, daughter of Armann Ericson, would be:

- *(Daughter's given name)* + *(father's given name + dottir)* = *Anna Armanndottir*

Many *family names* were originally *patronymic names* that now pass unchanged from generation to generation. *Family names* originating in patronymic names include those formed using:

- Arabic: *bin-, bint-, ibn-, Al-*
- Aramaic: *Bar-, ben*
- Armenian: *-ian, -yan*

- Danish: *-sen*
- Dutch: *de, der, in het van de, van* (lowercase letters in Dutch)
- English: *-son*
- Gaelic: *Fitz-, Ma-, Mac-, Mc-, O'-*
- Polish: *-ski, -ska, -cki, -dzki*
- Romanian: *-eanu, -escu*
- Russian: *-ev* and *-eva, -in* and *-ina, -ov* and *-ova, -ovich, et al.*
- Spanish: *-ez*
- Turkish: *-oglu*

PC
PC is the *post-nominal abbreviation* for Privy Council, an elite body in the United Kingdom and Commonwealth of Nations whose members (*privy counsellors*) advise a *monarch*.

See *Privy Council.*

p.c.
The abbreviation *p.c.* for *pour condoléance* is written on a *calling card* to express sympathy.

See also *Calling Card.*

Peer, Peerage, Peeress, Peers
Peers are the *nobles* of an imperial, royal, or noble state. In an imperial, royal, or noble state an individual is a *commoner*, a *peer*, or the *sovereign chief of state.*

Peer is the masculine form. *Peeress* is the feminine form used for a woman who holds the rank of *peeress* in her own right, or is the wife or widow of a *peer*. If the wife is not herself a *peer*, she uses the title as a *courtesy*. The husband of a *peer* is not given any of the *courtesies* of his wife's title and is addressed as Mr. *(name)*, unless he has his own title.

Life peers, appointed members of a *peerage*, are individuals of notable qualities, contributions, and ability who are designated *peers* for their lifetime. *Life peers* are ranked with *barons*.

The *peerage* includes all the *peers* in a particular country. In Great Britain the ranks of *peers* are: *duke/duchess, marquess/marchioness, earl/countess, viscount/viscountess,* and *baron/baroness*. In Spain, *grandee* is the equivalent term of *peer*.

Persona Non Grata
A *persona non grata* is an individual who is identified as unacceptable or unwelcome by the government.

p.f.
The abbreviation *p.f.* stands for *pour féliciter* (to congratulate).

The *p.f.* is written on the lower left-hand corner of a *calling card* to extend congratulations on national holidays and other special occasions.

See also *Calling Card.*

PFN – PP

p.f.n.a.

The abbreviation *p.f.n.a.* stands for *pour faire nouvel an* (Happy New Year).

The *p.f.n.a.* is written on the lower left-hand corner of a *calling card* to extend New Year greetings.

See also *Calling Card*.

Plenipotentiary

A *plenipotentiary* is a diplomatic representative who holds full power to conduct matters of state for his or her government. The term describes a representative sent by a *chief of state* who has been recognized by a receiving *chief of state*. The fully accredited diplomat is an *ambassador extraordinary and plenipotentiary*.

p.m.

The abbreviation *p.m.* stands for *pour memo ire* (to remind).

The *p.m.* is one of many abbreviations written on the lower left-hand corner of a *calling card*.

See also *Calling Card*.

Poet Laureate

A *poet laureate* is a designated official poet for a nation, state, or city. In the United States an office is appointed by the Librarian of Congress and titled the *Poet Laureate Consultant in Poetry to the Library of Congress*. In Canada the office is the *Canadian Parliamentary Poet Laureate*. In the United Kingdom the *Poet Laureate* is an honorary royal post awarded to a poet whose work is deemed to be of national significance.

The holders of the offices are addressed by their personal title or *Mr./Ms./Mrs./Professor/etc. (name)* and identified by *office*.

Police Officer, Policeman, Policewoman

A *police officer*, *policeman*, or *policewoman* is a member of a police department.

The highest administrative official in a department is usually a *commissioner of police* or *chief of police*. A *commissioner* is addressed as Mr./Madam Commissioner, or less formally as *Commissioner (name)*. A *chief* is addressed as *Chief (name)*.

Deputy commissioner, *deputy chief*, and *deputy chief (for portfolio)* are among the other ranks and honorifics used by police officials. The full title, *e.g.*, *deputy chief*, is used as an honorific.

The titles of lower administrative offices are not used as honorifics. Address these individuals as *Mr./Ms. (name)* and identify by *office*.

Police officers use various paramilitary ranks to structure their hierarchy: *captain*, *commander*, *lieutenant*, *sergeant*, and *officer*. Use the individual's rank as an honorific in every form of direct address.

Many former police officials use their ranked honorific for life, but such use is at the preference of the bearer.

See also *Sheriff*.

Pope, Pontiff

Pope and *pontiff* are equivalent titles for the *chief of state* of the *Holy See* (Vatican City) and head of the Roman Catholic Church. The office of the *pope* is formally called the *pontificate* and informally called the *papacy*. While the *pope* is elected, he is ranked as royalty.

Pope is an informal title. The *pope's* formal title is: Bishop of Rome, Vicar of Christ, Successor of the Prince of the Apostles, Supreme Pontiff of the Universal Church, Patriarch of the West, Primate of Italy, Archbishop and Metropolitan of the Roman Province, Sovereign of the State of Vatican City, and Servant of the Servants of God.

Pope of Rome is an infrequently used title for the *pope*, focusing on his authority as the *bishop* of Rome and his occupying the *see* of Rome.

Pope is sometimes used as an honorific in written forms of address, *Pope (name and number)*, but the most formal address is not by name but by title of the office.

Holy Father is used in place of his name in direct address with the *pope*.

Pope is also the title of the head of the Coptic Church, *e.g.*, the *Coptic Pope* or *Pope and Patriarch of Alexandria and All Africa*.

Portfolio, (*portfolio*)

An official's area of responsibility is called a *portfolio*.

Sometimes the *portfolio* is written as part of a title:

- Minister *of Foreign Affairs*
- Secretary *of Agriculture*
- Parliamentary Secretary *for Human Rights*

Other times the *portfolio* is written in parentheses, clarifying the range of office:

- Secretary of State (*Foreign Affairs and International Trade*)
- Secretary of State (*Parliamentary Affairs*)

Post Nominal, Post-nominal Abbreviation, PN

A *post nominal*, or *post-nominal abbreviation*, is a set of initials placed after a person's name to note honorary degrees, honors, decorations, medals, affiliations, and religious orders. *Post nominals* are usually written without periods, with a comma separating two or more sets of *post nominals*.

Post nominals are used with the full name in an address on an envelope or letter. Except for MP (member of Parliament) and PC (Privy Counsellor), they are rarely used socially or on place cards.

In an introduction, *post nominals* are never pronounced as a word or recited as letters. The honor they stand for is fully spoken.

p.p.

The abbreviation *p.p.* stands for *pour presenter*: to introduce or to present.

The *p.p.* is written on the lower left-hand corner of a senior officer's *calling card* when it accompanies the *calling card* of a subordinate officer.

See also *Calling Card*.

PPC – PRE

p.p.c.
The abbreviation *p.p.c.* stands for *pour prendre conge*: to say good bye.

The *p.p.c.* is written on the calling card to indicate one is leaving town. See also *Calling Card*.

p.r.
The abbreviation *p.r.* stands for *pour remercier*: to express thanks.

The *p.r.* is written on the lower left-hand corner of a calling card to express thanks for a gift or courtesy, or to acknowledge a message of congratulations. See also *Calling Card*.

Prebendary
In the Church of England/Anglican Church *prebendary* is an honorary title for a *canon* at a cathedral or collegiate church. The individual would be addressed by the hierarchical form of address he or she is entitled to and identified after his or her name as a *prebendary*.

Precedence
Precedence is the preferential order, rank, or importance granted to individuals in ceremonies and on social occasions.

At an event *precedence* determines the order in which individuals are received or seated, have their names listed in a program, or are dealt with in any situation where an order is established. In forms of address *precedence* determines who is introduced first among several individuals, who is introduced to whom, or who is listed first on a joint invitation.

Precedence is determined in a number of ways. Neither gender nor age are considerations. Among those who hold equivalent official positions, *precedence* is usually determined by length of service or longest history. Some examples follow:

- *Precedence* among officials of the same rank is often determined by which official has served the longest or has the earliest date of appointment: Precedence among members of the International Olympic Committee is determined by the date of their election to the committee.
- *Precedence* among officials of the same rank is often determined by the date of their organization's establishment. In the United States, among state officials of the same rank outside of their state, *precedence* is determined by the date of their state's admission to the union.
- *Precedence* among officials of the same rank is often determined by the location of the interaction. In the United States, a governor in his or her own state outranks all other officials.
- When all else is equal, *precedence* can be established alphabetically by surname.

For example, precedence in some groups is determined as follows:
- *Former Officials:* After current officials.
- *Active-duty Military:* By date of serving in the rank.
- *Retired Military:* After active-duty members of the same rank.
- *Senate-Confirmed Civilians:* By the date of appointment to the position.

- *State Officials:* States generally follow the federal model of precedence.
- *City Officials:* Elected officials first, followed by appointed officials, then city employees.
- *Foreign Officials:* Based on their U.S. counterparts.
- *American Indian Tribes:* By rank after federal, before state officials.

Prefect

A *prefect* is an official whose traditional authority is over a *prefecture*. However, not all *prefects* serve over that jurisdiction. For example, to *collectivities* of France, including Saint Barthelemy, Mayotte, or St. Martin, the appointed representative of the president of the Republic of France is a *prefect*. In Romania a *prefect* is the representative of the central government to local governments.

In an introduction *prefect* is sometimes used as an honorific: *Prefect (name)*, or *Mr./Mrs./etc. (name), the prefect of ...*

Prefecture

A *prefecture* is a geographic area and administrative division in many countries, comparable to a *state*. For example, Greece is divided into 51 *prefectures* and one *autonomous region*. Other countries divided into *prefectures* include the Central African Republic, Chad, Guinea, and Japan.

Traditionally a *prefecture* is the domain of a *prefect*; however, today *prefects* and *prefectures* exist independently.

In an introduction the *prefecture* would be included for specificity: *Member of the Greek Parliament from (name of prefecture)...*

Prelate

Prelate is not a specific office, title, or honorific but a senior member of the clergy with jurisdiction over an area or group. For example, an *archbishop* or *bishop* who has authority over the lower clergy is a *prelate*.

Premier

A *premier* is a high official in a *parliamentary government*.

In some instances *premier* is the title of the office. For example, in the Republic of China and Bermuda, a *premier* is the head of government. In Australian states such as Queensland, Tasmania, Victoria, and Western Australia, a *premier* is the head of the state government. In these cases, *premier* is sometimes used as an honorific, *Premier (surname)*, and is used in conversation in place of the name.

In other instances it is used as a generic term for a *head of government*, as a synonym for *prime minister* or *chancellor*. A newspaper might report that the "*Premier of Bhutan Visits the United Nations*," and in actuality the visiting *head of government* holds the office of *prime minister*.

Presbyter

A *presbyter* is an office held by a *priest* in a Christian Orthodox church, usually serving at a *parish*. A *presbyter* is addressed as a *priest*, and the office is included as identification after the name on an envelope or in an introduction.

PRE – PRI

A *presbyter* is also the title of a lay *elder* in the Presbyterian Church. In this case, the title is used after the name in an introduction or on an official envelope for identification, but not as an honorific.

President

President is an office and honorific with different precedence and duties in different situations.

A *president* is an officer, usually the highest, in a republic. Sometimes a president is *chief of state*, sometimes *head of government*, and sometimes both.

- A *president* is *chief of state* and *head of government* in Costa Rica, Mexico, and the United States.
- A *president* is the *chief of state* of the United Arab Emirates, with a *head of government* who is a prime minister.

A *president* is an executive officer, usually the highest, of an organization, firm, or corporation; college or university; state or republic.

- A *president* is the executive of the European Commission.
- *President* is the office of the highest judge of many national supreme courts.

A *vice president* is often the second highest officer after a president.

President is a title in the Church of Jesus Christ of Latter-day Saints for several offices:

- *President* is the title and honorific for the head of the church, and for the head of the Quorum of the Twelve Apostles.
- *President* is the honorific for the first and second counselors in the First Presidency.
- *President* is also the title and honorific for the head of a stake, which is a territorial division consisting of a group of congregations, with each congregation called a ward.

A *president*, or *vice president*, who holds a high governmental office is formally addressed not by name but as *Mr./Madame President,* or *Mr./Madame Vice President. LDS presidents* are addressed as *President (name)*. Presidents of secular organizations are addressed as *Mr./Ms./etc. (name), President of ...*

Presidium

A *presidium* is an executive committee or administrative body in government, *e.g.,* the Presidium of the Council of Ministers *(the cabinet)* in Belarus.

Primate

Primate is an ecclesiastical term for an *archbishop* or *bishop* of the highest rank in a country or region. It is neither a title nor an honorific.

Prime Minister

A *prime minister* is a member of a national assembly (a parliament) chosen to lead the majority party (or coalition of parties) and form a *government*. The *prime minister* chooses other members of parliament to be *ministers of (portfolio)* to direct the *executive departments* or *ministries*. The *prime ministers* and *ministers* form a *council of ministers* or a *cabinet*. The *prime minister* is most often *head of government*: the highest among equals.

Prince, Princess

Prince and *princess* are the masculine and feminine titles held by noble persons of high hereditary rank in various countries. *Prince* and *princess* are used neither as honorifics nor in direct address.

Often a *prince/princess* is the child of a *monarch*, with *crown prince/crown princess* being the title of the *heir apparent* or next in line to the throne. *Royal princess* is a title given a daughter of the *monarch* who is ranked above her siblings.

In a *grand duchy*, *prince/princess* is the title of the *heir apparent*. For example, a *Hereditary Grand Duke of Luxembourg* would be *Prince (name)*.

In a *principality*, *prince/princess* is the title of the *monarch*. The *heir apparent* in Monaco holds the title *Hereditary Prince/Hereditary Princess (name) of Monaco*, and in Liechtenstein, the *heir apparent* is the *Hereditary Prince/Hereditary Princess (name) of Liechtenstein*.

Prince is also the title for a noble *chief of state* (a hereditary prince) in an emirate. These *princes* are addressed in writing with the honorific *sheikh*.

Princess is the title for a woman who holds the title in her own right, or is the wife of a *hereditary prince* and receives the *courtesies* of a *princess*.

Principal

A *principal* is the academic and administrative head of an elementary, middle, or high school. In formal address *principal* is used after the name for identification, but not as an honorific. Address as Mr./Ms. *(name)* and identify as *principal of (school)*. Informally *principal* is used as an honorific or in place of the name in conversation.

In the United Kingdom a *principal* is the head of a constituent college of a university: A *principal* heads Hertford College of Oxford University. *Dear Principal of (college)* is used as a salutation, but otherwise *principal* is included for identification after the name, not used as an honorific.

Principal is also used to describe a main investor, partner, or important member in a business enterprise. For example, an architect might be referred to as being a *principal* in an architectural firm. As such, a *principal* is addressed as Mr./Ms./etc. *(name)*, with the organizational title included after his or her name for identification.

Prior, Prioress

Prior or *prioress* is a religious rank just below an *abbot* or *abbess*. A *prior* or *prioress* may be second in command at an *abbey*, or head of a *priory*: a monastic community below the rank of an *abbey*.

Prior is also the title and honorific of the head of certain monastic religious orders, *e.g.*, the Franciscans.

A *prior* is addressed in a salutation as *The Reverend Prior* or *Dear Father Prior*, and in conversation as *Father Prior*. A *prioress* is addressed in a salutation as *The*

PRI – PUB

Reverend Prioress or *Dear Mother Prioress*, and in conversation as *Mother Prioress*. Otherwise, address by the person's hierarchical title and identify after the name as a *prior* or *prioress*.

Private Member, Private Senator

In a parliamentary government, *ministers*, *deputy ministers*, and *parliamentary secretaries* are chosen from the members of the national assembly. A *private member* is a national assembly member, *e.g.*, a member of *the House of Representatives in the Commonwealth of Australia*, who is not a *minister* or the holder of any ministerial office.

A *private senator* is a member of a parliamentary senate, *e.g.*, *the Senate of Australia*, who is not a *minister* or *parliamentary secretary*.

Privy Council

The *Privy Council* is an elite body in the United Kingdom and Commonwealth of Nations whose members, *privy counsellors*, advise a *monarch*.

Members of the Privy Council in the United Kingdom are addressed with the courtesy title *the Right Honourable*. A *privy counsellor* who is already entitled to the courtesy title *the Right Honourable* due to a personal rank, adds the post-nomial initials *PC* after his or her name.

Members of the Privy Council in Canada are addressed with the courtesy title *the Honourable* and use the post-nominal *PC* for life.

In Australia a similar body is called the *Federal Executive Council*.

Professor

Professor is an honorific and courtesy title extended to a member of a university or college faculty in conversation, regardless of his or her actual graded rank: *professor*, *associate professor*, or *assistant professor*. Normally, outside academic situations professors are addressed as *Mr./Ms./Dr. (name)*.

Outside the United States, *professor* is commonly used as an honorific outside academia: Current and former faculty will be addressed as *Professor (name)* both at and away from their institution. If the person has another personal title, it is used with *professor* to form a compound honorific:

- Envelope: *Professor Lord (name)*
  In conversation: *Lord (name)*
- Envelope: *Professor the Honourable (full name)*
  In conversation: *Professor (name)*
- Envelope: *The Reverend Professor (full name)*
  In conversation: *Professor (name)*
- Envelope: *Deputy Professor (full name)* (a deputy in a Chamber of Deputies)
  In conversation: *Professor (name)*

Prosecutor General

Prosecutor General is a high office, title, and honorific in a *ministry*, *secretariat*, or *department of justice* who heads national law enforcement by prosecution in court. The office of *Prosecutor General* exists in Finland, Ukraine, Russia, and many other countries.

Protocol
Protocol is a collection of customs and defined regulations for conduct, courtesy, ceremonies, and official actions among nations, *chiefs of state*, *heads of governments*, judicial officials of the courts, the armed services, and other hierarchical groups. The academic, political, corporate, fraternal, religious, and social arenas all require knowledge of protocol.

   Diplomatic protocol is the code of international courtesies governing the conduct of those in the diplomatic service. It defines procedural matters and precedence among diplomats. *Protocols* are rules, and tend to be fixed over time.

Protocol Officer
Protocol officers focus on the adherence to correct *precedence*, conventions, established customs, and courtesies at official meetings, events, and celebratory ceremonies. *Protocol officer* is most often an established office and title in the diplomatic, military, and governmental arenas.

Province
A *province* is a subdivision of a country. In *Canada* it is the equivalent of a U.S. *state*: Canada is divided into 10 *provinces* and three *territories*. Other countries subdivided into *provinces* include Argentina, Ecuador, Indonesia, Mongolia, Poland, Syria, and Ukraine.

   In *Belgium* a province is a small area similar to a *county* in the United States.

   In an introduction *province* would be included for specificity: *Member of Canada's Parliament from (province), Mr./Ms. (surname)*.

Provost
A *provost* in U.S. academia is a chief academic official at a college or university, responsible for the faculty and courses. In the United Kingdom a *provost* is also the headmaster of a constituent college of a university. For example, a *provost* heads Queen's College of Oxford University.

   A *provost* in some monastic orders, such as the Dominicans, Carmelites, and Augustinians is the head of a monastery and its community of monks.

   Provost of (college) could be used as a very formal form of address or salutation, but normally the officeholder is addressed as *Dr./Professor (name)* and identified as the *provost*.

Public Health Service
The U.S. Public Health Service has officers that are uniformed and addressed in the same way as the officer ranks of the U.S. Navy:

	USPHS OFFICE	ADDRESSED AS
0-10	Assistant Secretary for Health	Admiral
0-9	Surgeon General	Vice-admiral

PUI – RAN

	USPHS OFFICE	ADDRESSED AS
0-8	Deputy Surgeon General	Rear admiral (*upper half*)
0-7	Assistant Surgeon General	Rear admiral (*lower half*)
0-6	Director	Captain
0-5	Senior	Commander
0-4	Full	Lieutenant commander
0-3	Senior assistant	Lieutenant
0-2	Assistant	Lieutenant junior grade
0-1	Junior assistant	Ensign

There are no warrant officers or non-commissioned officers in the USPHS. Address by *rank*, use the post-nominal *USPHS*, and identify by *office*.

Puisne Justice, Puisne Judge

A *puisne justice* or *puisne judge* is a *justice* or *judge* who serves on a high court, but is not the *chief justice* or *chief judge* of the court. Other courts call the same rank *associate justice* or *associate judge*.

Puisne describes the rank or status of a *judge*, but it is not used in direct address.

Quarter

A *quarter* is a geographic area and administrative division, which is most often a town. For example, Saint Lucia is composed of 11 *quarters*: Anse-la-Raye, Castries, Choiseul, Dauphin, Dennery, Gros-Islet, Laborie, Micoud, Praslin, Soufriere, and Vieux-Fort.

In an introduction the *quarter* would be included for specificity: *Member of the Saint Lucia National Assembly from (quarter), Mr./Ms. (surname)*.

Queen's Piper

The *Queen's Piper* is an honorary post in the United Kingdom for a bagpiper who is a member of the military. As the *Queen's Piper* he becomes a member of the royal household whose principal duty is to play every weekday at 9 a.m. for about 15 minutes under the Queen's window when she is in residence at Buckingham Palace, Windsor Castle, the Palace of Holyroodhouse, or Balmoral Castle. He is responsible for the coordination of the 12 Army pipers who play around the table after state banquets. The *Queen's Piper* is addressed by his military rank, and identified after his name by his office.

Queen's Representative

Queen's representative is the title of the representative of the Queen of New Zealand to the Cook Islands. Address the officeholder by personal rank or Mr./Mrs. (name) and identify by office.

PUI – RAN

R

Rabbi

Rabbi is the title and honorific of the chief official and spiritual leader at a synagogue.

A *rabbi* leads a congregation, is trained in Jewish law and traditions, and supervises the religious life of the community. *Rabbis* at Reform and Conservative congregations may also have pastoral and administrative duties.

Ragi

A *ragi* is a musician who performs at Sikh services.

Raion, Rayon

A *raion* is a geographic area and administrative division, which most directly translates as *district*. For example, members of the Republic of Moldova's Parliament come from 32 *raions*, three *municipalities*, and one *autonomous territorial unit*.

In an introduction the *raion* would be included for specificity: *Member of the Republic of Moldova's Parliament from (raion), Mr./Ms. (surname)*.

Other countries with raions include: Azerbaijan, Belarus, Latvia, Russia, and Ukraine.

Raja, Rajah, Rani

Raja is the noble title for the ruler of the state of Perlis in Malaysia. The *Raja* is addressed as *Your Royal Highness*.

Rajah or *raja* is a title and honorific for a Hindu king or for a princely ruler in India. A *rani* or *ranee* is a noblewoman who holds the title in her own right or as the wife of a *rajah*.

Ranger

Ranger is a title for a member of various organizations.

A *ranger* in the U.S. Army Airborne Rangers is a member of an elite quick-response infantry unit.

A Texas *ranger* is a state highway law-enforcement officer.

A *park ranger* or *forest ranger* is an official responsible for managing and protecting an area of a forest or parkland. An *interpretive ranger* may teach history, stewardship, or ecological principles to park visitors.

A *ranger* is addressed by his or her rank or rating in the hierarchy rather than as a *ranger*, but may be referred to in the third person as *Ranger (name)* or informally addressed as *ranger* in place of his or her name in conversation.

RAN – RES

Rank, Rating

Rank is the level a position holds in a *stepped hierarchy*. The term is most often used in relation to a high position or elevated station: *She has the rank of president*.

A related term, *rating*, is most often associated with a lower position or station. In the armed services both *rank* and *rating* are used to describe the separate classes in graded levels of personnel:

• *Rank* is used for the hierarchy of officers.
• *Rating* is used for the hierarchy of enlisted personnel.

Reader

A *reader* is a lay person who recites lessons or prayers in a church service. *Reader* in the Church of Christ, Scientist, for example, is used after the name in an introduction or on an official envelope for identification, but not as an honorific.

Realm

See *Monarchy* and *Commonwealth Realm*.

Rector

A *rector* is an administrator in academia or a religious organization.

A *rector* in the Episcopal Church is a cleric in charge of a *parish*.

A *rector* in the Roman Catholic Church is a priest who is the spiritual and administrative head of a seminary or educational institution.

A *rector* in academia is the administrative head of a supervisory board. For example, at the University of Virginia the *rector* of the *Board of Visitors* is chairman of the board of regents. A *rector* can also be the headmaster of a constituent college of a university: A *rector* heads Exeter College of Oxford University.

Rector is used after the name in an introduction or on a business envelope for identification, but not as an honorific. It can also be used informally as an honorific in spoken address and in place of the name in conversation.

Regent

In government, *regent* is a descriptive term for a person who is the *chief of state* or *head of government* during the minority, absence, or disability of a *monarch, ruler*, or *governor*. It is not used as a title or honorific.

In 2004 the *chief of state* of Liechtenstein, the *Prince*, assigned *head of government* duties to his son, the *Hereditary Prince*. With this action the *Hereditary Prince* is described as being the *regent* for his father, the *Prince*.

At an institution or organization such as a state university, a *board of regents* is made up of a *chairman* and *members*, not *regents*. *Chairman of the board of regents* or *member of the board of regents* are used for identification after the name in an introduction or on an envelope. Use the honorifics *Dr./Mr./Ms./etc.*

Captain regent is the title of the two *co-chiefs of state* in San Marino. The *captains regent* are addressed as members of the Great and General Council (parliament), and are identified after their names as *Captain Regent of the Republic San Marino*.

RAN – RES

Representative

A *representative* is a person elected to, or occasionally appointed to fill a vacancy in, a legislative body. While not traditionally an honorific, *representative* is correctly used to describe members of a House of Representatives: *The Honorable Joel Broyhill is the representative from Virginia's tenth district in the House of Representatives.*

See also *Congressman.*

Republic

A *republic* is a form of government with a *chief of state* whose power is derived from elected representatives of voting citizens.

A *federal republic* is a federation of self-governing regions that are united by a single *federal government*, such as the *Federal Republic of Germany* or the *Federative Republic of Brazil.*

In official country names modifications of *republic* are implied, but the adjectives do not denote unique forms of government. Rather, they seek to define the country's unique stature among neighboring rivals and previous regimes. Examples include:

- Arab Republic of Egypt
- Bolivarian Republic of Venezuela
- Cooperative Republic of Guyana
- Democratic Republic of South Korea
- Democratic Socialist Republic of Sri Lanka
- Islamic Republic of Pakistan
- Oriental Republic of Uruguay
- People's Democratic Republic of Algeria
- People's Republic of China
- Socialist Republic of Vietnam
- United Republic of Tanzania

Reserve Judge

A *reserve judge* is a retired *judge* who will temporarily substitute for a current *judge* when illness, a need to recuse, or other commitments require a replacement. *Reserve judge* describes the status of a *judge*. It is not a title or honorific.

Residence

A *residence* is the home of the ambassador in a foreign country's capital.

See also *Embassy* and *Chancery.*

Resident Commissioner

Resident commissioner is an office held by the elected representative from Puerto Rico to the U.S. House of Representatives.

REV – SEN

Reverend
Reverend is a courtesy title used with any member of the clergy, but most often with pastors of congregations. In formal usage *reverend* is preceded by *the* and always used with a full name: *The Reverend (full name)*.

RHIP
RHIP is an abbreviation for the phrase: *Rank Has Its Privileges*.

Righteous Among the Nations
Righteous Among the Nations is a *courtesy title* for non-Jewish rescuers of Jews during the Holocaust, awarded and used by a department at Yad Vashem, the main Holocaust memorial in Israel.

Royal, Royalty
Royal persons belong to a hereditary class with the highest social and political status in countries with a ruling or titular *monarch* because they are members of the family or lineage of a *king/queen* or other sovereign *chief of state*. They are collectively referred to as *royalty*.

Royal Highness
Royal highness is a title and form of address for a royal chief-of-state or a person with the rank of *king, queen, sultan, ruler, raja, grand duke*, and certain heirs apparent. It is used with the possessive pronouns *your, their, his*, and *her*. Abbreviated forms of *royal highness* include:

> H.R.H.   *His/Her Royal Highness*
> T.R.H.   *Their Royal Highnesses*

In some countries *royal highness* is only used with the *monarch* and the *heir apparent*; other members of the family are styled as *Your Highness*.

In other countries *royal highness* is a title and courtesy title used with members of the entire *royal family*: a brother, sister, child, grandchild, aunt, or uncle of a *king* or *queen*. The sovereign *chief of state* can also grant *royal highness* as a title to an individual considered to be a member of the *royal household*.

Ruler
Ruler is a title for the *chief of state* in certain Malaysian states, *e.g.*, Negeri Sembilan, or in one of the city-states in the United Arab Emirates, *e.g.*, Dubai.

S

Saint
In the Roman Catholic Church *saint* describes a deceased person, officially recognized by canonization as entitled to public veneration and capable of inter-

ceding for people on earth. It is used before the name when referring to the person: *Saint Sebastian*.

In the Church of Jesus Christ of Latter-day Saints, *saint* is an informal term used by church members to refer, in the third person, to any other member of the church.

Secretary

Secretary is an office, and sometimes an honorific, with different *precedence* and duties in different situations.

Secretary

Secretary is an office, and sometimes an honorific, with different *precedence* and duties in different situations.

A *secretary* is an executive officer, usually the highest, of a governmental body or political party.

In the U.S. federal and state governments *secretary* is a title and honorific for the head of an *executive department* and member of the *president's* or a *governor's cabinet*. It is the equivalent of a *minister* who is head of a *ministry*, the term used in parliamentary governments. With such high federal positions the officeholder's name is not used, and he or she is addressed in a salutation as *Dear Mr./Madam Secretary* and in conversation as *Mr./Madam Secretary*. At a state level *Secretary (surname)* is more frequently used.

A *secretary's* office or department is sometimes referred to as a *secretariat*.

General secretary (or *secretary general*) is a title and honorific for the head of an organization, *e.g.*, in the United Nations, or for the head of administration in an organization, *e.g.*, a national central bank.

In diplomacy, *first secretary*, *second secretary*, and *third secretary* are graded titles for positions at a *mission*. The titles are used after the name for identification in an introduction or on an official envelope, but not as honorifics.

In a *board of advisors* or *board of directors* at an organization or corporation, *secretary* is a title for an administrative and clerical member. The title is used after the name for identification in an introduction or on an official envelope, but not as an honorific.

In political parties, cooperatives, and trade unions, *secretary*, *general secretary*, *secretary general*, or *first secretary* are all titles held by high executive officers. These titles are used for identification, but not as honorifics.

Secretary General

See *Secretary*.

See

A *see* is the domain of a *bishop*. See also *Holy See*.

Senator

Senator is the office, title, and honorific for a member of a legislative body called a *senate*. Senators are addressed in conversation as *Senator (name)*, and in many of the world's senates, a senator is addressed as *Mr./Madame Senator (name)*.

SEN – SIR

Senior Executive Service (SES)

Members of the *Senior Executive Service* are government employees who hold positions at the top of the U.S. Civil Service just below Presidential appointees. Federal executive-level positions above GS-15 are referred to as being in the *Senior Executive Service* or more commonly the SES.

Serene Highness

Serene highness is a title and form of address used with a noble chief-of-state of a principality with the rank of *prince* or *princess*, and with members of the princely family including a *hereditary prince* and *hereditary princess*. It is used with the possessive pronouns *your*, *their*, *his*, and *her*. Abbreviated forms of *serene highness* include:

> H.S.H.   *His/Her Serene Highness*
> T.S.H.   *Their Serene Highnesses*

Sergeant at Arms

A *sergeant at arms* is an officer in an organization, court, or legislature who keeps order during meetings. *Sergeant at arms* is not used as an honorific. The officer is addressed as *Mr./Ms. (name)* and identified by his or her office.

Serjeant

Serjeant is a variant spelling of *sergeant*, as in the *serjeant-at-arms of the Australian House of Representatives*. The *serjeant-at-arms* is responsible for security and is the custodian of the mace, the symbol of authority of the House and the Speaker.

Sexton

Sexton is an office of a person charged with the maintenance of a church building and/or a cemetery. *Sextons* also serve at municipal cemeteries.

Sexton is used after the name in an introduction or on a business envelope for identification, but not as an honorific.

Shadow (Official)

A *shadow (official)* is an unofficial officeholder. In the government a member of an opposition party may hold an office of *shadow minister* to provide an opposition view to the party-in-power's *minister*. *Shadow ministers* form a shadow cabinet in parallel to the cabinet formed by the party-in-power's ministers.

For example, in the Parliament of New South Wales, Australia, Mr. James Constance, MP, a member of the Legislative Assembly, is *Shadow Minister for Aging*. He is a member of the Liberal Party while the party in power is the Australian Labor Party. *The Honourable Kristina Keneally*, MP, a member of the Australian Labor Party, is the *Minister for Aging*.

The District of Columbia, which has no representation in the U.S. Senate, has elected a *shadow senator* to highlight its lack of an official senator.

Sheikh, Sheikha

Sheikh, also spelled *shaikh*, *shaykh*, or *sheik*, is a masculine Arabic honorific and sometimes a title. A corresponding feminine honorific is *sheikha*. The precise use of *sheikh* varies from country to country, so check for local tradition.

Sheikh is often an honorific for any elder, scholar, or revered old man. For instance, any man more than 60 years of age might be addressed as *Sheikh (name)*.

Sheik is an honorific for a Shiite cleric.

Sheikh is also an honorific for a noble *prince* or *emir*, who is addressed as *His Highness Sheikh (name)*, or a member of the ruling family, who is addressed simply as *Sheikh (name)*.

Sheriff, High Sheriff, Deputy Sheriff

Sheriff is a title and honorific for a law enforcement officer of a city or county.

In some jurisdictions a *sheriff* is the highest law enforcement official.

Where a *chief of police* or *police commissioner* is the highest official, the *sheriff* assumes tasks such as keeping the jail, transporting prisoners, providing court-house security, serving summonses, and running auctions of foreclosed property.

In nearly every instance the *sheriff* is elected and is addressed as *the Honorable (full name)*, and identified as *Sheriff of (jurisdiction)*. Appointed sheriffs are also addressed as *the Honorable*.

A *deputy sheriff* is a law enforcement officer working for the *sheriff*. A *deputy sheriff* is hired by the sheriff and is not addressed as *the Honorable*. Many *deputy sheriffs* have ranks such as *lieutenant*, *sergeant*, and *corporal*. Address these officers as *(rank) + (name)* and identify them as being a *member of the office of the sheriff* or *sheriff's department*. If the officer's rank is *deputy sheriff*, he or she is addressed as *Deputy Sheriff (name)* in writing and in a formal introduction, and *Deputy (name)* in conversation.

A *high sheriff* is a law-enforcement official in Great Britain.

Shri, Shrimati

Shri and *shrimati* are the masculine and feminine Indian (Sanskrit) honorifics for Mr. and Mrs.

Sir, Lady, Dame

In the United Kingdom and Commonwealth, *sir* and *dame* are masculine and feminine honorifics for *knights* and *baronets*. The post nominals denoting the honor are separated by a comma from the name.

- Sir Winston Leonard Spencer Churchill, KG

  (KG = Knight of the Order of the Garter)

- Dame Carol Black, DBE

  (DBE = Dame Commander of the Order of the British Empire)

Sir, *lady*, and *dame* are used with the full name or first name only, but never with surname only: *Sir Elton John* or *Sir Elton*, but never *Sir John*.

The wife of a *Sir James Smith* is called *Lady Smith*, not using her given name. The husband of *Dame Sarah Walton* is called *Mr. (full name)* or *Mr. (surname)*.

Sir and *dame* are officially used only by subjects while in countries where the granting *monarch* is *chief of state*. Elsewhere use them as a *courtesy*.

SIR – SUP

Sir, Ma'am, Madam

Sir and *madam* are formal forms of address used in place of a person's name.

    Sir and *madam* are used in the salutation in a formal letter.

    Madam is also an honorific for a woman holding a high office: *Madam President, Madam Justice (surname), Madam Attorney General,* or *Madam Secretary.*

    Some children are taught to use *sir* and *ma'am* when referring to older men and women. However, in the business arena such usage sounds provincial or needlessly formal. Using the person's name shows a simple level of respect and puts others at ease.

- Say, *Thank you, Mr. Brent,* rather than *Thank you, sir.*
- Say, *No, Ms. Phelps,* rather than *No, ma'am.*

    Sometimes used in the military, government, and business arenas, *sir* and *ma'am* are a sign of deference by junior officers and staff to senior officers and officials.

- *Yes ma'am, your flight is confirmed.*
- *Sir, here is a copy of the agenda for your meeting.*

Solicitor, Solicitor General

Solicitor is a synonym for *attorney* or *lawyer.* The term is most often used in Commonwealth nations in conjunction with a *barrister.* A *solicitor* prepares legal documents, advises clients, and represents them in lower courts. A *barrister* represents clients in higher courts, arguing cases in front of a judge and jury.

    A *solicitor general* is the high legal official. In the United States the federal government's lawyer in the Supreme Court is the *Solicitor General of the United States.* A *solicitor general* usually serves under a higher official such as an *Attorney General.*

Sovereign

A *sovereign* is a hereditary *chief of state* of an independent state. *Sovereign* is neither a title nor an honorific.

Speaker

A *speaker* is a presiding officer over a legislative body, *e.g., Speaker of the House of Representatives* or *speaker of a national assembly.*

Sri

Sri is a masculine Indian (Sanskrit) honorific for *Mr.*

State

A *state* is a political entity or the governing institutions that rule a geographic area. It is also a part of many official names such as: State of New York, Independent State of Samoa, State of Qatar, Independent State of Papua New Guinea, State of Kuwait, State of Israel, and the State of Eritrea.

    See also *Country* and *Nation.*

Style, Styled

As a verb, *to style* someone with a title, or *to be styled* with a title, implies granting the use of a title one may (or may not) possess. An eldest son's use of a lesser title belonging to his father who has many titles, or a peer's untitled wife's use of a courtesy title based on her husband's rank, are examples of being *styled*. For example:

- A member of the Privy Council in the United Kingdom is addressed with the courtesy title *the Right Honourable*. However, a member of the Privy Council who also holds the title of *baron* has already been **styled** with the courtesy title *the Right Honourable* due to his noble title.
- The eldest son of a *duke* (a *duke* who also holds the lesser titles of *marquis* and *count*) may be **styled** a *marquis,* and that son's eldest son **styled** a *count.* Only the *duke* is actually a *peer:* The son and his son remain *commoners* until the titles descend.
- A *baron's* wife may be **styled** a *baroness,* but she is not a *peer* in her own right.

As a noun, a *style* is a generic synonym for title of the peerage, such as *duke* or *viscount.* Note the use of *style* in the following: No '*of*' is used between a *style* and a title. *Viscount Astor* is correct; *Viscount of Astor* is not correct.

The term *self-styled* is used when one grants oneself a title or honorific to which one may not be entitled.

Subordinate Officer

A *subordinate officer* is a *junior officer* in an armed force. For example, an officer cadet in the Canadian Air Force or Canadian Army or a Naval Cadet in the Canadian Navy is a *subordinate officer.*

Suffragan

See *Bishop.*

Sultan, Sultana, Sultanah, Sultanate

Sultan is the masculine title of a royal *chief of state* in Brunei and Oman. The area ruled by a *sultan* is a *sultanate.* The title is not used as an honorific: The royal person is addressed as *Your Majesty.*

Sultan is also the masculine title of a royal chief of state in many of the states within Malaysia. A Malaysian *sultan* is addressed as *Your Royal Highness.*

A *sultana* could be the wife of a *sultan,* but the wife of a sultan is not necessarily a *sultana; e.g.,* the *Sultan of Oman* has more than one wife, and none is designated as a *sultana.* In the Malaysian *sultanates* the consorts of the *sultan* are styled *sultana* or *sultanah.*

Superintendent

A *superintendent* is a senior administrator or officer in government or other institutions. There are *superintendents* in school systems, police departments, and government councils. A *superintendent* is also the person of authority on a construction site. *Superintendent* is sometimes used in conversation as an honorific with a surname, or in place of the name. Written address is usually: *Mr./Ms./etc. (name), Superintendent of (institution).*

SUP – TOW

A member of the *Board of General Superintendents* of the Church of the Nazarene is addressed, in his capacity as a member of the board, as *General Superintendent (name)*. When not acting in an official capacity, he is addressed by his own clerical or pastoral title.

Superior General

A *superior general* or *general superior* is the highest officer in a religious order. For example, the Society Jesus (the Jesuits) and the Society of St. Edmund are both led by *superior generals*.

A *superior general* is formally addressed as *The Reverend Superior General (full name)*, and less formally as *Father (name)*.

Supreme Court

A *supreme court* is the highest court in a country which has precedence over lower courts. The highest court has a variety of names:

- Common Court of Justice: Aruba
- Constitutional Court: Italy, Russia, South Africa, Turkey
- Court of Appeal: Kenya
- Court of Justice of the European Communities: European Union
- Federal Assembly Court: Switzerland
- Federal Constitutional Court: Germany
- High Civil Appeals Court: Bahrain
- High Court: Australia
- High Court of Appeal: Kuwait
- Privy Council: The Bahamas
- Summary Court: Cayman Islands
- Supreme Administrative Court: Bulgaria
- Supreme Constitutional Court: Egypt
- Supreme Council of Justice: Saudi Arabia
- Supreme Council of the Magistracy: Cambodia
- Supreme Court: United States
- Supreme Court of Appeal: Bhutan, Malawi
- Supreme Court of Appeals: France
- Supreme Court of Judicature: Barbados, Guyana
- Supreme Court of Justice: Belgium, East Timor, Honduras, Mexico, Romania
- Supreme Federal Tribunal: Brazil
- Supreme Judicial Court: Austria
- Supreme People's Court: China, Laos
- Tribunal of Judges: Andorra

SUP – TOW

Swami

Swami is an honorific for a Hindu religious teacher. It is used in front of the person's name, as in *Swami (name)*, or in conversation in place of the name, as in *Good morning, Swami.*

T

Take-in Card

A *take-in card, table card, seating card,* or *escort card* is a card received by a guest at a dinner event on which is written the name of another guest. At larger events it will also contain the number of the table at which these guests are seated.

The card is typically presented inside a small envelope with the name of the guest on the outside front. The addressee is to find the other guest and escort that guest from the pre-dinner reception to dinner, where they will be seated together.

At events where guests are not asked to escort other prescribed guests to dinner, the term is used for a card with only the number of the table at which the guest will be seated.

See also *YASA.*

TD

TD is a *post-nominal abbreviation* for *Teachta Dála*, Gaelic for a member of the *Dáil Éireann*, the lower house of the Irish Parliament. The *post nominals* are used in correspondence to and identification of a member.

Example: *Deputy John Smith, TD*

TDY

TDY is an abbreviation for a *temporary duty assignment.*

Tengku, Tunku

Tengku and *tunku* are varied spellings of a royal title and honorific that is equivalent to a *prince* in one of the Malaysian states. A *tunku mahkota* is a *crown prince*. Holders of these princely titles are addressed as *Your Highness*.

Town King

Town king is the title and honorific of the highest rank in certain Native American tribes. The domain of a *town king* is a *tribal town*.

Translator

A *translator* is a person who creates written translations, as opposed to an *interpreter* who orally translates conversation as it is being held.

TRA – VIE

Tun, Tun Sri, Tan Sri

Tun and *tun sri* or *tan sri* are chivalrous titles granted by the *Paramount Ruler of Malaysia*. In writing, these titled persons are addressed as *the Most Honorable*.

Union

Union is another name for a state, nation, or confederation, emphasizing its formation as a combination of members. Sometimes it is a part of the official name of a country such as the *Union of the Comoros*.

Verger

Verger is a title for a lay person who assists in ceremonial aspects and logistical details of a religious service.

The title *verger* is used after the name in an introduction or on a business envelope for identification, but not as an honorific.

Vestryman

Members of a *vestry*, *vestrymen*, are volunteer lay members of a church board. Identification of the office would be after the name in an introduction or on a business envelope, but *vestryman* is not used as an honorific. Address in writing as *Mr./Ms. (name)* and identify as a member of the *vestry of (organization)*.

Vicar

Vicar is a title for a cleric in charge of a chapel, or for certain parish *priests*.

A *vicar* or *vicar general* in the Roman Catholic Church is a priest who administers a *parish* or *diocese*, acts as an agent for another *priest*, or acts as a representative for a higher-ranking member of the clergy.

In writing, the title *vicar* is used after the name in an introduction or on a business envelope for identification, but not as an honorific. It is sometime used as an honorific or in place of the name verbally. In writing use *Mr./Ms./The Reverend (full name)* and identify as a *vicar of (institution)*.

The *Vicar of Christ* is a title for the *pope* of the Roman Catholic Church.

Vice

The prefix *vice* means *in place of*. So a *vice president* is a person who can act *in place of a president*, a *vice-chancellor* can act *in place of a chancellor*, a *viceroy* can act *in the place of a "roi"* or *king*.

In the United States Mr. *Vice President* is only used for the Vice President of the United States. For other officials, *vice-(office)* is used orally for identification in an introduction or in writing after the name, but not as an honorific: Address as *Mr./Ms./Dr./etc. (name)*.

Vice President

See *President*.

Vice-Consul

A *vice-consul* is a junior ranking member of a mission's consular office.

See also *Consul*.

Viceroy, Vicereine

Viceroy is a masculine title for a royal *governor* of a country, province, or colony, ruling as the representative of a *monarch*. The domain of a *viceroy* was a *viceroy-alty*. For example, under British rule, the *governor-general* of India's full title was the *governor-general and viceroy of India*.

A *vicereine* is a woman who is the *governor* of a country, province, or colony, ruling as the representative of a *monarch*, or the wife of a *viceroy*.

Vice-royal, Viceroyalty

Vice-royal describes a representative of a monarch. For example, a *governor-general* is a *vice-royal* office.

A *viceroyalty* is the province of a royally appointed official such as a *viceroy*, *governor-general, governor*, or *lieutenant governor* of a commonwealth state.

Vienna Convention on Diplomatic Relations, 1961

The *Vienna Convention on Diplomatic Relations*, adopted on April 18, 1961, by the United Nations Conference on Diplomatic Intercourse and Immunities held in Vienna, Austria, adapted and restated the rules for diplomatic relations originally formulated by the Congress of Vienna, 1815.

The 1961 document consists of 53 articles covering procedures of permanent diplomatic relations between States. Topics include: definitions of diplomatic relations; permanent and temporary establishment and breaking of diplomatic relations; procedures of arrival, accreditation, and departure of diplomats and members of missions; size and makeup of missions; rights, limitations, duties, and privileges of diplomats and members of missions; and details of diplomatic immunity.

See also *Congress of Vienna, 1815*.

VIS – YAS

Viscount, Viscountess

Viscount is the British spelling of the title for a nobleman of hereditary ranking below *count* in continental Europe or below *earl* in Great Britain. The domain of a *viscount* is said to be a *viscounty* or *viscountcy*.

Viscountess is the title for a noblewoman who holds the title in her own right, or is the wife or widow of a *viscount* using the title as a *courtesy*.

In other languages the equivalent titles are:

• French: *vicomte* and *vicomtesse*
• Italian: *visconte* and *viscontess*
• Spanish and Portuguese: *vizconde* and *vizcondesa*
• German: There is no equivalent title in Germany.

See also *Lord, Lady*.

Warden

A *warden* is an administrator or officer of an institution. Examples include: *prison warden, air-raid warden, game warden*, and *warden* of a park, church, or Masonic lodge. It is used in a salutation, and informally as an honorific or in place of the name in conversation. Address formally in writing as *Mr./Ms. (name)* and identify as *warden of (institution)*.

In the United Kingdom a *warden* is also the headmaster of a constituent college of a university. For example, a *warden* heads All Souls College of Oxford University. *Dear Warden of (college)* is used as a salutation, but otherwise the office is included after the name as identification, not as an honorific.

Westminster System

The *Westminster System* is the British system of government, named after the place where the British Parliament meets: the *Palace of Westminster*. The system is an operational plan of government with an elected legislature. Important features are a *chief of state* who is not the *head of government*, and an *executive government* created from the members of the the national assembly, most always called *parliament*.

Whip

In a legislative body a *whip* is the person responsible for organizing members of his or her political party to work in unison on issues, in debates, and in votes. It is not used as an honorific.

X

Y

YASA

YASA is an abbreviation for *You Are Seated At*. At an event with many tables and pre-assigned seating, a *YASA* is a card that has written on it the number of the table at which a guest will be seated. The cards, presented in an envelope with the guest's name written on it, are available before a guest enters the dining room.

See also *escort card* or *take-in card*.

Z

2 Honorifics & Titles

Honorifics

Use of Honorifics

An *honorific* or *honorific prefix* can define the title of the bearer's office, convey a rank, or denote a profession:

captain	*doctor*	*pastor*
chancellor	*judge*	*professor*
commissioner	*monsignor*	*senator*

Some specify gender:

mister	*lord*	*sir*
Ms.	*lady*	*dame*

Others specify gender and marital status:

missus	*miss*

Honorifics can be used in place of a name in direct address, as when addressing a woman as *miss* or a man as *mister* for emphasis, or because his or her name is not known. An *honorific prefix* always precedes the name.

Ms., while ubiquitous in the United States, is not universal in English-speaking countries: Mrs. and Miss are frequently the preferred forms. In Commonwealth countries married women frequently use Mrs. (*woman's first*) + (*surname*) and Mrs. (*surname*). Check for local preference and, most importantly, the preference of the bearer.

In writing, if the sex of your addressee is unknown (and you have no way to find out), use the honorific Mr. or use *no honorific*.

For example:

Mr. Chris Wolfe	Chris Wolfe
(Address)	(Address)
Dear Mr. Wolfe	Dear Chris Wolfe

A person does not give himself or herself an honorific such as Mr., Mrs., or Ms. For example on the corporate letterhead of an executive:

Correct: **John Renninger, Chief Executive Officer**
Incorrect: Mr. John Renninger, Chief Executive Officer

Honorifics and Academic Degrees

In the United States, using a high hierarchical title as an honorific supplants reference to academic degrees with holders of very high positions. For example, the office of *cardinal* in the Roman Catholic Church is considered to be so high that it is the *character of the individual* and not his *academic degrees* that is of note.

Example: Hillary Charnov, a senator with a *JD*
Correct: **Senator Hillary Charnov**
Incorrect: Senator Hillary Charnov, JD

Example: *Joseph Ahern, a cardinal with a PhD*
Correct: **His Eminence Cardinal Joseph Ahern**
Incorrect: His Eminence Cardinal Joseph Ahern, PhD

Reverend

The Reverend in the United States

The Reverend is the basic courtesy title for anyone who presents himself or herself as a member of the clergy. It is used before a *(full name)* or *(initial[s]) + (surname)*. Examples of correct forms include:

* *The Reverend Mark M. Phillips*
* *The Reverend C. M. Phillips*

The Reverend describes an individual: The person is *a reverend person*. It is not used with an office:

Correct: **The Reverend Mark M. Phillips**
Incorrect: *The Reverend Pastor of Grace Church*

While *Reverend* is sometimes used as an honorific in the manner of Mr./Ms./Mrs./Dr., such use is not traditional. In traditional use, *Reverend* is never used alone, never with only a first name or only a surname, and never with a hierarchical title.

For example, traditional use would exclude the following forms of address for the *Reverend Mark M. Phillips, pastor of St. Ann's Episcopal Church*:

NON-TRADITIONAL USES:	REASON
Good afternoon, Reverend.	Never alone
Good afternoon, Reverend Mark.	Never with only a first name
Good afternoon, Reverend Phillips.	Never with only a surname
The Reverend's sermon today will be …	Never alone
Reverend Mark's sermon today will be …	Never with only a first name
The Reverend Phillips's sermon today will be …	Never with only a surname
Reverend, may I introduce …	Never alone
Reverend Mark, may I introduce …	Never with only a first name
Reverend Phillips, may I introduce …	Never with only a surname

Some honorifics traditionally used when addressing clergy include:

Bishop (surname)	Clergy with a hierarchical title
Doctor (surname)	Clergy with a doctorate
Father/Mother (surname)	Roman Catholic, Episcopal, *etc.*
Imam (surname)	Islamic
Pastor (surname)	Basic honorific for any Christian
Mr./Ms./Mrs./Miss (surname)	Any, without other title or doctorate
Rabbi (surname)	Jewish

Traditionally correct forms include:

Good afternoon, Pastor.
Good afternoon, Pastor Phillips.
    The Pastor's sermon today will be …
    Pastor Phillips's sermon today will be …
    Pastor Phillips, may I introduce …

Good afternoon, Bishop (or other hierarchical title).
Good afternoon, Bishop Phillips.
    The Bishop's sermon today will be …
    Bishop Phillips's sermon today will be …
    Bishop Phillips, may I introduce …

Good afternoon, Doctor (clergy with doctorate).
Good afternoon, Doctor Phillips.
    The Doctor's sermon today will be …
    Doctor Phillips's sermon today will be …
    Doctor Phillips, may I introduce …

Good afternoon, Father/Mother/Brother/Sister (honorific only).
Good afternoon, Father/Mother/Brother/Sister Phillips.
    Father's sermon today will be …
    Father Phillips's sermon today will be …
    Father/Mother/Brother/Sister Phillips, may I introduce …

However, since personal preference is always taken into account, follow the example of your introducer or the preference of the bearer.

The Reverend Elsewhere in the World

Internationally, use of *the Reverend* is the same as outlined above with the following exception: *The Reverend* and other *courtesy titles* are combined with honorifics such as *professor* or *Dr.* or with personal titles such as *sir* or *lord* to create compound honorifics.

<table>
<tr>
<td>The Reverend Professor
Sir Joshua Stark
Department of Mathematics
St. Clare University</td>
<td>The Reverend
Dr. Zachary Tilden
Dean of the School of Theology
University of Leeds</td>
</tr>
</table>

Courtesy Titles for Clergy

Courtesy titles for clergy include:

- *His All Holiness*
- *His Holiness*
- *His Beatitude*
- *His Eminence*
- *The Most Reverend*
- *The Right Reverend*
- *The Venerable*
- *The Very Reverend*
- *The Reverend*

All are used in writing following the same pattern as *the Reverend*, but there are often special forms used in direct address. See the specific listing for each clerical office for the correct courtesy title.

Honorable

In the United States *the Honorable* is a courtesy title used with current and retired high-ranking federal and state officials and judges, and with some local officials. As a general rule, those *appointed by the President of the United States* and anyone *elected to public office* are entitled to be addressed as *the Honorable* for life.

Use *the Honorable* when addressing an envelope, in a letter's heading, or in introducing an official to a group. *The Honorable* is not used in a salutation or in conversation. In the United States it is not used on inside envelopes or on place cards.

The Honorable is always used before a full name. As a courtesy title *the Honorable* describes an individual: This person is *honorable*. As such it never precedes the name of an office in direct address.

Correct: **The Honorable William Stevenson, Mayor of Dayton**
Not ideal: *The Honorable Mayor of Dayton, William Stevenson*

> Correct: *The Mayor of Dayton*
> Incorrect: *The Honorable Mayor of Dayton*

In the United States *the Honorable* is never used with another honorific (*Mr.*, *Mrs.*, *Miss*, *Ms.*, *Dr.*), a post-nominal honorific (*Esq.*), a military rank, or post-nominal abbreviation for a scholastic degree.

> Correct: **The Honorable William Stevenson**
> Incorrect: *The Honorable Stevenson*
> *The Honorable Mr. Stevenson*
> *The Honorable Admiral Stevenson*
> *The Honorable William Stevenson, PhD*

Others use *the Honorable* when addressing an officeholder. An officeholder never uses *the Honorable* with his or her own name.

On an invitation issued by *the Speaker*:

> Correct: **The Speaker of the House of Representatives**
> **requests the pleasure of your company ...**
> Incorrect: *The Honorable Speaker of the House of Representatives*
> *requests the pleasure ...*

On a mayor's business card:

> Correct: **Victor Principe, Mayor of Bellport**
> Incorrect: *The Hon. Victor Principe, Mayor of Bellport*

The Honorable in Writing

The Honorable, frequently abbreviated as *the Hon.*, is most formally fully spelled out and placed on a line by itself, with the person's full name on a new line. In this form both the initial **T** and **H** are capitalized. It can share the line with the full name, or be abbreviated, for convenience or to save space.

> Most Formal: *The Honorable*
> *(Full name)*
> *(Address)*
>
> Formal: *The Honorable (full name)*
> *(Address)*
>
> Less Formal: *The Hon. (full name)*
> *(Address)*

U.S. Officeholders Addressed as *the Honorable*

The Honorable is used when addressing:

FEDERAL OFFICIALS

The Executive

- *Chief of staff to the President of the United States*
- *Assistant or counselor to the President of the United States*
- *Personal or special representative of the President of the United States*
- *President-elect*
- *Vice president-elect*

The cabinet and high officials in executive departments

- *The secretary of an executive department*
- *Deputy secretary, assistant secretary, and deputy assistant secretary*
- *Undersecretary, deputy undersecretary, and associate deputy undersecretary*
- *The Attorney General*
- *Deputy Attorney General, associate Attorney General*
- *Acting secretary, secretary ad-interim, and secretary-designate*

Certain other high positions appointed by the President

- *Solicitor General, Postmaster General, Surgeon General*
- *Chairman, administrator, commissioner, director, head, or member of a council, commission, agency, board, and authority*

The House of Representatives

- *Representative*
- *Delegate*
- *Representative-elect or delegate-elect*
- *Clerk of the House of Representatives*
- *Sergeant at arms*

The Senate

- *President pro tempore of the Senate*
- *Senator*
- *Senator-elect*
- *Sergeant at arms*

Department of Defense

- *Secretary of an armed service*
- *Undersecretary, assistant, and deputy-undersecretaries of an armed service*
- *Chairman, Joint Chiefs of Staff*
- *Vice chairman, Joint Chiefs of Staff*
- *Chiefs of staff of the Army and the Air Force*
- *Chief of Naval Operations*
- *Commandants of the Marine Corps and the Coast Guard*

The Judiciary
- *Judges*
- *Retired associate justice of the U.S. Supreme Court*
- *Chief judge, judge, presiding judge of lower U.S. federal courts*

DIPLOMATS
- *Ambassador*
- *Individual with the rank of ambassador*
- *High commissioner*
- *Diplomats with the rank of minister*

The Honorable in State and Local Governments

Every elected state and municipal official is entitled to be addressed as *the Honorable*. However, at the local level use of *the Honorable* varies, and many local officials are not addressed as *the Honorable*: Check for local preference.

STATE OFFICIALS
- *Governor, acting governor, governor-elect*
- *Lieutenant governor, acting lieutenant governor, lieutenant governor-elect*
- *Attorney General*
- *Secretary of state*
- *Governor-appointed secretary of (portfolio)*
- *Governor-appointed commissioner of a major state commission*
- *Governor's chief of staff*
- *President or Speaker of a state assembly*
- *State senator, representative, or delegate to a state assembly*
- *Clerk of the elected state assembly*
- *Associate justice of a state supreme court*
- *Chief judge, senior judge, and judges of lower state courts*

LOCAL OFFICIALS
- *Mayor, mayor-elect*
- *Elected member of county board of supervisors, city and town council*
- *Sheriff*
- *Other elected officials of a city or county*

The Honorable with Foreign Citizens

Many nations, from Argentina to the Kyrgyz Republic, address their officials as *the Honorable*. Others use *Your Excellency* for the chief of state, head of government, and officials of the rank of *minister*, and use *the Honorable* for legislators. In the United Kingdom some peers and the children of life peers are also addressed as *the Honourable*.

Internationally *the Honorable* is used in various orders and in combination with another courtesy title, honorific, rank, decorations, or personal title.

> *The Honourable*
> > *Dr. Ewart Brown, JP, MP*
> > > *Premier of Bermuda*

> ALSO WRITTEN *Dr. the Honourable Ewart Brown, JP, MP*
> > > *Premier of Bermuda*

> *Senator the Honourable*
> > *The Reverend Frederick A. McAlpine*
> > > *Government Senator, Commonwealth of the Bahamas*

> *The Right Honourable*
> > *General Sitiveni Rambuka*
> > > *Prime Minister of the Republic of Vanuatu*

See listings for specifics.

The Honourable

The Honourable, with a *U*, is the British spelling. Use this spelling with Commonwealth officials and officials of former Commonwealth countries because it is considerate to write a person's name exactly as he or she is accustomed to seeing it written. With U.S. officials and officials of non-English speaking countries that use *the Honorable* as a courtesy title, it is correct for an American to use the American spelling: *the Honorable*.

The Right Honourable

The Right Honourable is a courtesy title used with certain Canadian and British officials. Its placement and application are the same as *the Honourable*. It is typically abbreviated *the Right Hon.*

His/Her Honor, Your Honor

Your Honor is a diminutive form of *the Honorable*. In the United States it is not used in writing, but it is used in direct verbal address with a judge in court and a mayor of a city.

His/Her Honour is a courtesy title and form of address in Canada and Australia. In Canada the spouse of a provincial *governor* is addressed as *His/Her Honour*. The *administrator* of the Northern Territory of Australia is addressed in conversation as *Your Honour*.

Excellency

Your Excellency is a courtesy title used when addressing foreign officials including *president* and *cabinet minister*, and diplomats with the rank of *ambassador*. *Your Excellency* is also used with the *governors* of certain U.S. states.

Your Excellency is used in addressing:

Foreign officials of cabinet level and above
- *President*
- *Prime minister*
- *Cabinet ministers and secretaries of (portfolio)*
- *Other high officials of cabinet rank*

High-ranking diplomats and representatives to international organizations
- *Ambassadors of foreign powers*
- *Ministers of foreign powers*
- *Secretary general of the United Nations*
- *Secretary general of the Organization of American States*
- *Representatives to the Organization of American States*

Certain viceroyalty
- *Governor-General of the Commonwealth*
- *Governor of an Australian state*

Others, but never the officeholder, use *Excellency*. For example:

Correct: **The Ambassador of Japan requests the pleasure of...**
Incorrect: *His Excellency the Ambassador of Japan requests the pleasure of ...*

Foreign officials and diplomats use *His/Her Excellency* in combination with another courtesy title, an honorific, military rank, or a personal title. For example:

His Excellency
> *The Right Reverend Dr. Peter Hollingworth*, AC, OBE
> *Governor-General of Australia*

His Excellency
> *Dr. Rolf Heinz*
> *Ambassador of the Federal Republic of Germany*

His Excellency
> *General Jose Perez*
> *Ambassador of Spain to the United Nations*

His Excellency
> *The Earl of Somerset*, CMG
> *British Ambassador*

While *Excellency* is a courtesy title like *Honorable*, it is slightly different in that it is used as a title in direct address in place of the name.

Introduction, one person to another:
Your Excellency, may I present ...
... may I present His/Her Excellency the president of Sierra Leone ...

Conversation: *Your Excellency*

Foreign officials sometimes address American ambassadors as *Your Excellency* rather than *the Honorable* in correspondence or conversation since *Your Excellency* is the standard courtesy title of the diplomatic arena.

Excellency in U.S. State Governments

Traditionally in New Hampshire, South Carolina, and Massachusetts the governor is addressed as *Your Excellency*. See listings for *governor* for specifics.

International Forms

Honorifics for More Professions

Many languages include honorifics for professions not specifically acknowledged in English. Some examples from Spanish include:

- *Lic. (name)*   *for an attorney*
- *Econ. (name)*   *for an economist*
- *Ing. (name)*   *for an engineer*
- *Prof. (name)*   *for an academic*

Compound Honorifics

It is the custom in the United States to address an individual with just one honorific, post nominal, or courtesy title at a time:

- *The Honorable George Ashcroft*
- *Senator Ashcroft*
- *Dr. George Ashcroft*

Internationally, using every appropriate honorific and courtesy title is typical:

- *Senator the Honorable Dr. George Ashcroft*

Sometimes the name can include the styles of both office and personal rank, and post nominals for honors and decorations:

His/Her Excellency
The Right Honourable
Dr. Peter Hollingworth, AC, OBE
Governor-General of Australia
(Address)

Other international examples include:

- His Excellency Lord *(full name)*, PC
- Cardinal Sir *(full name)*, KBE
- General Dr. *(full name)*, AO
- Professor Dr. *(full name)*, Director of the Cabinet, Republic of Albania

When an individual both holds a *high office* and has a *personal rank*, the rule is: *Address by rank* and *identify by office*. For example, the *papal representative* is an *archbishop* who is also an *ambassador*.

[1] Following the U.S. practice to address with a single courtesy title, he is addressed as an *archbishop*, then identified as the papal representative:

> The Most Reverend
> (Full name), (post nominals for honors, decorations, order, etc.)
> Titular Archbishop of (place)
> The Apostolic Nuncio to the United States

[2] Following the international practice to address with all appropriate courtesy titles, he is addressed as:

> His Excellency
> The Most Reverend
> (Full name), (post nominals for honors, decorations, order, etc.)
> Titular Archbishop of (place)
> The Apostolic Nuncio to the United States

When an honorific and courtesy title are used together, a capital **T** is used on **The** when it begins a line, but a lower case **t** is used in the middle of a line.

> The Honourable Dr. (full name)
> (Address)

> Senator the Honourable (full name)
> (Address)

Honorifics and Personal Titles in Conversation

When addressing a person with a personal title in conversation, the title dictates the form:

Example:	Thomas Noyes, a viscount and a medical doctor:
Correct:	**Lord Noyes**
Incorrect:	Dr. Noyes
Example:	Michael Flynn, a knight and university professor:
Correct:	**Sir Michael Flynn** OR **Sir Michael**
Incorrect:	Professor Michael Flynn OR Professor Flynn

Honorifics and Courtesy Titles

Here is a comparison of U.S. Style and International Style:

U.S. STYLE	INTERNATIONAL STYLE
Senator	**Senator**
United States of America	**Federative Republic of Brazil**
Envelope, official:	Envelope, official:
The Honorable	*His/Her Excellency*
(Full name)	*Senator (full name)*
United States Senate	*Federal Senate*
(Address)	*(Address)*
Envelope, social:	Envelope, social:
The Honorable	*His/Her Excellency*
(Full name)	*Senator (full name)*
(Address)	*(Address)*
Invitation, inside envelope:	Invitation, inside envelope:
Senator (surname)	*H.E. Senator (full name)*
Place card:	Place card:
Senator (surname)	*H.E. Senator (full name)*

Address by (*Office*) or by Title Only

Certain very high officials are addressed in the most formal way in official correspondence and direct address: by *office/title*, never by *name*. In the United States, the *President, vice president, chief justice of the Supreme Court*, and members of the President's cabinet are among those addressed by their *office/title* rather than by their *name*. While the media refer to a current *President of the United States* in the third person as *President (name)* or even as Mr. *(surname)*, in direct address the President's name is never used.

> **Correct salutation:** **Dear Mr./Madam President**
> Incorrect salutation: *Dear President (surname)*
>
> **Correct in conversation:** **Mr./Madam President**
> Incorrect in conversation: *President (surname)*

Continued Use of Titles

Officially, neither holders of positions of which there is only one at a time, nor those who resign such positions, continue to use their titles.

Positions of which there is only one at a time include:

- *President of the United States*
- *Vice president of the United States*
- *Speaker of the House of Representatives*
- *Chief justice of the United States*
- *Secretaries of (portfolio)/Members of the President's cabinet*

For example, a former *Speaker of the House* is no longer Mr. *Speaker*: He or she reverts to *the Honorable (full name)* or Mr./Ms./etc. *(surname)*, and in each case is identified as *former Speaker of the House of the House of Representatives*.

Many former high officials do continue to use the honorific of their former office. Typically *governors, senators, ambassadors,* and *judges* continue to use the distinctive title for their position as a courtesy after they retire. However, such use is informal and at the preference of the bearer. Military officers (usually *captains* or *colonels* and above) continue to use their rank as an honorific and include *Retired* or *Ret.* post nominally on official correspondence.

Continued Use of *the Honorable* with Former U.S. Officials

In the United States, except in rare circumstances, once an *Honorable*, always an *Honorable*. A former *mayor* of a city is not officially addressed as *Mayor (name)*, but he or she is always *the Honorable (full name)*.

Envelope, official:
The Honorable
(Full name)
(Address)
Letter salutation: *Dear Mr./Ms. (surname):*
Introduction: *The Honorable (full name), former mayor of (municipality)*
Introduction, one person to another: Mr./Ms. *(surname)*

Continued Use of Courtesy Titles with Former Foreign Officials

Typically foreign government officials discontinue use of *Honorable* or *Excellency* when they leave office: They revert to simply Mr./Mrs./Professor/Dr./Sir/etc. *(name)*. Among the exceptions are individuals honored for their public service, or those appointed to a elite body such as the Queen's Privy Council in Canada, whose members are addressed as *the Honourable* for life. Check listing for specifics.

Graded and Basic Titles

Graded titles are ranks, or ratings, with stepped seniority. For example, the basic rank in a uniformed service *general* includes graded ranks *general, lieutenant general, major general,* and *brigadier general.*

In written address and formal introductions use the complete *graded rank*. In conversation and other instances use the *basic rank*. For example:

Envelope, official:

> *Lieutenant Colonel Todd Marks*, USA
> > *(Address)*

Introduction:

> *Lieutenant Colonel Todd Marks,(position/command/name of base/service)*

Letter salutation: *Dear Colonel Marks:*

Conversation: *Colonel Marks*

Other times the graded rank is used in every instance for clarity.

Envelope, official:

> *Gunnery Sergeant Linda di Marco*, USMC
> > *(Address)*

Introduction:

> *Gunnery Sergeant Linda di Marco,(position/command/name of base/service)*

Letter Salutation: *Dear Gunnery Sergeant di Marco*

Conversation: *Gunnery Sergeant di Marco*

3 Names

Names with Numbers

Spell out numbers of less than 100 in names of organizations, institutions, and houses of worship.

> Second Church of Christ, Scientist, Paris
> Quorum of the Seventy
> Seventh-day Adventist
> Appeals Court of the Eighth Circuit
> Twenty-second Precinct
>
> 121st Congress
> 327th Battalion

Names with Particles

A *particle* is a very short word, usually a preposition, that is part of a complete surname. Capitalization of the particle varies with the preference of the bearer. When only the *surname* is used with an honorific, capitalize the *particle* to match the capitalization of the name when it is used with a *full name*.

FULL NAME	WITH HONORIFIC
Mohammed al-Faisal	Mr. al-Faisal
Benyoussef Ben Khedda	Mr. Ben Khedda
Joyti De Laurey	Ms. De Laurey
Alicia de Larrocha	Ms. de Larrocha
Giulio Dell'Utri	Mr. Dell'Utri
Luca della Robbia	Mr. della Robbia
Aziz ibn-Saud	Mr. ibn-Saud

FULL NAME	WITH HONORIFIC
Gerard 't Hooft	Mr. 't Hooft
Ann MacKelway, MD	Dr. MacKelway
Dorothy McDonald	Ms. McDonald
James O'Donnell	Mr. O'Donnell
Lucien St. Vincent	Mr. St. Vincent
April Saint-Francis	Ms. Saint-Francis
Ruth Ten Eyck	Ms. Ten Eyck
Abigail Van Buren	Ms. Van Buren
Vincent van Gogh	Mr. van Gogh
Karl von Landen	Mr. von Landen

There are exceptions in use of the particle by personal preference of the bearer and customs in the country of origin. When in doubt, ask for the preferred form.

FULL NAME	WITH HONORIFIC
Suzette de Calais	Ms. Calais
Silvia de Las Nottas	Ms. Las Nottas

Compound Names

With a compound surname use both names, unless one is preferred by the bearer. When in doubt, ask for the correct form.

FULL NAME	WITH HONORIFIC
Luis Perez y Ortega	Mr. Perez y Ortega OR Mr. Perez
Sylvia Sanchez Iglesia	Ms. Sanchez Iglesia OR Ms. Sanchez

In Hispanic cultures the final name, *Ortega* in the first example and *Iglesia* in the second, is the maternal family name. It is used in formal introductions, and by personal preference in other circumstances, but it is not used without the penultimate, paternal family name: *Perez* in the first example and *Sanchez* in the second.

In Anglo-Saxon tradition, double names were formed when two land-owning families merged through marriage. Normally hyphenated, the names are always used as one.

FULL NAME	WITH HONORIFIC
Geoffrey Clifton-Brown	Mr. Clifton-Brown
Claire Curtis-Thomas	Ms. Curtis-Thomas

First Name Only

In official correspondence with high-ranking officials, use *(honorific)* + *(full name)* or *(honorific)* + *(surname)* even when on a *first-name basis* socially.

If in conversation with an official with whom one is socially on a *first-name basis*, but the conversation is taking place in an official situation or in the presence of others not on the same *first-name basis*, use *(honorific)* + *(full name)* or *(honorific)* + *(surname)*. Reserve the use of *first-name only* for private interactions.

Example:	On a first-name basis,
	in the presence of others not on a first-name basis
Conversation:	*Mr./Madam Mayor or Mayor (surname)*
Example:	On a first-name basis,
	in private or where everyone is on a first-name basis
Conversation:	*(First name)*

Nicknames

It is acceptable to address persons of equal or lower rank by a *nickname*. However, the time, place, and who is present determine whether it is appropriate to do so, and the name must not be objectionable to the person concerned.

Unnamed Guests on Invitations

Invitations should be addressed to a named person and his or her named guest. If you are inviting a woman to invite an escort of her choice, for example, address the invitation to the *invitee* and include a note that she is welcome to bring a guest.

Example:	An invitation is issued to Ann Noyes
	who is welcome to bring a guest to the event.
Correct:	**Ms. Ann Noyes**
Incorrect:	Ms. Ann Noyes and Guest
Include a note:	**Dear Ms. Noyes,**
	If you would like to bring a guest, please do so.
	Call me with his or her name so I can add
	the name to the guest list.
	Sincerely,
	(Name of host or hostess)

Names in Joint Forms of Address

In joint forms of official and business address, persons of the higher precedence are listed first without regard to gender.

In the United States the only courtesy accorded the spouse of a high-ranking official is in seating. Spouses take on neither the rank nor any form of address of the officials. Perhaps the only U.S. exception is a widowed spouse of a *former president of the United States* who has a high ranking on the precedence list at White House events (see page 122), but even she does not receive any special form of address. In the British Commonwealth spouses of *governor-generals, lord mayors,* and certain other officials have special forms of address.

Individuals presenting themselves as a couple, regardless of marital status, can be sent joint invitations. Individuals not presenting themselves as a couple should be sent separate invitations.

See *Joint Forms of Address*, page 139, for more information.

Common and Official Names

Countries, states, and territories have *common names* used for identification, but in formal forms of address use the *official name*. In the diplomatic arena special attention is given to names. For example, never address an ambassador from Germany as the *German ambassador* or the *ambassador of Germany*: The correct form is, the *ambassador of the Federal Republic of Germany*.

COMMON NAME	OFFICIAL NAME
Massachusetts	*Commonwealth of Massachusetts*
Rhode Island	*Rhode Island and the Plantation Province*
Guam	*Territory of Guam*
Bahrain	*Kingdom of Bahrain*
Germany	*Federal Republic of Germany*
Mexico	*United Mexican States*

Proper Order in Foreign Names

In some cultures, including Chinese, Hungarian, and Korean, the *family name* traditionally precedes the *given name*.

Frequently visitors from these countries, aware that in the United States the *given name* is first and the *family name* is last, may have already inverted their names for the benefit of English-speaking contacts. Use whichever name order the bearer presents, and clarify which is his or her *given name* and which is the *surname*, taking special care not to re-reverse the names.

	TRADITIONAL NAME ORDER	NAME ORDER FOR ENGLISH	WITH ENGLISH HONORIFIC
Chinese:	*Ku Tai*	*Tai Ku*	*Mr. Ku*
Hungarian:	*Mellor Vilar*	*Vilar Mellor*	*Mr. Mellor*
Korean:	*Cho Choong Hoon*	*Choong Hoon Cho*	*Mr. Cho*

Special Characters in Foreign Names and Titles

Many languages include characters and diacritical marks not used in English.

In languages using the Latin (roman) alphabet such as *Czech, Danish, Dutch, Finnish, French, German, Icelandic, Hungarian, Italian, Norwegian, Portuguese, Spanish,* and *Swedish,* reproduce the letters exactly as they were received in written address. If there is a mechanical problem in reproducing these special characters and marks, use the closest understandable letter.

Languages using other alphabets such as *Arabic, Chinese, Greek, Japanese, Korean,* and *Russian* are less likely to present a problem since one will typically receive the names transcribed into an English version.

4 Abbreviations & Post Nominals

Abbreviations

Abbreviating Honorifics

Except for *Dr.*, *Mr.*, *Mrs.*, *Ms.*, and some others, honorifics, military ranks, and names of offices are not normally abbreviated in *official* written forms of address. While *Ms.* is included, it is not considered an abbreviation since in its current use it has no spelled-out form.

Abbreviations are used in informal address and to save space on place cards:

Official: *Sister Carol Millerton, OP*

> Informal envelope: *Sr. Carol Millerton*
> Place card: *Sr. Carol*

Official: *General Christopher N. Westerhaven, USAF*

> Informal envelope, DOD abbreviation: *Gen Christopher N. Westerhaven*
> Place card, DOD abbreviation: *Gen Westerhaven*

> Informal envelope, civilian abbreviation: *Gen. Christopher N. Westerhaven*
> Place card, civilian abbreviation: *Gen. Westerhaven*

Official: *Captain Robert W. Thompson, USN*
>   *and Mrs. Thompson*

> Informal envelope, DOD abbreviation: *CAPT and Mrs. Robert W. Thompson*
> Place card, DOD abbreviation: *CAPT Thompson, Mrs. Thompson*

> Informal envelope, civilian abbreviation: *Capt. and Mrs. Robert W. Thompson*
> Place card, civilian abbreviation: *Capt. Thompson, Mrs. Thompson*

Abbreviating Courtesy Titles

Courtesy titles are routinely abbreviated on less formal correspondence, especially on place cards:

> Official: *His Highness Sheikh Khalifa bin Zayid Al-Nuhayyan*
> *President of the United Arab Emirates*
> Place card: *H.H. Sheikh Khalifa*

> Official: *The Right Honourable Gordon Brown, MP*
> *Prime Minister of the United Kingdom*
> Place card: *Rt. Hon. Gordon Brown, MP*

> Official: *The Honourable Professor Michael Bazik*
> Place card: *Hon. Prof. Michael Bazik*

Abbreviating Addresses

Highway, building, or house numbers are written in Arabic numerals:

> *Route 29*
> *234 Walnut Drive*

When a building number is part of the name, the building's number is often spelled out:

> *One Fifth Avenue*

When a building is on a numbered street, the building's number and street's number are sometimes adjacent. Spell out numbered streets of less than 100 to avoid confusion with the building number:

> *23 Ninth Avenue*
> *5 Fortieth Road*
> *8099 147th Street*

When the numbers are not adjacent, Arabic numerals can be used for both:

> *44 West 77th Street*
> *5 East 42nd Street*

Thoroughfare designations are most formally spelled out:

Avenue	*Drive*	*Road*
Boulevard	*Lane*	*Square*
Building	*Mews*	*Street*
Circle	*Path*	*Terrace*
Court	*Place*	*Way*

Single compass designations are not abbreviated when used with street names:

North Capitol Street	*East Williston Avenue*
South Eads Street	*West Palm Boulevard*

Double compass designations are abbreviated in an address without spaces or periods:

Montana Lane, NE   *SE Highway 240*
Wisconsin Avenue, NW   *SW 109th Street*

Abbreviating Names

First names are not abbreviated for any reason:

CORRECT   INCORRECT
Mr. William Miller   *Mr. Wm. Miller*
Ms. Elizabeth Toll   *Ms. Eliz. Toll*

Shortened names or nicknames are used at the preference of the bearer, but should be avoided unless the shortened name is known to be a legal name, or he or she never uses the full legal name:

Mr. Bill Henderson   (legal name is Bill, not William)
Ms. Nanci Walters   (never uses legal name, Nancy)

Do not abbreviate company names unless the company uses the abbreviation as a part of its name:

USE FULL NAME   AVOID
Henderson Associates   *Henderson Assoc.*
Wilson and Hobbs   *Wilson & Hobbs*

BUT
Tiffany & Co.
John Wiley & Sons Australia, Inc.

Names of cities and places are not abbreviated with the exception of those beginning with *saint*:

PREFERRED   AVOID
Washington, D.C.   *Wash., D.C.*
Vermont Avenue   *VT Avenue*
New York City   *N.Y.C.*
South Orange   *S. Orange*
St. Louis
St. Croix
Mount St. Helens

Saint, if part of a name, follows the preference of the bearer:

Lucien St. Vincent
April Saint-Francis

The names of states are not abbreviated except when the two-letter form is specified, as it is by the U.S. Postal Service for mailing envelopes:

ON THE LETTER   ON THE ENVELOPE
Nome, Alaska   *Nome, AK*
Huntington, West Virginia   *Huntington, WV*

Names of agencies, associations, companies, designations of ships, fraternal organizations, and unions can be abbreviated to conserve space or for simplicity. When abbreviating, use capital letters, without internal spaces or periods.

AFL-CIO	NATO	USAF
CBS	NBC	USMC
HMS	OPEC	USS
NAACP	UNESCO	YMCA

Punctuation and Spaces in Abbreviations

Initials as abbreviations for personal names are capitalized, with periods, with one space between initials:

Correct: Mr. C. R. Haber
Incorrect: Mr. C.R. Haber

Jr. and Sr. are set off from the name by commas; II and III are not:

Dr. Robert N. Buchanan, Jr.   Mr. Samuel R. Holt III
Robert N. Buchanan, Jr., MD   Samuel R. Holt III, CPA

Jr., Sr., II, III, and IV are not used without the full name:

Correct: Mr. Todd Keene, Jr.
Incorrect: Mr. Keene, Jr.

Middle names are included and abbreviated at the preference of the bearer. Even when the middle initial does not stand for a name, it is followed by a period for consistency:

Harry S. Truman

Abbreviations for the Armed Services

Branches of service are abbreviated by the Department of Defense without periods. Ranks can be abbreviated to save space on place cards or for simplicity.

BRANCHES OF SERVICE

U.S. Army	USA
U.S. Army Reserve	USAR
U.S. Army, Retired	USA, Retired/USA Ret.
U.S. Navy	USN
U.S. Navy Reserve	USNR
U.S. Navy, Retired	USN, Retired/USN Ret.
U.S. Marine Corps	USMC
U.S. Marine Corps Reserve	USMCR
U.S. Marine Corps, Retired	USMC, Retired/USMC Ret.
U.S. Air Force	USAF
U.S. Air Force Reserve	USAFR
U.S. Air Force, Retired	USAF, Retired/USAF Ret.

U.S. Coast Guard	USCG
U.S. Coast Guard Reserve	USCGR
U.S. Coast Guard, Retired	USCG, Retired/USCG Ret.

DOD Abbreviations for Ranks and Ratings

The Department of Defense (DOD) styles of abbreviations for ranks and ratings are listed below. Abbreviations used in civilian situations are punctuated and non-service-specific in form: Gen., Lt. Gen., Maj. Gen., Brig. Gen., and Col. But the use of the Department of Defense forms has the advantage of being service specific and correct in both civilian and military circumstances.

U.S. ARMY

General	GEN
Lieutenant general	LTG
Major general	MG
Brigadier general	BG
Colonel	COL
Lieutenant colonel	LTC
Major	MAJ
Captain	CPT
First lieutenant	1LT
Second lieutenant	2LT
Chief warrant officer	CW5, CW4, CW3, CW2
Warrant officer	WO1
Sergeant major of the Army	SMA
Command sergeant major	CSM
Sergeant major	SGM
First sergeant	1SG
Master sergeant	MSG
Sergeant first class	SFC
Staff sergeant	SSG
Sergeant	SGT
Corporal	CPL
Specialist	SPC
Private, first class	PFC
Private E-2	PV2
Private E-1	PV1

U.S. MARINE CORPS

General	Gen
Lieutenant general	LtGen
Major general	MajGen

| Brigadier general | BGen |
| Colonel | Col |

Lieutenant colonel	LtCol
Major	Maj
Captain	Capt
First lieutenant	1stLt
Second lieutenant	2ndLt

| Chief warrant officer | CWO5, CWO4, CWO3, CWO2 |
| Warrant officer | WO |

Sergeant major of the Marine Corps	SgtMajMC
Sergeant major	SgtMaj
Master gunnery sergeant	MGySgt
First sergeant	1stSgt
Master sergeant	MSgt

Gunnery sergeant	GySgt
Staff sergeant	SSgt
Sergeant	Sgt
Corporal	Cpl
Lance corporal	LCpl

| Private first class | PFC |
| Private | Pvt |

U.S. NAVY

Fleet admiral	FADM
Admiral	ADM
Vice admiral	VADM
Rear admiral, upper half	RADM OR RADM U
Rear admiral, lower half	RDML OR RADM L

Captain	CAPT
Commander	CDR
Lieutenant commander	LCDR
Lieutenant	LT
Lieutenant, junior grade	LTJG
Ensign	ENS

| Chief warrant officer | CWO2, CWO3, CWO4, CWO5 |
| Warrant officer | WO1 |

Master chief petty officer of the Navy	MCPON
Fleet command master chief petty officer	FLTMC
Force command master chief petty officer	FORMC
Master chief petty officer	MCPO
Senior chief petty officer	SCPO

Chief petty officer	CPO
Petty officer first class	PO1
Petty officer second class	PO2
Petty officer third class	PO3
Seaman	SN
Seaman apprentice	SA
Seaman recruit	SR

U.S. AIR FORCE

General	Gen
Lieutenant general	Lt Gen
Major general	Maj Gen
Brigadier general	Brig Gen
Colonel	Col
Lieutenant colonel	Lt Col
Major	Maj
Captain	Capt
First lieutenant	1st Lt
Second lieutenant	2nd Lt
Chief master sergeant of the Air Force	CMSAF
Command chief master sergeant	CCMSgt
First sergeant, E-9	1stSgt
Chief master sergeant	CMSgt
First sergeant, E-8	1stSgt
Senior master sergeant	SMSgt
First sergeant, E-7	1stSgt
Master sergeant	MSgt
Technical sergeant	TSgt
Staff sergeant	SSgt
Senior airman	SrA
Airman first class	A1C
Airman	Amn
Airman basic	AB

U.S. COAST GUARD

Admiral	ADM
Vice admiral	VADM
Rear admiral, upper half	RADM / RADM U
Rear admiral, lower half	RDML / RADM L
Captain	CAPT
Commander	CDR
Lieutenant commander	LCDR

Lieutenant	LT
Lieutenant, junior grade	LTJG
Ensign	ENS

Chief warrant officer	CWO2, CWO3, CWO4, CWO5
Warrant officer	WO1

Master chief petty officer of the Coast Guard	MCPO-CG
Command master chief	CMC
Master chief petty officer	MCPO
Senior chief petty officer	SCPO
Chief petty officer	CPO

Petty officer first class	PO1
Petty officer second class	PO2
Petty officer third class	PO3
Seaman	SN
Seaman apprentice	SA
Seaman recruit	SR

Post Nominals

When to Use Post-Nominal Abbreviations

Post-nominal abbreviations or *post-nominal initials* are formally used with a *full name* in a program, on an official envelope, and in the address block on a letter.

Post nominals always follow a full name. They are not used in a salutation or, with rare exception, socially.

If the honorary degree, honor, decoration, medal, affiliation, or religious order is to be mentioned in an introduction, say what the post nominal represents, not the letters in the abbreviation.

Academic Degrees

Post-nominal abbreviations for academic degrees are placed after the name in an address on an official envelope:

Clergy: *The Reverend*
Kyle Brandt, DD, LLD
Trinity Presbyterian Church
(Address)

Academia: *Kathryn Chew, PhD*
Department of Chemistry
Henderson College
(Address)

Professional: *Noah Miller, MSW*
Director
Portland Counseling Center
(Address)

In the style used in the United States, a post nominal for a doctorate is never used with the honorific *Dr.*:

Professional: *Vincent Mott, MD*
 (Address)

Social: *Dr. Vincent Mott*
 (Address)

In the United States with high officials, academic post nominals are not included. The reasoning is that the advanced degree is less important than the office. For example, the office of attorney general is so high that it is the individual's character, not his or her graduation from law school, that is of issue:

Correct: **The Honorable**
 Kenneth Klein
 Attorney General of Maryland
 (Address)

Incorrect: *The Honorable*
 Kenneth Klein, JurScD
 Attorney General of Maryland
 (Address)

Correct: **His Eminence**
 Richard Cardinal Lowe, OMI
 Archbishop of Chicago
 (Address)

Incorrect: *His Eminence*
 Richard Cardinal Lowe, OMI, PhD
 Archbishop of Chicago
 (Address)

Academic degrees are not used with military rank:

Correct: **Captain Benjamin Bond**
Incorrect: *Captain Benjamin Bond, PhD*

Academic degrees are not used with a courtesy title.

Correct: **The Honorable Marc Goodman**
Incorrect: *The Honorable Marc Goodman, MD*

Internationally, courtesy titles, honorifics, and post nominals are used in combination to create compound forms:

COURTESY TITLE/HONORIFIC + (NAME) + POST NOMINAL
- *His Excellency Dr. (full name), PhD*
- *Sir (full name), MD, PhD*

Academic degrees are not used with honorifics such as Dr./Mr./Mrs./Ms.:

CORRECT	CORRECT	INCORRECT
Ellen Berry, LittD	**Dr. Ellen Berry**	*Dr. Ellen Berry, LittD*
Adam Fox, MD	**Dr. Adam Fox**	*Dr. Adam Fox, MD*
Robin Kim, CPA	**Ms. Robin Kim**	*Ms. Robin Kim, CPA*

Abbreviations for academic degrees include:

DD   *Doctor of divinity*
DDS   *Doctor of dental surgery*
DO   *Doctor of osteopathy*
DVM   *Doctor of veterinary medicine*
JD   *Doctor of law*
LHD   *Doctor of humanities*
LittD   *Doctor of letters*
LLD   *Doctor of laws*
LPN   *Licensed practical nurse*
MD   *Doctor of medicine*
PhD   *Doctor of philosophy*
RN   *Registered nurse*

Honors, Decorations, Religious Orders

Post nominals for honorary degrees, honors, decorations, medals, affiliations, and religious orders are placed after a name:

> *His Excellency*
>> *The Right Honourable*
>>> *Brian Letts, GCB, CMG*
>>>> *British Ambassador*
>>>>> *(Address)*

> *The Reverend*
>> *James Healy, SJ*
>>> *Our Lady Queen of Peace Catholic Church*
>>>> *(Address)*

Sequence of Post Nominals

In the United States, when listing post-nominal abbreviations after a name, never list more than three, and do so in the following order:

First: *Religious orders*
Second: *Theological degrees*
Third: *Academic degrees*
Last: *Honorary degrees and decorations*

However, the order of post nominals varies from country to country. For example, in Australia, post-nominal abbreviations are placed in the following order:

First: *Orders, decorations, honours, and awards*
Second: *Queens Council, Senior Council, or Justice of the Peace*
Third: *Academic degrees: theological then academic*
Fourth: *Professional associations*
Fifth: *Member of Parliament, legislative assembly, or house of representatives*

In every case the safest course is to reproduce the order presented and follow the preference of the bearer.

Post Nominals in Social Address

In the U.S. Style, post nominals for honorary degrees, honors, decorations, medals, affiliations, and religious orders are not used on social envelopes, inside envelopes, or place cards:

Official:	*John Sheridan, MD*
Social Envelope:	*Dr. John Sheridan*
Place card:	*Dr. Sheridan*

Official:	*Captain John Montgomery, USN*
Social Envelope:	*Capt. John Montgomery*
Place card:	*Capt. Montgomery* (*Social Abbreviation*)
	OR *CAPT Montgomery* (*DOD Abbreviation*)

Official:	*The Reverend Malcolm Patton, OFM*
Social Envelope:	*Father Malcolm Patton*
Place card:	*Father Patton*

Internationally, the only exceptions to *no social use of post-nominals* are for a post nominal denoting membership in a parliamentary assembly such as *MP, MLA, TD, MNA, MHA,* or *MEP* or a high civilian award such as *PC, QC, VC,* or *CV.*

Official:	*Ms. Carolyn Millard, MP*
Social Envelope:	*Ms. Carolyn Millard, MP*
Place card:	*Ms. Carolyn Millard, MP*

Official:	*Rt. Hon. Beverley McLachlin, PC*
Social Envelope:	*Rt. Hon. Beverley McLachlin, PC*
Place card:	*Rt. Hon. Beverley McLachlin, PC*

Punctuation and Spaces in Post Nominals

Initials as abbreviations for words are capitalized, with or without periods according to the preferred style, but without internal spaces:

Correct:	**M.P.**	WITH PERIODS
Incorrect:	M. P.	
Correct:	**MP**	WITHOUT PERIODS
Incorrect:	M P	
Correct:	**Ph.D.**	WITH PERIODS
Incorrect:	Ph. D.	
Correct:	**PhD**	WITHOUT PERIODS
Incorrect:	Ph D	

5 Addresses, Salutations & Closings

Addresses

Addresses on Official Envelopes

The most formal format is spelling out every word in an address, except:

- Some honorifics are abbreviated: *Mr.*, *Mrs.*, *Dr.*, *Ms.*
- Names of states are abbreviated with the two-letter forms required by the United States Postal Service.

When writing a name with a courtesy title, or two names, the most formal way is to write each on a line by itself.

MOST FORMAL: *The Honorable*
Anthony Berrera

LESS FORMAL: *The Honorable Anthony Berrera*

MOST FORMAL: *Colonel Robert B. Neville*
and Mrs. Neville

LESS FORMAL: *Colonel and Mrs. Robert B. Neville*

Addresses on Social Mailing Envelopes

On a mailing envelope of social correspondence no reference is made to the office or rank of the addressee except in certain instances:

- The invitee is the holder of an office *so high* that he or she is addressed in every instance by *office* rather than by *name* as with the President of the United States or a royal or noble person.

- The invitee is the holder of an office, degree, or honor with a distinctive honorific used both professionally and socially such as *Senator, Judge, Commissioner, Dr.,* or *Sir.*

- The invitee is the holder of an office meriting address as *the Reverend, the Honorable, Your Excellency,* or other courtesy title.

- The invitee is a member of an assembly and uses a post-nominal abbreviation denoting membership: *MP, MEP, TD, MNA, MHA.*

Names on an Invitation's Inside Envelope

In the United States, except when the invitee is the holder of an office *so high* that he or she is addressed in every instance by *office* rather than by *name*, the guest's name is written on the inside envelope as the guest is addressed verbally:

- *Senator (surname)*
- *Judge (surname)*
- *Dr. (surname)*
- *Pastor/Father/Mother (surname)*
- *Mr./Ms. (surname)*

For a list of officials addressed by *office* in the United States, see page 142.

The inside envelope for invitations extended to close friends and family can be even more informal at the option of the host or hostess:

- *Grandma*
- *David*
- *Uncle Chris*

Outside of the United States *full names* are used on inside envelopes:

- *Senator (full name)*
  OR *The Honorable (full name)*
  OR *Senator the Hon. (full name)*
- *Air Vice-Marshall (full name)*
- *H.E. Cardinal (full name)*
- *H.B. Archbishop (full name)*
- *Bishop (full name)*
- *The Reverend Dr. (full name)*
- *Pastor (full name)*
- *Father/Mother (full name)*
- *Mr./Ms. (full name)*

Salutations

Official salutations are punctuated with a *colon*, social with a *comma*:

OFFICIAL: *Dear Dr. Baker:*

SOCIAL: *Dear Dr. Baker,*

Most private citizens can be addressed as *Dear (honorific) + (surname)*:

Dear Mr. (surname):
Dear Ms. (surname):
Dear Mrs. (surname):
Dear Miss (surname):

Not using the name is less personal and more formal:

Dear Sir:
Dear Madam:

The holder of an office with a special honorific is addressed as *Dear (honorific/rank) + (surname):* or more formally as *Dear (honorific only):*

FORMAL	MORE FORMAL
Dear Ambassador (surname):	*Dear Ambassador:*
Dear Captain (surname):	*Dear Captain:*
Dear Chancellor (surname):	*Dear Chancellor:*
Dear Governor (surname):	*Dear Governor:*
Dear Senator (surname):	*Dear Senator:*
Dear Judge (surname):	*Dear Judge:*
Dear Marshal (surname):	*Dear Marshal:*
Dear Pastor (surname):	*Dear Pastor:*

In salutations holders of very high positions, where the holder's name is not used in direct address, are addressed as *Dear (title):* or more formally by *(Title):*

FORMAL	MORE FORMAL
Dear Chief Justice:	*Chief Justice:*
Dear High Commissioner:	*High Commissioner:*
Dear Madame Secretary:	*Madame Secretary:*
Dear Mr. Attorney General:	*Mr. Attorney General:*
Dear Mr. President:	*Mr. President:*
Dear Mr. Speaker:	*Mr. Speaker:*
Dear Prime Minister:	*Prime Minister:*

Holders of very high ecclesiastical, royal, and vice royal titles are also addressed in a salutation by their titles:

Your Eminence:	*Your Holiness:*
Your Excellency:	*Your Majesty:*
Your Honour:	*Your Royal Highness:*

Complimentary Close

Choose the *complimentary close* to reflect the formality of the letter. The following chart arranges *closings* to show relative formality. There is no actual standard of formality: Choice of closings varies by industry, location, and relationship.

MORE FORMAL

MORE OFFICIAL

MORE CASUAL

MORE SOCIAL

Most respectfully
Very respectfully
Respectfully yours
Respectfully
Faithfully yours
Faithfully
Sincerely yours
Sincerely
Very truly yours
Yours truly
Cordially yours
Cordially
Regards
Warm regards
Best wishes
All the best
Take care
Until next time

In the United States *sincerely* is the basic business closing, but it is not standard everywhere. In Australia, *faithfully* is typical in business correspondence, so check for local tradition. For certain offices there are other customary *complimentary closings* such as:

- *I remain Your Majesty's faithful and devoted servant*
- *I have the honour to remain your Majesty's obedient servant*
- *I have the honor to remain Your Holiness's humble servant*

6 Name Badges & Place Cards

Name Badges

Name badges are worn to facilitate networking and business development. At social events they are provided at the preference of the host or hostess. A name badge can provide just the *given name* and *surname* or include an honorific, office, and organization. All of the guidelines for place cards in this section apply to writing names on name badges.

A name badge is worn on the right front lapel, in the upper chest or shoulder area. This placement makes the name badge easily read when the right hand is extended while shaking hands.

Place Cards

No *place cards*, or *seating cards*, are necessary at a seated event if it is so small that the host or hostess can provide individual guidance on where the guests are to sit. If giving such direction will delay the seating process, then place cards are appropriate. Lettering should be large enough to be read when standing near the table.

Types of Place Cards

Traditionally a *place card* simply identifies for a guest where he or she is to sit. The name appears on one side of a flat *place card* or on one face of a small folded *tent card* with the name facing the guest.

Place cards are less formally prepared as *tent cards* with the guest's name on both sides, acting as a name card for other guests at the table to see.

Even less formal *larger tent cards* include the guest's name, position, and company or organization on the side facing away from the guest. These are most often seen at events to facilitate networking and business development.

Consistent Style of Names on Place Cards

Preparing a person's name on a place card to match the style of all the other place cards is easy when the event is informal, or all the guests are from one country. However, when there is a mixture of nationalities and cultures among the guests, most protocol officers prefer to prepare the place card with a person's name the way he or she is accustomed to seeing it, rather than having all the cards match.

U.S. Style of Place Cards

The basic U.S. style for place cards is to *write the name* as you would *say the name* in conversation. Courtesy titles and post nominals are not included.

For offices where only *one person at a time holds the title*, or only *one person holding the title is at the event*, the place card can give the office rather than their name.

For example, The Honorable (full name), Governor of Alabama:
> At an event where the Governor is the only governor:
> PLACE CARD: *The Governor*

> But at a meeting of governors, more specificity is appropriate:
> PLACE CARD: *The Governor of Alabama*

For most guests, the formula is: (Honorific/title) + (surname).

> The Honorable Nancy Helton, Senator from the State of Illinois
> PLACE CARD: *Senator Helton*
> OR: *Sen. Helton*

> David Weiss, MD, Radiologist
> PLACE CARD: *Dr. Weiss*

> Laura Buchanan, Esq., Attorney at Law
> PLACE CARD: *Ms. Buchanan*

> Christopher Nolan, President of Kensington Consulting Co.
> PLACE CARD: *Mr. Nolan*

> Sister Carol Perry, SU
> PLACE CARD: *Sister Carol*
> OR: *Sr. Carol*

If following this guideline would produce identical place cards and seating would be confusing, it is appropriate to include more information.

PLACE CARD: *Ms. Anne Noyes*
PLACE CARD: *Ms. Heather Noyes*

PLACE CARD: *Mr. Thomas Hickey*
PLACE CARD: *Mr. Thomas Hickey, Jr.*

At intimate social and family events cards can be even more informal at the option of the host or hostess.

David Uslan, MD, Radiologist
PLACE CARD: *David*

Laura Buchanan, Esq., Attorney at Law
PLACE CARD: *Laura*

Ivan Franceus, President of Kensington Consulting Co.
PLACE CARD: *Uncle Ivan*

Carol Wallace
PLACE CARD: *Aunt Carol*

International Style of Place Cards

Internationally, the name on a place card is written in a more complete manner, as one would address a letter. A place card will include courtesy titles, full ranks, honorifics, full names, and post-nominal abbreviations.

A U.S. official and a U.S.-style place card

Example: The Honorable James Smith, Representative of (district)
Member of the House of Representatives,
United States of America

PLACE CARD 1: *Mr. Smith*
PLACE CARD 2: *Congressman Smith*   (honorific because Congressman *is his preference*)

A foreign official and an international-style place card

Example: The Right Honourable James Smith, member for (district)
Member of the House of Commons, and Privy Counsellor,
United Kingdom

PLACE CARD: *Rt. Hon. James Smith, MP*

A U.S. official and a U.S.-style place card

Example: The Honorable Mary Jones, Senator from (state)
Member of the Senate, United States of America

PLACE CARD: *Senator Jones*

A foreign official and an international-style place card

    Example: Senator Mary Jones
                    Member of the Senate of the Commonwealth of Australia

   PLACE CARD: *Senator Mary Jones*

And there are always a variety of correct ways to write a place card.

    Example: His/Her Excellency the Honourable (full name), AC, CVO, MC
                    Governor-General of the Commonwealth of Australia

PLACE CARD 1:	*The Governor-General*	*(By office, short version)*
PLACE CARD 2:	*The Governor-General of Australia*	*(By office, long version)*
PLACE CARD 3:	*H.E. the Hon. (full name)*	*(Complete name)*

    Example: The Honourable Paul Lennon, MHA, Premier of Tasmania

PLACE CARD 1:	*Premier of Tasmania*	*(By name of office)*
PLACE CARD 2:	*The Hon. Paul Lennon, MHA*	*(Complete name)*

Post Nominals on Place Cards

In the U.S. style, post-nominal abbreviations are not included on place cards. Neither the U.S. style nor the international style include abbreviations for honors or academic degrees on place cards.

The international style includes certain post-nominal abbreviations. When they do appear, they follow the name, never the office.

Examples of post nominals that do appear on place cards include:

    Member of a national or state parliament or legislative body
        MdB, Member of Parliament, Federal Republic of Germany (*Bundestag*)
        MEP, Member of the European Parliament
        MHA, Member of the House Assembly (*Australia, Canada*)
        MLC, Member of the Legislative Council (*Australia*)
        MLA, Member of the Legislative Assembly (*Australia, Canada*)
        MPP, Member of the Provincial Parliament (*Canada*)
        MNA, Member of the National Assembly (*Canada*)
        MP, Member of Parliament (*ubiquitous*)
        TD, Member of the Parliament of Ireland (*Teachta Dála*)

    Highest civilian awards, for example:
        QC, Queen's Counsel (*United Kingdom, Canada*)
        PC, Member of a Privy Council, Privy Counsellor (*Australia*)
        VC, Victoria Cross for Australia
        CV, Cross of Valor (*Australia, Canada, Greece*)

7 Introductions

Official Introductions

Very High Officials

In the United States, with certain very high positions such as *President, Vice President,* and *chief justice of the Supreme Court,* the individual's name is not used in an introduction or in the response to an introduction:

CORRECT INTRODUCTION:	CORRECT RESPONSE:
The President of the United States	**Mr. President**
His Majesty the King	**Your Majesty**

INCORRECT INTRODUCTION:	INCORRECT RESPONSE:
(Full name), President of the United States	*President (surname)*
King (name)	*King (name)*

When introducing an officeholder whose name is used with reference to his or her office, there are two equally correct forms:

HONORIFIC + FULL NAME + POSITION

The Honorable	Dennis Kucinich,	*representative from the 10th District of Ohio*
The Reverend	Todd Ames,	*pastor of St. Peter's Episcopal Church*
Ms.	Angela Cho,	*president of the Sunbelt Bank*

POSITION + HONORIFIC + SURNAME

The representative from the 10th District of Ohio,	Mr.	Kucinich
The pastor of St. Peter's Episcopal Church,	Dr.	Ames
The president of the Sunbelt Bank,	Ms.	Cho

Announced *vs.* Introduced

Certain very high officials, such as a *royal chief of state* or the *Pope*, are never introduced to anyone: Everyone is introduced to them. At an audience they are announced.

Use of *Surname Only* in Introductions

Use of the *surname only* creates a more formal introduction. In keeping with the formality of their offices, use *(honorific)* + *(surname only)* in introductions of elected officials, judges, members of the armed services, diplomats, and other high officials. For example:

> *(Former high elected official)*, may I present *(judge)*
>> Mr. Clinton, may I present *Judge Barker* ...
>
> *(Military officer)*, may I introduce *(military officer)*
>> Admiral McCaw, may I introduce *Captain Montgomery* ...
>
> *(Diplomat)*, may I introduce to you *(elected official)*
>> Ambassador Huang, may I introduce to you *Councilman Snyder* ...

Use of the surname only is appropriate in any formal situation:

> *Pastor Jones, may I present Dr. Smith* ...
> *Chancellor Lucia, may I introduce Ms. Harrison* ...
> *Mayor Keller, may I introduce to you Officer Lyle* ...
> *Ms. Henderson, I would like to introduce to you Mr. Barker* ...

Symmetric Use of Names

When introducing two people using *(honorific)* + *(name)*, apply the same formula for both.

> *(Honorific)* + *(surname only)*, may I present *(honorific)* + *(surname only)*
>> Doctor Garcia, may I present Ms. Helm ...
>> Mr. Wilson, I would like to introduce Ms. Jones ...
>> Ms. Lowe, I would like to introduce to you Mr. Kirk ...
>
> *(Honorific)*+*(full name)*, may I introduce *(honorific)* + *(full name)*
>> Doctor Iris Garcia, may I present Ms. Ann Helm ...
>> Mr. John Wilson, I would like to introduce Ms. Emily Jones ...
>> Ms. Alice Lowe, I would like to introduce to you Mr. Thomas Kirk ...

When not using honorifics, use:

> *(Full name)*, may I introduce *(full name)*
>> John Wilson, may I introduce Emily Jones ...
>> Alice Lowe, may I present Thomas Kirk ...

Asymmetric Forms

When introducing a private citizen to a well known person or very high official, it is reasonable to use only the well known person's or the official's *surname*, since the person you are introducing will already know the *full name* of the official.

Mr./Ms. *(well-known person, surname only)*,
>> may I introduce to you
>>> Mr./Ms. *(full name)*...

Mr. *Gates*,
>> I would like to introduce to you
>>> Mr. *Alan Todd*,
>>>> a computer science major ...

Ms. *Couric*,
>> may I present
>>> Ms. *Doris Pooser*,
>>>> the author of a new book on ...

First-Name-Only Introductions

Children may be introduced to one another with *given names* only, but when introducing adults, always use the *given name* and *surname*.

Respond with *Last Name Only* When Introduced

In non-official situations in the United States, it often is assumed that everyone is on a *first-name basis*. However, differences in age, professional stature, cultural background, accomplishment, or simply personal preference will influence the most appropriate form of address.

A cautious approach is recommended: Even if your introducer provides *both given name* and *surname*, use the more formal form, Mr./Ms. *(surname)*, and wait to be invited to be on a *first-name basis* by the other person.

FOR EXAMPLE:

Introducer:	*Carolyn Hill, I would like to introduce to you Gary Kroc.*
Carolyn Hill:	*I am glad to meet you, Mr. Kroc.*
Gary Kroc:	*It is nice to meet you, Ms. Hill.*

ANOTHER SCENARIO:

Introducer:	*Carolyn Hill, I would like to introduce to you Gary Kroc.*
Carolyn Hill:	*I am glad to meet you, Mr. Kroc.*
Gary Kroc:	*It is nice to meet you, Ms. Hill. Please call me Gary.*
Carolyn Hill:	*Thank you Gary. Please call me Carolyn.*

References to the Country in Formal Introductions

Use of the *official country name* is always the most formal option, but when only one official of a rank is present it may not be necessary to include the official country name. In the United States, high officials are introduced *with* or *without* reference to the *United States*.

In the United States:

The Vice President OR *The Vice President of the United States*
The Attorney General OR *The Attorney General of the United States*

Abroad, full reference to the United States of America is included:

The Vice President of the United States of America
The Attorney General of the United States of America

In diplomatic circumstances *American* is used as an adjective:

American Ambassador
American Ambassador to (country)
American Consul-general

However, in the western hemisphere *American* is not used for U.S. officials:

Ambassador of the United States of America
Ambassador of the United States of America to (country)
Consul-general of the United States of America

Designation of Service in Military Introductions

Circumstances will dictate whether it is necessary to include the designations of branch of service in formal introductions.

- Designation frequently **is not made** at military events.
  Those present will be able to recognize the uniform and insignia and will know the branch of service.

- Designation **is made** at civilian functions for the information of those who may not recognize the uniforms and insignia, or to identify personnel who may be out of uniform.

Introduction at military events:

Captain Mark Clark, (position/command/base)

Introduction at civilian events:

Captain Mark Clark, United States Navy, (position/command/base)

Business Introductions

Precedence in Business Introductions

Precedence determines who is introduced to whom. Neither gender nor age is a consideration in official or business situations.

The name of the person of higher precedence is always spoken *first*. The name of the person with lower precedence is always spoken *last*. For information on precedence in establishing name order, see page 139.

Greater Authority

Persons of greater authority receive/have presented to them persons of lower authority.

(Greater authority) receives *(lower authority)*
    (Chairman of the board), may I present *(new board member)*...
    (National sales manager), may I introduce *(local sales associate)*...

Elected and Appointed Officials

Official persons receive/have introduced to them *non-official persons*. Military, police, fire department, and other officials *in uniform* receive/have introduced to them persons *not in uniform*. If an official's duties are well known, the position does not need to be explained.

    (Official persons) receive *(non-official persons)*
        Mayor Hughes, may I present *Michael McNabb, principal of ...*
        Rabbi Green, may I introduce Ms. *Vick, president of Vick Exports ...*
        Officer Hastings, this is Mr. *Kim, owner of a deli in your precinct ...*

Clients

Clients receive, or have introduced to them, *one's colleagues* and *business associates*. *Clients* are considered more important than anyone in the organization. The higher precedence granted to a client holds true even if the client is *very junior* and one's colleague is *very senior*.

    (Clients) receive *(your business associates)*
        Matt Hopkins, I'd like to introduce *Ben Grossman*, president
        of our company. Ben, Matt is our client from Chicago.

Precedence and Phrasing in Introductions

The formality of an introduction is influenced by the phrasing.

    Formal:
        Mr. *Greater Authority*, may I present Ms. *Lesser Authority ...*
        Ms. *Greater Authority*, may I introduce Mr. *Lesser Authority ...*

    Less formal:
        Mr. *Greater Authority*, I'd like to introduce to you Ms. *Lesser Authority ...*
        Ms. *Greater Authority*, I'd like to introduce Mr. *Lesser Authority ...*

    Casual/informal:
        Mr./Ms. *Greater Authority*, this is Mr./Ms. *Lesser Authority ...*

    Don't use expressions such as:
        ... shake hands with ...
        ... make the acquaintance of ...

    Never use:
        *... I would like to introduce **you to** ...*
        *... I would like **you to** meet ...*
    These phrasings change an introduction from:
        CORRECT: *A greater authority receiving a lesser authority*
        TO INCORRECT: *A greater authority being introduced to a lesser authority.*

Group Introductions

When introducing a client or an important person to a group, the client or important person's name is said first:

> Ms. Client, I'd like to introduce the members of our research team.

Then, introduce each team member by name:
> Mark Bechara, our team leader.

Ms. Client shakes Mark Bechara's hand.

Then, introduce others in order of their positions on the research team.
> Carol Depew, head of our accounting department.

Ms. Client shakes Carol Depew's hand.

Include each team member and treat each one as a valued asset. Be mindful that overlooking someone may be viewed as a slight. If this happens, correct your oversight immediately.

Another option is to invite each team member to tell his or her name and position on the team.

Introductions of Colleagues: A Casual Option

Colleagues, friends, and peers can be introduced in a casual way; however, the introduction should not be sloppy. If one person is higher ranking, he or she should be introduced first. If the precedence of everyone is equal, introduce in the most convenient order. Slow down and pronounce each name clearly. Even where everyone is on a first-name basis, use *given name* and *surname*.

Introducer:	*Angela Gomez, this is Mark Vidal.*
Angela Gomez:	*I am glad to meet you, Mark.*
Mark Vidal:	*It is nice to meet you, Angela.*

In the United States use of *first name only* is so broadly accepted, the importance of surnames may seem reduced. But providing only the *given name* (no surname) as the introducer indicates one is casual about names in general, lacking confidence in one's ability to make an introduction, and does not want to make the effort.

Social Introductions

Precedence in Social Introductions

In most circumstances asking oneself a few questions will help in deciding who has higher precedence in social situations:

> *Who is older?*
> *Is one more accomplished?*
> *Are you introducing a man and a woman?*

The name of the person of higher precedence is always spoken first. The name of the person with lower precedence is always spoken last.

Age

An older person receives a younger person:

Mr. Smith, I'd like to introduce Mary Johnson, my daughter …

Mrs. Wagstaff, may I present Mrs. Giles. Mrs. Giles is Mary's teacher. Mrs. Wagstaff is my grandmother.

Accomplishment

A more distinguished person receives a less distinguished person:

Ms. Doe, may I introduce Ms. Jones. Ms. Jones chairs our floral committee. Ms. Doe's company underwrote tonight's event …

Mr. Niles, may I present Mr. Clark. Mr. Clark is a new resident here in Fairfax. Mr. Niles in a member of the Fairfax County Board …

Gender

A woman receives a man:

Mrs. Cho, may I present Mr. Hixon …

Jennifer Hill, may I introduce Claude Barnett …

Some Exceptions

According to diplomatic protocol, *women* are introduced (or presented) to *ambassadors, ministers* or *minister-counselors in charge of legations, chiefs of state, royalty,* and *dignitaries* of a church:

Mr. Ambassador, may I present Mrs. John Hill, organizer of tonight's event …

Mr. President, may I present Jane Rowan, director of the Heyward School …

Your Eminence, may I present Helen Flynn, from St. Vincent's Hospital …

Phrasing in Introductions

The phrasing influences the formality of an introduction. See page 115 for suggested forms to use and forms to avoid.

GROUP INTRODUCTIONS

When introducing a number of persons, say the new person's name and then give the names of the others in the group. If one can't remember all of their names, it is correct, acceptable, and practical to say the new person's name and suggest that the others introduce themselves:

Hello, everyone. This is Helga Schade from Germany. Please introduce yourselves to Helga.

If introducing new arrivals at a party, a round-the-room tour isn't necessary. Introduce the newcomers to the closest group of persons, and check back from time to time to make sure they are circulating.

INTRODUCING ONE'S SPOUSE

One should never refer to one's own husband or wife as Mr. (*surname*) or Mrs. (*surname*) in social introductions. If everyone knows the surname, all one needs say is:

This is Tom, my husband. .
I'd like you to meet Mary, my wife.

A man should never say:

Meet the missus.
Meet the wife.

A woman should never say:

Meet the husband.

If a woman is known by a professional name, or has a different surname from that of her husband, she should mention her husband's surname when introducing him:

I would like to introduce Tom Williams, my husband ...

This avoids the awkwardness of the husband being called by the wife's surname.

INTRODUCING RELATIVES

Clarify their relationship to you.

I'd like to present Margaret Hickey, my mother ...
I'd like to introduce to you Thomas Hickey, my brother ...

If one's mother has remarried:

Mary Cameron, my mother
Harry Cameron, my stepfather

Conversation Tips

Forgetting Names

It's so easy to forget someone's name, even though you can remember the time and the place you met. You can easily avoid embarrassment by being calm and sincere:

I recall our meeting, but I simply can't recall your name.
Please tell me your name again.
I'm having trouble recalling your name.

Never say:

I've forgotten your name.
What's that name again?
I can't remember your name.

These phrases clearly give the impression that the person simply wasn't important enough to remember.

Pronouncing Difficult Names

Pronouncing a person's name correctly shows respect and consideration. This requires only a little extra effort on your part. It's not only appropriate but also very flattering to say: "I'm not sure how to pronounce your name correctly. Please tell me the correct way to say it."

Never say:

What an unusual name!

Even worse is:

Your name sounds so foreign. Where are you from?

If you have a difficult name, help the person who is trying to pronounce it. Create an association to make it easier for others to say your name correctly:

It's Chai, which rhymes with pie.

If someone mispronounces your name, correct it immediately, but gently:

It's Johansen, not Johnson. The names sound so much alike, it's confusing.

Don't Point

Often the introducer points first to one person and then the other. Clearly, both know who they are; therefore, pointing communicates little more than the nervousness and uncertainty of the introducer.

Look at each person as you say his or her name. This focuses attention on the individual. It also makes him or her feel important while you appear in control.

One Introduction Is Enough

Don't follow up an introduction with a reciprocal introduction.

Don't say: Mr. Doe, may I present Ms. Gill; Ms. Gill, may I present Mr. Doe ...
Say: Mr. Doe, may I present Ms. Gill ...

Start the Conversation

Always include a conversational clue to provide a basis for their opening a conversation.

At a business meeting:

Bradley Hunter, I'd like to introduce Silvia Ortiz, my regional manager.
Brad is originally from your hometown, Chicago ...

In a social setting:

Angela Gomez, this is Mark Vidal. Mark and I met at the Chamber of Commerce meeting a few weeks ago. Angela and I work together ...

Mary Smith, I'd like to introduce Tom Jones. Tom and I were classmates in college, and he's here on business. Mary and I share an office.

Don't give a lavish biography to impress the other guests. Don't tack on "my friend" to one of the names when introducing two persons. It implies that the other person is not a friend.

Incorrect Introductions

When you are misintroduced, correct the person immediately, but do so in a friendly way:

My surname is Johnson, not Johansen

When your firm is misidentified, smile and include the corrected information in your reply to the introduction:

I'm with the International Monetary Fund, not the World Bank.

8 Precedence

Precedence and Forms of Address
In forms of address, precedence determines:

* Who is introduced first when several people are present
* Who is introduced to whom
* Whose name is listed first in an address on an envelope or letter

United States of America
Unofficial Order, Lists, or Tables of Federal Precedence
The President of the United States determines the rank of all American federal officials. Other federal departments make adjustments to include officials who attend their events.

However, any precedence list should be considered unofficial because each administration has the option to establish its own order of precedence, and sometimes an administration does so as circumstances alter the hierarchy.

Prototype Federal Precedence List
No official precedence list is issued in the United States, but there are many unofficial versions. This is a compendium of lists *The Protocol School of Washington*® believes to be up-to-date at the time of publication.

VIP CODE 1 (HEADS OF STATE)
1. President of the United States
   Heads of state and reigning royalty

VIP CODE 2 (FIVE-STAR EQUIVALENTS)

2. Vice President of the United States

3. Governor of a state in his or her own state

4. Speaker of the House of Representatives
   Chief Justice of the United States

5. Former presidents of the United States by earliest assumption of office
   American ambassadors to foreign governments at post

6. Secretary of State

7. President, United Nations General Assembly, in session
   Secretary General of the United Nations
   President, United Nations General Assembly, not in session
   President, International Court of Justice

8. Ambassadors of foreign governments accredited to the United States,
   by date of presentation of credentials

9. Widows of former presidents of the United States

10. Associate justices of the Supreme Court
    Retired chief justices of the United States
    Retired associate justices of the Supreme Court

11. Members of the cabinet, other than the secretary of state. (See item 6.)
    Secretary of the Treasury
    Secretary of Defense
    Attorney General
    Secretary of the Interior
    Secretary of Agriculture
    Secretary of Commerce
    Secretary of Labor
    Secretary of Health and Human Services
    Secretary of Housing and Urban Development
    Secretary of Transportation
    Secretary of Energy
    Secretary of Education
    Secretary of Veterans Affairs
    Secretary of Homeland Security
    Chief of Staff to the President
    Director, Office of Management and Budget
    U.S. Trade Representative
    Administrator, Environmental Protection Agency
    Director, Office of National Drug Control Policy
    Director of National Intelligence

12. President pro tempore of the Senate
    Senators by length of service. When length is the same, by state's date of
    admission to the Union, or alphabetically by state's name

13. Governors of states outside their own states by their state's date
    of admission to the Union or alphabetically by state's name

122

14. Acting heads of executive departments
    Former vice presidents of the United States or their widows

15. Members of the House of Representatives by length of service, then by
    state's date of admission to the Union, or alphabetically by state's name

16. Delegates to the House of Representatives (non-voting members) from
    Territory of American Samoa, District of Columbia, Territory of Guam,
    Commonwealth of Puerto Rico, and U.S. Virgin Islands,
    by date of election of delegate
    Governors of Commonwealth of Puerto Rico, Territory of Guam,
    Territory of American Samoa, U.S. Virgin Islands, and the
    Commonwealth of the Northern Mariana Islands, by territory's date
    of entering United States jurisdiction, or alphabetically by territory

17. Assistant to the President for National Security Affairs
    Senior Advisor to the President
    Assistant to the President and Deputy Chief of Staff
    Assistants to the President by seniority
    Chief of Staff to the Vice President
    Chairman, Council of Economic Advisors
    Chairman, Council on Environmental Quality
    Director, Office of Science and Technology Policy
    Chief of Protocol at the White House or accompanying the President

18. *Chargés d'affaires* assigned to diplomatic missions in Washington, D.C.
    Chargés d'affaires ad interim assigned to diplomatic missions
    in Washington, D.C.

19. Former secretaries of state, by seniority of assuming office
    Former cabinet members, by seniority of assuming office

20. Deputy to members of the cabinet by date of establishment of
    the department and others as added by the President:
    > Deputy Secretary of State
    > Deputy Secretary of the Treasury
    > Deputy Secretary of Defense
    > Deputy Attorney General
    > Deputy Secretary of the Interior
    > Deputy Secretary of Agriculture
    > Deputy Secretary of Commerce
    > Deputy Secretary of Labor
    > Deputy Secretary of Health and Human Services
    > Deputy Secretary of Housing and Urban Development
    > Deputy Secretary of Transportation
    > Deputy Secretary of Energy
    > Deputy Secretary of Education
    > Deputy Secretary of Veterans Affairs
    > Deputy Secretary of Homeland Security
    > Deputy Director, Office of Management and Budget
    > Deputy U.S. Trade Representative

Deputy Administrator, Environmental Protection Agency
Deputy Director, Office of National Drug Control Policy
Deputy Director of National Intelligence

21. Permanent Representative of the United States to the United Nations
U.S. Permanent Representative on the Council of the North
Atlantic Treaty Organization at post
Representative of the United States to the European Union at post
Ambassadors at large

22. Undersecretaries of State and the Counselor of the Department of State,
as ranked by the Department of State
Undersecretaries of executive departments and the Associate Attorney
General, according to date of establishment of the department.
If more than one from a department, then as ranked within the
department. In the Defense Department, undersecretaries are after
the Chairman of the Joint Chiefs of Staff. (See item 23.)
Secretary of the Army
Secretary of the Navy
Secretary of the Air Force
Postmaster General
Director, Federal Bureau of Investigation
Chairman, Board of Governors of the Federal Reserve
Chairman, Export-Import Bank
Director, Central Intelligence Agency
Administrator, Small Business Administration
Administrator, Agency for International Development

23. Chairman, Joint Chiefs of Staff
Vice Chairman, Joint Chiefs of Staff
Retired Chairman, Joint Chiefs of Staff
Chief of Staff of the Air Force, Chief of Staff of the Army,
Commandant of the Marine Corps, and Chief of Naval Operations,
by date of appointment
Commandant of the Coast Guard
Combatant commanders by date of appointment

24. Lieutenant governors in their own states

25. Permanent representatives of foreign governments to the United Nations
Secretary General of the Organization of American States
Chairman, Permanent Council of the Organization of American States
Representative of the United States to the European Office of
the United Nations, Geneva
Representative of the United States to the Vienna Office of
the United Nations
Permanent Representative of the United States to the
Organization of American States
Permanent Representatives of foreign governments to the
Organization of American States

124

Representative of the United States to the Organization for
Economic Cooperation and Development
Heads of international organizations, including:
International Monetary Fund
World Bank
North Atlantic Treaty Organization

26. Administrator, General Services Administration
Administrator, National Aeronautics and Space Administration
Chairman, Merit Systems Protection Board
Director, Office of Personnel Management
Administrator, Federal Aviation Administration
Chairman, Nuclear Regulatory Commission
Director of the Peace Corps

27. Deputy Permanent Representative to the United Nations
Deputy Administrator, Small Business Administration
Deputy Director, Central Intelligence Agency

28. American ambassadors, on state and official visits to the United States
Chief of Protocol at the Department of State or outside the White House
Career ambassadors

VIP CODE 3   (FOUR-STAR EQUIVALENTS)

29. Chief judges and circuit judges of the U.S. Courts of Appeals,
by length of service
Solicitor General
Chief judges and district judges, U.S. District Courts, by length of service
Chief judges and judges of the U.S. Court of Military Appeals
for the Armed Forces
Chief judges and judges of the U.S. Court of Appeals for Veterans Claims

30. Mayors of U.S. cities and the District of Columbia in their own cities

31. American *chargé d'affaires* at post
Principal deputy undersecretaries of executive departments
Undersecretaries of the Army, Navy, and Air Force

32. Assistant secretaries, assistant Attorneys General, counselors, and legal
advisers of executive departments by date of establishment of the
department. If more than one from a department, then as ranked
within the department.
Deputy assistants to the President, by seniority
Deputy Administrator, Agency for International Development

33. Undersecretaries General of the United Nations
Administrator, National Oceanographic and Atmospheric Administration
Deputy Director, General Services Administration
Deputy Director, National Aeronautics and Space Administration
Deputy Director, Office of Personnel Management

34. Assistant administrators, Agency for International Development
    Assistant U.S. trade representatives

35. U.S. Comptroller General
    Members of the Council of Environmental Quality
    Members of the Council of Economic Advisors

36. American ambassadors-designate, in the United States under normal orders, or on leave

37. Mayors of U.S. cities and the District of Columbia, when not in own city

38. Four-star military officers – General or admiral, by seniority
        Retired officers by rank with but after active officers
    Officers of the U.S. Senate and U.S. House of Representatives
    Assistant secretaries of the Army, Navy and Air Force and general counsels
        of the military departments, by date of appointment
    Executive Secretary, National Security Council

VIP CODE 4 (THREE-STAR EQUIVALENTS)

39. Deputy undersecretaries of executive departments
    Directors of defense agencies by establishment date of the agency
    Directors of Department of Defense field activities by establishment
        date of the agency
    Three-star military officers – Lieutenant general, vice admiral, by seniority
        Retired officers by rank with but after active members
    State senators and representatives in their own states
    Former American Ambassadors/Chiefs of Diplomatic Missions,
        in order of presentation of credentials at first post

40. Acting assistant secretaries of executive departments
    President, Overseas Private Investment Corporation
    Treasurer of the United States
    Director of the Mint
    Chairman, Federal Communications Commission
    Director, National Bureau of Standards
    Other chairmen of bureaus, boards, and commissions not previously listed
    Librarian of Congress
    Vice chairmen and members of the board of governors of the
        Federal Reserve System
    Secretary of the Smithsonian Institution
    Chairman, National Endowment for the Humanities
    Chairman, National Endowment for the Arts
    Director, National Science Foundation
    Surgeon General, U.S. Public Health Service
    Heads of independent agencies not mentioned previously,
        by date of establishment of the agency

41. Special assistants to the President
    Chairman of the American Red Cross

Ministers of foreign governments assigned to diplomatic missions
   in Washington, D.C.
Deputy chief of protocol
Commissioner of the U.S. Customs Service
Commissioners: Level IV Executives

42. Deputy undersecretaries of executive departments, according to date of
      establishment of the department; if more than one from a department,
      then as ranked within the department. (See item 40.)
   Deputy assistant secretaries of executive departments, according to date of
      establishment of the department; if more than one from a department,
      then as ranked within the department
   Deputy counsels of executive departments, according to date of
      establishment of the department; if more than one from a department,
      then as ranked within the department.

VIP CODE 5 (TWO-STAR EQUIVALENTS)

43. Two-star military – Major general, rear admiral, by seniority
      Retired officers by rank with but after active officers
   Assistant chiefs of protocol
   Directors of offices of executive departments
   Counselors of foreign governments assigned to diplomatic missions
      in Washington, D.C.
   Consuls general of foreign governments
   Deputy assistant secretaries of the Army, Navy, and Air Force and deputy
      general counsels, by date of establishment of the department; if more
      than one from a department, then as ranked within the department

44. Chief judge and judges, U.S. Court of International Trade
   Chief judge and associate judges, U.S. Court of Claims
   Chief judge and associate judges, U.S. Tax Court
   The deputy or principal deputy director for a Defense agency
   The deputy or principal deputy director for a Defense field activity

VIP CODE 6 (ONE-STAR EQUIVALENTS)

45. One-star military – Brigadier generals, rear admirals, by seniority
      Retired officers by rank with but after active officers
   Members of the Senior Executive Service
   Desk officers of executive departments
   First secretaries of foreign governments assigned to diplomatic missions
      in Washington, D.C. when there is no counselor
   Members of federal bureaus, board, and commissions

VIP CODE 7

46. Colonels and captains

Order of the States by Entry into the Union, Alphabetical

STATE	DATE OF ENTRY	SEQUENCE
Alabama	December 14, 1819	22
Alaska	January 3, 1959	49
Arizona	February 14, 1912	48
Arkansas	June 15, 1836	25
California	September 9, 1850	31
Colorado	August 1, 1876	38
Connecticut	January 9, 1788	5
Delaware	December 7, 1787	1
Florida	March 3, 1845	27
Georgia	January 2, 1788	4
Hawaii	August 21, 1959	50
Idaho	July 3, 1890	43
Illinois	December 3, 1818	21
Indiana	December 11, 1816	19
Iowa	December 28, 1846	29
Kansas	January 29, 1861	34
Kentucky	June 1, 1792	15
Louisiana	April 30, 1812	18
Maine	March 15, 1820	23
Maryland	April 28, 1788	7
Massachusetts	February 6, 1788	6
Michigan	January 26, 1837	26
Minnesota	May 11, 1858	32
Mississippi	December 10, 1817	20
Missouri	August 10, 1821	24

STATE	DATE OF ENTRY	SEQUENCE
Montana	November 8, 1889	41st
Nebraska	March 1, 1867	37
Nevada	October 31, 1864	36
New Hampshire	June 21, 1788	9
New Jersey	December 18, 1787	3
New Mexico	January 6, 1912	47
New York	July 26, 1788	11
North Carolina	November 21, 1789	12
North Dakota	November 2, 1889	39
Ohio	March 1, 1803	17
Oklahoma	November 16, 1907	46
Oregon	February 14, 1859	33
Pennsylvania	December 12, 1787	2
Rhode Island	May 29, 1790	13
South Carolina	May 23, 1788	8
South Dakota	November 2, 1889	40
Tennessee	June 2, 1796	16
Texas	December 29, 1845	28
Utah	January 4, 1896	45
Vermont	March 4, 1791	14
Virginia	June 26, 1788	10
Washington	November 11, 1889	42
West Virginia	June 20, 1863	35
Wisconsin	May 29, 1848	30
Wyoming	July 10, 1890	44

Order of the States by Entry into the Union, Chronological

SEQUENCE	STATE	DATE OF ENTRY
1	Delaware	December 7, 1787
2	Pennsylvania	December 12, 1787
3	New Jersey	December 18, 1787
4	Georgia	January 2, 1788
5	Connecticut	January 9, 1788
6	Massachusetts	February 6, 1788
7	Maryland	April 28, 1788
8	South Carolina	May 23, 1788
9	New Hampshire	June 21, 1788
10	Virginia	June 26, 1788
11	New York	July 26, 1788
12	North Carolina	November 21, 1789
13	Rhode Island	May 29, 1790
14	Vermont	March 4, 1791
15	Kentucky	June 1, 1792
16	Tennessee	June 2, 1796
17	Ohio	March 1, 1803
18	Louisiana	April 30, 1812
19	Indiana	December 11, 1816
20	Mississippi	December 10, 1817
21	Illinois	December 3, 1818
22	Alabama	December 14, 1819
23	Maine	March 15, 1820
24	Missouri	August 10, 1821
25	Arkansas	June 15, 1836

SEQUENCE	STATE	DATE OF ENTRY
26	Michigan	January 26, 1837
27	Florida	March 3, 1845
28	Texas	December 29, 1845
29	Iowa	December 28, 1846
30	Wisconsin	May 29, 1848
31	California	September 9, 1850
32	Minnesota	May 11, 1858
33	Oregon	February 14, 1859
34	Kansas	January 29, 1861
35	West Virginia	June 20, 1863
36	Nevada	October 31, 1864
37	Nebraska	March 1, 1867
38	Colorado	August 1, 1876
39	North Dakota	November 2, 1889
40	South Dakota	November 2, 1889
41	Montana	November 8, 1889
42	Washington	November 11, 1889
43	Idaho	July 3, 1890
44	Wyoming	July 10, 1890
45	Utah	January 4, 1896
46	Oklahoma	November 16, 1907
47	New Mexico	January 6, 1912
48	Arizona	February 14, 1912
49	Alaska	January 3, 1959
50	Hawaii	August 21, 1959

Precedence Order of Territories
51 District of Columbia
52 Puerto Rico
53 Guam
54 American Samoa
55 Commonwealth of Northern Marianas
56 Trust Territories
57 Virgin Islands

Prototype Order of Precedence in a State
Note: Most states follow the federal model, as in this list.

Governor
Lieutenant governor
Attorney General
Members of the Cabinet
U.S. Senators for the state by date of taking office

U.S. Representatives for the state by date of taking office
Speaker of the state's lower legislative house:
    State Assembly, House of Representatives, or House of Delegates
Chief justice of the state's supreme court
President of the state's upper house

Former governors by date of taking office
Active justices of the state's supreme court
Retired justices of the state's supreme court
Federal judges
Widows of former governors by date of taking office

Members of the state's upper house
Members of the state's lower house
Judges of the state court of appeals
Judges of other state courts
Mayors by city population

Chairmen of boards of supervisors by jurisdiction population
Former lieutenant governors
Former Attorneys General
Appointed heads of a state department or institution
Chairmen of boards, of a state department or institution
Executive assistants to a governor

United Kingdom

Unofficial British Order of Precedence

The Sovereign
The Consort of a Queen
The Prince of Wales
The Sovereign's male family members in precedence order

The Archbishop of Canterbury
The Lord Chancellor (The Lord High Chancellor)
The Archbishop of York
The Prime Minister

The Lord High Treasurer
The Lord President of the Council (President of the Privy Council)
The Speaker of the House of Commons
The Lord Speaker (Speaker of the House of Lords)
The Lord Chief Justice

The Lord Privy Seal
Ambassadors and high commissioners
The Lord Chamberlain
The Earl Marshal
The Lord Steward

The Master of the Horse
Ministers of (portfolio)
Bishops of London, Durham, and Winchester
Diocesan bishops by seniority as a bishop
Suffragan bishops by seniority as a bishop

Secretaries of State, holding the rank of Baron
Members of the House of Lords
Commissioner of the Great Seal
Treasurer of the royal household
Comptroller of the royal household

Vice-chamberlain of the royal household
Master of the Rolls
Privy counsellors, not holding a current office
Chancellor of the Exchequer
Chancellor of the Duchy of Lancaster

Lord Chief Justice of England
President of the Family Division
The Lord(s) Justice of Appeal
Judges of the High Court

Order of Precedence among Peers

Note: In the United Kingdom, *peers* are ranked among the government officials. Check for their precedence as necessary. Precedence among peers of the same rank can depend on many circumstances beyond the scope of this book.

Check for additional information as necessary.

Peers of countries:
- Peers of England
- Peers of Scotland
- Peers of Great Britain (1603-1707)
- Peers of Ireland
- Peers of United Kingdom and Ireland

Precedence among those with honours and titles:
- Dukes
- Marquesses
- Earls
- Viscounts
- Barons
- Knights of the Garter
- Baronets
- Knights
- Companions

Commonwealth of Australia

Unofficial Australian Order of Precedence

1. The Sovereign
2. The Governor-general
3. Governor of a state
   The governor of a state in his or her own state
   Administrator of a territory in his or her own territory
   Governors not in their own state by date of taking office
4. The Prime Minister
5. The Premier in his or her own state
   or a chief minister in his or her own territory
6. The President of the Senate and Speaker of the House of Representatives
   by date of taking office. The President of the Senate has higher
   ranking if date of taking office is the same.
7. The Chief Justice of Australia
8. Foreign diplomats by date of presentation of credentials
   Ambassadors and high commissioners
   Chargés d'affaires
   Acting high commissioners and *chargés d'affaires ad interim*
9. Members of the Federal Executive Council
   Deputy Prime Minister
   Ministers
   Treasurer
10. Administrators of Northern Territory and Norfolk Island

134

11. The Leader of the Opposition

12. Former governors-general by last date of holding office
    Former prime ministers by last date of holding office
    Former chief justices of Australia by last date of holding office

13. Premier or chief minister in his or her own state or territory, followed by:
    Premier of New South Wales
    Premier of Victoria
    Premier of Queensland
    Premier of Western Australia
    Premier of South Australia
    Premier of Tasmania
    Chief minister of the Northern Territory
    Chief minister of Norfolk Island

14. The lord mayor of a city in his or her own city

15. Justices of the High Court by seniority
    The Chief Justice of the Federal Court of Australia
        The President of the Australian Industrial Relations Commission
    The chief justice of a state in his or her own state
        Chief justices of states by date of taking office

16. Members of the Privy Council

17. The Chief of the Defence Force

18. Chief judges of federal courts by seniority

19. Members of Australian Parliament

20. Judges of federal courts and deputy presidents of the Australian
        Conciliation and Arbitration Commission by seniority

21. Lord mayors of cities in order of city population

22. Heads of churches and religious communities
        by date of taking current office in Australia

23. Presiding officers of state legislatures in their own states
        Presiding officer, then officers of state legislatures
            by date of taking office
        Presiding officer, then officers of the Northern Territory Legislature
        Presiding officer, then officers of the Norfolk Island Legislature

24. Members of a state Executive Council by date of taking office
    Members of the Territorial Executive Council by date of taking office

25. The Leader of the Opposition of a state or territorial legislature
        in his or her own state or territory, followed by:
            Leader of the Opposition of New South Wales
            Leader of the Opposition of Victoria
            Leader of the Opposition of Queensland
            Leader of the Opposition of Western Australia
            Leader of the Opposition of South Australia
            Leader of the Opposition of Tasmania

> Leader of the Opposition of Northern Territory

26. Judges of state and territorial Supreme Courts by date of taking office

27. Members of the Federal Executive Council, not currently in office

28. Members of state or territorial legislatures in their own states or territories, followed by:

> Members of state legislature of New South Wales
> Members of state legislature of Victoria
> Members of state legislature of Queensland
> Members of state legislature of Western Australia
> Members of state legislature of South Australia
> Members of state legislature of Tasmania
> Members of the Northern Territory Legislative Assembly
> Members of the Norfolk Island Legislative Assembly

29. Secretaries of the Air Force, Army, and Navy by date of appointment
Chief of the Army, Air Force, Navy by date of appointment

30. Consuls-general by date of recognition
Consuls by date of recognition
Vice-consuls by date of recognition

31. Holders of honours granted by the sovereign in order of precedence

Canada

Unofficial Canadian Order of Precedence

1. The Sovereign

2. The Governor-general

3. The Prime Minister

4. The Chief Justice

5. Former governors-general by last date of holding office
Spouses of deceased governors-general by last date of holding office
Former prime ministers by last date of holding office
Former chief justices by date of appointment

6. The Speaker of the Senate
The Speaker of the House of Commons

7. Ambassadors by the date of presentation of their credentials
High commissioners by the date of presentation of their credentials
Ministers plenipotentiary by the date of presentation of their credentials
Chargés d'affaires by the date of presentation of their credentials

8. Minister by date of appointment to the Privy Council
Secretaries of State by date of appointment to the Privy Council

9. Leader of the Opposition

10. The lieutenant governors of the provinces by their province's entry into the confederation

11. Members of the Privy Council who are not ministers by the date of appointment to the Privy Council. Precedence to those addressed as the Right Honourable by the date of appointment.

12. Premiers of the provinces by the province's entry into the confederation

13. Commissioners of the territories by the territory's entry into the confederation

14. The Government Leaders of the territories by the territory's entry into the confederation

15. National heads of religious denominations by date of appointment to their current office in Canada

16. Puisne judges of the Supreme Court
    The chief justice and the associate chief justice of a federal court
    The chief justices of the provincial and territorial courts in Ottawa. (See item 22.)
    The chief justices and associate justices of provincial and territorial superior courts in Ottawa. (See item 31.)
    Judges of a federal court
    Puisne judges of the superior courts
    The Chief Judge, Associate Chief Judge, and judges of the Tax Court by rank, then by the date of appointment

17. Senators in Ottawa. (See item 26.)
    Members of the House of Commons in Ottawa. (See item 26.)

18. Diplomatic representatives of countries without diplomatic relations with Canada

19. Clerk of the Privy Council and secretary to cabinet

20. The Chief of the Defence Staff
    Commissioner of the Royal Canadian Mounted Police

21. The Speakers of provincial legislative assemblies
    The Speakers of territorial legislative assemblies

22. Chief justices of provincial supreme courts in their own province. (See item 16.)
    Chief justices of territorial supreme courts in their own territory. (See item 16.)

23. Ministers/members of provincial executive councils
    Ministers/members of territorial executive councils

24. The Leader of the Opposition in provincial legislative assemblies
    The Leader of the Opposition in territorial legislative assemblies

25. Members of provincial legislative assemblies by seniority
    Members of territorial legislative assemblies by seniority

26. Senators in the Canadian Senate in their own province. (See item 17.)
    Senator in the Canadian Senate in their own territory. (See item 17.)
    Members of the Canadian House of Commons in their own province. (See item 17.)
    Members of the Canadian House of Commons in their own territory. (See item 17.)

27. Tribal leaders

28. Regional heads of religious denominations by date of appointment
    to their current office
29. Divisional commanders of the Royal Canadian Mounted Police
    Regional commanders of Canadian Armed Services
30. Judges of provincial courts by seniority. (See item 16.)
    Judges of territorial courts by seniority. (See item 16.)
31. Mayor of the capital city of the province or territory in his or her own city
32. Deputy ministers of a territory or province

Order of the Provinces by Entry into the Confederation

SEQUENCE	STATE	DATE OF ENTRY
1.	Ontario	July 1, 1867
2.	Quebec	July 1, 1867
3.	Nova Scotia	July 1, 1867
4.	New Brunswick	July 1, 1867
5.	Manitoba	July 15, 1870
6.	British Columbia	July 20, 1871
7.	Prince Edward Island	July 1, 1873
8.	Saskatchewan	September 1, 1905
9.	Alberta	September 1, 1905
10.	Newfoundland and Labrador	March 31, 1949

Order of the Territories by Entry into the Confederation

SEQUENCE	TERRITORY	DATE OF ENTRY
1.	Northwest Territories	July 15, 1870
2.	Yukon	June 13, 1898
3.	Nunavut	April 1, 1999

9 Joint Forms of Address

Precedence in Joint Forms of Address

Precedence, the preferential order, rank, or privileges granted to individuals in ceremonies and social formalities, also determines name order in joint forms of address. *Precedence* in the world of business and diplomacy is determined by position, power, seniority, and personal stature. Neither age nor gender are considerations.

Considerations When Establishing Name Order

Higher official before a lower official
  A person holding a high office, or having a title, before an unofficial person

Higher military rank or rating before a lower rank or rating
  A person with military rank or rating before a civilian

Higher hierarchical religious title before a lower hierarchical religious title
  A person with a hierarchical religious title before a layperson

Higher hereditary title before a lower hereditary title
  A person with a hereditary title before a person without a hereditary title

Higher importance at the event to which the persons are being invited
  The invited person before his or her spouse, escort, or guest

Name Order When Precedence Is Less Defined

When none of the ways of establishing rank listed on the previous page are pertinent, here are some guidelines to follow.

SHARED SURNAME

Among private citizens with a shared surname, follow the order in *Mr. and Mrs.*: *Man first, woman second.* For example, a married couple named *Robert and Sarah Buchanan* could be addressed in the following ways:

FORMAL	*Mr. and Mrs. Robert N. Buchanan*
	Robert and Sarah Buchanan
CASUAL	*Robert and Sarah*

DIFFERENT SURNAMES

One option is to follow the *Mr. and Mrs.* order: *Man first, woman second.*

FORMAL	*Mr. Peter Rusk and Ms. Linda Lenny*
	Peter Lenny and Linda Rusk
CASUAL	*Peter and Linda*

Or list in alphabetical order.

*Ms. Linda **Lenny** and Mr. Peter **Rusk***
*Mr. Frank **Baker** and Mr. Tom **Wilson***
*Ms. Susan **Clifton** and Ms. Maria **Yeonas***

Invitations to Unnamed Guests

Invitations are not correctly addressed to a named person and the person's unnamed guest. The invitation should be addressed to the intended guest and include a note that he or she is welcome to bring a guest. The host should ask the intended guest to provide the name of his or her guest so the host can prepare for the event.

Correct: **Ms. Ann Noyes**
Incorrect: *Ms. Ann Noyes and Guest*

Private Citizens

When both guests use the basic honorifics *Mr., Mrs., Ms.,* or *Miss,* use the following forms. If either uses any other honorific, see the following sections.

SHARED LAST NAME

Envelope, social: *Mr. and Mrs. Joshua Silver*
(Address)
Inside envelope: *Mr. and Mrs. Silver*

DIFFERENT LAST NAMES

Envelope, social: *Mr. Brian Neville*
and Ms. Susan Webb
(Address)

Inside envelope: *Mr. Neville and Ms. Webb*

Envelope, social: *Mr. Clyde Clark*
and Mr. Paul Tuffs
(Address)
Inside envelope: *Mr. Clark and Mr. Tuffs*

Envelope, social: *Ms. Diane Smith*
and Ms. Jennifer Thompson
(Address)
Inside envelope: *Ms. Smith and Ms. Thompson*

Doctors and Academics

Examples: *Dr. (name)*   *Chancellor (name)*   *President (name)*
                       Dean (name)   *Professor (name)*

SHARED SURNAME

Envelope, social: *(Honorific) Roger Phelps*
and Mrs. Phelps
(Address)
(Honorific only) and Mrs. Roger Phelps
(Address)
Inside envelope: *(Honorific only) and Mrs. Phelps*

Envelope, social: *(Honorific) Alice Shah*
and Mr. Tariq Shah
(Address)
Inside envelope: *(Honorific only) and Mr. Shah*

DIFFERENT SURNAMES

Envelope, social: *(Honorific) Roger Fox*
and Ms. Jane Goss
(Address)
Inside envelope: *(Honorific) Fox and Ms. Goss*

Envelope, social: *(Honorific) Lucy Khin*
and Mr. David Patel
(Address)
Inside envelope: *(Honorific) Khin and Mr. Patel*

Two Doctors, Two Academics

The person with higher precedence is listed first in every instance.

SHARED SURNAME

Envelope, social: *(Honorific) Ivan Kraus*   *(man higher precedence)*
    and (honorific) Susan Kraus
    (Address)

Inside envelope: *(Honorific) Kraus and (honorific) Kraus*

For two individuals with the same honorific and a shared last name, consider the following. This form is less formal and implies equal precedence.

Envelope, social: *(Plural honorific) Ivan and Susan Kraus*
    (Address)

Inside envelope: *(Plural honorific) Kraus*

DIFFERENT SURNAMES

Envelope, social: *(Honorific) Lucy French*   *(woman higher precedence)*
    and (honorific) Roger Betts
    (Address)

Inside envelope: *(Honorific) French and (honorific) Betts*

Officials Addressed by Title Only

Certain very high officials are addressed in social correspondence by the *title of their office* rather than by *their name*. In the United States, officials who are addressed on an invitation by *title only* include:

Chief of State, Head of Government
- *President of the United States*
- *Vice President of the United States*

Speaker or President of a National Assembly
- *Speaker of the House of Representatives*

Supreme Court
- *Chief Justice of the Supreme Court*
- *Associate justice of the Supreme Court*

Member of the Cabinet or Council of Ministers
- *Secretary of State*
- *Secretary of the Treasury*
- *Secretary of Defense*
- *Attorney General*
- *Secretary of (other departments)*

Certain Other High Offices
- *Deputy secretaries of a cabinet-level department*
- *Postmaster General*

142

Head of State Government

- *Governors*
- *Acting governors*
- *Governors-elect*
- *Lieutenant governors*

Member of a State Cabinet

- *Members of a governor's cabinet*

Head of Municipal Government

- *Mayors*

To determine name order when addressing two officeholders, see *Considerations When Establishing Name Order* on page 139.

Shared Surname

WIVES

Wives are addressed with honorific and surname only.

Envelope, social: *The President*
and Mrs. Kennedy
(Address)

Inside envelope: *The President and Mrs. Kennedy*

Envelope, social: *His Excellency*
The Prime Minister of Canada (whose surname is Doe)
and Dr. Doe
(Address)

Inside envelope: *The Prime Minister and Dr. Doe*

Envelope, social: *The Secretary of Energy* (whose surname is Perez)
and Mrs. Perez
(Address)

Inside envelope: *The Secretary of Energy and Mrs. Perez*

Envelope, social: *The Mayor of Cincinnati* (whose surname is Timmons)
and Mrs. Timmons
(Address)

Inside envelope: *The Mayor of Cincinnati and Mrs. Timmons*

HUSBANDS

On a social envelope, a husband is addressed as Mr. *(full name)*. On the invitation's inside envelope, a husband is addressed as Mr. *(surname)*.

Envelope, social: *The Chief of Protocol*
and Mr. Thomas R. Tucker
(Address)

Inside envelope: *The Chief of Protocol and Mr. Tucker*

Different Surnames

Envelope, social: *The Governor of Maine* (surname is not Ferguson)
and Ms. Harriet Ferguson
(Address)

Inside envelope: *The Governor of Maine and Ms. Ferguson*

Envelope, social: *The Mayor of Cleveland* (surname is not Mott)
and Dr. Lisa Mott
(Address)

Inside envelope: *The Mayor of Cleveland and Dr. Mott*

Officials Addressed With a Courtesy Title and as Title (Name)

Some high officials are addressed as *The Honorable (full name)*, *His/Her Excellency* or another courtesy title on a mailing envelope, and *(honorific of their office) (name)* on the inside envelope. For example:

- *Senators are addressed with the honorific* Senator.
- *Judges of lower courts are addressed with the honorific* Judge.
- *Other officials are addressed with a special honorific such as* Ambassador *or* Commissioner.

To address two officeholders, see page 139.

Shared Surname

On the social envelope the wife of a man with higher precedence is addressed as *Mrs. (surname)*. The husband of a woman with higher precedence is addressed as *Mr. (first and surname)*.

EXAMPLE: Judge

Envelope, social: *The Honorable*
Arnold Zapf
and Mrs. Zapf
(Address)

Inside envelope: *Judge Zapf and Mrs. Zapf*

EXAMPLE: U.S. Senator

Envelope, social: *The Honorable*
Judith Pratt
and Mr. Clive Pratt
(Address)

Inside envelope: *Senator Pratt and Mr. Pratt*

Different Surnames

EXAMPLE: Judge

Envelope, social: *The Honorable*
Scott Chin
and Ms. Nora Lee
(Address)
Inside envelope: *Judge Chin and Ms. Lee*

EXAMPLE: U.S. Senator

Envelope, social: *The Honorable*
Ann Polk
and Mr. Henry Rusk
(Address)
Inside envelope: *Senator Polk and Mr. Rusk*

Officials Addressed With a Courtesy Title and Mr. or Ms.

Most holders of high office who are addressed as *the Honorable (full name)*, *His/Her Excellency*, or another courtesy title on mailing envelopes are addressed as Mr. or Ms. *(surname)* on inside envelopes.

Shared Surname

On a social envelope, the wife of a man with higher precedence is addressed as Mrs. *(surname)*. The husband of a woman with higher precedence is addressed as Mr. *(full name)*.

On an invitation's inside envelope, when the surnames are the same, the name order of the social form Mr. *and* Mrs. *(surname)*, man first, woman second, is used regardless of precedence.

Envelope, social: *The Honorable*
Thomas Kline
and Mrs. Kline
(Address)
Inside envelope: *Mr. and Mrs. Kline*

Envelope, social: *The Honorable*
Judith Pratt
and Dr. Terry Pratt
(Address)
Inside envelope: *Dr. and Mrs. Pratt*

Mrs. *and Dr. Pratt* is an option that maintains official precedence, but most protocol officers suggest that following the social Mr. *and Mrs.* order is appropriate.

Different Surnames

When the addressees' surnames are different, the person with higher precedence is always listed first.

> Envelope, social: *The Honorable*
> > *Scott Pelosi*
> > *and Dr. Nina Gold*
> > *(Address)*
> Inside envelope: *Mr. Pelosi and Dr. Gold*

> Envelope, social: *The Honorable*
> > *Linda Ortiz*
> > *and Mr. Jose Mela*
> > *(Address)*
> Inside envelope: *Ms. Ortiz and Mr. Mela*

Two Officials, Both Addressed With a Courtesy Title

Shared Surname

On the mailing envelope, follow the order prescribed by the precedence of the positions held. See more on precedence on page 121.

On an invitation's inside envelope, when the surnames are the same, use the name order of the social form *Mr. and Mrs.*, man first, woman second, regardless of precedence.

MAN HIGHER PRECEDENCE

> Envelope, social: *The Honorable*
> > *Tariq Habib*
> > *and the Honorable*
> > *Linda Habib*
> > *(Address)*
> Inside envelope: *Mr. and Mrs. Habib*

WOMAN HIGHER PRECEDENCE

> Envelope, social: *The Honorable*
> > *Sybille Millard*
> > *and the Honorable*
> > *Howard Millard*
> > *(Address)*
> Inside envelope: *Mr. and Mrs. Millard*

Different Surnames

Follow the order prescribed by the precedence of the positions held in every instance.

MAN HIGHER PRECEDENCE

> Envelope, social: *The Honorable*
> > *Henry Wren*
> > > *and the Honorable*
> > > > *Sarah Miller*
> > > > > *(Address)*
>
> Inside envelope: Mr. *Wren and Ms. Miller*

WOMAN HIGHER PRECEDENCE

> Envelope, social: *The Honorable*
> > *Sarah Miller*
> > > *and the Honorable*
> > > > *Henry Wren*
> > > > > *(Address)*
>
> Inside envelope: Ms. *Miller and Mr. Wren*

Members of the Armed Services

Spouse of a Member of the Armed Services

Civilian wives are addressed as *Mrs. (surname).* Nonmilitary husbands are addressed as Mr. *(full name)* on a social envelope, with Mr. *(surname)* on an invitation's inside envelope.

Both Guests Are in the Armed Services

The higher-ranking member of the armed forces is listed first. *Full names* are used on social envelopes, *surnames only* on the invitation's inside envelope.

> Envelope, social: *(Higher graded rank/rating) (first and surname)*
> > *and (lower graded rank/rating) (first and surname)*
> > > *(Address)*
>
> Inside envelope: *(Higher basic rank/rating) (surname)*
> > *and (lower basic rank/rating) (surname)*

Only One in the Armed Services: Officers and Warrant Officers

SHARED SURNAME

> Envelope, social: *(Graded rank/rating) Joshua Downes*
> > *and Mrs. Downes*
> > > *(Address)*
>
> > *(Graded rank/rating) and Mrs. Joshua Downes*
> > > *(Address)*

Inside envelope: *(Basic rank/rating) and Mrs. Downes*

Envelope, social: *(Graded rank/rating) Susan Henson*
and Mr. Steven Henson
(Address)
Inside envelope: *(Basic rank/rating) and Mr. Henson*

DIFFERENT SURNAMES

Envelope, social: *(Graded rank/rating) Paul Bridwell*
and Ms. Cynthia Lenny
(Address)
Inside envelope: *(Basic rank/rating) Bridwell and Ms. Lenny*

Envelope, social: *(Graded rank/rating) Lucy Palmer*
and Mr. Douglas Granito
(Address)
Inside envelope: *(Basic rank/rating) Palmer and Mr. Granito*

Only One in the Armed Services: Noncommissioned Officers in the Army, Air Force, and Marine Corps

SHARED SURNAME

Envelope, social: *(Graded rating) Todd Smith*
and Mrs. Smith
(Address)
(Graded rating) and Mrs. Todd Smith
(Address)
Inside envelope: *Mr. and Mrs. Smith*
Envelope, social: *(Graded rating) Jill Watts*
and Mr. Harold Watts
(Address)
Inside envelope: *Mr. and Mrs. Watts*

DIFFERENT SURNAMES

Envelope, social: *(Graded rating) James Watson*
and Ms. Rachel Perez
(Address)
Inside envelope: *Mr. Watson and Ms. Perez*

Envelope, social: *(Graded Rating) Diana Guzman*
and Mr. Thomas King
(Address)
Inside envelope: *Ms. Guzman and Mr. King*

148

Only One in the Armed Services: Noncommissioned Officers in the Navy and Coast Guard

Ratings are not used on social envelopes in the Navy and Coast Guard.

SHARED SURNAME

When the surnames are the same, list the names *man first, woman second.*

Envelope, social: Mr. and Mrs. Todd Smith
(Address)
Inside envelope: Mr. and Mrs. Smith

DIFFERENT SURNAMES

When the surnames are different, the service member is named first on an invitation to an official event where the service member is the invited guest.

When the invited guest is a noncommissioned male officer:

Envelope, social: Mr. John Kramer
and Ms. Jennifer Hughes
(Address)
Inside envelope: Mr. Kramer and Ms. Hughes

When the invited guest is a noncommissioned female officer:

Envelope, social: Ms. Jennifer Hughes
and Mr. John Kramer
(Address)
Inside envelope: Ms. Hughes and Mr. Kramer

Clergy Addressed as *the Reverend*

Shared Surname

A person with a hierarchical title is listed before a lay person. On a social envelope, wives of clergy are addressed as Mrs. (*surname*). Husbands are addressed as Mr. (*full name*) on the social envelope, with Mr. (*surname*) on the invitation's inside envelope.

ONE IS CLERGY

Envelope, social: The Reverend John Poe
and Mrs. Poe
(Address)
The Reverend and Mrs. John Poe
(Address)
Inside envelope: Dr./Father/Pastor/etc. and Mrs. Poe
OR Mr. and Mrs. Poe

Envelope, social: *Rabbi Craig Land*
and Mrs. Land
(Address)
Rabbi and Mrs. Craig Land
(Address)

Inside envelope: *Rabbi and Mrs. Land*

Envelope, social: *The Reverend Mary Havel*
and Mr. Milo Havel
(Address)

Inside envelope: *Dr./Deacon/Pastor/etc. and Mr. Havel*
OR *Mr. and Mrs. Havel*

Envelope, social: *Rabbi Lisa Stein*
and Mr. Geoffrey Stein
(Address)

Inside envelope: *Rabbi and Mr. Stein*

BOTH ARE CLERGY
Man Higher Precedence

Envelope, social: *The Reverend David Jones*
and the Reverend Alice Jones
(Address)

The Reverends David and Alice Jones
(Address)

Inside envelope: Use their personal honorifics as appropriate
Dr./Father/Pastor/etc. and Mrs. Jones
OR *Mr. and Mrs. Jones*
OR *Drs. Jones*
OR *Pastors Jones*

Equal Precedence (less formal than the above)

Precedence is technically never equal: One person was ordained before another, one holds a higher hierarchical office, *etc*. The order in *Mr. and Mrs.* (man first, woman second) is typically followed for couples using the same surname.

Envelope, social: *The Reverends David and Alice Jones*
(Address)

Woman Higher Precedence

Envelope, social: *The Reverend Alice Jones*
and The Reverend David Jones
(Address)

Inside envelope: Use their personal honorifics as appropriate
Dr./Mother/Pastor/etc. and Mr. Jones
OR *Mr. and Mrs. Jones*
OR *Drs. Jones*
OR *Pastors Jones*

Different Surnames

ONE IS CLERGY

A person with a hierarchical title is listed before a lay person.

Envelope, social: *The Reverend George Brent*
and Ms. Hilda Phelps
(Address)
Inside envelope: *Dr./Father/Pastor/etc. Brent and Ms. Phelps*

Envelope, social: *Rabbi Judith Marcus*
and Mr. Milton Bookman
(Address)
Inside envelope: *Rabbi Marcus and Mr. Bookman*

Envelope, social: *Rabbi Lawrence Coleman*
and Ms. Carol Schecter
(Address)
Inside envelope: *Rabbi Coleman and Ms. Schecter*

Envelope, social: *The Reverend Ann Krell*
and Mr. Carl Moss
(Address)
Inside envelope: *Dr./Mother/Pastor/etc. Krell and Mr. Moss*
Ms. Krell and Mr. Moss

BOTH ARE CLERGY

The person with higher precedence is listed first.

Man with Higher Precedence

Envelope, social: *The Reverend Kevin Ross*
and The Reverend Jane Peters
(Address)

Inside envelope: Use their personal honorifics as appropriate.
Father Ross and Mother Peters
OR *Drs./Pastors Ross and Peters*
OR *Mr. Ross and Ms. Peters*

Woman with Higher Precedence

Envelope, social: *The Reverend Jane Peters*
and The Reverend Kevin Ross
(Address)

Inside envelope: Use their personal honorifics as appropriate.
Dr. Peters and Father Ross
OR *Mother Peters and Mr. Ross*

PART II

Forms of Address

10 Private Citizens

Corporate President, Chief Executive, Executive
Envelope, official:
> Mr./Ms. *(full name)*
>> *(Title/position)*
>>> *(Name of company)*
>>> *(Address)*

Letter salutation: *Dear Mr./Ms. (surname):*
Complimentary close: *Sincerely yours,* OR *Sincerely,*
Envelope, social:
> Mr./Ms. *(full name)*
>> *(Address)*

Invitation, inside envelope: Mr./Ms. *(surname)*
Place card: Mr./Ms. *(surname)*
Introduction:
> Mr./Ms. *(full name)*, *(title/position)* of *(name of company)*
> OR *(Full name)*, *(title/position)* of *(name of company)*
> OR *(Title/position)*, *(name of company)*, Mr./Ms. *(surname)*

Introduction, one person to another:
> Mr./Ms. *(full name or surname only)*
> OR *(Full name)*

Conversation: Mr./Ms. *(surname)*

Man or Woman, Business
Envelope, official:
> Mr./Ms. *(full name)*
>> *(Company name)*
>>> *(Address)*

Letter salutation: *Dear Mr./Ms. (surname):*
Complimentary close: *Sincerely yours,* OR *Sincerely,*
Introduction:
> Mr./Ms. *(full name)*, *(title/position) of (name of company)*
> OR *(Title/position)*, *(name of company)*, Mr./Ms. *(surname)*

Introduction, less formal: *(Full name)*, *(title/position) of (name of company)*
Introduction, one person to another:
> Mr./Ms. *(full name or surname only)*
> OR *(Full name)*

Conversation: Mr./Ms. *(surname)*

Man, Social
Envelope:
> Mr. *(full name)*
>> *(Address)*

Letter salutation: *Dear Mr. (surname):*
Complimentary close: *Sincerely yours,* OR *Sincerely,*
Invitation, inside envelope: Mr. *(surname)*
Place card: Mr. *(surname)*
Introduction (only children are introduced by first name only):
> Mr. *(full name or surname only)*
> OR *(Full name)*

Conversation: Mr. *(surname)*

Woman, Undefined Marital Status, Social
Envelope:
> Ms. *(full name)*
>> *(Address)*

Letter salutation: *Dear Ms. (surname):*
Complimentary close: *Sincerely yours,* OR *Sincerely,*
Invitation, inside envelope: Ms. *(surname)*
Place card: Ms. *(surname)*
Introduction:
> Ms. *(full name or surname only)*
> OR *(Full name)*

Conversation: Ms. *(surname)*

156

Woman, Married, Contemporary, Social

Envelope:
>Mrs. (woman's first name) (surname)
>>(Address)

Letter salutation: Dear Mrs. (surname):
Complimentary close: Sincerely yours, OR Sincerely,
Invitation, inside envelope: Mrs. (surname)
Place card: Mrs. (surname)
Introduction: Mrs. (woman's first name) (surname) OR (Full name)
Conversation: Mrs. (surname)

Woman, Married, Traditional, Social

Envelope:
>Mrs. (husband's full name)
>>(Address)

Letter salutation: Dear Mrs. (surname):
Complimentary close: Sincerely yours, OR Sincerely,
Invitation, inside envelope: Mrs. (surname)
Place card: Mrs. (surname)
Introduction: Mrs. (husband's full name) OR Mrs. (surname)
Conversation: Mrs. (surname)

Woman, Widow, Traditional, Social

Envelope:
>Mrs. (husband's full name)
>>(Address)

Letter salutation: Dear Mrs. (surname):
Complimentary close: Sincerely yours, OR Sincerely,
Invitation, inside envelope: Mrs. (surname)
Place card: Mrs. (surname)
Introduction (only children are introduced by first name only):
>Mrs. (husband's full name) OR Mrs. (surname) OR (Woman's full name)
Conversation: Mrs. (surname)

Woman, Divorced, Traditional, Social

Envelope:
>Mrs. (woman's first name) (former husband's surname)
>>(Address)

Letter salutation: Dear Mrs. (surname):
Complimentary close: Sincerely yours, OR Sincerely,
Invitation, inside envelope: Mrs. (surname)
Place card: Mrs. (surname)
Introduction: Mrs. (woman's first name) (former husband's surname)

Introduction, less formal: *(Woman's first name) (former husband's surname)*
Introduction, one person to another:
　Mrs. *(woman's first name) (former husband's surname)*
　OR Mrs. *(surname)*
　OR *(Woman's full name)*
Conversation: Mrs. *(surname)*

Woman, Single, Traditional, Social
Envelope:
　Miss *(full name)*
　　(Address)
Letter salutation: *Dear Miss (surname):*
Complimentary close: *Sincerely yours,* OR *Sincerely,*
Invitation, inside envelope: Miss *(surname)*
Place card: Miss *(surname)*
Introduction: Miss *(full name or surname only)* OR *(Full name)*
Conversation: Miss *(surname)*

Children: Girls, Traditional
Envelope:
　Miss *(full name)*
　　(Address)
Letter salutation: *Dear Miss (surname):*
Complimentary close: *Sincerely yours,* OR *Sincerely,*
Invitation, inside envelope: Miss *(surname)*
Place card: Miss *(surname)*
Introduction: Miss *(full name)*
Introduction, less formal: *(Full name)*
Introduction, one person to another:
　Miss *(full name or surname only)* OR *(Full name)*
Conversation: Miss *(surname)* OR *(First name)*

Children: Boys, Traditional
NOTE: Use of *master* outside conservative circles is considered old fashioned.
Envelope:
　Master *(full name)*
　　(Address)
Letter salutation: *Dear Master (surname):*
Complimentary close: *Sincerely yours,* OR *Sincerely,*
Invitation, inside envelope: Master *(surname)*
Place card: Master *(surname)*
Introduction: Master *(full name)*
Introduction, less formal: *(Full name)*
Introduction, one person to another: Master *(surname)* OR *(Full name)*
Conversation: Master *(surname)* OR *(First name)*

11 Professionals & Academics

Professionals

Doctor

Example: *Doctor of dentistry, medicine,* or *osteopathy*
            Doctor of veterinary medicine
Envelope, official:
    (Full name), DDS, MD, DO, DVM (or other degree)
        (Name of practice, hospital, or clinic)
            (Address)
Letter salutation: *Dear Dr. (surname):*
Complimentary close: *Sincerely yours,* OR *Sincerely,*
Envelope, social:
    Dr. (full name)
        (Address)
Invitation, inside envelope: *Dr. (surname)*
Place card: *Dr. (surname)*
Introduction:
    Dr. (full name), a (name of medical specialty), (name and location of
        practice, institution, hospital, or clinic)
    OR *(Title/position), (name of institution, hospital, or clinic), Dr. (surname)*
Introduction, one person to another: *Dr. (full name or surname only)*
Conversation, initially: *Dr. (surname)*
Conversation, subsequently: *Dr.*

Nurse

Envelope, official:
> *(Full name), (RN, LPN, or other post nominal)*
> > *(Name of practice, hospital, or clinic)*
> > > *(Address)*

Letter salutation: Dear Mr./Ms. *(surname)*:
Complimentary close: *Sincerely yours,* OR *Sincerely,*
Envelope, social:
> Mr./Ms. *(full name)*
> > *(Address)*

Invitation, inside envelope: Mr./Ms. *(surname)*
Place card: Mr./Ms. *(surname)*
Introduction:
> Mr./Ms. *(full name), (degree/area of specialization), (name and location of practice, hospital, or clinic)*
> OR *(Title/position), (name and location of institution, hospital, or clinic),* Mr./Ms. *(surname)*

Introduction, one person to another:
> Mr./Ms. *(full name or surname only)*
> > *(Full name)*

Conversation: Mr./Ms. *(surname)*

Doctorate: Not Medical, Outside Academia, and Honorary

NOTE: Those not in teaching or research positions and those who are the recipients of honorary doctorates typically do not use Dr., but personal preference should be taken into account.

See also *Academics,* page 162.
Envelope, official:
> Mr./Ms./Dr. *(full name)*
> > *(Address)*

Letter salutation: Dear Mr./Ms./Dr. *(surname)*:
Complimentary close: *Sincerely yours,* OR *Sincerely,*
Envelope, social:
> Mr./Ms./Dr. *(full name)*
> > *(Address)*

Invitation, inside envelope: Mr./Ms./Dr. *(surname)*
Place card: Mr./Ms./Dr. *(surname)*
Introduction:
> Mr./Ms./Dr. *(full name), (position), (company/institution)*
> OR *(Title/position), (company/institution).* Mr./Ms./Dr. *(surname)*

Introduction, one person to another:
> Mr./Ms. *(full name or surname only)*
> OR Dr. *(full name or surname only)*
> OR *(Full name)*

Conversation: Mr./Ms./Dr. *(surname)*

Attorney

NOTE: *Attorney* is not traditionally an honorific in address, but sometimes attorneys will informally answer the phone *Attorney (surname)*, or will be identified in the third person as *Attorney (surname)* for clear identification.

For attorneys using *JD*, see *Academics*, page 162.

Envelope, official:
> Mr./Ms. *(full name)*
>> *Attorney at Law*
>>> *(Name of firm)*
>>>> *(Address)*
> *(Full name)*, *Esq.*
>> *(Name of firm)*
>>> *(Address)*

Letter salutation: *Dear Mr./Ms. (surname):*
Complimentary close: *Sincerely yours,* OR *Sincerely,*
Envelope, social:
> Mr./Ms. *(full name)*
>> *(Address)*

Invitation, inside envelope: Mr./Ms. *(surname)*
Place card: Mr./Ms. *(surname)*
Introduction:
> Mr./Ms. *(full name)*, *attorney at law with (firm name and location)*
> OR *Attorney at law with (firm name and location)*, Mr./Ms. *(surname)*

Introduction, one person to another:
> Mr./Ms. *(full name or surname only)* OR *(Full name)*

Conversation: Mr./Ms. *(surname)*

Accountant, Architect, Designer, or Other Professionals

Examples: *(Full name)*, CPA
> *(Full name)*, ASID
> *(Full name)*, AIA

Envelope, official:
> *(Full name)*, *(post nominal for professional accreditation)*
>> *(Name of firm)*
>>> *(Address)*

Letter salutation: *Dear Mr./Ms. (surname):*
Complimentary close: *Sincerely yours,* OR *Sincerely,*
Envelope, social:
> Mr./Ms. *(full name)*
>> *(Address)*

Invitation, inside envelope: Mr./Ms. *(surname)*
Place card: Mr./Ms. *(surname)*
Introduction:
> Mr./Ms. *(full name)*, *(position held/profession) (name and location of firm)*
> OR *(Position held/profession)*, *(name and location of firm)*, Mr./Ms. *(surname)*

Introduction, one person to another:
> Mr./Ms. *(full name or surname only)* OR *(Full name)*

Conversation: Mr./Ms. *(surname)*

Academics

Academic Degrees

NOTE: Degrees other than doctorates (*e.g.*, bachelor's and master's degrees) are rarely used outside academic publications and have no special forms of address.

Academic degrees are not normally used with the name when the individual is addressed as *president* or *chancellor*: The office is judged to outrank the degree.

Chancellor/President of a College/University

Envelope, official:
> *Chancellor/President (full name)*
> > *(College/university)*
> > > *(Address)*

> *Dr.* can be used if the person has a doctorate, although this is less common.
> *Dr. (full name)*
> > *Chancellor/President*
> > > *(College/university)*
> > > > *(Address)*

Letter salutation: *Dear Dr./Chancellor/President (surname):*
Complimentary close: *Sincerely yours,* OR *Sincerely,*
Envelope, social:
> *Dr./Chancellor/President (full name)*
> > *(Address)*

Invitation, inside envelope: *Dr./Chancellor/President (surname)*
Place card: *Dr./Chancellor/President (surname)*
Introduction:
> *(Full name), (chancellor/president) of (college/university)*
> OR *Dr. (full name), (chancellor/president) of (college/university)*
> OR *(Chancellor/president) of (college/university) Dr./Mr./Ms. (surname)*

Introduction, one person to another:
> *Dr./Chancellor/President (full name or surname only)*

Conversation, initially: *Dr./Chancellor/President (surname)*
Conversation, subsequently: *Dr./Chancellor/President*

Dean of a College or of the Faculty

Envelope, official:
> *Dean (full name)*
> > *(College/university)*
> > > *(Address)*
> *Professor (full name)*
> > *Dean of (students/college/faculty)*
> > > *(College/university)*
> > > > *(Address)*

Dr./Mr./Ms. *(full name)*
    Dean of *(students/college/faculty)*
      (College/university)
      (Address)
(Full name) (post nominal for degrees held)
    Dean of *(students/college/faculty)*
      (College/university)
      (Address)

Letter salutation: *Dear Dr./Dean/Professor (surname):*
Complimentary close: *Sincerely yours,* OR *Sincerely,*
Envelope, social:
    Dr./Dean/Professor (full name)
      (Address)
Invitation, inside envelope: *Dr./Dean/Professor (surname)*
Place card: *Dr./Dean/Prof. (surname)*
Introduction:
    Dr. (full name), dean of (students, college, etc.), (college/university)
    OR *Dean of (students, college, etc.), (college/university), Dr. (surname)*
Introduction, one person to another:
    Dr./Dean/Professor (full name or surname only)
Conversation, initially: *Dr./Dean/Professor (surname)*
Conversation, subsequently: *Dr./Dean/Professor*

Professor, Assistant Professor, Associate Professor

NOTE: *Dr.* is used if the person has a doctorate. *Professor/Mr./Ms.* is used if an individual does not hold a doctoral degree. Graded levels of *professor, e.g., assistant professor* or *associate professor,* are not used verbally and seldom used in writing in direct address.
Envelope, official:
    Professor/Mr./Ms. (full name)
      (College/university)
      (Address)
    (Full name) (post nominal for degrees held)
      (College/university)
      (Address)
Letter salutation:
    Dear Dr. (surname):
    Dear Professor (surname):
Complimentary close: *Sincerely yours,* OR *Sincerely,*
Envelope, social:
    Dr./Professor/Mr./Ms. (full name)
      (Address)
Invitation, inside envelope: *Dr./Professor/Mr./Ms. (surname)*
Place card: *Dr./Prof./Mr./Ms. (surname)*

Introduction:
> Dr./Professor/Mr./Ms. *(full name)*, *department of (discipline)*,
> *(college/university)*
>
> OR *Dr./Mr./Ms. (full name)*, *(graded level of professor)*, *department of*
> *(discipline)*, *(college/university)*
>
> OR *(Graded level of professor)*, *department of (discipline)*, *(college/university)*,
> *Dr./Mr./Ms. (surname)*

Introduction, one person to another:
> *Dr./Professor (full name or surname only)*

Conversation, initially: *Dr./Professor (surname)*

Conversation, subsequently: *Dr./Professor*

Professor of an Endowed Chair

Envelope, official:
> Dr./Professor/Mr./Ms. *(full name)*
> > *(Name of endowed chair)*
> > > *(College/university)*
> > > > *(Address)*

Introduction:
> Dr./Professor/Mr./Ms. *(full name)*, *the (name of endowed chair)*,
> *(college/university)*
>
> OR *The (name of endowed chair)*, *(college/university)*,
> *Dr./Professor/Mr./Ms. (surname)*

Instructors

Use Mr./Ms. *(name)* and identify by position after the name.

12 Federal, State & Municipal Officials

U.S. Federal Government

FEDERAL EXECUTIVE

President of the United States
NOTE: While the President is referred to as *President (surname)* in the media, the President's name is never used in his or her presence.
Envelope, official:
> *The President*
> > *The White House*
> > > *Washington, DC 20500*

Letter salutation: *Dear Mr./Madam President:*
Complimentary close: Most respectfully,
Envelope, social:

The President	*The President*
(Address)	*and Mrs. (surname)*
	(Address)
	The President
	and Mr. (full name)
	(Address)

Invitation, inside envelope:
> *The President*
> OR *The President and Mrs. (surname)*
> OR *The President and Mr. (surname)*

Place card: *The President* OR *The President of the United States*

Announced: *The President* OR *The President of the United States*
Introduction, one person to another:
    In the United States everyone is introduced to the President.
        Mr./Madam President, may I present ...
Conversation: Mr./Madam President

Wife or Husband of the President, *Contemporary Form*

NOTE: It is not necessary to specify that he or she is married to the President.
Envelope, official:
    Mrs. *(surname)*
        The White House
           Washington, DC 20500
    Mr. *(full name)*
        The White House
           Washington, DC 20500
Letter salutation: *Dear Mrs./Mr. (surname):*
Complimentary close: *Sincerely yours,* OR *Sincerely,*
Envelope, social (if the President is not invited):
    Mrs. *(surname)*   Mr. *(full name)*
    (Address)   *(Address)*
Invitation if the President is not invited (inside envelope): Mrs./Mr. *(surname)*
Place card: Mrs./Mr. *(surname)*
Introduction: Recent First Ladies have requested to be introduced by their own
names, *e.g.*, Hillary Rodham Clinton and Laura Bush.
    First Lady, (preferred full name)
    Mr. *(full name)*
Introduction, one person to another:
    Mrs. *(surname)*
    Mr. *(surname)*
Conversation: Mrs./Mr. *(surname)*

Wife of the President, *Traditional Form*

NOTE: It is not necessary to specify that she is married to the President.
Envelope, official:
    Mrs. *(surname)*
        The White House
           Washington, DC 20500
Letter salutation: *Dear Mrs. (surname):*
Complimentary close: *Sincerely yours,* OR *Sincerely,*
Envelope, social (if the President is not invited):
    Mrs. *(surname)*
        (Address)
Invitation if the President is not invited (inside envelope): Mrs. *(surname)*
Place card: Mrs. *(surname)*
Introduction: *First Lady, Mrs. (surname)*
Introduction, one person to another: Mrs. *(surname)*
Conversation: Mrs. *(surname)*

President-Elect of the United States

Envelope, official:
> The Honorable
>> (Full name)
>>> The President-elect
>>> (Address)

Letter salutation: *Dear Mr./Ms. (surname):*
Complimentary close: *Most respectfully,* OR *Respectfully yours,*
Envelope, social:
> The Honorable
>> (Full name)
>> (Address)

Invitation, inside envelope: *Mr./Ms. (surname)*
Place card: *Mr./Ms. (surname)*
Introduction: *The Honorable (full name), the president-elect*
Introduction, one person to another: *Mr./Ms. (surname)*
Conversation: *Mr./Ms. (surname)*

Former President of the United States

Envelope, official:
> The Honorable
>> (Full name)
>> (Address)

Letter salutation: *Dear Mr./Ms. (surname):*
Complimentary close: *Most respectfully,* OR *Respectfully yours,*
Envelope, social:
> The Honorable
>> (Full name)
>> (Address)

Invitation, inside envelope: *Mr./Ms. (surname)*
Place card: *Mr./Ms. (surname)*
Introduction: *The Honorable (full name)*
Introduction, less formal: *Mr./Ms. (surname)*
Introduction, one person to another: *Mr./Ms. (surname)*
Conversation: *Mr./Ms. (surname)*

Vice President of the United States

Envelope, official:
> The Vice President
>> Old Executive Office Building
>> Washington, DC 20501

Letter salutation: *Dear Mr./Madam Vice President:*
Complimentary close: *Most respectfully,* OR *Respectfully yours,*
Envelope, social:
> The Vice President
>> (Address)

> The Vice President
> and Mrs. (surname)
> (Address)
> The Vice President
> and Mr. (full name)
> (Address)

Invitation, inside envelope:
> The Vice President
> OR The Vice President and Mrs./Mr. (surname)

Place card: The Vice President OR The Vice President of the United States
Introduction: The Vice President OR The Vice President of the United States
Introduction, one person to another:
> Mr./Madam Vice President, may I present …
> … may I present the Vice President …

Conversation: Mr./Madam Vice President

Vice President as President of the Senate

Envelope, official:
> The Vice President
> United States Senate
> Washington, DC 20510

Letter salutation: Dear Mr./Madam President:
Complimentary close: Most respectfully, OR Respectfully yours,
Place card: Mr. President
Introduction: Mr. President of the Senate
Introduction, one person to another: Mr. President, may I present …
Conversation: Mr./Madam President

Wife or Husband of the Vice President of the United States

NOTE: It is not necessary to specify that he or she is married to the Vice President. See also note under Introduction, in Wife of the President, Contemporary Form, page 166.

Envelope, official:
> Mrs. (husband's full name)/Mr. (full name)
> (Address)

Letter salutation: Dear Mrs./Mr. (surname):
Complimentary close: Sincerely yours, OR Sincerely,
Envelope, social (if the Vice President is not invited):
> Mrs. (husband's full name)/Mr. (full name)
> (Address)

Invitation (if the Vice President is not invited): Mrs./Mr. (surname)
Place card: Mrs./Mr. (surname)
Introduction: Mrs. (surname) OR Mr. (full name)
Introduction, one person to another:
> Mrs. (surname)
> OR Mr. (surname)

Conversation: Mrs./Mr. (surname)

168

Vice President-elect of the United States
Envelope, official:
> The Honorable
> (Full name)
>> The Vice President-elect
>> (Address)

Letter salutation: *Dear Mr./Ms. (surname):*
Complimentary close: *Most respectfully,* OR *Respectfully yours,*
Envelope, social:
> The Honorable
> (Full name)
> (Address)

Invitation, inside envelope: *Mr./Ms. (surname)*
Place card: *Mr./Ms. (surname)*
Introduction: *The Honorable (full name), vice president-elect*
Introduction, one person to another: *Mr./Ms. (surname)*
Conversation: *Mr./Ms. (surname)*

Former Vice President of the United States
Envelope, official:
> The Honorable
> (Full name)
> (Address)

Letter salutation: *Dear Mr./Ms. (surname):*
Complimentary close: *Most respectfully,* OR *Respectfully yours,*
Envelope, social:
> The Honorable
> (Full name)
> (Address)

Invitation, inside envelope: *Mr./Ms. (surname)*
Place card: *Mr./Ms. (surname)*
Introduction: *The Honorable (full name)*
Introduction, less formal: *Mr./Ms. (surname)*
Introduction, one person to another: *Mr./Ms. (surname)*
Conversation: *Mr./Ms. (surname)*

Secretary (of Portfolio)
Examples: *Secretary of Defense*
         Secretary of an armed service
Envelope, official:
> The Honorable
> (Full name)
>> Secretary of (department)
>> (Address)

Letter salutation: *Dear Mr./Madam Secretary:*
Complimentary close: *Respectfully yours,* OR *Respectfully,*

Envelope, social:
>*The Secretary of (department)*
>>*(Address)*

Invitation, inside envelope: *The Secretary of (department)*
Place card: *The Secretary of (department)*
Introduction: *The Honorable (full name), secretary of (department)*
Introduction, one person to another:
>*Mr./Madam Secretary, may I present ...*
>*... may I present Secretary (surname) ...*

Conversation: *Mr./Madam Secretary*

Attorney General

Envelope, official:
>*The Honorable*
>>*(Full name)*
>>>*Attorney General*
>>>>*(Address)*

Letter salutation: *Dear Mr./Madam Attorney General:*
Complimentary close: *Respectfully,* OR *Sincerely yours,*
Envelope, social:
>*The Attorney General*
>>*(Address)*

Invitation, inside envelope: *The Attorney General*
Place card: *The Attorney General*
Introduction: *The Honorable (full name), the Attorney General*
Introduction, less formal: *Attorney General (surname)*
Introduction, one person to another:
>*Mr./Madam Attorney General, may I present ...*
>*... may I present Mr./Ms. (surname), the Attorney General...*
>*... may I present Mr./Ms.(surname) ...*

Conversation: *Mr./Madam Attorney General or Mr./Ms. (surname)*

Acting Secretary

Examples:　*Secretary-designate*
　　　　　Secretary ad-interim
　　　　　Acting Attorney General
　　　　　Attorney General-designate
　　　　　Attorney General ad-interim

Envelope, official:
>*The Honorable*
>>*(Full name)*
>>>*(Title)*
>>>>*(Address)*

Letter salutation: *Dear Mr./Ms. (surname):*
Complimentary close: *Sincerely yours,* OR *Sincerely,*
Envelope, social:
>*The (title)*
>>*(Address)*

170

Invitation, inside envelope: *The (title)*
Place card: *The (title)*
Introduction:
  The Honorable (full name), (title)
  (Title), Mr./Ms. (surname)
Introduction, one person to another:
  Mr./Ms. (surname), may I present ...
  ... may I present Mr./Ms. (surname), (position) ...
  ... may I present Mr./Ms. (surname) ...
Conversation: *Mr./Ms. (surname)*

Solicitor General
Envelope, official:
  The Honorable
    (Full name)
      Solicitor General
        (Address)
Letter salutation:
  Dear Mr./Madam Solicitor General:
  Dear Mr./Ms. (surname):
Complimentary close: *Sincerely yours,* OR *Sincerely,*
Envelope, social:
  The Honorable
    (Full name)
      (Address)
Invitation, inside envelope: *The Solicitor General*
Place card: *The Solicitor General*
Introduction:
  The Honorable (full name), Solicitor General
  OR *The Solicitor General, Mr./Ms. (surname)*
Introduction, one to another:
  Mr./Ms. (surname), may I present ...
  ... may I present Mr./Ms. (surname), the Solicitor General...
Conversation, formally: *Mr./Madam Solicitor General*
Conversation, less formal: *Mr./Ms. (surname)*

Postmaster General
Envelope, official:
  The Honorable
    (Full name)
      Postmaster General
        (Address)
Letter salutation: *Dear Mr./Madam Postmaster General:*
Complimentary close: *Sincerely yours,* OR *Sincerely,*
Envelope, social:
  The Postmaster General
    (Address)
Invitation, inside envelope: *The Postmaster General*

Place card: *The Postmaster General*
Introduction:
>*The Honorable (full name), postmaster general*
>OR *The Postmaster General, Mr./Ms. (surname)*

Introduction, one to another:
>*Mr./Madam Postmaster General may I present …*
>*… may I present Mr./Ms. (surname), the Postmaster General …*
>*… may I present Mr./Ms. (surname) …*

Conversation formally: *Mr./Madam Postmaster General*
Conversation, less formal: *Mr./Ms. (surname)*

Surgeon General

NOTE: The *surgeon general* will be a *physician* and have the rank of *rear admiral, upper half* as commander of the officers of the U.S. Public Health Service.
Envelope, official:
>*The Honorable*
>>*(Full name)*
>>>*Surgeon General*
>>>>*(Address)*

Letter salutation: *Dear Dr. (surname):*
Complimentary close: *Sincerely yours,* OR *Sincerely,*
Envelope, social:
>*The Honorable*
>>*(Full name)*
>>>*(Address)*

Invitation, inside envelope: *Dr./Admiral (surname)*
Place card: *Dr./Admiral (surname)*
Introduction:
>*The Honorable (full name), surgeon general*
>OR *The Surgeon General, Dr./Admiral (surname)*

Introduction, one person to another: *Dr./Admiral (surname)*
Conversation: *Dr./Admiral (surname)*

Chief of Protocol with the Rank of Ambassador

Envelope, official:
>*The Honorable*
>>*(Full name)*
>>>*The Chief of Protocol*
>>>>*(Address)*

Letter salutation: *Dear Ambassador (surname):*
Complimentary close: *Sincerely yours,* OR *Sincerely,*
Envelope, social:
>*The Chief of Protocol*
>>*(Address)*

Invitation, inside envelope: *The Chief of Protocol*
Place card: *The Chief of Protocol*

Introduction:
> *Ambassador (full name), chief of protocol*
> OR *The chief of protocol, Ambassador (surname)*

Introduction, one person to another: *Ambassador (surname)*
Conversation: *Ambassador (surname)*

Chief of Protocol without the Rank of Ambassador
Envelope, official:
> *The Honorable*
> > *(Full name)*
> > > *The Chief of Protocol*
> > > > *(Address)*

Letter salutation: *Dear Mr./Ms.(surname):*
Complimentary close: *Sincerely yours,* OR *Sincerely,*
Envelope, social:
> *The Chief of Protocol*
> > *(Address)*

Invitation, inside envelope: *The Chief of Protocol*
Place card: *The Chief of Protocol*
Introduction:
> *The Honorable (full name), chief of protocol*
> OR *The chief of protocol, Mr./Ms. (surname)*

Introduction, one person to another: Mr./Ms. *(surname)*
Conversation: Mr./Ms. *(surname)*

Commissioner of an Agency or Commission
Example: *Commissioner of the Internal Revenue*
Envelope, official:
> *The Honorable*
> > *(Full name)*
> > > *Commissioner of (agency or name of commission)*
> > > > *(Address)*

Letter salutation: *Dear Mr./Madam Commissioner:*
Complimentary close: *Sincerely yours,* OR *Sincerely,*
Envelope, social:
> *The Honorable*
> > *(Full name)*
> > > *(Address)*

Invitation, inside envelope: Mr./Ms. *(surname)*
Place card: Mr./Ms. *(surname)*
Introduction:
> *The Honorable (full name), commissioner of (agency or name of commission)*
> OR *The commissioner of (agency or name of commission),* Mr./Ms. *(surname)*

Introduction, one person to another: Mr./Ms. *(surname)*
Conversation:
> *Mr./Madam Commissioner or Commissioner*
> OR Mr./Ms. *(surname)*

Chairman of a Commission or Board
Envelope, official:
> The Honorable
> (Full name)
> > (Full title of position held)
> > (Address)

Letter salutation, more formal: *Dear Mr./Madam Chairman:*
Letter salutation, less formal: *Dear Mr./Ms. (surname):*
Complimentary close: *Sincerely yours,* OR *Sincerely,*
Envelope, social:
> The Honorable
> (Full name)
> > (Address)

Invitation, inside envelope: Mr./Ms. *(surname)*
Place card: Mr./Ms. *(surname)*
Introduction:
> *The Honorable (full name), (full title of position held)*
> OR *(Full title of position held)*, Mr./Ms. *(surname)*

Introduction, one to another: Mr./Ms. *(surname)*
Conversation: Mr./Ms. *(surname)*

Other Positions Appointed by the President, Addressed as *The Honorable*
Examples:
> *Administrator of a federal council, commission, agency, board, or authority*
> *Assistant secretary of an executive department or an armed force*
> *Assistant to the president*
> *Associate Attorney General*
> *Associate deputy undersecretary of an executive department*
> *Chairman of a federal council, commission, agency, board, or authority*
> *Commissioner of a federal council, commission, agency, board, or authority*
> *Comptroller General*
> *Counsellor to the president (or to another very high ranking official)*
> *Deputy assistant secretary of an executive department*
> *Director of a federal council, commission, agency, board, or authority*
> *Head of a federal agency, board, or authority*
> *Legal advisor to a very high ranking federal official*
> *Librarian of Congress*
> *Member of a federal council, commission, agency, board, or authority*
> *President of a federal council, commission, agency, board, or authority*
> *Public Printer, U.S. Government Printing Office*
> *Special assistant to the President*
> *Undersecretary of an executive department*
> *U.S. Attorney*

Envelope, official:
>The Honorable
>>(Full name)
>>>(Full title of position held)
>>>>(Address)

Letter salutation: Dear Mr./Ms. (surname):
Complimentary close: Sincerely yours, OR Sincerely,
Envelope, social:
>The Honorable
>>(Full name)
>>>(Address)

Invitation, inside envelope: Mr./Ms. (surname)
Place card: Mr./Ms. (surname)
Introduction:
>The Honorable (full name), (full title of position held)
>OR The (full title of position held), Mr./Ms. (surname)

Introduction, one person to another: Mr./Ms. (surname)
Conversation: Mr./Ms. (surname)

Positions Appointed by the President, Not Addressed as *The Honorable*

Examples: District Director (e.g., of the Internal Revenue)
>>Collector of Customs

Envelope, official:
>Mr./Ms. (full name)
>>(Title)
>>>(Address)

Letter salutation: Dear Mr./Ms. (surname):
Complimentary close: Sincerely yours, OR Sincerely,
Envelope, social:
>Mr./Ms. (full name)
>>(Address)

Invitation, inside envelope: Mr./Ms. (surname)
Place card: Mr./Ms. (surname)
Introduction:
>Mr./Ms. (full name), (title)
>OR (Title), Mr./Ms. (surname)

Introduction, one person to another: Mr./Ms. (surname)
Conversation: Mr./Ms. (surname)

Marshal for a Judicial District

NOTE: *Marshals* are appointed by the President and approved by the Senate. See also forms for *deputy marshals* and *inspectors* on page 188. Use of *marshal* as an honorific socially is at the preference of the bearer.

Envelope, official:
> The Honorable
>> (Full name)
>>> United States Marshal
>>> (Judicial District)
>>> (Address)

Letter salutation: *Dear Marshal (surname):*
Complimentary close: *Sincerely yours,* OR *Sincerely,*
Envelope, social:
> The Honorable
>> (Full name)
>> (Address)

Invitation, inside envelope: Mr./Ms. *(surname)*
Place card social: Mr./Ms. *(surname)*
Place card official: *Marshal (surname)*
Introduction: *The Honorable (full name), United States Marshal of the (district)*
Introduction, one person to another:
> *Marshal (surname)* or Mr./Ms. *(surname)*

Conversation: *Marshal (surname)* OR Mr./Ms. *(surname)*

FEDERAL LEGISLATIVE

SENATE

Senator

Envelope, official:
> The Honorable
>> (Full name)
>>> United States Senate
>>> (Address)

Envelope to a senator as *president pro tempore* of the senate:
> The Honorable
>> (Full name)
>>> President pro Tempore of the Senate
>>> (Address)

Envelope to a senator as a committee or subcommittee chairman:
> The Honorable
>> (Full name)
>>> Chairman
>>>> (Committee or subcommittee)
>>>> (Address)

Letter salutation: *Dear Senator (surname)*:
Complimentary close: *Sincerely yours,* OR *Sincerely,*
Envelope, social:
> *The Honorable*
> *(Full name)*
> *(Address)*

Invitation, inside envelope: *Senator (surname)*
Place card: *Senator (surname)*
Introduction: *The Honorable (full name), United States senator from (state)*

Introduction as *president pro tempore* of the senate:
> *The Honorable (full name), president pro tempore of the Senate*
> *The president pro tempore of the Senate, Senator (surname)*

Introduction, one person to another: *Senator (surname)*
Conversation, initially: *Senator (surname)*
Conversation, subsequently: *Senator*

Majority/Minority Leader of the Senate
NOTE: Senate majority and minority leaders do not use additional titles in direct address as party leaders.

Senator-elect
Envelope, official:
> *The Honorable*
> *(Full name)*
> > *United States Senator-elect*
> > *(Address)*

Letter salutation: *Dear Mr./Ms. (surname)*:
Complimentary close: *Sincerely yours,* OR *Sincerely,*
Envelope, social:
> *The Honorable*
> *(Full name)*
> *(Address)*

Invitation, inside envelope: *Mr./Ms. (surname)*
Place card: *Mr./Ms. (surname)*
Introduction:
> *The Honorable (full name), United States senator-elect from (state)*
> OR *The United States senator-elect from (state), Mr./Ms. (surname)*

Introduction, one to another: *Mr./Ms. (surname)*
Conversation: *Mr./Ms. (surname)*

Former Senator
NOTE: A former senator could be addressed as *Mr./Ms./etc. (name)*, and identified as a former senator, but continued use of the honorific *senator* is the norm.
Envelope, official:
> *The Honorable*
> *(Full name)*
> *(Address)*

Letter salutation: *Dear Senator (surname):*
Complimentary close: *Sincerely yours,* OR *Sincerely,*
Envelope, social:
   The Honorable
     (Full name)
      (Address)
Invitation, inside envelope: *Senator (surname)*
Place card: *Senator (surname)*
Introduction:
   The Honorable (full name), former United States senator from (state)
   OR *The former United States senator from (state), Senator (surname)*
Introduction, one person to another: *Senator (surname)*
Conversation: *Senator (surname)*

Secretary of the Senate
Envelope, official:
   The Honorable
     (Full name)
      Secretary of the Senate
      (Address)
Letter salutation: *Dear Mr./Ms. (surname):*
Complimentary close: *Sincerely yours,* OR *Sincerely,*
Envelope, social:
   The Honorable
     (Full name)
      (Address)
Invitation, inside envelope: *Mr./Ms. (surname)*
Place card: *Mr./Ms. (surname)*
Introduction:
   The Honorable (full name), Secretary of the United States Senate
   OR *The Secretary of the United States Senate, Mr./Ms. (surname)*
Introduction, one person to another: *Mr./Ms. (surname)*
Conversation: *Mr./Ms. (surname)*

Sergeant at Arms of the Senate
Envelope, official:
   The Honorable
     (Full name)
      Sergeant at Arms
      (Address)
Letter salutation: *Dear Mr./Ms. (surname):*
Complimentary close: *Sincerely yours,* OR *Sincerely,*
Envelope, social:
   The Honorable
     (Full name)
      (Address)

178

Invitation, inside envelope: Mr./Ms. (*surname*)
Place card: Mr./Ms. (*surname*)
Introduction:
> The Honorable (*full name*), *sergeant at arms of the United States Senate*
> OR *The sergeant at arms of the United States Senate*, Mr./Ms. (*surname*)

Introduction, one person to another: Mr./Ms. (*surname*)
Conversation: Mr./Ms. (*surname*)

Member of the Staff of a Senator
Envelope, official:
> Mr./Ms. (*full name*)
>> (*Position if senior staff*) *to the Honorable* (*senator's full name*)
>>> *United States Senate*
>>> (*Address*)
>
> OR   Mr./Ms. (*full name*)
>> *Office of the Honorable* (*senator's full name*)
>>> *United States Senate*
>>> (*Address*)

Letter salutation: *Dear* Mr./Ms. (*surname*):
Complimentary close: *Sincerely yours,* OR *Sincerely,*
Envelope, social:
> Mr./Ms. (*full name*)
>> (*Address*)

Invitation, inside envelope: Mr./Ms. (*surname*)
Place card: Mr./Ms. (*surname*)
Introduction:
> Mr./Ms. (*full name*), (*position if senior staff*) *to*
>> *the Honorable* (*senator's full name*)
>
> OR (*Position if senior staff*) *to the Honorable* (*senator's full name*),
>> Mr./Ms. (*surname*)
>
> OR Mr./Ms. (*full name*) *of the office of the Honorable* (*senator's full name*)

Introduction, one person to another: Mr./Ms. (*full name or surname only*)
Conversation: Mr./Ms. (*surname*)

Chaplain of the Senate
NOTE: *Dr.* is used if the chaplain has a doctorate, *Pastor/Father/Rabbi* if not. See form of address for specific denominations for additional options, and check for personal preference.
Envelope, official:
> *The Reverend*
>> (*Full name*), (*degrees held*)
>>> *Chaplain of the Senate*
>>> (*Address*)

Letter salutation: *Dear* Dr./Pastor/*etc.* (*surname*):
Complimentary close: *Sincerely yours,* OR *Sincerely,*

Envelope, social:
> The Reverend
>> (Full name)
>>> (Address)

Invitation, inside envelope: *Dr./Pastor/etc. (surname)*
Place card: *Dr./Pastor/Father/etc. (surname)*
Introduction:
> The Reverend (full name), chaplain of the United States Senate
> OR The chaplain of the United States Senate, *Dr./Pastor/etc. (surname)*

Introduction, one person to another:
> Dr./Pastor/etc. (surname)

Conversation: *Dr./Pastor/etc. (surname)*

HOUSE OF REPRESENTATIVES

Speaker of the House of Representatives
Envelope, official:
> The Speaker of the House of Representatives
>> United States Capitol
>>> Washington, DC 20515

Letter salutation: *Dear Mr./Madam Speaker:*
Complimentary close: *Respectfully yours,* OR *Respectfully,*
Envelope, social:
> The Speaker of the House of Representatives
>> (Address)

Invitation, inside envelope: *The Speaker of the House of Representatives*
Place card:
> The Speaker of the House
> OR The Speaker of the House of Representatives

Introduction:
> The Honorable (full name), the Speaker of the House of Representatives

Introduction. one person to another:
> Mr./Madam Speaker, may I present ...
> ... may I present the Speaker of the House of Representatives ...

Conversation: *Mr./Madam Speaker*

Representative
While *representative, congressman,* and *congresswoman* are not traditional honorifics for members of the House of Representatives, they are the informal honorifics of choice of some members. Follow the preference of the bearer.
Envelope, official:
> The Honorable
>> (Full name)
>>> United States House of Representatives
>>>> (Address)

Envelope as chairman of a committee or subcommittee:
>The Honorable
>>(Full name)
>>>Chairman
>>>>(Committee or subcommittee name)
>>>>(Address)

Letter salutation: *Dear Mr./Ms. (surname):*
Letter salutation if chairman of a committee: *Dear Mr. Chairman:*
Complimentary close: *Sincerely yours,* OR *Sincerely,*
Envelope, social:
>The Honorable
>>(Full name)
>>>(Address)

Invitation, inside envelope: *Mr./Ms. (surname)*
Place card: *Mr./Ms. (surname)*
Introduction:
>*The Honorable (full name), representative from (state)*
>OR *The Honorable (full name), representative from (district) (state)*
>OR *Representative from (state), Mr./Ms. (surname)*
>OR *Representative from (district) (state), Mr./Ms. (surname)*

Introduction, one person to another: *Mr./Ms. (surname)*
Conversation: *Mr./Ms. (surname)*

Majority/Minority Leaders
NOTE: Majority and minority leaders in the House of Representatives are addressed as *Representative* and do not use additional titles in regard to their party leadership positions.

Resident Commissioner of Puerto Rico
Envelope, official:
>The Honorable
>>(Full name)
>>>Resident Commissioner from Puerto Rico
>>>>United States House of Representatives
>>>>(Address)

Letter salutation: *Dear Mr./Ms. (surname):*
Complimentary close: *Sincerely yours,* OR *Sincerely,*
Envelope, social:
>The Honorable
>>(Full name)
>>>(Address)

Invitation, inside envelope: *Mr./Ms. (surname)*
Place card: *Mr./Ms. (surname)*

Introduction:

> The Honorable (full name), resident commissioner from Puerto Rico
>> to the House of Representatives
>
> OR The resident commissioner from Puerto Rico to the House of Representatives,
>> Mr./Ms. (surname)

Introduction, one person to another: Mr./Ms. (surname)

Conversation:

> Mr./Madam Commissioner
> OR Resident Commissioner
> OR Mr./Ms. (surname)

Delegate to the House of Representatives

Envelope, official:

> The Honorable
>> (Full name)
>>> Delegate of (jurisdiction)
>>> (Address)

Letter salutation: *Dear Mr./Ms. (surname):*

Complimentary close: *Sincerely yours,* OR *Sincerely,*

Envelope, social:

> The Honorable
>> (Full name)
>>> (Address)

Invitation, inside envelope: Mr./Ms. (surname)

Place card: Mr./Ms. (surname)

Introduction:

> The Honorable (full name), delegate of (jurisdiction) to the
>> House of Representatives
>
> OR The delegate of (jurisdiction) to the House of Representatives,
>> Mr./Ms. (surname)

Introduction, one person to another: Mr./Ms. (surname)

Conversation: Mr./Ms. (surname)

Representative-elect

Envelope, official:

> The Honorable
>> (Full name)
>>> Representative-elect
>>> (Address)

Letter salutation: *Dear Mr./Ms. (surname):*

Complimentary close: *Sincerely yours,* OR *Sincerely,*

Envelope, social:

> The Honorable
>> (Full name)
>>> (Address)

Invitation, inside envelope: Mr./Ms. *(surname)*
Place card: Mr./Ms. *(surname)*
Introduction:
> The Honorable *(full name)*, *representative-elect from (state)*
> OR The Honorable *(full name)*, *representative-elect from (district) (state)*
> OR *The representative-elect from (state)*, Mr./Ms. *(surname)*
> OR *The representative-elect from (district) (state)*, Mr./Ms. *(surname)*

Introduction, one person to another: Mr./Ms. *(surname)*
Conversation: Mr./Ms. *(surname)*

Former Representative
Envelope, official:
> The Honorable
> *(Full name)*
> *(Address)*

Letter salutation: *Dear Mr./Ms. (surname)*:
Complimentary close: *Sincerely yours,* OR *Sincerely,*
Envelope, social:
> The Honorable
> *(Full name)*
> *(Address)*

Invitation, inside envelope: Mr./Ms. *(surname)*
Place card: Mr./Ms. *(surname)*
Introduction:
> The Honorable *(full name)*, *former representative from (state)*
> OR The Honorable *(full name)*, *former representative from (district) of (state)*
> OR *The former representative from (state)*, Mr./Ms. *(surname)*
> OR *The former representative from (district) (state)*, Mr./Ms. *(surname)*

Introduction, one person to another: Mr./Ms. *(surname)*
Conversation: Mr./Ms. *(surname)*

Clerk of the House of Representatives *or*
Sergeant at Arms of the House of Representatives
Envelope, official:
> The Honorable
> *(Full name)*
> *(Full title)*
> *(Address)*

Letter salutation: *Dear Mr./Ms. (surname)*:
Complimentary close: *Sincerely yours,* OR *Sincerely,*
Envelope, social:
> The Honorable
> *(Full name)*
> *(Address)*

Invitation, inside envelope: Mr./Ms. *(surname)*
Place card: Mr./Ms. *(surname)*

Introduction:
> *The Honorable (full name), (full title)*
> OR *(Full title), Mr./Ms. (surname)*

Introduction, one person to another: Mr./Ms. *(surname)*
Conversation: Mr./Ms. *(surname)*

Member of the Staff of a Representative

Envelope, official:
> Mr./Ms. *(full name)*
>> *(Position if senior staff) to the Honorable (representative's full name)*
>>> *United States House of Representatives*
>>> *(Address)*
>
> OR Mr./Ms. *(full name)*
>> *Office of the Honorable (representative's full name)*
>>> *United States House of Representatives*
>>> *(Address)*

Letter salutation: *Dear Mr./Ms. (surname):*
Complimentary close: *Sincerely yours,* OR *Sincerely,*
Envelope, social:
> Mr./Ms. *(full name)*
>> *(Address)*

Invitation, inside envelope: Mr./Ms. *(surname)*
Place card: Mr./Ms. *(surname)*
Introduction:
> Mr./Ms. *(full name), (position if senior staff) to*
>> *the Honorable (representative's full name)*
>
> OR Mr./Ms. *(full name) of the office of*
>> *the Honorable (representative's full name)*
>
> OR *(Position if senior staff) to the Honorable (representative's full name),*
>> Mr./Ms. *(surname)*
>
> OR *From the office of the Honorable (representative's full name),*
>> Mr./Ms. *(surname)*

Introduction, one person to another: Mr./Ms. *(surname)*
Conversation: Mr./Ms. *(surname)*

Chaplain of the House of Representatives

NOTE: *Dr.* is used if the chaplain has a doctorate, *Pastor/Father/Rabbi* if not. See form of address for specific denominations for additional options, and check for personal preference.
Envelope, official:
> *The Reverend*
>> *(Full name), (degrees held)*
>>> *Chaplain of the House of Representatives*
>>> *(Address)*

Letter salutation: *Dear Dr./Pastor/etc. (surname):*
Complimentary close: *Sincerely yours,* OR *Sincerely,*

Envelope, social:
>   *The Reverend*
>   >   *(Full name)*
>   >   >   *(Address)*

Invitation, inside envelope: *Dr./Pastor/etc. (surname)*
Place card: *Dr./Pastor/etc. (surname)*
Introduction:
>   *The Reverend (full name), chaplain of the House of Representatives*
>   OR *The chaplain of the House of Representatives,*
>   >   *Dr./Pastor/etc. (surname)*

Introduction, one person to another: *Dr./Pastor/etc. (surname)*
Conversation: *Dr./Pastor/etc. (surname)*

FEDERAL JUDICIARY

Chief Justice of the Supreme Court
Envelope, official:
>   *The Chief Justice*
>   >   *The Supreme Court*
>   >   >   *One First Street, NE*
>   >   >   >   *Washington, DC 20543*

Letter salutation: *Dear Chief Justice:*
Complimentary close: *Sincerely yours,* OR *Sincerely,*
Envelope, social:
>   *The Chief Justice*
>   >   *(Address)*

Invitation, inside envelope: *The Chief Justice*
Place card: *The Chief Justice*
Introduction: *The Chief Justice of the Supreme Court of the United States*
Introduction, one person to another:
>   *Mr./Madam Chief Justice may I present …*
>   *… may I present the Chief Justice …*

Conversation, initially: *Mr./Madam Chief Justice*
Conversation, subsequently: *Chief Justice*

Associate Justice of the Supreme Court
NOTE: The *given name* of an associate justice is not used unless there are two justices with the same *surname*.
Envelope, official:
>   *Justice (surname)*
>   >   *The Supreme Court*
>   >   >   *One First Street, NE*
>   >   >   >   *Washington, DC 20543*

Letter salutation: *Dear Justice (surname):*
Complimentary close: *Sincerely yours,* OR *Sincerely,*

Envelope, social:
  Justice (surname)
  (Address)
Invitation, inside envelope: *Justice (surname)*
Place card: *Justice (surname)*
Introduction: *Justice (surname) of the Supreme Court of the United States*
Introduction, one person to another: *Justice (surname)*
Conversation, initially: *Justice (surname)*
Conversation, subsequently: *Justice*

Retired Chief Justice of the Supreme Court
Envelope, official:
  Chief Justice (surname)
  (Address)
Letter salutation: *Dear Chief Justice (surname):*
Complimentary close: *Sincerely yours,* OR *Sincerely,*
Envelope, social:
  Chief Justice (surname)
  (Address)
Invitation, inside envelope: *Chief Justice (surname)*
Place card: *Chief Justice (surname)*
Introduction:
  The Honorable (full name), former chief justice
  of the Supreme Court of the United States
  OR *Former chief justice of the Supreme Court of the United States,*
  Chief Justice (surname)
Introduction, one person to another: *Chief Justice (surname)*
Conversation: *Chief Justice*

Retired Associate Justice of the Supreme Court
Envelope, official:
  The Honorable
  (Full name)
  (Address)
Letter salutation: *Dear Mr./Madam Justice (surname):*
Complimentary close: *Sincerely yours,* OR *Sincerely,*
Envelope, social:
  The Honorable
  (Full name)
  (Address)
Invitation, inside envelope: *Mr./Madam Justice (surname)*
Place card: *Mr./Madam Justice (surname)*
Introduction:
  Mr./Madam Justice (full name), former associate justice
  of the Supreme Court of the United States

186

OR *Former associate justice of the Supreme Court of the United States,*
  Mr./Madam Justice (surname)
Introduction, one person to another: *Mr./Madam Justice (surname)*
Conversation: *Mr./Madam Justice (surname)*

Chief Judge of a Court *or* Senior Judge of a Court
Envelope, official:
  The Honorable
  (Full name)
      Chief Judge/Senior Judge
      (Court)
        (Address)
Letter salutation: *Dear Judge (surname):*
Complimentary close: *Sincerely yours,* OR *Sincerely,*
Envelope, social:
  The Honorable
  (Full name)
      (Address)
Invitation, inside envelope: *Judge (surname)*
Place card: *Judge (surname)*
Introduction:
  The Honorable (full name), chief judge/senior judge, (court)
  OR *Chief judge/senior judge, (court), Judge (surname)*
Introduction, one person to another: *Judge (surname)*
Conversation: *Judge (surname)*

Judge of a Court
Envelope, official:
  The Honorable
  (Full name)
      (Court)
        (Address)
Letter salutation: *Dear Judge (surname):*
Complimentary close: *Sincerely yours,* OR *Sincerely,*
Envelope, social:
  The Honorable
  (Full name)
      (Address)
Invitation, inside envelope: *Judge (surname)*
Place card: *Judge (surname)*
Introduction:
  The Honorable (full name), judge of the (court)
  OR *Judge of the (court), Judge (surname)*
Introduction, one person to another: *Judge (surname)*
Conversation: *Judge (surname)*

Deputy Marshal, Chief Deputy Marshal, Inspector, Chief Inspector

NOTE: *United States marshals* are appointed by the President, approved by the Senate, and are addressed as *the Honorable*. See form on *page 176*.

Envelope, official:

Mr./Ms. *(full name)*
(Title)
(Judicial district)
(Address)

Letter salutation: *Dear (title) (surname):*
Complimentary close: *Sincerely yours,* OR *Sincerely,*

Envelope, social:

Mr./Ms. *(full name)*
(Address)

Invitation, inside envelope: Mr./Ms. *(surname)*
Place card: Mr./Ms. *(surname)*
Introduction:

Mr./Ms. *(full name)*, *(title)*, *(district)*
OR *(Title)*, *(district)*, Mr./Ms. *(surname)*

Introduction, one person to another: Mr./Ms. *(surname)*
Conversation: Mr./Ms. *(surname)*

Clerk of a Lower Court

Envelope, official:

Mr./Ms. *(full name)*
Clerk of the *(court)*
(Address)

Letter salutation: *Dear Mr./Ms. (surname):*
Complimentary close: *Sincerely yours,* OR *Sincerely,*

Envelope, social:

Mr./Ms. *(full name)*
(Address)

Invitation, inside envelope: Mr./Ms. *(surname)*
Place card: Mr./Ms. *(surname)*
Introduction:

Mr./Ms. *(full name)*, *clerk of the (court)*
OR *Clerk of the (court)*, Mr./Ms. *(surname)*

Introduction, one person to another: Mr./Ms. *(full name or surname only)*
Conversation: Mr./Ms. *(surname)*

U.S. State Governments

STATE EXECUTIVE

Governor, Addressed as *The Honorable*

NOTE: *The Honorable* is the most frequently used courtesy title for governors. However, Massachusetts, New Hampshire, and South Carolina officially address their governor as *Your Excellency*. See that listing, which follows.

Envelope, official:
> The Honorable
> (Full name)
>> Governor of (state)
>> (Address)

Letter salutation: *Dear Governor (surname):*
Complimentary close: *Sincerely yours,* OR *Sincerely,*
Envelope, social:

The Governor of (state)	The Governor
(Address)	(Address)

Invitation, inside envelope:
> The Governor of (state) OR The Governor

Place card: *The Governor of (state)* OR *The Governor*
Introduction: *The Honorable (full name), governor of (state)*
Introduction, one person to another: *Governor (surname)*
Conversation, initially: *Governor (surname)*
Conversation, subsequently: *Governor*

Governor, Addressed as *His/Her Excellency*

NOTE: Massachusetts, New Hampshire, and South Carolina officially address their governor with the courtesy title *Your Excellency:* Official documents and proclamations currently issued by these governors identify the governors as *His Excellency (full name)*. However, such use is perhaps waning. Spokespersons in the offices of the current gubernatorial administrations in New Hampshire and South Carolina state *the Honorable* is now equally acceptable.

Envelope, official:
> His/Her Excellency
> (Full name)
>> Governor of (state)
>> (Address)

Letter salutation: *Your Excellency:* OR *Dear Governor (surname):*
Complimentary close: *Sincerely yours,* OR *Sincerely,*
Envelope, social:

The Governor of (state)	The Governor
(Address)	(Address)

Invitation, inside envelope:
> The Governor of (state) OR The Governor

Place card: *The Governor of (state)* OR *The Governor*
Introduction: *His/Her Excellency (full name), governor of (state)*
Introduction, one person to another: *Governor (surname)*
Conversation, initially: *Governor (surname)*
Conversation, subsequently: *Your Excellency* OR *Governor*

Acting Governor of a State
Envelope, official:
> *The Honorable*
>> *(Full name)*
>>> *Acting Governor of (state)*
>>> *(Address)*

Letter salutation: *Dear Mr./Ms. (surname):*
Complimentary close: *Sincerely yours,* OR *Sincerely,*
Envelope, social:
> *The Acting Governor of (state)*
>> *(Address)*
> *The Acting Governor*
>> *(Address)*

Invitation, inside envelope:
> *The Acting Governor of (state)* OR *The Acting Governor*

Place card: *The Acting Governor of (state)* OR *The Acting Governor*
Introduction:
> *The Honorable (full name), acting governor of (state)*
> OR *The acting governor of (state), Mr./Ms. (surname)*

Introduction, one person to another: *Mr./Ms. (surname)*
Conversation: *Mr./Ms. (surname)*

Governor-elect of a State
Envelope, official:
> *The Honorable*
>> *(Full name)*
>>> *Governor-elect of (state)*
>>> *(Address)*

Letter salutation: *Dear Mr./Ms. (surname):*
Complimentary close: *Sincerely yours,* OR *Sincerely,*
Envelope, social:
> *The Governor-elect of (state)*
>> *(Address)*
> *The Governor-elect*
>> *(Address)*

Invitation, inside envelope: *Mr./Ms. (surname)*
Place card: *The Governor-elect of (state)* OR *The Governor-elect*
Introduction:
> *The Honorable (full name), governor-elect of (state)*
> OR *The governor-elect of (state), Mr./Ms. (surname)*

Introduction, one person to another: *Mr./Ms. (surname)*
Conversation: *Mr./Ms. (surname)*

190

Former Governor of a State

Envelope, official:
> The Honorable
> > (Full name)
> > > (Address)

Letter salutation: Dear Mr./Ms. (surname):
Complimentary close: Sincerely yours, OR Sincerely,
Envelope, social:
> The Honorable
> > (Full name)
> > > (Address)

Invitation, inside envelope: Mr./Ms. (surname)
Place card: Mr./Ms. (surname)
Introduction:
> The Honorable (full name), former governor of (state)
> OR Former governor of (state), Mr./Ms. (surname)

Introduction, one person to another: Mr./Ms. (surname)
Conversation: Mr./Ms. (surname)

Lieutenant Governor of a State

Envelope, official:
> The Honorable
> > (Full name)
> > > Lieutenant Governor of (state)
> > > > (Address)

Letter salutation: Dear Mr./Ms. (surname):
Complimentary close: Sincerely yours, OR Sincerely,
Envelope, social:
> The Lieutenant Governor of (state)
> > (Address)
> The Lieutenant Governor
> > (Address)

Invitation, inside envelope: Mr./Ms. (surname)
Place card: The Lieutenant Governor OR The Lieutenant Governor of (state)
Introduction:
> The Honorable (full name), lieutenant governor of (state)
> OR The lieutenant governor of (state), Mr./Ms. (surname)

Introduction, one person to another: Mr./Ms. (surname)
Conversation: Mr./Ms. (surname)

Secretary of (Portfolio) *or*
Member of a Governor's Cabinet with the Title of Secretary

Example: (*Full name*), *the secretary of* (*portfolio*) *of the State of Vermont*
Envelope, official:
> The Honorable
> > (*Full name*)
> > > Secretary of (*department*) of (*name of state*)
> > > (*Address*)
> OR The Honorable
> > (*Full name*)
> > > Secretary of (*department*)
> > > (*Address*)

Letter salutation: *Dear Mr./Madam Secretary:*
Complimentary close: *Respectfully yours,* OR *Respectfully,*
Envelope, social:
> The Secretary of (*department*) of (*state*)
> > (*Address*)
> OR   The Secretary of (*department*)
> > (*Address*)

Invitation, inside envelope: *The Secretary of* (*department*)
Place card:
> The Secretary of (*department*) of (*state*)
> OR The Secretary of (*department*)

Place card, less formal: *Secretary* (*surname*)
Introduction: *The Honorable* (*full name*), *secretary of* (*department*) *of* (*state*)
Introduction, one person to another:
> Mr./Madam Secretary, may I present ...
> ... may I present the secretary of (*department*) of (*state*) ...

Conversation, initially: *Mr./madam secretary*
Conversation, subsequently: *Secretary* (*surname*)

State Attorney General

Example: (*Full name*), *the attorney general of Michigan*
Envelope, official:
> The Honorable
> > (*Full name*)
> > > The Attorney General of (*state*)
> > > (*Address*)
> OR   The Honorable
> > (*Full name*)
> > > The Attorney General
> > > (*Address*)

Letter salutation: *Dear Mr./Madam Attorney General:*
Complimentary close: *Sincerely yours,* OR *Sincerely,*
Envelope, social:

Honor & Respect

The Attorney General of (state)
  (Address)
OR *The Attorney General*
    (Address)
Invitation, inside envelope: *The Attorney General*
Place card: *The Attorney General of (state)* OR *The Attorney General*
Place card, less formal: *Attorney General (surname)*
Introduction: *The Honorable (full name), attorney general of the state of (state)*
Introduction, one person to another: *Attorney General (surname)*
Conversation, initially: *Mr./Madam Attorney General*
Conversation, subsequently: *Attorney General (surname)*

State Treasurer, Comptroller, or Auditor
Envelope, official:
  The Honorable
  (Full name)
    (Title of office) of (state)
      (Address)
Letter salutation: *Dear Mr./Ms. (surname):*
Complimentary close: *Sincerely yours,* OR *Sincerely,*
Envelope, social:
  The Honorable
  (Full name)
    (Address)
Invitation, inside envelope: *Mr./Ms. (surname)*
Place card: *Mr./Ms. (surname)*
Introduction:
  The Honorable (full name), (title of office) of (state)
  OR *(Title of office) of (state), Mr./Ms. (surname)*
Introduction, one to another: *Mr./Ms. (surname)*
Conversation: *Mr./Ms. (surname)*

Member of the Staff of an Elected State Official
Envelope, official:
  Mr./Ms. (full name)
    (Position if senior staff) to the Honorable (official's full name)
      (Address)
  OR *Mr./Ms. (full name)*
        Office of the Honorable (official's full name)
          (Address)
Letter salutation: *Dear Mr./Ms. (surname):*
Complimentary close: *Sincerely yours,* OR *Sincerely,*
Envelope, social:
  Mr./Ms. (full name)
    (Address)
Invitation, inside envelope: *Mr./Ms. (surname)*
Place card: *Mr./Ms. (surname)*

Introduction:
> Mr./Ms. (full name), (position if senior staff) to
>> the Honorable (official's full name)
>
> OR (Position if senior staff) to the Honorable (official's full name),
>> Mr./Ms. (surname)
>
> OR Mr./Ms. (full name), office of the Honorable (official's full name)
>
> OR From the office of the Honorable (official's full name), Mr./Ms. (surname)

Introduction, one person to another: Mr./Ms. (surname)
Conversation: Mr./Ms. (surname)

STATE LEGISLATURE

Names of Legislatures
In most states the upper house is the Senate, and the lower house is the House of Representatives.

- In some states (e.g., California and New York) the lower house is an *Assembly* or *State Assembly*.
- In other states (e.g., Maryland, Virginia, and West Virginia) the lower house is the *House of Delegates*.
- In Nebraska there is only one legislative house and its members use the honorific *senator*.

Adapt the following formats using the appropriate name of the legislature.

Names of States
Most states are called the *State of (name)*, but the official names vary. For example, Pennsylvania, Kentucky, Massachusetts, and Virginia are *the Commonwealth of (name)* rather than *State of (name)*. Rhode Island is correctly *Rhode Island and the Province Plantation*. See page 90 for more common and official names.

President or Speaker of a State Assembly
Envelope, official:
> The Honorable
>> (Full name)
>>> (Title) of the (assembly)
>>>> (Address)

Letter salutation:
> Dear Mr./Madam President: OR Dear Mr./Madam Speaker:
> OR Mr./Madam President: OR Mr./Madam Speaker:

Complimentary close: *Sincerely yours,* OR *Sincerely,*
Place card: (Title)
Introduction: *The Honorable (full name), (title) of the (assembly) of (state)*
Introduction, one person to another:
> Mr./Madam President
> Mr./Madam Speaker

Conversation: Mr./Madam President OR Mr./Madam Speaker

State Senator, Representative, or Delegate

NOTE: *State senators* will use *senator* as an honorific. *State senators* may be addressed as Mr./Ms. *(name)* in Washington, DC, especially in the presence of *U.S. Senators*. *Delegates* may use *delegate* as an honorific. Otherwise, use Mr./Ms. *(name)* and identify as a *member of (name of assembly)*.

Envelope, official:
> The Honorable
>> (Full name)
>>> (Name of assembly)
>>> (Address)

Letter salutation: Dear Mr./Ms. *(surname)*:
Complimentary close: Sincerely yours, OR Sincerely,
Envelope, social:
> The Honorable
>> (Full name)
>>> (Address)

Invitation, inside envelope: Mr./Ms. *(surname)*
Place card: Mr./Ms. *(surname)*
Introduction:
> The Honorable *(full name)*, *(name of state)* state *(title of elected position)*

Introduction, one person to another: Mr./Ms. *(surname)*
Conversation: Mr./Ms. *(surname)*

Staff of a State Senator, Representative, or Delegate

Envelope, official:
> Mr./Ms. *(full name)*
>> (Position if senior staff) to the Honorable (official's full name)
>> (Address)
> OR Mr./Ms. *(full name)*
>> Office of the Honorable (official's full name)
>> (Address)

Letter salutation: Dear Mr./Ms. *(surname)*:
Complimentary close: Sincerely yours, OR Sincerely,
Envelope, social:
> Mr./Ms. *(full name)*
>> (Address)

Invitation, inside envelope: Mr./Ms. *(surname)*
Place card: Mr./Ms. *(surname)*
Introduction:
> Mr./Ms. *(full name)*, *(position if senior staff)* to
>> the Honorable *(official's full name)*
> OR *(Position if senior staff)* to the Honorable *(official's full name)*,
>> Mr./Ms. *(surname)*
> OR Mr./Ms. *(full name)* of the office of the Honorable *(official's full name)*
> OR From the office of the Honorable *(official's full name)*, Mr./Ms. *(surname)*

Introduction, one person to another: Mr./Ms. *(full name or surname only)*
Conversation: Mr./Ms. *(surname)*

STATE JUDICIARY

Chief Justice of a State Supreme Court

NOTE: *Judges* are addressed as *the Honorable (full name)*, but a *chief justice* and *justices* of a supreme court are not.

Envelope, official:
    Chief Justice (full name)
        The Supreme Court of (state)
            (Address)
Letter salutation: *Dear Chief Justice (surname):*
Complimentary close:
    Sincerely yours,
    OR *Sincerely,*
Envelope, social:
    Chief Justice (full name)
        (Address)
Invitation, inside envelope: *Chief Justice (surname)*
Place card: *Chief Justice (surname)*
Introduction: *Chief Justice (full name) of the Supreme Court of (state)*
Introduction, one person to another: *Chief Justice (surname)*
Conversation: *Chief Justice (surname)*

Associate Justice of a State Supreme Court

Envelope, official:
    Justice (full name)
        The Supreme Court of (state)
            (Address)
Letter salutation: *Dear Justice (surname):*
Complimentary close: *Sincerely yours,* OR *Sincerely,*
Envelope, social:
    Justice (full name)
        (Address)
Invitation, inside envelope: *Justice (surname)*
Place card: *Justice (surname)*
Introduction: *Justice (full name) of the Supreme Court of (state)*
Introduction, one person to another: *Justice (surname)*
Conversation: *Justice (surname)*

Chief Judge of a State Court

Envelope, official:
    The Honorable
        (Full name)
            Chief Judge of the (Court)
                (Address)
Letter salutation: *Dear Judge (surname):*
Complimentary close: *Sincerely yours,* OR *Sincerely,*

196

Envelope, social:
>   The Honorable
>   (Full name)
>   (Address)
Invitation, inside envelope: *Judge (surname)*
Place card: *Judge (surname)*
Introduction:
>   The Honorable *(full name)*, *chief judge, (court)*
>   OR *Chief judge, (court)*, *Judge (surname)*
Introduction, one person to another: *Judge (surname)*
Conversation: *Judge (surname)*

Judge of a State Court
NOTE: If addressing a *senior judge, resident judge,* or other type of *judge,* include the full title on the envelope and in an introduction.
Envelope, official:
>   The Honorable
>   (Full name)
>   (Court)
>   (Address)
Letter salutation: *Dear Judge (surname):*
Complimentary close:
>   Sincerely yours,
>   OR *Sincerely,*
Envelope, social:
>   The Honorable
>   (Full name)
>   (Address)
Invitation, inside envelope: *Judge (surname)*
Place card: *Judge (surname)*
Introduction:
>   The Honorable *(full name)*, *judge of the (court)*
>   OR *Judge of the (court)*, *Judge (surname)*
Introduction, one person to another: *Judge (surname)*
Conversation: *Judge (surname)*

Chief Magistrate, Magistrate
NOTE: A *magistrate* is a *judge* in *Magistrate Court.* If the judge is a *chief magistrate,* use the complete title in the introduction.
Envelope, official:
>   The Honorable
>   (Full name)
>   (Court)
>   (Address)
Letter salutation: *Dear Judge (surname):*
Complimentary close: *Sincerely yours,* OR *Sincerely,*

Envelope, social:
>The Honorable
>>(Full name)
>>>(Address)

Invitation, inside envelope: Judge (surname)
Place card: Judge (surname)
Introduction: The Honorable (full name), magistrate of the (court)
Introduction, one person to another: Judge (surname)
Conversation: Judge (surname)

Clerk of a State Court

Envelope, official:
>Mr./Ms. (full name)
>>Clerk of the (court)
>>>(Address)

Letter salutation: Dear Mr./Ms. (surname):
Complimentary close: Sincerely yours, OR Sincerely,
Envelope, social:
>Mr./Ms. (full name)
>>(Address)

Invitation, inside envelope: Mr./Ms. (surname)
Place card: Mr./Ms. (surname)
Introduction:
>Mr./Ms. (full name), clerk of the (court)
>OR Clerk of the (court), Mr./Ms. (surname)

Introduction, one person to another: Mr./Ms. (full name or surname only)
Conversation: Mr./Ms. (surname)

Texas Rangers: Chief, Captain, Lieutenant, or Sergeant

Envelope, business:
>(Rank) (full name)
>>Texas Department of Public Safety
>>>(Company No. or office)
>>>>(Address)

Letter salutation: Dear (rank) (surname):
Complimentary close: Sincerely yours, or Sincerely,
Envelope, social:
>Mr./Ms. (full name)
>>(Address)

Invitation, inside envelope: Mr./Ms. (surname)
Official place card: (Rank) (surname)
Social place card: Mr./Ms. (surname)
Introduction:
>Texas Ranger (rank) (full name), (name of office, headquarters, company)
>>of (county/city)

198

Introduction, one person to another:
  (Rank) (surname), may I present ...
  ... may I present (rank) (surname) ...
Conversation, initially: (Rank) (surname)
Conversation, subsequently: (Rank only)

U.S. Muncipal Governments

Mayor
Envelope, official:
  The Honorable
    (Full name)
      Mayor of (municipality)
        (Address)
Letter salutation: Dear Mayor (surname):
Complimentary close: Sincerely yours, OR Sincerely,
Envelope, social:
  The Mayor of (municipality)
    (Address)
Invitation, inside envelope: The Mayor of (municipality)
Place card: Mayor (surname)
Introduction:
  The Honorable (full name), mayor of (municipality)
  OR Mayor of (municipality), Mayor (surname)
Introduction, one person to another: Mayor (surname)
Conversation: Mr./Madam Mayor OR Mayor (surname)

Former Mayor
Envelope, official:
  The Honorable
    (Full name)
      (Address)
Letter salutation: Dear Mr./Ms. (surname):
Complimentary close: Sincerely yours, OR Sincerely,
Envelope, social:
  The Honorable
    (Full name)
      (Address)
Invitation, inside envelope: Mr./Ms. (surname)
Place card: Mr./Ms. (surname)
Introduction:
  The Honorable (full name), former mayor of (city)
  OR The former mayor of (city), Mr./Ms. (surname)
Introduction, one person to another: Mr./Ms. (surname)
Conversation: Mr./Ms. (surname)

Mayor-elect
Envelope, official:
The Honorable
(Full name)
(Address)
Letter salutation: *Dear Mr./Ms. (surname):*
Complimentary close: *Sincerely yours,* OR *Sincerely,*
Envelope, social:
The Honorable
(Full name)
(Address)
Invitation, inside envelope: *Mr./Ms. (surname)*
Place card: *Mr./Ms. (surname)*
Introduction:
The Honorable (full name), mayor-elect of (city)
OR *The mayor-elect of (city), Mr./Ms. (surname)*
Introduction, one person to another: *Mr./Ms. (surname)*
Conversation: *Mr./Ms. (surname)*

City/County Council *or* Board Member
NOTE: In many communities elected officials below the rank of *mayor* are not addressed as *the Honorable. Alderman, councilman, councilwoman,* or *councilperson* describe members of councils, and are not formally used as honorifics. However, they are informally used as honorifics and in place of the name in conversation. Check for the local protocol.
Envelope, business:
The Honorable
(Full name)
(Full title of position) of (county/city)
(Address)
Letter salutation: *Dear Mr./Ms. (surname):*
Complimentary close: *Sincerely yours,* OR *Sincerely,*
Envelope, social:
The Honorable
(Full name)
(Address)
Invitation, inside envelope: *Mr./Ms. (surname)*
Place card: *Mr./Ms. (surname)*
Introduction:
The Honorable (full name), (city) (assembly) member
OR *(City or county) (assembly) member, Mr./Ms. (surname)*
Introduction, one person to another: *Mr./Ms. (full name or surname only)*
Conversation: *Mr./Ms. (surname)*

Elected City and County Commissioners

Examples: *County Commissioner*
              Commissioner of the Water Board
              Police Commissioner

NOTE: In some communities elected officials below the rank of mayor are not addressed as *the Honorable*. Check for the local protocol.

Envelope, business:
   The Honorable
      (Full name)
         (Full title of position) of (county/city)
            (Address)
Letter salutation:
   Dear Mr./Ms. (surname):
   OR *Dear Commissioner (surname):*
Complimentary close: *Sincerely yours,* OR *Sincerely,*
Envelope, social:
   The Honorable
      (Full name)
         (Address)
Invitation, inside envelope: *Mr./Ms. (surname)*
Place card social: *Mr./Ms. (surname)*
Place card official: *Commissioner (surname):*
Introduction: *The Honorable (full name), (full title) of (county/city)*
Introduction, one person to another:
   (Commissioner) (surname), may I present ...
   ... may I present Commissioner (surname) ...
   Mr./Ms. (full name OR surname only), may I present ...
   ... may I present Mr./Ms. (surname) ...
Conversation:
   Mr./Madam Commissioner
   OR *Commissioner (surname)*
   OR *Mr./Ms. (surname)*
Conversation, subsequently: *Commissioner*

Elected City or County District Attorney

NOTE: In some communities elected officials below the rank of mayor are not addressed as *the Honorable*. Check for the local protocol.

Envelope, business:
   The Honorable
      (Full name)
         (Full title of position) of (county/city)
            (Address)
Letter salutation:
   Dear Mr./Madam District Attorney:
   OR *Dear Mr./Ms. (surname):*
Complimentary close: *Sincerely yours,* OR *Sincerely,*

Envelope, social:
> *The Honorable*
> *(Full name)*
> *(Address)*

Invitation, inside envelope: Mr./Ms. *(surname)*
Place card: Mr./Ms. *(surname)*
Introduction: *The Honorable (full name), (full title) of (county/city)*
Introduction, one person to another:
> Mr./Madam District Attorney, may I present ...
> Mr./Ms. *(surname only),* may I present ...
> ... may I present Mr./Ms. *(surname)* ...

Conversation, initially: Mr./Madam District Attorney
Conversation, subsequently: Mr./Ms. *(surname)*

Sheriff

Envelope, business:
> *The Honorable*
> *(Full name)*
> > *Sheriff of (county/city)*
> > *(Address)*

Letter salutation: *Dear Sheriff (surname):*
Complimentary close: *Sincerely yours,* OR *Sincerely,*
Envelope, social:
> *The Honorable*
> *(Full name)*
> *(Address)*

Invitation, inside envelope: Mr./Ms. *(surname)*
Place card social: Mr./Ms. *(surname)*
Place card official: *Sheriff (surname)*
Introduction: *The Honorable (full name), Sheriff of (county/city)*
Introduction, one person to another:
> *Sheriff (surname),* may I present ...
> ... may I present *Chief/Sheriff (surname)* ...

Conversation, initially: *Sheriff (surname)*
Conversation, subsequently: *Sheriff*

Chief of Police

NOTE: Most chiefs of police are appointed municipal officials and would not be addressed as *the Honorable.* However, check for local tradition.
Envelope, business:
> Mr./Ms. *(full name)*
> > *(Full title of position) of (county/city)*
> > *(Address)*

Letter salutation:
> *Dear Chief (surname):*
> OR *Dear Mr./Ms. (surname):*

202

Complimentary close: *Sincerely yours,* OR *Sincerely,*
Envelope, social:
 Mr./Ms. *(full name)*
  (Address)
Invitation, inside envelope: Mr./Ms. *(surname)*
Place card social: Mr./Ms. *(surname)*
Place card official: Chief *(surname)*
Introduction:
 Mr./Ms. *(full name), (full title of position) of (county/city)*
  OR *(Full title of position) of (county/city),* Mr./Ms. *(surname)*
Introduction, one person to another:
 Chief *(surname), may I present ...*
 ... may I present Chief *(surname) ...*
Conversation, initially: Chief *(surname)*
Conversation, subsequently: *Chief*

City or County Judge: Appointed or Elected
Envelope, official:
 The Honorable
  (Full name)
   Judge of *(name of court) (city or county)*
    (Address)
Letter salutation: *Dear* Judge *(surname):*
Complimentary close: *Sincerely yours,* OR *Sincerely,*
Envelope, social:
 The Honorable
  (Full name)
   (Address)
Invitation, inside envelope: Judge *(surname)*
Place card: Judge *(surname)*
Introduction:
 The Honorable *(full name), judge of the (name of court) (city or county)*
Introduction, one person to another: Judge *(surname)*
Conversation: Judge *(surname)*

13 Armed Services

Secretary of Defense
See *Secretary of (portfolio)* page 169.

Secretary of an Armed Force
See *Secretary of (portfolio)* page 169.

Undersecretary of an Armed Force
See *Other Positions Appointed by the President* page 174.

Chairman, Joint Chiefs of Staff
NOTE: Address by *rank* and identify as *chairman*.
Envelope, official:
(*Full rank*) (*full name*), (*post nominal for branch of service*)
    Chairman of the Joint Chiefs of Staff
        (*Address*)
Letter salutation: *Dear (basic rank) (surname):*
Complimentary close: *Sincerely yours,* OR *Sincerely,*
Envelope, social:
(*Full rank*) (*full name*)
    (*Address*)
Invitation, inside envelope: (*Basic rank*) (*surname*)
Place card: (*Basic rank*)/(*service-specific abbreviated rank*) (*surname*)
Introduction:
(*Full rank*) (*full name*), Chairman of the Joint Chiefs of Staff
OR Chairman of the Joint Chiefs of Staff, (*basic rank*) (*surname*)
Introduction, one person to another: (*Basic rank*) (*surname*)

Conversation: *(Basic rank) (surname)*
Conversation, less formal: *(Basic rank)*

Chaplain in the Armed Services
See page 246.

Army, USA; Air Force, USAF; and Marine Corps, USMC

Chief of Staff of the Army
NOTE: Address by *rank* and identify as *chief of staff*.
Envelope, official:
(Full rank) (full name)
Chief of Staff of the Army
(Address)
Letter salutation: Dear *(basic rank) (surname)*:
Complimentary close: *Sincerely yours,* OR *Sincerely,*
Envelope, social:
(Full rank) (full name)
(Address)
Invitation, inside envelope: *(Basic rank) (surname)*
Place card: *(Basic rank)/(service-specific abbreviated rank) (surname)*
Introduction:
(Full rank) (full name), Chief of Staff of the Army
OR *The Chief of Staff of the Army, (basic rank) (surname)*
Introduction, one person to another: *(Basic rank) (surname)*
Conversation: *(Basic rank) (surname)*
Conversation, less formal: *(Basic rank)*

Chief of Staff of the Air Force
NOTE: Address by *rank* and identify as *chief of staff*.
Envelope, official:
(Full rank) (full name)
Chief of Staff of the Air Force
(Address)
Letter salutation: Dear *(basic rank) (surname)*:
Complimentary close: *Sincerely yours,* OR *Sincerely,*
Envelope, social:
(Full rank) (full name)
(Address)
Invitation, inside envelope: *(Basic rank) (surname)*
Place card: *(Basic rank)/(service-specific abbreviated rank) (surname)*

206

Introduction:
(Full rank) *(full name)*, Chief of Staff of the Air Force
OR The Chief of Staff of the Air Force, *(basic rank)* *(surname)*
Introduction, one person to another: *(Basic rank)* *(surname)*
Conversation: *(Basic rank)* *(surname)*
Conversation, less formal: *(Basic rank)*

Commandant of the Marine Corps

NOTE: Address by *rank* and identify as *commandant*.
Envelope, official:
(Full rank) *(full name)*
    Commandant of the Marine Corps
      (Address)
Letter salutation: Dear *(basic rank)* *(surname)*:
Complimentary close: Sincerely yours, OR Sincerely,
Envelope, social:
(Full rank) *(full name)*
    (Address)
Invitation, inside envelope: *(Basic rank)* *(surname)*
Place card: *(Basic rank)/(service-specific abbreviated rank)* *(surname)*
Introduction:
(Full rank) *(full name)*, Commandant of the Marine Corps
OR The Commandant of the Marine Corps, *(basic rank)* *(surname)*
Introduction, one person to another: *(Basic rank)* *(surname)*
Conversation: *(Basic rank)* *(surname)*
Conversation, less formal: *(Basic rank)*

General, Lieutenant General, Major General, Brigadier General

Envelope, official:
(Full rank) *(full name)*, USA/USAF/USMC
    (Title/position)
      (Address)
Letter salutation: Dear General *(surname)*:
Complimentary close: Sincerely yours, OR Sincerely,
Envelope, social:
(Full rank) *(full name)*
    (Address)
Invitation, inside envelope: General *(surname)*
Place card: General/*(service-specific abbreviated rank)* *(surname)*
Introduction:
(Full rank) *(full name)*, *(position/command/name of base/service)*
OR *(Position/command/name of base)*, General *(surname)*
Introduction, one person to another: General *(surname)*
Conversation: General *(surname)*
Conversation, less formal: General

Colonel
Envelope, official:
Colonel (full name), USA/USAF/USMC
(Address)
Letter salutation: *Dear Colonel (surname):*
Complimentary close: *Sincerely yours,* OR *Sincerely,*
Envelope, social:
Colonel (full name)
(Address)
Invitation, inside envelope: *Colonel (surname)*
Place card: *Colonel/(service-specific abbreviated rank) (surname)*
Introduction:
Colonel (full name), (position/command/name of base/service)
OR *(Position/command/name of base), Colonel (surname)*
Introduction, one person to another: *Colonel (surname)*
Conversation: *Colonel (surname)*
Conversation, less formal: *Colonel*

Lieutenant Colonel
Envelope, official:
Lieutenant Colonel (full name), USA/USAF/USMC
(Address)
Letter salutation: *Dear Colonel (surname):*
Complimentary close: *Sincerely yours,* OR *Sincerely,*
Envelope, social:
Lieutenant Colonel (full name)
(Address)
Invitation, inside envelope: *Colonel (surname)*
Place card: *Colonel/(service-specific abbreviated rank) (surname)*
Introduction:
Lieutenant colonel (full name), (position/command/name of base/service)
OR *(Position/command/name of base), Colonel (surname)*
Introduction, one person to another: *Colonel (surname)*
Conversation: *Colonel (surname)*
Conversation, less formal: *Colonel*

Major or Captain
Envelope, official:
(Rank) (full name), USA/USAF/USMC
(Address)
Letter salutation: *Dear (rank) (surname):*
Complimentary close: *Sincerely yours,* OR *Sincerely,*
Envelope, social:
(Rank) (full name)
(Address)
Invitation, inside envelope: *(Rank) (surname)*
Place card: *(Rank)/(service-specific abbreviated rank) (surname)*

Introduction:
>   (Rank) (full name), (position/command/name of base/service)
>   OR (Position/command/name of base), (rank) (surname)

Introduction, one person to another: (Rank) (surname)
Conversation: (Rank) (surname)
Conversation, less formal: (Rank)

First Lieutenant or Second Lieutenant

NOTE: In the past, forms of address for Army lieutenants varied slightly from Air Force and Marine Corps lieutenants, but current directives show forms of address to be identical in all services.

Envelope, official:
>   (First/Second) Lieutenant (full name), USA/USAF/USMC
>>   (Address)

Letter salutation: Dear Lieutenant (surname):
Complimentary close: Sincerely yours, OR Sincerely,
Envelope, social:
>   (First/Second) Lieutenant (full name)
>>   (Address)

Invitation, inside envelope: Lieutenant (surname)
Place card: Lieutenant/(service-specific abbreviated rank) (surname)
Introduction:
>   First/Second Lieutenant (full name), (position/command/name of base/service)
>   OR (Position/command/name of base), Lieutenant (surname)

Introduction, one person to another: Lieutenant (surname)
Conversation: Lieutenant (surname)
Conversation, less formal: Lieutenant

Retired Officer, USA, USAF, or USMC

NOTE: Retired active duty officers may continue to use their ranks; circumstances will determine continued use of ranks by retired reserve officers.

Envelope, official:
>   (Full rank) (full name), USA/USAF/USMC, Retired
>>   (Address)

Letter salutation: Dear (basic rank) (surname):
Complimentary close: Sincerely yours, OR Sincerely,
Envelope, social:
>   (Full rank) (full name)
>>   (Address)

Invitation, inside envelope: (Basic rank) (surname)
Place card: (Basic rank)/(service-specific abbreviated rank) (surname)
Introduction:
>   (Full rank) (full name), United States Army, Retired
>   (Full rank) (full name), United States Air Force, Retired
>   (Full rank) (full name), United States Marine Corps, Retired

Introduction, one person to another: (Basic rank) (surname)
Conversation: (Basic rank) (surname)
Conversation, less formal: (Basic rank)

Cadet, United States Military Academy
Envelope:
> Cadet (full name), USA
>> Company (___), Corp of Cadets
>>> United States Military Academy
>>> West Point, NY 10996

Letter salutation: *Dear Cadet (surname):*
Complimentary close: *Sincerely yours,* OR *Sincerely,*
Invitation, inside envelope: *Cadet (surname)*
Place card: *Cadet (surname)*
Introduction: *Cadet (full name), United States Military Academy*
Introduction, one person to another: *Cadet (surname)*
Conversation: *Cadet (surname)*

Cadet, United States Air Force Academy
NOTE: *Cadet First Class* is abbreviated as C1C
  Cadet Second Class is abbreviated as C2C
Envelope, official:
> Cadet (full name), USAF
>> Room (___), (____) Hall
>>> United States Air Force Academy
>>> Colorado Springs, CO 80840

Letter salutation: *Dear Cadet (surname):*
Complimentary close: *Sincerely yours,* OR *Sincerely,*
Invitation, inside envelope: *Cadet (surname)*
Place card: *Cadet (surname)* OR *C1C/C2C (surname)*
Introduction: *Cadet (full name), United States Air Force Academy*
Introduction, one person to another: *Cadet (surname)*
Conversation: *Cadet (surname)*

Chief Warrant Officer or Warrant Officer, USA or USMC
Envelope, official:
> Chief Warrant Officer (full name), USA/USMC
>> (Position/command/name of base)
>>> (Address)
> Warrant Officer (full name), USA/USMC
>> (Position/command/name of base)
>>> (Address)

Letter salutation:
> Dear Chief Warrant Officer (surname):
> Dear Warrant Officer (surname):

Complimentary close: *Sincerely yours,* OR *Sincerely,*
Envelope, social:
> Chief Warrant Officer (full name)
>> (Address)
> Warrant Officer (full name)
>> (Address)

210

Invitation, inside envelope:
  Dear Chief Warrant Officer (surname):
  Dear Warrant Officer (surname):
Place card: *(Rank)/(service-specific abbreviated rank)/Mr./Ms. (surname)*
Introduction:
  (Full rank) (full name), (position/command/name of base/service)
  (Position/command/name of base), Chief Warrant Officer (surname)
  (Position/command/name of base), Warrant Officer (surname)
Introduction, one person to another:
  Chief Warrant Officer (surname) OR *Warrant Officer (surname)*
Conversation:
  Chief Warrant Officer (surname) OR *Warrant Officer (surname)*

Sergeant Major of the Army, USA
Command Sergeant Major, USA
Sergeant Major, USA
Envelope, official:
  (Full rank) (full name), USA
    (Address)
Letter salutation: *Dear Sergeant Major (surname):*
Complimentary close: *Sincerely yours,* OR *Sincerely,*
Envelope, social:
  Sergeant Major (full name)
    (Address)
Invitation, inside envelope: *Sergeant Major (surname)*
Place card: *Sergeant Major (surname)* OR SMA/CSM/SGM *(surname)*
Introduction:
  Sergeant Major (full name), (position/command/name of base/USA)
    OR *(Position/command/name of base/etc.), Sergeant Major (surname)*
Introduction, one person to another: *Sergeant Major (surname)*
Conversation: *Sergeant Major (surname)*

First Sergeant and Master Sergeant, USA
Envelope, official:
  (Full rating) (full name), USA
    (Address)
Letter salutation: *Dear (full rating) (surname):*
Complimentary close: *Sincerely yours,* OR *Sincerely,*
Envelope, social:
  (Full rating) (full name)
    (Address)
Invitation, inside envelope: *(Full rating) (surname)*
Place card: *(Full rating) (surname)* OR 1SG/MSG *(surname)*
Introduction:
  (Full rating) (full name), (position/command/name of base/USA)
    OR *(Position/command/name of base), (full rating) (surname)*
Introduction, one person to another: *(Full rating) (surname)*
Conversation: *(Full rating) (surname)*

Platoon Sergeant, Sergeant First Class, Staff Sergeant, USA
Sergeant, USA

Envelope, official:
> (Full rating) (full name), USA
>> (Address)

Letter salutation: *Dear Sergeant (surname):*
Complimentary close: *Sincerely yours,* OR *Sincerely,*
Envelope, social:
> (Full rating) (full name)
>> (Address)

Invitation, inside envelope: *Sergeant (surname)*
Place card: *Sergeant (surname)* OR *PSG/SFC/SSG/SGT (surname)*
Introduction:
> (Full rating) (full name), (position/command/name of base/USA)
> OR (Position/command/name of base), Sergeant (surname)

Introduction, one person to another: *Sergeant (surname)*
Conversation: *Sergeant (surname)*

Corporal, Specialist, Private, USA

Envelope, official:
> (Rank) (full name), USA
>> (Address)

Letter salutation: *Dear (Rank) (surname):*
Complimentary close: *Sincerely yours,* OR *Sincerely,*
Envelope, social:
> (Rank) (full name)
>> (Address)

Invitation, inside envelope: *(Rank) (surname)*
Place card: *(Rank) (surname)* OR *CPL/SPC/PV2/PV1 (surname)*
Introduction:
> (Rank) (full name), (position/command/name of base/USA)
> OR (Position/command/name of base), (rank) (surname)

Introduction, one person to another: *(Rank) (surname)*
Conversation: *(Rank) (surname)*

Private First Class, USA

Envelope, official:
> Private First Class (full name), USA
>> (Address)

Letter salutation: *Dear Private (surname):*
Complimentary close: *Sincerely yours,* OR *Sincerely,*
Envelope, social:
> Private (full name)
>> (Address)

Invitation, inside envelope: *Private (surname)*
Place card: *Private (surname)* OR PFC *(surname)*
Introduction:
   Private (full name), *(position/command/name of base/USA)*
   OR *(Position/command/name of base)*, *Private (surname)*
Introduction, one person to another: *Private (surname)*
Conversation: *Private (surname)*

Chief Master Sergeant of the Air Force, Chief Master Sergeant, Command Chief Master Sergeant, USAF

Envelope, official:
   (Full rating) (full name), USAF
   (Address)
Letter salutation: *Dear Chief (surname):*
Complimentary close: *Sincerely yours,* OR *Sincerely,*
Envelope, social:
   (Full rating) (full name)
   (Address)
Invitation, inside envelope: *Chief (surname)*
Place card: *Chief (surname)* OR CMSAF/SMSgt *(surname)*
Introduction:
   (Full rating) (full name), *(position/command/name of base/USAF)*
   OR *(Position/command/name of base)*, *(full rating) (surname)*
Introduction, one person to another: *Chief (surname)*
Conversation: *Chief (surname)*

Senior Master Sergeant, Master Sergeant, Technical Sergeant, Staff Sergeant, and First Sergeant, USAF

Envelope, official:
   (Full rating) (full name), USAF
   (Address)
Letter salutation: *Dear Sergeant (surname):*
Complimentary close: *Sincerely yours,* OR *Sincerely,*
Envelope, social:
   (Full rating) (full name)
   (Address)
Invitation, inside envelope: *Sergeant (surname)*
Place card: *Sergeant (surname)* OR SMSgt/MSgt/TSgt/SSgt/Sgt *(surname)*
Introduction:
   (Full rating) (full name), *(position/command/name of base/USAF)*
   OR *(Position/command/name of base)*, *(full rating) (surname)*
Introduction, one person to another: *Sergeant (surname)*
Conversation: *Sergeant (surname)*

Senior Airman, Airman First Class, Airman, Airman Basic, USAF

Envelope, official:
  (Full rating) (full name), USAF
  (Address)
Letter salutation: *Dear Airman (surname):*
Complimentary close: *Sincerely yours,* OR *Sincerely,*
Envelope, social:
  (Full rating) (full name)
  (Address)
Invitation, inside envelope: *Airman (surname)*
Place card: *Airman (surname)* OR *SrA/A1C/Amn/AB (surname)*
Introduction:
  (Full rating) (full name), *(position/command/name of base/USAF)*
  OR *(Position/command/name of base)*, *(full rating) (surname)*
Introduction, one person to another: *Airman (surname)*
Conversation: *Airman (surname)*

Sergeant Major of the Marine Corp, USMC
Sergeant Major, USMC

Envelope, official:
  (Full rank) (full name), USMC
  (Address)
Letter salutation: *Dear Sergeant Major (surname):*
Complimentary close: *Sincerely yours,* OR *Sincerely,*
Envelope, social:
  (Full rank) (full name)
  (Address)
Invitation, inside envelope: *Sergeant Major (surname)*
Place card: *Sergeant Major (surname)* or *SgtMaj (surname)*
Introduction:
  (Full rank) (full name), *(position/command/name of base/USMC)*
  OR *(Position/command/name of base)*, *(full rating) (surname)*
Introduction, one person to another: *Sergeant Major (surname)*
Conversation: *Sergeant Major (surname)*

First Sergeant, Master Sergeant, Gunnery Sergeant, Staff Sergeant, Sergeant, Private First Class, and Private, USMC

Envelope, official:
  (Full rank) (full name), USMC
  (Address)
Letter salutation: *Dear (Full rank) (surname):*
Complimentary close: *Sincerely yours,* OR *Sincerely,*
Envelope, social:
  (Full rank) (full name)
  (Address)

214

Invitation, inside envelope: *(Full rating) (surname)*
Place card: *(Full rank)/(service-specific abbreviated rating) (surname)*
Introduction:
> *(Full rank) (full name)*, *(position/command/name of base/service)*
> OR *(Position/command/name of base)*, *(full rank) (surname)*

Introduction, one person to another: *(Full rank) (surname)*
Conversation: *(Full rank) (surname)*

Corporal, Lance Corporal, USMC

Envelope, official:
> *(Full rank) (full name)*, USMC
> *(Address)*

Letter salutation: *Dear Corporal (surname):*
Complimentary close: *Sincerely yours,* OR *Sincerely,*
Envelope, social:
> *(Full rank) (full name)*
> *(Address)*

Invitation, inside envelope: *Corporal (surname)*
Place card: *Corporal (surname)* OR *Cpl/LCpl (surname)*
Introduction:
> *(Full rank) (full name)*, *(position/command/name of base/USMC)*
> OR *(Position/command/name of base)*, *Corporal (surname)*

Introduction, one person to another: *Corporal (surname)*
Conversation: *Corporal (surname)*

Navy, USN: Coast Guard, USCG

Chief of Naval Operations

NOTE: Address by *rank* and identify as *chief of Naval Operations.*
Envelope, official:
> *(Full rank) (full name)*
> *Chief of Naval Operations*
> *(Address)*

Letter salutation: *Dear (basic rank) (surname):*
Complimentary close: *Sincerely yours,* OR *Sincerely,*
Envelope, social:
> *(Full rank) (full name)*
> *(Address)*

Invitation, inside envelope: *(Basic rank) (surname)*
Place card: *(Basic rank)/(service-specific abbreviated rank) (surname)*
Introduction:
> *(Full rank) (full name)*, *Chief of Naval Operations*
> OR *The Chief of Naval Operations,* *(basic rank) (surname)*

Introduction, one person to another: *(Basic rank) (surname)*
Conversation: *(Basic rank) (surname)*
Conversation, less formal: *(Basic rank)*

Commandant of the Coast Guard
NOTE: Address by *rank* and identify as the *commandant*.
Envelope, official:
> *(Full rank) (full name)*
>> Commandant of the Coast Guard
>> *(Address)*

Letter salutation: *Dear (basic rank) (surname)*:
Complimentary close: *Sincerely yours*, OR *Sincerely*,
Envelope, social:
> *(Full rank) (full name)*
>> *(Address)*

Invitation, inside envelope: *(Basic rank) (surname)*
Place card: *(Basic rank)/(service-specific abbreviated rank) (surname)*
Introduction:
> *(Full rank) (full name)*, Commandant of the Coast Guard
> OR *The Commandant of the Coast Guard, (basic rank) (surname)*

Introduction, one person to another: *(Basic rank) (surname)*
Conversation: *(Basic rank) (surname)*
Conversation, less formal: *(Basic rank)*

Admiral, Vice-Admiral, or Rear Admiral
Envelope, official:
> *(Full rank) (full name)*, USN/USCG
>> *(Title/position)*
>> *(Address)*

Letter salutation: *Dear Admiral (surname)*:
Complimentary close: *Sincerely yours*, OR *Sincerely*,
Envelope, social:
> *(Full rank) (full name)*
>> *(Address)*

Invitation, inside envelope: *Admiral (surname)*
Place card: *Admiral/(service-specific abbreviated rank) (surname)*
Introduction:
> *(Full rank) (full name)*, *(position/command/name of base/service)*
> OR *(Position/command/name of base)*, *Admiral (surname)*

Introduction, one person to another: *Admiral (surname)*
Conversation: *Admiral (surname)*
Conversation, less formal: *Admiral*

Captain or Commander
Envelope, official:
> *(Rank) (full name)*, USN/USCG
> > *(Address)*

Letter salutation: *Dear (rank) (surname)*:
Complimentary close: *Sincerely yours,* OR *Sincerely,*
Envelope, social:
> *(Rank) (full name)*
> > *(Address)*

Invitation, inside envelope: *(Rank) (surname)*
Place card: *Captain/CAPT* OR *Commander/CDR (surname)*
Introduction:
> *(Rank) (full name)*, *(position/command/name of base/service)*
> OR *(Position/command/name of base)*, *(rank) (surname)*

Introduction, one person to another: *(Rank) (surname)*
Conversation: *(Rank) (surname)*
Conversation, less formal: *(Rank)*

Lieutenant Commander
Envelope, official:
> *Lieutenant Commander (full name)*, USN/USCG
> > *(Address)*

Letter salutation: *Dear Commander (surname)*:
Complimentary close: *Sincerely yours,* OR *Sincerely,*
Envelope, social:
> *Lieutenant Commander (full name)*
> > *(Address)*

Invitation, inside envelope: *Commander (surname)*
Place card: *Commander/LCDR (surname)*
Introduction:
> *Lieutenant Commander (full name)*, *(position/command/name of base)*
> OR *(Position/command/name of base)*, *Commander (surname)*

Introduction, one person to another: *Commander (surname)*
Conversation: *Commander (surname)*
Conversation, less formal: *Commander (surname)*

Lieutenant or Lieutenant Junior Grade
NOTE: Addressing a lieutenant as *Mr./Ms. (surname)* is an internal practice of the Navy used aboard ship. In every other circumstance military personnel should be addressed by rank.
Envelope, official:
> *Lieutenant/Lieutenant, jg (full name)*, USN/USCG
> > *(Address)*

Letter salutation: *Dear Lieutenant (surname)*:
Complimentary close: *Sincerely yours,* OR *Sincerely,*

Envelope, social:
  Lieutenant/Lieutenant, jg (full name)
    (Address)
Invitation, inside envelope: *Lieutenant (surname)*
Place card: *Lieutenant/LT/LTJG (surname)*
Introduction:
  Lieutenant/Lieutenant, jg (full name), *(position/command/name of base/service)*
    OR *(Position/command/name of base)*, *Lieutenant (surname)*
Introduction, one person to another: *Lieutenant (surname)*
Conversation: *Lieutenant (surname)*
Conversation, one person to another: *Lieutenant*

Ensign
Envelope, official:
  Ensign (full name), USN/USCG
    (Address)
Letter salutation: *Dear Ensign (surname):*
Complimentary close: *Sincerely yours,* OR *Sincerely,*
Envelope, social:
  Ensign (full name)
    (Address)
Invitation, inside envelope: *Ensign (surname)*
Place card: *Ensign/ENS (surname)*
Introduction:
  Ensign (full name), *(position/command/name of base/service)*
    OR *(Position/command/name of base)*, *Ensign (surname)*
Introduction, one person to another: *Ensign (surname)*
Conversation: *Ensign (surname)*
Conversation, less formal: *Ensign*

Retired Officer, USN or USCG
NOTE: Retired active duty officers may continue to use their ranks. Circumstances will determine continued use of ranks by retired reserve officers.
Envelope, official:
  (Full rank) (full name), USN/USCG
    Retired
      (Address)
Letter salutation: *Dear (basic rank) (surname):*
Complimentary close: *Sincerely yours, or Sincerely,*
Envelope, social:
  (Full rank) (full name)
    (Address)
Invitation, inside envelope: *(Basic rank) (surname)*
Place card: *(Basic rank)/(service-specific abbreviated rank) (surname)*
Introduction:
  (Full rank) (full name), *United States Navy, Retired*
  (Full rank) (full name), *United States Coast Guard, Retired*

218

Introduction, one person to another: *(Basic rank)* *(full name)*
Conversation: *(Basic rank)* *(surname)*
Conversation, less formal: *(Basic rank)*

Cadet, United States Naval Academy
Envelope, official:
> Midshipman *(full name)*, USN
>> Room (___), (_____) Hall
>> United States Naval Academy
>> Annapolis, MD 21402

Letter salutation: *Dear Midshipman (surname):*
Complimentary close: *Sincerely yours,* OR *Sincerely,*
Invitation, inside envelope: *Midshipman (surname)*
Place card: *Midshipman (surname)*
Introduction: *Midshipman (full name),* United States Naval Academy
Introduction, one person to another: *Midshipman (surname)*
Conversation: *Midshipman (surname)*

Cadet, United States Coast Guard Academy
Envelope, official:
> Cadet *(full name)*, USCG
>> United States Coast Guard Academy
>> New London, CT 06320

Letter salutation: *Dear Cadet (surname):*
Complimentary close: *Sincerely yours,* OR *Sincerely,*
Invitation, inside envelope: *Cadet (surname)*
Place card: *Cadet (surname)*
Introduction: *Cadet (full name),* United States Coast Guard Academy
Introduction, one person to another: *Cadet (surname)*
Conversation: *Cadet (surname)*

Chief Warrant Officer, Warrant Officer
Envelope, official:
> Chief Warrant Officer *(full name)*, USN/USCG
>> *(Address)*
> Warrant Officer *(full name)*, USN/USCG
>> *(Address)*

Letter salutation: *Dear Mr./Ms. (surname):*
Complimentary close: *Sincerely yours,* OR *Sincerely,*
Envelope, social:
> Chief Warrant Officer *(full name)*
>> *(Address)*
> Warrant Officer *(full name)*
>> *(Address)*

Invitation, inside envelope: *Mr./Ms. (full name)*

United States Armed Services

Commissioned Personnel

	ARMY	MARINE CORPS	NAVY	AIR FORCE	COAST GUARD
	General	(no equivalent)	Fleet Admiral	General	(no equivalent)
0-10	General	General	Admiral	General	Admiral
0-9	Lieutenant General	Lieutenant General	Vice Admiral	Lieutenant General	Vice Admiral
0-8	Major General	Major General	Rear Admiral (*upper*)	Major General	Rear Admiral
0-7	Brigadier General	Brigadier General	Rear Admiral (*lower*)	Brigadier General	(*no current equivalent*)
0-6	Colonel	Colonel	Captain	Colonel	Captain
0-5	Lieutenant Colonel	Lieutenant Colonel	Commander	Lieutenant Colonel	Commander
0-4	Major	Major	Lieutenant Commander	Major	Lieutenant Commander
0-3	Captain	Captain	Lieutenant	Captain	Lieutenant
0-2	First Lieutenant	First Lieutenant	Lieutenant Junior Grade	First Lieutenant	Lieutenant Junior Grade
0-1	Second Lieutenant	Second Lieutenant	Ensign	Second Lieutenant	Ensign

Warrant Officers

	ARMY	MARINE CORPS	NAVY	AIR FORCE	COAST GUARD
W-4	Chief Warrant Officer 4	Chief Warrant Officer 4	Chief Warrant Officer 4	*There are no Warrant Officers in the Air Force*	Chief Warrant Officer 4
W-3	Chief Warrant Officer 3	Chief Warrant Officer 3	Chief Warrant Officer 3		Chief Warrant Officer 3

	ARMY	MARINE CORPS	NAVY	AIR FORCE	COAST GUARD
W-2	Warrant Officer 2	Chief Warrant Officer 2	Chief Warrant Officer 2		Chief Warrant Officer 2
W-1	Warrant Officer 1	Warrant Officer 1	Warrant Officer 1		Warrant Officer 1

Enlisted Personnel

	ARMY	MARINE CORPS	NAVY	AIR FORCE	COAST GUARD
E-9	Sergeant Major of the Army Command Sergeant Major OR Sergeant Major	Sergeant Major of the Marine Corps Sergeant Major OR Master Gunnery Sergeant	Master Chief Petty Officer of the Navy Master Chief Petty Officer OR Fleet/Command Master Chief Petty Officer	Chief Master Sergeant of the Air Force Chief Master Sergeant OR First Sergeant OR Command Chief Master Sergeant	Master Chief Petty Officer of the Coast Guard Master Chief Petty Officer OR Command Chief Petty Officer
E-8	First Sergeant OR Master Sergeant	First Sergeant OR Master Sergeant	Senior Chief Petty Officer	Senior Master Sergeant OR First Sergeant	Senior Chief Petty Officer
E-7	Sergeant First Class OR Platoon Sergeant	Gunnery Sergeant	Chief Petty Officer	Master Sergeant OR First Sergeant	Chief Petty Officer
E-6	Staff Sergeant	Staff Sergeant	Petty Officer First Class	Technical Sergeant	Petty Officer First Class
E-5	Sergeant	Sergeant	Petty Officer Second Class	Staff Sergeant	Petty Officer Second Class
E-4	Corporal OR Specialist	Corporal	Petty Officer Third class	Senior Airman	Petty Officer Third Class
E-3	Private First Class	Lance Corporal	Seaman	Airman First Class	Seaman
E-2	Private E-2	Private First Class	Seaman Apprentice	Airman	Seaman Apprentice
E-1	Private E-1	Private	Seaman Recruit	Airman Basic	Seaman Recruit

Place card:
Chief Warrant Officer (surname) OR *CWO2,3,4 or 5 (surname)*
Warrant Officer (surname) OR *WO1 (surname)*
Introduction:
(Full rank) (full name), (position/command/name of base/service)
OR *(Position/command/name of base), (full rank) (surname)*
OR *(Position/command/name of base), Mr./Ms. (surname)*
Introduction, one person to another: Mr./Ms. *(surname)*

Master Chief Petty Officer of the Navy
Master Chief Petty Officer of the Coast Guard
Fleet/Command Master Chief Petty Officer, USN or USCG
Master Chief Petty Officer, USN or USCG

Envelope, official:
(Full rating) (full name), USN/USCG
(Address)
Letter salutation: *Dear Master Chief (surname):*
Complimentary close: *Sincerely yours,* OR *Sincerely,*
Envelope, social:
(Full rating) (full name)
(Address)
Invitation, inside envelope: *Master Chief (surname)*
Place card: *Master Chief (surname)* OR MCPO-N/MCPO/MCPO-CG *(surname)*
Introduction:
(Full rating) (full name), (position/command/name of base/etc.)
OR *(Position/command/name of base), (full rating) (surname)*
Introduction, one person to another: *Master Chief (surname)*
Conversation: *Master Chief (surname)*

Senior Chief Petty Officer

Envelope, official:
Senior Chief Petty Officer (full name), USN/USCG
(Address)
Letter salutation: *Dear Senior Chief (surname):*
Complimentary close: *Sincerely yours,* OR *Sincerely,*
Envelope, social:
Senior Chief Petty Officer (full name)
(Address)
Invitation, inside envelope: *Senior Chief (surname)*
Place card: *Senior Chief (surname)* OR SCPO/ *(surname)*
Introduction:
Senior Chief Petty Officer (full name), (position/command/name of base/etc.)
OR *(Position/command/name of base), Senior Chief Petty Officer (surname)*
Introduction, one person to another: *Senior Chief (surname)*
Conversation: *Senior Chief (surname)*

222

Chief Petty Officer

Envelope, official:
> Chief Petty Officer (full name), USN/USCG
> > (Address)

Letter salutation: Dear Chief (surname):
Complimentary close: Sincerely yours, OR Sincerely,
Envelope, social:
> Chief Petty Officer (full name)
> > (Address)

Invitation, inside envelope: Chief (surname)
Place card: Chief (surname) OR CPO (surname)
Introduction:
> Chief Petty Officer (full name), (position/command/name of base/etc.)
> OR (Position/command/name of base), Chief Petty Officer (surname)

Introduction, one person to another: Chief (surname)
Conversation: Chief (surname)

Petty Officer First Class, Second Class, Third Class

Envelope, official:
> (Full rating) (full name), USN/USCG
> > (Address)

Letter salutation: Dear Petty Officer (surname):
Complimentary close: Sincerely yours, OR Sincerely,
Envelope, social:
> (Full rating) (full name)
> > (Address)

Invitation, inside envelope: Petty Officer (surname)
Place card: Petty Officer (surname) OR PO1/PO2/PO3 (surname)
Introduction:
> (Full rating) (full name), (position/command/name of base/etc.)
> OR (Position/command/name of base), (full rating) (surname)

Introduction, one person to another: Petty Officer (surname)
Conversation: Petty Officer (surname)

Seaman, Seaman Apprentice, Seaman Recruit

Envelope, official:
> (Full rating) (full name), USN/USCG
> > (Address)

Letter salutation: Dear Seaman (surname):
Complimentary close: Sincerely yours, OR Sincerely,
Envelope, social:
> (Full rating) (full name)
> > (Address)

Invitation, inside envelope: Seaman (surname)
Place card: Seaman (surname) OR SN/SA/SR (surname)

Introduction:
   (Full rating) (full name), (position/command/name of base/etc.)
   OR *(Position/command/name of base), (full rating) (surname)*
Introduction, one person to another: *Seaman (surname)*
Conversation: *Seaman (surname)*

14 Diplomats & International Representatives

U. S. Diplomats

NOTE: Citizens of the United States address U.S. ambassadors and ministers as *the Honorable*. When U.S. diplomats travel abroad, they are typically addressed as *His/Her Excellency* by foreign citizens.

Diplomats Addressed as *The Honorable*
Ambassador
Minister

Diplomats Not Addressed as *The Honorable*
Minister-Counselor
Counselor
Attaché
First Secretary
Second Secretary
Assistant Attaché
Third Secretary
Assistant Attaché

Ambassador at Post, Except in the Western Hemisphere
Envelope, official:
> *The Honorable*
> > *(Full name)*
> > > *American Ambassador*
> > > > *(Address)*

Letter salutation: *Dear Mr./Madam Ambassador:*
Complimentary close: *Sincerely yours,* OR *Sincerely,*
Envelope, social:
> *The American Ambassador*
> > *(Address)*

Invitation, inside envelope: *The American Ambassador*
Place card:
> *The American Ambassador*
> OR *The American Ambassador to (country)*
> OR *Ambassador (surname)*

Introduction: *The Honorable (full name), American ambassador*
Introduction, one person to another: *Ambassador (surname)*
Conversation: *Mister/Madam Ambassador*
Conversation, less formal: *Ambassador (surname)*

Ambassador at Post in the Western Hemisphere

Envelope, official:
> *The Honorable*
> > *(Full name)*
> > > *Ambassador of the United States of America*
> > > > *(Address)*

Letter salutation: *Dear Mr./Madam Ambassador:*
Complimentary close: *Sincerely yours,* OR *Sincerely,*
Envelope, social:
> *The Ambassador of the United States of America*
> > *(Address)*

Invitation, inside envelope: *The Ambassador of the United States*
Place card:
> *The Ambassador of the United States of America*
> OR *The Ambassador of the United States of America to (country)*
> OR *Ambassador (surname)*

Introduction:
> *The Honorable (full name), Ambassador of the United States of America*

Introduction, one person to another: *Ambassador (surname)*
Conversation: *Mister/Madam Ambassador*
Conversation, less formal: *Ambassador (surname)*

Ambassador Away from Post

NOTE: Use *Ambassador of the United States of America* in the Western Hemisphere. Use *American Ambassador* elsewhere.
Envelope, official:
> *The Honorable*
> > *(Full name)*
> > > *American Ambassador to (country)*
> > > > *(Address)*

226

Letter salutation: *Dear Mr./Madam Ambassador:*
Complimentary close: *Sincerely yours,* OR *Sincerely,*
Envelope, social:
> The American Ambassador
> (Address)

Invitation, inside envelope: *The American Ambassador*
Place card:
> The American Ambassador
> OR *The American Ambassador to (country)*
> OR *Ambassador (surname)*

Introduction: *The Honorable (full name), American ambassador*
Introduction, one person to another: *Ambassador (surname)*
Conversation: *Mister/Madam Ambassador*
Conversation, less formal: *Ambassador (surname)*

Ambassador with a Military Rank

NOTE: *Members of the U.S. Armed Services,* beginning on page 205, has information on each rank's use in writing and conversation.
Envelope, official:
> At post
> > (Full rank) (full name)
> > > The American Ambassador
> > > (Address)

> OR at post in the Western Hemisphere
> > (Full rank) (full name)
> > > The Ambassador of the United States of America
> > > (Address)

> OR away from post
> > (Full rank) (full name)
> > > The American Ambassador to (country)
> > > (Address)

> OR away from post in the Western Hemisphere
> > (Full rank) (full name)
> > > The Ambassador of the United States of America to (country)
> > > (Address)

Letter salutation: *Dear (basic rank) (surname):*
Complimentary close: *Same as other ambassadors*
Envelope, social: *Same as other ambassadors*
Invitation, inside envelope: *Same as other ambassadors*
Place card: *Same as other ambassadors*
Introduction:
> (Full rank) (full name), The American ambassador
> OR *(Full rank) (full name), The American Ambassador to (country)*
> OR *(Full rank) (full name), The Ambassador of the United States of America*
> OR *(Full rank) (full name), The Ambassador of the United States of America to (country)*

Introduction, one person to another: *Same as other ambassadors*
Conversation: *Same as other ambassadors*

Ambassador at Large

NOTE: Use *ambassador, American ambassador,* or *Ambassador of the United States* as appropriate for clarity.
Envelope, official:
> The Honorable
> > (Full name)
> > > Ambassador at Large
> > > > (Address)

Letter salutation: *Dear Mr./Madam Ambassador:*
Complimentary close: *Sincerely yours,* OR *Sincerely,*
Envelope, social:
> The Honorable
> > (Full name)
> > > (Address)

Invitation, inside envelope: *Ambassador (surname)*
Place card: *Ambassador (surname)*
Introduction:
> The Honorable (full name), ambassador at large
> OR Ambassador at large, Ambassador (surname)

Introduction, one person to another: *Ambassador (surname)*
Conversation: *Mister/Madam Ambassador*

High Commissioner of the United States

Envelope, official, at post:
> The Honorable
> > (Full name)
> > > United States High Commissioner for (country)
> > > > (Address)

Letter salutation: *Dear Mr./Ms. (surname):*
Complimentary close: *Sincerely yours,* OR *Sincerely,*
Envelope, social:
> The Honorable
> > (Full name)
> > > (Address)

Invitation, inside envelope: *Mr./Ms. (surname)*
Place card: *Mr./Ms. (surname)*
Introduction:
> The Honorable (full name), United States high commissioner for (country)
> OR The United States high commissioner for (country), Mister/Ms. (surname)

Introduction, one person to another: *Mister/Ms. (surname)*
Conversation: *Mister/Ms. (surname)*

Consul General
Envelope, official:
At post:
> *(Full name), Esq.*
>> *American Consul General*
>> *(Address)*

OR at post in the Western Hemisphere
> *(Full name), Esq.*
>> *Consul General of the United States of America*
>> *(Address)*

OR away from post
> *(Full name), Esq.*
>> *American Consul General for (place)*
>> *(Address)*

OR away from post in the Western Hemisphere
> *(Full name), Esq.*
>> *Consul General of the United States of America for (place)*
>> *(Address)*

Letter salutation: *Dear Mr./Ms. (surname):*
Complimentary close: *Sincerely yours,* OR *Sincerely,*
Envelope, social:
> *Mr./Ms. (full name)*
> *(Address)*

Invitation, inside envelope: *Mr./Ms. (surname)*
Place card: *Mr./Ms. (surname)*

Introduction:
> *Mister/Ms. (full name), the American Consul General*
> OR *The American Consul General, Mister/Ms. (surname)*

NOTE: Use *American Consul General* OR *Consul General of the United States of America* as appropriate.

Introduction, one person to another: *Mister/Ms. (surname)*
Conversation: *Mister/Ms. (surname)*

Consul or Vice-Consul
Use form for *Consul General* and identify as a *consul* or *vice-consul.*

Chargé d'affaires
NOTE: A chargé is addressed by personal rank and identified as a *chargé; e.g.,* a chargé with the rank of minister will be addressed as *the Honorable (full name).*
Envelope, official:
> *Mr./Ms. (full name)*
>> *Chargé d'affaires of the United States of America*
>> *(Address)*

Letter salutation: *Sir/Madam:* OR *Dear Mr./Ms. (surname):*
Complimentary close: *Sincerely yours,* OR *Sincerely,*

Envelope, social:
Chargé d'affaires of the United States of America
    (Address)
Invitation, inside envelope: Mr./Ms. *(surname)*
Place card: Mr./Ms. *(surname)*
Introduction:
    Mister/Ms. (full name), the chargé d'affaires of the United States of America
    OR *The chargé d'affaires of the United States of America, Mister/Ms. (surname)*
Introduction, one person to another: *Mister/Ms. (surname)*
Conversation: *Mister/Ms. (surname)*

Chargé d'affaires ad Interim
Use form under *Chargé d'affaires* and identify as a *chargé d'affaires ad interim.*

Deputy Chief of Mission
NOTE: A deputy chief of mission is addressed by personal rank and identified as a *deputy chief of mission; A* DCM with the rank of minister and will be addressed as *the Honorable (full name).*
Envelope, official:
    Mr./Ms. *(full name)*
        Deputy Chief of Mission of the (embassy of country)
        (Address)
Letter salutation: *Sir/Madam:* OR *Dear Mr./Ms. (surname):*
Complimentary close: *Sincerely yours,* OR Sincerely,
Envelope, social:
    Mr./Ms. *(surname)*
        (Address)
Invitation, inside envelope: Mr./Ms. *(surname)*
Place card: Mr./Ms. *(surname)*
Introduction:
    Mister/Ms. (full name), the Deputy Chief of Mission...
    The deputy chief of mission of the (embassy of country), Mister/Ms. (surname)
Introduction, one person to another: *Mister/Ms. (surname)*
Conversation: *Mister/Ms. (surname)*

Personal or Special Representative of the President
Special Assistant or Advisor to the President
Envelope, official, in the USA:
    The Honorable
        Mr./Ms. *(full name)*
            (Specific title) to the President
            (Address)
    OR if abroad:
    The Honorable
        Mr./Ms. *(full name)*
            (Specific title) to the President of the United States
            (Address)
Letter salutation: *Dear Mr./Ms. (surname):*

Complimentary close: *Sincerely yours,* OR *Sincerely,*
Envelope, social:
> The Honorable
>> Mr./Ms. *(full name)*
>> *(Address)*

Invitation, inside envelope: Mr./Ms. *(surname)*
Place card: Mr./Ms. *(surname)*
Introduction:
> The Honorable *(full name)*, *(specific title)*
> OR The *(specific title)*, *Mister/Ms. (surname)*

Introduction, one person to another: *Mister/Ms. (surname)*
Conversation: *Mister/Ms. (surname)*

Former Career Ambassador

Envelope, official:
> The Honorable
>> *(Full name)*
>> *(Address)*

Letter salutation: *Dear Ambassador (surname):*
Complimentary close: *Sincerely yours,* OR *Sincerely,*
Envelope, social:
> The Honorable
>> *(Full name)*
>> *(Address)*

Invitation, inside envelope: *Ambassador (surname)*
Place card: *Ambassador (surname)*
Introduction:
> The Honorable *(full name)*, *former ambassador of the United States of America*

Introduction, one person to another: *Ambassador (surname)*
Conversation: *Ambassador (surname)*

Former Ambassador

NOTE: A former career diplomat who has held the rank of ambassador uses *ambassador* as an honorific for life. Another individual who has held the rank of ambassador for a period of time may revert to Mr./Ms./*etc.* Check for the preference of the bearer.

Envelope, official:
> The Honorable
>> *(Full name)*
>> *(Address)*

Letter salutation: *Dear Ambassador (surname):*
Complimentary close: *Sincerely yours,* OR *Sincerely,*
Envelope, social:
> The Honorable
>> *(Full name)*
>> *(Address)*

Invitation, inside envelope: *Ambassador (surname)*
Place card: *Ambassador (surname)*

Introduction:
> The Honorable (full name), former ambassador of the United States of America
> OR Former ambassador of the United States of America, Ambassador (surname)

Introduction, one person to another: Ambassador (surname)
Conversation: Ambassador (surname)

International Organizations

Representative to an International Organization, with the Rank of Ambassador

Envelope, official:
> The Honorable
> (Full name)
>> The United States Ambassador to (organization)
>> (Address)

Letter salutation: Dear Mr./Madam Ambassador:
Complimentary close: Sincerely yours, OR Sincerely,
Envelope, social:
> The Honorable
>> The United States Ambassador to (organization)
>> (Address)

Invitation, inside envelope: Mr./Ms. (surname)
Place card: Mr./Ms. (surname)
Introduction:
> Ambassador (full name), the United States representative to (organization)

Introduction, one person to another: Ambassador (surname)
Conversation: Mister/Madam Ambassador

Representative to an International Organization

Envelope, official:
> The Honorable
> (Full name)
>> The United States Representative to (organization)
>> (Address)

Letter salutation: Dear Mr./Ms. (surname):
Complimentary close: Sincerely yours, OR Sincerely,
Envelope, social:
> The Honorable
> (Full name)
>> (Address)

Invitation, inside envelope: Mr./Ms. (surname)
Place card: Mr./Ms. (surname)
Introduction: Mister/Ms. (full name), the United States representative to …
Introduction, one person to another: Mister/Ms. (surname)
Conversation: Mister/Ms. (surname)

Representative to an International Organization, with a Military Rank

NOTE: See listing under *Members of the U.S. Armed Forces* for more information on how to use each rank's full rank and basic rank in writing and conversation.

Envelope, official:
> *(Rank) (full name)* USA/USN/USAF/USMC/USCG
> > *(Position and organization)*
> > *(Address)*

Letter salutation: *Dear (rank) (surname):*
Complimentary close: *Sincerely yours,* OR *Sincerely,*
Envelope, social:
> *(Rank) (full name)*
> > *(Address)*

Invitation, inside envelope: *(Rank) (surname)*
Place card: *(Rank) (surname)*
Introduction: *(Rank) (full name), the (position and title) to (organization)*
Introduction, one person to another: *(Rank) (surname)*
Conversation: *(Rank) (surname)*

15 Tribal Officials

There are more than 560 Native American tribes in the United States that are officially recognised by the federal government, each with its own laws and traditions. While there are similarities among tribal entities, each tribal government maintains it own unique structure. Some sources suggest that tribal officials are not addressed with the courtesy title *the Honorable*, but most tribes use the courtesy title *the Honorable* when addressing their own officials. Check the preference of the bearer and the tradition of a tribe to assure the most acceptable form of address.

Tribal Executive

Chief	First Chief	Assistant Chief
	Head Chief	Assistant Principal Chief
	Honorary Chief	Deputy Principal Chief
	Principal Chief	Second Chief
		Sub Chief

Examples: (*Full name*), Sub Chief, *Narragansett Indian Tribal Council*
(*Full name*), Head Chief, (*name of tribe*)

NOTE: Elected tribal officials are typically addressed as *the Honorable*, but not every tribe uses a courtesy title when addressing its leaders. Check for specific tradition. If there there are stepped ranks of chief, check to see if lower chiefs are addressed with the (basic rank) "*chief*" or if they are addressed with (*full rank*). Chief is sometimes reserved for the highest chief only.

Chief, *continued:*

Envelope, official:
> The Honorable
>> (Full name)
>>> (Full title) of the (tribe)
>>>> (Address)

Letter salutation: *Dear Mr./Ms./etc. (surname):* OR *Dear Chief (surname):*
Complimentary close: *Sincerely yours,* OR *Sincerely,*
Envelope, social:
> The Honorable
>> (Full name)
>>> (Address)

Invitation, inside envelope:
> Mr./Ms./etc. (surname) OR Chief (surname)

Place card:
> Mr./Ms./etc. (surname) OR Chief (surname)

Introduction: *The Honorable (full name), (full title) of the (tribe)*
Introduction, one person to another:
> Mr./Ms./etc. (surname) OR Chief (surname)

Conversation: Mr./Ms./etc. (surname) OR Chief (surname)
Conversation, less formal: *Chief, sir* OR *ma'am*

President   Vice President
Chair   Vice-chair
Chairperson   Vice-chairperson
Chairman   Vice-chairman
Chairwoman   Vice-chairwoman

Examples: *(Full name), Chairperson, (name of tribe)*
            (Full name), President (name of tribe)
            (Full name), Tribal President, (name of tribe)

NOTE: Elected tribal officials are typically addressed as *the Honorable*, but not every tribe uses a courtesy title when addressing tribal officials. Check for specific tradition.

Envelope, official:
> The Honorable
>> (Full name)
>>> (Title) of the (tribe)
>>>> (Address)

Letter salutation: *Dear Mr./Ms./etc. (surname):* OR *Dear (title) (surname):*
Complimentary close: *Sincerely yours,* OR *Sincerely,*
Envelope, social:
> The Honorable
>> (Full name)
>>> (Address)

Invitation, inside envelope: Mr./Ms./etc. (surname)
Place card: Mr./Ms./etc. (surname)

236

Introduction: *The Honorable (full name), (title) of the (tribe)*
Introduction, one person to another:
  Mr./Ms./etc. (surname) OR *(Title) (surname)*
Conversation: Mr./Ms./etc. *(surname)* OR *(Title) (surname)*
Conversation, less formal: *(Title), sir* OR *ma'am*

Secretary   Counsellor
Treasurer   Councilman
Councilwoman

Example: *(Full name), Treasurer of the (name of tribe)*
NOTE: Elected tribal officials are typically addressed as *the Honorable*, but not every tribe uses a courtesy title when addressing tribal officials. Check for specific tradition.
Envelope, official:
  The Honorable
    (Full name)
      (Title) of the (tribe)
        (Address)
Letter salutation: *Dear Mr./Ms./etc. (surname):*
Complimentary close: *Sincerely yours,* OR *Sincerely,*
Envelope, social:
  The Honorable
    (Full name)
      (Address)
Invitation, inside envelope: Mr./Ms./etc. *(surname)*
Place card: Mr./Ms./etc. *(surname)*
Introduction: *The Honorable (full name), (title) of the (tribe)*
Introduction, one person to another: Mr./Ms./etc. *(surname)*
Conversation: Mr./Ms./etc. *(surname)*
Conversation, less formal: *(Title), sir* OR *ma'am*

Governor
Example: *(Full name), Governor, Pueblo of Cochiti*
Envelope, official:
  The Honorable
    (Full name)
      Governor of the (tribe)
        (Address)
Letter salutation: *Dear Governor (surname):*
Complimentary close: *Sincerely yours,* OR *Sincerely,*
Envelope, social:
  The Honorable
    (Full name)
      (Address)
Invitation, inside envelope: *Governor (surname)*
Place card: *Governor (surname)*
Introduction: *The Honorable (full name), governor of the (tribe)*

Introduction, one person to another: *Governor (surname)*
Conversation: *Governor (surname)*
Conversation, less formal: *Governor, sir* OR *ma'am*

First Lieutenant Governor
Second Lieutenant Governor
Envelope, official:
The Honorable
    (Full name)
       (Full title) of the (tribe)
       (Address)
Letter salutation: *Dear Lieutenant Governor (surname):*
Complimentary close: *Sincerely yours,* OR *Sincerely,*
Envelope, social:
The Honorable
    (Full name)
       (Address)
Invitation, inside envelope: *Lt. Governor (surname)*
Place card: *Lt. Governor (surname)*
Introduction: *The Honorable (full name), (full title) of the (tribe)*
Introduction, one person to another: *Lieutenant Governor (surname)*
Conversation: *Lieutenant Governor (surname)*
Conversation, less formal: *Lieutenant Governor, sir* OR *ma'am*

Traditional Leader   War Captain
Spiritual Leader   First Warrior
Second Warrior
Examples: *(Full name), Spiritual Leader of the (name of tribe)*
            (Full name), War Captain, (name of tribe)
NOTE: Elected tribal officials are typically addressed as *the Honorable*, but not every tribe uses a courtesy title when addressing tribal officials. Check for specific tradition.
Envelope, official:
The Honorable
    (Full name)
       (Title) of the (tribe)
       (Address)
Letter salutation: *Dear Mr./Ms./etc. (surname):* OR *Dear (title) (surname):*
Complimentary close: *Sincerely yours,* OR *Sincerely,*
Envelope, social:
The Honorable
    (Full name)
       (Address)
Invitation, inside envelope: *Mr./Ms./etc. (surname)*
Place card: *Mr./Ms./etc. (surname)*
Introduction: *The Honorable (full name), (full title) of the (tribe)*

Introduction, one person to another: Mr./Ms./etc. (surname)
Conversation: Mr./Ms./etc. (surname)
Conversation, less formal: (Title), sir OR ma'am

Peacemaker
Elder
Example: (Full name), Peacemaker, (name of tribe) (peacemaker council)
NOTE: Elected tribal officials are typically addressed as the Honorable, but not every tribe uses a courtesy title when addressing tribal officials. Check for specific tradition.
Envelope, official:
    The Honorable
    (Full name)
        (Title) of the (tribe)
            (Address)
Letter salutation: Dear (title) (surname):
Complimentary close: Sincerely yours, OR Sincerely,
Envelope, social:
    The Honorable
    (Full name)
        (Address)
Invitation, inside envelope: (Title) (surname)
Place card: (Title) (surname)
Introduction: The Honorable (full name), (full title) of the (tribe)
Introduction, one person to another: (Title) (surname)
Conversation: (Title) (surname)
Conversation, less formal: (Title), sir OR ma'am

Mekko, Micco
Examples: (Full name), Mekko, Kialegee Tribal Town of Okalahoma
             (Full name), Micco, Coushatta Tribe of Louisiana
NOTE: Elected tribal officials are typically addressed as the Honorable, but not every tribe uses a courtesy title when addressing tribal officials. Check for specific tradition.
Envelope, official:
    The Honorable
    (Full name)
        Mekko/Micco
            (Tribal town)
                (Address)
Letter salutation: Dear Mekko/Micco (surname):
Complimentary close: Sincerely yours, OR Sincerely,
Envelope, social:
    The Honorable
    (Full name)
        (Address)
Invitation, inside envelope: Mekko/Micco (surname)

Place card: *Mekko/Micco (surname)*
Introduction: *The Honorable (full name), Mekko/Micco, (tribal town)*
Introduction, one person to another: *Mekko/Micco (full name)*
Conversation: *Mekko/Micco (surname)*
Conversation, less formal: *Mekko/Micco, sir* OR *ma'am*

Town King

Example: *(Full name), Town King, Thlopthlocco Tribal Town*
NOTE: *Town king* is the same rank and office as *micco* or *mekko* but is the English equivalent of the tribal title. Elected tribal officials are typically addressed as *the Honorable*, but not every tribe uses a courtesy title when addressing tribal officials. Check for specific tradition.
Envelope, official:
> *The Honorable*
> > *(full name)*
> > > *Town King*
> > > > *(Tribal town)*
> > > > > *(Address)*

Letter salutation: *Dear Town King (surname):*
Complimentary close: *Sincerely yours,* OR *Sincerely,*
Envelope, social:
> *The Honorable*
> > *(Full name)*
> > > *(Address)*

Invitation, inside envelope: *Town King (surname)*
Place card: *Town King (surname)*
Introduction: *The Honorable (full name), Town King, (tribal town)*
Introduction, one person to another: *Town King (surname)*
Conversation: *Town King (surname)*
Conversation, less formal: *Town King, sir* OR *ma'am*

Tribal Judiciary

Chief Justice of a Tribal Court

Example: *(Full name), Chief Justice of the (name of tribe) Supreme Court*
Envelope, official:
> *The Honorable*
> > *(Full name)*
> > > *Chief Justice of the (name of court)*
> > > > *Address*

Letter salutation: *Dear Chief Justice:*
Complimentary close: *Sincerely yours,* OR *Sincerely,*
Envelope, social:
> *The Honorable*
> > *(Full name)*
> > > *(Address)*

Invitation, inside envelope: *Justice (surname)*
Place card: *Justice (surname)*
Introduction:
> The Honorable *(full name)*, Chief Justice of the *(name of court)*
> OR Chief Justice of the *(name of court)*, Justice *(surname)*

Introduction, one person to another:
> *Justice (surname), may I present ....*
> *... may I present the Justice (surname)...*

Conversation: *Justice (surname)*
Conversation, less formal: *Justice, sir* OR *ma'am*

Chief Judge of a Tribal Court
Example: *(Full name)*, Chief Judge of the *(name of tribe)* Tribal Court
Envelope, official:
> The Honorable
> *(Full name)*
> > Chief Judge of the *(name of court)*
> > Address

Letter salutation: *Dear Chief Judge:*
Complimentary close: *Sincerely yours,* OR *Sincerely,*
Envelope, social:
> The Honorable
> *(Full name)*
> > *(Address)*

Invitation, inside envelope: *Judge (surname)*
Place card: *Judge (surname)*
Introduction:
> The Honorable *(full name)*, Chief Judge of the *(name of court)*
> OR Chief Judge of the *(name of court)*, Judge *(surname)*

Introduction, one person to another:
> *Judge (surname), may I present ....*
> *... may I present the Judge (surname)...*

Conversation: *Judge (surname)*
Conversation, less formal: *Judge, sir* OR *ma'am*

Associate Justice of a Tribal Court
Justice of a Tribal Court
Example: *(Full name)*, Associate Justice of the Cherokee Nation Supreme Court
Envelope, official:
> The Honorable
> *(Full name)*
> > *(Full title)* of the *(name of court)*
> > *(Address)*

Letter salutation: *Dear Justice (surname):*
Complimentary close: *Sincerely yours,* OR *Sincerely,*

Envelope, social:
> The Honorable
>> (Full name)
>>> (Address)

Invitation, inside envelope: *Justice (surname)*
Place card: *Justice (surname)*
Introduction:
> The Honorable *(full name)*, *(full title)* of the *(name of court)*
> OR *(Full title)* the *(name of court)* Justice *(surname)*

Introduction, one person to another: *Justice (surname)*
Conversation: *Justice (surname)*
Conversation, less formal: *Justice, sir* OR *ma'am*

Associate Judge of a Tribal Court
Deputy Judge of a Tribal Court
Judge of a Tribal Court
Administrative Law Judge of a Tribal Court
Chief Magistrate of a Tribal Court
Magistrate of a Tribal Court

Examples: *(Full name), Administrative Law Judge of the Kalispel Tribal Court*
> *(Full name), Associate Judge of the Ho-Chunk Nation Court*
> *(Full name), Chief Magistrate, Court of Indian Offenses, Apache Tribe*
> *(Full name), Magistrate, Court of Indian Offenses, Eastern Shawnee Tribe*

Envelope, official:
> The Honorable
>> (Full name)
>>> (Full title) of the (name of court)
>>> (Address)

Letter salutation: *Dear Judge (surname):*
Complimentary close: *Sincerely yours,* or *Sincerely,*
Envelope, social:
> The Honorable
>> (Full name)
>>> (Address)

Invitation, inside envelope: *Judge (surname)*
Place card: *Judge (surname)*
Introduction:
> The Honorable *(full name)*, *(full title)* of the *(name of court)*
> OR *(Full title)* the *(name of court)* Judge *(surname)*

Introduction, one person to another: *Judge (surname)*
Conversation: *Judge (surname)*
Conversation, less formal: *Judge, sir* OR *ma'am*

16 Clergy & Religious Officials

Forms of Address for Western and Eastern Clergy

In many sects a member of the clergy is a peer in, an official of, and a spokesperson for a faith community. Hierarchical offices and titles define responsibility and territory of influence. As a sign of respect a cleric is acknowledged with reverent form of address.

However, a definitive form of address for all clerics is problematic:

* Officials are not ranked in a hierarchical manner.
* Congregations are autonomous and develop their own forms of address.
* A religion's name for the same rank of clergy changes from language to language and dialect to dialect.
* In some religions there is no clergy. For example, Jain ceremonies are led by members of the lay community who require no special form of address. There are Jain monks, but they do not lead services or attend secular public or social events.

In these and other circumstances it is essential to both research the local customs and follow the lead of your introducer.

Forms of Address for Members and Nonmembers

Religious communities frequently have traditions for addressing their own clergy. For example, a Roman Catholic may choose to close a letter to a Roman Catholic bishop with *Your humble servant*. However, anyone of any religion or denomination can close a letter to a Roman Catholic bishop with *Sincerely yours*. Therefore, *Sincerely yours* is listed here as the recommended form.

Baha'i

The Baha'i faith has no clergy and no specific terminology to be used when addressing members. While Baha'i has elected local, national, and international assemblies, ranking members do not receive special forms of address.

Buddhist

Dalai Lama

Envelope:
> His Holiness
>> The Dalai Lama
>>> (Address)

Letter salutation: *Your Holiness:*
Complimentary close: *Respectfully yours,*
Wedding invitation, inside envelope:
> His Holiness
>> The Dalai Lama

Place card: *H.H. The Dalai Lama* OR *The Dalai Lama*
Introduction: *His Holiness the Dalai Lama*
Introduction, one person to another:
> *Your Holiness, may I present...*
> *... may I present His Holiness the Dalai Lama*

Conversation: *Your Holiness*

Geshe

Examples: *Kelsang Gyeltsen*
             Tsultim Rinpoche
             Sopa Gyatso

NOTE: A full name is a combination of (*given name of person who ordained this teacher*) + (*given name of this teacher*).
Envelope:
> The Venerable
>> (Full name)
>>> (Address)
> OR The Venerable
>> Geshe (full name)
>>> (Address)

Letter salutation: *Dear Geshe (given name of this teacher):*
Complimentary close: *Sincerely yours,* OR *Sincerely,*
Wedding invitation, inside envelope: Geshe (*given name of this teacher*)

244

Place card:
> The Ven. Geshe (given name of this teacher)
> OR Geshe (given name of this teacher)

Introduction:
> The Venerable Geshe (full name) of (temple) in (location)

Introduction, one person to another: Geshe (given name of this teacher)

Conversation:
> Geshe (given name of teacher)
> OR Geshe

Gen

Examples: Kelsang Khedrub
Kelsang Lekma

NOTE: A full name is a combination of (given name of person who ordained this teacher) + (given name of this teacher).

Envelope:
> Gen (full name)
> (Address)

Letter salutation: Dear Gen (given name of this teacher):

Complimentary close: Sincerely yours, OR Sincerely,

Wedding invitation, inside envelope: Gen (given name of this teacher)

Place card: Gen (given name of this teacher)

Introduction: Gen (full name) of (temple) in (location)

Introduction, one person to another: Gen (given name of this teacher)

Conversation: Gen (given name of teacher) OR Gen

Kadam

Examples: Carol Heyes
Chris Clausen

NOTE: A kadam may have a traditional name (given name of person who ordained this teacher) + (given name of this teacher), or use his or her given and surname. Check for preference of the bearer.

Envelope:
> Kadam (full name)
> (Address)

Letter salutation: Dear Kadam (given name of teacher):

Complimentary close: Sincerely yours, OR Sincerely,

Place card: Kadam (given name of teacher)

Introduction: Kadam (full name) of (temple) in (location)

Conversation: Kadam (given name of teacher)

Chaplain

Chaplain in the Armed Services

NOTE: For more on the use of full rank and basic rank, see listing for the rank held by the chaplain by branch of service.

Envelope, official:
> Chaplain (full name)
>> (Full rank), (post nominal for branch of service)
>> (Address)
> OR Chaplain (full rank) (full name), (post nominal for branch of service)
>> (Address)

Letter salutation: Dear Chaplain (surname):
Complimentary close: Sincerely yours, OR Sincerely,
Envelope, social:
> Chaplain (full name)
>> (Address)

Wedding invitation, inside envelope: Chaplain (surname)
Place card: Chaplain (surname)
Introduction:
> Chaplain (full name), (full rank), (branch of service),
>> (current assignment and location)

Introduction, one person to another: Chaplain (surname)
Conversation: Chaplain (surname)

Chaplain

Examples: Dr. (full name), Episcopal Chaplain, University of Arizona
Father (full name), Associate Catholic University Chaplain
Imam (full name), University Chaplain for the Muslim Community
Rabbi (full name), Chaplain, Princeton University

NOTE: Address by his or her hierarchical (rank) and identify by (office).

Christian Orthodox

Ecumenical Patriarch, Patriarch of Constantinople

Example: Bartholomew, Archbishop
> of Constantinople, New Rome and Ecumenical Patriarch

Envelope:
> His All Holiness
>> The Ecumenical Patriarch
>> (Address)

Letter salutation: Your All Holiness:
Complimentary close: Respectfully yours, OR Respectfully,
Wedding invitation, inside envelope:
> His All Holiness
>> The Ecumenical Patriarch

Place card: *H.A.H. The Ecumenical Patriarch* OR *The Ecumenical Patriarch*
Announced: *His All Holiness, the Ecumenical Patriarch*
Conversation: *Your All Holiness*

Pope COPTIC ORTHODOX
Example: *Shenouda III*
Envelope:
> *His Holiness*
>> *Pope (name and number)*
>> *Pope of Alexandria*
>>> *Patriarch of the See of St. Mark*
>>> *(Address)*

Letter salutation: *Your Holiness:*
Complimentary close: *Respectfully yours,* OR *Respectfully,*
Wedding invitation, inside envelope:
> *His Holiness*
>> *Pope (name and number)*

Place card: *H.H. Pope (name)*
Announced:
> *His Holiness Pope (name and number),*
>> *Pope of Alexandria, Patriarch of the See of St. Mark*

Conversation: *Your Holiness*

Patriarch CHRISTIAN ORTHODOX
NOTE: Both *Your Beatitude* and *Your Holiness* are used to address patriarchs. The courtesy titles are roughly equivalent, and which is used is a matter of tradition and translation. For example, in Slavonic, the liturgical language of the Eastern Orthodox Church, the Patriarch of Moscow is addressed with the courtesy title *Blazhenstvo.* Blazhenstvo translates as blessed, which might have implied use of *Beatitude,* but *Holiness* is traditionally used in English for this patriarch.

ADDRESSED AS HIS BEATITUDE

Examples: *Ignatius IV, Patriarch of Antioch and All the East*
Theodoros II, Pope and Patriarch of Alexandria and All Africa
Theophilos III, Patriarch of the Holy City of Jerusalem and All Palestine
Envelope, official:
> *His Beatitude*
>> *Patriarch of (place)*
>> *(Address)*

Letter salutation: *Your Beatitude:*
Complimentary close: *Respectfully yours,* OR *Respectfully,*
Wedding invitation, inside envelope:
> *His Beatitude*
>> *Patriarch (name and number)*

Place card: *H.B. Patriarch (name and number)* OR *Patriarch (name and number)*
Announced: *His Beatitude, Patriarch (name and number) of (place)*
Conversation: *Your Beatitude*

ADDRESSED AS HIS HOLINESS

Examples: *Alexy II, Patriarch of Moscow*
Maxim, Patriarch of Bulgaria
The patriarchs of Georgia, Serbia, and Romania
Envelope:
His Holiness
Patriarch (name and number) of (place)
(Address)
Letter salutation: *Your All Holiness:*
Complimentary close: *Respectfully yours,* OR *Respectfully,*
Wedding invitation, inside envelope:
His Holiness
Patriarch (name and number)
Place card: *H.H. Patriarch (name and number)*
Announced: *His Holiness, Patriarch (name and number) of (place)*
Conversation: *Your Holiness*

Archbishop CHRISTIAN ORTHODOX

NOTE: Most archbishops are addressed as *Your Eminence*. However a few archbishops are addressed as *Your Beatitude*. Check for the preference of the bearer.

ADDRESSED AS HIS EMINENCE

Examples: *Alypy, Archbishop of Chicago and Detroit Diocese*
Hilarion, Archbishop of Sydney, Australia, and New Zealand Diocese
Timotheos, Archbishop of Crete
Envelope, official:
His Eminence
Archbishop (name) of (place)
(Position)
(Address)
Letter salutation: *Your Eminence:*
Complimentary close: *Sincerely yours,* OR *Sincerely,*
Wedding invitation, inside envelope: *Archbishop (name)*
Place card: *H.E. Archbishop (name)* OR *Archbishop (name)*
Introduction: *His Eminence Archbishop (name) of (place)*
Introduction, one person to another:
Your Eminence OR *Archbishop (name)*
Conversation: *Your Eminence*

ADDRESSED AS HIS BEATITUDE

Examples: *Herman, Archbishop of Washington and New York,*
Metropolitan of All America and Canada
Anastasios, Archbishop of Tirana and All Albania
Christodoulos, Archbishop of Athens and All Greece
Chrysostomos II, Archbishop of New Justiniana and All Cyprus

Envelope, official:
> *His Beatitude*
>> *Archbishop (name and number)*
>>> *(Address)*

Letter salutation: *Your Beatitude:*
Complimentary close: *Sincerely yours,* OR *Sincerely,*
Wedding invitation, inside envelope: *Archbishop (name and number)*
Place card:
> *H.B. Archbishop (name and number)* OR *Archbishop (name and number)*

Introduction: *His Beatitude, Archbishop (name and number) of the (place)*
Introduction, one person to another: *Your Beatitude* OR *Archbishop (name)*
Conversation: *Your Beatitude*

Metropolitan or Titular Metropolitan   CHRISTIAN ORTHODOX

ADDRESSED AS HIS EMINENCE

Examples: *Benedict, Metropolitan of Philadelphia*
Laurus, Metropolitan of Eastern America and New York Diocese
Envelope, official:
> *His Eminence*
>> *Metropolitan (name) of (place)*
>>> *(Position, diocese, and place)*
>>> *(Address)*

Letter salutation: *Your Eminence:*
Complimentary close: *Sincerely yours,* OR *Sincerely,*
Wedding invitation, inside envelope: *Metropolitan (name)*
Place card: *H.E. Metropolitan (name)* OR *Metropolitan (name)*
Introduction: *His Eminence Metropolitan (name) of (place)*
Introduction, one person to another: *Your Eminence* OR *Metropolitan (name)*
Conversation: *Your Eminence*

ADDRESSED AS HIS BEATITUDE

Examples: *Sawa, Metropolitan of Warsaw and All Poland*
Metropolitan Krystof of the Czech Lands and Slovakia
Envelope, official:
> *His Beatitude*
>> *Metropolitan (name) of (place)*
>>> *(Position, diocese, and place)*
>>> *(Address)*

Letter salutation: *Your Beatitude:*
Complimentary close: *Sincerely yours,* OR *Sincerely,*
Wedding invitation, inside envelope: *Metropolitan (name)*
Place card: *H.B. Metropolitan (name)* OR *Metropolitan (name)*
Introduction: *His Beatitude Metropolitan (name) of (place)*

Introduction, one person to another:
Your Beatitude OR *Metropolitan (name)*
Conversation: *Your Eminence*

Bishop or Titular Bishop CHRISTIAN ORTHODOX

Examples: *Daniel, Bishop of Erie*
    Mark, Bishop of London
Envelope, official:
    The Right Reverend
        Bishop of (area)
        (Address)
Letter salutation: *Your Grace:*
Complimentary close: *Sincerely yours,* OR *Sincerely,*
Wedding invitation, inside envelope: *Bishop (name)*
Place card: *Rt. Rev. Bishop (name)* OR *Bishop (name)*
Introduction:
    The Right Reverend (name), bishop of (place)
    OR *His Grace Bishop (name)*
Introduction, one person to another: *Your Grace* OR *Bishop (name)*
Conversation: *Your Grace*

Archimandrite

Envelope, official:
    The Very Reverend Father
        (Name)
            Archimandrite
            (Address)
Letter salutation: *Dear Reverend:* OR *Dear Father:* OR *Dear Father (surname):*
Complimentary close: *Sincerely yours,* OR *Sincerely,*
Envelope, social:
    The Very Reverend Father
        (Name)
            (Address)
Wedding invitation, inside envelope: *Father (surname)*
Place card: *Very Rev. Father (surname)* OR *Father (surname)*
Introduction: *The Very Reverend (full name), archimandrite of (place)*
Introduction, one person to another: *Father (surname)*
Conversation: *Father (surname)* OR *Father*

Abbot CHRISTIAN ORTHODOX

Envelope, official:
> The Right Reverend Abbot
>> (Full name)
>>> (Monastery)
>>> (Address)

Letter salutation: Dear Reverend Father (surname): OR Dear Father:
Complimentary close: Sincerely yours, OR Sincerely,
Envelope, social:

> The Right Reverend Abbot   The Right Reverend Abbot
>> (Full name)   (Full name)
>>> (Address)   and Mrs. (surname)
>>>   (Address)

Wedding invitation, inside envelope: Father (surname)
Place card: Rt. Rev. Father (surname) OR Father (surname)
Introduction: The Right Reverend Abbot (full name), of (monastery) in (location)
Introduction, one person to another: Father (surname)
Conversation: Father (surname) OR Father

Archpriest, Deacon, Presbyter, Priest CHRISTIAN ORTHODOX

NOTE: Address as noted and identify by (office) as appropriate.
Envelope, official:

> The Reverend   The Reverend (full name)
>> (Full name)   (Church)
>>> (Church)   (Address)
>>> (Address)

Letter salutation: Dear Father (surname): OR Dear Reverend:
Complimentary close: Sincerely yours, OR Sincerely,
Envelope, social:

> The Reverend   The Reverend (full name)
>> (Full name)   (Address)
>>> (Address)

Wedding invitation, inside envelope: Father (surname)
Place card:
> Deacon (surname)
> Father (surname)
> Presbyter (surname)

Introduction: The Reverend (full name), of (church) in (location)
Introduction, one person to another:
> Deacon (surname)
> Father (surname)
> Presbyter (surname)

Conversation:
Deacon (given name) OR *Deacon*
Father (given name) OR *Father*
Presbyter (given name) OR *Presbyter*

Abbess, Mother Superior CHRISTIAN ORTHODOX
Envelope, official:
The Reverend Mother
    (Name)
       (Convent)
         (Address)
Letter salutation: *Dear Reverend Mother:*
Complimentary close: *Sincerely yours,* OR *Sincerely,*
Envelope, social:
The Reverend Mother
    (Name)
       (Address)
Wedding invitation, inside envelope: *Reverend Mother (name)*
Place card: *Reverend Mother (name)*
Introduction: *The Reverend Mother (name), of (convent) in (location)*
Introduction, one person to another: *Reverend Mother (name)*
Conversation: *Reverend Mother (name)* OR *Reverend Mother*

Monk, Brother CHRISTIAN ORTHODOX
Examples: *(Name)*
         (Given name)(surname)
Envelope, official:
Brother (name)   *Brother (full name)*
  (Monastery)   *(Monastery)*
    (Address)   *(Address)*
Letter salutation: *Dear Brother (name):* OR *Dear Brother (given name):*
Complimentary close: *Sincerely yours,* OR *Sincerely,*
Envelope, social:
Brother (name)   *Brother (full name)*
  (Address)   *(Address)*
Wedding invitation, inside envelope: *Brother (name)* OR *Brother (given name)*
Place card: *Brother (name)* OR *Brother (given name)*
Introduction: *Brother (full name), of (monastery) in (location)*
Introduction, one person to another: *Brother (name)* OR *Brother (given name)*
Conversation: *Brother (name), Brother (given name)* OR *Brother*

Nun ORTHODOX

Examples: *(Name)*
              (Given name)(surname)

Envelope, official:

Sister (name)	*Sister (full name)*
(Convent)	*(Convent)*
(Address)	*(Address)*

Letter salutation: *Dear Sister (name):* OR *Dear Sister (surname):*

Complimentary close: *Sincerely yours,* OR *Sincerely,*

Envelope, social:

Sister (name)	*Sister (full name)*
(Address)	*(Address)*

Wedding invitation, inside envelope: *Sister (name)* OR *Sister (surname)*

Place card: *Sister (name)* OR *Sister (surname)*

Introduction: *Sister (name/full name), of (convent) in (location)*

Introduction, one person to another: *Sister (name)* OR *Sister (surname)*

Conversation: *Sister (name), Sister (surname),* OR *Sister*

Christian Science

There are no ordained clergy in Christian Science.

The church is composed of The First Church of Christ, Scientist, in Boston, Massachusetts (also known as the Mother Church) and its branches. The First Church of Christ, Scientist, in Boston, which is the worldwide headquarters, is the only church of the denomination whose name is preceded by *The*. The name of the branch churches begin with a number, *e.g.*, Second Church of Christ, Scientist, Paris; Fifth Church of Christ, Scientist, Los Angeles.

Practitioner

NOTE: Letters are addressed to the home or office address, not to a church, except for officers or employees of The First Church of Christ, Scientist, in Boston.

Envelope, official:

    (Full name), C.S.

        (Home or office address)

Letter salutation: *Dear Mr./Ms. (surname):*

Complimentary close: *Sincerely yours,* OR *Sincerely,*

Envelope, social:

    Mr./Ms. *(full name)*

        (Home or office address)

Wedding invitation, inside envelope: Mr./Ms. *(surname)*

Place card: Mr./Ms. *(surname)*

Introduction: Mr./Ms. *(full name)*, *a Christian Science practitioner*
Introduction, one person to another: Mr./Ms. *(surname)*
Conversation: Mr./Ms. *(surname)*

Teacher

NOTE: Letters are addressed to the home or office address, not a church, except for officers or employees of The First Church of Christ, Scientist, in Boston. C.S.B. stands for Christian Science Board (teacher).
Envelope, official:
(Full name), C.S.B.
(Home or office address)
Letter salutation: *Dear Mr./Ms. (surname):*
Complimentary close: *Sincerely yours*, OR *Sincerely,*
Envelope, social:
Mr./Ms. (full name)
(Home or office address)
Wedding invitation, inside envelope: Mr./Ms. *(surname)*
Place card: Mr./Ms. *(surname)*
Introduction: Mr./Ms. *(full name)*, *a Christian Science practitioner and teacher*
Introduction, one person to another: Mr./Ms. *(surname)*
Conversation: Mr./Ms. *(surname)*

First Reader, Second Reader
President, Board Member

Envelope, official:
Mr./Ms. (full name)
(Position)
(Name of church)
(Address)
Letter salutation: *Dear Mr./Ms. (surname):*
Complimentary close: *Sincerely yours*, OR *Sincerely,*
Envelope, social:
Mr./Ms. (full name)
(Address)
Wedding invitation, inside envelope: Mr./Ms. *(surname)*
Place card: Mr./Ms. *(surname)*
Introduction: Mr./Ms. *(full name)*, *(position) at (name of church)*, *(location)*
Introduction, one person to another: Mr./Ms. *(surname)*
Conversation: Mr./Ms. *(surname)*

The Church of Jesus Christ of Latter-day Saints

NOTE: Use of the full name on the inside envelope and place card is traditional in the church. Elder and sister do not denote an official position.

President LDS

Envelope, official:
> President (full name)
>> The Church of Jesus Christ of Latter-day Saints
>>> (Address)

Letter address line:
> President (full name)
>> The Church of Jesus Christ of Latter-day Saints
>>> (Address)

Letter salutation: Dear President (surname):
Complimentary close: Sincerely,

Envelope, social:
> President (full name)   President and Sister (president's full name)
>> (Address)   (Address)

Wedding invitation, inside envelope:
> President (full name)   President and Sister (president's full name)

Place card:
> President (full name)   Sister (president's full name)

Introduction:
> (Full name), president of The Church of Jesus Christ of Latter-day Saints

Introduction, one person to another: President (surname)
Conversation: President (surname)

First or Second Counselor, First Presidency

NOTE: A counselor in the First Presidency is addressed with the honorific President. In formal introductions his position should be noted as either First Counselor in the First Presidency or Second Counselor in the First Presidency.

Envelope, official:
> President (full name)
>> (First/Second) Counselor in the First Presidency
>>> The Church of Jesus Christ of Latter-day Saints
>>>> (Address)

Letter address line:
> President (full name)
>> (First/Second) Counselor in the First Presidency
>>> The Church of Jesus Christ of Latter-day Saints
>>>> (Address)

Letter salutation: Dear President (surname):
Complimentary close: Sincerely,

Envelope, social:

President *(full name)*   President and Sister *(president's full name)*
    (Address)   *(Address)*

Wedding invitation, inside envelope:

President *(full name)*   President and Sister *(president's full name)*

Place card:

President *(full name)*   Sister *(president's full name)*

Introduction:

(Full name), *(first/second counselor)* in the First Presidency of
    The Church of Jesus Christ of Latter-day Saints

Introduction, one person to another: President *(surname)*

Conversation: President *(surname)*

President or Acting President
The Quorum of the Twelve Apostles

Envelope, official:

(Full name)
    (President/Acting President) of the Quorum of the Twelve Apostles
        The Church of Jesus Christ of Latter-day Saints
        (Address)

Letter address line:

President *(full name)*
    (President/Acting President) of the Quorum of the Twelve Apostles
        The Church of Jesus Christ of Latter-day Saints
        (Address)

Letter salutation: *Dear President (surname):*

Complimentary close: *Sincerely,*

Envelope, social:

President *(full name)*   President and Sister *(president's full name)*
    (Address)   *(Address)*

Wedding invitation, inside envelope:

President *(full name)*   President and Sister *(president's full name)*

Place card:

President *(full name)*   Sister *(president's full name)*

Introduction:

(Full name), *(first/second counselor)* in the First Presidency of
    The Church of Jesus Christ of Latter-day Saints

Introduction, one person to another: President *(surname)*

Conversation: President *(surname)*

Member, Quorum of the Twelve Apostles

Envelope, official:

Elder *(full name)*
    The Quorum of the Twelve Apostles
        The Church of Jesus Christ of Latter-day Saints
        (Address)

256

Letter address line:
　Elder (full name)
　　The Quorum of the Twelve Apostles
　　　The Church of Jesus Christ of Latter-day Saints
　　　　(Address)
Letter salutation: *Dear Elder (surname):*
Complimentary close: *Sincerely,*
Envelope, social:
　Elder (full name) 　　　　*Elder and Sister (husband's full name)*
　　(Address) 　　　　　　　　*(Address)*
Wedding invitation, inside envelope:
　Elder (full name) 　　　　*Elder and Sister (husband's full name)*
Place card:
　Elder (full name) 　　　　*Sister (husband's full name)*
Introduction:
　(Full name), member of the Quorum of the Twelve Apostles of
　　The Church of Jesus Christ of Latter-day Saints
Introduction, one person to another: *Elder (surname)*
Conversation: *Elder (surname)*

Member, Presidency of the Seventy
Envelope, official:
　Elder (full name)
　　The Presidency of the Seventy
　　　The Church of Jesus Christ of Latter-day Saints
　　　　(Address)
Letter address line:
　Elder (full name)
　　The Presidency of the Seventy
　　　The Church of Jesus Christ of Latter-day Saints
　　　　(Address)
Letter salutation: *Dear Elder (surname):*
Complimentary close: *Sincerely,*
Envelope, social:
　Elder (full name) 　　　　*Elder and Sister (husband's full name)*
　　(Address) 　　　　　　　　*(Address)*
Wedding invitation, inside envelope:
　Elder (full name) 　　　　*Elder and Sister (husband's full name)*
Place card:
　Elder (full name) 　　　　*Sister (husband's full name)*
Introduction:
　(Full name), member of the Presidency of the Seventy of
　　The Church of Jesus Christ of Latter-day Saints
Introduction, one person to another: *Elder (surname)*
Conversation: *Elder (surname)*

Member, First or Second Quorums of the Seventy

Envelope, official:
> Elder (full name)
>> The Church of Jesus Christ of Latter-day Saints
>>> (Address)

Letter address line:
> Elder (full name)
>> The (First/Second) Quorum of the Seventy
>>> The Church of Jesus Christ of Latter-day Saints
>>>> (Address)

Letter salutation: Dear Elder (surname):
Complimentary close: Sincerely,
Envelope, social:
> Elder (full name)   Elder and Sister (husband's full name)
>> (Address)   (Address)

Wedding invitation, inside envelope:
> Elder (full name)   Elder and Sister (husband's full name)

Place card:
> Elder (full name)   Sister (husband's full name)

Introduction:
> (Full name), member of the (First/Second) Quorum of the Seventy of
>> The Church of Jesus Christ of Latter-day Saints

Introduction, one person to another: Elder (surname)
Conversation: Elder (surname)

Member, Third through the Sixth Quorums of the Seventy

Envelope, official:
> Elder (full name)
>> The Church of Jesus Christ of Latter-day Saints
>>> (Address)

Letter address line:
> Elder (full name)
>> Area Authority Seventy
>>> The Church of Jesus Christ of Latter-day Saints
>>>> (Address)

Letter salutation: Dear Elder (surname):
Complimentary close: Sincerely,
Envelope, social:
> Elder (full name)   Elder and Sister (husband's full name)
>> (Address)   (Address)

Wedding invitation, inside envelope:
> Elder (full name)   Elder and Sister (husband's full name)

Place card:
> Elder (full name)   Sister (husband's full name)

258

Introduction:
> (Full name), Area Authority Seventy of
>> The Church of Jesus Christ of Latter-day Saints

Introduction, one person to another: Elder (surname)
Conversation: Elder (surname)

Presiding Bishop LDS

Envelope, official:
> Bishop (full name)
>> Presiding Bishop
>>> The Church of Jesus Christ of Latter-day Saints
>>>> (Address)

Letter address line:
> Bishop (full name)
>> Presiding Bishop
>>> The Church of Jesus Christ of Latter-day Saints
>>>> (Address)

Letter salutation: Dear Bishop (surname):
Complimentary close: Sincerely,
Envelope, social:

Bishop (full name)	Bishop and Sister (husband's full name)
(Address)	(Address)

Wedding invitation, inside envelope:

Bishop (full name)	Bishop and Sister (husband's full name)

Place card:

Bishop (full name)	Sister (husband's full name)

Introduction:
> (Full name), presiding bishop of The Church of Jesus Christ of Latter-day Saints

Introduction, one person to another: Bishop (surname)
Conversation: Bishop (surname)

Counselor in the Presiding Bishopric

Envelope, official:
> Bishop (full name)
>> (First/Second) Counselor of the Presiding Bishopric
>>> The Church of Jesus Christ of Latter-day Saints
>>>> (Address)

Letter address line:
> Bishop (full name)
>> (First/Second) Counselor of the Presiding Bishopric
>>> The Church of Jesus Christ of Latter-day Saints
>>>> (Address)

Letter salutation: Dear Bishop (surname):
Complimentary close: Sincerely,
Envelope, social:

Bishop (full name)	Bishop and Sister (husband's full name)
(Address)	(Address)

Wedding invitation, inside envelope:
    Bishop (full name)
    Bishop and Sister (husband's full name)
Place card:
    Bishop (full name)
    Sister (husband's full name)
Introduction:
    (Full name), first/second counselor in the presiding bishopric of
        The Church of Jesus Christ of Latter-day Saints
Introduction, one person to another: *Bishop (surname)*
Conversation: *Bishop (surname)*

President of a Stake
Envelope, official:
    President (full name)
    (Name of stake)
    (Address)
Letter address line:
    President (full name)
    (Name of stake)
        The Church of Jesus Christ of Latter-day Saints
        (Address)
Letter salutation: *Dear President (surname):*
Complimentary close: *Sincerely,*
Envelope, social:
    President (full name)   *President and Sister (husband's full name)*
    (Address)   *(Address)*
Wedding invitation, inside envelope:
    President (full name)   *President and Sister (husband's full name)*
Place card:
    President (full name)   *Sister (husband's full name)*
Introduction:
    (Full name), president of the (name of stake) of
        The Church of Jesus Christ of Latter-day Saints, in (location)
Introduction, one person to another: *President (surname)*
Conversation: *President (surname)*

Bishop LDS
Envelope, official:
    Bishop (full name)
    (Name of ward)
        The Church of Jesus Christ of Latter-day Saints
        (Address)

Letter address line:
  Bishop (full name)
    (Name of ward)
      The Church of Jesus Christ of Latter-day Saints
        (Address)
Letter salutation: *Dear Bishop (surname):*
Complimentary close: *Sincerely,*
Envelope, social:
  Bishop (full name)   *Bishop and Sister (husband's full name)*
    (Address)   *(Address)*
Wedding invitation, inside envelope:
  Bishop (full name)   *Bishop and Sister (husband's full name)*
Place card:
  Bishop (full name)   *Sister (husband's full name)*
Introduction:
  (Full name), Bishop of the (name of ward) of
    The Church of Jesus Christ of Latter-day Saints in (location)
Introduction, one person to another: *Bishop (surname)*
Conversation: *Bishop (surname)*

Missionary LDS
Envelope, official:
  Elder/Sister (surname)
    (Mission headquarters)
      (Address)
Letter salutation: *Dear Elder (surname):*
Complimentary close: *Sincerely,*
Envelope, social:
  Elder/Sister (surname)
    (Address)
Wedding invitation, inside envelope: *Elder/Sister (surname)*
Place card: *Elder/Sister (surname)*
Introduction: *Elder/Sister (surname), a missionary of*
                    The Church of Jesus Christ of Latter-day Saints
Introduction, one person to another: *Elder/Sister (surname)*
Conversation: *Elder/Sister (surname)*

Hindu

NOTE: Pandit is a courtesy title used to address a learned person. Maharaj (more often used in the north of India) and Swami (used in both the north and south of India) are also used, but Pandit is suggested since it is accepted everywhere. Sri is a Sanskrit honorific, used like Mr. is used in English. The letters ji are added to the name without a hyphen.

Chief Priest, Priest HINDU
Envelope:

Pandit	Pandit Sri (name)ji
Sri (name)ji	(Temple)
(Temple)	(Address)
(Address)	

Letter salutation: *Respected Pandit (name)ji:*
Complimentary close: *Sincerely yours,* OR *Sincerely,*
Invitation: *Pandit Sri (name)ji*
Place card: *Pandit Sri (name)ji*
Introduction, formal: *Pandit Sri (name)ji of (temple) in (location)*
Introduction, one person to another: *Pandit Sri (name)ji*
Conversation: *Sri (name)ji*
Conversation, less formal: *Pandit-ji*

Temple Trustees
Hindu temple trustees do not receive special forms of address. Address as *Dr./Mr./Mrs./Ms./etc. (name)* and identify by *(office)*.

Jehovah's Witnesses

Elder
NOTE: A contact or representative may be a man or a woman, but elders are men.
Envelope, official:
    Elder (full name)
        (Kingdom Hall)
            (Address)
Letter salutation: *Dear Elder (surname):*
Complimentary close: *Sincerely yours,* OR *Sincerely,*
Invitation (inside envelope): *Elder (surname)*
Place card: *Elder (surname)*
Introduction:
    Elder (full name), (position) at (Kingdom Hall) in (location)
    OR *(Full name), (position) at (Kingdom Hall) in (location)*
Introduction, one person to another: *Elder (surname)*
Conversation: *Elder (surname)* OR Mr. *(surname)* OR *Elder*

Brother, Sister
Brother and sister are both used as honorifics by Witnesses, but are not usually used by non-Witness visitors. Forms of direct address among members include:
- *Brother (surname)* OR *Brother*
- *Sister (surname)* OR *Sister*

Jewish

NOTE: The Reverend is not used in the United States when addressing rabbis. In the United Kingdom address a chief rabbi as the Very Reverend, and address a rabbi as the Reverend.

Rabbi

Envelope, official:
> Rabbi (full name)
> (Congregation)
> (Address)

Envelope, social:
> Rabbi (full name)
> (Address)

Letter salutation: Dear Rabbi (surname):
Complimentary close: Sincerely yours, OR Sincerely,
Wedding invitation, inside envelope: Rabbi (surname)
Place card: Rabbi (surname)
Introduction: Rabbi (full name), of (congregation) in (location)
Introduction, one person to another: Rabbi (surname)
Conversation: Rabbi (surname)

Rabbi with a Doctorate

NOTE: Use of rabbi usually supplants use of Dr. but sometimes in academia, or by personal preference, Rabbi Dr. is used. Follow the lead of your introducer or personal preference of the bearer.

Envelope, official:
> Rabbi Dr. (full name)
> (Congregation)
> (Address)

Envelope, social:
> Rabbi Dr. (full name)
> (Address)

Letter salutation: Dear Rabbi Dr. (surname):
Complimentary close: Sincerely yours, OR Sincerely,
Wedding invitation, inside envelope: Rabbi Dr. (surname)
Place card: Rabbi Dr. (surname)
Introduction: Rabbi Doctor (full name), of (congregation) in (location)
Introduction, one person to another: Rabbi Doctor (surname)
Conversation: Rabbi Doctor (surname) OR Rabbi

Cantor

Envelope, official:
> Cantor (full name)
> (Congregation)
> (Address)

Envelope, social:
  Cantor (full name)
    (Address)
Letter salutation: Dear Cantor (surname):
Complimentary close: Sincerely yours, OR Sincerely,
Wedding invitation, inside envelope: Cantor (surname)
Place card: Cantor (surname)
Introduction: Cantor (full name), of (congregation) in (location)
Introduction, one person to another: Cantor (surname)
Conversation: Cantor (surname)

Muslim

SHIA ISLAM

Shia Islam, the second largest branch of Islam, regards Ali (cousin and brother to Mohammed, Prophet of Islam) and his descendants to be the honored and rightful successors to Mohammed. In the Shiite tradition, Sayyid and Sayida (meaning leader) are the masculine and feminine honorifics for descendants of the Prophet. There are many other variant spellings of Sayyid and Sayida, so follow the spelling presented. If the wife of a Shiite cleric is entitled to use Sayida use it like Mrs. Sometimes a Muslim woman continues to use her family name after marriage, but currently in the United States using her husband's family name as a surname is not infrequent: Check for personal preference.

Grand Ayatollah
Examples: Grand Ayatollah al-Sayyid Ali al-Hussani al-Sistani
            Grand Ayatollah Sayyid Ali Husaini Sistani
Envelope, official:
  His Eminence
    Grand Ayatollah (full name)
      (Mosque or other official address)
        (Address)
Envelope, social:
  His Eminence   His Eminence
    Grand Ayatollah (full name)   Grand Ayatollah (full name)
      (Address)   and Mrs. (surname)
                                              (Address)
                                        OR IF APPROPRIATE
                                        His Eminence
                                          Grand Ayatollah (full name)
                                            and Sayida (surname)
                                              (Address)
Letter salutation: Your Eminence:
Complimentary close: Respectfully yours, OR Respectfully,

Invitation (inside envelope):

    H.E. Grand Ayatollah *(surname)*   H.E. Grand Ayatollah *(surname)*
                                                and Mrs. *(surname)*

                                            OR IF APPROPRIATE

                                      H.E. Grand Ayatollah *(surname)*
                                                and Sayida *(surname)*

Place card: H.E. Grand Ayatollah *(surname)* OR Grand Ayatollah *(surname)*

Introduction:

    His Eminence Grand Ayatollah (full name)
        of (mosque or other official institution) in (location)

Introduction, one person to another: *His Eminence Grand Ayatollah (full name)*

Conversation: *Sayyid (surname)*

Conversation, less formal: *Sayyid*

Ayatollah

Example: *Ayatollah Muhammad Taqi Misbah Yazdi*

Envelope, official:

    His Eminence
        Ayatollah (full name)
            (Mosque or other official address)
                (Address)

Envelope, social:

    His Eminence   *His Eminence*
        Ayatollah (full name)   *Ayatollah (full name)*
            (Address)   *and Mrs. (surname)*
                                     (Address)

                                 OR IF APPROPRIATE

                                 His Eminence
                                    Ayatollah (full name)
                                       and Sayida (surname)
                                         (Address)

Letter salutation: *Your Eminence:*

Complimentary close: *Respectfully yours,* OR *Respectfully,*

Invitation (inside envelope):

    H.E. Ayatollah *(surname)*   H.E. Ayatollah *(surname)*
                                            and Mrs. *(surname)*

                                        OR IF APPROPRIATE

                                   H.E. Ayatollah *(surname)*
                                   and Sayida *(surname)*

Place card: H.E. Ayatollah *(surname)* OR Ayatollah *(surname)*

Introduction:

    His Eminence Ayatollah (full name)
        of (mosque, seminary, or institution) in (location)

Introduction, one person to another: *His Eminence Ayatollah (full name)*

Conversation: *Sayyid (surname)*

Conversation, less formal: *Sayyid*

Hajjatul Islam, Hojat-ol-Islam, Hojatoleslam

Hajjatul Islam is an honorific and academic degree of Shiite clerics. Sometimes the honorific is used with the full or family name:

- *Hajjatul Islam (full name)*
- *Hajjatul Islam (surname)*

It is also used in combination with *Sayyid* or *Sheikh*.

- *Sayyid*, among the Shiite, is the honorific for a descendant of the Prophet.
- *Sheikh*, among the Shiite, is the honorific for man who is not a descendant.

HAJJATUL ISLAM + SAYYID

Example: *Hajjatul Islam Sayyid Musa Sadr*
Envelope, official:
Hajjatul Islam Sayyid (full name)
    (Mosque)
        (Address)
Envelope, social:

Hajjatul Islam Sayyid (full name)	*Hajjatul Islam Sayyid (full name)*
(Address)	*and Mrs. (surname)*
	(Address)
	OR IF APPROPRIATE
	Hajjatul Islam Sayyid (full name)
	and Sayyida (surname)
	(Address)

Letter salutation: *Dear Sayyid (surname):*
Complimentary close: *Sincerely yours,* OR *Sincerely,*
Invitation (inside envelope):

Sayyid (surname)	*Sayyid (surname)*
	and Mrs. (surname)
	OR IF APPROPRIATE
	Sayyid (surname)
	and Sayyida (surname)

Place card: *Sayyid (surname)*
Introduction: *Hajjatul Islam Sayyid (full name) of (mosque) in (location)*
Introduction, one person to another: *Sayyid (full name)*
Conversation: *Sayyid (surname)*
Conversation, less formal: *Sayyid*

HAJJATUL ISLAM + SHEIKH

Example: *Hujjatul Islam Sheikh Haleem Al-Behbahani*
Envelope, official:
Hajjatul Islam Sheikh (full name)
    (Mosque)
        (Address)

Envelope, social:
> Hajjatul Islam Sheikh (full name)
> (Address)

> Hajjatul Islam Sheikh (full name)
> and Mrs. (surname)
> (Address)
> OR IF APPROPRIATE
> Hajjatul Islam Sheikh (full name)
> and Sayyida (surname)
> (Address)

Letter salutation: *Dear Sheikh (surname):*
Complimentary close: *Sincerely yours,* OR *Sincerely,*
Invitation (inside envelope):
> Sheikh (surname)

> Sheikh (surname)
> and Mrs.(surname)
> OR IF APPROPRIATE
> Sheikh (surname)
> and Sayyida (surname)

Place card: *Sheikh (surname)*
Introduction: *Hajjatul Islam Sheikh (full name) of (mosque) in (location)*
Introduction, one person to another: *Sheikh (surname)*
Conversation: *Sheikh (surname)*
Conversation less formal: *Sheikh*

Imam SHIITE

NOTE: Imam is not used as an honorific for Shiite clerics.
* *Sayyid* is the honorific for a descendant of the Prophet among the Shiite.
* *Sheikh* is the honorific for man who is not a descendant among the Shiite.

Check for preference of the bearer, then address as *Sayyid (full name)* or *Sheikh (full name)*.
Envelope, official:
> Sayyid/Sheikh (full name)
> (Mosque)
> (Address)

Letter salutation: *Dear Imam (surname):*
Complimentary close: *Sincerely yours,* OR *Sincerely,*
Envelope, social:
> Sayyid/Sheikh (full name)
> (Address)

> Sayyid/Sheikh (full name)
> and Sayyida (surname)
> (Address)

Wedding invitation, inside envelope:
> Sayyid/Sheikh (surname)

> Sayyid/Sheikh (surname)
> and Sayyida (surname)

Place card: *Sayyid/Sheikh (surname)*
Introduction: *Sayyid/Sheikh (full name), Imam of (mosque) in (location)*
Introduction, one person to another: *Sayyid/Sheikh (full name)*
Conversation: *Sayyid/Sheikh (surname)*
Conversation, less formal: *Sayyid/Sheikh*

SUNNI ISLAM

In the Sunni tradition, *sayyida* or *sayida* is the honorific for all women, while the Shiites use the honorific only for those descended from Mohammed, the Prophet.

Traditionally a Muslim woman continues to use her *family name* after marriage, but use of her *husband's family name* as the *surname* is not unusual, especially in the West: Check for personal preference.

Grand Sheikh, Grand Imam

Examples: Dr. *Mohammed Sayed Tantawi, the Grand Sheik of Al-Azhar*
            Sheikh Mohamed Sayed Tantawi, Grand Imam of Al Azhar

Envelope, official:
   His Eminence
      (Honorific if presented) (full name)
         (Title)
            (Address)

Letter salutation: *Your Eminence:*

Complimentary close: *Respectfully yours,* OR *Respectfully,*

Envelope, social:

His Eminence	*His Eminence*
(Honorific) (full name)	*(Honorific) (full name)*
(Title)	*(Title)*
(Address)	*and Sayyida (surname)*
	(Address)

Invitation (inside envelope):

His Eminence	*His Eminence*
The (title)	*The (title)*
	and Sayyida (surname)

Place card: *H.E. The (title)* OR *The (title)*

Announced: *His Eminence (personal honorific if presented) (name), the (title)*

Conversation: *Your Eminence*

Grand Mufti

Examples: Dr. *Ahmad Badr Al-Din Hassoun, Grand Mufti of the Syrian Republic*
            Sheikh Ahmad Badr Al-Din Hassoun, the Grand Mufti of Syria

Envelope, official:
   His Eminence
      (Honorific if presented) (full name)
         The Grand Mufti of (place)
            (Address)

Letter salutation: *Your Eminence:*

Complimentary close: *Respectfully yours,* OR *Respectfully,*

Envelope, social :

His Eminence	His Eminence
(Honorific) (full name)	(Honorific) (full name)
The Grand Mufti of (place)	The Grand Mufti of (place)
(Address)	and Sayyida (surname)
	(Address)

Wedding invitation, inside envelope:

His Eminence	His Eminence
The Grand Mufti of (place)	The Grand Mufti of (place)
	and Sayyida (surname)

Place card: H.E. The Grand Mufti of (place) OR The Grand Mufti of (place)
Announced: His Eminence (full name), the Grand Mufti of (place)
Conversation: Your Eminence

Imam SUNNI

NOTE: Imam is used as an honorific for a Sunni cleric, but not for a Shiite cleric. Check for the preference of the bearer.
Envelope, official:
  Imam (full name)
    (Mosque)
      (Address)
Letter salutation: Dear Imam (surname):
Complimentary close: Sincerely yours, OR Sincerely,
Envelope, social:

Imam (full name)	Imam (full name)
(Address)	and Sayyida (surname)
	(Address)

Wedding invitation, inside envelope:

Imam (surname)	Imam (surname)
	and Sayyida (surname)

Place card: Imam (surname)
Introduction: Imam (full name) of (mosque) in (location)
Introduction, one person to another: Imam (full name)
Conversation: Imam (surname)
Conversation, less formal: Imam

Protestant Christian

ANGLICAN CHURCH

Archbishops of Canterbury and York

Example: Dr. (full name), Archbishop of Canterbury

NOTE: Archbishops are normally addressed as *the Most Reverend*. These two arch-bishops are additionally addressed *as the Right Honourable* due to membership in the Privy Council.

Envelope:

> The Most Rev. and Right Hon.
>> Archbishop of (place)
>>> (Address)

Letter salutation: *Your Grace:* OR *My Lord Archbishop:*
Complimentary close: *Yours Respectfully,*
Wedding invitation, inside envelope: *The Archbishop of (place)*
Place card: *The Archbishop of (place)*
Introduction: *The Most Reverend and Right Honourable Archbishop of (place)*
Introduction, one person to another:

> *Your Grace, may I present...*
> *... may I present the Archbishop of (place)*

Conversation: *Your Grace*

Archbishop ANGLICAN

Example: Dr. (full name), Archbishop of Brisbane
Envelope:

> The Most Reverend
>> Archbishop of (place)
>>> (Address)

Letter salutation: *Your Grace:* OR *Dear Archbishop:* OR *Most Reverend Sir:*
Complimentary close: *Yours Respectfully,*
Wedding invitation, inside envelope: *The Archbishop of (place)*
Place card: *The Archbishop of (place)*
Introduction: *The Most Reverend Archbishop of (place)*
Introduction, one person to another:

> *Your Grace, may I present...*
> *... may I present the Archbishop of (place)*

Conversation: *Your Grace*

Retired Archbishop ANGLICAN

Example: Dr. (full name)

NOTE: Addressed as a bishop. Retired archbishops who are members of the Privy Council are addressed as *the Right Reverend and Right Honourable*.

270

Envelope:
>   The Right Reverend
>   (Full name)
>   (Address)

Letter salutation: *Dear Bishop:*
Complimentary close: *Yours Respectfully,*
Wedding invitation, inside envelope: *Bishop (surname)*
Place card: *Bishop (surname)*
Introduction: *Bishop (full name)*
Introduction, one person to another:
>   *Bishop (surname), may I present...*
>   *... may I present the Bishop (surname), retired archbishop of (place)*

Conversation: *Your Grace* OR *Bishop (surname)* OR *Bishop*

Bishop ANGLICAN

Example: *Dr. (full name), Bishop of Durham*
NOTE: A bishop is also less formally addressed by name: *the Right Reverend (full name), Bishop of (place).*
Envelope:
>   The Right Reverend
>   Bishop of (place)
>   (Address)

Letter salutation: *My Lord:* OR *My Lord Bishop:*
Complimentary close: *Yours Respectfully,*
Wedding invitation, inside envelope: *The Bishop of (place)*
Place card: *The Bishop of (place)*
Introduction: *The Right Reverend Bishop of (place)*
Introduction, one person to another: *The Bishop of (place)* OR *Bishop (place)*
Conversation: *My Lord*
Conversation, less formal: *Bishop* OR *Bishop (place)*

Retired Bishop ANGLICAN

Use form for *Retired Archbishop*, page 270.

Dean ANGLICAN

Example: *Dr. (full name), Dean of St. Peter's Cathedral*
NOTE: A dean is also less formally addressed by name: *the Very Reverend (full name), Dean of (church).*
Envelope:
>   The Very Reverend
>   Dean of (church)
>   (Address)

Letter salutation: *Dear Dean:*

Complimentary close: *Yours Respectfully,*
Wedding invitation, inside envelope: *The Dean of (church)*
Place card: *The Dean of (church)*
Introduction: *The Very Reverend Dean of (church) in (location)*
Introduction, one person to another: *Dean*
Conversation: *Dean* OR *Dean (surname)*

Retired Dean ANGLICAN
Address as a *Priest*, page 274.

Provost ANGLICAN
Example: *Dr. (full name), Provost of Glasgow Cathedral*
NOTE: A provost is also less formally addressed by name: *the Very Reverend (full name), Provost of (church).*
Envelope:
> *The Very Reverend*
> > *Provost of (church)*
> > > *(Address)*

Letter salutation: *Dear Provost:*
Complimentary close: *Yours Respectfully,*
Wedding invitation, inside envelope: *The Provost of (church)*
Place card: *The Provost of (church)*
Introduction: *The Very Reverend Provost of (church) in (location)*
Introduction, one person to another: *Provost*
Conversation: *Provost* OR *Provost (surname)*

Retired Provost ANGLICAN
Address as a *Priest*, page 274.

Archdeacon ANGLICAN
Example: *Dr. (full name), Archdeacon of St. Paul's Church*
NOTE: An archdeacon is also less formally addressed by name: *the Venerable (full name), Archdeacon of (diocese).*
Envelope:
> *The Venerable*
> > *Archdeacon of (place)*
> > > *(Address)*

Letter salutation: *Dear Archdeacon:*
Complimentary close: *Yours Respectfully,*
Wedding invitation, inside envelope: *The Archdeacon of (place)*
Place card: *The Archdeacon of (diocese)*
Introduction: *The Venerable Archdeacon of (place)*
Introduction, one person to another: *The Archdeacon of (place)*
Conversation: *Archdeacon* OR *Archdeacon (surname)*

Retired Archdeacon ANGLICAN
Address as a *Priest*, page 274.

Canon ANGLICAN
Example: Dr. *(full name)*, *Huron University College*
Envelope:
> *The Reverend Canon*
> > *(Full name)*
> > > *(Place)*
> > > > *(Address)*

Letter salutation: *Dear Canon:*
Complimentary close: *Yours Respectfully,*
Wedding invitation, inside envelope: *Canon (surname)*
Place card: *Canon (surname)*
Introduction: *The Reverend Canon (full name), of (church) in (location)*
Introduction, one person to another: *Canon (surname)*
Conversation: *Canon (surname)* OR *Canon*

Retired Canon ANGLICAN
Address as a *Priest*.

Prebendary ANGLICAN
Example: Dr. *(full name)*, *the Parish Church of St. James*
Envelope:
> *The Reverend Prebendary*
> > *(Full name)*
> > > *(Place)*
> > > > *(Address)*

Letter salutation: *Dear Prebendary (surname):*
Complimentary close: *Yours Respectfully,*
Wedding invitation, inside envelope: *Prebendary (surname)*
Place card: *Prebendary (surname)*
Introduction: *The Reverend Prebendary (full name), of (church) in (location)*
Introduction, one person to another: *Prebendary (surname)*
Conversation: *Prebendary (surname)* OR *Prebendary*

Retired Prebendary ANGLICAN
Address as a *Priest*.

Vicar, Rector ANGLICAN
Address as a *Priest*. Identify as *Vicar of (church)* or *Rector of (Church)*.

Priest ANGLICAN
Examples: Dr. (full name)
            Father (name)
Envelope:
   The Reverend
     (Full name), (post nominals as appropriate)
     (Church)
      (Address)
   The Reverend
     (Full name)
      (Position)
       (Institution/organization)
        (Address)
Letter salutation: *Dear Reverend Father:* OR *Dear Father/Dr. (surname):*
Complimentary close: *Yours Respectfully,*
Wedding invitation, inside envelope: *Father /Dr. (surname)*
Place card: *Father/Dr. (surname)*
Introduction:
   The Reverend (full name), pastor of (church) in (location)
   The Reverend (full name), (position)
Introduction, one person to another: *Father/Doctor (surname)*
Conversation: *Father/Doctor (surname)* OR *Father*

Mother ANGLICAN
Envelope:
   The Reverend
     Mother Superior (full name), (post nominals as appropriate)
      (Community)
       (Address)
Letter salutation: *Dear Reverend Mother:*
Complimentary close: *Yours faithfully,*
Wedding invitation, inside envelope: *Reverend Mother*
Place card: *Reverend Mother*
Introduction: *The Reverend Mother (full name), of (community)*
Introduction, one person to another: *Reverend Mother*
Conversation: *Reverend Mother*

Brother ANGLICAN
Example: Brother (full name)
Envelope:
   Brother (full name), (initials of order)
     (Monastery/institution)
      (Address)
Letter salutation: *Dear Brother (given name):*
Complimentary close: *Yours faithfully,*
Wedding invitation, inside envelope: *Brother (given name)*
Place card: *Brother (given name)*

Introduction:
> Brother (full name), of the (order) of the (monastery/institution) in (location)

Introduction, one person to another: *Brother (given name)*

Conversation: *Brother (given name)*

Conversation, less formal: *Brother*

Sister ANGLICAN

Envelope:
> Sister (full name), (post nominals as appropriate)
>> (Community)
>>> (Address)

Letter salutation: *Dear Sister (given name):*

Complimentary close: *Yours faithfully,*

Wedding invitation, inside envelope: *Sister (given name)*

Place card: *Sister (given name)*

Introduction: *Sister (full name) of (community)*

Introduction, one person to another: *Sister (given name)*

Conversation: *Sister (given name)*

Curate ANGLICAN

Use same form as *Priest*, and identify as a *curate*, or *curate at (church)*.

Abbot ANGLICAN

Envelope:
> The Right Reverend
>> The Lord Abbot (full name), (post nominal as appropriate)
>>> Abbey of (name)
>>> (Address)

Letter salutation: *Dear Abbot:*

Complimentary close: *Respectfully yours,*

Wedding invitation, inside envelope: *Father Abbot*

Place card: *Father Abbot*

Introduction: *The Right Reverend the Lord Abbot, (full name), Abbot of (place)*

Introduction, one person to another: *Father Abbot*

Conversation: *Father Abbot*

Chancellor of an Episcopal Court

Example: *Sir (full name), Chancellor*

NOTE: Address the chancellor by *(rank)*. This example is for a *knight*, but rank could be different.

Envelope:
> The Worshipful
>> (Personal honorific if any) (full name)
>>> (Address)

Letter salutation: *Sir:*
Complimentary close: *Yours Respectfully,*
Wedding invitation, inside envelope: *Mr./Madame Chancellor*
Place card: *Mr./Madame Chancellor* OR *Chancellor (surname)*
Introduction:
    The Worshipful (personal honorific if any) (full name), Chancellor of ...
Introduction, one person to another:
    Mr./Madame Chancellor, may I present...
    ... may I present Chancellor (surname)
Conversation: *Your worshipful* OR *Learned chancellor*
Conversation, less formal: *Mr./Madame Chancellor* OR *Chancellor*

Chancellor of a Cathedral
NOTE: Address by the clerical *(rank)* and identify by *(office)*.

EPISCOPAL CHURCH

Presiding Bishop EPISCOPAL
Example: *Dr. (full name)*
Envelope, official:
    The Most Reverend
        (Full name), (post nominals as appropriate)
            Presiding Bishop of the Episcopal Church
            (Address)
Letter salutation: *Dear Bishop (surname):*
Complimentary close: *Sincerely yours,* OR *Sincerely,*
Envelope, social:
    The Most Reverend
        (Full name)
            (Address)
Wedding invitation, inside envelope: *Bishop (surname)*
Place card: *Bishop (surname)*
Introduction:
    The Most Reverend (full name), presiding bishop of the Episcopal Church
Introduction, one person to another: *Bishop (surname)*
Conversation: *Bishop (surname)*

Bishop EPISCOPAL
Example: *Dr. (full name)*
Envelope, official:
    The Right Reverend
        (Full name), (post nominals as appropriate)
            Bishop of (diocese)
            (Address)
Letter salutation: *Dear Bishop (surname):*
Complimentary close: *Sincerely yours,* OR *Sincerely,*

276

Envelope, social:
>The Right Reverend
>>(Full name)
>>(Address)

Wedding invitation, inside envelope: Bishop (surname)
Place card: Bishop (surname)
Introduction: The Right Reverend (full name), bishop of (area)
Introduction, one person to another: Bishop (surname)
Conversation: Bishop (surname) OR Bishop

Archdeacon EPISCOPAL

Example: Dr. (full name)
Envelope, official:
>The Venerable
>>(Full name), (post nominals as appropriate)
>>Archdeacon of (diocese or deanery)
>>>(Address)

Letter salutation: Dear Archdeacon (surname):
Complimentary close: Sincerely yours, OR Sincerely,
Envelope, social:
>The Venerable
>>(Full name)
>>(Address)

Wedding invitation, inside envelope: Archdeacon (surname)
Place card: Archdeacon (surname)
Introduction: The Venerable (full name), archdeacon of (diocese or deanery)
Introduction, one person to another: Archdeacon (surname)
Conversation: Archdeacon (surname) OR Archdeacon

Dean EPISCOPAL

Envelope, official:
>The Very Reverend
>>(Full name)
>>>Dean of (cathedral, church, etc)
>>>(Address)

Letter salutation: Dear Dean (surname):
Complimentary close: Sincerely yours, OR Sincerely,
Envelope, social:
>The Very Reverend
>>(Full name)
>>(Address)

Wedding invitation, inside envelope: Dean (surname)
Place card: Dean (surname)
Introduction: The Very Reverend (full name), dean of (place) in (location)
Introduction, one person to another: Dean (surname)
Conversation: Dean (surname) OR Dean

Deacon/Deaconess EPISCOPAL

NOTE: Deacon as an honorific abbreviated as *Dcn*.
Envelope, official:
> *The Reverend*
> > *(Full name)*
> > > *Deacon/Deaconess of (cathedral, diocese, deanery, etc.)*
> > > > *(Address)*

Letter salutation: *Dear Deacon/Deaconess (surname):*
Complimentary close: *Sincerely yours*, OR *Sincerely,*
Envelope, social:
> *The Reverend*
> > *(Full name)*
> > > *(Address)*

Wedding invitation, inside envelope: *Deacon/Deaconess (surname)*
Place card: *Deacon/Deaconess (surname)*
Introduction: *The Reverend (full name), deacon/deaconess of (place)*
Introduction, one person to another: *Deacon/Deaconess (surname)*
Conversation: *Deacon/Deaconess (surname)* OR *Deacon/Deaconess*

Canon EPISCOPAL

Examples: *Dr. (full name)*
            Cannon (full name), M.*Div*
            (Full name), S.T.M.
Envelope, official:
> *The Reverend Canon*
> > *(Full name), (degrees held)*
> > > *(Title) of (church)*
> > > > *(Address)*

Letter salutation: *Dear Canon (surname):*
Complimentary close: *Sincerely yours*, OR *Sincerely,*
Envelope, social:
> *The Reverend Canon*
> > *(Full name)*
> > > *(Address)*

Wedding invitation, inside envelope: *Canon (surname)*
Place card: *Canon (surname)*
Introduction: *The Reverend Canon (full name), of (church) in (location)*
Introduction, one person to another: *Canon (surname)*
Conversation: *Canon (surname)* OR *Canon*

Vicar, Rector EPISCOPAL
Examples: Dr. (full name)
           Father (full name), DMA
Envelope, official:
  The Reverend
    (Full name), (degrees held)
      (Title) of (church)
        (Address)
Letter salutation: Dear Father/Mother/Dr. (surname):
Complimentary close: Sincerely yours, OR Sincerely,
Envelope, social:
  The Reverend
    (Full name)
      (Address)
Wedding invitation, inside envelope: Father/Mother/Dr. (surname)
Place card: Father/Mother/Dr. (surname)
Introduction: The Reverend (full name), (title) of (church) in (location)
Introduction, one person to another: Father/Mother/Doctor (surname)
Conversation: Father/Mother/Mr./Doctor (surname) OR Father/Mother

Priest EPISCOPAL
Example: Dr. (full name)
           Father (full name)
           Mother (full name)
Envelope:
  The Reverend   The Reverend (full name), (degrees held)
    (Full name), (degrees held)   (Church)
      (Church)   (Address)
        (Address)
Letter salutation: Dear Father/Mother/Dr. (surname):
Complimentary close: Sincerely yours, OR Sincerely,
Wedding invitation, inside envelope: Father /Mother/Dr. (surname)
Place card: Father/Mother/Dr. (surname)
Introduction: The Reverend (full name), (title) of (church) in (location)
Introduction, one person to another: Father/Mother/Doctor (surname)
Conversation: Father/Mother/Doctor (surname) OR Father/Mother

Seminarian EPISCOPAL
NOTE: Address as Mr./Ms. (name) and identify as a seminarian of (seminary).

Protestant Denominations

Chairman, Leader, or President of a Denomination

Examples: Dr. (full name), President of the ...
The Reverend (full name), Presiding Pastor, American Association of ...
The Reverend (full name), General Minister and President of ...
Bishop (full name), Presiding Bishop of ...

NOTE: Address as a *pastor* or *minister*, page 281, and identify (*office*).

EXAMPLE: GENERAL SUPERINTENDENT

NOTE: Typically general superintendents hold doctorates and are addressed as *Dr. (name)*. However, if a general superintendent does not hold a doctorate, use *Pastor (name)*.

Envelope, official:

The Reverend (full name)	The Reverend (full name), (degrees held)
General Superintendent	(Title of office)
Church of the Nazarene	(Denomination)
(Address)	(Address)

Letter salutation: Dear Dr. (*surname*):
Complimentary close: Sincerely yours, OR Sincerely,
Place card: Dr. (*surname*)
Introduction: The Reverend (full name), General Superintendent of ...
Introduction, one person to another: Dr. (*surname*)
Conversation: Dr. (*surname*)

Methodist Bishop

Example: Dr. (full name)
Envelope, official:
The Reverend
(Full name), (degrees held)
Methodist Bishop
(Address)
Letter salutation:
Reverend Sir: OR Dear Bishop (*surname*): OR Dear Dr. (*surname*):
Complimentary close: Sincerely yours, OR Sincerely,
Envelope, social:
The Reverend
(Full name)
(Address)
Wedding invitation, inside envelope: Bishop (*surname*)
Place card: Bishop (*surname*)
Introduction:
The Reverend (full name), bishop of (area) of the (church)
Introduction, one person to another: Bishop (*surname*)
Conversation: Bishop (*surname*)

Pastor or Minister

WITH A DOCTORATE

Examples: Dr. (full name)
Reverend Dr. (full name)
(Full name), Ph.D., D.D., LL.D.

NOTE: Use of The Reverend Dr. (full name) is not traditionally correct in American usage. Address as either The Reverend (full name) or Dr. (full name). But use of the combined (courtesy title) + (academic honorific) is widely seen in contemporary correspondence.

Envelope, official:

The Reverend
(Full name), (degrees held)
(Church)
(Address)

The Reverend (full name), (degrees held)
(Church)
(Address)

Letter salutation: Dear Dr. (surname):
Complimentary close: Sincerely yours, OR Sincerely,

Envelope, social:

The Reverend
(Full name)
(Address)

The Reverend (full name)
(Address)

Wedding invitation, inside envelope: Dr. (surname)
Place card: Dr. (surname)
Introduction:

The Reverend (full name), (position) of (church) in (location)
OR The Reverend Doctor (full name), (position) of (church) in (location)

Introduction, one person to another: Doctor (surname)
Conversation (follow the form used by the introducer):

Doctor/Pastor (surname)
OR Pastor/Doctor

WITHOUT A DOCTORATE

Examples: Rev. (full name)
Pastor (full name)
Mr. (full name)

Envelope, official:

The Reverend
(Full name)
(Church)
(Address)

The Reverend (full name)
(Church)
(Address)

Letter salutation: Dear Pastor/Mr./Ms. (surname):
Complimentary close: Sincerely yours, OR Sincerely,

Envelope, social:
>   *The Reverend*
>   *(Full name)*
>   *(Address)*

Wedding invitation, inside envelope: *Pastor/Mr./Ms. (surname)*
Place card: *Pastor/Mr./Ms. (surname)*
Introduction:
>   *The Reverend (full name), (position) of (church) in (location)*
>   OR *(Position) of (church) in (location), Pastor/Mr./Ms. (surname)*

Introduction, one person to another: *Pastor/Mr./Ms. (surname)*
Conversation: *Pastor (surname)* OR *Mr./Ms. (surname)*

Roman Catholic

Pope/Pontiff

Example: *Benedict XVI*
Envelope:
>   *His Holiness*
>   > *The Pope*
>   > > *The Apostolic Palace*
>   > > *00120 Vatican City*

Letter salutation: *Your Holiness:* OR *Most Holy Father:*
Complimentary close (laity, clerics):
>   *Most respectfully,*
>   OR *I have the honor to remain Your Holiness's humble servant,*

Complimentary close (bishops): *Devotedly yours in Christ,*
Place card:
>   *His Holiness*
>   OR *H.H. the Pope*
>   OR *H.H. Pope (name and number)*

Announced: *His Holiness*
Conversation: *Your Holiness* OR *Holy Father*

Cardinal

Examples: *Edward Cardinal Egan, Archdiocese of New York*
>   *His Eminence Justin F. Rigali, Archbishop of Philadelphia*

NOTE: In Great Britain a Roman Catholic cardinal is addressed as *My Lord Cardinal*, offering the same courtesy offered to the Archbishop of Canterbury and the Archbishop of York.
Envelope:
>   *His Eminence*
>   > *(Given name) Cardinal (surname)*
>   > > *Archbishop of (place)*
>   > > *(Address)*

OR *His Eminence*
> *Cardinal (given name) (surname)*
>> *Archbishop of (place)*
>>> *(Address)*

Letter salutation: *Your Eminence:*
Letter salutation, less formal: *Dear Cardinal (surname):*
Complimentary close: *Respectfully yours,* OR *Respectfully,*
Wedding invitation, inside envelope:
> *His Eminence*
>> *Cardinal (surname)*

Place card: *H.E. Cardinal (surname)*
Announced:
> *His Eminence (given name) Cardinal (surname), the archbishop of (place)*

Conversation: *Your Eminence*
Conversation, less formal: *Cardinal (surname)*

Cardinals who are Patriarchs

Example: *Dom José Policarpo, Cardinal Patriarch of Lisbon*
NOTE: Patriarchs who are also cardinals, traditionally from Venice and Lisbon, take the title, precedence, and rank of the cardinalate. These patriarchs are also addressed as *Your Eminence.*
Envelope:
> *His Eminence*
>> *(Given name) Cardinal (surname)*
>>> *The Patriarch of (place)*
>>>> *(Address)*

Letter salutation: *Your Eminence*
Letter salutation, less formal: *Dear Cardinal (surname):*
Complimentary close: *Respectfully yours,* OR *Respectfully,*
Wedding invitation, inside envelope:
> *His Eminence*
>> *Cardinal (surname)*

Place card: *H.E. Cardinal (surname)* OR *Cardinal (surname)*
Introduction:
> *His Eminence (given name) Cardinal (surname), the Patriarch of (place)*

Introduction, one person to another:
> *Your Eminence, may I present …*
> *… may I present His Eminence (given name) Cardinal (surname)*

Conversation: *Your Eminence*
Conversation, less formal: *Cardinal (surname)*

Patriarchs who hold a rank between Cardinal and Archbishop

Example: *Michael Sabbah, Patriarch of Jerusalem*
Envelope:
> *His Beatitude*
>> *(Full name) (post nominals as appropriate)*
>>> *The Patriarch of (place)*
>>> *(Address)*

Letter salutation: *Your Beatitude:*
Letter salutation, less formal: *Dear Archbishop (surname):*
Complimentary close: *Respectfully yours,* OR *Respectfully,*
Wedding invitation, inside envelope:
> *His Beatitude*
>> *Archbishop (surname)*

Place card: *H.B. Archbishop (surname)* OR *Archbishop (surname)*
Introduction: *His Beatitude the Patriarch of (place)*
Introduction, one person to another:
> *Your Beatitude, may I present …*
> *… may I present His Beatitude Archbishop (surname)*

Conversation: *Your Beatitude*
Conversation, less formal: *Archbishop (surname)*

Apostolic Delegate, Papal Nuncio, Pro-Nuncio, Nuncio

Examples: *Archbishop (full name), Apostolic Nuncio to the United States*
His Excellency Archbishop (full name), Apostolic Nuncio
Notes:
(1) A papal representative will hold a hierarchical rank such as cardinal, archbishop, or bishop, and the diplomatic rank of ambassador. Since he will not have an archdiocese or diocese to supervise, he may have the title of *Titular Archbishop/Bishop of (place)*.
(2) Following the rule to address by *(rank)* and identify by *(office)*, in the example below he is addressed by *hierarchical rank* (titular archbishop) and identified by *diplomatic office* (ambassador).
(3) For pro-nuncio or nuncio, adapt the form below.
Envelope:
> *The Most Reverend*
>> *(Full name), (post nominals as appropriate)*
>>> *Titular Archbishop of (place)*
>>> *The Apostolic Nuncio to the United States*
>>> *(Address)*

Letter salutation as an archbishop: *Most Reverend Sir:*
Letter salutation as an ambassador: *Your Excellency:*
Complimentary close: *Respectfully yours,* OR *Respectfully,*

Wedding invitation, inside envelope, as an ambassador:
> *His Excellency*
>> *The Apostolic Nuncio*

Place card, as an ambassador: *H.E. The Apostolic Nuncio*

Announced:
> *The Most Reverend (full name), titular archbishop of (place),*
>> *the apostolic nuncio to the (place)*
> OR *His Excellency (full name) The Apostolic Nuncio to (place)*

Conversation: *Your Excellency*

Archbishop CATHOLIC

Example:　　*(Full name), Archbishop of Oklahoma City*

Envelope:
> *The Most Reverend*
>> *(Full name)*
>>> *Archbishop of (diocese)*
>>>> *(Address)*
> Envelope in the British style:
>> *His Grace*
>>> *The Most Reverend*
>>>> *(Full name), (post nominals as appropriate)*
>>>>> *Archbishop of (diocese)*
>>>>>> *(Address)*

Letter salutation: *Dear Archbishop (surname):*

Complimentary close: *Respectfully yours,* OR *Respectfully,*

Wedding invitation, inside envelope:
> *The Most Reverend*
>> *Archbishop (surname)*

Place card: *Archbishop (surname)*

Introduction: *The Most Reverend (full name), archbishop of (place)*

Introduction, one person to another:
> *Archbishop (surname), may I present ...*
> *... may I present Archbishop (surname) ...*

Conversation: *Archbishop (surname)*

Titular Archbishop CATHOLIC

Envelope:
> *The Most Reverend*
>> *(Full name)*
>>> *Titular Archbishop of (diocese)*
>>>> *(Address)*

Letter salutation: *Dear Archbishop (surname):*

Complimentary close: *Respectfully yours,* OR *Respectfully,*

Wedding invitation, inside envelope:
> The Most Reverend
>> Archbishop (surname)

Place card: Archbishop (surname)

Introduction:
> The Most Reverend (full name), Titular Archbishop of (place)

Introduction, one person to another:
> Archbishop (surname), may I present ...
> ... may I present Archbishop (surname) ...

Conversation: Archbishop (surname)

Bishop CATHOLIC

Examples: *(Full name), D.D., J.C.L., Bishop of Palm Beach*

NOTE: Sometimes Catholic bishops are addressed as *Your Grace* in the Anglican style.

Envelope:
> The Most Reverend
>> (Full name)
>>> Bishop of (place)
>>> (Address)

Letter salutation: *Dear Bishop (surname):*

Complimentary close: *Respectfully yours,* OR *Respectfully,*

Wedding invitation, inside envelope:
> The Most Reverend
>> Bishop (surname)

Place card: Bishop (surname)

Introduction: The Most Reverend (full name), bishop of (place)

Introduction, one person to another:
> Bishop (surname), may I present ...
> ... may I present Bishop (surname) ...

Conversation: Bishop (surname)

Conversation, less formal: Bishop (surname)

Abbot CATHOLIC

Example: *(Full name), OSB, Abbot of St. Meinrad's Benedictine Abbey*

Envelope:
> The Right Reverend
>> (Full name), (post nominals as appropriate)
>>> Abbot of (place)
>>>> Abbey of (name)
>>>> (Address)

Letter salutation: *Dear Reverend Abbot:* OR *Dear Father Abbot:*

Letter salutation, less formal: *Dear Abbot (surname):*

Complimentary close: *Respectfully yours,*

Wedding invitation, inside envelope:
> The Right Reverend
>> (Full name)

Place card: *Father Abbot*
Introduction: *The Right Reverend (full name), Abbot of (place)*
Introduction, one person to another: *Abbot (surname)*
Conversation: *Father Abbot* OR *Father*

Canon, Provost, Dean CATHOLIC

NOTE: Address by *(rank)* and identify by *(office)*. The names of the offices are sometimes used as honorifics in conversation.

Monsignor: Higher and Lower Ranks

NOTE: Traditionally certain "higher" monsignors have been addressed as *the Right Reverend Monsignor (full name)*; Other "lower" monsignors have been addressed as *the Very Reverend Monsignor (full name)*. Check for preference of the bearer and adapt the form for Monsignor that follows.

Monsignor

Envelope:
> *The Reverend Monsignor*
> > *(Full name), (post nominals as appropriate)*
> > *(Address)*

Letter salutation: *Dear Monsignor (surname):*
Complimentary close: *Sincerely yours,* OR *Sincerely,*
Wedding invitation, inside envelope: *Monsignor (surname)*
Place card: *Msgr. (surname)*
Introduction: *The Reverend Monsignor (full name) of (church) in (location)*
Introduction, one person to another: *Monsignor (surname)*
Conversation: *Monsignor (surname)*
Conversation, less formal: *Monsignor*

Priest CATHOLIC

Example: *Fr. (full name), SJ*
Envelope:

The Reverend	*The Reverend (full name), (initials…)*
(Full name), (initials of order)	*(Church)*
(Church)	*(Address)*
(Address)	

Letter salutation: *Dear Father (surname):*
Complimentary close: *Sincerely yours,* OR *Sincerely,*
Wedding invitation, inside envelope: *Father (surname)*
Place card: *Father (surname)*
Introduction: *The Reverend (full name), of the (order), of (church) in (location)*
Introduction, one person to another: *Father (surname)*
Conversation: *Father (surname)*
Conversation, less formal: *Father*

Deacon/Deaconess CATHOLIC

Examples: *Deacon (full name), Ph.D.*
               Deaconess (full name), NOSB, VIC, AIC

Envelope:
   Deacon/Deaconess (full name)
      (Address)

Letter salutation: *Dear Deacon/Deaconess (surname):*
Complimentary close: *Sincerely yours,* OR *Sincerely,*
Wedding invitation, inside envelope: *Deacon/Deaconess (surname)*
Place card: *Deacon/Deaconess (surname)*
Introduction: *Deacon/Deaconess (full name) of the (place and location)*
Introduction, one person to another: *Deacon/Deaconess (surname)*
Conversation: *Deacon/Deaconess (surname)*
Conversation, less formal: *Deacon/Deaconess*

Brother CATHOLIC

Example: *(Full name), FMS*
Envelope:
   Brother (full name), (initials of order)
      (Monastery/institution)
      (Address)

Letter salutation: *Dear Brother (given name):*
Complimentary close: *Sincerely yours,* OR *Sincerely,*
Wedding invitation, inside envelope: *Brother (given name)*
Place card: *Brother (given name)*
Introduction:
   Brother (full name), of the (order) of the (monastery/institution) in (location)
Introduction, one person to another: *Brother (given name)*
Conversation: *Brother (given name)*
Conversation, less formal: *Brother*

Friar

Examples: *Fr. (full name)*
               (Full name), OP

Envelope:
   Fr. (full name), (initials of order)
      (Monastery/institution)
      (Address)

Letter salutation: *Dear Fr. (given name):*
Complimentary close: *Sincerely yours,* OR *Sincerely,*
Wedding invitation, inside envelope: *Fr. (given name)*
Place card: *Fr. (given name)*
Introduction:
   Friar (full name), of the (order) of the (monastery/institution) in (location)
Introduction, one person to another: *Friar (given name)*
Conversation: *Friar (given name)*
Conversation, less formal: *Friar*

288

Mother Superior Using Her First and Family Name CATHOLIC

NOTE: Some orders address their Superior as *Sister Servant*, which is used in place of *Mother* in every instance.

Envelope:
> *Mother (full name), (initials of order)*
>> *Superior*
>>> *(Convent/institution)*
>>> *(Address)*

Letter salutation: *Dear Mother:* OR *Dear Mother (full name):*
Complimentary close: *Sincerely yours,* OR *Sincerely,*
Wedding invitation, inside envelope: *Mother (full name)*
Place card: *Mother (full name)*
Introduction:
> *Mother (full name) of the (order), of the (convent/institution) in (location)*

Introduction, one person to another: *Mother (full name)*
Conversation: *Mother (given name)*
Conversation, less formal: *Mother*

Mother Superior Using a Chosen Religious Name CATHOLIC

NOTE: Some orders address their Superior as *Sister Servant*, which is used in place of *Mother* in every instance.

Envelope:
> *Mother (full name), (initials of order)*
>> *Superior*
>>> *(Convent/institution)*
>>> *(Address)*

Letter salutation: *Dear Mother:* OR *Dear Mother (full name):*
Complimentary close: *Sincerely yours,* OR *Sincerely,*
Wedding invitation, inside envelope: *Mother (full name)*
Place card: *Mother (full name)*
Introduction:
> *Mother (full name) of the (order), of the (convent/institution) in (location)*

Introduction, one person to another: *Mother (full name)*
Conversation: *Mother (full name)*
Conversation, less formal: *Mother*

Nun Using Her Given Name and Family Name CATHOLIC

Envelope:
> *Sister (full name), (initials of order)*
>> *(Convent/institution)*
>>> *(Address)*

Letter salutation: *Dear Sister:* OR *Dear Sister (given name):*
Complimentary close: *Sincerely yours,* OR *Sincerely,*
Wedding invitation, inside envelope: *Sister (given name)*
Place card: *Sister (given name)*
Introduction:
> *Sister (full name), of the (order) of the (convent/institution) in (location)*

Introduction, one person to another: *Sister (given name)*
Conversation: *Sister (given name)*
Conversation, less formal: *Sister*

Nun Using a Chosen Religious Name CATHOLIC

Envelope:
> *Sister (full name), (initials of order)*
> > *(Convent/institution)*
> > > *(Address)*

Letter salutation: *Dear Sister:* OR *Dear Sister (full name):*
Complimentary close: *Sincerely yours,* OR *Sincerely,*
Wedding invitation, inside envelope: *Sister (full name)*
Place card: *Sister (full name)*
Introduction:
> *Sister (full name), of the (order) of the (convent/institution) in (location)*

Introduction, one person to another: *Sister (full name)*
Conversation: *Sister (full name)*
Conversation, less formal: *Sister*

The Salvation Army

General

Examples: *General (full name), General of the Salvation Army*
Envelope, official:
> *General (full name)*
> > *General of the Salvation Army*
> > > *(Address)*

Letter salutation: *Dear General (surname):*
Complimentary close: *Sincerely yours,* OR *Sincerely,*
Envelope, social:
> *General (full name)*
> > *(Address)*

Wedding invitation, inside envelope: *General (surname)*
Place card: *General (full name)*
Introduction from a dais: *General (full name), General of the Salvation Army*
Introduction, one person to another: *General (surname)*
Conversation: *General (surname)*
Conversation, less formal: *General*

National or Territorial Commander

Examples: Commissioner *(full name)*, National Commander
Commissioner *(full name)*, National President of Women's Ministries
Commissioner *(full name)*, Territorial Commander

NOTE: Address a *National* or *Territorial Commander* as *Commissioner (name)*.

Envelope, official:
Commissioner *(full name)*
(Title of office held)
(Address)

Letter salutation: *Dear Commissioner (surname):*
Complimentary close: *Sincerely yours,* OR *Sincerely,*

Envelope, social:
Commissioner *(full name)*
(Address)

Wedding invitation, inside envelope: *Commissioner (surname)*
Place card: *Commissioner (surname)*

Introduction from a dais:
Commissioner *(full name)*, *(title of office held)* of the Salvation Army

Introduction, one person to another: *Commissioner (surname)*
Conversation: *Commissioner (surname)*
Conversation, less formal: *Commissioner*

Colonel, Lieutenant Colonel, Major, Captain

Examples: Colonel *(full name)*, Commander of the USA Eastern Territory
Lt. Colonel *(full name)*, Southern California Divisional Commander
Major *(full name)*, Corps Officer
Captain *(full name)*, Corps Officer

Envelope, official:
(Rank) (full name)
(Title of office held)
(Address)

Letter salutation: *Dear (Rank) (surname):*
Complimentary close: *Sincerely yours,* OR *Sincerely,*

Envelope, social:
(Rank) (full name)
(Address)

Wedding invitation, inside envelope: *(Rank) (surname)*
Place card: *(Rank) (full name)*

Introduction from a dais:
(Rank) (full name), *(title of office held)* of the Salvation Army

Introduction, one person to another: *(Rank) (surname)*
Conversation: *(Rank) (surname)*
Conversation, less formal: *(Rank)*

Seventh-day Adventist

NOTE: The honorific Dr. is typically not used by Adventist clergy holding *Ph.D.*, *D.D.*, *LL.D.*, or other advanced degrees. However, the personal preference of the bearer should be taken into account.

USAGE IN THE USA

Minister ADVENTIST
Envelope, official:
  Elder (full name)
    (Church)
      (Address)
Letter salutation: *Dear Elder (surname):*
Complimentary close: *Sincerely yours,* OR *Sincerely,*
Envelope, social:
  Elder (full name)
    (Address)
Wedding invitation, inside envelope: *Elder (surname)*
Place card: *Elder (surname)*
Introduction, one person to another: *Elder (surname)*
Introduction: *Elder (full name), of (church) in (location)*
Conversation: *Elder (surname)*
Conversation, less formal: *Elder*

USAGE IN OTHER COUNTRIES

Minister ADVENTIST
Envelope, official:
  Pastor (full name)
    (Church)
      (Address)
Letter salutation: *Dear Pastor (surname):*
Complimentary close: *Sincerely yours,* OR *Sincerely,*
Envelope, social:
  Pastor (full name)
    (Address)
Wedding invitation, inside envelope: *Pastor (surname)*
Place card: *Pastor (surname)*
Introduction, one person to another: *Pastor (surname)*
Introduction: *Pastor (full name), of (church) in (location)*
Conversation: *Pastor (surname)*
Conversation, less formal: *Pastor*

Sikh

NOTE: Traditionally Sikh men have the surname *Singh*, and Sikh women the surname *Kaur*. However, in current Sikh usage in the United States many Sikh men adopt a name other than *Singh* as surname, or adopt *Singh* as a family name. Sikh women sometimes use their husband's surname, and include *Kaur* in their complete name.

Giani
Example: *Giani Gurdit Singh*
Envelope, official:
   Giani (full name)
      (Temple)
         (Address)
Letter salutation: *Dear Giani (full name)*:
Complimentary close: *Sincerely yours,* OR *Sincerely,*
Envelope, social:

Giani (full name)	*Giani (full name)*
(Address)	*and Mrs. (surname)*
	(Address)

Wedding invitation, inside envelope: *Giani (surname)*
Place card: *Giani (surname)*
Introduction: *Giani (full name) of the (temple) in (location)*
Introduction, one person to another:
   Giani (surname) OR *Giani (full name)*
Conversation:
   Giani (surname) OR *Giani (given name)* OR *Giani (given name)-ji*
   OR *Giani-ji*

Zoroastrian

Ervad or Dastur with a Doctorate

Examples: Dr. (full name)
           (Full name), Ph.D.

Envelope, official:
  The Reverend
      Ervad/Dastur Dr. (full name)
          (Temple)
              (Address)
Letter salutation: Dear (title) Dr. (surname):
Letter ending: Sincerely yours, OR Sincerely,
Envelope, social:
  The Reverend
      (Title) Dr. (full name)
          (Address)

Invitation, inside envelope: (Title) Dr. (surname)
Place card: (Title) Dr. (surname)
Introduction: The Reverend Dr. (full name), (title) of the (temple) in (location)
Introduction, one person to another: (Title) Dr. (full name)
Conversation: Doctor (surname) OR (title) (surname)
Conversation, less formal: Doctor OR (title only)

Ervad or Dastur without a Doctorate

Envelope, official:
  The Reverend
      Ervad/Dastur (full name)
          (Temple)
              (Address)
Letter salutation: Dear (title) (surname)
Letter ending: Sincerely yours, OR Sincerely,
Envelope, social:
  The Reverend
      (Title) (full name)
          (Address)
Invitation, inside envelope: (Title) (surname)
Place card: (Title) (surname)
Introduction: The Reverend (title) (full name) of the (temple) in (location)
Introduction, one person to another: (Title) (full name)
Conversation: (Title) (surname)
Conversation, less formal: (Title only)

17 Canadian Officials

Canadian Chief of State

King/Queen of Canada

NOTE: The king/queen of Canada is also the hereditary monarch of the United Kingdom: Elizabeth the Second, by the Grace of God, Queen of the United Kingdom, Canada and Her Other Realms and Territories, Head of the Commonwealth, Defender of the Faith. Forms of address are to *His/Her Majesty* without reference to the domain. For more information on royalty and peers see page 393.
Envelope:
> *His/Her Majesty*
> > *The King/Queen*
> > *(Address)*

Letter salutation: *Your Majesty:*
Complimentary close: *Respectfully yours*, OR *Respectfully,*
Complimentary close by subjects:
> *I remain Your Majesty's faithful and devoted servant,*

Invitation, inside envelope:
> *His/Her Majesty*
> > *The King/Queen*

Place card: H.M. *The King/Queen*
Announced/Introduction: *His/Her Majesty the King/Queen*
In Canada, all persons are presented to the monarch: *Your Majesty, may I present …*
Conversation: *Your Majesty*
Conversation, less formal: *Sir/ma'am*

Canadian Federal Parliament

Governor-General

NOTE: Address a former Governor-General as *the Right Honourable (special honorific or hierarchical title if any) (name)* and identify as the *former governor-general of Canada.*

Envelope, official:
> *His/Her Excellency*
>> *The Right Honourable*
>>> *(Full name), (post nominals for decorations and honors)*
>>>> *Governor-General of Canada*
>>>>> *(Address)*

Letter salutation: *Your Excellency:*
Complimentary close: *Yours sincerely,*
Envelope, social:
> *The Governor-General*
>> *(Address)*

Invitation, inside envelope: *The Governor-General*
Place card: *The Governor-General*
Introduction:
> *His/Her Excellency the Right Honourable (full name),*
>> *Governor-General of Canada*

Introduction, one person to another:
> *Your Excellency, may I present ...*
> *... may I present the Governor-General*

Conversation: *Your Excellency* OR *Excellency*
Conversation, less formal: *Sir* OR *madam*

Spouse of the Governor-General

NOTE: The spouse of a governor-general is addressed with the courtesy title *Your Excellency* only in Canada. It is not necessary to identify him or her as married to the governor-general.

The name used by a wife of a governor-general is her preference: while the traditional form is *Mrs. (husband's first and surname)*, recent wives have preferred *Mrs. (woman's first and surname)*, or simply *(woman's first and surname)* without an honorific. Check for preference of the bearer.

Envelope, official:

Her Excellency	*His Excellency*
Mrs. (husband's full name)	*Mr. (full name)*
(Address)	*(Address)*

Letter salutation: *Dear Mr./Mrs. (surname):* OR *Your Excellency:*
Complimentary close: *Yours sincerely,*
Envelope, social (if the governor-general is not invited):

Her Excellency	*His Excellency*
Mrs. (husband's full name)	*Mr. (full name)*
(Address)	*(Address)*

Invitation (if the governor-general is not invited) inside envelope:

Her Excellency His Excellency
Mrs. (surname) Mr. (surname)

Place card: Mr./Mrs./etc. (surname)
Introduction:
His Excellency Mr. (full name) ...
Her Excellency Mrs. (surname) ...
OR Her Excellency (other form of her name) ...
Introduction, one person to another:
Your Excellency, may I present ...
... may I present His Excellency Mr. (surname) ...
... may I present Her Excellency Mrs. (surname) ...
OR ... may I present Her Excellency (other form of her name) ...
Conversation: Your Excellency OR Excellency
Conversation, less formal: Sir/madam, OR Mr./Mrs./etc. (surname)

Privy Counsellor: Member of the Queen's Privy Council

NOTE: The Queen's Privy Council for Canada is frequently referred to as simply the Privy Council. Members of the Privy Council are addressed as the Honourable and use the post-nominals PC for life.

Envelope, official:
The Honourable
(Special honorific if any) (full name), PC
(Address)
Letter salutation: Dear Mr./Mrs./Dr./etc. (surname):
Complimentary close: Yours sincerely,
Envelope, social:
The Honourable
(Special honorific if any) (full name), PC
(Address)
Invitation, inside envelope:
The Honourable
(Special honorific if any) (full name), PC
Place card:
The Hon. (special honorific if any) (full name), PC
Introduction:
The Honourable (special honorific if any) (full name),
(identification of office held as appropriate)
Introduction, one person to another:
Mr./Ms./Dr./etc. (surname), may I present ...
... may I present Mr./Ms./Dr./etc. (surname) ...
Conversation: Sir/madam, OR Mr./Ms./Dr./etc. (surname)

SENATE

Speaker of the Senate, Privy Counsellor

Envelope, official:
  Senator the Honourable
     (Full name), (post nominals for decorations and honors), PC
        Speaker of the Senate
           The Senate
              (Address)
Letter salutation: *Dear Mr./Madam Speaker:*
Complimentary close: *Yours sincerely,*
Envelope, social:
  The Speaker of the Senate
     (Address)
Invitation, inside envelope: *The Speaker of the Senate*
Place card: *The Speaker of the Senate*
Introduction:
  Senator the Honourable (full name), the Speaker of the Senate of Canada
Introduction, one person to another:
  Mr./Madam Speaker, may I present ...
  ... may I present the Speaker of the Senate
Conversation: *Mr./Madam Speaker*

Speaker of the Senate, Not a Privy Counsellor

Envelope, official:
  The Honourable
     (Full name), Senator
        Speaker of the Senate
           The Senate
              (Address)
Letter salutation: *Dear Mr./Madam Speaker:*
Complimentary close: *Yours sincerely,*
Envelope, social:
  The Honourable
     (Full name)
        (Address)
Invitation, inside envelope:
  The Honourable
     (Full name)
Place card: *The Hon. (full name)*
Introduction: *The Honourable (full name), Speaker of the Senate of Canada*
Introduction, one person to another: *Mr./Madam Speaker*
Conversation: *Mr./Madam Speaker*

298

Senator, Privy Counsellor

NOTE: Address a former senator as a *Privy Counsellor* and identify as a *former senator*. Continued use of *Senator* as an honorific is informal: Address in conversation as *Mr./Ms./etc. (name)*.

Envelope, official:
> Senator the Honourable
>> (Full name), PC
>>> (Address)

Letter salutation: *Dear Senator (surname):*
Complimentary close: *Yours sincerely,*
Envelope, social:
> Senator the Honourable
>> (Full name), PC
>>> (Address)

Invitation, inside envelope:
> Senator the Honourable
>> (Full name), PC

Place card: *Senator The Hon. (full name), PC*
Introduction:
> Senator the Honourable (full name) of (province) in the Senate of Canada ...

Introduction, one person to another: *Senator (surname)*
Conversation: *Senator (surname)*
Conversation, less formal: *Senator*

Senator, Not a Privy Counsellor

NOTE: Address a former senator as *the Honourable (full name)* and identify as a *former senator*. Continued use of *Senator* as an honorific is informal: Address in conversation as *Mr./Ms./etc. (name)*.

Envelope, official:
> The Honourable
>> (Full name), Senator
>>> (Address)

Letter salutation: *Dear Senator (surname):*
Complimentary close: *Yours sincerely,*
Envelope, social:
> The Honourable
>> (Full name), Senator
>>> (Address)

Invitation, inside envelope:
> The Honourable
>> (Full name), Senator

Place card: *The Hon. (full name), Senator*

Introduction:
  The Honourable (full name), senator of (province) in the Senate of Canada ...
Introduction, one person to another: *Senator (surname)*
Conversation: *Senator (surname)*
Conversation, less formal: *Senator*

HOUSE OF COMMONS

Speaker of the House of Commons
NOTE: Address a speaker as *the Honourable* only while in office. Address a former Speaker as *Mr./Ms./etc. (name)* and identify as *former Speaker of the House of Commons.* If the individual is a member of the Privy Council, see *Privy Counsellor,* page 296.
Envelope, official:
  The Honourable
    (Full name), (post nominals for decorations and honors), MP
      Speaker of the House of Commons
      (Address)
Letter salutation: *Dear Mr./Madam Speaker:*
Complimentary close: *Yours sincerely,*
Envelope, social:
  The Speaker of the House of Commons
    (Address)
Invitation, inside envelope:
  The Speaker of the House of Commons of Canada
Place card: *The Speaker of the House of Commons*
Introduction:
  Mr./Madam Speaker, may I present ...
  ... may I present the Speaker of the House of Commons
Conversation: *Mr./Madam Speaker*

Member of House of Commons, Privy Counsellor
NOTE: Address a former member as a *Privy Counsellor* and identify as *former member of the House of Commons.* See form for *Privy Counsellor,* page 296.
Envelope, official:
  The Honourable
    (Full name), (post nominals for decorations and honors), PC, MP
      (Address)
Letter salutation: *Dear Mr./Ms./etc. (surname):*
Complimentary close: *Yours sincerely,*
Envelope, social:
  The Honourable
    (Full name), PC, MP
      (Address)

Invitation, inside envelope:
> The Honourable
> > (Full name), PC, MP

Place card: The Hon. (full name), PC, MP

Introduction:
> The Honourable (full name), member of the House of Commons of Canada
> OR Member of the House of Commons of Canada, Mr./Ms./etc. (surname)

Introduction, one person to another: Mr./Ms./etc. (surname)

Conversation: Mr./Ms./etc. (surname)

Member of House of Commons, Not a Privy Counsellor

NOTE: Address a former member as Mr./Ms./etc. (name) and identify as a former member of the House of Commons.

Envelope, official:
> Mr./Ms./etc. (full name), MP
> > (Address)

Letter salutation: Dear Mr./Ms./etc. (surname):

Complimentary close: Yours sincerely,

Envelope, social:
> Mr./Ms./etc. (full name), MP
> > (Address)

Invitation, inside envelope: Mr./Ms./etc. (full name), MP

Place card: Mr./Ms./etc. (full name), MP

Introduction:
> Mr./Ms./etc. (full name), member of the House of Commons of Canada
> OR Member of the House of Commons of Canada, Mr./Ms./etc. (surname)

Introduction, one person to another: Mr./Ms./etc. (surname)

Conversation: Mr./Ms./etc. (surname)

Canadian Federal Executive

Prime Minister

NOTE: Address a former prime minister as a Privy Counsellor and identify as the former prime minister. See form for Privy Counsellor, page 296.

Envelope, official:
> The Right Honourable
> > (Full name), (post nominals for decorations and honors), PC, MP
> > > Prime Minister
> > > > (Address)

Letter salutation: Dear Prime Minister: OR Prime Minister:

Complimentary close: Yours sincerely,

Envelope, social:
> The Prime Minister
> > (Address)

Invitation, inside envelope: The Prime Minister

Place card: The Prime Minister

Introduction: *The Right Honourable (full name), the Prime Minister of Canada*
Introduction, one person to another:
> *Mr./Madam Prime Minister, may I present ...*
> *... may I present the Prime Minister ...*

Conversation: *Prime Minister*
Conversation, less formal: *Sir/madam*

Deputy Prime Minister

NOTE: Address a former deputy prime minister as a *Privy Counsellor* and identify as the *former deputy prime minister*. See form for *Privy Counsellor*, page 296.
Envelope, official:
> *The Right Honourable*
>> *(Full name), (post nominals for decorations and honors)*, PC, MP
>>> *Deputy Prime Minister*
>>> *(Address)*

Letter salutation: *Dear Deputy Prime Minister:*
Complimentary close: *Yours sincerely,*
Envelope, social:
> *The Right Honourable*
>> *(Full name)*, PC, MP
>>> *(Address)*

Invitation, inside envelope:
> *The Right Honourable*
>> *(Full name)*, PC, MP

Place card: *The Right Hon. (full name)*, PC, MP
Introduction:
> *The Right Honourable (full name), the Deputy Prime Minister of Canada*

Introduction, one person to another:
> *Mr./Ms./etc. (surname) may I present ...*
> *... may I present the Deputy Prime Minister, Mr./Ms./etc. (surname)...*

Conversation: *Mr./Ms./etc. (surname)*

Minister: Member of the House of Commons

NOTE: Address a former minister as a *Privy Counsellor* and identify as a *former minister* or *former secretary*. See form for *Privy Counsellor*, page 296.
Envelope, official:
> *The Honourable*
>> *(Full name), (post nominals for decorations and honors)*, PC, MP
>>> *Minister of (portfolio)*
>>> *(Address)*

Letter salutation: *Dear Minister:*
Complimentary close: *Yours sincerely,*
Envelope, social:
> *The Minister of (portfolio)*
>> *(Address)*

Invitation, inside envelope: *The Minister of (portfolio)*

Place card: *The Minister of (portfolio)*
Introduction: *The Honourable (full name), the Minister of (portfolio) of Canada*
Introduction, one person to another:
    Minister, may I present ...
    ... may I present the Minister of (portfolio) ...
    OR *... may I present the Minister of (portfolio), (Minister) (surname) ...*
Conversation: *Minister* OR *Minister (surname)*

Minister: Senator

NOTE: Address a former minister as a *Privy Counsellor* and identify as a *former minister* or *former secretary*. See form for *Privy Counsellor*, page 296.
Envelope, official:
    Senator the Honourable
        (Full name), (post nominals for decorations and honors), PC
            Minister of (portfolio)
            (Address)
Letter salutation: *Dear Minister:*
Complimentary close: *Yours sincerely,*
Envelope, social:
    The Minister of (portfolio)
        (Address)
Invitation, inside envelope: *The Minister of (portfolio)*
Place card: *The Minister of (portfolio)*
Introduction:
    Senator the Honourable (full name), the Minister of (portfolio) of Canada
Introduction, one person to another:
    Minister, may I present ...
    ... may I present the Minister of (portfolio) ...
    OR *... may I present the Minister of (portfolio), Minister (surname) ...*
Conversation: *Minister* OR *Minister (surname)*

Deputy Minister, Assistant Deputy Minister

NOTE: Address as a member of Parliament and identify as *deputy minister* or *assistant minister of (portfolio)*. *Deputy Minister* and *Assistant Deputy Minister* are used in salutation and for identification.

Secretary of State: House of Commons

Envelope, official:
    The Honourable
        (Full name), (post nominals for decorations and honors), PC, MP
            Secretary of State (portfolio)
            (Address)
Letter salutation: *Dear Secretary of State:* OR *Dear Mr./Ms./etc.(surname):*
Complimentary close: *Yours sincerely,*
Envelope, social:
    The Secretary of State (portfolio)
        (Address)

Invitation, inside envelope: *The Secretary of State (portfolio)*
Place card: *The Secretary of State (portfolio)*
Introduction: *The Honourable (full name), the Secretary of State of Canada*
Introduction, one person to another:
>   *Secretary of State, may I present …*
>   OR *Mr./Ms./etc.(surname), may I present …*
>   *… may I present the Secretary of State …*
>   OR *… may I present the Secretary of State, Mr./Ms./etc.(surname) …*

Conversation: *Secretary of State* OR *Mr./Ms./etc.(surname)*

Canadian Federal Judiciary

Chief Justice of Canada

NOTE: A former chief justice, as a member of the Privy Council, is addressed as *the Honourable* for life. Formal use of a judicial honorific ceases upon retirement: Address as *Mr./Mrs./etc. (surname)* and identify as a *former chief justice.*
Envelope, official:
>   *The Right Honourable*
>>   *(Full name), (post nominals for decorations and honors),* PC
>>>   *Chief Justice of Canada*
>>>>   *(Address)*

Letter salutation: *Dear Chief Justice:*
Complimentary close: *Yours sincerely,*
Envelope, social:
>   *The Chief Justice of Canada*
>>   *(Address)*

Invitation, inside envelope: *The Chief Justice*
Place card: *The Chief Justice*
Introduction: *The Right Honourable (full name), Chief Justice of Canada*
Introduction, one person to another:
>   *Mr./Madam Chief Justice, may I present …*
>   *… may I present the Chief Justice …*

Conversation: *Mr./Madam Chief Justice*
Conversation, less formal: *Sir/madam*

Chief Justice of the Federal Court of Canada
Associate Chief Justice of the Federal Court of Canada

NOTE: Use form of *Puisne Judges of the Supreme Court of Canada* and identify as *Chief Justice* OR *Associate Chief Justice.*

Puisne Judges of the Supreme Court of Canada
Judges of the Federal Court

NOTE: Former judges of high courts continue to be addressed with the courtesy title *the Honourable* for life. Formal use of a judicial honorific ceases upon retirement: Address as *Mr./Ms./etc. (surname)* and identify as a former judge.

Envelope, official:
> The Honourable
>> Mr./Madame Justice (full name), (post nominal decorations/honors)
>>> (Name of court)
>>> (Address)

Letter salutation: *Dear Mr./Madam Justice (surname):*
Complimentary close: *Yours sincerely,*

Envelope, social:
> The Honourable
>> Mr./Madame Justice (full name)
>>> (Address)

Invitation, inside envelope:
> The Honourable
>> Mr./Madame Justice (full name)

Place card: *The Hon. Mr./Madame Justice (full name)*

Introduction:
> The Honourable Mr./Madam Justice (full name),
> Judge of the (name of court) of Canada

Introduction, one person to another:
> Mr./Madam Justice, may I present ...
> ... may I present Mr./Madame Justice (surname) ...

Conversation: *Mr./Madam Justice*

Chief Judge or Judge of the Tax Court of Canada

NOTE: Former judges of high courts continue to be addressed with the courtesy title *the Honourable* for life. Formal use of a judicial honorific ceases upon retirement: Address as *Mr./Mrs./etc. (surname)* and identify as a former judge.

Envelope, official:
> The Honourable
>> (Full name), (post nominals for decorations and honors)
>>> Chief Judge
>>>> Tax Court of Canada
>>>> (Address)
> The Honourable
>> (Full name)
>>> Tax Court of Canada
>>> (Address)

Letter salutation: *Dear Chief Judge:* OR *Dear Judge (surname):*
Complimentary close: *Yours sincerely,*
Envelope, social:
> *The Honourable*
>> *(Full name)*
>>> *(Address)*

Invitation, inside envelope:
> *The Honourable*
>> *(Full name)*

Place card: *The Hon. (full name)*
Introduction:
> *The Honourable (full name), chief judge of the Tax Court of Canada*
> *The Honourable (full name), judge of the Tax Court of Canada*

Introduction, one person to another:
> *Chief Judge, may I present ...*
> *... may I present the chief judge of the Tax Court ...*
> *Judge (surname), may I present ...*
> *... may I present Judge (surname) ...*

Conversation: *Chief Judge* OR *Judge (surname)*

Judge of a Superior Court:
Appeal Court, Superior Court, Court of the Queen's Bench

NOTE: Former judges of high courts continue to be addressed with the courtesy title *the Honourable* for life. Formal use of a judicial honorific ceases upon retirement: Address as Mr./Mrs./Ms./*hierarchical title/etc. (surname).*
Envelope, official:
> *The Honourable*
>> *(Full name)*
>>> *(Name of court)*
>>> *(Address)*

Letter salutation: *Dear Mr./Madam Justice (surname):*
Complimentary close: *Yours sincerely,*
Envelope, social:
> *The Honourable*
>> *(Full name)*
>>> *(Address)*

Invitation, inside envelope:
> *The Honourable*
>> *(Full name)*

Place card: *The Hon. (full name)*
Introduction: *The Honourable (full name), judge of the (name of court) of Canada*
Introduction, one person to another:
> *Mr./Madam Justice (surname), may I present ...*
> *... may I present Mr./Madam Justice (surname) ...*

Conversation: *Mr./Madam Justice (surname)*

306

Canadian Provincial & Territorial Officials

Lieutenant Governor
Envelope, official:
> His/Her Honour
>> The Honourable
>>> (Full name), (post nominals for decorations and honors)
>>>> Lieutenant Governor
>>>>> (Address)

Letter salutation: *Your Honour:* or *My Dear Lieutenant Governor:*
Complimentary close: *Yours sincerely,*
Envelope, social:
> The Honourable
>> (Full name)
>>> (Address)

Invitation, inside envelope:
> The Honourable
>> (Full name)

Place card:
> His/Her Honour or The Hon. (full name)
> or The Lieutenant Governor of (province)

Introduction:
> His/Her Honour the Honourable (full name),
>> Lieutenant Governor of (province)

Introduction, one person to another:
> Your Honour, may I present ...
> ... may I present His/Her Honour the Honourable (full name),
>> Lieutenant Governor of (province) ...

Conversation: *Your Honour*
Conversation, less formal: *Sir/madam,* or *Mr./Ms./etc. (surname)*

Spouse of the Lieutenant Governor
NOTE: The spouse of a lieutenant governor is addressed with the courtesy title *His/Her Honour* only in Canada.
Envelope, official:
> His/Her Honour
>> (Full name)
>>> (Address)

Letter salutation: *Your Honour:* or *Dear Mr./Mrs./etc. (surname):*
Complimentary close: *Yours sincerely,*
Envelope, social:
> His/Her Honour
>> (Full name)
>>> (Address)

Invitation, inside envelope:
>His/Her Honour
>>(Full name)

Place card: His/Her Hon. (full name) OR Mr./Mrs./etc. (full name)
Introduction:
>His/Her Honour, Mr./Ms. (full name)
>Her Honour, Mrs. (surname)

Introduction, one person to another:
>Your Honour, may I present ...
>... may I present His/Her Honour, Mr. (full name) ...
>OR ... may I present His/Her Honour, Mrs. (surname) ...

Conversation: Your Honour
Conversation, less formal: Sir/madam, OR Mr./Mrs./Ms. (surname)

Former Lieutenant Governor

Envelope, official:
>The Honourable
>>(Full name), (post nominals for decorations and honors)
>>>(Address)

Letter salutation: Dear Mr./Ms./etc. (surname):
Complimentary close: Yours sincerely,
Envelope, social:
>The Honourable
>>(Full name)
>>>(Address)

Invitation, inside envelope:
>The Honourable
>>(Full name)

Place card: The Hon. (full name)
Introduction: The Honourable (full name), former Lieutenant Governor of (province)
Introduction, one person to another:
>Mr./Ms./etc. (surname), may I present ...
>... may I present Mr./Ms./etc. (surname), former Lieutenant Governor of (province)

Conversation: Mr./Ms./etc. (surname)

Premier

NOTE: A former premier does not continue to be addressed as the Honourable.
Envelope, official:
>The Honourable
>>(Full name), MLA/MPP/MNA
>>>Premier
>>>>(Address)

Letter salutation: Dear Premier:
Complimentary close: Yours sincerely,

308

Envelope, social:
> *The Honourable*
>> *(Full name)*, MLA/MPP/MNA
>> *(Address)*

Invitation, inside envelope:
> *The Honourable*
>> *(Full name)*, MLA/MPP/MNA

Place card: *The Hon. (full name)*, MLA/MPP/MNA

Introduction: *The Honourable (full name), Premier of (province)*

Introduction, one person to another:
> *Premier, may I present ...*
> *... may I present Mr./Ms./etc. (surname), Premier of (province)*

Conversation: *Premier*

Conversation, less formal: *Mr./Ms./etc. (surname)*

Commissioner

NOTE: *Commissioner* is not used as an honorific for this office. Former commissioners do not continue to be addressed as *the Honourable*.

Envelope, official:
> *The Honourable*
>> *(Full name), (post nominals for decorations and honors)*
>> *Commissioner*
>> *(Address)*

Letter salutation: *Commissioner (surname):*

Complimentary close: *Yours sincerely,*

Envelope, social:
> *The Honourable*
>> *(Full name)*
>> *(Address)*

Invitation, inside envelope:
> *The Honourable*
>> *(Full name)*

Place card: *The Hon. (full name)*

Introduction: *The Honourable (full name), Commissioner of (territory)*

Introduction, one person to another:
> *Your Honour, may I present ...*
> OR *Mr./Mrs./etc. (surname), may I present...*
> *... may I present Mr./Mrs./etc. (surname), Commissioner of (territory)*

Conversation: *Mr./Mrs./etc. (surname)*

Government Leader

Example: (Full name), MLA
NOTE: A former government leader is not addressed as the Honourable.
Envelope, official:
> The Honourable
>> (Full name), MLA
>>> Government Leader
>>> (Address)

Letter salutation: Dear Mr./Mrs./etc. (surname):
Complimentary close: Yours sincerely,
Envelope, social:
> The Honourable
>> (Full name), MLA
>>> (Address)

Invitation, inside envelope:
> The Honourable
>> (Full name), MLA

Place card: The Hon. (full name), MLA
Introduction: The Honourable (full name), government leader of (territory)
Introduction, one person to another:
> Premier, may I present ...
> ... may I present Mr./Mrs./etc. (surname), government leader of (territory)

Conversation: Mr./Mrs./etc. (surname)
Conversation, less formal: Mr./Mrs./etc. (surname)

Provincial or Territorial Minister

NOTE: A former provincial or territorial minister is not addressed as the Honourable after leaving office.
Envelope, official:
> The Honourable
>> (Full name), MLA/MPP/MNA/MHA
>>> Minister of (portfolio)
>>> (Address)

Letter salutation: Dear Minister:
Complimentary close: Yours sincerely,
Envelope, social:
> The Minister of (portfolio)
>> (Address)

Invitation, inside envelope: The Minister of (portfolio)
Place card: The Minister of (portfolio)
Introduction:
> The Honourable (full name), the Minister of (portfolio) of (province or territory)

Introduction, one person to another:
> Minister, may I present ...
> ... may I present the Minister of (portfolio) ...
> OR ... may I present the Minister of (portfolio), Mr./Ms./etc. (surname) ...

Conversation: Minister
Conversation, less formal: Mr./Ms./etc.(surname)

Speaker of a Legislative Assembly of a Province and Territory

NOTE: The Speaker of a Legislative Assembly is addressed as *the Honourable* only while in office.

Envelope, official:
> *The Honourable*
> > *(Full name)*, MLA/MPP/MNA/MHA
> > > *Speaker of (name of assembly)*
> > > > *(Address)*

Letter salutation: *Dear Mr./Madam Speaker:*
Envelope, social:
> *The Speaker of (name of assembly)*
> > *(Address)*

Invitation, inside envelope: *The Speaker of (name of assembly)*
Place card: *The Speaker of (name of assembly)*
Introduction:
> *Mr./Madam Speaker, may I present ...*
> *... may I present the Speaker of the (name of assembly) of (province/territory),*
> > *Speaker (surname)*

Conversation: *Mr./Madam Speaker*
Conversation, less formal: *Speaker (surname)*

Member of a Provincial or Territorial Legislative Assembly

Envelope, official:
> *Mr./Ms./etc. (full name)*, MLA/MPP/MNA/MHA
> > *(Address)*

Letter salutation: *Dear Mr./Ms./etc. (surname):*
Complimentary close: *Yours sincerely,*
Envelope, social:
> *Mr./Ms./etc. (full name)*, MLA/MPP/MNA/MHA
> > *(Address)*

Invitation, inside envelope:
> *Mr./Ms./etc. (full name)*, MLA/MPP/MNA/MHA

Place card: *Mr./Ms./etc. (full name)*, MLA/MPP/MNA/MHA
Introduction:
> *Mr./Ms./etc. (full name), member of the (name of legislative assembly)*
> > *of (province or territory)*
> OR *Member of the (name of legislative assembly) of (province or territory),*
> > *Mr./Ms./etc. (surname)*

Introduction, one person to another: *Mr./Ms./etc. (surname)*
Conversation: *Mr./Ms./etc. (surname)*

Chief Judge or Judge of a Provincial or Territorial Court

NOTE: Former judges of provincial and territorial courts do not continue to be addressed with *the Honourable* or formally use a judicial honorific. Address as *Mr./Mrs./etc. (surname)* and identify as a former judge. To retain use of the courtesy title *the Honourable*, retired judges have to go to the Governor-General for approbation. If approved (which is almost always the case), the precedence list is updated.

Envelope, official:
  The Honourable
  (Full name)
      Provincial/territorial (name of court)
      (Address)
Letter salutation, more formal: *Dear Chief Judge:*
Letter salutation, less formal: *Dear Judge (surname):*
Complimentary close: *Yours sincerely,*
Envelope, social:
  The Honourable
  (Full name)
      (Address)
Invitation, inside envelope:
  The Honourable
  (Full name)
Place card: *The Hon. (full name)*
Introduction:
  The Honourable (full name), chief judge of the (name of court)
  The Honourable (full name), judge of the (name of court)
Introduction, one person to another:
  Judge (surname), may I present
  ... may I present Judge (surname) ...
Conversation: *Judge (surname)*

Canadian Diplomats

Ambassador of Canada by a Canadian Citizen

NOTE: Canada sends ambassadors to foreign (non-Commonwealth) countries. Canadian citizens do not address a Canadian ambassador as *His/Her Excellency*. A Canadian ambassador would be accorded *His/Her Excellency* by a receiving government. For that form, see listing for *Ambassador of a Foreign Country by a Canadian Citizen*, page 314.

Envelope, official:
  Mr./Ms./etc. (full name)
      Ambassador of Canada
      (Address)

Letter salutation: *Dear Ambassador:*
Complimentary close: *Yours sincerely,*
Envelope, social:
>*Mr./Ms./etc. (full name)*
>>*(Address)*

Invitation, inside envelope: *Mr./Ms./etc. (full name)*
Place card: *Mr./Ms./etc. (full name)*
Introduction: *(Full name), ambassador of Canada to (country)*
Introduction, one person to another: *Mr./Madam Ambassador*
Conversation: *Mr./Madam Ambassador*

High Commissioner of Canada by a Canadian Citizen

NOTE: Canada sends high commissioners to Commonwealth countries. Canadian citizens do not address a high commissioner of Canada as *His/Her Excellency.* In a foreign country, a Canadian high commissioner would be addressed as *His/Her Excellency* by the receiving government.
Envelope, official:
>*Mr./Ms./etc. (full name)*
>*High Commissioner for Canada*
>>*(Address)*

Letter salutation: *Dear High Commissioner:*
Complimentary close: *Yours sincerely,*
Envelope, social:
>*Mr./Ms./etc. (full name)*
>>*(Address)*

Invitation, inside envelope: *Mr./Ms./etc. (full name)*
Place card: *Mr./Ms./etc. (full name)*
Introduction: *(Full name), high commissioner for Canada to (country)*
Introduction, one person to another: *Mr./Madam High Commissioner*
Conversation: *Mr./Madam High Commissioner*

High Commissioner of a Commonwealth Country by a Canadian Citizen

Envelope, official:
>*His/Her Excellency*
>>*(Full name)*
>>*High Commissioner for (country)*
>>>*(Address)*
>*His/Her Excellency*
>>*(Full name)*
>>>*British High Commissioner*
>>>>*(Address)*

Letter salutation: *Dear High Commissioner:*
Complimentary close: *Yours sincerely,*

Envelope, social:
  His/Her Excellency
    (Full name)
    (Address)
Invitation, inside envelope:
  His/Her Excellency
    (Full name)
Place card: *His/Her Excellency (full name)*
Introduction:
  His/Her Excellency (full name), the high commissioner for (country)
  His/Her Excellency (full name), the British high commissioner
Introduction, one person to another: *Mr./Madam High Commissioner*
Conversation: *Mr./Madam High Commissioner*

Ambassador of a Foreign Country by a Canadian Citizen
Envelope, official:
  His/Her Excellency
    (Full name)
      The Ambassador of (country)
        (Address)
Letter salutation: *Excellency:* OR *Dear Mr./Madam Ambassador:*
Complimentary close: *Yours Sincerely,*
Envelope, social:
  His/Her Excellency
      The Ambassador of (country)
        (Address)
Invitation, inside envelope: *The Ambassador of (country)*
Place card: *The Ambassador of (country)*
Introduction:
  His/Her Excellency (full name), ambassador of (country)
  OR *Ambassador of (country), Ambassador (surname)*
Introduction, one person to another: *Ambassador (surname)*
Conversation: *Your Excellency* OR *Mr./Madam Ambassador*

Canadian Armed Services

Chief of Defence Staff – CDS
Vice-Chief of Defence Staff – VCDS
Chief of Maritime Staff – CMS
Chief of Land Staff – CLS
Chief of Air Staff – CAS

Examples: *General (full name)*, CMM, MSC, CD
Lieutenant-General (full name), CMM, CD
Vice-Admiral (full name), OMM, MSM, CD

Envelope, official:
(Full rank) (full name), *(post nominals for decorations and honors)*
(Office)
(Address)

Introduction:
(Full rank) (full name), *(office)*
OR *(Office)*, *(full rank) (surname)*

Commissioned Officer: 010 to 03

Examples: *Lieutenant-General (full name)*, CD
Lieutenant-General (full name), CD *(Ret'd)*
Brigadier-General (full name), OMM, CD
Major-General (full name), MD, CD
Admiral (full name), CD
Admiral (full name), CD *(Ret'd)*
Vice-Admiral (full name), CMM, CD
Rear-Admiral (full name), OMM, CD

Envelope, official:
(Full rank) (full name), *(post nominals for decorations and honors)*
(Position/command/name of base/service)
(Address)

Letter salutation:
Dear (full rank) (surname):
OR *Dear (basic rank) (surname):*

Complimentary close: *Yours faithfully,*

Envelope, social:
(Full rank) (full name)
(Address)

Invitation, inside envelope: *(Full rank) (full name)*

Place card: *(Abbreviated rank) (full name)*

Introduction:
(Full rank) (full name), *(position/command/name of base/service)*
OR *(Position/command/name of base/service)*, *(full rank) (surname)*

Canadian Armed Services

National Defence and the Canadian Forces
Canadian Forces Land Command (LFC)
Canadian Forces Maritime Command (MARCOM)
Canadian Forces Air Command (AIRCOM)

	ARMY (LFC)	NAVY (MARCOM)	AIR FORCE (AIRCOM)
Commissioned Officers			
010			
09	Gen — General	Adm — Admiral	Gen — General
08	LGen — Lieutenant-General	VAdm — Vice-Admiral	LGen — Lieutenant-General
07	MGen — Major-General	RAdm — Rear-Admiral	MGen — Major-General
06	BGen — Brigadier-General	Cmdre — Commodore	BGen — Brigadier-General
05	Col — Colonel	Capt(N) — Captain	Col — Colonel
04	LCol — Lieutenant-Colonel	Cdr — Commander	LCol — Lieutenant-Colonel
03	Maj — Major	LCdr — Lieutenant-Commander	Maj — Major
02	Capt — Captain	Lt(N) — Lieutenant	Capt — Captain
01	Lt — Lieutenant	SLt — Sub-Lieutenant	Lt — Lieutenant
01	2Lt — Second-Lieutenant	A/SLt — Acting Sub-Lieutenant	2Lt — Second-Lieutenant
	OCdt — Officer Cadet	NCdt — Naval Cadet	OCdt — Officer Cadet

Canadian Armed Services

National Defence and the Canadian Forces

Canadian Forces Land Command (LFC)
Canadian Forces Maritime Command (MARCOM)
Canadian Forces Air Command (AIRCOM)

Enlisted Personnel

	ARMY (LFC)		NAVY (MARCOM)		AIR FORCE (AIRCOM)	
E9	CWO	Chief Warrant Officer	CPO-1	Chief Petty Officer 1st Class	CWO	Chief Warrant Officer
E8	MWO	Master Warrant Officer	CPO-2	Chief Petty Officer 2nd Class	MWO	Master Warrant Officer
E7	WO	Warrant Officer	PO-1	Petty Officer 1st Class	WO	Warrant Officer
E6	Sgt	Sergeant	PO-2	Petty Officer 2nd Class	Sgt	Sergeant
E5	MCpl	Master Corporal	MS	Master Seaman	MCpl	Master Corporal
E4	Cpl	Corporal	LS	Leading Seaman	Cpl	Corporal
E3	Pte	Private	AB	Able Seaman	Pte	Private
E2	Pte (Recruit)	Private Recruit	OS	Ordinary Seaman	Pte (Recruit)	Private Recruit

Commissioned ranks *O10-O1* and non-commissioned grades *E9-E2* notations are provided for comparison to U.S. ranks and ratings only.

Introduction, one person to another: *(Full rank) (surname)*
Conversation: *(Full rank) (surname)*
Conversation, less formal: *(Basic rank) (surname)* OR *(Basic rank)*
Conversation, by a junior: *Sir/ma'am*

Commissioned Officer: 02 to 01

Examples: *Lieutenant (full name)*, DC
            Sub-Lieutenant (full name)
            Acting Lieutenant (full name)

NOTE: Higher-ranking officers address these ranks of officers verbally as Mr./Ms. *(surname)*. Non-commissioned officers address these officers as *(full rank) (surname)* or *sir/ma'am*. Civilians should use *(full rank) (surname)*.

Envelope, official:
    (Full rank) (full name), (post nominals for decorations and honors)
        (Position/command/name of base/service)
            (Address)
Letter salutation:
    Dear (full rank) (surname):
    OR *Dear (basic rank) (surname):*
Complimentary close: *Yours faithfully,*
Envelope, social:
    (Full rank) (full name)
        (Address)
Invitation, inside envelope: *(Full rank) (full name)*
Place card: *(Abbreviated rank) (full name)*
Introduction:
    (Full rank) (full name), (position/command/name of base/service)
    OR *(Position/command/name of base), (full rank) (surname)*
Introduction, one person to another: *(Full rank) (surname)*
Conversation: *(Full rank) (surname)* OR *(Full rank)*
Conversation, by a junior: *Sir/ma'am*

Warrant Officers: E7, E8, and E9

Examples: *Chief Warrant Officer (full name)*, MSM, CD
            Master Warrant Officer (full name), CD
            Warrant Officer (full name)

Notes:

(1) It is the custom for commissioned officers to address warrant officers verbally as Mr./Ms. *(surname)*. Non-commissioned officers address warrant officers as *(full rank) (surname)* or *sir/ma'am*. Civilians can use either as *(full rank) (surname)* or Mr./Ms. *(surname)*.

(2) Army and Air Force chief warrant officers are not informally addressed as *Chief* or *Chief (name)*. *Chief* is used in this manner for *Naval Chief Petty Officers* CPO-1 and CPO-2.

Envelope, official:
> (*Full rank*) (*full name*), (*post nominals for decorations and honors*)
>> (*Position/command/name of base*)
>>> (*Address*)

Letter salutation: *Dear Mr./Ms. (surname)*:
Complimentary close: *Yours Sincerely,*
Envelope, social:
> (*Full rank*) (*full name*)
>> (*Address*)

Invitation, inside envelope: *Mr./Ms. (full name)*
Place card: (*Abbreviated rank*) (*full name*) OR *Mr./Ms. (full name)*
Introduction:
> (*Full rank*) (*full name*), (*position/command/name of base*)
> OR (*Position/command/name of base*), (*full rank*) (*surname*)

Introduction, one person to another: (*Full rank*) (*surname*)
Conversation: (*Full rank*) (*surname*)
Conversation, less formal: *Mr./Ms. (surname)*

Chief Petty Officers: E8 and E9

Examples: *Chief Petty Officer 1st Class (full name)*, CD
> *Chief Petty Officer 2nd Class (full name)*

Envelope, official:
> (*Full rank*) (*full name*), (*post nominals for decorations and honors*)
>> (*Position/command/name of base/service*)
>>> (*Address*)

Letter salutation: *Dear (full rank) (surname)*: OR *Dear Chief (surname)*:
Complimentary close: *Yours sincerely,*
Envelope, social:
> (*Full rank*) (*full name*)
>> (*Address*)

Invitation, inside envelope: (*Full rank*) (*full name*)
Place card: (*Abbreviated rank*) (*full name*)
Introduction:
> (*Full rank*) (*full name*), (*position/command/name of base/service*)
> OR (*Position/command/name of base*), (*full rank*) (*surname*)

Introduction, one person to another: (*Full rank*) (*surname*)
Conversation: (*Full rank*) (*surname*)
Conversation, less formal: *Chief (surname)* OR *Chief*

Non-Commissioned Officers: E7 to E2

Examples: *Sergeant (full name)*
               Master Seaman (full name)
               Corporal (full name)

Envelope, official:
    (Full rank) (full name)
        (Position/command/name of base)
        (Address)

Letter salutation: *Dear (full rank) (surname):*
Complimentary close: *Yours faithfully,*
Envelope, social:
    (Full rank) (full name)
        (Address)

Invitation, inside envelope: *(Full rank) (full name)*
Place card: *(Abbreviated rank) (full name)*
Introduction:
    (Full rank) (full name), (position/command/name of base)
    OR *(Position/command/name of base), (full rank) (surname)*

Introduction, one person to another: *(Full rank) (surname)*
Conversation: *(Full rank) (surname)*
Conversation, informal: *(Basic rank) (surname)*

Royal Canadian Mounted Police, RCMP

NOTE: The following abbreviations are used in the RCMP

i/c	*in charge of a detachment, unit, etc.*
O.I.C.	*Officer in Charge*
O.C.	*Officer commanding*
C.O.	*Commanding Officer*

Commissioned Officers

LEVEL	ABBREVIATED RANK	FULL RANK	
D/M - O2	Commr	*Commissioner*	Rank is equivalent to a Deputy Minister
E/M - O5	D/Commr	*Deputy Commissioner*	
E/M - O4 E/M - O3	A/Commr	*Assistant Commissioner*	
E/M - O2	C/Supt	*Chief Superintendent*	
	Supt	*Superintendent*	
	Insp	*Inspector*	

Envelope, official:
    (Full rank) (full name)
        (Position/division)
        (Address)

Letter salutation: *Dear (full rank) (surname):*

Complimentary close: *Yours faithfully,*
Envelope, social:
    (Full rank) (full name)
      (Address)
Invitation, inside envelope: *(Full rank) (full name)*
Place card: *(Abbreviated rank) (full name)*
Introduction:
    (Full rank) (full name), *(position/division)*, Royal Canadian Mounted Police
    (Position/division) of the Royal Canadian Mounted Police, *(full rank) (surname)*
Introduction, one person to another: *(Full rank) (surname)*
Conversation:
    (Full rank) (surname)
    OR *(Full rank)*
Conversation, by a junior: *Sir/ma'am*

Non-Commissioned Officers E9 and E8

LEVEL	ABBREVIATED RANK	FULL RANK
E9	C/S/M	*Corps Sergeant Major*
E8	S/M	*Sergeant Major*
E7	S/S/M	*Staff Sergeant Major*

Envelope, official:
    (Full rank) (full name)
      (Position/division)
        (Address)
Letter salutation: *Dear (full rank) (surname):*
Complimentary close: *Yours faithfully,*
Envelope, social:
    (Full rank) (full name)
      (Address)
Invitation, inside envelope: *(Full rank) (full name)*
Place card: *(Abbreviated rank) (full name)*
Introduction:
    (Full rank) (full name), *(position/division)*, Royal Canadian Mounted Police
    (Position/division) of the Royal Canadian Mounted Police, *(full rank) (surname)*
Introduction, one person to another: *(Full rank) (surname)*
Conversation:
    (Full rank) (surname)
    OR *(Full rank)*
Conversation, by a junior: *Sir/ma'am*

Non-Commissioned Officer

LEVEL	ABBREVIATED RANK	FULL RANK
E6	S/Sgt	Staff Sergeant
E5	Sgt	Sergeant
E4	Cpl	Corporal
E3	Cst	Constable
E2	S/Cst	Special Constable

NOTE: A staff sergeant is formally addressed in conversation as *(Full rank) (surname)*, and informally addressed as *Staff (surname)*.

Envelope, official:
> *(Full rank) (full name)*
> *(Position/division)*
> *(Address)*

Letter salutation: *Dear (full rank) (surname):*

Complimentary close: *Yours faithfully,*

Envelope, social:
> *(Full rank) (full name)*
> *(Address)*

Invitation, inside envelope: *(Full rank) (full name)*

Place card: *(Abbreviated rank) (full name)*

Introduction:
> *(Full rank) (full name), (position/division), Royal Canadian Mounted Police*
> *(Position/division) of the Royal Canadian Mounted Police, (full rank) (surname)*

Introduction, one person to another: *(Full rank) (surname)*

Conversation:
> *(Full rank) (surname)*
> OR *(Full rank)*

18 Australian Officials

Australian Chief of State

King/Queen of Australia

NOTE: The king/queen of Australia is also the hereditary monarch of the United Kingdom (Elizabeth the Second, by the Grace of God, Queen of Australia and Her other Realms and Territories, Head of the Commonwealth). Forms of address are to *His/Her Majesty* without reference to the domain. For more information on royalty see page 393.

Envelope:
> His/Her Majesty
>> The King/Queen
>>> (*Address*)

Letter salutation: *Your Majesty:*
Complimentary close: *Respectfully yours*, OR *Respectfully*,
Complimentary close by subjects:
> *I remain Your Majesty's faithful and devoted servant*,

Invitation, inside envelope: *His/Her Majesty The King/Queen*
Place card: *Her Majesty* OR *H.M. The King/Queen*
Announced/Introduction: *His/Her Majesty, The King/Queen*
Presentation (*In Australia all persons are presented to the monarch*):
> *Your Majesty may I present* ...

Conversation: *Your Majesty*
Conversation, less formal: *Sir/ma'am*

Australian Federal Parliament

Governor-General

Examples: *(Full name)*, AC
           The Right Reverend Dr. (full name), AC, OBE
           Major-General (full name), AC, CVO, MC
           Sir (full name), AC, CVO, MC

Envelope, official:
   His/Her Excellency
      (Rank, title, special honorific) (full name), *(post nominals decorations)*
      Governor-General of Australia
         (Address)

Letter salutation: *Your Excellency:*
Complimentary close: *Yours faithfully,*

Envelope, social:
   His/Her Excellency
      (Rank, title, special honorific) (full name)
         (Address)

Invitation, inside envelope:
   His/Her Excellency
      (Rank, title, special honorific) (full name)

Place card: *The Governor-General*

Introduction:
   His/Her Excellency (Rank, title, special honorific)
      (full name), governor-general of Australia

Introduction, one person to another:
   Your Excellency, may I present …
   … may I present His/Her Excellency (Rank, title, special honorific)
      (full name), governor-general

Conversation, initially: *Your Excellency* OR *Excellency*
Conversation, subsequently: *Sir* OR *madam*

Spouse of the Governor-General

NOTE: The spouse of a governor-general of the Commonwealth of Australia is addressed with the courtesy title *his/her Excellency* in Australia. It is not necessary to identify him or her as married to the governor-general.

Current Australian style suggests that it is no longer customary to address the wife of an official as Mrs. *(husband's first and surname)*. The name used by a wife is at her preference: She may prefer Mrs. *(woman's first and surname)* or simply *(woman's first and surname)* without an honorific. Check for the preference of the bearer.

Envelope, official:
   His Excellency
      Mr. (full name)
         (Address)

324

Her Excellency
> Mrs. (woman's first and surname)
> > (Address)

Her Excellency
> (other form of full name)
> > (Address)

Letter salutation: Your Excellency: OR Dear Mr./Mrs. (surname):
Complimentary close: Yours faithfully,
Envelope, social (if the governor-general is not invited):
His Excellency
> Mr. (full name)
> > (Address)

Her Excellency
> Mrs. (woman's first and surname)
> > (Address)

Her Excellency
> (Other form of full name)
> > (Address)

Invitation (if the governor-general is not invited), inside envelope:
His Excellency, Mr. (full name)
OR Her Excellency, Mrs. (full name)
OR Her Excellency, (other form of full name)
Place card:
Mr./Mrs. (full name) OR Mrs. (surname)
Introduction:
His/Her Excellency, Mr. (full name) ...
OR Her Excellency, Mrs. (surname) ...
OR Her Excellency, (other form of her name) ...
Introduction, one person to another:
Your Excellency, may I present ...
... may I present His Excellency, Mr. (surname) ...
OR ... may I present Her Excellency, Mrs. (surname) ...
OR ... may I present Her Excellency, (other form of her name) ...
Conversation, initially: Your Excellency OR Excellency
Conversation, less formal: Mr./Mrs. (surname) OR Mrs. (surname)
Conversation, subsequently: Sir OR madam

Former Governor-General

Examples: (Full name), AC
> Sir (full name), AC
> Dr. (full name), AC

NOTE: A former governor-general continues to be addressed with the courtesy title the Honourable for life: Address as the Honourable (Rank, title, special honorific) (full name) and identify as a former governor-general of the Commonwealth of Australia. or verbally as (Rank, title, special honorific) (surname).

Members of the Privy Council

NOTE: New members of the Privy Council are no longer being appointed in Australia, but those previously appointed are addressed as *the Right Honourable* for life. See format for member of the Privy Council on pages 362-363.

Members of the Federal Executive Council

NOTE: The Federal Executive Council is made up of current and former members in executive government. This includes the prime minister, ministers, and parliamentary secretaries. The forms below for president of the Senate, senator, speaker of the House of Representatives, and ministers reflect their membership in the Federal Executive Council and their address with the courtesy title *the Honourable* for life.

Former Member of the Federal Executive Council

Examples: *(Full name)*
             Sir (full name)
             Dame (full name)

Envelope:

  The Honourable
       (Rank, title, special honorific) (full name)
       (Address)

Letter salutation: *Dear (Rank, title, special honorific) (surname):*
Complimentary close: *Yours faithfully,*
Invitation, inside envelope:

  The Hon. (Rank, title, special honorific) (full name)

Place card: *The Hon. (Rank, title, special honorific) (full name)*
Introduction: *The Honourable (Rank, title, special honorific) (full name)*
Introduction, one person to another:

  (Rank, title, special honorific) (full name), may I present ...
  ... may I present the Honourable (Rank, title, special honorific) (surname)...

Conversation: *(Rank, title, special honorific) (surname)*

SENATE

President of the Senate

Example: *(Full name), President of the Senate and Senator for (state)*
Envelope, official:

  Senator the Honourable
       (Full name)
            President of the Senate
            The Senate
              (Address)

Letter salutation: *Dear Mr./Madame President:*

Complimentary close: *Yours faithfully,*
Envelope, social:
 Senator the Honourable
 (Full name)
 (Address)
Invitation, inside envelope: *Senator the Hon. (full name)*
Place card:
 The President of the Senate OR *Senator The Hon. (full name)*
Introduction:
 The Honourable (full name), president of the Senate
 of the Commonwealth of Australia
Introduction, one person to another: *Mr./Madame President*
Conversation: *Mr./Madame President*

Senator
Example: *(Full name), senator for (state)*
Envelope, official:
 Senator (full name)
 (Address)
Letter salutation: *Dear Senator:* OR *Dear Senator (surname):*
Complimentary close: *Yours faithfully,*
Envelope, social:
 Senator (full name)
 (Address)
Invitation, inside envelope: *Senator (full name)*
Place card: *Senator (full name)*
Introduction: *Senator (full name)*
Introduction, one person to another: *Senator (surname)*
Conversation, initially: *Senator (surname)*
Conversation, subsequently: *Senator*

Clerk of the Senate
Deputy Clerk of the Senate
Usher of the Black Rod
Address with Mr./Mrs./etc. *(name)* and identify by office held.

HOUSE OF REPRESENTATIVES

Speaker of the House of Representatives
Example: *(Full name), MP, Speaker of the House of Representatives,*
 and member for (electorate division)
Envelope, official:
 The Honourable
 (Full name), MP
  Speaker of the House of Representatives
  (Address)
Letter salutation: *Dear Mr./Madam Speaker:*

Complimentary close: *Yours faithfully,*
Envelope, social:
> The Honourable
> > (Full name), MP
> > > (Address)

Invitation, inside envelope: *The Hon. (full name), MP*
Place card: *The Speaker* OR *The Hon. (full name), MP*
Introduction:
> The Honourable (full name), *speaker of the House of Representatives*
> > *of the Commonwealth of Australia*

Introduction, one person to another: *Mr./Madam Speaker*
Conversation: *Mr./Madam Speaker*

Former Speaker of the House of Representatives
Address as Mr./Mrs./etc. *(name)* or with a hierarchical title as is appropriate, and identify as *former speaker of the House of Representatives.* Speakers of the Australian House of Representatives are granted continued use of the courtesy title *the Honourable (e.g.,* as a member of the Federal Executive Council) on a case-by-case basis. Check for the status of the individual.

Member of House of Representatives
Examples: *(Full name), MP, member for (electorate division)*
> > *Dr. (full name), MP, member for (electorate division)*

Envelope, official:
> Mr./Mrs./etc. *(full name), MP*
> > (Address)

Letter salutation: *Dear Sir/Madam:*
Complimentary close: *Yours faithfully,*
Envelope, social:
> Mr./Mrs./etc. *(full name), MP*
> > (Address)

Invitation, inside envelope: Mr./Mrs./etc. *(full name), MP*
Place card: Mr./Mrs./etc. *(full name), MP*
Introduction:
> Mr./Mrs./etc. *(full name), member of the House of Representatives*
> > *of the Commonwealth of Australia*
> OR *Member of the House of Representatives of the*
> > *Commonwealth of Australia,* Mr./Mrs./etc. *(surname)*

Introduction, one person to another: Mr./Mrs./etc. *(surname)*
Conversation: Mr./Mrs./etc. *(surname)*

Clerk of the House of Representatives
Serjeant-at-Arms
Address as Mr./Mrs./etc. *(name)* and identify with the office held.

Australian Federal Executive

Prime Minister

Example: (*Full name*), MP, *member for* (*electorate division*)

NOTE: A former prime minister, as a former member of the Federal Executive Council, is addressed with the courtesy title *the Honourable* for life.

Envelope, official:
> *The Honourable*
>> (*Full name*), MP
>>> *Prime Minister*
>>>> (*Address*)

Letter salutation: *Prime Minister:*
Complimentary close: *Yours faithfully,*
Envelope, social:
> *The Honourable*
>> (*Full name*), MP
>>> (*Address*)

Invitation, inside envelope: *The Hon.* (*full name*), MP
Place card: *The Hon.* (*full name*), MP
Introduction:
> *The Honourable* (*full name*), *the prime minister of the*
>> *Commonwealth of Australia*

Introduction, one person to another:
> *Prime Minister, may I present* ...
> ... *may I present the Honourable* (*full name*), *the prime minister.*

Conversation: *Prime Minister* OR *Mr./Mrs./etc.* (*surname*)

Deputy Prime Minister

Example: (*Full name*), MP, *deputy prime minister, minister for Trade,*
>> *and member for* (*electorate division*)

NOTE: A former deputy prime minister, as a former member of the Federal Executive Council, is addressed with the courtesy title *the Honourable* for life.

Envelope, official:
> *The Honourable*
>> (*Full name*), MP
>>> *The Deputy Prime Minister*
>>>> (*Address*)

Letter salutation: *Dear Minister:*
Complimentary close: *Yours faithfully,*
Envelope, social:
> *The Honourable*
>> (*Full name*), MP
>>> (*Address*)

Invitation, inside envelope: *The Hon.* (*full name*), MP
Place card: *The Hon.* (*full name*), MP

Introduction:

> The Honourable (full name), the deputy prime minister
> of the Commonwealth of Australia

Introduction, one person to another:

> Minister may I present ... OR Mr./Mrs./etc. (surname) may I present ...
> ... may I present the Honourable (full name), the deputy prime minister ...

Conversation: Minister OR Mr./Mrs./etc. (surname)

Cabinet Minister, Attorney General, or Treasurer: Senator

Examples: (Full name), Minister for Finance and Administration,
>   member for (electorate division)
>   (Full name), SC, Minister for Arts and Sport,
>   member for (electorate division)

NOTE: Adapt this form for the treasurer or Attorney General. The officeholder will also be a senator for a state: Introductions may include some or all of those details. As former members of the Federal Executive Council these officials are addressed with the courtesy title the Honourable for life.

Envelope, official:

> Senator the Honourable
>   (Full name), (post nominals for decorations and honors)
>   Minister for (portfolio)
>   (Address)

Letter salutation: Dear Minister: OR Dear Senator (surname):
Complimentary close: Yours faithfully,
Envelope, social:

> Senator the Honourable
>   (Full name)
>   (Address)

Invitation, inside envelope: Senator the Hon. (full name)
Place card: Senator the Hon. (full name)
Introduction:

> Senator the Honourable (full name), the Minister for (portfolio)
> of the Commonwealth of Australia...

Introduction, one person to another:

> Senator (surname), may I present ... OR Minister, may I present ...
> ... may I present the Minister for (portfolio), Senator (surname)...

Conversation: Minister OR Senator (surname) OR Senator

Cabinet Minister, Attorney General, or Treasurer: MP

Examples: *(Full name), MP, Minister for Defence, member for (electorate division)*
               (Full name), MLA, Treasurer, member for (electorate division)
               (Full name), MLC, Attorney-General, member for (electorate division)
               Dr. (Full name), MLC, Minister for the Aging and Health,
                    member for (electorate division)

NOTE: Adapt this form for the treasurer or Attorney General. The officeholder will also be a member of parliament for a district: Introductions may include some or all of those details. As former members of the Federal Executive Council these officials are addressed with the courtesy title *the Honourable* for life.

Envelope, official:
    The Honourable
        (Full name), (post nominals for decorations and honors)
            (Office)
            (Address)
    The Honourable
        Mr./Mrs./etc. (full name), (post nominals for decorations and honors)
            (Office) of the Commonwealth of Australia
            (Address)

Letter salutation: *Dear Minister/Treasurer/Attorney General/etc.:*
Complimentary close: *Yours faithfully,*

Envelope, social:
    The Honourable
        (Full name), (post nominals for decorations and honors)
            (Address)
    The Honourable
        Mr./Mrs./etc. (full name), (post nominals for decorations and honors)
            (Address)

Invitation, inside envelope:
    The Hon. (full name), (post nominals for decorations and honors)
Place card: *The Hon. (full name), (post nominals for decorations and honors)*
Introduction: *The Honourable (full name), the Minister for (portfolio) of the Commonwealth of Australia...*
Introduction, one person to another:
    Minister/Treasurer/Attorney General, may I present ...
    OR *Mr./Mrs./etc. (surname), may I present ...*
    ... may I present the (exact title of office), Mr./Mrs./etc. (surname)
Conversation: *Minister/Treasurer/Attorney General* OR *Mr./Mrs./etc. (surname)*

Assistant Minister, Attorney General, or Treasurer: Senator

Example: (*Full name*), *Minister for Immigration and Citizenship,*
                        member for (electorate division)

NOTE: Adapt this form for an assistant Attorney General or assistant treasurer. An assistant minister will also be a senator for a state: Introductions may include some or all of those details. Assistant ministers are addressed with the courtesy title *the Honourable* only while in office.

Envelope, official:
    Senator the Honourable
        (*Full name*), (*post nominals for decorations and honors*)
            Assistant Minister for (portfolio)
                (*Address*)

Letter salutation: *Dear Senator (surname):*
Complimentary close: *Yours faithfully,*

Envelope, social:
    Senator the Honourable
        (*Full name*)
            (*Address*)

Invitation, inside envelope: *Senator the Hon. (full name)*
Place card: Senator *The Hon. (full name)*

Introduction:
    Senator the Honourable (full name), the Minister for (portfolio)
        of the Commonwealth of Australia...

Introduction, one person to another:
    Senator, may I present ...
    OR *Senator (surname), may I present ...*
    OR *Minister, may I present ...*
    ... may I present the Assistant Minister for (portfolio), Senator (surname) ...

Conversation, initially: *Senator (surname)*
Conversation, subsequently: *Senator*

Assistant Minister, Attorney General, or Treasurer: MP

Example: (*Full name*), *MP, Assistant Minister for the Environment and*
                        Water Resources and member for (electorate division)

NOTE: Adapt this form for an assistant treasurer or assistant Attorney General. An assistant minister will also be a member of parliament for a district: Introductions may include some or all of those details. Assistant ministers are addressed with the courtesy title *the Honourable* only while in office.

Envelope, official:
    The Honourable
        (*Full name*), *MP*
            Assistant Minister for (portfolio)
                (*Address*)

Letter salutation: *Dear Assistant Minister:*
Complimentary close: *Yours faithfully,*

332

Envelope, social:
> *The Honourable*
>> *(Full name)*, MP
>>> *(Address)*

Invitation, inside envelope: *The Hon. (full name)*, MP
Place card: *The Hon. (full name)*, MP
Introduction:
> *The Honourable (full name), the Assistant Minister for (portfolio)*
>> *of the Commonwealth of Australia...*

Introduction, one person to another:
> *Assistant Minister may I present ...*
> OR *Mr./Mrs./etc. (surname) may I present ...*
> *... may I present the Assistant Minister for (portfolio), Mr./Mrs./etc. (surname) ...*

Conversation: *Assistant Minister* OR *Mr./Mrs./etc. (surname)*

Parliamentary Secretary: Senator

Example: *(Full name), Parliamentary Secretary to the Minister for Ageing and Health*
NOTE: The officeholder will also be a senator for a state: Introductions may include some or all of the details. Parliamentary secretaries are addressed with the courtesy title *the Honourable* only while in office.
Envelope, official:
> *Senator the Honourable*
>> *(Full name)*
>>> *Parliamentary Secretary to the Minister for (portfolio)*
>>>> *(Address)*

Letter salutation: *Dear Senator (surname):*
Complimentary close: *Yours faithfully,*
Envelope, social:
> *Senator the Honourable*
>> *(Full name)*
>>> *(Address)*

Invitation, inside envelope: *Senator the Hon. (full name)*
Place card: *Senator the Hon. (full name)*
Introduction:
> *Senator the Honourable (full name), the Parliamentary Secretary to the*
>> *Minister for (portfolio) of the Commonwealth of Australia*

Introduction, one person to another:
> *Senator (surname), may I present ...*
> *... may I present the Parliamentary Secretary to the Minister for (portfolio),*
>> *Senator (surname) ...*

Conversation, initially: *Senator (surname)*
Conversation, subsequently: *Senator*

Parliamentary Secretary: MP

Examples:　(Full name), MP, Parliamentary Secretary to the Minister of Foreign Affairs
(Full name), MLA, Parliamentary Secretary to the Minister of Tourism
(Full name), MLC, Parliamentary Secretary, Roads and Ports

NOTE: The officeholder will also be a member of parliament for a district:
Introductions may include some or all of those details. Parliamentary secretaries
are addressed with the courtesy title the Honourable only while in office.

Envelope, official:
The Honourable
(Full name), (post nominals for decorations and honors)
Parliamentary Secretary to the Minister for (portfolio)
(Address)

Letter salutation: Dear Mr./Mrs./etc. (surname):
Complimentary close: Yours faithfully,

Envelope, social:
Mr./Mrs./etc. (full name), (post-nominal as appropriate)
(Address)

Invitation, inside envelope:
Mr./Mrs./etc. (full name), (post-nominal as appropriate)

Place card: Mr./Mrs./etc. (full name), (post-nominal as appropriate)

Introduction:
Mr./Mrs./etc. (surname), parliamentary secretary to the
minister of (portfolio) of the Commonwealth of Australia...
OR Parliamentary Secretary to the Minister for (portfolio) of the
Commonwealth of Australia, Mr./Mrs./etc. (surname)

Introduction, one person to another: Mr./Mrs./etc. (surname)
Conversation: Mr./Mrs./etc. (surname)

Shadow Minister

NOTE: A shadow minister is introduced as the Honorable (full name), Shadow minister for (portfolio) and addressed as Mr./Mrs./etc. (name).

Australian Federal Judiciary

Chief Justice of the High Court/Chief Justice of Australia

Examples: (Full name), AC
(Full name), AC, KBE

NOTE: The chief justice of the High Court is addressed with the courtesy title *the Honourable* for life. Use of a judicial honorific does not officially continue for life: Address as Mr./Mrs. *(name)* and identify as a former chief justice.

Envelope, official:
The Honourable
(Full name), (post-nominals as appropriate)
Chief Justice
High Court of Australia
(Address)

Letter salutation: *Dear Chief Justice:* OR *Dear Chief Justice (surname):*
Complimentary close: *Yours faithfully,*
Envelope, social:
The Chief Justice
(Address)

Invitation, inside envelope: *The Chief Justice*
Place card: *The Chief Justice* OR *Chief Justice (surname)*
Introduction:
The Honourable (full name), Chief Justice of Australia
OR *His/Her Honour (full name), Chief Justice of Australia*
Introduction, one person to another:
Chief Justice, may I present OR *Chief Justice (surname), may I present*
... may I present the Chief Justice of Australia, the Honourable (full name) ...
Conversation: *Chief Justice (surname)*
Conversation, less formal: *Chief Justice*
Conversation, when on the bench: *Your Honour*

Chief Justice of the Federal Court or the Family Court

Examples: (Full name), AC
(Full name), AC, KBE

NOTE: A chief justice of the Federal or Family Court is addressed with the courtesy title *the Honourable* for life. Use of a judicial honorific does not officially continue for life: Address as Mr./Mrs. *(name)* and identify as a former chief justice.

Envelope, official:
The Honourable
(Full name), (post-nominals as appropriate)
Chief Justice of (name of court)
(Address)

Letter salutation: *Dear Chief Justice:* OR *Dear Chief Justice (surname):*
Complimentary close: *Yours faithfully,*
Envelope, social:
The Chief Justice
(Address)

Invitation, inside envelope: *The Chief Justice*
Place card:
    The Chief Justice or Chief Justice (surname)
Introduction:
    The Honourable (full name), Chief Justice of (name of court)
        of the Commonwealth of Australia
    OR *His/Her Honour (full name), Chief Justice of (name of court)*
        of the Commonwealth of Australia
Introduction, one person to another:
    Chief Justice, may I present OR *Chief Justice (surname), may I present*
    … may I present the Chief Justice of (name of court),
        the Honourable (full name) …
Conversation: *Chief Justice (surname)*
Conversation, less formal: *Chief Justice*
Conversation, when on the bench: *Your Honour*

Justice of the High Court, Federal Court, or Family Court (Pusine Judges)

Examples: *(Full name)*
           (Full name), AC, QC
           Sir (full name), AC, KBE, CB
NOTE: Justices of the High Court, Federal Court, and Family Court are addressed with the courtesy title *the Honourable* for life. Use of a judicial honorific does not officially continue for life: Address as *Mr./Mrs. (name)* and identify as a former justice.
Envelope, official:
    The Honourable
        (Full name), (post-nominals as appropriate)
           Justice of the (name of court)
           (Address)
Letter salutation: *Dear Justice (surname):*
Complimentary close: *Yours faithfully,*
Envelope, social:
    The Honourable
    Justice (full name)
        (Address)
Invitation, inside envelope: *The Hon. Justice (full name)*
Place card (use last-name-only unless there are two judges with same surname):
    Justice (surname) OR *Justice (full name)*
Introduction:
    The Honourable (full name), Justice of the (name of court),
        of the Commonwealth of Australia
    OR *His/Her Honour (full name), Justice of the (name of court),*
        of the Commonwealth of Australia
Introduction, one person to another:
    Justice (name) may I present … OR *Your Honour may I present …*
    … may I present Justice (surname) …

Conversation, initially: *Justice (surname)*
Conversation, subsequently: *Judge*

Chief Federal Magistrate
Federal Magistrate

Envelope, official:
>(*Title*) (*full name*)
>>(*Name of court*)
>>>(*Address*)

Letter salutation: *Dear (title) (surname):*
Complimentary close: *Yours faithfully,*
Place card: (*Title*) (*full name*)
Introduction:
>(*Title*) (*full name*) *of the (name of court) of the Commonwealth of Australia*

Introduction, one person to another:
>(*Title*) (*surname*), *may I present …*
>… *may I present (title) (surname) …*

Conversation, on the bench: *Your Honor*
Conversation: (*Title*) (*surname*) OR (*Title*) OR Mr./Mrs./etc. (*name*)

Australian State Executive

Governor

Examples: (*Full name*), AC
              Professor (full name), AC
              Dr. (full name), AM
              Rear Admiral (full name), AO, CSC, RANR
              The Honourable (full name), AC

Envelope, official:
>*His/Her Excellency*
>>(*Honorific, rank or title*) (*full name*), (*post-nominals as appropriate*)
>>>*Governor*
>>>>(*Address*)

Letter salutation: *Your Excellency:*
Complimentary close: *Yours faithfully,*
Envelope, social:
>*His/Her Excellency*
>>(*Honorific, rank or title*) (*full name*)
>>>(*Address*)

Invitation, inside envelope:
>*His/Her Excellency*
>>(*Honorific, rank or title*) (*full name*)

Place card: *The Governor of (state)*
Introduction:
>*His/Her Excellency (honorific, rank or title) (full name), governor of (state)*

Introduction, one person to another:
> *Your Excellency, may I present …*
> *… may I present His/Her Excellency*
>> *(honorific, rank or title) (full name), governor of (state) …*

Conversation: *Your Excellency*
Conversation, less formal: *(Honorific, rank or title) (surname)* OR *Governor*
Conversation, subsequently: *Sir* OR *ma'am*

Spouse of the Governor

NOTE: The spouse of the governor of a state receives no special form of address due to being the spouse of a governor in Australia.

Former Governor

NOTE: A former governor does not continue to use the courtesy title *the Honourable* after leaving office. Address with *Mr./Mrs./etc.*, a rank or title as appropriate, and identify as a *former governor of (state)*. Some former officeholders may be knighted: Use *Sir/Dame* before the name.

Lieutenant Governor

Examples: *(Full name),* AC
            Sir (full name), KBE

NOTE: When officiating in place of the governor, a lieutenant governor is introduced and addressed as: *His/Her Excellency the Lieutenant Governor of (State)*. Otherwise, a lieutenant governor is neither addressed with the courtesy title *his/her Excellency* nor the honorific *lieutenant governor*. Address as *Mr./Mrs./Mrs./Miss (name)* and identify as the *lieutenant governor of (state)*.

    In some states the lieutenant governor is also the state's chief justice of the Supreme Court. Check for specifics of the individual.

Premier

Example: *(Full name),* MLA
           Sir (full name), MHA
           Dr. (full name), MHA

Envelope, official:
> *The Honourable*
>> *(Special honorific if provided) (full name), (post-nominals as appropriate)*
>> *Premier*
>>> *(Address)*

Letter salutation: *Dear Premier:* OR *Dear Mr./Madam Premier:*
Complimentary close: *Yours faithfully,*
Envelope, social:
> *The Honourable*
>> *(Full name), (post-nominals as appropriate)*
>> *(Address)*

Invitation, inside envelope: *The Hon. (full name)*
Place card:
> *The Premier*
> OR *The Premier of (state)*
> OR *The Honourable (full name), (post-nominals as appropriate)*

338

Introduction: *The Honourable (full name), premier of (state)*
Introduction, one person to another:
    Premier, may I present ...
    Mr./Madam Premier, may I present ...
    ... may I present (special honorific as provided) (surname) premier of (state)
Conversation, initially: *Premier (surname)* OR *Premier*
Conversation, subsequently: *Sir* OR *ma'am*

Former Premier

NOTE: A former premier does not continue to be addressed with the courtesy title *the Honourable* because of his or her service as premier. However, a former premier may retain use of *the Honourable* on a case-by-case basis. Check for the individual situation. Otherwise, address as *Mr./Mrs./etc. (name)* and identify as the *former premier of (state)*.

Deputy Premier

Examples: *(Full name), MP*
              (Full name), MLC
              Dr. (full name), MLA
NOTE: A deputy premier is often additionally minister of *(portfolio)*. Address as *the Honourable* is not continued after leaving office solely by virtue of service as a deputy premier.
Envelope, official:
    The Honourable
        (Full name), (post nominals for decorations and honors)
            Deputy Premier
                (Address)
Letter salutation: *Dear Mr./Mrs./etc. (surname):*
Complimentary close: *Yours faithfully,*
Envelope, social:
    The Honourable
        (Full name), (post nominals for decorations and honors)
            (Address)
Invitation, inside envelope:
    The Hon. (full name), (post nominals for decorations and honors)
Place card: *The Hon. (full name), (post nominals for decorations and honors)*
Introduction: *The Honourable (full name), deputy premier of (state)*
Introduction, one person to another:
    Premier, may I present ...
    ... may I present (Rank, title, special honorific) (surname)
        deputy premier of (state)
Conversation: *Mr./Mrs./etc. (surname)*

State Minister: Member of Parliament

Examples: *(Full name)*, MP, *Treasurer*
(Full name), MLC, *Minister for Consumer Protection*
Dr. *(full name)*, MLA, *Attorney General*

NOTE: A minister will also be an elected official of a jurisdiction: Introductions may include some or all of the details. Address as *the Honourable* is not continued after leaving office by virtue of service as a minister.

Envelope, official:
The Honourable
(Full name), *(post nominals for decorations and honors)*
Minister for (portfolio)
(Address)

Letter salutation: *Dear Minister:*
Complimentary close: *Yours faithfully,*
Envelope, social:
The Honourable
(Full name), *(post nominals for decorations and honors)*
(Address)

Invitation, inside envelope:
The Hon. (full name), *(post nominals for decorations and honors)*
Place card: *The Hon. (full name)*, *(post nominals for decorations and honors)*
Introduction: *The Honourable (full name)*, *the Minister for (portfolio) of (state)*
Introduction, one person to another:
Minister, may I present...
OR *Mr./Mrs./etc. (surname), may I present ...*
... may I present the Minister for (portfolio) ...
OR *... may I present the Minister for (portfolio), Mr./Mrs./etc. (surname) ...*
Conversation: *Minister* OR *Mr./Mrs./etc. (surname)*

Administrator of the Northern Territory

Examples: Mrs. *(full name)*, AC
Dr. *(full name)*, AM

NOTE: Address as *his/her Honour* is not continued after leaving office by virtue of service as the administrator.

Envelope, official:
His/Her Honour the Administrator
Mr./Mrs./etc. (full name), *(post-nominal letters as appropriate)*
(Address)

Letter salutation: *Dear Administrator:*
Complimentary close: *Yours faithfully,*
Envelope, social:
His/Her Honour the Administrator
Mr./Mrs./etc. (full name)
(Address)

Invitation, inside envelope:
His/Her Honour the Administrator
Mr./Mrs./etc. (full name)

340

Place card:
> His/Her Hon. the Administrator
> Mr./Mrs./etc. (full name)

Introduction:
> His/Her Honour the Administrator Mr./Mrs./etc. (full name),
>   Administrator of Northern Territory
> OR His/Her Honour the Administrator of Northern Territory,
>   Mr./Mrs./etc. (surname)

Introduction, one person to another: Mr./Mrs./etc. (surname)
Conversation: Mr./Mrs./etc. (surname)
Conversation, when on the bench: Your Honour

Chief Minister of Australian Capital Region
Chief Minister of Norfolk Island
Chief Minister of Northern Territory
Example: (Full name), MLA

NOTE: Use the same form for a member of a Legislative Assembly, page 343, and identify as Chief Minister of ... Only a current chief minister is addressed with the courtesy title the Honourable.

Australian State Legislative

President of a Legislative Council
Example: (Full name), MLC
NOTE: Only current members are addressed as the Honourable.
Envelope, official:
> The Honourable
>   (Full name), MLC
>   President of the Legislative Council
>   (Address)

Letter salutation: Dear Mr./Madam President:
Complimentary close: Yours faithfully,
Envelope, social:
> The Honourable
>   (Full name), MLC
>   (Address)

Invitation, inside envelope: The Hon. (full name), MLC
Place card: Mr./Madam President OR The Hon. (full name), MLC
Introduction:
> The Honourable (full name), president of the Legislative Council of (state)
> OR President of the (state) Legislative Council of (state), Mr./Mrs./etc. (surname)

Introduction, one person to another: Mr./Mrs./etc. (surname)
Conversation: Mr./Mrs./etc. (surname)

Member of the Legislative Council
Examples: *(Full name)*, MLC
NOTE: Only current members are addressed as *the Honourable*.
Envelope, official:
> *The Honourable*
>> *(Full name), (post-nominals as appropriate)*
>>> *(Address)*

Letter salutation: *Dear Mr./Mrs./etc. (surname):*
Complimentary close: *Yours faithfully,*
Envelope, social:
> *The Honourable*
>> *(Full name)*
>>> *(Address)*

Invitation, inside envelope: *The Hon. (full name)*
Place card: *The Hon. (full name)*
Introduction:
> *The Honourable (full name), member of the (state) Parliament*
> *Member of the (state) parliament, Mr./Mrs./etc. (surname)*

Introduction, one person to another: *Mr./Mrs./etc. (surname)*
Conversation: *Mr./Mrs./etc. (surname)*

Speaker of a Legislative Assembly or House of Assembly
Example: *(Full name)*, MP, *Speaker of the Legislative Assembly*
NOTE: A speaker will also be an elected representative of a jurisdiction: Introductions may include some or all of those details. The speaker is addressed with the courtesy title *the Honourable* while in office, not for life. The speaker of the legislative assembly *(MLA)* in the Australian Capital Territory is not accorded the courtesy title *the Honourable*: Address as Mr./Mrs./etc. *(name)*.
Envelope, official:
> *The Honourable*
>> *(Full name), (post nominals for decorations and honors)*
>>> *Speaker of the (name of assembly)*
>>>> *(Address)*

Letter salutation: *Dear Speaker:*
Complimentary close: *Yours faithfully,*
Envelope, social:
> *The Honourable*
>> *(Full name)*
>>> *(Address)*

Invitation, inside envelope: *The Hon. (full name)*
Place card: *The Speaker* OR *The Hon. (full name)*
Introduction:
> *The Honourable (full name), speaker of the (name of assembly) of (state)*

Introduction, one person to another:
> *Speaker, may I present ...*
> *... may I present the Speaker, the Honourable (full name) ...*

Conversation: *Speaker*

Member of a Legislative Assembly
Member of a Legislative House of Assembly
Member of a State Parliament (lower house)

Examples: Dr. *(full name)*, MP
Mr. *(full name)*, MLA
Mrs. *(full name)*, MLC
Mrs. *(full name)*, MHA

Envelope, official:
Mr./Mrs./etc. *(full name)*, *(post nominals for decorations and honors)*
(Address)
Letter salutation: *Dear Mr./Mrs./etc. (surname):*
Complimentary close: *Yours faithfully,*
Envelope, social:
Mr./Mrs./etc. *(full name)*, *(post nominals for decorations and honors)*
(Address)
Invitation, inside envelope:
Mr./Mrs./etc. *(full name)*, *(post nominals for decorations and honors)*
Place card: Mr./Mrs./etc. *(full name)*, *(post nominals for decorations and honors)*
Introduction: Mr./Mrs./etc. *(full name)*, *member of the (state) parliament*
Introduction, one person to another: Mr./Mrs./etc. *(surname)*
Conversation: Mr./Mrs./etc. *(surname)*

Leader of the Opposition in Tasmanian House of Assembly
NOTE: The current officeholder is addressed with the courtesy title *the Honourable*.
Address as Mr./Mrs./etc. *(surname)* in conversation.

Australian State Judiciary

Chief Justice of a State Supreme Court
Example: *(Full name)*, AC, *Chief Justice of (state)*
NOTE: The chief justice is addressed with the courtesy title *the Honourable* for life.
Use of a judicial honorific does not officially continue for life: Address as
Mr./Mrs./etc. *(name)* and identify as a *former chief justice*.
Envelope, official:
The Honourable
(full name), *(post nominals for decorations and honors)*
The Chief Justice
Supreme Court of (state)
(Address)
Letter salutation: *Your Honour:* OR *Dear Chief Justice:*
Complimentary close: *Yours faithfully,*
Envelope, social:
The Chief Justice
(Address)
Invitation, inside envelope: *The Chief Justice*

Place card:
>   *The Chief Justice or Chief Justice (surname)* OR *The Chief Justice of (state)*

Introduction:
>   *The Honourable (full name), Chief Justice of (state)*
>   OR *His/Her Honour (full name), Chief Justice of (state)*

Introduction, one person to another:
>   *Chief Justice, may I present ...*
>   OR *Chief Justice (surname), may I present ...*
>   OR *Your Honour, may I present ...*
>   *... may I present the Chief Justice of (state), the Honourable (full name) ...*

Conversation, initially: *Chief Justice (surname)*
Conversation, subsequently: *Chief Justice*

Justice of a State Supreme Court

NOTE: A justice is addressed with the courtesy title *the Honourable* for life upon application and approval. Use of a judicial honorific does not officially continue for life: Address as *Mr./Mrs./etc. (name)* and identify as a *former justice*.

Envelope, official:
>   *The Honourable*
>   *(Full name)*
>   *(Name of court)*
>   *(Address)*

Letter salutation: *Dear Justice (surname):*
Letter salutation, old style: *Dear Mr. Justice (surname):*
Complimentary close: *Yours faithfully,*

Envelope, social:
>   *The Honourable*
>   *Justice (full name)*
>   *(Address)*

Invitation, inside envelope: *The Hon. Justice (full name)*
Place card: *The Hon. Justice (full name)*

Introduction:
>   *The Honourable (full name), Justice of the (name of court), Court of Australia*
>   OR *His/Her Honour (full name), Justice of the (name of court), Court of Australia*

Introduction, one person to another:
>   *Justice (surname), may I present* OR *Your Honour, may I present ...*
>   *... may I present Justice (surname) ...*

Conversation: *Justice (surname)*
Conversation, old style: *Mr. Justice (surname)*
Conversation, when on the bench: *Your Honour*

Chief Judge, Senior Judge, Judges: District and County Courts

NOTE: Chief judges and senior judges are addressed as *Judge (name)* and their higher status is included after the name for identification: *His Honour Judge (full name), Senior Judge, District Court of (state)*.

These judges are addressed with the courtesy title *his/her Honour* for life upon

344

application and approval. Use of a judicial honorific does not officially continue for life: Address as *Mr./Mrs. (name)* and identify as a *former judge.*
Envelope, official:
> *His/Her Honour*
>> *Judge (full name)*
>>> *(name of court)*
>>>> *(Address)*

Letter salutation: *Dear Judge (surname):*
Complimentary close: *Yours faithfully,*
Envelope, social:
> *His/Her Honour*
>> *Judge (full name)*
>>> *(Address)*

Invitation, inside envelope: *His/Her Honour Judge (full name)*
Place card: *His/Her Honour Judge (surname)*
Introduction:
> *His/Her Honour (full name), Judge of the (name of court), Court of Australia*

Introduction, one person to another:
> *Your Honour, may I present ...*
> OR *Judge (surname), may I present ...*
> *... may I present His/Her Honour Judge (surname) ...*

Conversation, initially: *Judge (surname)*
Conversation, subsequently: *Judge*
Conversation, when on the bench: *Your Honour*

Magistrate

NOTE: While the judicial honorific magistrate is often used in official situations, some magistrates prefer *Mr./Mrs./etc. (name).* In social settings address the office-holder as *Mr./Mrs./etc (full name).*
Envelope, official:
> *Magistrate (full name)*
>> *(Name of court)*
>>> *(Address)*

Letter salutation: *Dear Magistrate:* OR *Dear Magistrate (name):*
Complimentary close: *Yours faithfully,*
Place card: *Magistrate (full name)*
Introduction: *Magistrate (full name)*
Introduction, one person to another:
> *Magistrate (surname), may I present ...*
> *... may I present Magistrate (surname) ...*

Conversation, on the bench: *Your Honor*
Conversation, initially: *Magistrate (surname)*
Conversation, subsequently: *Magistrate*

Australian Municipal Officials

Lord Mayor of Darwin, Newcastle, and Wollongong
Form is the same as next listing, but courtesy title is *The Right Worshipful.*

Lord Mayor
Examples: Mr./Mrs. *(full name)*
Alderman *(full name)*
Councillor *(full name)*

NOTE: A woman who holds the office is also addressed as the *Lord Mayor.* The wife of a *lord mayor* is traditionally addressed in the city as *The Lady Mayoress of (city).*
Envelope, official:
   The Right Honourable the Lord Mayor of *(city)*
      (Honorific) (full name), (post nominals for decorations and honors)
         (Address)
Letter salutation: *Dear Lord Mayor:*
Complimentary close: *Yours faithfully,*
Envelope, social:
   The Right Honourable the Lord Mayor
      (Address)
Invitation, inside envelope: *The Right Hon. the Lord Mayor*
Place card: *The Right Hon. the Lord Mayor*
Introduction: *The Right Honourable the Lord Mayor of (city) (full name)*
Introduction, one person to another:
   Lord Mayor, may I present …
   OR *Your Honour, may I present …*
   … may I present the Right Honourable the Lord Mayor of (city),
      (honorific) (surname) …
Conversation: *Lord Mayor*

Mayor, addressed as *His/Her Worship*
Examples: Mrs. *(full name)*
Councillor *(full name)*
Alderman *(full name)*
Envelope, official:
   His/Her Worship the Mayor of *(city)*
      Mr./Mrs./Cr./etc. *(full name)*
         (Address)
Letter salutation:
   Dear Mr./Madam Mayor:
   or *Dear Mayor:*
Complimentary close: *Yours faithfully,*

Envelope, social:
>*His/Her Worship the Mayor of (city)*
>>*Mr./Mrs./Cr./etc. (full name)*
>>>*(Address)*

Invitation, inside envelope: *Mr./Mrs./Cr./etc. (full name)*
Place card: *Mr./Mrs./Cr./etc. (full name)*
Introduction: *His/Her Worship the Mayor of (city)*, *Mr./Mrs./Cr./etc. (full name)*
Introduction, one person to another:
>*Mr./Mrs./Cr./etc. (surname)*, *may I present ...*
>*... may I present His/Her Worship the Mayor of (city)*,
>>*Mr./Mrs./Cr./etc. (surname) ...*

Conversation: *Mr./Madam Mayor*

Mayor, not addressed as *His/Her Worship*

Example: *Mrs. (full name)*
>*Councillor (full name)*
>*Alderman (full name)*

Envelope, official:
>*Mr./Mrs./Cr./etc. (full name)*
>>*Mayor of (city)*
>>>*(Address)*

Letter salutation: *Dear Mayor:*
Complimentary close: *Yours faithfully,*
Envelope, social:
>*Mr./Mrs./Cr./etc. (full name)*
>>*Mayor of (city)*
>>>*(Address)*

Invitation, inside envelope: *Mr./Mrs./Cr./etc. (full name)*
Place card: *Mr./Mrs./etc. (full name)*
Introduction: *The Mayor of (city)*, *Mr./Mrs./Cr./etc. (full name)*
Introduction, one person to another:
>*Mr./Mrs./Cr./etc. (surname)*, *may I present ...*
>*... may I present the Mayor of (city)*, *Mr./Mrs./Cr./etc. (full name) ...*

Conversation: *Mr./Mrs./Cr./etc. (surname)*

Shire President

Examples: *Councillor (full name)*
Envelope, official:
>*Mr./Mrs./Cr./etc. (full name)*
>>*Shire President of (place)*
>>>*(Address)*

Letter salutation: *Dear Mr./Madam President:*
Complimentary close: *Yours faithfully,*
Envelope, social:
>*Mr./Mrs./Cr./etc. (full name)*
>>*(Address)*

Invitation, inside envelope: *Mr./Mrs./Cr./etc. (full name)*
Place card, official: *Councillor (full name)*
Place card, social: *Mr./Mrs./Cr./etc. (full name)*
Introduction:
> *Councillor (full name), Shire President of (place)*
> *The Shire President of (place), Councillor (surname)*

Introduction, one person to another:
> *Mr./Madam President* OR *Councillor (surname)*

Conversation, more formal: *Mr./Madam President*
Conversation, less formal: *Councillor (surname)*

Alderman, Commissioner, Councillor

Examples: *Councillor (full name)*
> *Commissioner (full name)*
> *Mr. (full name)*

NOTE: Use the *(name of office)* as an honorific in the salutation or conversation. When giving a complete introduction use *Mr./Mrs. (name)* to avoid using the *(name of office)* twice.

Envelope, official:
> *Mr./Mrs./Cr./etc. (full name)*
> > *(Name of office) of (organization)*
> > > *(Address)*

Letter salutation:
> *Dear Councillor/Commissioner/Alderman (full name):*
> OR *Dear Mr./Mrs./Cr./etc. (full name):*

Complimentary close: *Yours faithfully,*
Envelope, social:
> *Mr./Mrs./Cr./etc. (full name)*
> > *(Address)*

Invitation, inside envelope: *(Office) (full name)*
Place card: *(Office) (full name)*
Introduction:
> *Mr./Mrs./etc. (full name), (office) of (organization)*
> OR *(Office) of (organization), Mr./Mrs./etc. (surname),*

Introduction, one person to another:
> *Councillor/Commissioner/Alderman (full name)*

Conversation: *Councillor/Commissioner/Alderman (full name)*

Australian Diplomats

Ambassador, High Commissioner

Examples: (Full name), Ambassador of the Republic of...
(Full name), High Commissioner for...
(Full name), Australian High Commissioner

Envelope, official:
His/Her Excellency
Mr./Mrs./etc. (full name)
Ambassador of...
(Address)
His/Her Excellency
Mr./Mrs./etc. (full name)
High Commissioner for...
(Address)

Letter salutation:
Your Excellency: OR Dear Ambassador: OR Dear High Commissioner:

Complimentary close: Yours faithfully,

Envelope, social:
His/Her Excellency
Mr./Mrs./etc. (full name)
(Address)
His/Her Excellency
Ambassador (full name)
(Address)

Invitation, inside envelope:
The Ambassador of (country) OR The High Commissioner for (country)
H.E. Mr./Mrs./etc. (full name) OR Ambassador (full name)

Place card:
The Ambassador of (country) OR The High Commissioner for (country)
H.E. Mr./Mrs./etc. (full name) OR Ambassador (full name)

Introduction:
His/Her Excellency Mr./Mrs./etc. (full name), ambassador of...
His/Her Excellency Mr./Mrs./etc. (full name), high commissioner for...

Introduction, one person to another:
Your Excellency, may I present ...
... may I present His/Her Excellency Mr./Mrs./etc. (full name), (office) ...

Conversation initially: Your Excellency

Conversation subsequently: Sir OR ma'am

Spouse of an Ambassador or High Commissioner

NOTE: Australians accord the courtesy title Your Excellency to the spouse of a foreign ambassador accredited to Australia in Australia. See Australian form for Spouse of a Governor-General, page 324.

Minister

Example: (*Full name*), *Minister of the* ...
Envelope, official:
>   His/Her Excellency
>   Mr./Mrs./etc. (*full name*)
>   Minister of...
>   (*Address*)

Letter salutation: *Your Excellency:* OR *Dear Minister:*
Complimentary close: *Yours faithfully,*
Envelope, social:
>   His/Her Excellency
>   Mr./Mrs./etc. (*full name*)
>   (*Address*)

Invitation, inside envelope: H.E. Mr./Mrs./etc. (*full name*)
Place card: H.E. Mr./Mrs./etc. (*full name*)
Introduction: *His/Her Excellency Mr./Mrs./etc. (full name)*, minister of...
Introduction, one person to another:
>   *Your Excellency, may I present* ...
>   ... *may I present His/Her Excellency Mr./Mrs./etc. (full name)*, (*office*) ...

Conversation: *Your Excellency*

Peers

Knight, Dame

NOTE: See also page 404 for expanded format.
Envelope:
>   Sir (*full name*), (*initials of the order*)
>   (*Address*)
>   Dame (*full name*), (*initials of the order*)
>   (*Address*)

Letter salutation: *Dear Sir/Dame (first name):*
Complimentary close: *Yours sincerely,*
Invitation, inside envelope: *Sir/Dame (full name)*
Place card: *Sir/Dame (full name)*
Introduction: *Sir/Dame (full name)*
Introduction, one person to another: *Sir/Dame (first name)*
Conversation: *Sir/Dame (first name)*

Australian Defence Force, ADF

NOTE: ADF rank abbreviations (all capital letters) shown on pages 354 and 355 are reserved for use by the Australian Defence Force.

Chief of the Defence Force (CDF)
Chief Executive Officer
of the Defence Materiel Organization (CEO DMO)
Vice-Chief of Defence Force (VCDF)
Australian Army
    Chief of the Army (CA)
    Deputy Chief of Army, (DCA)
    Land Commander Australia
Royal Australian Navy (RAN)
    Chief of the Navy (CN)
    Deputy Chief of the Navy (DCN)
    Commander Australian Fleet (COMAUSFLTA)
Royal Australian Air Force (RAAF)
    Chief of the Air Force (CAF)
    Deputy Chief of the Air Force (DCAF)
    Air Commander Australia (ACAUST)

NOTE: Address the officers above by *(rank)* and identify by *(office)*. Adapt form for Commissioned Officers that follows.

Commissioned Officer: 011 to 03

Examples: *Major-General (full name)*, AO
                Rear-Admiral (full name), AC, RAN
                Air Vice-Marshal (full name), AO (Ret'd), RAAF

NOTE: No post-nominal branch of service abbreviation is used for the Army. For lieutenant-general, major-general, lieutenant-colonel, vice-admiral, and rear-admiral use (basic rank) in oral address and a salutation. Air chief marshal, air vice-marshal, and air marshal are all addressed as *Air Marshal (name)* orally or in a salutation. Use *(full rank)* in every instance for lieutenant-commander, air commodore, group captain, wing commander, and squadron leader.

Envelope, official, Army:
    (Full rank) (full name), *(post nominals for decorations and honors)*
        (Position/command/name of base)
            (Address)

Envelope, official, Navy or Air Force:
    (Full rank) (full name), *(post nominals for decorations and honors)*, *RAN/RAAF*
        (Position/command/name of base)
            (Address)

Letter salutation, formal: *Dear Sir/Madam:*
Letter salutation, social: *Dear (basic rank):* OR *Dear (basic rank) (surname):*
Complimentary close: *Yours faithfully,*
Envelope, social:
  (Full rank) (full name), (post nominals for decorations and honors)
    (Address)
Invitation, inside envelope: *(Full rank) (full name)*
Place card:
   (Full rank) (full name) OR *(ADF abbreviated rank) (full name)*
Introduction:
  (Full rank) (full name), (position/command/name of base)
  OR *(Position/command/name of base), (full rank) (surname)*
Introduction, one person to another: *(Full rank) (surname)*
Conversation: *(Full rank) (surname)*
Conversation, by their juniors: *Sir/ma'am*

Commissioned Officer Army and Air Force: 02 to 01
Examples: *Lieutenant (full name)*
        (Full name), Flying Officer
Envelope, official:
  Mr./Mrs./Ms. (full name)
    (Position/command/name of base)   + , RAAF *(if Air Force)*
      (Address)
Letter salutation: *Dear Sir/Madam:*
Complimentary close: *Yours faithfully,*
Envelope, social:
  Mr./Mrs./Ms. (full name)
    (Address)
Invitation, inside envelope: Mr./Mrs./Ms. *(full name),*
Place card: Mr./Mrs./Ms. *(full name),* or *(ADF abbreviated rank) (full name)*
Introduction:
  Mr./Mrs./Ms. *(full name), (position/command/name of base)*
  OR *(Position/command/name of base),* Mr./Mrs./Ms. *(surname)*
Introduction, one person to another: Mr./Mrs./Ms. *(surname)*
Conversation: Mr./Mrs./Ms. *(surname)*

Commissioned Officer Navy: 02 – Sub Lieutenant
Examples: *Sub Lieutenant (full name)*
NOTE: Adapt this form for *acting sub lieutenant.*
Envelope, official:
  Sub Lieutenant (full name), RAN
    (Position/command/name of base)
      (Address)
Letter salutation: *Dear Sir/Madam:*
Complimentary close: *Yours faithfully,*

Envelope, social:
> Sub Lieutenant (full name),
> > (Address)

Invitation, inside envelope: Sub Lieutenant (full name),
Place card: Sub Lieutenant (full name), or SBLT (full name)
Introduction:
> Sub Lieutenant (full name), (position/command/name of base)
> OR (Position/command/name of base), Sub Lieutenant (surname)

Introduction, one person to another: Sub Lieutenant (surname)
Conversation: Sub Lieutenant (surname)

Commissioned Officer Navy: 01 – Midshipman

Examples: (Full name), Midshipman
Envelope, official:
> Mr./Mrs./Ms. (full name), (post nominals for decorations and honors), RAN
> > (Position/command/name of base)
> > > (Address)

Letter salutation: Dear Sir/Madam:
Complimentary close: Yours faithfully,
Envelope, social, Navy:
> Mr./Mrs./Ms. (full name),
> > (Address)

Invitation, inside envelope: Midshipman (full name),
Place card: Mr./Mrs./Ms. (full name), or MIDN (full name)
Introduction:
> Mr./Mrs./Ms. (full name), (position/command/name of base)
> OR (Position/command/name of base), Mr./Mrs./Ms. (surname)

Introduction, one person to another: Mr./Mrs./Ms. (surname)
Conversation: Mr./Mrs./Ms. (surname)

Warrant Officers

Examples: Warrant Officer (full name), AM
             (Full name), Warrant Officer Class 2
NOTE: In the Navy, warrant officers are addressed as Mr./Mrs./Miss./Ms. (name). See form for Commissioned Officer 02 to 01 on page 352. In the Army and Air Force warrant officers are addressed as Warrant Officer (surname) or sir/ma'am. Identify a Warrant Officer of the Navy and Warrant Officer of the Air Force by (office) after Warrant Officer (name).
Envelope, official:
> Warrant Officer (full name), (post nominals for decorations and honors)
> > (Position/command/name of base)
> > > (address)

Letter salutation: Dear Sir/Madam:
Complimentary close: Sincerely yours, or Sincerely,

Australian Armed Services

COMMISSIONED PERSONNEL

	Army		Navy		Air Force
011	FM	Field Marshal	ADM	Admiral of the Fleet	AFM	Marshal of the Air Force
010	GEN	General	ADM	Admiral	ACM	Air Chief-Marshal
09	LTGEN	Lieutenant-General	VADM	Vice-Admiral	AIRMSHL	Air Marshal
08	MAJGEN	Major-General	RADM	Rear-Admiral	AVM	Air Vice-Marshal
07	BRIG	Brigadier	CDRE	Commodore	AIRCDRE	Air Commodore
06	COL	Colonel	CAPT	Captain	GPCAPT	Group Captain
05	LTCOL	Lieutenant-Colonel	CMDR	Commander	WGCDR	Wing Commander
04	MAJ	Major	LCDR	Lieutenant-Commander	SQNLDR	Squadron Leader
03	CAPT	Captain	LEUT	Lieutenant	FLTLT	Flight Lieutenant
02	LT	Lieutenant	SBLT	Sub Lieutenant	FLGOFF	Flying Officer
01	2LT	Second Lieutenant	MIDN	Midshipman	PLTOFF	Pilot Officer

Commissioned 011-01 and non-commissioned E9-E2 grades are provided for comparison to U.S. ranks and ratings only. ADF rank abbreviations are reserved for use by the Australian Defence Force.

Australian Armed Services

ENLISTED PERSONNEL

	Army		**Navy**		**Air Force**	
E9	WO	Warrant Officer	WO-N	Warrant Officer of the Navy	WOFF-AF	Warrant Officer of the Air Force
	RSM-A	Regimental Sergeant Major of the Army				
E8	WO1	Warrant Officer 1	WO	Warrant Officer	WOFF	Warrant Officer
E8	WO2	Warrant Officer 2	CPO	Chief Petty Officer		
E7	SSGT	Staff Sergeant	N/A		FSGT	Flight Sergeant
E6	SGT	Sergeant	PO	Petty Officer	SGT	Sergeant
E5	CPL	Corporal	LS	Leading Seaman	CPL	Corporal
	BDR	Bombardier				
E4	LCPL	Lance Corporal	N/A		N/A	
	LBDR	Lance Bombardier				
E3	PTE(P)	Private Proficient	AB	Able Seaman	LAC	Leading Aircraftman
					LACW	Leading Aircraftwoman
E2	PTE	Private	SMN	Seaman	AC	Aircraftman
					ACW	Aircraftwoman

Envelope, social:
> *Warrant Officer (full name)*
>> *(address)*

Invitation, inside envelope: Mr./Mrs. *(surname)*

Place card:
> *Warrant Officer (surname)*
> OR *(ADF abbreviated rank) (surname)*
> OR Mr./Mrs. *(surname)*

Introduction:
> *Warrant Officer (full name)*, *(position/command/name of base)*
> OR *(Position/command/name of base)*, *Warrant Officer (surname)*

Introduction, one person to another: *Warrant Officer (surname)*

Conversation: *Warrant Officer (surname)*

Non-Commissioned Officers E9 to E2

NOTE: Chief petty officers are informally addressed as *Chief* or *Chief (surname)* orally and in salutation.

Envelope, official:
> *(Full rank) (full name)*
>> *(Position/command/name of base)*
>>> *(Address)*

Letter salutation: Dear *(full rank)*: OR Dear *(full rank) (surname)*:

Complimentary close: *Yours faithfully,*

Envelope, social:
> *(Full rank) (full name)*
>> *(Address)*

Invitation, inside envelope: *(Full rank) (full name)*

Place card:
> *(Full rank) (full name)* or *(ADF abbreviated rank) (full name)*

Introduction:
> *(Full rank) (full name)*, *(position/command/name of base)*
> OR *(Position/command/name of base)*, *(full rank) (surname)*

Introduction, one person to another: *(Full rank) (surname)*

Conversation: *(Full rank) (surname)*

Conversation, informal: *(Full rank) (surname)*

19 British Officials

United Kingdom Chief of State

King/Queen of the United Kingdom

NOTE: Forms of address for *His/Her Majesty* make no reference to the domain.
Envelope:
>*The Private Secretary to*
>>*His/Her Majesty the King/Queen*
>>>*(Address)*

Letter salutation to a letter to the King/Queen:
>*Your Majesty:* OR *May it please Your Majesty:*

Complimentary close by non-subjects:
>*Respectfully yours,* OR *Respectfully,*

Complimentary close by subjects:
>*I remain Your Majesty's faithful and devoted servant,*

Place card:
>*Your Majesty* OR *His/Her Majesty the King/Queen*
>OR *H.M. The King/Queen*

Announced/Introduction: *His/Her Majesty the King/Queen*
Introduction, one person to another (In the United Kingdom all persons are presented to the monarch): *Your Majesty may I present …*
Conversation, initially: *Your Majesty*
Conversation, subsequently: *Sir/ma'am*

United Kingdom Executive

Prime Minister
Example: (Full name), MP
Envelope, official:
> The Right Hon.
>> (Full name), MP
>>> Prime Minister
>>>> (Address)

Letter salutation: *Dear Prime Minister:*
Complimentary close: *Yours faithfully,*
Envelope, social:
> The Prime Minister
>> (Address)

Invitation, inside envelope: *The Prime Minister*
Place card: *The Right Hon. the Prime Minister*
Introduction: *The Right Honourable (full name), the Prime Minister*
Introduction, one person to another:
> Mr./Madam Prime Minister, may I present …
> … may I present the Prime Minister

Conversation, initially: *Mr./Madam Prime Minister*
Conversation, subsequently: *Sir/madam*

The Cabinet
NOTE: Members of the Cabinet are not addressed as *the Right Honourable* because of service in the Cabinet: It is their appointment to the Privy Council that grants them this courtesy title. The precise composition of the Cabinet can vary, but it recently included:
> **Secretaries:**
>> Secretary of State for (portfolio)
>> Chief Secretary to the Treasury
>
> **Ministers:**
>> Minister for (portfolio)
>> Deputy Prime Minister
>
> **Chancellors:**
>> Lord Chancellor/Lord High Chancellor
>> Chancellor of Exchequer
>
> **Leaders:**
>> Leader of the House of Commons
>> Leader of the House of Lords/Lord Speaker
>
> **Lords:**
>> Lord Privy Seal
>> Lord High Treasurer/First Lord of the Treasury
>
> **Chief Whip**

358

Cabinet: Member of the House of Commons/MP

Examples: *(Full name)*, QC, MP
            Sir (full name), KBE, MP

Notes:

(1) Privy Counsellors in the House of Commons do not use the post-nominal abbreviation PC: Use of *the Right Honourable* suffices to note their membership.

(2) In an introduction or conversation it is acceptable to use a shortened version of the name of office held, such as *Minister (name)* or *Minister*, but, as member's of Parliament, their basic form of oral address is *Mr./Mrs./etc. (name)*.

Envelope, official:

>   *The Right Hon.*
>>   *(Full name)*, *(post nominals for decorations and honors)*, MP
>>>   *(Cabinet office held)*
>>>>   *(Address)*

>   *The Right Hon.*
>>   *Sir (full name)*, *(post nominals for decorations and honors)*, MP
>>>   *(Cabinet office held)*
>>>>   *(Address)*

Letter salutation (as appropriate):

>   *Dear Chancellor:* OR *Dear Chief Secretary:* OR *Dear Deputy Minister:*
>   OR *Dear Lord:* OR *Dear Minister:* OR *Dear Secretary of State:*

Complimentary close: *Yours faithfully,*

Envelope, social:

>   *The Right Hon.*
>>   *(Full name)*, MP
>>>   *(Address)*

Invitation, inside envelope: *The Right Hon. (full name)*, MP

Place card: *The Right Hon. (full name)*, MP

Introduction: *The Right Honourable (full name), (name of office held)*

Introduction, one person to another:

>   *(Honorific for their office) (surname)*, *may I present ...*
>   OR *Mr./Mrs./etc. (surname)*, *may I present ...*
>   *... may I present Mr./Ms./etc. (surname), (name of office*

Conversation, initially:

>   *(Honorific for their office) (surname)* OR *Mr./Mrs./etc. (surname)*

Conversation, subsequently: *(Honorific for their office)*

Cabinet: Member of the House of Lords

Examples: *Duke of (name)*, PC
            Lord (name), KCMG, PC
            Sir (name), QC, PC

NOTE: Privy Counsellors in the House of Lords use the post-nominal abbreviation PC. For a sample of how a name and forms of address for each title are written, see the listing for the specific title.

Envelope, official:
> *The Right Hon.*
>> *(Title) (name), (post nominals for decorations and honors), PC*
>>> *(Cabinet office held)*
>>>> *(Address)*

Letter salutation:
> *Dear (Cabinet office held):* OR *Dear (Standard salutation for the title):*

Introduction: *The Right Honourable (title) (name), (Cabinet office held)*

Introduction, one person to another:
> *(Title) (name), may I present …*
> *… may I present (title) (name), (Cabinet office held)*

All other forms of address: *Use standard form for his or her title.*

Other High Officials

> *Secretary of State for (portfolio)*
> *Secretary of the Exchequer*
> *Minister of State*
> *Minister of State for (portfolio)*
> *Parliamentary Undersecretary of State*
> *Parliamentary Undersecretary of State for (portfolio)*

Privy Counsellor, House of Commons/MP

Example: *The Right Hon. (full name),* MP
              The Rt. Hon. (full name), MP

NOTE: Use form for *Cabinet: Member of the House of Commons/MP,* page 359. As members of the Privy Council they are addressed as *the Right Honourable.* As members of the House of Commons they use the post-nominal abbreviation MP, and are addressed in conversation as *Mr./Mrs./etc. (name).*

Privy Counsellor, House of Lords

Examples: *Duke of (name),* PC
             Lord (name), KCMG, PC
             Sir (name), QC, PC

NOTE: Use form for *Cabinet: Member of the House of Lords,* page 359. For a sample of how a name and forms of address for each title are written, see the listing for the specific title.

House of Commons/MP

Example: *(Full name),* MP

NOTE: Use form for a *Member of the House of Commons,* page 359, except he or she may be addressed by *(office)* in the salutation or conversation, and identified as *holder of the (office)* in a writing or in a complete introduction. As a member of the House of Commons address as *Mr./Mrs./etc (name).*

Member of the House of Lords

Examples: *Baroness (name)*
Lady (name)
Lord (name), CBE
Sir (full name)

NOTE: Use form for a *Member of the House of Lords*, page 364, additionally identifying him or her by *(office)* in the address line and in an introduction. For a sample of how a name and forms of address for each title are written, see the listing for the specific title.

Not a Member of Parliament

NOTE: For a high official who is not a member of Parliament, address as Mr./Mrs. *(name)*. Identify by *(office)* in the address line and in an introduction.

Lord Chamberlain

NOTE: The Lord Chamberlain is a Privy Counsellor and a peer. Adapt form for *Privy Councellors: Peer* on page 362. Identify as the *Lord Chamberlain* in written address and in an introduction.

Chancellor of the Duchy of Lancaster

NOTE: Use form for a *Cabinet: Member of the House of Commons/MP*, page 359. Identify as the *Chancellor of the Duchy of Lancaster* in written address and in an introduction.

Privy Council

Lord President of the Council

NOTE: The Lord President of the Privy Council is a peer and Privy Counsellor. Address by *(the title he or she holds)* and identify by *(office)* in written forms of address and in a complete introduction.

Privy Counsellors: Peers

NOTE: Privy Counsellors are addressed with the courtesy title *the Right Honourable* for life. But some peers are already addressed as *the Right Honourable* because of their title. Peer Privy Counsellors may use the post-nominal abbreviation PC so their membership will not be overlooked.

Example of an envelope for a duke, who is a Privy Counsellor:

> His Grace
>> The Duke of (place), PC
>>> (Address)

Example of an envelope for a marquess, who is a Privy Counsellor:

> The Most Hon.
>> The Marquess of (name), PC
>>> (Address)

Envelope for other peers who is a Privy Counsellor:

> (Standard courtesy title for his or her title)
>> (Standard title and name), PC
>>> (Address)

All other forms of address:

> Use standard form for his or her title without reference to Privy Council.

Privy Counsellors: Commoners

Examples: Mr. *(full name)*
Mrs. *(full name)*
(Full name), PhD
(Full name), Esq.

NOTE: Privy Counsellors are addressed with the courtesy title *the Right Honourable* for life. Commoners do not use the post-nominal abbreviation *PC*, since the use of *the Right Honourable* denotes membership.

Envelope:
The Right Hon.
(Full name)
(Address)

Letter salutation: *Dear Sir:* OR *Dear Mr./Mrs./etc. (surname):*
Complimentary close: *Yours sincerely,*
Invitation, inside envelope: *The Right Hon. (full name)*
Place card: *The Right Hon. (full name)*
Introduction: *The Right Honourable Mr./Mrs./etc. (full name)*
Introduction, one person to another:
Mr./Mrs./etc. *(surname)*, *may I present …*
… may I present Mr./Mrs./etc. (surname)
Conversation: *Mr./Mrs./etc. (surname)*

Privy Counsellors: Military

Examples: Admiral *(full name)*
Air Marshal *(full name)*

NOTE: Privy Counsellors are addressed with the courtesy title *the Right Honourable* for life.

Envelope:
(Full rank) The Right Hon.
(Full name)
(Address)

Letter salutation: *Dear Sir:* OR *Dear (Full rank) (surname):*
Complimentary close: *Yours sincerely,*
Invitation, inside envelope: *(Rank) The Right Hon. (full name)*
Place card: *(Rank) The Right Hon. (full name)*
Introduction: *(Rank) The Right Honourable (full name)*
Introduction, one person to another:
(Rank) (surname), *may I present …*
… may I present (rank) (surname)
Conversation: *(Rank) (surname)*

United Kingdom Legislative

HOUSE OF LORDS

Lord Speaker of the House of Lords

Example: *The Right Hon. The Baroness (name)*

NOTE: Use *Lord Speaker of the House of Lords* for identification on the line beneath the name, above the address in the form appropriate for his or her title and membership in the House of Lords.

Envelope, official:

The Right Hon.
>   *The (title) (name)*
>>   *Lord Speaker of the House of Lords*
>>   *(Address)*

Introduction: *Use form of the name appropriate for his or her title, followed by* the Lord Speaker of the House of Lords *for identification.*

Letter salutation: *Dear Lord Speaker:*

All other forms of address: *Use standard form for his or her title.*

Duke: Member of the House of Lords

Examples: *Duke of Montrose*
                    Duke of Norfolk

NOTE: The given name of the titled person in never used.

Envelope:

His Grace
>   *The Duke of (place)*
>>   *(Address)*

Letter salutation: *Dear Duke of (place):*

Complimentary close: *Yours sincerely,*

Place card: *The Duke of (place)*

Introduction: *His Grace the Duke of (place), member of the House of Lords*

Introduction, one person to another:

>   *Your Grace, may I present ...*
>   *... may I present the Duke of (place)*

Conversation: *Your Grace*

Marquess: Member of the House of Lords

Example: *Marquess of Cholmondeley*

NOTE: The given name of the titled person in never used.

Envelope:

The Most Hon.
>   *The Marquess of Cholmondeley*
>>   *(Address)*

Letter salutation: *Dear Lord Cholmondeley:*

Complimentary close: *Yours sincerely,*
Place card: *The Most Hon. Lord Cholmondeley*
Introduction:
> *The Most Honourable the Marquess of Cholmondeley,*
> *member of the House of Lords*

Introduction, one person to another: *Lord Cholmondeley*
Conversation, initially: *Lord Cholmondeley*
Conversation, subsequently: *My Lord*

Earl: Member of the House of Lords

Examples: *Earl Ferrers*
            Earl of Rosslyn
            Earl of Mar and Kellie

NOTE: When an earldom's name has the compound form *(name one)* + *(name two)*, use the earldom's name in the following way: When *(complete name)* is called for, use *(name one)* + *(name two)*; when *(name)* is called for, use only *(name one)*. For example, *The Earl of Mar and Kellie* is addressed as *Lord Mar* in conversation. The given name of the titled person in never used. *The Right Honourable* is routinely abbreviated to *The Right Hon.* in the United Kingdom.
Envelope:
> *The Right Hon.*
> > *The Earl of (complete name)*
> > *(Address)*

Letter salutation: *Dear Lord (name):*
Complimentary close: *Yours sincerely,*
Place card: *The Right Hon. Lord (name)*
Introduction:
> *The Right Honourable the Earl of (complete name), member of the House of Lords*

Introduction, one person to another: *Lord (name)*
Conversation: *Lord (name)*

Countess: Member of the House of Lords

Example: *Countess of Mar*

NOTE: The given name of the titled person in never used. *The Right Honourable* is routinely abbreviated to *The Right Hon.* in the United Kingdom.
Envelope:
> *The Right Hon.*
> > *The Countess of Mar*
> > *(Address)*

Letter salutation: *Dear Lady Mar:*
Complimentary close: *Yours sincerely,*
Place card: *The Right Hon. Lady Mar*
Introduction:
> *The Right Honourable the Countess of Mar, member of the House of Lords*

Introduction, one person to another: *Lady Mar*
Conversation: *Lady Mar*

Viscount: Member of the House of Lords

Examples: *Viscount Astor*
              Viscount Colville of Culross

NOTE: When a viscountcy's name has the compound form *(name one)* of *(name two)*, use the viscountcy's name in the following way: When **(complete name)** is called for, use *(name one)* of *(name two)*; when **(name)** is called for, use only *(name one)*. For example, *Viscount Colville of Culross* is addressed as *Lord Colville* in conversation. The given name of the titled person is never used. *The Right Honourable* is routinely abbreviated to *The Right Hon.* in the United Kingdom.

Envelope:
>   *The Right Hon.*
>>   *The Viscount (complete name)*
>>   *(Address)*

Letter salutation: *Dear Lord (name):*
Complimentary close: *Yours sincerely,*
Place card: *The Right Hon. Lord (name)*
Introduction:
>   *The Right Honourable the Viscount (complete name), member of the House of Lords*

Introduction, one person to another: *Lord (name)*
Conversation: *Lord (name)*

Viscountess: Member of the House of Lords

Example: *Viscountess (name)*

NOTE: When a viscountcy's name has the compound form *(name one)* of *(name two)*, use the viscountcy's name in the following way: When **(complete name)** is called for, use *(name one)* of *(name two)*; when **(name)** is called for, use only *(name one)*. For example, the *Viscountess Wright of Topsdown* would be addressed as *Lady Wright* in conversation. *The Right Honourable* is routinely abbreviated to *The Right Hon.* in the United Kingdom.

Envelope:
>   *The Right Hon.*
>>   *The Viscountess (complete name)*
>>   *(Address)*

Letter salutation: *Dear Lady (name):*
Complimentary close: *Yours sincerely,*
Place card: *The Right Hon. Lord (name)*
Introduction:
>   *The Right Honourable the Viscountess (complete name),*
>>   *member of the House of Lords*

Introduction, one person to another: *Lady (name)*
Conversation: *Lady (name)*

Baron: Member of the House of Lords

Example 1: William Plinkerville, raised to the peerage (life peer) as Baron Plinkerville, is addressed as *Lord Plinkerville*.

366

Example 2: Philip Smith, raised to the peerage (life peer) as Baron Smith of Peckham, is addressed as *Lord Smith of Peckham* rather than *Lord Smith* because there is already another member who is *Lord Smith: Lord Smith of Haringey*.

NOTE: The title baron is never used in direct address. If a baron's title is in the form *(name one) of (name two)*, see examples above. The given name of the life peer is never used. *The Right Honourable* is routinely abbreviated to *The Right Hon.* in the United Kingdom.

Envelope:
> *The Right Hon.*
>> *The Lord (complete name)*
>>> *(Address)*

Letter salutation: *Dear Lord (name):*
Complimentary close: *Yours sincerely,*
Place card: *The Right Hon. The Lord (name)*
Introduction:
> *The Right Honourable the Lord (complete name), member of the House of Lords*

Introduction, one person to another: *Lord (name)*
Conversation: *Lord (name)*

Baroness: Member of the House of Lords

Examples: *Baroness Kingsmill*
Baroness Oppenheim-Barnes
Baroness Young of Hornsey
Baroness James of Holland Park

Notes: The title baroness is sometimes, but not always, used in address. A life peeress, and peeress who holds the title in her own right, can choose to be addressed as *baroness* rather than *lady*. Check for personal preference. If the peeress does not prefer *baroness*, see sample for *Lady, Member of the House of Lords*, page 368. When a baroness's name has the compound form *(name one) of (name two)*, use the *baronetcy's* name in the following way: When **(complete name)** is called for, use *(name one) of (name two)*; when **(name)** is called for, use only *(name one)*. For example, Baroness James of Holland Park is addressed as *Baroness James* in conversation. The given name of the titled person is never used.

Envelope:
> *The Right Hon.*
>> *The Baroness (complete name)*
>>> *(Address)*

Letter salutation: *Dear Baroness (name):*
Complimentary close: *Yours sincerely,*
Place card: *The Right Hon. Baroness (name)*
Introduction:
> *The Right Honourable the Baroness (complete name), member of the House of Lords*

Introduction, one person to another: *Baroness (name)*
Conversation: *Baroness (name)*

Lady: Member of the House of Lords

Example: *Lady Saltoun of Abernethy*

NOTE: A life peeresses, or peeress who holds the title in her own right, can choose to be addressed with the honorific *baroness*. Check for personal preference. When a baronetcy's name has the compound form *(name one) of (name two)*, use the baronetcy's name in the following way: When **(complete name)** is called for, use *(name one) of (name two)*; when **(name)** is called for, use only *(name one)*. For example, Lady Saltoun of Abernethy is addressed as *Lady Saltoun* in conversation. The given name of the titled person in never used.

Envelope:

> *The Right Hon.*
>> *Lady (complete name)*
>> *(Address)*

Letter salutation: *Dear Lady (name):*

Complimentary close: *Yours sincerely,*

Place card: *The Right Hon. Lady (name)*

Introduction: *The Right Honourable Lady (name), member of the House of Lords*

Introduction, one person to another: *Lady (name)*

Conversation: *Lady (name)*

Lord: Member of the House of Lords (Life Peer)

See *Baron*.

Archbishop: Member of the House of Lords

Examples: *Archbishop of Canterbury*
             Archbishop of York

NOTE: *The Right Hon.* and *the Most Rev.* are routinely abbreviated in the United Kingdom.

Envelope:

> *The Most Rev. and The Right Hon.*
>> *The Lord Archbishop of (place)*
>> *(Address)*

Letter salutation: *Dear Lord Archbishop:* OR *Your Grace:*

Complimentary close: *Yours faithfully,*

Place card: *The Archbishop of (place)*

Introduction:

> *The Most Reverend and the Right Honourable the Lord Archbishop of (place),*
>> *member of the House of Lords*

Introduction, one person to another:

> *Your Grace, may I present ...*
> *... may I present the Archbishop of (place)*

Conversation: *Your Grace*

368

Bishop: Member of the House of Lords

Examples: *Bishop of Durham*
            Bishop of Ripon and Leeds

Envelope:
   The Right Rev.
      The Lord Bishop of (place)
         (Address)

Letter salutation: *My Lord:* OR *Dear Lord Bishop:*
Complimentary close: *Yours faithfully,*
Place card: *The Lord Bishop of (place)*
Introduction:
   The Most Reverend and the Right Honourable the Lord Bishop of (place),
      member of the House of Lords
Introduction, one person to another: *The Lord Bishop of (place)* OR *Bishop (place)*
Conversation: *Your Grace, Bishop* OR *Bishop (place)* OR *Bishop (surname)*

Privy Counsellor Bishop

NOTE: Bishop members of the Privy Council are addressed with the both courtesy titles: *The Right Rev.* and *The Right Hon.*
Envelope:
   The Right Hon.
      The Right Rev.
         The Lord Bishop of (place)
            (Address)

Doctor Bishop

Example: *Bishop of Worcester* who uses *Dr.*
Envelope:
   The Right Rev.
      Dr. The Lord Bishop of (place)
         (Address)

HOUSE OF COMMONS

Speaker of the House of Commons

Example: *(Full name)*, MP
Envelope, official:
   Mr./Mrs./etc *(full name)*, *(post nominals for decorations and honors)*, MP
      Speaker of the House of Commons
         (Address)

Letter salutation: *Mr./Madam Speaker:*
Complimentary close: *Yours faithfully,*
Envelope, social:
   Mr./Mrs./etc. *(full name)*, *(post nominals)*, MP
      (Address)

Invitation, inside envelope:
    Mr./Mrs./etc. (full name), (post nominals), MP
Place card, official: Mr./Madam Speaker
Place card, social: Mr./Mrs./etc. (full name), (post nominals), MP
Introduction:
    The Right Honourable (full name), Speaker of the House of Commons
Introduction, one person to another:
    Mr./Madam Speaker, may I present …
    … may I present the Speaker of the House of Commons,
        Mr./Mrs./etc. (surname)
Conversation: Mr./Madam Speaker OR Mr./Mrs./etc. (surname)

Member of House of Commons
Examples: (Full name), MP
             (Full name), QC, MP
Envelope, official:
    Mr./Mrs./etc. (full name), (post nominals for decorations and honors), MP
      (Address)
Letter salutation: Mr./Mrs./etc. (surname):
Complimentary close: Yours faithfully,
Envelope, social:
    Mr./Mrs./etc. (full name), (post nominals), MP
      (Address)
Invitation, inside envelope:
    Mr./Mrs./etc. (full name), (post nominals), MP
Place card: Mr./Mrs./etc. (full name), (post nominals), MP
Introduction: The Right Honourable (full name), (name of office held)
Introduction, one person to another:
    Mr./Mrs./etc. (surname), may I present …
    … may I present Mr./Mrs./etc. (surname), member of Parliament
Conversation: Mr./Mrs./etc. (surname)

United Kingdom Judiciary

Senior Lord of Appeal in Ordinary
Lord of Appeal in Ordinary

Example: *Lord (name), PC*

NOTE: Peers, except dukes, are addressed in conversation as *Lord/Lady (name)*. Baronets and knights are addressed in conversation as *Sir/Dame (name)*. Check for the exact title of the officeholder.

Envelope, official:
> *The Rt. Hon.*
>> *The Lord (name), PC*
>>> *(Name of office)*
>>> *(Address)*

Introduction: *The (name of office), (form of name for his or her title)*
All other forms of address: *Use standard form for his or her title.*

Lord Chief Justice of England and Wales

Example: *Lord (name), PC*

NOTE: Peers, except dukes, are addressed in conversation as *Lord/Lady (name)*. Baronets and knights are addressed in conversation as *Sir/Dame (name)*. Check for the exact title of the officeholder.

Envelope, official:
> *The Rt. Hon.*
>> *Lord Chief Justice of England and Wales*
>>> *(Address)*

Salutation: *My Lord:* OR *Dear Lord Chief Justice:*
Introduction:
> *The Lord Chief Justice of England and Wales, (form of name for the title) …*
All other forms of address: *Use standard form for his or her title.*

Deputy Lord Chief Justice of England and Wales

NOTE: Peers, except dukes, are addressed in conversation as *Lord/Lady (name)*. Baronets and knights are addressed in conversation as *Sir/Dame (name)*. Check for the exact title of the officeholder.

Envelope, official:
> *The Rt. Hon.*
>> *Deputy Lord Chief Justice of England and Wales*
>>> *(Address)*

Salutation: *My Lord:*
Introduction:
> *The Deputy Lord Chief Justice of England and Wales, (form of name for the title) …*
All other forms of address: *Use standard form for his or her title.*

Master of the Roll: Court of Appeal, Civil Division

Example: *Sir (name)*

NOTE: Peers, except dukes, are addressed in conversation as *Lord/Lady (name)*. Baronets and knights are addressed in conversation as *Sir/Dame (name)*. For a sample of how a name and forms of address for each title are written, see the listing for the specific title.

Envelope, official:

> *The Rt. Hon.*
>> *The Master of the Roll*
>> *Court of Appeal*
>> *(Address)*

Salutation: *Dear Master of the Roll:*

Introduction: *The Master of the Roll, the (form of name for his or her title) …*

All other forms of address: *Use standard form for his or her title.*

Vice President of the Court of Appeal, Civil Division

Example: *Sir (full name)*

NOTE: Peers, except dukes, are addressed in conversation as *Lord/Lady (name)*. Baronets and knights are addressed in conversation as *Sir/Dame (name)*. Check for the exact title of the officeholder. Justices are addressed with surname only unless there are two justices with the same surname.

Envelope, official:

> *The Rt. Hon.*
>> *Lord Justice (surname)*
>>> *Vice President of the Court of Appeal*
>>> *(Address)*

Introduction:

> *The Vice President of the Court of Appeal, the (form of name for his or her title) …*

All other forms of address: *Use standard form for his or her title.*

Senior Presiding Judge For England and Wales
Judge of the Court of Appeal of England and Wales

Examples: *Lord (full name)*
Baroness (name)
Sir (full name)
Sir (full name), CVO
Lady (full name), DBE

NOTE: Peers, except dukes, are addressed in conversation as *Lord/Lady (name)*. Baronets and knights are addressed in conversation as *Sir/Dame (name)*. Check for the exact title of the officeholder. Justices are addressed with *surname only* unless there are two justices with the same surname.

Envelope, official:

> *The Rt. Hon.*
>> *Lord/Lady Justice (surname), (post nominals for decorations and honors)*
>>> *(Name of court)*
>>> *(Address)*

372

Introduction: *The Right Honourable Lord/Lady Justice (surname)* ...
All other forms of address: *Use standard form for his or her title.*

Lord High Chancellor
Lord Chancellor of the High Court of Justice

Examples: *The Right Hon. (full name)*, MP
            Sir (name), QC, PC
            Lord (name), KCMG, PC

NOTE: Peers, except dukes, are addressed in conversation as *Lord/Lady (name)*. Baronets and knights are addressed in conversation as *Sir/Dame (name)*. Check for the exact title of the officeholder.
Envelope, official:
   The Right Hon.
      The Lord Chancellor
         (Address)
Letter salutation: *Dear Lord Chancellor:* OR *My Lord:*
Introduction: *The Right Honourable Lord Chancellor*
All other forms of address: *Use standard form for his or her title.*

The Chancellor of the High Court

Example: *Sir (full name)*, CVO, PC

NOTE: Peers, except dukes, are addressed in conversation as *Lord/Lady (name)*. Baronets and knights are addressed in conversation as *Sir/Dame (name)*. Check for the exact title of the officeholder. Justices are addressed with *surname only* unless there are two justices with the same surname.
Envelope, official:
   The Right Hon.
      Lord/Lady Justice (surname), *(post nominals for decorations and honors)*
         Chancellor of the High Court
            (Address)
Introduction: *The Chancellor of the High Court, (form of name for his/her title)* ...
All other forms of address: *Use standard form for his or her title.*

President of the Family Division of the High Court

Examples: *Sir (full name)*, Kt
            Dame (full name), GBE

NOTE: Peers, except dukes, are addressed in conversation as *Lord/Lady (name)*. Baronets and knights are addressed in conversation as *Sir/Dame (name)*. Check for the exact title of the officeholder. Justices are addressed with *surname only* unless there are two justices with the same surname.
Envelope, official:
   The Right Hon.
      Lord/Lady Justice (surname), *(post nominals for decorations and honors)*
         President of the Family Division
            (Address)
Introduction: *The President of the Family Division, (form of name for his/her title)* ...
All other forms of address: *Use standard form for his or her title.*

The Official Guide to Names, Titles, and Forms of Address   **373**

President of the Queen's Bench of the High Court

Example: Sir (full name)

NOTE: Peers, except dukes, are addressed in conversation as Lord/Lady (name). Baronets and knights are addressed in conversation as Sir/Dame (name). Check for the exact title of the officeholder. Justices are addressed with surname only unless there are two justices with the same surname.

Envelope, official:

> The Right Hon.
>> Lord/Lady Justice (surname), (post nominals for decorations and honors)
>>> President of the Queen's Bench
>>> (Address)
>
> OR   The Right Hon.
>> Mr./Madame Justice (surname), (post-nominals)
>>> President of the Queen's Bench
>>> (Address)

Introduction:

> The President of the Queen's Bench, (form of name for his/her title) ...

All other forms of address: Use standard form for his or her title.

Justice of the High Court, Chancery Division
Justice of the High Court, Family Division
Justice of the High Court, Queen's Bench

Examples: Sir (full name), OBE
              Dame (full name), DBE

NOTE: Justices are addressed by surname only unless there are two justices with the same surname, in which case they are addressed with their full name. Women justices are addressed as Mrs. Justice (surname) regardless of marital status. Peers, except dukes, are addressed in conversation as Lord/Lady (name). Baronets and knights are addressed in conversation as Sir/Dame (name). Check for title of the officeholder.

Envelope, official:

> The Hon.
>> Mr./Mrs. Justice (surname), (post nominals for decorations and honors)
>>> (Name of court)
>>> (Address)

Introduction:

> His/Her Honourable Mr./Mrs. Justice (surname), of the (name of court) ...

Conversation, official: My Lord OR Your Lordship

All other forms of address: Use standard form for his or her title.

Presiding Judge of a Crown or Circuit Court
Senior Circuit Judge of a Crown or County Court
Circuit Judge of a Crown or County Court

Examples: *(Full name)*
Sir (full name)
(Full name), QC

NOTE: If addressing a judge as a presiding or senior judge, include the designation on an official envelope and in an introduction. Judges are addressed with *surname only* unless there are two justices with the same surname. If the judge is a knight, forms of address for his or her title also apply.

Envelope, official:
His/Her Honour
Judge (surname), (post nominals for decorations and honors)
(Name of court)
(Address)

Letter salutation: *Dear Sir/Madam:*
Complimentary close: *Yours faithfully,*
Envelope, social:
Mr./Mrs./etc. (full name)
(Address)

Invitation, inside envelope: *Mr./Mrs./etc. (surname)*
Place card, social: *Mr./Mrs./etc. (full name)*
Place card, official: *Judge (surname)*
Introduction:
His/Her Honour Judge (surname), of the (name of court) ...
Introduction, one person to another:
Judge (surname), may I present ...
... may I present Judge (surname)
Conversation, on the bench: *Your Honour*
Conversation: *Judge (surname)* OR *Judge*

Judge of a Lower Court

NOTE: If addressing a judge as a presiding, resident, or senior judge, include the full name of office on an official envelope and in an introduction. Judges are addressed with *surname only* unless there are two justices with the same surname. If the judge is a knight, the forms of address for his or her title also apply.

Envelope, official:
His/Her Honour
Judge (surname)
(Name of court)
(Address)

Letter salutation: *Dear Sir/Madam:*
Complimentary close: *Yours faithfully,*

Envelope, social:
> Mr./Mrs./etc. (full name)
>> (Address)

Invitation, inside envelope: Mr./Mrs./etc. (surname)
Place card, social: Mr./Mrs./etc. (name)
Place card, official: Judge (surname)
Introduction:
> His/Her Honour Judge (surname), of the (name of court) ...

Introduction, one person to another:
> Your Honour, may I present ...
> ... may I present His/Her Honour Judge (surname)

Conversation, on the bench: Your Honour
Conversation: Judge (surname), Judge, Sir or Ma'am

Magistrate
Envelope, official:
> (Full name), Esq.
>> (Name of court)
>>> (Address)

Letter salutation: Dear Sir:
Complimentary close: Yours faithfully,
Envelope, social:
> (Full name), Esq.
>> (Address)

Invitation, inside envelope: Mr./Mrs./etc. (surname)
Place card, social: Mr./Mrs./etc. (full name)
Place card, official: (Full name), Esq.
Introduction: His/Her Worship (full name), of the (name of court) ...
Introduction, one person to another:
> Mr./Mrs./etc. (surname), may I present ...
> ... may I present His/Her Worship (surname)

Conversation, on the bench: Your worship
Conversation: Mr./Mrs./etc. (surname)

Municipal Officials

Lord-Lieutenant

NOTE: Address in writing by his or her personal title and identify as *H.M. Lord-Lieutenant of (place)*. Address in conversation initially as *My Lord-Lieutenant* and subsequently by the form appropriate for his or her personal title.

High Sheriff

NOTE: The office of high sheriff is appointed for a county by the sovereign, in contrast with an appointed or elected sheriff who serves a town or village.
Envelope, official:
> *(Full name), Esq.*
>> *High Sheriff of (place)*
>>> *(Address)*

Letter salutation: *Dear Sir:*
Complimentary close: *Yours faithfully,*
Envelope, social:
> *(Full name), Esq.*
>> *(Address)*

Invitation, inside envelope: *Mr./Mrs./etc. (surname)*
Place card, social: *Mr./Mrs./etc. (full name)*
Place card, official: *(Full name), Esq.*
Introduction:
> *Mr./Mrs./etc. (full name), of the High Sheriff of (place)*

Introduction, one person to another:
> *Mr./Mrs./etc. (surname), may I present ...*
> *... may I present Mr./Mrs./etc. (surname)*

Conversation: *Sheriff* OR *Mr./Mrs. Sheriff* OR *Mr./Mrs./etc. (surname)*

Lord Mayor

NOTE: Belfast, Dublin, Edinburgh, Glasgow, the City of London, and many other cities have lord mayors. A woman who holds the office is also addressed as *the Lord Mayor*. The wife of a lord mayor is traditionally addressed in the city as *the Lady Mayoress of (city)*.
Envelope, official:
> *The Right Honourable the Lord Mayor of (city)*
>> *(Honorific if presented) (full name), (post nominal decorations or honors)*
>>> *(Address)*

Letter salutation: *Dear Lord Mayor:*
Complimentary close: *Yours faithfully,*
Envelope, social:
> *The Right Honourable the Lord Mayor*
>> *(Address)*

Invitation, inside envelope:
> *The Right Hon. the Lord Mayor*

Place card:
> *The Right Hon. the Lord Mayor*
> OR *The Lord Mayor of (city)*

Introduction: *The Right Honourable, the Lord Mayor of (city) (full name)*
Introduction, one person to another:
> *Lord Mayor, may I present ...*
> *... may I present the Right Honourable, the Lord Mayor of (city),*
> > *(Honorific) (surname)*

Conversation: *Lord Mayor*

Mayor of a City

Envelope, official:
> *The Right Worshipful the Mayor of (city)*
> > *(Honorific if presented) (full name)*
> > > *(Address)*

Letter salutation: *Dear Sir/Madam:*
Complimentary close: *Yours faithfully,*
Envelope, social:
> *The Right Worshipful the Mayor of (city)*
> > *(Address)*

Invitation, inside envelope: *Mr./Mrs./Cr./etc. (full name)*
Place card:
> *The Right Worshipful the Mayor*
> OR *The Mayor of (city)*

Introduction:
> *The Right Worshipful the Mayor of (city), Mr./Mrs./Cr./etc. (full name)*
Introduction, one person to another:
> *Mr./Madam Mayor, may I present ...*
> *... may I present His/Her Worship the Mayor of (city), (Honorific) (surname)*

Conversation: *Mr./Madam Mayor*

Mayor of a Town

Example: *Mr./Mrs./etc. (full name)*
Envelope, official:
> *The Worshipful the Mayor of (town)*
> > *(Honorific if presented) (full name)*
> > > *(Address)*

Letter salutation: *Dear Sir/Madam:*
Complimentary close: *Yours faithfully,*
Envelope, social:
> *The Worshipful the Mayor of (town)*
> > *(Address)*

Invitation, inside envelope: *(Honorific) (full name)*
Place card: *The Worshipful the Mayor* OR *The Mayor of (town)*
Introduction: *The Worshipful the Mayor of (town), (Honorific) (full name)*

378

Introduction, one person to another:
>Mr./Madam Mayor, may I present ...
>... may I present His/Her Worship the Mayor of (town), (Honorific) (surname)

Conversation: Mr./Madam Mayor

President or Chairman of a County Council
Example: Cr. (full name)
Envelope, official:
>The President/Chairman of the (name) County Council
>>Cr./etc. (full name)
>>>(Address)

Letter salutation: Dear Mr./Madam President/Chairman:
Complimentary close: Yours faithfully,
Envelope, social:
>Cr./etc. (full name)
>>(Address)

Invitation, inside envelope: Cr./etc. (full name)
Place card: Cr./etc. (full name)
Introduction:
>Councillor (full name), president/chairman of the (name) County Council
>The president/chairman of the (name) County Council, Councillor (surname)

Introduction, one person to another:
>Mr./Madam President/Chairman OR Councillor (surname)

Conversation: Mr./Madam President/Chairman

Deputy Mayor
Example: Mr./Mrs./etc. (full name)
Envelope, official:
>Mr./Mrs./etc. (full name)
>>Deputy Mayor of (town)
>>>(Address)

Letter salutation: Dear Sir/Madam:
Complimentary close: Yours faithfully,
Envelope, social:
>Mr./Mrs./etc. (full name)
>>(Address)

Invitation, inside envelope: Mr./Mrs./etc. (full name)
Place card: The Deputy Mayor OR Mr./Mrs./etc. (full name)
Introduction: Mr./Mrs./etc. (full name)
Introduction, one person to another:
>Mr./Mrs./etc. (surname), may I present ...
>... may I present the Deputy Mayor of (town), Mr./Mrs./etc. (surname)

Conversation: Mr./Mrs./etc. (full name)

Alderman

Example: *Mr./Mrs./etc. (full name)*
              Sir (full name)

Envelope, official:
    Mr./Mrs./etc. Alderman (full name)
        (Address)
    Alderman Sir/Dame (full name)
        (Address)

Letter salutation: *Dear Alderman:* OR *Dear Madam Alderman:*, OR *Dear Sir/Madam:*

Complimentary close: *Yours faithfully,*

Envelope, social:
    Mr./Mrs./etc. (full name)
        (Address)
    Sir/Dame (full name)
        (Address)

Invitation, inside envelope:
    Mr./Mrs./etc. (full name)
    Sir/Dame (full name)

Place card, official:
    Mr./Mrs./etc. Alderman (full name)
    Alderman Sir/Dame (full name)

Place card, social:
    Mr./Mrs./etc. (full name)
    Sir/Dame (full name)

Introduction:
    Mr./Mrs./etc. Alderman (full name)
    Alderman Sir/Dame (full name)

Introduction, one person to another:
    Mr./Mrs./etc. Alderman (full name), may I present ...
    ... may I present Mr./Mrs./etc. Alderman (full name)
    OR *Alderman Sir/Dame (full name), may I present ...*
        ... may I present Alderman Sir/Dame (full name)

Conversation:
    Mr./Mrs./etc. Alderman (full name)
    Alderman Sir/Dame (full name)

Councillor

Examples: *Cr. (full name)*
                Sir (full name)

Envelope, official:
    Councillor (full name)
        (Address)
    Councillor Mrs./Miss (full name)
        (Address)
    Councillor Sir/Dame (full name)
        (Address)

Letter salutation: *Dear Councillor:*
Complimentary close: *Yours faithfully,*

Envelope, social:
    Mr./Mrs./Miss/etc. (full name)
        (Address)
    Sir/Dame (full name)
        (Address)

Invitation, inside envelope:
    Mr./Mrs./etc. (full name)
    Sir/Dame (full name)

Place card, official:
    Councillor (full name)
    Councillor Mrs./Miss (full name)
    Councillor Sir/Dame (full name)

Place card, social:
    Mr./Mrs./etc. (full name)
    Sir/Dame (full name)

Introduction:
    Councillor (full name)
    Councillor Mrs./Miss (full name)
    Councillor Sir/Dame (full name)

Introduction, one person to another:
    Councillor (full name), may I present ...
    ... may I present Councillor (full name)
    Councillor Mrs./Miss (full name), may I present ...
    ... may I present Mrs./Miss Councillor (full name)
    Councillor Sir/Dame (full name), may I present ...
    ... may I present Councillor Sir/Dame (full name)

Conversation:
    Councillor (full name)
    Councillor Mrs./Miss (full name)
    Councillor Sir/Dame (full name)

Justice of the Peace
NOTE: If the justice of the peace has a personal title, address in writing by his or her personal title and add the post-nominal abbreviation *JP* after the name.
Envelope, official:
>*(Full name)*, *JP*
>>*(Address)*

Letter salutation: *Dear Sir/Madam:*
Complimentary close: *Yours faithfully,*
Envelope, social:
>*(Full name)*
>>*(Address)*

Invitation, inside envelope: *Mr./Mrs./etc. (surname)*
Place card, official: *(Full name)*, *JP*
Place card, social: *Mr./Mrs./etc. (full name)*
Introduction: *His/Her Worship (full name)*, *Justice of the Peace ...*
Introduction, one person to another:
>*Mr./Mrs./etc. (surname)*, *may I present ...*
>*... may I present His/Her Worship (surname)*

Conversation, on the bench: *Your Worship*
Conversation: *Mr./Mrs./etc. (surname)*

Clerk of a County Council
Town Clerk
NOTE: Address in writing as *Mr./Mrs./etc. (name)* and identify by office.

Heads of Department of Law Enforcement
Offices: *Commissioner*
Deputy Commissioner OR *Assistant Commissioner*
Chief Superintendent OR *Superintendent*
Chief Constable
Deputy Chief Constable OR *Assistant Chief Constable*

Examples: *(Full name)*, *Esq. OBE*
(Full name), *Esq. QPM*
Sir (full name), *CBE*

Envelope, official:
>*(Full name)*, *Esq.*, *(post nominals for decorations and honors)*
>>*(Name of office)*
>>>*(Name of police department)*
>>>>*(Address)*
>*Sir/Dame (full name)*, *(post nominals for decorations and honors)*
>>*(Name of office)*
>>>*(Name of police department)*
>>>>*(Address)*

Letter salutation: *Dear (name of office):*
Complimentary close: *Yours faithfully,*

Envelope, social:
  Mr./Mrs./etc. *(full name)*
    (Address)
  Sir/Dame (full name)
    (Address)
Invitation, inside envelope:
  Mr./Mrs./etc. *(surname)*
  Sir/Dame (full name)
Place card, social:
  Mr./Mrs./etc. *(full name)*
  Sir/Dame (full name), *(Name of office)* ...
Place card, official: *(Name of office)*
Introduction:
  Mr./Mrs./etc. *(full name)*, *(name of office)* of the *(name of police department)* ...
  Sir/Dame (full name), *(name of office)* of the *(name of police department)* ...
Introduction, one person to another:
  Mr./Mrs./etc. *(surname)*, *may I present* ...
  Sir/Dame (name), *may I present* ...
Conversation, formally: *(Name of office)*
Conversation, less formally:
  Mr./Mrs./etc. *(full name)*
  Sir/Dame (name)

Chief Inspector, Constable, Detective, Inspector, Sergeant

NOTE: Ranks may or may not be used socially: Check for preference.
Envelope, official:
  (Rank) (full name)
    (Name of police department)
      (Address)
Letter salutation: Dear *(rank) (surname)*:
Complimentary close: *Yours faithfully,*
Envelope, social:
  Mr./Mrs./etc. *(full name)*
    (Address)
Invitation, inside envelope: Mr./Mrs./etc. *(surname)*
Place card, social: Mr./Mrs./etc. *(full name)*
Place card, official: *(Rank) (full name)*
Introduction: *(Rank) (full name)* of the *(name of police department)* ...
Introduction, one person to another: Mr./Mrs./etc. *(surname)*, *may I present* ...
Conversation, formally: *(Rank) (surname)*
Conversation, less formally: *(Rank only)*

United Kingdom Armed Services

Commissioned Officer with a Personal Title

Example: Lord (name), (post-nominal initials)
NOTE: A titled woman would be addressed as *Lady* in place of *Lord*. For details on the use of a noble name see the listing for the specific title under *British Royalty and Nobility*. Social forms are included in that listing.
Envelope:
> *(Full rank) Lord (name), (post nominals for decorations and honors)*
> > *(Address)*

Letter salutation: *Dear Lord (name):*
Complimentary close: *Yours sincerely,*
Official invitation, envelope:
> *(Full rank) Lord (name), (post nominals for decorations and honors)*
> > *(Address)*

Official invitation, inside envelope: *(Full rank) Lord (name)*
Official place card: *(Full rank) Lord (name)*
Introduction: *(Full rank) Lord (name)*
Introduction, one person to another:
> *Lord (name), may I present ...*
> *... may I present Lord (name)*

Conversation: *Lord (name)*

Example: The Hon. (full name), (post-nominal initials)
NOTE: For details on use of a noble name, see the listing for the specific title under *British Royalty and Nobility*. Social forms are included in that listing.
Envelope:
> *(Full rank) the Hon. (full name), (post nominals for decorations and honors)*
> > *(Address)*

Letter salutation: *Dear (full rank) (surname):*
Complimentary close: *Yours sincerely,*
Official invitation, envelope:
> *(Full rank) the Hon. (full name), (post nominals for decorations and honors)*
> > *(Address)*

Official invitation, inside envelope: *(Full rank) (surname)*
Official place card: *(Full rank) (surname)*
Introduction: *(Full rank) the Hon. (full name)*
Introduction, one person to another:
> *(Full rank) (surname), may I present ...*
> *... may I present (Full rank) (surname)*

Conversation: *(Full rank) (surname)* OR *(Rank only)*

Example: Sir (full name), (post-nominal initials)

NOTE: A titled woman would be addressed as *Dame* in place of *Sir*. Use of the forms of address by military rank or by personal title varies. Check for the preference of the bearer.

Envelope:
(Full rank) Sir (full name), *(post nominals for decorations and honors)*
(Address)

Letter salutation: *Dear (full rank) (surname):* OR *Dear Sir (first name):*
Complimentary close: *Yours sincerely,*
Official invitation, envelope:
(Full rank) Sir (full name), *(post nominals for decorations and honors)*
(Address)

Official invitation, inside envelope: *(Full rank) (surname)* OR *Sir (first name)*
Official place card: *(Full rank) (surname)* OR *Sir (first name)*
Introduction: *(Full rank) Sir (full name)*
Introduction, one person to another:
(Full rank) (surname), may I present ...
OR *Sir (first name), may I present ...*
... may I present (Full rank) (surname)
OR *... may I present Sir (first name)*
Conversation: *(Full rank) (surname)* OR *Sir (first name)*

Example: Sir (full name), Bt., (post-nominal initials)

NOTE: A woman holding a baronetcy is addressed as *Dame (full name)*, *Btss*.

Envelope:
(Full rank) Sir (full name), *Bt.*, *(post nominals for decorations and honors)*
(Address)

Letter salutation: *Dear (full rank) (surname):* OR *Dear Sir (first name):*
Complimentary close: *Yours sincerely,*
Official invitation, envelope:
(Full rank) Sir (full name), *Bt.*, *(post nominals for decorations and honors)*
(Address)

Official invitation, inside envelope: *(Full rank) (surname)* OR *Sir (first name)*
Official place card: *(Full rank) (surname)* OR *Sir (first name)*
Introduction: *(Full rank) Sir (full name)*
Introduction, one person to another:
(Full rank) (surname), may I present ...
OR *Sir (first name), may I present ...*
... may I present (Full rank) (surname)
OR *... may I present Sir (first name)*
Conversation: *(Full rank) (surname)* OR *Sir (first name)*

British Army and Royal Marines: OI1 to O3

Examples: General *(full name)*
             Lieutenant-General *(full name)*
             Major-General *(full name)*
             Brigadier *(full name)*
             Colonel *(full name)*
             Lieutenant-Colonel *(full name)*
             Major *(full name)*
             Captain *(full name)*

Army envelope, official:
    (Full rank) (full name), (post nominals for decorations and honors)
        (Position/command/name of base)
            (Address)

Marines envelope, official:
    (Full rank) (full name), (post nominals for decorations and honors), RM
        (Position/command/name of base)
            (Address)

Letter salutation:
    Dear Sir/Madam: OR *Dear (full rank) (surname):*

Complimentary close: *Yours faithfully,*

Envelope, social:
    (Full rank) (full name), (post nominals for decorations and honors)
        (Address)

Invitation, inside envelope: *(Full rank) (full name)*

Place card:
    (Full rank) (full name) OR *(Abbreviated rank) (full name)*

Introduction:
    (Full rank) (full name), (position/command/name of base)
    OR *(Position/command/name of base), (full rank) (surname)*

Introduction, one person to another: *(Full rank) (surname)*

Conversation: *(Full rank) (surname)*

Conversation, by their juniors: *Sir/ma'am*

British Army and Royal Marines: O2 to O1

NOTE: It is a custom for higher-ranking officers to address sub-lieutenants in conversation as *Mr./Mrs. (surname)*. Civilians should use *(full rank) (surname)*.

Examples: Lieutenant *(full name)*
             Second Lieutenant *(full name)*

Army envelope, official:
    (Full rank) (full name), (post nominals for decorations and honors)
        (Position/command/name of base)
            (Address)

Marines envelope, official:
> *(Full rank) (full name)*, *(post nominals for decorations and honors)*, RM
>> *(Position/command/name of base)*
>>> *(Address)*

Letter salutation: *Dear (full rank) (surname):*
Complimentary close: *Yours faithfully,*
Envelope, social:
> *(Full rank) (full name)*, *(post nominals for decorations and honors)*
>> *(Address)*

Invitation, inside envelope: *(Full rank) (full name)*
Place card:
> *(Full rank) (full name)* OR *(Abbreviated rank) (full name)*

Introduction:
> *(Full rank) (full name)*, *(position/command/name of base)*
> OR *(Position/command/name of base)*, *(full rank) (surname)*

Introduction, one person to another: *(Full rank) (surname)*
Conversation: *(Full rank) (surname)*
Conversation, by their juniors: *Sir* OR *ma'am*

Royal Navy and Royal Air Force: O11 to O8

Examples: *Admiral (full name)*
> *Vice-Admiral (full name)*, OBE
> *Rear-Admiral (full name)*
> *Air Chief-Marshal (full name)*, VC
> *Air Marshal (full name)*
> *Air Vice-Marshal (full name)*

NOTE: Air Chief-Marshal, Air Marshal, and Air Vice-Marshal are all addressed as *Air Marshal (name)* orally, but by *(full rank)(name)* in writing. Post nominals for branch of service, *RN* and *RAF*, are not used with these ranks.

Envelope, official:
> *(Full rank) (full name)*, *(post nominals for decorations and honors)*
>> *(Position/command/name of base)*
>>> *(Address)*

Letter salutation: *Dear Sir/Madam:* OR *Dear (full rank) (surname):*
Complimentary close: *Yours faithfully,*
Envelope, social:
> *(Full rank) (full name)*, *(post nominals for decorations and honors)*
>> *(Address)*

Invitation, inside envelope: *(Full rank) (full name)*
Place card:
> *(Full rank) (full name)* OR *(Abbreviated rank) (full name)*

continues on page 34

British Armed Services

Ranks and Ratings of the Services (O11-O1 grades at left are U.S. grades are for comparison to U.S. ranks only)

	BRITISH ARMY & ROYAL MARINES	ROYAL NAVY	ROYAL AIR FORCE
O11	FM Field Marshal (Army only)	Admiral of the Fleet	MRAF Marshal of the Royal Air Force
O10	Gen General	Adm Admiral	Air Chf Mshl Air Chief-Marshal
O9	Lt-Gen Lieutenant-General	VAdm Vice-Admiral	Air Mshl Air Marshal
O8	Maj-Gen Major-General	RAdm Rear-Admiral	AVM Air Vice-Marshal
O7	Brig Brigadier	Cdre Commodore	Air Cdre Air Commodore
O6	Col Colonel	Capt Captain	Gp Capt Group Captain
O5	Lt-Col Lieutenant-Colonel	Cdr Commander	Wg Cdr Wing Commander
O4	Maj Major	Lt Cdr Lieutenant-Commander	Sqn Ldr Squadron Leader
O3	Capt Captain	Lt Lieutenant	Flt Lt Flight Lieutenant
O2	Lt Lieutenant	SLt Sub-Lieutenant	Fg Off Flying Officer
O1	2Lt Second Lieutenant	MIDN Midshipman	Plt Off Pilot Officer
	OCdt Cadet	O/C Cadet	OCdt Officer Cadet

British Armed Services

Ranks and Ratings of the Services
(E9-E1 grades at left are U.S. grades and are for comparison to U.S. ratings only)

	BRITISH ARMY & ROYAL MARINES	ROYAL NAVY	ROYAL AIR FORCE
E9	WO1 Warrant Officer Class 1 / Regimental Sergeant Major	WO-1 Warrant Officer Class 1	WO Warrant Officer
E8	WO2 Warrant Officer Class 2	WO2 Warrant Officer Class 2	N/A N/A
E7	SSgt Staff Sergeant (Army) / CSgt Color Sergeant (Marines)	CPO Chief Petty Officer	FS Flight Sergeant / Chf Tech Chief Technician
E6	Sgt Sergeant	PO Petty Officer	Sgt Sergeant
E5	N/A N/A	N/A N/A	N/A N/A
E4	LCpl Lance Sergeant / Cpl Corporal	N/A Leading Seaman	Cpl Corporal
E3	LCpl Lance Corporal / LBdr Lance Bombardier	N/A N/A	Jnr Tech Junior Technician
E2	Pte Private	N/A Able Seaman	SAC Tech Senior Aircraft Technician / SAC Senior Aircraftman/woman / LAC Leading Aircraftman/woman
E1	Pte Private	N/A New Entry	

continued

Introduction:
    (Full rank) (full name), *(position/command/name of base)*
    OR *(Position/command/name of base)*, *(full rank) (surname)*
Introduction, one person to another: *(Full rank) (surname)*
Conversation: *(Full rank) (surname)*
Conversation, by their juniors: *Sir/ma'am*

Royal Navy and Royal Air Force: 07 to 04

Examples: *Commodore (full name), RN*
             Captain (full name), RN
             Commander (full name), RN
             Lieutenant-Commander (full name), RN
             Lieutenant (full name), RN
             Air Commodore (full name), RAF
             Group Captain (full name), RAF
             Wing Commander (full name), RAF
             Squadron Leader (full name), RAF
             Flight Lieutenant (full name), RAF

NOTE: Navy lieutenants are addressed socially as Mr./Mrs. *(name)*.
Envelope, official:
    (Full rank) (full name), *(post nominals for decorations and honors)*, *RN/RAF*
        (Position/command/name of base)
        (Address)
Letter salutation: *Dear Sir/Madam:* OR *Dear (full rank) (surname):*
Complimentary close: *Yours faithfully,*
Envelope, social:
    (Full rank) (full name), *(post nominals for decorations and honors)*
        (Address)
Invitation, inside envelope: *(Full rank) (full name)*
Place card:
    (Full rank) (full name) OR *(Abbreviated rank) (full name)*
Introduction:
    (Full rank) (full name), *(position/command/name of base)*
    OR *(Position/command/name of base)*, *(full rank) (surname)*
Introduction, one person to another: *(Full rank) (surname)*
Conversation: *(Full rank) (surname)*
Conversation, by their juniors: *Sir/ma'am*

Royal Navy and Royal Air Force: 02, 01, and Cadets

Examples: *Sub-Lieutenant (full name), RN*
             Midshipman (full name), RN
             Cadet (full name), RN

Flying Officer (full name), RAF
Pilot Officer (full name), RAF
Officer Cadet (full name), RAF

NOTE: It is a custom for higher-ranking officers to address sub-lieutenants, mid-shipman, flight officers and pilot officers in a salutation and conversation as Mr./Mrs. *(surname)*. Civilians should use *(full rank) (surname)*.

Envelope, official:
   (Full rank) (full name), (post nominals for decorations and honors), RN/RAF
      (Position/command/name of base)
         (Address)

Letter salutation:
   Dear (full rank) (surname):

Complimentary close: *Yours faithfully,*

Envelope, social:
   Mr./Mrs. (full name)
      (Address)

Invitation, inside envelope: Mr./Mrs. *(full name)*

Place card:
   (Full rank) (full name) or (Service-specific abbreviated full rank) (full name)

Introduction:
   (Full rank) (full name), (position/command/name of base)
   OR *(Position/command/name of base), (full rank) (surname)*

Introduction, one person to another: *(Full rank) (surname)*

Conversation: *(Full rank) (surname)*

Warrant Officers: E9 and E8

NOTE: Warrant officers Class II in the British Army are addressed by *(full rank) (name)* rather than as Mr./Mrs. *(name)*.

Envelope, official:
   (Full rank) (full name)
      (Position/command/name of base)
         (address)

Marine envelope, official:
   (Full rank) (full name), RM
      (Position/command/name of base)
         (address)

Air Force envelope, official:
   (Full rank) (full name), RAF
      (Position/command/name of base)
         (address)

Letter salutation: *Dear Mr./Mrs. (surname):*

Complimentary close:
   Sincerely yours, or Sincerely,

Envelope, social:
>Mr./Mrs. *(full name)*, *(post nominals for decorations and honors)*
>>*(address)*

Invitation, inside envelope: Mr./Mrs. *(surname)*
Place card: Mr./Mrs. *(surname)*
Introduction:
>*(Full rank) (full name)*, *(position/command/name of base)*
>OR *(Position/command/name of base)*, *(full rank) (surname)*

Introduction, one person to another: Mr./Mrs. *(surname)*
Conversation: Mr./Mrs. *(surname)*

Non-Commissioned Rates: E7 to E2

Examples: *Chief Petty Officer (full name)*
>>*Lance Corporal (full name)*
>>*Petty Officer (full name)*
>>*Leading Aircraftman (full name)*, RAF

NOTE: Chief petty officers are informally addressed in conversation as *Chief* or *Chief (surname)* and in salutation as *Chief (surname)*. Basic ranks are sometimes informally used as honorifics in conversation: However, since there is an E3 lance corporal in the Army, and an E4 corporal in the Air Force, it is most accurate to use *(full rank)(name)*.

Envelope, official:
>*(Full rank) (full name)*
>>*(Position/command/name of base)*
>>*(Address)*

Letter salutation: *Dear (full rank) (surname)*:
Complimentary close: *Yours faithfully,*
Envelope, social:
>*(Full rank) (full name)*, *(post nominals for decorations and honors)*
>>*(Address)*

Invitation, inside envelope: *(Full rank) (full name)*
Place card:
>*(Full rank) (full name)* OR *(Abbreviated rank) (full name)*

Introduction:
>*(Full rank) (full name)*, *(position/command/name of base)*
>OR *(Position/command/name of base)*, *(full rank) (surname)*

Introduction, one person to another: *(Full rank) (surname)*
Conversation: *(Full rank) (surname)*
Conversation, informal: *(Basic rank) (surname)*

British Royalty and Nobility

THE ROYAL FAMILY

NOTE: Unless from someone personally acquainted with the Royal Family member, letters are addressed to the private secretary with a request that the letter be brought to the attention of the intended Royal person.

Examples: *The Duke of Edinburgh*
The Prince of Wales
The Duke of York
The Princess Royal
The Duke of Gloucester
The Duchess of Gloucester
The Duke of Kent
The Duchess of Kent

Envelope:
The Private Secretary to
(Followed by the form given in the appropriate listing that follows)

Letter salutation to the Private Secretary:
Dear Sir/Madam:
Dear Mr./Mrs./Lord/Lady/etc. (surname):

King or Queen

Envelope:
The Private Secretary to
His/Her Majesty the King/Queen
(Address)

Salutation in a letter to the private secretary: *Dear Sir:*

Complimentary close to the private secretary: *Respectfully yours,* OR *Respectfully,*

Salutation in a letter to the sovereign:
Madam: OR *May it please Your Majesty:*

Complimentary close by non-subjects: *Respectfully yours,* OR *Respectfully,*

Complimentary close by subjects:
I remain Your Majesty's faithful and devoted servant,
I have the honour to remain Your Majesty's obedient servant,

Place card:
His/Her Majesty
OR *H.M. The King/Queen*

Announced:
His/Her Majesty the King/Queen
His/Her Majesty (name), the King/Queen

Presentation: *Your Majesty, may I present ...*

Conversation, initially: *Your Majesty*

Conversation, subsequently: *Sir/ma'am*

Her Majesty Queen Elizabeth II
Envelope:
> The Private Secretary to
>> Her Majesty the Queen
>> (Address)
>
> OR The Private Secretary to
>> Her Majesty the Queen
>> and His Royal Highness
>>> The Duke of Edinburgh
>>> (Address)

Letter salutation: *May it please Your Majesty:*
Complimentary close: *Respectfully yours,* OR *Respectfully,*
Complimentary close by subjects:
> *I remain Your Majesty's faithful and devoted servant,*

Invitation:
> Her Majesty the Queen
> and H.R.H. the Prince Philip

Place card:
> *Her Majesty* OR *H.M. The Queen*

Place card outside the UK/Commonwealth: *H.M. Queen Elizabeth II*
Announced: *Her Majesty the Queen*
Introduction outside the United Kingdom: *Her Majesty Queen Elizabeth II*
Introduction, one person to another (in the United Kingdom all persons would be presented to the Queen): *Your Majesty, may I present …*
Conversation, initially: *Your Majesty*
Conversation, subsequently: *Ma'am*

His Royal Highness The Prince Philip
Envelope:
> His Royal Highness
>> The Prince Philip
>> Duke of Edinburgh
>> (Address)

Letter salutation: *Your Royal Highness:*
Complimentary close: *Yours very truly,*
Invitation, inside envelope:
> His Royal Highness
>> The Prince Philip

Place card: *H.R.H. The Prince Philip*
Introduction: *His Royal Highness the Prince Philip, Duke of Edinburgh*
Introduction, one person to another:
> *Your Royal Highness, may I present …*
> *… may I present His Royal Highness the Prince Philip, Duke of Edinburgh*

Conversation, initially: *Your Royal Highness*
Conversation, subsequently: *Sir*

394

His Royal Highness The Prince of Wales
Envelope:
> *His Royal Highness*
>> *The Prince of Wales*
>>> *(Address)*

Letter salutation: *Your Royal Highness:*
Complimentary close: *Yours very truly,*
Invitation, inside envelope:
> *His Royal Highness*
>> *The Prince of Wales*

Place card: *H.R.H. The Prince of Wales*
Introduction: *His Royal Highness the Prince of Wales*
Introduction, one person to another:
> *Your Royal Highness, may I present ...*
> *... may I present His Royal Highness the Prince of Wales*

Conversation, initially: *Your Royal Highness*
Conversation, subsequently: *Sir*

His Royal Highness The Duke of York
Envelope:
> *His Royal Highness*
>> *The Duke of York*
>>> *(Address)*

Letter salutation: *Your Royal Highness:*
Complimentary close: *Yours very truly,*
Invitation, inside envelope:
> *His Royal Highness*
>> *The Duke of York*

Place card: *H.R.H. The Duke of York*
Introduction: *His Royal Highness the Duke of York*
Introduction, one person to another:
> *Your Royal Highness, may I present ...*
> *... may I present His Royal Highness the Duke of York*

Conversation, initially: *Your Royal Highness*
Conversation, subsequently: *Sir*

His Royal Highness The Earl of Wessex
Envelope:
> *His Royal Highness*
>> *The Earl of Wessex*
>>> *(Address)*

Letter salutation:
> *Your Royal Highness:* OR *Lord Wessex:*

Complimentary close: *Yours very truly,*

Invitation, inside envelope:
　His Royal Highness
　　The Earl of Wessex
Place card: *H.R.H. The Earl of Wessex*
Introduction: *His Royal Highness the Earl of Wessex*
Introduction, one person to another:
　Your Royal Highness, may I present …
　… may I present His Royal Highness the Earl of Wessex
Conversation, initially: *Your Royal Highness*
Conversation, subsequently: *Sir*

Her Royal Highness The Princess Royal
Envelope:
　Her Royal Highness
　　The Princess Royal
　　　(Address)
Letter salutation: *Your Royal Highness:*
Complimentary close: *Yours very truly,*
Invitation, inside envelope:
　Her Royal Highness
　　The Princess Royal
Place card: *H.R.H. The Princess Royal*
Introduction: *Her Royal Highness the Princess Royal*
Introduction, one person to another:
　Your Royal Highness, may I present …
　… may I present Her Royal Highness the Princess Royal
Conversation, initially: *Your Royal Highness*
Conversation, subsequently: *Ma'am*

HEREDITARY PEERS

Duke/Duchess
Examples:　　*Duke of Abercorn*
　　　　　　Duke of Argyll
　　　　　　Duke of Beaufort
NOTE: The given name of the titled person in never used in formal address.
Envelope:
　His/Her Grace
　　The Duke/Duchess of (place)
　　　(Address)
　Their Graces
　　The Duke and Duchess of (place)
　　　(Address)
Letter salutation:
　My Lord Duke:

396

Dear Duke/Duchess of (place):
Dear Duke/Duchess:
Complimentary close: *Yours sincerely,*
Invitation, inside envelope:
    The Duke/Duchess of (place)
    The Duke and Duchess of (place)
Place card: *The Duke/Duchess of (place)*
Introduction:
    The Duke/Duchess of (place)
    His/Her Grace the Duke/Duchess of (place)
Introduction, one person to another:
    Your Grace, may I present …
    … may I present the Duke/Duchess of (place)
Conversation: *Your Grace*

Eldest Son of a Duke

NOTE: The eldest son of a duke is styled as his father's second title, *e.g.*, *The Marquess of (place)*, and in this example would follow forms of address for a marquess.

Younger Sons of a Duke

    Envelope: *Lord (first and surname)*
    Letter salutation: *Dear Lord (first name):*
    Complimentary close: *Yours sincerely,*
    Invitation, inside envelope:
        Lord (first name) or *Lord and Lady (husband's first name)*
    Place card: *Lord (first and surname)*
    Introduction: *Lord (first and surname)*
    Introduction, one person to another: *Lord (first name)*
    Conversation: *Lord (first name)*

Wife of a Younger Son of a Duke

    Envelope: *Lady (husband's first and surname)*
    Letter salutation: *Dear Lady (husband's first name):*
    Complimentary close: *Yours sincerely,*
    Invitation, inside envelope: *Lady (husband's first name)*
    Place card: *Lady (husband's first name)*
    Introduction: *Lady (husband's first and surname)*
    Introduction, one person to another: *Lady (husband's first name)*
    Conversation: *Lady (husband's first name)*

Daughters of a Duke

    Envelope: *Lady (first and surname)*
    Letter salutation: *Dear Lady (first name):*
    Complimentary close: *Yours sincerely,*
    Invitation, inside envelope: *Lady (first name)*
    Place card: *Lady (first name)*
    Introduction: *Lady (first and surname)*
    Introduction, one person to another: *Lady (first name)*
    Conversation: *Lady (first name)*

Marquess/Marchioness

Examples: *The Marquess Townshend*
            The Marquess of Bute
            The Marquess of Aberdeen and Temair

NOTE: When a marquessate has a compound name, *(name one) of/and (name two)*, use *name one* when *(name)* is specified and the *compound name* when the *(complete name)* is specified. The given name of the titled person in never used in formal address.

Envelope, official:
> *The Most Hon.*
>> *The Marquess/Marchioness (complete name)*
>> *(Address)*
> *The Most Hon.*
>> *The Marquess and Marchioness (complete name)*
>> *(Address)*

Letter salutation: *My Lord/Madam:* or *Dear Lord/Lady (name):*
Complimentary close: *Yours sincerely,*
Envelope, social:
> *The Marquess/Marchioness (complete name)*
> *(Address)*
> *The Marquess and Marchioness (complete name)*
> *(Address)*

Invitation, inside envelope:
> *Lord/Lady (name)*
> *Lord and Lady (name)*

Place card: *Lord/Lady (name)*
Introduction: *The Most Honourable the Marquess/Marchioness (complete name)*
Introduction, one person to another: *Lord/Lady (name)*
Conversation: *Lord/Lady (name)*

Eldest Son of a Marquess

The eldest son of a marquess is styled as his father's second title, *e.g.: The Earl (name)*, and in this example would follow forms of address for a earl.

Younger Sons of a Marquess

> Envelope: *Lord (first and surname)*
> Letter salutation: *Dear Lord (first name):*
> Complimentary close: *Yours sincerely,*
> Invitation, inside envelope:
>> *Lord (first name)* or *Lord and Lady (husband's first name)*
> Place card: *Lord (first name)*
> Introduction: *Lord (first and surname)*
> Introduction, one person to another: *Lord (first name)*
> Conversation: *Lord (first name)*

Wife of a Younger Son of a Marquess
    Envelope: *Lady (husband's first and surname)*
    Letter salutation: *Dear Lady (husband's first name):*
    Complimentary close: *Yours sincerely,*
    Invitation, inside envelope: *Lady (husband's first name)*
    Place card: *Lady (husband's first name)*
    Introduction: *Lady (husband's first and surname)*
    Introduction, one person to another: *Lady (husband's first name)*
    Conversation: *Lady (husband's first name)*

Daughters of a Marquess
    Envelope: Lady *(first and surname)*
    Letter salutation: *Dear Lady (first name):*
    Complimentary close: *Yours sincerely,*
    Invitation, inside envelope: *Lady (first name)*
    Place card: *Lady (first name)*
    Introduction: *Lady (first and surname)*
    Introduction, one person to another: *Lady (first name)*
    Conversation: *Lady (first name)*

Earl/Countess

Examples: *The Earl Ferrers*
              The Earl of Coventry
              The Earl of Shrewsbury and Waterford

NOTE: When an *earldom* has a compound name, *(name one) of/and (name two)*, use *name one* when *(name)* is specified and the *compound name* when the *(complete name)* is specified. The *given name* of the titled person in never used in formal address.

Envelope:
    The Right Hon.
        The Earl/Countess (complete name)
           (Address)
    The Right Hon.
        The Earl and Countess (complete name)
           (Address)
Letter salutation: *Dear Lord/Lady (name):*
Complimentary close: *Yours sincerely,*
Envelope, social:
    The Earl/Countess (complete name)
        (Address)
    The Earl and Countess (complete name)
        (Address)
Invitation, inside envelope: *Lord/Lady (name)* or *Lord and Lady (name)*
Place card: *Lord/Lady (name)*
Introduction: *The Right Honourable the Earl/Countess (complete name)*
Introduction, one person to another: *Lord/Lady (name)*
Conversation: *Lord/Lady (name)*

Eldest Son of Earl

The eldest son of an earl is styled as his father's second title, *e.g., The Viscount (name)* and in this example would follow forms of address for a viscount.

Younger Sons of an Earl
Envelope: *The Honourable (first and surname)*
Letter salutation: *Dear Mr. (surname):*
Complimentary close: *Yours sincerely,*
Invitation, inside envelope: *Mr. (surname)* or *Mr. and Mrs. (surname)*
Place card: *The Hon. (surname)*
Introduction: *The Honourable (first and surname)*
Introduction, one person to another: *Mister (surname)*
Conversation: *Mister (surname)*

Wife of a Younger Son of an Earl
Envelope: *The Honourable Mrs. (husband's first name and surname)*
Letter salutation: *Dear Mrs. (surname):*
Complimentary close: *Yours sincerely,*
Invitation, inside envelope: *Mrs. (surname)*
Place card: *The Hon. Mrs. (surname)*
Introduction: *The Honourable Mrs. (husband's first name and surname)*
Introduction, one person to another: *Mrs. (surname)*
Conversation: *Mrs. (surname)*

Daughters of an Earl
Envelope: *Lady (first and surname)*
Letter salutation: *Dear Lady (first name):*
Complimentary close: *Yours sincerely,*
Invitation, inside envelope: *Lady (first name)*
Place card: *Lady (first name)*
Introduction: *Lady (first and surname)*
Introduction, one person to another: *Lady (first name)*
Conversation: *Lady (first name)*

Viscount/Viscountess

Examples: *The Viscount Falmouth*
            The Viscount of Arbuthnott
            The Viscount Massereen and Ferrard
            The Viscount Colville of Culross

NOTE: When a viscountcy has a compound name, *(name one) of/and (name two)*, use *name one* when *(name)* is specified and the *compound name* when the *(complete name)* is specified. The given name of the titled person in never used in formal address.

Envelope, official:
 The Right Hon.
     The Viscount/Viscountess (complete name)
         (Address)
 The Right Hon.
     The Viscount and Viscountess (complete name)
         (Address)

400

Letter salutation: *Dear Lord/Lady (name one)*:
Complimentary close: *Yours sincerely,*
Envelope, social:
    The Viscount/Viscountess (complete name)
        (Address)
    The Viscount and Viscountess (complete name)
        (Address)
Invitation, inside envelope:
    Lord/Lady (name one)
    Lord and Lady (name)
Place card: *Lord/Lady (name)*
Introduction: *The Right Honourable the Viscount/Viscountess (complete name)*
Introduction, one person to another: *Lord/Lady (name)*
Conversation: *Lord/Lady (name)*

Sons of a Viscount
    Envelope: *The Honourable (first and surname)*
    Letter salutation: *Dear Mr. (surname)*:
    Complimentary close: *Yours sincerely,*
    Invitation, inside envelope: Mr. *(surname)* or Mr. *and Mrs. (surname)*
    Place card: *The Hon. (surname)*
    Introduction: *The Honourable (first and surname)*
    Introduction, one person to another: *Mister (surname)*
    Conversation: *Mister (surname)*

Wife of a Son of a Viscount
    Envelope: *The Honourable Mrs. (husband's first name and surname)*
    Letter salutation: *Dear Mrs. (surname)*:
    Complimentary close: *Yours sincerely,*
    Invitation, inside envelope: Mrs. *(surname)*
    Place card: *The Hon. Mrs. (surname)*
    Introduction: *The Honourable Mrs. (husband's first name and surname)*
    Introduction, one person to another: *Missus (surname)*
    Conversation: *Missus (surname)*

Daughters of a Viscount
    Envelope: *The Honourable (first and surname)*
    Letter salutation: *Dear Miss (surname)*:
    Complimentary close: *Yours sincerely,*
    Invitation, inside envelope: Miss *(surname)*
    Place card: *The Hon. (first and surname)*
    Introduction: *The Honourable (first and surname)*
    Introduction, one person to another: *Miss (surname)*
    Conversation: *Miss (surname)*

Baron/Baroness

Examples: *The Baron Clinton*
            The Baron Hale of Richmond
            The Baroness Willoughby de Eresby
            The Baron of Henley and Northington

NOTE: Baron and baroness are not traditionally used in direct address with hereditary peers. With baronies with a compound name, *(name one) of/and (name two)*, use *name one* when *(name)* is specified and the *compound name* when the *(complete name)* is specified. The given name of the titled person in never used in formal address.

Envelope, official:
   The Right Hon.
      Lord/Lady (complete name)
         (Address)
   The Right Hon.
      Lord and Lady (complete name)
         (Address)
Letter salutation: *Dear Lord/Lady (name):*
Complimentary close: *Yours sincerely,*
Envelope, social:
   Lord/Lady (complete name)
      (Address)
   Lord and Lady (complete name)
      (Address)
Invitation, inside envelope:
   Lord/Lady (name)
   Lord and Lady (name)
Place card: *Lord/Lady (name)*
Introduction: *The Right Honourable Lord/Lady (complete name)*
Introduction, one person to another: *Lord/Lady (full name)*
Conversation: *Lord/Lady (name)*

Son of a Baron

   Envelope: *The Honourable (first and surname)*
   Letter salutation: *Dear Mr. (surname):*
   Complimentary close: *Yours sincerely,*
   Invitation, inside envelope: *Mr. (surname)*
   Place card: *The Hon. (surname)*
   Introduction: *The Honourable (first and surname)*
   Introduction, one person to another: *Mister (surname)*
   Conversation: *Mister (surname)*

Wife of a Son of a Baron

   Envelope: *The Honourable Mrs. (husband's first and surname)*
   Letter salutation: *Dear Mrs. (surname):*
   Complimentary close: *Yours sincerely,*
   Invitation, inside envelope: *Mrs. (surname)*

402

Place card: *The Hon. Mrs. (husband's first and surname)*
Introduction: *The Honourable Mrs. (husband's first and surname)*
Introduction, one person to another: *Missus (surname)*
Conversation: *Missus (surname)*

Daughter of a Baron
Envelope: *The Honourable (first and surname)*
Letter salutation: *Dear Miss (surname):*
Complimentary close: *Yours sincerely,*
Invitation, inside envelope: *Miss (surname)*
Place card: *The Hon. (first and surname)*
Introduction: *The Honourable (first and surname)*
Introduction, one person to another: *Miss (surname)*
Conversation: *Miss (surname)*

Widows of Peers
NOTE: Dowager before a title is traditionally used for a hereditary peer's widow. However, widows have styled themselves in other ways. Confirm the preference of the bearer.

FORMULA: *The Dowager (full title)*
Examples: The Dowager Duchess of (place)
The Dowager Marchioness (name or of name[s])
The Dowager Countess of (name[s])
The Dowager Viscountess (complete name)
The Dowager Lady (complete name)

FORMULA: *(First name), (full title)*
Example: Mary, Viscountess Lister

BARONETS AND KNIGHTS

Baronet
Envelope:
    Sir (full name), Bt.   *Dame (full name), Btss.*
      (Address)   *(Address)*
    Sir (full name), Bt.
      and Lady (surname)
        (Address)
Letter salutation: *Dear Sir/Dame (first name):*
Complimentary close: *Yours sincerely,* OR *Sincerely,*
Invitation, inside envelope: *Sir/Dame (first name)*
Place card: *Sir/Dame (full name)*
Introduction: *Sir/Dame (full name)*
Introduction, one person to another: *Sir/Dame (first name)*
Conversation: *Sir/Dame (first name)*

Knight

Examples: *Knight Grand Cross (full name)*, GBC
Knight Commander (full name), KCMG

NOTE: Wives of knights are addressed as *Lady (surname)*. Husbands of knights receive none of the courtesies of the wife's honour. Peers who are knighted continue to use their hereditary title, and add the post-nominal initials of the order.

Envelope:
Sir (full name), (initials of the order)
(Address)
Sir (full name), (initials of the order)
and Lady (surname only)
(Address)

Letter salutation: *Dear Sir (first name):*
Complimentary close: *Yours sincerely,* OR *Sincerely,*
Invitation, inside envelope: *Sir (first name)*
Place card: *Sir (first name)*
Introduction: *Sir (full name)*
Introduction, one person to another: *Sir (first name)*
Conversation: *Sir (first name)*

Dame

Examples: *Dame Grand Cross (full name)*, GBC
Dame Commander (full name), KCMG

NOTE: Dame is the female equivalent of address to *Sir* for a British knighthood. Husbands of dames receive none of the courtesies of the wife's honour. Peers who are knighted continue to use their hereditary title, and add the post-nominal initials of the order.

Envelope:
Dame (full name), (initials of the order)
(Address)
Dame (full name), (initials of the order)
and Mr. (full name)
(Address)

Letter salutation: *Dear Dame (first name):*
Complimentary close: *Yours sincerely,* OR *Sincerely,*
Invitation, inside envelope: *Dame (first name)*
Place card: *Dame (first name)*
Introduction: *Dame (full name)*
Introduction, one person to another: *Dame (first name)*
Conversation: *Dame (first name)*

Knighted Non-Subjects

Envelope:
>   Mr. *(full name)*, *(initials of the order)*
>   *(Address)*
>   Ms./Mrs./etc. *(full name)*, *(initials of the order)*
>   *(Address)*

Letter salutation: *Dear Mr./Mrs./etc. (surname):*
Complimentary close: *Yours sincerely,* OR *Sincerely,*
Invitation, inside envelope: Mr./Mrs./etc. *(surname)*
Place card: Mr./Mrs./etc. *(surname)*
Introduction: Mr./Mrs./etc. *(full name)*
Introduction, one person to another: Mr./Mrs./etc. *(surname)*
Conversation: Mr./Mrs./etc. *(surname)*

LIFE PEERS

Life Peers

Envelope, official:
>   *The Right Hon.*
>   *Lord/Lady (full name)*
>   *(Address)*
>   *The Right Hon.*
>   *Lord and Lady (male peer's full name)*
>   *(Address)*
>   *The Right Hon.*
>   *Lady (female peer's full name)*
>   *and Mr. (husband's full name)*
>   *(Address)*

Letter salutation: *Dear Lord/Lady (name):*
Complimentary close: *Yours sincerely,*
Envelope, official:
>   *Lord/Lady (full name)*
>   *(Address)*
>   *Lord and Lady (male peer's full name)*
>   *(Address)*
>   *Lady (female peer's full name)*
>   *and Mr. (husband's full name)*
>   *(Address)*

Invitation, inside envelope: *Lord/Lady (name)* OR *Lord and Lady (name)*
Place card: *The Right Hon. Lord/Lady (name)*
Introduction: *The Right Honourable Lord/Lady (name)*
Conversation: *Lord/Lady (name)*

20 International Officials

Chief of State/Head of Government

President

Examples: (Full name), President of (country)
             Dr. (full name), President of (country)

NOTE: Address by (office only) is more formal than any form that includes the person's (name). Many presidents are addressed domestically as His/Her Excellency (name), and sometimes presidents not addressed as His/Her Excellency domestically are addressed His/Her Excellency when traveling abroad.

ADDRESSED BY OFFICE

Envelope, official:
    The President of the (full name of country)
        (Address)
    OR The President of the (full name of country)
            (Personal honorific if presented) (full name)
                (Address)
Letter salutation: Dear Mr./Madam President:
Complimentary close: Respectfully yours,
Envelope, social:
    The President of (full name of country)
        (Address)
Invitation, inside envelope: The President of (full name of country)
Place card: The President of (full name of country)
Introduction: The President of (full name of country)

Introduction, one person to another:
    Mr./Madam President, may I present ...
    ... may I present the President of (full name of country) ...
Conversation, initially: *Mr./Madam President*
Subsequently in conversation: *Sir/madam*

ADDRESSED AS HIS/HER EXCELLENCY

Envelope, official:
    His/Her Excellency
        (Personal honorific if presented) (full name), (post nominals as presented)
            President of the (full name of country)
                (Address)
Letter salutation: *Your Excellency:*
Complimentary close: *Respectfully yours,*
Envelope, social:
    The President of (full name of country)
        (Address)
Invitation, inside envelope: *The President of (full name of country)*
Place card: *The President of (full name of country)*
Introduction:
    His/Her Excellency (personal honorific if presented) (full name),
        the President of (full name of country)
Introduction, one person to another:
    Your Excellency, may I present ...
    ... may I present His/Her Excellency (personal honorific) (full name) ...
Conversation, initially: *Your Excellency*
Subsequently in conversation: *Sir/madam*

Chairman
    of the Council of Ministers (*e.g., Bosnia and Herzegovina*)
    of the Presidency (*e.g., Bosnia and Herzegovina*)
    of the State Peace and Development Council (*e.g., Myanmar*)

Chancellor (*e.g., Austria, Germany*)

Executive President (*e.g., Zimbabwe*)

Premier (*e.g., China*)

Supreme Leader (*e.g., Iran*)

Examples: *(Full name), (title of office) of (country)*
             Dr. (full name), (title of office) of (country)

NOTE: Address by *(office only)* is more formal than any form that includes the person's *(name)*. Some chiefs of state/heads of government are addressed domestically as *His/Her Excellency*, but often officials of these ranks not addressed as *His/Her Excellency* domestically are addressed as *His/Her Excellency* abroad.

ADDRESSED BY OFFICE

Envelope, official:
> The *(title of office) of (full name of country)*
> *(Address)*
> OR   The *(title of office) of (full name of country)*
>> *(Personal honorific if presented) (full name)*
>> *(Address)*

Letter salutation: *Dear Mr./Madam (title of office):*
Complimentary close: *Respectfully yours,*
Envelope, social:
> The *(title of office) of (full name of country)*
> *(Address)*

Invitation, inside envelope: The *(title of office) of (full name of country)*
Place card: The *(title of office) of (full name of country)*
Introduction: The *(title of office) of (full name of country)*
Introduction, one person to another:
> Mr./Madam *(title of office),* may I present...
> ... may I present the *(title of office) of (full name of country)*...

Conversation, initially: Mr./Madam *(title of office)*
Subsequently in conversation: *Sir/madam*

ADDRESSED AS HIS/HER EXCELLENCY

Envelope, official:
> *His/Her Excellency*
>> *(Personal honorific if presented) (full name)*
>> The *(title of office) of (full name of country)*
>> *(Address)*

Letter salutation: *Your Excellency:*
Complimentary close: *Respectfully yours,*
Envelope, social:
> The *(title of office) of (full name of country)*
> *(Address)*

Invitation, inside envelope: The *(title of office) of (full name of country)*
Place card: The *(title of office) of (full name of country)*
Introduction:
> *His/Her Excellency (personal hononorific if presented) (full name),*
>> *(title of office) of (full name of country)*

Introduction, one person to another:
> *Your Excellency,* may I present...
> ... may I present His/Her Excellency *(personal honorific if presented)*
>> *(full name), (title of office) of (full name of country)*...

Conversation, initially: *Your Excellency*
Subsequently in conversation: *Sir/madam*

Prime Minister

Examples: (Full name), Prime Minister of (country)
              Dr. (full name), Prime Minister of (country)
NOTE: Addressing a head of government by (office) is the most formal form and is never incorrect. Prime ministers in various countries are addressed domestically as *His/Her Excellency, the Honorable, the Right Honourable*, and without any courtesy title. Check for specific tradition.

ADDRESSED BY OFFICE

NOTE: Adapt form for *Chairman, Chancellor* by (office) on pages 408-409.

ADDRESSED AS *HIS/HER EXCELLENCY*

Envelope, official:
   His/Her Excellency
      (Personal honorific if presented) (full name), (post nominals as presented)
         Prime Minister of (full name of country)
            (Address)
Letter salutation: *Your Excellency:*
Complimentary close: *Respectfully yours,*
Envelope, social:
   The Prime Minister of (full name of country)
      (Address)
Invitation, inside envelope:
   The Prime Minister of (full name of country)
Place card: *The Prime Minister of (full name of country)*
Introduction:
   His/Her Excellency (full name), the Prime Minister of (full name of country)
   OR *The Prime Minister of (full name of country), His/Her Excellency (full name)*
Introduction, one person to another:
   Your Excellency, may I present ...
   ... may I present the Prime Minister of (full name of country) ...
Conversation, initially: *Your Excellency* OR *Mr./Madam Prime Minister*
Subsequently in conversation: *Sir/madam*

ADDRESSED AS *THE RIGHT HONOURABLE*

See form for prime minister of the United Kingdom, page 358.

ADDRESSED AS *THE HONORABLE*

See form for prime minister of Australia, page 329.

Departments, Ministries, and Secretariats

Cabinet Ministers and Secretaries

Examples: (Full name), Minister for (portfolio) of (country)

Mr. (full name), Minister for (portfolio) of (country)

Dr. (full name), Minister for (portfolio) of (country)

Professor (full name), Minister for (portfolio) of (country)

NOTE: Although His/Her Excellency is the courtesy title most frequently used when addressing a member of a foreign cabinet, it is not universal. Some nations address a cabinet member as the Honourable, others as the Right Honourable, still others without a courtesy title. Check for specific tradition.

ADDRESSED AS HIS/HER EXCELLENCY

Envelope, official:

His/Her Excellency

(Personal honorific if presented) (full name), (post nominals)

(Title of office) of (full name of country)

(Address)

Letter salutation: Your Excellency:

Complimentary close: Respectfully yours,

Envelope, social:

The (title of office) of (full name of country)

(Address)

Invitation, inside envelope: The (title of office)

Place card:

The (title of office)

OR H.E. (personal honorific if presented) (full name)

Introduction:

His/Her Excellency (full name), the (title of office) of (full name of country)

OR The (title of office) of (full name of country), His/Her Excellency (full name)

Introduction, one person to another:

Your Excellency, may I present ...

... may I present His/Her Excellency (full name) ...

Conversation: Your Excellency

Subsequently in conversation: Sir/madam

Less formal introduction, one person to another:

Minister/Secretary (surname), may I present ...

... may I present Minister/Secretary (surname) ...

Less formal conversation: Minister/Secretary (surname) OR Minister/Secretary

ADDRESSED AS THE RIGHT HONOURABLE

See form for Cabinet Member, MP of the United Kingdom, page 359.

ADDRESSED AS *THE HONORABLE*

See form for *Cabinet Minister, MP* of Australia, page 331.

Deputy Minister, Undersecretary

Examples: *(Full name), Deputy Minister for (portfolio) of (country)*
            Dr. (full name), Undersecretary of (portfolio) of (country)

NOTE: Frequently only ministers, secretaries, and other officials of cabinet rank are addressed with a courtesy title. For deputy, assistant, and under- ranked officials, check for the specific tradition.

ADDRESSED AS *HIS/HER EXCELLENCY*

Adapt form for *Cabinet Ministers and Secretaries*, page 411.

ADDRESSED AS *THE HONOURABLE*

See forms for *Australian Assistant Minister*, page 332.

ADDRESSED WITHOUT A COURTESY TITLE

Envelope, official:
  Mr./Mrs./etc. *(full name)*
       (Title of office) of (full name of country)
       (Address)
Letter salutation:
  Dear (title of office):
  OR *Dear Mr./Mrs./etc. (surname):*
Complimentary close: *Respectfully yours,*
Envelope, social:
  The (title of office) of (full name of country)
       (Address)
Invitation, inside envelope: *The (title of office)*
Place card: *The (title of office)* OR Mr./Mrs./etc. *(full name)*
Introduction:
  Mr./Mrs./etc. *(full name), the (title of office) of (full name of country)*
  OR *The (title of office) of (full name of country),* Mr./Mrs./etc. *(surname)*
More formal introduction, one person to another:
  (Title of office) (surname), may I present ...
  ... may I present (title of office) (surname) ...
More formal conversation: *(Title of office) (surname)*
Less formal introduction, one person to another:
  Mr./Mrs./etc. *(surname), may I present ...*
  ... may I present Mr./Mrs./etc. *(surname), the (title of office) ...*
Less formal conversation: Mr./Mrs./etc. *(surname)*

Members of Elected Assemblies

National Assemblies:

- Advisory Council
- Assembly, Assembly of the Union
- Chamber of Representatives
- Council: General Council, Grand Council
- Council of: the European Union, States, Representatives
- Federal: Assembly, Council
- House of: Assembly, Federation, Representatives
- Legislative Assembly
- Knesset
- Legislative Council
- Legislature
- National: Assembly, Congress, Council
- People's: Assembly, Congress, Council
- States (Staten) or States General
- Second Chamber
- Supreme: Assembly, Council

NOTE: Traditions in the use of courtesy titles for members of national assemblies vary by country. Perhaps the most frequent pattern is only the speaker or president of the assembly or chamber is addressed with a courtesy title; members are not.

However, other traditions include:

- All members of a national assembly are addressed with a courtesy title.
- A members of the upper chamber is addressed as *the Venerable*;
  A member of the lower house is addressed as *the Honourable*.
- A member of the upper chamber is addressed with a courtesy title;
  A member of a lower chamber is not.
- No member of the assembly is addressed with a courtesy title.

In countries where officials are addressed with a courtesy title, it is typically only while they are in office. Continued use of any courtesies of an office by a former officeholder is unusual.

Speaker or President of an Assembly

Examples: Dr. *(full name)*, *President of the (assembly)*
            Professor (full name), *Speaker of the (assembly)*

NOTE: Address as a *member* and identify after the name as *speaker* or *president*. Sometimes in assemblies where a member is not addressed with a courtesy title, the speaker or president is. Check for specific tradition.

Members of Parliament

Examples: Dr. *(full name)*, *President of the (assembly)*
            Professor (full name), *Speaker of the (assembly)*
            (Full name), *Member of the (assembly)*

NOTE: More than 50 nations in which the head of government is a prime minister call their national assembly *parliament* in the same way the combined House of Representatives and Senate in the United States is called *congress*. Frequently members of a unicameral parliament, or members of a lower house of a bicameral parliament, are addressed without a courtesy title, but with a post nominal such as MP: The form for Australian House of Representatives, page 328, illustrates this style. For a member of a parliamentary senate, see page 327; for a chamber of deputies, see page 417; or for a house of lords, see page 364.

ADDRESSED AS *HIS/HER EXCELLENCY*

Envelope, official:
  His/Her Excellency
    (Personal honorific if presented) (full name), (post nominals as presented)
      (Name of assembly) of (full name of country)
      (Address)
Letter salutation: *Your Excellency:*
Complimentary close: *Sincerely yours*, OR *Sincerely,*
Envelope, social:
  His/Her Excellency
    (Personal honorific if presented) (full name)
      (Address)
Invitation, inside envelope:
  His/Her Excellency
    (Personal honorific if presented) (full name)
Place card: *H.E. (personal honorific if presented) (full name)*
Introduction:
  His/Her Excellency (personal honorific if presented) (full name),
    member of the (name of assembly) of (full name of country)
  OR *(Member) of the (name of assembly) of the (full name of country),*
    His/Her Excellency (full name)
Introduction, one person to another:
  Your Excellency, may I present …
  … may I present His/Her Excellency (honorific if presented) (full name)…
Conversation: *Your Excellency*

ADDRESSED AS *THE HONOURABLE*

Modify the form for Representative, page 180. Identify as a *member of the (name of assembly) of (full name of country)*. Members may also use a post nominal such as MP to note their legislative office.

ADDRESSED WITHOUT A COURTESY TITLE

Envelope, official:
  Mr./Mrs./etc. (full name)
    (Name of assembly) of (full name of country)
      (Address)

Letter salutation: *Dear Mr./Mrs./etc. (surname)*:
Complimentary close: *Respectfully yours*,
Envelope, social:
    Mr./Mrs./etc. (full name)
        (Address)
Invitation, inside envelope: *Mr./Mrs./etc. (full name)*
Place card: *Mr./Mrs./etc. (full name)*
Introduction:
    Mr./Mrs./etc. (full name), member of the (assembly) of (country)
    OR *Member of the (assembly) of the (country), Mr./Mrs./etc. (surname)*
Introduction, one person to another: *Mr./Mrs./etc. (surname)*
Conversation: *Mr./Mrs./etc. (surname)*

Speaker or President of a Senate

Examples: *Dr. (full name), President of the Senate of (country)*
               Professor (full name), Speaker of the Senate of (country)
NOTE: Address as a *member of parliament* and identify after the name as *speaker* or *president*. Note that sometimes in assemblies where a member is not addressed with a courtesy title, the speaker or president is. Check for the specific tradition.

Senator

Examples: *Dr. (full name), President of the Senate of (country)*
               Professor (full name), member of the Senate of (country)
               (Full name), Senator of (name of province), Senate of (country)
NOTE: Some countries use courtesy titles when addressing all *senators*; others extend the courtesy only to a *president* or *speaker* of a senate. Check for the specific tradition.

ADDRESSED AS *HIS/HER EXCELLENCY*

Envelope, official:
    His/Her Excellency
        (Personal honorific if presented) (full name), (post nominals as presented)
            Senate of the (full name of country)
               (Address)
Letter salutation:
    Your Excellency:
    OR *Dear Senator (personal honorific if presented) (surname):*
Complimentary close: *Sincerely yours,* OR *Sincerely,*
Envelope, social:
    His/Her Excellency
        (Personal honorific if presented) (full name)
            (Address)
Invitation, inside envelope:
    His/Her Excellency
        (Personal honorific if presented) (full name)
Place card: *H.E. (personal honorific if presented) (full name)*

Introduction:
> *Senator from (full name of country)*, *His/Her Excellency*
>> *(personal honorific if presented) (full name)*

Introduction, one person to another:
> *Your Excellency, may I present …*
> *… may I present His/Her Excellency*
>> *Senator (personal honorific if presented) (full name)*

Conversation: *Your Excellency*

Subsequently in conversation: *Sir/madam*

Conversation, less formal:
> *Senator (personal honorific if presented) (surname)*
> OR *Senator*

ADDRESSED AS *THE HONOURABLE*

NOTE: See form for Senator, page 176, and include post nominals and compound honorifics, *e.g.*, *Senator Dr. (name)* or *Senator Professor (name)*. See also the form for the President of the Senate of Australia, page 326.

ADDRESSED WITHOUT A COURTESY TITLE

Envelope, official:
> *Senator (personal honorific if presented) (full name)*
>> *Senate of the (full name of country)*
>>> *(Address)*

Letter salutation: *Dear Senator (personal honorific if presented) (surname):*

Complimentary close: *Sincerely yours* OR *Sincerely,*

Envelope, social:
> *Senator (personal honorific if presented) (full name)*
>> *(Address)*

Invitation, inside envelope:
> *Senator (personal honorific if presented) (full name)*

Place card: *Senator (full name)*

Introduction:
> *Senator (personal honorific if presented) (full name) from (full name of country)*
> *The Senator from (full name of country), (personal honorific if presented) (surname)*

Introduction, one person to another: *Senator (surname)*

Conversation: *Senator (personal honorific if presented) (surname)*

Subsequently in conversation: *Sir/madam*

Less formal conversation: *Senator*

Deputy in a Chamber of Deputies

Examples: Dr. *(full name)*, *speaker of the Chamber of Deputies of (country)*
(Full name), *chairperson of the Chamber of Deputies of (country)*
(Full name), *member of the Chamber of Deputies of (country)*

NOTE: For a president or speaker, address as a *deputy* and identify by *(office)* on an official envelope and in a formal introduction. Many countries extend a courtesy title only to the president or speaker of a Chamber of Deputies, not to the members. Check for the specific tradition.

ADDRESSED AS *HIS/HER EXCELLENCY*

Envelope, official:
　His/Her Excellency
　　Deputy *(personal honorific if presented) (full name)*
　　　Chamber of Deputies of *(full name of country)*
　　　　(Address)
Letter salutation: *Your Excellency:* OR *Dear Deputy (surname):*
Complimentary close: *Sincerely yours,* OR *Sincerely,*
Envelope, social:
　His/Her Excellency
　　Deputy *(personal honorific if presented) (full name)*
　　　(Address)
Invitation, inside envelope:
　His/Her Excellency
　　Deputy *(personal honorific if presented) (full name)*
Place card: H.E. *(personal honorific is presented) (full name)*
Introduction:
　His/Her Excellency Deputy *(personal honorific if presented) (full name)*,
　　member of the Chamber of Deputies of *(full name of country)*
　OR *Member of the Chamber of Deputies of (full name of country)*
　　His/Her Excellency Deputy *(personal honorific if presented) (full name)*
Introduction, one person to another:
　Your Excellency, may I present …
　… may I present His/Her Excellency Deputy (surname) …
Conversation: *Your Excellency*
Conversation, less formal: *Deputy (surname)* OR *Deputy*
Subsequently in conversation: *Sir/madam*

ADDRESSED AS *THE HONOURABLE*

NOTE: Adapt the form above, or see Representatives, page 180. See also form for Speaker of the Australian House of Representatives, page 327.

ADDRESSED WITHOUT A COURTESY TITLE

Examples: Dr. *(full name)*, *Speaker of the Chamber of Deputies of (country)*
(Full name), *member of the Chamber of Deputies of (country)*

Envelope, official:
> Deputy (personal honorific if presented) (full name)
>> Chamber of Deputies of (full name of country)
>>> (Address)

Letter salutation: Dear Deputy (surname):
Complimentary close: Sincerely yours, OR Sincerely,
Envelope, social:
> Deputy (personal honorific if presented) (full name)
>> (Address)

Invitation, inside envelope:
> Deputy (personal honorific if presented) (full name)

Place card: Deputy (personal honorific if presented) (full name)
Introduction:
> Deputy (personal honorific if presented) (full name),
>> member of the Chamber of Deputies of (full name of country)
> OR Member of the Chamber of Deputies of (full name of country),
>> Deputy (personal honorific if presented) (surname)

Introduction, one person to another: Deputy (surname)
Conversation: Deputy (surname)
Conversation, less formal: Deputy
Subsequently in conversation: Sir/madam

Noble Chief of State/Head of Government

Correspondence to a Member of a Ruling Family

NOTE: Unless from someone is personally acquainted with the family member, correspondence is not directly addressed to the royal person but rather to a court official. The title for this official will be specific to the court.
Envelope addressed could include:
> The Private Secretary to
>> His/Her Majesty the King/Queen

> OR His Excellency
>> The Head of the Royal Protocol Office

> OR His Excellency
>> The Chief of the Royal Protocol

Letter salutation: Dear Sir: OR Dear Mr./Mrs./etc. (surname):

Emperor/Empress

Example: Akihito, Emperor of Japan
Envelope:
> His/Her Imperial Majesty
>> The Emperor/Empress of (country)
>>> (Address)

Letter salutation: Your Imperial Majesty:

418

Complimentary close: *Most Respectfully,*
Complimentary close by subjects:
    I remain Your Imperial Majesty's faithful and devoted servant,
Invitation, inside envelope:
    His/Her Imperial Majesty
        The Emperor/Empress of (country)
Place card: H.I.M. *The Emperor/Empress of (country)*
Introduction: *His/Her Imperial Majesty, the Emperor/Empress of (country)*
Conversation: *Your Imperial Majesty*
Subsequently in conversation: *Sir/ma'am*

King/Queen

Examples: *Beatrix, Queen of the Netherlands*
            Elizabeth II, Queen of Great Britain and Northern Ireland
            Harald V, King of Norway
            Margrethe II, Queen of Denmark
            Mohammed VI, King of Morocco
            Norodom Sihamoni, Kingdom of Cambodia
            Taufa'ahau Tupou V, King of Tonga
Envelope:
    His/Her Majesty
        The King/Queen of (full name of country)
            (Address)
    OR *Their Majesties*
        The King and Queen of (country/people)
            (Address)
Letter salutation: *Your Majesty:*
Complimentary close: *Most Respectfully,*
Complimentary close by subjects:
    I remain Your Majesty's faithful and devoted servant,
    OR *I have the honor to remain Your Majesty's obedient servant,*
Invitation, inside envelope:
    His/Her Majesty
        The King/Queen
    Their Majesties
        The King and Queen of (country/people)
Place card: H.M. *The King/Queen of (country/people)*
Introduction:
    His/Her Majesty the King/Queen of (country/people)
    Their Majesties the King and Queen of (country/people)
Introduction, one person to another
    Your Majesty, may I present ...
    ... may I present His/Her Majesty the King/Queen of ...
Conversation: *Your Majesty*
Subsequently in conversation: *Sir/ma'am*

King of Saudi Arabia

Example: *Abdullah, King of Saudi Arabia*
Envelope:
> *The Custodian of the Two Holy Mosques*
> *King Abdullah bin Abdul Aziz Al Saud*
> *(Address)*

Letter salutation: *Your Majesty:*
Letter salutation, less formal: *Dear King Abdullah:*
Complimentary close: *Most Respectfully,*
Place card: H.M. *King Abdullah*
Introduction:
> *The Custodian of the Two Holy Mosques*
> *The King of Saudi Arabia*

Introduction, one person to another:
> *Your Majesty, may I present ...*
> *... may I present The Custodian of the Two Holy Mosques,*
> *the King of Saudi Arabia*

Introduction, one person to another, less formal: *King Abdullah, may I present ...*
Conversation: *Your Majesty*
Subsequently in conversation: *Sir*

Sultan

Examples: *Qaboos, The Sultan of Oman*
> FULL NAME: *Qaboos bin Sa'id Al 'Bu Sa'id*
> *Hassanal Bolkiah, The Sultan of Brunei*
> FULL NAME: *Hassanal Bolkiah Mu'izzaddin Waddaulah*

Envelope:
> *His Majesty*
> *The Sultan of (country)*
> *(Address)*

Letter salutation: *Your Majesty:*
Complimentary close: *Most Respectfully,*
Invitation, inside envelope:
> *His Majesty*
> *The Sultan of (country)*

Place card: H.M. *The Sultan of (country)*
Introduction: *His Majesty the Sultan of (country)*
Introduction, one person to another:
> *Your Majesty, may I present ...*
> *... may I present His Majesty the Sultan of ...*

Conversation: *Your Majesty*
Subsequently in conversation: *Sir*

Paramount Ruler

Example: *Mizan Zainal Abidin, Yang di-Pertuan Agong of Malaysia*
NOTE: The consort of the Paramount Ruler is addressed in conversation as *Your Majesty* and subsequently as *ma'am*.
Envelope:
> *His Majesty*
>> *The Paramount Ruler of Malaysia*
>>> *(Address)*

Letter salutation: *Your Majesty:*
Complimentary close: *Most Respectfully*, OR *Your Humble Servant,*
Invitation, inside envelope:
> *His Majesty*
>> *The Paramount Ruler of Malaysia*

Place card: H.M. *The Paramount Ruler of Malaysia*
Introduction: *His Majesty the Paramount Ruler of Malaysia*
Introduction, one person to another:
> *Your Majesty, may I present …*
> *… may I present His Majesty the Paramount Ruler of Malaysia …*

Conversation: *Your Majesty*
Subsequently in conversation: *Sir*

Sultan of a Malay State

Examples: *Abdul Halim, Sultan of Kedah, Yang di-Pertuan Agong V*
Envelope:
> *His Royal Highness*
>> *Sultan of (state)*
>>> *(Address)*

Letter salutation: *Your Majesty:*
Complimentary close: *Most Respectfully,*
Invitation, inside envelope:
> *His Royal Highness*
>> *Sultan of (state)*

Place card: H.R.H. *The Sultan of (state)*
Introduction: *His Royal Highness the Sultan of (state)*
Introduction, one person to another:
> *Your Royal Highness, may I present …*
> *… may I present His Royal Highness, the Sultan of (state) …*

Conversation: *Your Royal Highness*
Subsequently in conversation: *Sir*

Ruler of a Malay State

Example: *Yang di-Pertuan Besar, Ruler of Negeri Sembilian*
Envelope:
> *His Royal Highness*
>> *Ruler of (state)*
>>> *(Address)*

Letter salutation: *Your Majesty:*
Complimentary close: *Most Respectfully,*
Invitation, inside envelope:
> *His Royal Highness*
>> *Ruler of (state)*

Place card: *H.R.H. The Ruler of (state)*
Introduction: *His Royal Highness the Ruler of (state)*
Introduction, one person to another:
> *Your Royal Highness, may I present ...*
> *... may I present His Royal Highness the Ruler of (state) ...*

Conversation: *Your Royal Highness*
Subsequently in conversation: *Sir*

Raja

Example: *Yang di-Pertuan Besar, Raja of Perlis*
Envelope:
> *His Royal Highness*
>> *The Raja of Perlis*
>>> *(Address)*

Letter salutation: *Your Majesty:*
Complimentary close: *Most Respectfully,*
Invitation, inside envelope:
> *His Royal Highness*
>> *The Raja of Perlis*

Place card: *H.R.H. The Raja of Perlis*
Introduction: *His Royal Highness the Raja of Perlis*
Introduction, one person to another:
> *Your Royal Highness, may I present ...*
> *... may I present His Royal Highness the Raja of Perlis ...*

Conversation: *Your Royal Highness*
Subsequently in conversation: *Sir*

Grand Duke/Duchess of a Grand Duchy

Example: *Henri, Grand Duke of Luxembourg*
Envelope:
> *His/Her Royal Highness*
>> *(Name)*
>>> *Grand Duke/Duchess of Luxembourg*
>>>> *(Address)*

Letter salutation: *Your Royal Highness:*

Complimentary close: *Most Respectfully,*
Invitation, inside envelope:
> *His/Her Royal Highness*
> > *(Name)*

Place card: *H.R.H. (name)*
Introduction:
> *His/Her Royal Highness the Grand Duke/Duchess of Luxembourg*
> *His/Her Royal Highness (name), the Grand Duke/Duchess of Luxembourg*
> *The Grand Duke/Duchess of Luxembourg His/Her Royal Highness (name)*

Introduction, one person to another:
> *Your Royal Highness, may I present …*
> *… may I present His/Her Royal Highness (name) …*

Conversation: *Your Royal Highness*

Prince/Princess of a Principality

Examples: *Albert II, Prince of Monaco*
             Hans-Adam II, Prince of Liechtenstein

Envelope:
> *His/Her Serene Highness*
> > *Prince/Princess (name and number)*
> > *(Address)*

Letter salutation: *Your Serene Highness:*
Complimentary close: *Most Respectfully,*
Invitation, inside envelope:
> *His/Her Serene Highness*
> > *Prince/Princess (name and number)*

Place card: *H.S.H. Prince/Princess (name and number)*
Introduction: *His/Her Serene Highness the Prince/Princess of (country)*
Introduction, one person to another:
> *Your Serene Highness, may I present …*
> *… may I present His/Her Serene Highness (name and number) …*

Conversation: *Your Serene Highness*
Subsequently in conversation in Monaco: *Monseigneur*

Emir

Example: *Sheihk Hamad, The Emir of Qatar*
            FULL NAME: *Hamad Bin Khalifa Al-Thani*
            FAMILY NAME: *Al-Thani*

Envelope:
> *His Highness*
> > *Sheikh (name)*
> > > *Emir of (state/country)*
> > > *(Address)*

Letter salutation: *Your Highness:*
Complimentary close: *Most Respectfully,*

Complimentary close by subjects:
I remain Your Highness's faithful and devoted servant,
OR *I have the honor to remain Your Highness's obedient servant,*
Invitation, inside envelope:
His Highness
The Emir of (state/country)
Place card: *H.H. Sheikh (name)*
Introduction:
His Highness the Emir of (state/country)
OR *His Highness Sheikh (name), the prince of (state/country)*
OR *The Prince of (state/country), His Highness Sheikh (name)*
Introduction, one person to another:
Your Highness, may I present ...
... may I present His Highness the Emir of ...
OR *... may I present His Highness Sheikh (name) ...*
Conversation: *Your Highness*
Subsequently in conversation: *Sir*

Prince of an Emirate
Example: *Sheikh Sabah, The Prince of Kuwait*
            FULL NAME: *Sheikh Sabah Al-Ahmad Al-Jaber Al-Sabah*
            FAMILY NAME: *Al-Sabah*
Envelope:
His Highness
Sheikh (name)
Prince of (state/country)
(Address)
Letter salutation: *Your Highness:*
Complimentary close: *Most Respectfully,*
Complimentary close by subjects:
I remain Your Highness's faithful and devoted servant,
OR *I have the honor to remain Your Highness's obedient servant,*
Invitation, inside envelope:
His Highness
The Prince of (state/country)
Place card: *H.H. Sheikh (name)*
Introduction:
His Highness the Prince of (state/country)
OR *His Highness Sheikh (name) the prince of (state/country)*
OR *The Prince of (state/country) His Highness Sheikh (name)*
Introduction, one person to another:
Your Highness, may I present ...
... may I present His Highness the Prince of ...
OR *... may I present His Highness Sheikh (name) ...*
Conversation: *Your Highness*
Subsequently in conversation: *Sir*

424

President of the United Arab Emirates

Example: *Sheikh Khalifa, The Ruler of Abu Dhabi*
                     FULL NAME: *Khalifa bin Zayid Al-Nuhayyan*

Envelope:
>   *His Highness*
>   *Sheikh (full name)*
>   *President of the United Arab Emirates*
>   *The Presidential Palace*
>   *Address*

Letter salutation: *President Sheikh (given name):*
Complimentary close: *Most Respectfully,*
Invitation, inside envelope:
>   *His Highness*
>   *President Sheikh (full name)*

Place card: *H.H. President Sheikh (full name)*
Introduction:
>   *His Highness President Sheikh (full name) of the United Arab Emirates*
>   *The President of the United Arab Emirates, His Highness Sheikh (full name)*

Introduction, one person to another:
>   *Your Highness, may I present …*
>   *… may I present His Highness President Sheikh (full name) …*

Conversation: *President* OR *Your Highness*
Subsequently in conversation: *Sir*

Ruler of an Emirate

Example: *Sheikh Mohammed bin Rashid Al-Maktoum, Ruler of Dubai*
Envelope:
>   *His Highness*
>   *Sheikh (full name)*
>   *Ruler of (state)*
>   *Address*

Letter salutation: *Your Highness:*
Complimentary close: *Most Respectfully,*
Invitation, inside envelope:
>   *His Highness*
>   *The Ruler of (state)*

Place card: *H.H. Sheikh (name)*
Introduction:
>   *His Highness the Ruler of (state)*
>   OR *His Highness Sheikh (full name), the ruler of (state)*
>   OR *The Ruler of (state), His Highness Sheikh (full name)*

Introduction, one person to another:
>   *Your Highness, may I present …*
>   *… may I present His Highness the Ruler of (state) …*
>   OR *… may I present His Highness Sheikh (full name) …*

Conversation: *Your Highness*
Subsequently in conversation: *Sir*

Other Official Royalty and Nobility

Crown Prince/Princess of a Royal Family

Examples: *Prince Haji Al-Muhtadee Billah, Crown Prince of Brunei Darussalam*
Prince Philippe, Duke of Brabant, Crown Prince of the Belgians
Prince Willem-Alexander, Crown Prince of the Netherlands

NOTE: For the crown prince and crown princess of the **Japanese imperial throne**, modify form to *His/Her Imperial Highess*.

Envelope:
His/Her Royal Highness
(Title) (name)
Crown Prince/Princess of (country)
(Address)

Letter salutation: *Your Royal Highness:*
Complimentary close: *Respectfully,*
Invitation, inside envelope:
His/Her Royal Highness
(Title) (name)

Place card: *H.R.H. (title) (name)*
Introduction:
His/Her Royal Highness (title) (name), crown prince/princess of (country)
OR *The crown prince/princess of (country) His/Her Royal Highness (title) (name)*
Introduction, one person to another:
Your Royal Highness, may I present …
… may I present His/Her Royal Highness …
Conversation: *Your Royal Highness*
Subsequently in conversation: *Sir/ma'am*

Crown Prince of Saudi Arabia

Examples: *Sultan bin Abdulaziz Al-Saud*
Envelope:
His/Her Royal Highness
Crown Prince Sultan (name)
(Office)
(Address)

Letter salutation: *Your Royal Highness:*
Complimentary close: *Respectfully,*
Invitation, inside envelope:
His Royal Highness
Crown Prince Sultan (name)

Place card: *H.R.H. Crown Prince Sultan (name)*
Introduction: *His/Her Royal Highness Crown Prince Sultan (name) of Saudi Arabia*
Introduction, one person to another:
Your Royal Highness, may I present …
… may I present His Royal Highness …

426

Conversation: *Your Royal Highness*
Subsequently in conversation: *Sir*

Crown Prince of an Emirate

Examples: *General Sheikh Mohammed Bin Zayed Al-Nahyan,*
                        Crown Prince of Abu Dhabi
                Sheikh Tameen Bin Hamad Al-Thani, Crown Prince of Qatar
                Shaikh Hamdan Bin Mohammad Al Maktoum, Crown Prince of Dubai
NOTE: Include all honorifics, titles, and ranks presented.
Envelope:
    His Highness
        Sheikh (name)
            Crown Prince of (emirate)
                (Address)
Letter salutation: *Your Highness:*
Complimentary close: *Respectfully,*
Invitation, inside envelope:
    His Highness
        Sheikh (name)
Place card: *H.H. Sheikh (name)*
Introduction:
    His Highness Sheikh (name), the crown prince of (emirate)
    OR *The crown prince of (emirate), His Highness Sheikh (name)*
Introduction, one person to another:
    Your Highness, may I present …
    … may I present His Highness Sheikh (name) …
Conversation: *Your Highness*
Subsequently in conversation: *Sir*

Heir Apparent of an Emirate

Envelope:
    His Highness
        Sheikh (name)
            The Heir Apparent of (emirate)
                (Address)
Letter salutation: *Your Highness:*
Complimentary close: *Respectfully,*
Invitation, inside envelope:
    His Highness
        Sheikh (name)
Place card: *H.H. Sheikh (name)*
Introduction:
    His Highness Sheikh (name), the Heir Apparent of (emirate)
    OR *The Heir Apparent of (country), His Highness Sheikh (name)*

Introduction, one person to another:
> Your Highness, may I present ...
> ... may I present His Highness Sheikh (name) ...

Conversation: Your Highness
Subsequently in conversation: Sir

Royal Heir Apparent of a Malaysian State

Examples: DYTM Tuanku Syed Faizuddin Putra, the Crown Prince of Perlis
> DYTM Tuanku Syed Faizuddin Putra, the Raja Muda of Perlis
> DYTM Tuanku Syed Faizuddin Putra
>> ibni Tuanku Syed Sirajuddin Putra Jamalullail, D.K., S.P.M.P.

NOTE: DYTM Tuanku Raja Muda is short for Duli Yang Teramat Mulia Tuanku Raja Muda, a courtesy title which roughly translates to His Royal Highness the Crown Prince. Syed is the masculine honorific and sharifah is the feminine honorific for descendants of the Prophet. The spouse of the heir is styled DYTM Tanku (name).

Envelope:
> His Royal Highness
>> The Crown Prince of (state)
>> (Address)

Letter salutation: Your Royal Highness:
Complimentary close: Respectfully,
Invitation, inside envelope:
> His Royal Highness
>> (Syed if presented) (name)

Place card: H.R.H. (Syed if presented) (name)
Introduction:
> His Royal Highness (Syed if presented) (name), the Crown Prince of (state)
> OR The crown prince of (state),
>> His Royal Highness (Syed if presented) (name)

Introduction, one person to another:
> Your Royal Highness, may I present ...
> ... may I present His Royal Highness (Syed if presented) (name) ...

Conversation: Your Royal Highness
Subsequently in conversation: Sir

Heir Apparent of a Malaysian State

Examples: Tengku Muhammad Faris Petra ibni Sultan Ismail Petra, D.K.,
> Yang Teramat Mulia Tengku Mahkota of Kelantan
> Duli Yang Teramat Mulia Paduka Putra
>> Tengku Mahkota Johor Dar ul-Takzim

NOTE: Yang Teramat Mulia is a courtesy title which roughly translates to His Highness. Tengku Mahkota translates as crown prince.

Envelope:
> His Highness
>> The Crown Prince of (state)
>> (Address)

Letter salutation: Your Highness:

428

Complimentary close: *Respectfully,*
Invitation, inside envelope:
> His Highness
> > (name)

Place card: *H.H. (name)*
Introduction:
> His Highness (name), the Crown Prince of (state)
> OR The Crown Prince of (state), His Highness (name)

Introduction, one person to another:
> Your Highness, may I present …
> … may I present His Highness (name) …

Conversation: *Your Highness*
Subsequently in conversation: *Sir*

Hereditary Grand Duke/Duchess of a Grand Duchy
Example: *Prince Guillaume, Hereditary Grand Duke of Luxembourg*
Envelope:
> His/Her Royal Highness
> > Prince/Princess (name)
> > > Hereditary Grand Duke/Duchess of Luxembourg
> > > > (Address)

Letter salutation: *Your Royal Highness:*
Complimentary close: *Respectfully,*
Invitation, inside envelope:
> His/Her Royal Highness
> > Prince/Princess (name)

Place card: *H.R.H. Prince/Princess (name)*
Introduction:
> His/Her Royal Highness Prince/Princess (name),
> > the Hereditary Grand Duke/Duchess of Luxembourg
> OR The Hereditary Grand Duke/Duchess of Luxembourg,
> His/Her Royal Highness Prince/Princess (name)

Introduction, one person to another:
> Your Royal Highness, may I present …
> … may I present His/Her Royal Highness Prince/Princess (name). …

Conversation: *Your Royal Highness*

Hereditary Prince/Princess of a Principality
Example: *Prince Alois, Hereditary Prince of Liechtenstein*
Envelope:
> His/Her Serene Highness
> > Hereditary Prince
> > > (name) of (country)
> > > > (Address)

Letter salutation: *Your Serene Highness:*
Complimentary close: *Respectfully,*

Invitation, inside envelope:
  His/Her Serene Highness
    Prince/Princess (name)
Place card: *H.S.H. Prince/Princess (name)*
Introduction:
  His/Her Serene Highness Prince/Princess (name),
    the Hereditary Prince of (country)
  OR *The Hereditary Prince of (country),*
    His/Her Serene Highness Prince/Princess (name)
Introduction, one person to another:
  Your Serene Highness, may I present …
    … may I present His/Her Serene Highness Prince/Princess (name) …
Conversation: *Your Serene Highness*

Prince/Princess of a Royal Family
Examples: *Prince Christian, Prince of Denmark*
       Princess Leonor, Princess of Spain
Envelope:
  His/Her Royal Highness
    Prince/Princess (name)
      (Address)
Letter salutation: *Your Royal Highness:*
Complimentary close: *Respectfully,*
Invitation, inside envelope:
  His/Her Royal Highness
    Prince/Princess (name)
Place card: *H.R.H. Prince/Princess (name)*
Introduction: *His/Her Royal Highness Prince/Princess (name)*
Introduction, one person to another:
  Your Royal Highness, may I present …
    … may I present His/Her Royal Highness Prince/Princess (name) …
Conversation: *Your Royal Highness*
Subsequently in conversation: *Sir/ma'am*

Prince/Princess of a Princely Family
Examples: *Prince Maximilian, Prince of Liechtenstein*
       Princess Stephanie, Princess of Monaco
Envelope:
  His/Her Serene Highness
    Prince/Princess (name)
      (Address)
Letter salutation: *Serene Highness:*
Complimentary close: *Respectfully,*

430

Invitation, inside envelope:
    His/Her Serene Highness
       Prince/Princess (name)
Place card: *H.S.H. Prince/Princess (name)*
Introduction: *His/Her Serene Highness Prince/Princess (name)*
Introduction, one person to another:
    Your Serene Highness, may I present …
    … may I present His/Her Serene Highness Prince/Princess (name) …
Conversation: *Your Serene Highness*
Subsequently in conversation: *Sir/ma'am*

Diplomats

Ambassador Extraordinary and Plenipotentiary
Examples: *Sir (full name), The Ambassador of …*
               Admiral (full name), The Ambassador of …
               General (full name), The Ambassador of …
               Dr. (full name), Ambassador of …
               Mrs. (full name), Ambassador of …
               (Full name), The Ambassador of …
Envelope, official:
    His/Her Excellency
       (Personal honorific if presented) (full name), (post nominals as appropriate)
           The Ambassador of (full name of country)
           (Address)
Letter salutation: *Your Excellency:* OR *Dear Mr./Madam Ambassador:*
Complimentary close: *Sincerely yours,* OR *Sincerely,*
Envelope, social:
    The Ambassador of (full name of country)
       (Address)
Invitation, inside envelope: *The Ambassador of (full name of country)*
Place card: *The Ambassador of (full name of country)*
Introduction:
    His/Her Excellency (personal honorific if presented) (full name),
       Ambassador of (full name of country)
    OR *Ambassador of (full name of country), Ambassador (surname)*
Introduction, one person to another:
    Your Excellency, may I present …
    … may I present Ambassador (surname) …
Conversation: *Your Excellency* OR *Mr./Madam Ambassador*
Conversation, less formal: *Ambassador (surname)*

Ambassador with a Personal Title
Envelope, official:
> *His/Her Excellency*
>> *(Appropriate form for their title) (full name)*
>>> *The Ambassador of (full name of country)*
>>>> *(Address)*

Introduction:
> *His/Her Excellency (appropriate form for their title) (full name),*
>> *Ambassador of (full name of country)*

All other forms of address: Use standard forms for his or her title.

Appointed Ambassador
Envelope, official:
> *His/Her Excellency*
>> *(Full name)*
>>> *The Appointed Ambassador of (full name of country)*
>>>> *(Address)*

Letter salutation: *Your Excellency:* OR *Dear Mr./Madam Ambassador:*
Complimentary close: *Sincerely yours,* OR *Sincerely,*
Envelope, social:
> *The Appointed Ambassador of (full name of country)*
>> *(Address)*

Invitation, inside envelope: *The Appointed Ambassador of (full name of country)*
Place card: *The Appointed Ambassador of (full name of country)*
Introduction:
> *His/Her Excellency (full name), Appointed Ambassador of (full name of country)*

Introduction, one person to another: *Ambassador (surname)*
Conversation: *Your Excellency* OR *Mr./Madam Ambassador*

Minister Plenipotentiary
NOTE: *His/Her Excellency* is reserved for an accredited minister.
Envelope, official:
> *His/Her Excellency*
>> *(Full name)*
>>> *Embassy of (full name of country)*
>>>> *(Address)*

Letter salutation: *Your Excellency:* OR *Dear Minister:*
Complimentary close: *Sincerely yours,* OR *Sincerely,*
Envelope, social:
> *His/Her Excellency*
>> *(Full name)*
>>> *(Address)*

Invitation, inside envelope: *H.E. (full name)*
Place card: *H.E. (full name)*

432

Introduction:
> His/Her Excellency (full name), Minister of (full name of country)
> OR His/Her Excellency (full name), Minister of (full name of country)

Introduction, one person to another:
> Your Excellency, may I present …
> … may I present the Minister of (full name of country),
>> His/Her Excellency (full name)
> OR … may I present Minister (surname) …

Conversation: Your Excellency OR Minister (surname)

Minister-Counselor

NOTE: His/Her Excellency is reserved for officials of the ranks of accredited ambassador or accredited minister. Check for preference and tradition of the bearer. If addressed as His/Her Excellency, modify form for minister and identify as a *minister-counselor of (country)*. If no courtesy title is to be used identify as *minister-counselor of (country)* and address as Mr./Mrs./etc. (name).

Chargé d'Affaires
Chargé d'Affaires ad interim
Chargé d'Affaires ad hoc
Chargé d'Affaires pro tempore

NOTE: Address as Mr./Mrs./Ms. (name) unless the chargé has the rank of minister and is addressed as His/Her Excellency. If a minister-counselor see note above. Identify as a *chargé* after the name.

Counselor
Attaché, Assistant Attaché
First Secretary, Second Secretary, Third Secretary
General Consul, Consul, Vice Consul

NOTE: Address as Mr./Mrs./etc. (name) and identify by (office). Some consuls are addressed as *the Honorable*. Check for preference of the bearer.

International Organizations

Secretary General of the United Nations
Envelope, official:
> His/Her Excellency
>> (Personal honorific if presented) (full name)
>>> Secretary General of the United Nations
>>>> (Address)

Letter salutation:
> Your Excellency:
> OR Dear Mr./Madam Secretary General:
> OR Dear (personal honorific if presented) (surname):

Complimentary close: Sincerely yours, OR Sincerely,
Envelope, social:
> His/Her Excellency
>> The Secretary General of the United Nations
>>> (Address)

Invitation, inside envelope: The Secretary General of the United Nations
Place card:
> The Secretary General of the United Nations
> OR H.E. (Personal honorific if presented) (full name)

Introduction:
> His/Her Excellency (full name), Secretary General of the United Nations
> The Secretary General of the United Nations, Mr./Mrs./Dr./etc. (surname)

Introduction, one person to another:
> Your Excellency, may I present ...
> OR Mr./Madam Secretary General, may I present ...
> ... may I present the Secretary General ...
> OR ... may I present (Personal honorific if presented) (surname) ...

Conversation:
> Your Excellency OR Mr./Madam Secretary General
> OR (Personal honorific if presented) (surname)

Secretary General of the Organization of American States
Envelope, official:
> His/Her Excellency
>> (Personal honorific if presented) (full name)
>>> Secretary General of the Organization of American States
>>>> (Address)

Letter salutation: Your Excellency: OR Dear Mr./Madam Secretary General:
Complimentary close: Sincerely yours, OR Sincerely,
Envelope, social:
> His/Her Excellency
>> The Secretary General of the Organization of American States
>>> (Address)

OR *His/Her Excellency*
>> *(Personal honorific if presented) (full name)*
>> *(Address)*

Invitation, inside envelope:
The Secretary General of the Organization of American States

Place card:
The Secretary General of the Organization of American States
OR *H.E. (full name)*

Introduction:
His/Her Excellency (full name),
>> *Secretary General of the Organization of American States*

Introduction, one person to another:
Mr./Madam Secretary General, may I present ...
... may I present the Secretary General ...

Conversation: *Your Excellency* OR *Mr./Madam Secretary General*

Ambassador to an International Organization

Envelope, official:
His/Her Excellency
>> *(Full name)*
>>> *(Position & organization)*
>>> *(Address)*

Letter salutation: *Your Excellency:* or *Dear Mr./Madam Ambassador:*

Complimentary close: *Sincerely yours,* OR *Sincerely,*

Envelope, social:
His/Her Excellency
>> *(Full name)*
>>> *(Address)*

Invitation, inside envelope: *The (position & organization)*

Place card: *The (position & organization)* OR *H.E. (full name)*

Introduction:
His/Her Excellency (full name), representative of (country) to (organization)
OR *The representative of (country) to (organization), Ambassador (surname)*

Introduction, one person to another: *Ambassador (surname)*

Conversation: *Mr./Madam Ambassador* OR *Ambassador (surname)*

PART III

Country Names & Officials

21 Country Names & Officials

Titles and Forms of Address
There are more than 200 governmental entities; each has its own unique structure and hierarchy. While similarities exist, each has its own traditions. Thus, it
is important to check the preference of the bearer and the tradition of a country
to assure the most successful outcome.

Precedence
National officials in this section are not necessarily listed in precedence order.

Afghanistan
Official name: Islamic Republic of Afghanistan
    Embassy of Afghanistan
    Noun and adjective: Afghan
    Chief of state and head of government: President
    Other high officials:
        First and second vice presidents
        Ministers of *(portfolio)*
        Deputy ministers of *(portfolio)*
        Members of the House of Elders
        Members of the House of the People
        Justices of the Supreme Court
        Judges of the High Courts and Appeals Courts
        Governor of the Central Bank
NOTE: Address the president by *(office)* or as *His/Her Excellency.* Address other officials
by *(honorific)* + *(name)* and identify by *(office).*

Akrotiri

Official name: Akrotiri Sovereign Base Area
   An overseas territory of the United Kingdom
   Diplomatic representation by the United Kingdom
   Chief of state and head of government: King/Queen
        (hereditary monarch of the United Kingdom)
   Other high official: Administrator

Albania

Official name: Republic of Albania
   Embassy of the Republic of Albania
   Noun and adjective: Albanian
   Chief of state: President
   Head of government: Prime minister
   Other high officials:
        Deputy prime minister
        Ministers of *(portfolio)* in the Council of Ministers
        Speaker and deputies of the Kuvendi/Parliament
        Chief justice and justices of the Supreme Court
        Justices of the Constitutional Court
        Governor of the Bank of Albania

Algeria

Official name: People's Democratic Republic of Algeria
   Embassy of the People's Democratic Republic of Algeria
   Noun and adjective: Algerian
   Chief of state: President
   Head of government: Prime minister
   Other high officials:
        Ministers of *(portfolio)*
        Members of the Council of Nations
        Members of the National People's Assembly
        Chief justice and justices of the Supreme Court
        Governor of the Central Bank
NOTE: Address the president by *(office)* or as *His/Her Excellency.* Also address the prime
minister, speaker of the National People's Assembly, or chief justice of the Supreme
Court as *His/Her Excellency.* Address members of the National People's Assembly as *the
Honorable.* Address other officials with an honorific *(Mr./Mrs./etc.)* + *(name)* and iden-
tify by *(office).*

American Samoa

Official name: Territory of American Samoa
   An unincorporated, unorganized territory of the United States
   Diplomatic representation by the United States
   Noun and adjective: American Samoan
   Chief of state: President of the United States
   Head of government: Governor
   Other high officials:
        Departmental directors
        Senators in the Senate

440

Members of the House of Representatives
Chief justice and associate justices in the High Court

Andorra
Official name: Principality of Andorra
Embassy of Andorra/Permanent Mission of the Principality of Andorra to the
United Nations
Noun and adjective: Andorran
Chief of state:
French co-prince (President of the French Republic)
Spanish co-prince (Episcopal co-prince, the Bishop of Urgell, Spain)
Head of government: President of the Executive Council
Other high officials:
Members of the Executive Council
Members of the General Council of the Valleys
Justices and judges of the Tribunal of Judges, Tribunal of Courts,
Supreme Court of Justice of Andorra, Supreme Council of Justice,
and Constitutional Tribunal
NOTE: Address the president by *(office)* or as *His/Her Excellency.* Also address a member
of the Executive Council or a judge of a high court as *His/Her Excellency.* Address members
of the General Council of the Valleys and other elected officials as *the Honourable.*
Address other officials by *(honorific)* + *(name)* and identify by *(office).*

Angola
Official name: Republic of Angola
Embassy of the Republic of Angola
Noun and adjective: Angolan
Chief of state and head of government: President
Head of government: Prime minister and president
Other high officials:
Deputy prime minister
Ministers in the office of the presidency for *(portfolio)*
Ministers of *(portfolio)* in a Council of Ministers
Secretary of state for *(portfolio)*
Deputies of the National Assembly
President and judges of the Constitutional Court
Justices of the Supreme Court
Governor of the National Bank of Angola
NOTE: Address the president by *(office)* or as *His/Her Excellency.* Also address the prime
minister, a minister, or secretary as *His/Her Excellency.* Address a deputy of the National
Assembly as *Deputy (name).* Address other officials with an appropriate honorific
(Justice/Judge/Mr./Mrs./etc.) + *(name)* and identify by *(office).*

Anguilla
Official name: Anguilla
An overseas territory of the United Kingdom
Diplomatic representation by the United Kingdom
Noun and adjective: Anguillian
Chief of state: King/Queen (hereditary monarch of the United Kingdom)
Vice-royal representative: Governor

Head of government: Chief minister
Other high officials:
Deputy Governor
Members of the Executive Council
Speaker and members of the House of Assembly
Chief justice and justices of the Eastern Caribbean Supreme Court
President and judges of the Caribbean Court of Justice
Judge of the High Court

NOTE: Address the governor as *His/Her Excellency.* Address the chief minister, deputy governor, or a minister as *the Honourable.* Address the chief justice as *His Lordship, the Honourable Chief Justice,* or as *the Honourable (name).* Address a justice or judge of a high court as *the Honourable (name).* Address other officials by *(honorific) + (name)* and identify by *(office).*

Antigua and Barbuda
Official name: Antigua and Barbuda
Embassy of Antigua and Barbuda
Noun and adjective: Antiguan, Barbudan
Chief of state: The King/Queen of Antigua and Barbuda
Elizabeth the Second, by the Grace of God, Queen of Antigua and Barbuda and of Her Other Realms and Territories, Head of the Commonwealth.
Vice-royal representative: Governor-general
Head of government: Prime minister
Other high officials:
Deputy prime minister
Ministers of *(portfolio)* in the Council of Ministers
Attorney General
Senators in the Senate
Speaker and members of the House of Representatives
Chief justice and justices of appeal of the Eastern Caribbean Supreme Court
President and judges of the Caribbean Court of Justice
Judge of the High Court

NOTE: Address the governor-general as *His/Her Excellency.* Address the prime minister, members of the Cabinet, and members of the legislature as *the Honourable.* Address the chief justice as *His Lordship, the Honorable Chief Justice,* or *the Honourable (name).* Address a justice or judge of a high court as *the Honourable (name).* Address other officials by *(honorific) + (name)* and identify by *(office).* Include *Sir* or *Dame* in the forms of address of knighted officials.

Argentina
Official name: Argentine Republic
Embassy of the Argentine Republic
Noun and adjective: Argentine
Chief of state and head of government: President
Other high officials:
Vice president
Chief of the Cabinet
Ministers of *(portfolio)*
General secretary for the Presidency

President and vice-presidents of the Senate
President of the Senate
Senators in the Senate
President and vice-presidents of the Chamber of Deputies
Secretaries of (*portfolio*) of the Chamber of Deputies
Deputies in the Chamber of Deputies
President and justices of the Supreme Court
President of the Central Bank
Governors of the provinces

NOTE: Address the president by (*office*) or as *the Honorable*. Address the vice president, leadership in the Senate and Chamber of Deputies, a member of the Cabinet, senator, deputy, or judge of a high court as *the Honorable*. Address other officials by (*honorific*) + (*name*) and identify by (*office*).

Armenia

Official name: Republic of Armenia
Embassy of the Republic of Armenia
Noun and adjective: Armenian
Chief of state: President
Head of government: Prime minister
Other high officials:
Chief of staff of the Council of Ministers
Ministers of (*portfolio*) in the Council of Ministers
Members of the National Assembly/Parliament
Judges of the Constitutional Court and the Court of Cassation
Chairman of the National Bank

NOTE: Address the president and prime minister by (*office*) or as *His/Her Excellency*. Also address a member of the Cabinet, member of Parliament, or judge of a high court as *His/Her Excellency*. Address other officials by (*honorific*) + (*name*) and identify by (*office*).

Aruba

Official name: Aruba
Diplomatic representation by the Royal Netherlands Embassy
Minister Plenipotentiary for Aruba at the Embassy of the Kingdom of
the Netherlands
Noun and adjective: Aruban
Chief of state: King/Queen (hereditary monarch of the Netherlands)
Vice-royal representative: Governor
Head of government: Prime minister
Other high officials:
Ministers of (*portfolio*) in the Council of Ministers
Attorney General in the Council of Ministers
Members of the Staten
Judges of the Common Court of Justice of Aruba
President of the Central Bank of Aruba

NOTE: Address the governor as *His/Her Excellency*.

Ashmore and Cartier Islands
Official name: Territory of Ashmore and Cartier Islands
    A territory of Australia
    Diplomatic representation by the Commonwealth of Australia
    Administered by the Australian Department of Transport and Regional Services

Australia
Official name: Commonwealth of Australia
    Embassy of Australia
    Noun and adjective: Australian
    Chief of state: King/Queen of Australia
        Elizabeth the Second, by the Grace of God, Queen of Australia and
        Her Other Realms and Territories, Head of the Commonwealth
    Vice-royal representative: Governor-general
    Head of government: Prime minister
    Other high officials:
        Deputy prime minister
        Members of the Federal Executive Council
        Minister for (*portfolio*)
        Attorney General
        Treasurer
        Special Minister of State
        Deputy ministers
        Assistant ministers
        Parliamentary secretaries
        President of the Senate
        Senators in the Senate
        Speaker and members of the House of Representatives
        Chief justice of Australia
        Justices of the High Court
        Chief justice and justices of the Federal Court of Australia
        Chief justice and justices of the High Court
        Governor of the Reserve Bank
NOTE: See page 323.

Austria
Official name: Republic of Austria
    Embassy of Austria
    Noun and adjective: Austrian
    Chief of state: President
    Head of government: Chancellor
    Other high officials:
        Vice chancellor
        Ministers for (*portfolio*) in the Council of Ministers
        State Secretaries
        Deputy secretaries, and undersecretaries of executive departments
        President and members of the Federal Council/Bundesrat
        President and members of National Council/Nationalrat

Judges of the Supreme Judicial Court and the Constitutional Court
President of the Austrian National Bank

NOTE: Address the president and chancellor by *(office)* or *the Honorable*. Also address the vice chancellor, a minister, president of the Federal Council and National Council, deputy secretary, or undersecretary as *the Honorable*. Address a member of the Federal and National Councils, judge of a high court, or other official with an appropriate honorific *(Judge/Mr./Mrs./etc.)* + *(name)* and identify by *(office)*.

Azerbaijan

Official name: Republic of Azerbaijan
Embassy of the Republic of Azerbaijan
Noun and adjective: Azerbaijani, Azeri
Chief of state: President
Head of government: Prime minister
Other high officials:
First deputy prime minister
Deputy prime ministers
Ministers of *(portfolio)* in the Council of Ministers
Members of the Milli Mejlis/National Assembly
Justices of the Supreme Court
Chairman of the National Bank

NOTE: Address the president by *(office)* or as *His/Her Excellency*. Also address the prime minister, deputy prime minister, or a minister in the Council of Ministers as *His/Her Excellency*. Address a member of the National Assembly, a judge, or other officials by *(honorific)* + *(name)* and identify by *(office)*.

The Bahamas

Official name: Commonwealth of the Bahamas
Embassy of the Commonwealth of the Bahamas
Noun and adjective: Bahamian
Chief of state: The King/Queen of the Commonwealth of the Bahamas
Elizabeth the Second, by the Grace of God, Queen of the Commonwealth of the Bahamas and of Her Other Realms and Territories, Head of the Commonwealth
Vice-royal representative: Governor-general
Head of government: Prime minister
Other high officials:
Deputy prime minister
Ministers of *(portfolio)*
Attorney General
President of the Senate
Senators in the Senate
Speaker and members of the House of Assembly/Parliament
President, chief justice, and justices of the Court of Appeal
Lord justice and justices of the Supreme Court
Governor of the Central Bank

NOTE: Address the governor-general as *His/Her Excellency*; the prime minister as *the Right Honourable*; the Attorney General or a minister in the cabinet as *the Honourable*; a senator as *Senator (name)* without a courtesy title; and, member of the House of

Assembly as *Mr./Mrs./Dr./etc. (name)*, MP without a courtesy title. The lord justice is *the Right Honourable*, and a justice is *the Honourable*. Address the governor of the Central Bank and other officials by *(honorific)* + *(name)* and identify by *(office)*. Include *Sir* or *Dame* in the forms of address of knighted officials.

Bahrain

Official name: Kingdom of Bahrain
    Embassy of the Kingdom of Bahrain
    Noun and adjective: Bahraini
    Chief of state: King (hereditary monarch)
    Head of government: Prime minister
    Other high officials:
        Crown prince (the heir apparent)
        Deputy prime ministers
        Ministers of *(portfolio)*
        Members of the Consultative Council
        Members in the Council of Representatives
        Judges of the High Civil Appeal Court
        Chairman of the Central Bank of Bahrain
NOTE: Address the chief of state as *His Royal Highness*. The prime minister, deputy prime minister, and perhaps other officials will have a noble title and are addressed as *His Excellency Sheikh (name)* and identified by *(office)*. Otherwise address the deputy prime minister, minister, member of the Consultative Council, or chairman of the Central Bank as *His/Her Excellency*. Address a high judge as *the Honorable*. Address a member in the Council of Representatives, governor of a board, and other officials by *(honorific)* + *(name)* and identify by *(office)*.

Bangladesh

Official name: People's Republic of Bangladesh
    Embassy of the People's Republic of Bangladesh
    Noun and adjective: Bangladeshi
    Chief of state: President
    Head of government: Prime minister
    Other high officials:
        Chief advisors for *(portfolio)* in the cabinet
        Members of Parliament
        Chief justice and justices of the Supreme Court
        Governor of the Central Bank

Barbados

Official name: Barbados
    Embassy of Barbados
    Noun and adjective: Barbadian, Bajan
    Chief of state: The King/Queen of Barbados
        Elizabeth the Second, by the Grace of God, Queen of Barbados
        and of Her Other Realms and Territories, Head of the Commonwealth
    Vice-royal representative: Governor-general
    Head of government: Prime minister

Other high officials:
>Deputy prime minister
>Ministers of *(portfolio)*
>Attorney General
>Senators in the Senate
>Speaker and deputy speaker of the House of Assembly
>Members of the House of Assembly
>Justices of the Court of Appeal of the Supreme Court
>Judges of the High Court of the Supreme Court
>President and judges of the Caribbean Court of Justice
>Governor of the Central Bank

NOTE: Address the governor-general as *His/Her Excellency*. Address the prime minister as *the Right Honourable*. Address a minister in the cabinet and all members of both assemblies as *the Honourable*. Address other officials by *(honorific)* + *(name)* and identify by *(office)*. Include *Sir* or *Dame* in the forms of address of knighted officials.

Bassas da India
See *Iles Eparses*.

Barbuda
See *Antigua and Barbuda*.

Belarus
Official name: Republic of Belarus
>Embassy of the Republic of Belarus
Noun and adjective: Belarusian
Chief of state: President
Head of government: Prime minister
Other high officials:
>First deputy prime minister
>Deputy prime ministers
>Ministers in the Presidium of the Council of Ministers
>Ministers of *(portfolio)*
>Head of the Presidential Administration
>Members of the Council of the Republic
>Members of the Chamber of Representatives
>Chairman of the State Control Committee
>Chairman and justices of the Supreme Court
>Chairman and justices of the Constitutional Court
>Chairman of the Board of the National Bank

NOTE: Address the president and prime minister by *(office)* or as *His/Her Excellency*. Also address a deputy prime minister as *His/Her Excellency*. Address a minister or head of Presidential Administration as *the Honorable*. Address other officials by *(honorific)* + *(name)* and identify by *(office)*.

Belgium

Official name: Kingdom of Belgium
> Embassy of Belgium
> *Noun and adjective:* Belgian
> *Chief of state:* King (hereditary monarch)
> *Head of government:* Prime minister
> *Other high officials:*
>> Prince/princess/the heir apparent
>> Prince/princess
>> Deputy prime ministers
>> Ministers of *(portfolio)* in the Council of Ministers
>> Senators in the Senate
>> Deputies in the Chamber of Deputies
>> Justices of the Supreme Court of Justice
>> Governor of the National Bank

NOTE: Address the chief of state and heir apparent as *Your Royal Highness*, but other members of the ruling family as *Your Highness*. Address the prime minister, a deputy prime minister, or minister as *His/Her Excellency*. Address all other officials by *(honorific)* + *(name)* and identify by *(office)*.

Belize

Official name: Belize
> Embassy of Belize
> *Noun and adjective:* Belizean
> *Chief of state:* The King/Queen of Belize
>> Elizabeth the Second, by the Grace of God, Queen of Belize and of Her Other Realms and Territories, Head of the Commonwealth
> *Vice-royal representative:* Governor-general
> *Head of government:* Prime minister
> *Other high officials:*
>> Deputy prime minister
>> Ministers of *(portfolio)*
>> Attorney General
>> Senators in the Senate
>> Members of the House of Representatives
>> Chief justice and justices of the Supreme Court
>> President and judges of the Caribbean Court of Justice
>> Governor of the Central Bank

NOTE: Address the governor-general as *His/Her Excellency*. Address the prime minister, the deputy prime minister, the Attorney General, a minister, a senator, a member of the House of Representatives, and officials of equal or higher rank as *the Honourable*. Address the governor of the Central Bank and other officials by *(honorific)* + *(name)* and identify by *(office)*. Include *Sir* or *Dame* in the forms of address of knighted officials.

Benin

Official name: Republic of Benin
> Embassy of the Republic of Benin
> *Noun and adjective:* Beninese
> *Chief of state and head of government:* President

448

Other high officials:
    Ministers of *(portfolio)* in the Council of Ministers
    Deputies of the National Assembly
    President and justices of the Supreme Court
    President and justices of the Constitutional Court
    Judges of the High Court of Justice
    Governor of the Central Bank of Benin
NOTE: Address the president by *(office)* or as *His/Her Excellency.* Address a minister, deputy, or justice of a high court as *the Honorable.* Address other officials by *(honorific)* + *(name)* and identify by *(office).*

Bermuda

Official name: Bermuda
    An overseas territory of the United Kingdom
    Diplomatic representation by the United Kingdom
    Noun and adjective: Bermudian
    Chief of state: King/Queen (hereditary monarch of the United Kingdom)
    Vice-royal representative: Governor
    Head of government: Premier
    Other high officials:
        Deputy premier
        Chairman of the Royal Advisory Council
        Ministers of *(portfolio)*
        Junior ministers
        President, vice-president, and senators in the Senate
        Speaker, deputy speaker, government house leader of the House of Assembly
        Members of the House of Assembly
        Chief justice and justices of the Supreme Court
        Justices of the Court of Appeal
NOTE: Address the governor as *His/Her Excellency.* Address the premier by *(office)* or as *the Honourable.* Also address the prime minister, deputy premier, chairman of the RAC, a minister, or leader in the House of Assembly as *the Honourable.* Address a senator as *Senator (name)* and a member of the House of Assembly as *Mr./Mrs. (name),* MP. Address other officials by *(honorific)* + *(name)* and identify by *(office).* Include *Sir* or *Dame* in the forms of address of knighted officials. The use of the post-nominal JP, for Justice of the Peace, is widespread by officials in Bermuda where it is an appointed administrative, rather than judicial, designation.

Bhutan

Official name: Kingdom of Bhutan
    Consulate General of Bhutan
    Noun and adjective: Bhutanese
    Chief of state: King
    Head of government: Prime minister
    Other high officials:
        Ministers of *(portfolio)* in the Council of Ministers
        Members of the Royal Advisory Council
        Members of the National Assembly
        Judges of the High Court

Bolivia

Official name: Republic of Bolivia
>	Embassy of the Republic of Bolivia
>	*Noun and adjective:* Bolivian
>	*Chief of state and head of government:* President
>	*Other high officials:*
>>		Vice president
>>		Ministers of *(portfolio)*
>>		Senators in the Senate
>>		Deputies in the Chamber of Deputies
>>		Justices of the Supreme Court of Justice
>>		Judges of District Courts (departmental courts)
>>		President of the Central Bank

NOTE: Bolivians do not use courtesy titles when addressing their national leaders. Officials are directly addressed as Mr./Madam *(office)*: *Mr. President, Madam Minister, Mr. Senator, Madam Deputy,* etc. When the official's name is used in writing, the *(honorific)* *(full name)* is on the second line. Address other officials by *(honorific)* + *(name)* and identify by *(office)*. When the president, vice president, or a minister travels abroad he or she is often addressed as *His/Her Excellency.*

Bosnia and Herzegovina

Official name: Bosnia and Herzegovina
>	Embassy of Bosnia and Herzegovina
>	*Noun and adjective:* Bosnian, Herezegovinian
>	*Chief of state:* Chairman of the Presidency
>>		The office rotates every eight months among three members.
>	*Head of government:* Chairman of the Council of Ministers
>	*Other high officials:*
>>		Chairman of the Council of Ministers
>>		Ministers of *(portfolio)* in the Council of Ministers
>>		Members of the Constitutional Court
>>		Members of the House of Representatives
>>		Members of the House of Peoples
>>		Judges of the State Court
>>		Governor of the Central Bank
>	*Members of the Federation Government*
>	*Members of the Republika Srpska Government*

NOTE: Address the chairman of the Presidency and chairman of the Council of Ministers by *(office)* or as *His/Her Excellency.* Also address members in the Cabinet as *His/Her Excellency.* Address members of both houses of Parliament as *the Honorable.* Address other officials by *(honorific)* + *(name)* and identify by *(office).*

Botswana

Official name: Republic of Botswana
>	Embassy of the Republic of Botswana
>	*Singular noun and adjective:* Motswana
>	*Plural noun and adjective:* Botswana
>	*Chief of state and head of government:* President

450

Other high officials:
> Vice president
> Ministers of (*portfolio*)
> Attorney General
> Chiefs, sub-chiefs, and members of the House of Chiefs
> Speaker and members of the National Assembly
> Chief justice/president and justices of the Court of Appeal
> Governor of the Bank of Botswana

NOTE: Address the president and vice president by (*office*) or as *His/Her Excellency*. Also address a member of the Cabinet as *His/Her Excellency*. Address other officials by (*honorific*) + (*name*) and identify by (*office*).

Brazil

Official name: Federative Republic of Brazil
> Brazilian Embassy
> *Noun and adjective:* Brazilian
> *Chief of state and head of government:* President
> *Other high officials:*
>> Vice president
>> Chiefs of (*portfolio*)
>> Ministers of (*portfolio*)
>> President of the Senate
>> Senators in the Senate
>> President of the Chamber of Deputies
>> Federal deputies in the Chamber of Deputies
>> President and justices of the Supreme Federal Tribunal
>> Judges of the Higher Tribunal of Justice
>> President of the Central Bank

NOTE: Address the president by (*office*) or as *His/Her Excellency*. Also address a vice president, chief, or ministers as *His/Her Excellency*. Address other officials by (*honorific*) + (*name*) and identify by (*office*).

British Indian Ocean Territory

Official name: British Indian Ocean Territory
> An overseas territory of the United Kingdom
> Diplomatic representation by the United Kingdom
> Chief of state and head of government:
>> King/Queen (hereditary monarch of the United Kingdom)
> *Other high officials:*
>> Commissioner
>> Administrator

NOTE: The commissioner and administrator are addressed as Mr./Mrs./etc. (*name*) and identified by (*office*).

British Virgin Islands

Official name: British Virgin Islands
> An overseas territory of the United Kingdom
> Diplomatic representation by the United Kingdom
> *Noun and adjective:* British Virgin Islander
> *Chief of state:* King/Queen (hereditary monarch of the United Kingdom)

Vice-royal representative: Governor
Head of government: Premier
Other high officials:
> Deputy premier
> Ministers
> Attorney General
> Speaker and members of the House of Assembly
> Chief justice and justices of appeal of the Eastern Caribbean Supreme Court
> President and judges of the Caribbean Court of Justice
> Judge of the High Court

NOTE: Address the governor as *His/Her Excellency*. Address the premier, deputy premier, Attorney General, and speaker of the House of Assembly as *the Honourable*. Address the chief justice as *His Lordship, the Honourable Chief Justice,* or *the Honourable (name)*. Address a justice or judge as *the Honourable (name)*. Address other officials by *(honorific)* + *(name)* and identify by *(office)*. Include *Sir* or *Dame* in the forms of address of knighted officials.

Brunei

Official name: State of Brunei Darussalam
> Embassy of the State of Brunei Darussalam
> *Noun and adjective:* Bruneian
> *Chief of state and head of government:* Sultan (hereditary monarch)
> *Other high officials:*
>> Crown prince/senior minister
>> Ministers of *(portfolio)*
>> Members of the Religious Council
>> Members of the Council of Succession
>> Members of the Legislative Council
>> Chief justice and justices of the Supreme Court

NOTE: Address the sultan as *Your Majesty* and the crown prince as *Your Royal Highness*. Also address a prince in the royal family holding a high office as *Your Royal Highness* and identify by *(office)*. Address ministers as *the Honourable Pehin Dato (name)* or *the Honourable (name)*. Address other officials by *(honorific)* + *(name)* and identify by *(office)*.

Bulgaria

Official name: Republic of Bulgaria
> Embassy of the Republic of Bulgaria
> *Noun and adjective:* Bulgarian
> *Chief of state:* President
> *Head of government:* Prime minister
> *Other high officials:*
>> Vice president
>> Deputy prime ministers
>> Ministers of *(portfolio)* in the Council of Ministers
>> Chairman and members of the National Assembly
>> Justices of the Supreme Administrative and the Constitutional Courts
>> Justices of the Supreme Court of Cassation
>> Chairman of the Bulgarian National Bank

452

NOTE: Address the president by *(office)* or as *His/Her Excellency*. Also address the prime minister, vice president, chairman of the National Assembly, or a minister as *His/Her Excellency*. Address other officials by *(honorific)* + *(name)* and identify by *(office)*.

Burkina Faso

Official name: Burkina Faso
    Embassy of Burkina Faso
    Noun and adjective: Burkinabe
    Chief of state: President
    Head of government: Prime minister
    Other high officials:
        Ministers of *(portfolio)* in the Council of Ministers
        Delegate ministers of *(portfolio)*
        Speaker and members of the Chamber of Representatives
        Speaker and deputies of the National Assembly
        President, vice president, and justices of the Supreme Court
        Governor of the Central Bank of Burkina Faso

NOTE: Address the president by *(office)* or as *His/Her Excellency*. Also address the prime minister or a speaker of a legislature as *His/Her Excellency*. Address other officials by *(honorific)* + *(name)* and identify by *(office)*.

Burma

    See *Myanmar (Union of Myanmar)*, page 498.

Burundi

Official name: Republic of Burundi
    Embassy of the Republic of Burundi
    Noun and adjective: Burundian
    Chief of state and head of government: President
    Other high officials:
        First vice president
        Second vice president
        Ministers of *(portfolio)* in the Council of Ministers
        President of and senators in the Senate
        Speaker of and members of the National Assembly
        Judges of the courts and tribunals
        Governor and executive board of the Bank of Burundi

NOTE: Address the president by *(office)* or as *His/Her Excellency*. Also address a vice president, minister, or other high official as *His/Her Excellency*. Address other officials by *(honorific)* + *(name)* and identify by *(office)*.

Cambodia

Official name: Kingdom of Cambodia
    Royal Embassy of Cambodia
    Noun and adjective: Cambodian
    Chief of state: King (hereditary monarch)
    Head of government: Prime minister
    Other high officials:
        Deputy prime ministers
        Ministers of *(portfolio)*

President of and senators in the Senate
President and members of National Assembly
Justices of the Supreme Court
Judges of the Supreme Council of the Magistracy
Governor of the State Bank of Cambodia

NOTE: Address the chief of state as *Your Majesty*. Address the prime minister, a deputy prime minister, minister, senator, member of the National Assembly, or judge of a high court as *His/Her Excellency*. Address an official holding the honorary title Samdech as *Samdech (name)* and identify by *(office)*: The prime minister, presidents of the legislatures, and chief justice of the Supreme Court frequently hold this title. Address other officials by *(honorific)* + *(name)* and identify by *(office)*.

Cameroon

Official name: Republic of Cameroon
    Embassy of the Republic of Cameroon
    Noun and adjective: Cameroonian
    Chief of state: President
    Head of government: Prime minister
    Other high officials:
        Deputy prime ministers
        Secretary General of the Presidency
        Secretary of state
        Ministers of *(portfolio)*
        Delegate Minister of *(portfolio)*
        President, vice presidents, and deputy of the National Assembly
        President and advisor (justices) of the Supreme Court
        Judges of the High Court of Justice
        Governor, Secretary General, and vice governor of the
            Bank of the Central African States

NOTE: Address only the president and minister of foreign affairs as *His/Her Excellency*. Address the prime minister, a secretary, or minister as Mr./*Madam (office)*, without a courtesy title. Address members of the National Assembly as *the Honourable*. Address the president of the Supreme Court by *(office)*, not by name. Address the advisors (associate judges) of the Supreme Court as *Judge (name)* and identify by *(office)*. Address other officials by *(honorific)* + *(name)* and identify by *(office)*.

Canada

Official name: Canada
    Embassy of Canada
    Noun and adjective: Canadian
    Chief of state: The King/Queen of Canada
        Elizabeth the Second, by the Grace of God, Queen of the United Kingdom, Canada and Her Other Realms and Territories, Head of the Commonwealth, Defender of the Faith
    Vice-royal representatives:
        Governor-general
        Lieutenant governors
    Head of government: Prime minister

454

Other high officials:
> Ministers of *(portfolio)* in the Federal Ministry
> President of the Treasury Board
> President of the Queen's Privy Council
> Leader of government and senators in the Senate
> Leader of government in and members of the House of Commons
> Justices of the Supreme Court of Canada and the Federal Court of Canada
> Judges of the Federal Court of Appeal
> Judges of provincial courts such as the Court of Appeal,
>> Court of the Queen's Bench, Superior Court, and Court of Justice
> Commissioners, premiers and government leaders
> Governor of the Bank of Canada

NOTE: See page 295.

Cape Verde

Official name: Republic of Cape Verde
> Embassy of the Republic of Cape Verde
> *Noun and adjective:* Cape Verdean
> *Chief of state:* President
> *Head of government:* Prime minister
> *Other high officials:*
>> Ministers of *(portfolio)* in the Council of Ministers
>> Secretaries of *(portfolio)* in the Council of Ministers
>> President and deputies in the National Assembly
>> President, vice presidents, and judge counselors of
>>> the Supreme Tribunal of Justice
>> Governor of the Bank of Cape Verde

NOTE: Address the president by *(office)* or as *His/Her Excellency*. Also address the prime minister, minister, secretary, president of the National Assembly, and president of the Supreme Tribunal of Justice as *His/Her Excellency*. Address high judges as *the Honorable*. Address deputies in the National Assembly, and the governor of the central bank by *(honorific)* + *(name)*, and identify by *(office)*.

Cayman Islands

Official name: Cayman Islands
An overseas territory of the United Kingdom
> Diplomatic representation by the United Kingdom
> *Noun and adjective:* Caymanian
> *Chief of state and head of government:*
>> King/Queen (hereditary monarch of the United Kingdom)
> *Vice-royal representative:* Governor
> *Other high officials:*
>> Leader of Government Business
>> Ministers of *(portfolio)*
>> Official Members of the Legislative Assembly
>> Speaker, Leader of the Opposition, and members of the Legislative Assembly
>> Judges of the Summary Court, Grand Court, and the Cayman Court of Appeal

NOTE: Address the governor as *His/Her Excellency*. Address a minister as *His/Her Excellency*. Also address the Leader of Government Business, speaker, Leader of the

Opposition, or an Official Member of the Legislative Assembly as *the Honourable*. Address other officials by *(honorific)* + *(name)* and identify by *(office)*. Include *Sir* or *Dame* in the forms of address of knighted officials. The use of the post-nominal JP, for Justice of the Peace, is widespread by officials in the Cayman Islands where it is an appointed administrative, rather than judicial, designation.

Central African Republic
Official name: Central African Republic
    Embassy of Central African Republic
    Noun and adjective: Central African
    Chief of state: President of the Republic
    Head of government: Prime minister
    Other high officials:
        Ministers of *(portfolio)* in the Council of Ministers
        President and deputies in the National Assembly
        President and justices of the Supreme Court of Appeal/Court of Cassation
        Governor of the Central Bank of the Central African Republic
NOTE: Address the president by *(office)* or as *the Honorable*. Also address the prime minister, president of the National Assembly, president of the Supreme Court, or a minister as *the Honorable*. Address other officials by *(honorific)* + *(name)* and identify by *(office)*.

Chad
Official name: Republic of Chad
    Embassy of the Republic of Chad
    Noun and adjective: Chadian
    Chief of state: President
    Head of government: Prime minister
    Other high officials:
        Ministers of *(portfolio)* in the Council of State
        Ministers of state for *(portfolio)*
        Minister-delegates
        President of and deputies in the National Assembly
        Justices of the Supreme Court, and the Court of Appeal
        Judges of the Criminal Courts
NOTE: Address the president by *(office)* or as *the Honourable*. Also address the prime minister or minister as *the Honourable*. Address other officials by *(honorific)* + *(name)* and identify by *(office)*.

Chile
Official name: Republic of Chile
    Embassy of the Republic of Chile
    Noun and adjective: Chilean
    Chief of state and head of government: President
    Other high officials:
        Ministers of *(portfolio)*
        Minister Secretary General of government
        Minister Secretary General of the presidency
        President of and senators in the Senate
        President and first and second vice presidents of the Chamber of Deputies
        Deputies in the Chamber of Deputies

456

President and justices of the Supreme Court
Judges of the Constitutional Tribunal
President of the Central Bank

NOTE: Address the president by *(office)* or as *the Honorable*. Also address a minister or Minister Secretary General as *the Honorable*. Address other officials by *(honorific)* + *(name)* and identify by *(office)*.

China

Official name: People's Republic of China
    Embassy of the People's Republic of China
    Noun and adjective: Chinese
    Chief of state: President
    Head of government: Premier
    Other high officials:
        Vice president
        Executive vice premier, State Council (cabinet)
        Vice premiers (more than one), State Council (cabinet)
        State Councilor, State Council (cabinet)
        Ministers of *(portfolio)*, State Council (cabinet)
        General secretary of the Party
        President/chairman of the Central Military Commission
        Chairman of the Standing Committee of the National People's Congress
        Members of the National People's Congress
        President and vice president of the Supreme People's Court
        Governor of the People's Bank of China

NOTE: Address the president and premier by *(office)* or as *His/Her Excellency*. Also address the vice president, general secretary, or a councilor, chairman, minister, official of the National People's Congress, or other high official as *His/Her Excellency*. Address members of the People's Congress and other officials by *(honorific)* + *(name)* and identify by *(office)*.

Christmas Island

Official name: Territory of Christmas Island
    A territory of Australia
    Representation by the Commonwealth of Australia
    Noun: Christmas Islander
    Adjective: Christmas Island
    Chief of state: King/Queen (hereditary monarch of the United Kingdom)
    Vice-royal representative: Governor-general of Australia
    Head of government: Administrator
    Other high officials:
        Members of the Christmas Island Shire Council
        Justices of the Supreme Court
        Judges of the District Court

Cocos (Keeling) Islands

Official name: Territory of Cocos (Keeling) Islands
    A territory of Australia
    Representation by the Commonwealth of Australia
    Noun and adjective: Cocos Islander

Chief of state: King/Queen (hereditary monarch of the United Kingdom)
Vice-royal representative: Governor-general of Australia
Head of government: Administrator
Other high officials:
>   Members of the Cocos (Keeling) Islands Shire Council
>   Justices of the Supreme Court

Colombia

Official name: Republic of Colombia
>   Embassy of the Republic of Colombia
>   *Noun and adjective:* Colombian
>   *Chief of state and head of government:* President
>   *Other high officials:*
>>   Vice president
>>   Ministers of *(portfolio)*
>>   Director of National Planning
>>   Prosecutor General
>>   President of and senators in Senate
>>   President of and representatives in the House of Representatives
>>   President and justices of the Supreme Court of Justice
>>   President and justices of the Supreme Constitutional Court
>>   President and judges of the Superior Judicial Council
>>   President, Bank of the Republic

NOTE: Colombians do not use courtesy titles when addressing their national leaders. Officials are directly addressed as Mr./Madam *(office)*: Mr. *President;* Madam Vice President, Mr. Minister, Madam Senator, etc. When the official's name is used in writing, the *(office)* is on the first line and the *(honorific)* *(full name)* is on the second line. Address other officials by *(honorific)* + *(name)* and identify by *(office)*. When the president, vice president, or a minister travels abroad he or she is often addressed as His/Her Excellency.

Comoros

Official name: Union of the Comoros
>   Embassy of the Union of Comoros
>   *Noun and adjective:* Comoran
>   *Chief of state and head of government:* President
>   *Other high officials:*
>>   President of Anjouan
>>   President of Grand Comore
>>   President of Moheli
>>   Vice president for *(portfolio)*
>>   Ministers of *(portfolio)* in the Council of Ministers
>>   Deputies in the Assembly of the Union
>>   Justices of the Supreme Court
>>   Governor of the Central Bank of Comoros

NOTE: Address the president by *(office)* or as His/Her Excellency. Also address a regional president, vice president, or minister as His/Her Excellency. Address other officials by *(honorific)* + *(name)* and identify by *(office)*.

Congo (DRC, Kinshasa)

Official name: Democratic Republic of Congo
> Embassy of the Democratic Republic of the Congo
> *Noun and adjective:* Congolese
> *Chief of state:* President
> *Head of government:* Prime minister
> *Other high officials:*
>> Ministers of *(portfolio)*
>> President, deputy presidents, and senators in the Senate
>> President, deputy president, vice presidents,
>>> and members of the National Assembly
>> President and justices of the Supreme Court
>> Governor of the Central Bank

NOTE: Address the president and prime minister by *(office)* or as *His/Her Excellency*. Also address a minister as *His/Her Excellency*. Address a parliamentary official, senator, or member of the National Assembly as *the Honorable*. Address other officials by *(honorific)* + *(name)* and identify by *(office)*.

Congo (RC, Brazzaville)

Official name: Republic of Congo
> Embassy of the Republic of the Congo
> *Noun and adjective:* Congolese
> *Chief of state and head of government:* President
> *Other high officials:*
>> Prime minister
>> Ministers at the presidency in charge of *(portfolio)*
>> Ministers of *(portfolio)*
>> Attorney General
>> President and senators in the Senate
>> President and members of the National Assembly
>> President and justices of the Supreme Court of Justice
>> Director of the Central Bank of the Republic of Congo

NOTE: Address the president and prime minister by *(office)* or as *His/Her Excellency*, and a minister as *His/Her Excellency*. Address a president of the senate or senator as *the Venerable*, and a president or member of the National Assembly as *the Honourable*. Address other officials by *(honorific)* + *(name)* and identify by *(office)*.

Cook Islands

Official name: Cook Islands
> Diplomatic representation by New Zealand
> *Noun and adjective:* Cook Islander
> *Chief of state:* The King/Queen of New Zealand
>> Elizabeth the Second, by the Grace of God, Queen of New Zealand and
>> Her Other Realms and Territories, Head of the Commonwealth
> *Head of government:* Prime minister
> *Other high officials:*
>> Queen's representative
>> New Zealand high commissioner
>> Deputy prime minister

Ministers of (*portfolio*) in the Cabinet
Speaker, deputy speaker and members of the Legislative Assembly/Parliament
Traditional leaders in the House of Ariki
Judges of the High Court

NOTE: Address the prime minister, deputy prime minister, or a minister as *the Honorable*. Address a member of Parliament as *Mr./Mrs. (name)*, MP. Address other officials by (*honorific*) + (*name*) and identify by (*office*).

Coral Sea Islands

Official name: Coral Sea Islands Territory
A territory of Australia
Diplomatic representation by the Commonwealth of Australia
Government: Department of the Transport and Regional Services, in Canberra

Costa Rica

Official name: Republic of Costa Rica
Embassy of Costa Rica
Noun and adjective: Costa Rican
Chief of state and head of government: President
Other high officials:
First and second vice presidents
Ministers of (*portfolio*) of the Cabinet
President and vice president of the Legislative Assembly
First and second secretaries of the Legislative Assembly
Deputies in the Legislative Assembly
President and magistrates of the Supreme Court
President of the Central Bank

NOTE: Costa Ricans do not use courtesy titles when addressing their national leaders. An official is directly addressed as *Mr./Madam (office)*. Address as *Mr. President of the Republic, Madam Vice President, Mr. Deputy*, etc. When the official's name is used in writing, the (*office*) is on the first line, the (*honorific*) (*full name*) is on the second line. When the president, a vice president, or minister travels abroad he or she is often addressed as *His/Her Excellency*. Address other officials by (*honorific*) + (*name*) and identify by (*office*).

Cote d'Ivoire

Official name: Republic of Cote d'Ivoire
Embassy of the Republic of Cote d'Ivoire
Noun and adjective: Ivoirian
Chief of state: President
Head of government: Prime minister
Other high officials:
Ministers of (*portfolio*)
Members of the National Assembly
President and justices of the Supreme Court
Judges of the Judicial, Audit, Constitutional, and Administrative Chambers

NOTE: Address the president, prime minister, and president of the Supreme Court by (*office*) or as *His/Her Excellency*. Address a member of the National Assembly as *the Honourable*. Address other officials by (*honorific*) + (*name*) and identify by (*office*).

460

Croatia

Official name: Republic of Croatia
Embassy of the Republic of Croatia
Noun: Croat, Croatian
Adjective: Croatian
Chief of state: President
Head of government: Prime minister
Other high officials:
Deputy prime ministers for *(portfolio)* in the Council of Ministers
Ministers of *(portfolio)* in the Council of Ministers
Representatives of the Assembly
Justices of the Supreme Court
Governor of the National Bank of Croatia

NOTE: Address the president by *(office)* or as *His/Her Excellency.* Also address the prime minister as *His/Her Excellency.* Address a justice of the Supreme Court as *the Honorable.* Address members of the legislature and other officials by *(honorific)* + *(name)* and identify by *(office).*

Cuba

Official name: Republic of Cuba
Diplomatic representation by an Interests Section in the Swiss Embassy
Noun and adjective: Cuban
Chief of state and head of government: President of the Council of State
and President of the Council of Ministers
Other high officials:
First vice president of the Council of State
First vice president of the Council of Ministers
Vice presidents of the Council of State
Vice presidents of the Council of Ministers
Secretary of the Executive Committee of the Council of Ministers
Ministers of *(portfolio)* in the Council of Ministers
Attorney General in the Council of Ministers
Members of National Assembly of the People's Power
Justices of the People's Supreme Court
President of the Central Bank of Cuba

Cyprus

Official name: Republic of Cyprus
Embassy of the Republic of Cyprus
Noun and adjective: Cypriot
Chief of state and head of government: President
Other high officials:
Undersecretary to the President
Ministers of *(portfolio)* in the Council of Ministers
Members of the House of Representatives/Parliament
Justices of the Supreme Court
Governor of the Central Bank

NOTE: Address the president by *(office)* or as *His/Her Excellency.* Also address the minister of foreign affairs as *His/Her Excellency.* Address a minister, member of Parliament, or justice of the Supreme Court as *the Honourable*. Address other officials by *(honorific)* + *(name)* and identify by *(office)*.

Czech Republic

Official name: Czech Republic
　　Embassy of the Czech Republic
　　Noun and adjective: Czech
　　Chief of state: President
　　Head of government: Prime minister
　　Other high officials:
　　　　Deputy prime ministers
　　　　Ministers of *(portfolio)*
　　　　Senators in the Senate
　　　　Deputies in the Chamber of Deputies
　　　　Chairman, deputy chairman, and justices of the Supreme Court
　　　　Chairman, deputy chairman, and judges of the Constitutional Court
　　　　Governor of the Czech National Bank
NOTE: Address the president and prime minister by *(office)* or as *His/Her Excellency*. Also address a deputy prime minister or minister as *His/Her Excellency*. Address other officials by *(honorific)* + *(name)* and identify by *(office)*.

Denmark

Official name: Kingdom of Denmark
　　Royal Danish Embassy
　　Noun: Dane
　　Adjective: Danish
　　Chief of state: King/Queen (hereditary monarch)
　　Head of government: Prime minister
　　Other high officials:
　　　　Prince/princess consort
　　　　Crown prince/crown princess
　　　　Prince/princess
　　　　Ministers of *(portfolio)* in the Council of State
　　　　Speaker and members of the People's Assembly
　　　　Chief justice/president and justices of the Supreme Court
　　　　Chairman of the Board of Governors of the Danish National Bank
NOTE: Address the chief of state as *Your Majesty*. Address other members of the ruling family by the form appropriate for their titles. Address the speaker of People's Assembly, chief justice of the Supreme Court, or a minister as *His/Her Excellency*. Address other officials by *(honorific)* + *(name)* and identify by *(office)*.

Dhekelia

Official name: Dhekelia Sovereign Base Area
　　An overseas territory of the United Kingdom
　　Diplomatic representation by the United Kingdom
　　Chief of state and head of government: King/Queen
　　　　(hereditary monarch of the United Kingdom)
　　Other high official: Administrator (Commander of the British Forces, Cyprus)

Djibouti

Official name: Republic of Djibouti
    Embassy of the Republic of Djibouti
    Noun and adjective: Djiboutian
    Chief of state: President
    Head of government: Prime minister
    Other high officials:
        Ministers of *(portfolio)* in the Council of Ministers
        Deputies in the Chamber of Deputies
        Justices of the Supreme Court
        Governor of the Central Bank

NOTE: Address the president and prime minister by *(office)* or as *His/Her Excellency.* Also address ministers as *His/Her Excellency.* Address justices in the Supreme Court as *the Honourable.* Address other officials by *(honorific)* + *(name)* and identify by *(office).*

Dominica

Official name: Commonwealth of Dominica
    Embassy of the Commonwealth of Dominica
    Noun and adjective: Dominican
    Chief of state: President
    Head of government: Prime minister
    Other high officials:
        Ministers of *(portfolio)*
        Attorney General
        Parliamentary secretary of *(portfolio)*
        Senators in the House of Assembly
        Representatives in the House of Assembly
        Chief justice and justices of appeal of the Eastern Caribbean Supreme Court
        President and judges of the Caribbean Court of Justice
        Judge of the High Court

NOTE: Address the president by *(office)* or as *His/Her Excellency.* Address a member of the cabinet or member of Parliament as *the Honourable.* Address the chief justice as *His Lordship, the Honourable Chief Justice,* or as *the Honourable (name).* Address a justice or judge of a high court as *the Honourable (name).* Address lower officials by *(honorific)* + *(name)* and identify by *(office).*

Dominican Republic

Official name: Dominican Republic
    Embassy of the Dominican Republic
    Noun and adjective: Dominican
    Chief of state and head of government: President
    Other high officials:
        Vice president
        Secretaries of state of *(portfolio)*
        Attorney General
        President of the Senate
        Senators in the Senate
        President of the Chamber of Deputies
        Deputies in the Chamber of Deputies

President and justices of the Supreme Court of Justice
Governor of the Central Bank

NOTE: Address the president by (office) or as His/Her Excellency. Address the president of the Senate, president of the Chamber of Deputies, and president of the Supreme Court as the Honourable. Address a senator, deputy, justice, or other officials by (honorific) + (name) and identify by (office).

East Timor

See Timor-Leste.

Ecuador

Official name: Republic of Ecuador
Embassy of Ecuador
Noun and adjective: Ecuadorian
Chief of state and head of government: President
Other high officials:
Vice president
Ministers of (portfolio)
Secretary Generals of (portfolio)
President of the National Congress
First and second vice presidents of the National Congress
Members of the National Congress
President of the Central Bank
President and justices of the Supreme Court of Justice

NOTE: Address the president by (office) or as His/Her Excellency. Ecuadorians do not use courtesy titles when addressing ministers. Ministers are addressed in writing by (office) or orally as Mr./Madam Minister. Address the leaders and members of the National Congress as the Honorable. Address other officials by (honorific) + (name) and identify by (office).

Egypt

Official name: Arab Republic of Egypt
Embassy of the Arab Republic of Egypt
Noun and adjective: Egyptian
Chief of state: President
Head of government: Prime minister
Other high officials:
Ministers of (portfolio)
Speaker and members of the People's Assembly
Members of the Advisory Council
President and justices of the Supreme Constitutional Court
Governor of the Central Bank

NOTE: Address the president and prime minister by (office) or as His/Her Excellency. Also address a minister, or the president or a justice of the Supreme Court as His/Her Excellency. Address members of the People's Assembly, Advisory Council, and other officials by (honorific) + (name) and identify by (office).

El Salvador
Official name: Republic of El Salvador
>Embassy of El Salvador
>*Noun and adjective:* Salvadoran
>*Chief of state and head of government:* President
>*Other high officials:*
>>Vice president
>>Ministers of *(portfolio)* in the Council of Ministers
>>Secretaries of *(portfolio)*
>>Particular secretary of the Presidency
>>Private secretary of the Presidency
>>Technical secretary of the Presidency
>>President and deputies of the Legislative Assembly
>>Chief justice and justices of the Supreme Court of Justice
>>President and judges of the Constitutional and Civil Courts
>>President of the Central Reserve Bank

NOTE: Address the president by *(office)* or as *His/Her Excellency.* Also address the vice president, a minister, secretary, or other member of the Cabinet as *His/Her Excellency.* Address other officials by *(honorific)* + *(name)* and identify by *(office).*

Equatorial Guinea
Official name: Republic of Equatorial Guinea
>Embassy of the Republic of Equatorial Guinea
>*Noun and adjective:* Equatorial Guinean, Equatoguinean
>*Chief of state:* President
>*Head of government:* Prime minister
>*Other high officials:*
>>First and second vice prime ministers of *(portfolio)*
>>Secretary General of *(portfolio)*
>>Ministers of *(portfolio)* in the Council of Ministers
>>Members of the House of People's Representatives
>>Justices of the Supreme Tribunal

NOTE: Address the president and prime minister by *(office)* or as *His/Her Excellency.* Also address a minister or justice of the Supreme Tribunal as *His/Her Excellency.* Address members of the House of People's Representative as *the Honourable.* Address other officials by *(honorific)* + *(name)* and identify by *(office).*

Eritrea
Official name: State of Eritrea
>Embassy of the State of Eritrea
>*Noun and adjective:* Eritrean
>*Chief of state and head of government:* President
>*Other high officials:*
>>Vice president
>>Director, Office of the President
>>Ministers of *(portfolio)* of the State (or Executive) Council
>>Members of the National Assembly
>>Judges of the High Court
>>Governor of the National Bank of Eritrea

NOTE: Address the president by (office) or as His/Her Excellency, and members of the cabinet as His/Her Excellency. Address members of the National Assembly as the Honourable. Address other officials by (honorific) + (name) and identify by (office).

Estonia

Official name: Republic of Estonia
    Embassy of Estonia
    Noun and adjective: Estonian
    Chief of state: President
    Head of government: Prime minister
    Other high officials:
        Ministers of (portfolio) in the Council of Ministers
        Speaker and members of Parliament
        Chief of Justice
        Chancellor of Justice
        Judges of the National Court
        President of the Bank of Estonia
NOTE: Estonians do not use courtesy titles when addressing their national officials. Officials are directly addressed as Mr./Madam (office): Mr. President, Madam Minister, Mr. Speaker, Madam Chief of Justice, Mr. Chancellor, etc. When the official's name is used in writing, the (office) is on the first line, the (honorific) (full name) is on the second line. However, the president, prime minister, speaker of Parliament, chief of justice, chancellor of justice, or a minister are frequently addressed as His/Her Excellency when outside of Estonia.

Ethiopia

Official name: Federal Democratic Republic of Ethiopia
    Embassy of Federal Democratic Republic of Ethiopia
    Noun and adjective: Ethiopian
    Chief of state: President
    Head of government: Prime minister
    Other high officials:
        Deputy prime minister
        Ministers of (portfolio) in the Council of Ministers
        Vice ministers of (portfolio)
        Speaker and members of the House of Federation
        Speaker and members of the House of Peoples Representatives
        President, vice president, and justices of the Supreme Court
        Governor of the National Bank of Ethiopia
NOTE: Address the president by (office) or as the Honorable. Also address the prime minister or a minister as the Honorable. Address lower officials by (honorific) + (name) and identify by (office).

European Union

Official name: European Union
    Chief of union: President of the European Commission
    Other high officials:
        Vice presidents for (portfolio) of the European Commission
        Commissioners for (portfolio) of the European Commission
        Director-generals for (portfolio)

Representatives of the European Commission in the member states
Representatives of the European Commission outside the European Union
President, vice president, and members of the European Parliament
President, high representative, ministers, and permanent representatives
     in the Council of the European Union
Heads, deputy heads of Representation
President, presidents of the Chambers, Advocate General and judges in
     the European Court of Justice
President and members of the Court of Auditors

Commission of the European Communities

• Address the president in writing as *His/Her Excellency Mr./Mrs./etc. (name)*, *President of the Commission of the European Communities*. Introduce by *(office)*, and address in conversation as either *Mr./Mrs. President* or *President (name)*.

• Address a vice president, commissioner, director-general, or representative of the commission from a member state in writing as *Mr./Mrs./etc. (name)* and identify by *(office)*. Introduce by *(office)* and in conversation address as *Vice-president/Commissioner/Mr./Mrs./etc. (name)*. Director-general and representative are not used as honorifics.

• A Permanent Representative of the Commission outside the European Union holds the rank of ambassador. Use the standard form for an ambassador and identify as the *Head of the Representation of the European Commission to (country)*.

European Parliament

• Address the president or a vice president in writing as *Mr./Mrs./etc. (name)* and identify by *(office)*. Introduce by *(office)*. Address in conversation as *Mr./Mrs. President* or *President (name)*, or *Mr./Mrs. Vice-president* or *Vice-president (name)*.

• Address members as *Mr./Mrs./etc. (name)*, MEP.

Council of the European Union

• Address the president or a minister for *(portfolio)* in writing as *His/Her Excellency Mr./Mrs. (name)*, and identify by *(office)*. Introduce by *(office)*. Address in conversation as *Mr./Mrs. President* or *President (name)*, *Minister* or *Minister (name)*.

• A *Permanent Representative* of a member state holds the rank of *ambassador*. Use the standard forms for an *ambassador* and identify as the *Permanent Representative of (country) to the European Union*.

• Address the High Representative for the Common Foreign and Security Policy, and Secretary-general of the Council of the European Union in writing as *Mr./Mrs./etc. (name)* and identify by *(office)*. Introduce by *(office)*, and address in conversation as *Mr./Mrs./etc. (name)* or *Sir/Madam*.

European Court of Justice

• Address the president in writing as *His/Her Excellency Mr./Mrs./etc. (name)*, *President of the European Court of Justice*: Introduce by *(office)*, and address in conversation as *Mr./Mrs. President* or *President (name)*.

• Address and introduce a president of a chamber in writing as *Judge (name)*, *President of (name of chamber) of the European Court of Justice*. Address in conversation as *Mr./Mrs. President*.

• Address an Advocate-General in writing as *Advocate-General (name)*, *European Court of Justice*. Introduce as *(given name) + (surname)*, *(office)*, and address in conversation as *Advocate-General*.

• Address and introduce a judge in writing as *Judge (name) of the European Court of Justice.* Address in conversation as *Judge (name)* or *Judge.*

European Court of Auditors

• Address the president in writing as *Mr./Mrs./etc. (name), President of the European Court of Auditors.* Introduce by *(name)* and by *(office)* and address in conversation as *Mr./Mrs. President* or *President (name).*

• Address and introduce members in writing as *Mr./Mrs./etc. (name), member of the European Court of Auditors,* and address in conversation as *Mr./Mrs. (name)* or *Sir/Madam.*

Falkland Islands/Islas Malvinas

Official name: Falkland Islands (Islas Malvinas)
An overseas territory of the UK, also claimed by Argentina
Diplomatic representation by the United Kingdom
Noun: Falkland Islander
Adjective: Falkland Island
Chief of state: King/Queen (hereditary monarch of the United Kingdom
Head of government: Governor (appointed by the monarch)
Other high officials:
> Councillors of the Legislative Council
> Chief justice and justices of the Supreme Court
> Senior magistrates of the Magistrates Court
> Judges of the Court of Summary Jurisdiction

NOTE: Address the governor as *His/Her Excellency.* Address councillors as *Mr./Mrs./etc. (name),* and identify the area they represent. Address judges as *the Honourable.*

Faroe Islands

Official name: Faroe Islands
A self-governing overseas administrative district of Denmark
Diplomatic representation by the Kingdom of Denmark
Noun and adjective: Faroese
Chief of state: King/Queen (hereditary monarch of Denmark)
Head of government: Prime minister
Other high officials:
> High commissioner
> Ministers of *(portfolio)*
> Members of the Longting/Parliament

Fiji

Official name: Republic of the Fiji Islands
Embassy of the Republic of Fiji Islands
Noun and adjective: Fijian
Chief of state: President
Head of government: Prime minister
Other high officials:
> Ministers for *(portfolio)*
> Attorney General
> Senators in the Senate
> Members of the House of Representatives
> Justices of the Supreme Court and Court of Appeal

Judges of the High Court
Governor of the Reserve Bank

NOTE: Address the president by *(office)* or as *His/Her Excellency.* Address a member of the Cabinet, senator, member of the House of Representatives, or justice of a high court as *the Honourable.* Address lower officials by *(honorific)* + *(name)* and identify by *(office).*

Finland

Official name: Republic of Finland
Embassy of Finland
Noun: Finn
Adjective: Finnish
Chief of state: President
Head of government: Prime minister
Other high officials:

Deputy prime minister
Ministers of *(portfolio)* in the Council of State
Members of Eduskunta/Parliament
Justices of the Supreme Court
Governor of the Bank of Finland

NOTE: Address the president by *(office)* or as *His/Her Excellency.* Also address the prime minister, deputy prime minister, or a minister as *His/Her Excellency.* Address justices of the Supreme Court, members of Parliament, and other officials by *(honorific)* + *(name)* and identify by *(office).*

France

Official name: French Republic
Embassy of France
Nouns: French, Frenchman, and Frenchwoman
Adjective: French
Chief of state: President
Head of government: Prime minister
Other high officials:

Vice president of the Council of State
Ministers of *(portfolio)* in the Council of Ministers
Secretaries of state for *(portfolio)* in the Council of Ministers
High commissioners for *(portfolio)*
President and members of the Constitutional Council
President of the Economic and Social Council
Chancellor of the Legion of Honor
Chancellor of the Order of Merit
Chancellor of the Order of the Libération
President of the Senate
Senators in the Senate
President and deputies of the National Assembly
First president, presidents, and judges of the Court of Cassation
First president, presidents, and judges of the Revenue Court
Justices of the Supreme Court of Appeals
Governor of the Bank of France

NOTE: French citizens do not address their national officials as *His/Her Excellency* or *the*

Honorable. Officials are formally addressed as Mr./Madam *(office)* as in Mr. *President of the Republic (Monsieur le President de la République)*, Mr. *Prime Minister (Monsieur le Premier Ministre)*, Mr. *President* for a president of council or chamber in the legislature *(Monsieur le Président)*, Mr. *Senator (Monsieur le Sénateur)*, or Mr. *Deputy (Monsieur le Député)*.

An exception is to address a woman who is a deputy in the National Assembly, a mayor, or a town counselor simply as *Madame* rather than as *Madam Deputy (Madame le Député)*, *Madam Mayor (Madame le Maire)*, or *Madam Counselor (Madame le Conseiller municipale)*.

When the official's name is used in writing, *the (office)* is on the first line, the *(honorific) (full name)* is on the second line.

Address other officials by *(honorific)* + *(name)* and identify by *(office)*.

French Polynesia
Official name: Overseas Lands of French Polynesia
> An overseas collectivity of France
> Diplomatic representation by the French Republic
> *Noun and adjective:* French Polynesian
> *Chief of state:* President of the French Republic
>> Representative of the chief of state: High commissioner of the Republic
> *Head of government:* President of French Polynesia
> *Other high officials:*
>> Ministers of *(portfolio)* in the Council of Ministers
>> President and members of the Territorial Assembly
>> Justices of the Court of Appeal

Gabon
Official name: Gabonese Republic
> Embassy of the Gabonese Republic
> *Noun and adjective:* Gabonese
> *Chief of state:* President
> *Head of government:* Prime minister
> *Other high officials:*
>> Vice president
>> Deputy prime ministers (vice prime ministers)
>> Ministers of state for *(portfolio)* in the Council of Ministers
>> Ministers of *(portfolio)* in the Council of Ministers
>> President and senators in the Senate
>> President and members of the National Assembly
>> Justices of the Supreme Court
>> Director of the Central Bank of Gabon

NOTE: Address the president by *(office)* or as *His/Her Excellency.* Also address the vice president, prime minister, a deputy prime minister, or a minister as *His/Her Excellency.* Address a senator as *the Venerable.* Address a member of the National Assembly or a justice in the Supreme Court as *the Honorable.* Address other officials by *(honorific)* + *(name)* and identify by *(office)*.

The Gambia

Official name: Republic of the Gambia
   Embassy of the Gambia
   Noun and adjective: Gambian
   Chief of state and head of government: President
   Other high officials:
      Vice president
      Secretaries of state for *(portfolio)*
      Attorney General
      Speaker and members of the National Assembly
      Chief justice and justices of the Supreme Court
      Governor of the Central Bank of the Gambia
NOTE: Address the president by *(office)* or as *His/Her Excellency*. Address the vice president, the Attorney General, a secretary in the cabinet, or member of the National Assembly as *the Honourable*. Address the chief justice and justices as *My Lord Chief Justice* and *My Lord Justice (name)*, respectively. Address other officials by *(honorific)* + *(name)* and identify by *(office)*.

Georgia

Official name: Georgia
   Embassy of the Republic of Georgia
   Noun and adjective: Georgian
   Chief of state and head of government: President
   Other high officials:
      Prime minister
      Ministers of *(portfolio)*
      State ministers for *(portfolio)*
      Prosecutor General
      Speaker and members of Parliament (Supreme Council)
      Judges of the Supreme and Constitutional Courts
      Chairman of the National Bank
NOTE: Address the president by *(office)* or as *His/Her Excellency*. Also address the prime minister or a minister as *His/Her Excellency*. Address members of Parliament, members of the judiciary, and other high officials by *(honorific)* + *(name)* and identify by *(office)*.

Germany

Official name: Federal Republic of Germany
   Embassy of the Federal Republic of Germany
   Noun and adjective: German
   Chief of state: President
   Head of government: Chancellor
   Other high officials:
      Vice chancellor
      Federal Ministers of *(portfolio)*
      President and members of the Bundestag/Federal Assembly/Parliament
      President and members of the Bundesrat/Federal Council/Parliament
      President and judges of the Federal Constitutional Court
      President of the Bundesbank
NOTE: Germans do not address their national officials with courtesy titles. Address the

very highest officials in writing by *(name of office)*, Mr./Mrs. *(name)*. For example, address the president as *The President of the Federal Republic of Germany, Mr./Mrs. (name)*, and the chancellor as *The Chancellor of the Federal Republic of Germany, Mr./Mrs. (name)*. Address these officials in a salutation or conversation as Mr./Madam *(office)*: Mr./Madam President or Mr./Madam Chancellor. When the official's name is used in writing, the *(office)* is on the first line and the *(honorific)* *(full name)* is on the second line. A member of the Bundestag is addressed in writing as *Member of the Federal Assembly, Mr./Mrs. (name)*, MdB, in a salutation as Mr./Madam Representative, and in conversation as Mr./Mrs. *(name)*. Address other officials by *(honorific)* + *(name)* and identify by *(office)*.

Ghana

Official name: Republic of Ghana
> Embassy of Ghana
> *Noun and adjective:* Ghanaian
> *Chief of state and head of government:* President
> *Other high officials:*
>> Vice president
>> Senior minister
>> Ministers of *(portfolio)* in the Council of State
>> Attorney General
>> Speaker, deputy speakers, and members of Parliament
>> Chief justice and justices of the Supreme Court
>> Governor and deputy governors of the Bank of Ghana

NOTE: Address the president and vice president by *(office)* or as *His/Her Excellency*. Address the speaker of Parliament as *the Right Honourable*. Address a minister in the Council of State as *the Honourable*, and a member of Parliament as *the Honourable* with the post-nominal abbreviation MP. Formally address the chief justice of the Supreme Court in writing as *the Honourable Chief Justice*. Address the chief justice and justices of the Supreme Court in conversation as *His Lordship (name)* or *Her Ladyship (name)*. Address a tribal king (such as an Ashanti king) as *His Royal Highness* rather than *His Majesty*. Address chiefs in Akan-speaking areas as *Nana (name)*. Address other officials by *(honorific)* + *(name)* and identify by *(office)*.

Gibraltar

Official name: Gibraltar
> An overseas territory of the United Kingdom
> Diplomatic representation by the United Kingdom
> *Noun:* Gibraltarian
> *Adjective:* Gibraltar
> *Chief of state:* King/Queen (hereditary monarch of the United Kingdom)
> *Vice-royal representative:* Governor
> *Head of government:* Chief minister
> *Other high officials:*
>> Ministers in the Council of Ministers
>> Members of the House of Assembly

NOTE: Address the governor as *His/Her Excellency*. Address the chief minister as *the Honourable*.

Greece

Official name: Hellenic Republic
 Embassy of Greece
 Noun and adjective: Greek
 Chief of state: President
 Head of government: Prime minister
 Other high officials:
  Ministers of (*portfolio*)
  Deputies of Parliament
  Justices of the Supreme Judicial Court and Special Supreme Tribunal
  Governor of the Bank of Greece
NOTE: Address the president by (*office*) or as *His/Her Excellency.* Also address the prime minister or a minister as *His/Her Excellency.* Address a deputy or justice of a high court as *the Honourable.* Address other officials by (*honorific*) + (*name*) and identify by (*office*).

Greenland

Official name: Greenland
 A self-governing overseas administrative division of Denmark
 Diplomatic representation by Kingdom of Denmark
 Noun: Greenlander
 Adjective: Greenlandic
 Chief of state: King/Queen (hereditary monarch of Denmark)
 Vice-royal representative: High commissioner
 Head of government: Prime minister
 Other high officials:
  Members of the Home Rule Government
  Members of Parliament
  Judges of the High Court

Grenada

Official name: Grenada
 Embassy of Grenada
 Noun and adjective: Grenadian
 Chief of state: The King/Queen of Grenada
  Elizabeth the Second, by the Grace of God, Queen of Grenada and Her Other Realms and Territories, Head of the Commonwealth
 Vice-royal representative: Governor-general
 Head of government: Prime minister
 Other high officials:
  Ministers of (*portfolio*)
  Attorney General
  Senators in the Senate
  Members of the House of Representatives
  Chief justice and justices of the Eastern Caribbean Supreme Court
  President and judges of the Caribbean Court of Justice
  Judge of the High Court
NOTE: Address the governor-general as *His/Her Excellency.* Address the prime minister and a minister who is a member of the House of Representatives as *the Honourable (name),* MP, and a minister who is a senator as *Senator the Honourable (name),* and iden-

tify by (office). If an official is a member of the Privy Council, address him or her as *the Right Honourable*. Address the chief justice as *His Lordship, the Honorable Chief Justice*, or as *the Honourable (name)*. Address a justice or judge of a high court as *the Honourable (name)*. Address other officials by (honorific) + (name) and identify by (office). Include *Sir* or *Dame* in the forms of address of knighted officials.

Guam

Official name: Territory of Guam
    Territory of the United States
    Diplomatic representation by the United States of America
    Noun and adjective: Guamanian
    Chief of state: President of the United States
    Head of government: Governor
    Other high officials:
        Lieutenant governor
        Heads of executive departments
        Members of the legislature
        Judge of the Federal District Court
        Judges of the Territorial Superior Court

Guatemala

Official name: Republic of Guatemala
    Embassy of Guatemala
    Noun and adjective: Guatemalan
    Chief of state and head of government: President
    Other high officials:
        Vice president
        Ministers of (portfolio) in the Council of Ministers
        Attorney General
        Solicitor General
        President of the Congress of the Republic
        First, second, and third vice presidents of the Congress of the Republic
        First, second, third, fourth, and fifth secretaries of the
            Congress of the Republic
        Deputies of the Congress of the Republic
        President and justices of the Supreme Court of Justice
        President and judges of the Constitutional Court
        President of the Bank of Guatemala

NOTE: Address the president by (office) or as *His/Her Excellency*. Also address the vice president, Attorney General, Solicitor General, president of Congress, president of the Supreme Court, president of the Constitutional court, a justice of either high court, or minister as *His/Her Excellency*. Address a congressional vice president, congressional secretary, or deputy as *the Honorable*. Address other officials by (honorific) + (name) and identify by (office).

Guernsey

Official name: Bailiwick of Guernsey
    A British crown dependency
    Diplomatic representation by the United Kingdom
    Noun and adjective: Channel Islander
    Chief of state: King/Queen (hereditary monarch of the United Kingdom)
    Vice-royal representative: Lieutenant governor
    Head of government: Chief minister
    Other high officials:
        Ministers and deputy ministers of *(portfolio)*
        Presiding officer, deputy presiding officer of the States of Deliberation
        Deputies of the States of Deliberation
        Bailiffs of the Royal Court

NOTE: With the exception of the lieutenant governor, who is addressed as *His/Her Excellency*, address all Channel Island officials without courtesy titles. Address judges of the Royal Court as *Mr. Bailiff (name)*, *Mr. Deputy Bailiff (name)*, and *Mr. Lieutenant Bailiff (name)*. Use the name of office as an honorific: *Chief Minister (name)*, *Minister (name)*, *Deputy (name)*, etc. Address presiding officers in the States of Deliberation as *Deputy (name)*, and identify by *(office)*. Address other officials by *(honorific)* + *(name)* and identify by *(office)*.

Guinea

Official name: Republic of Guinea
    Embassy of the Republic of Guinea
    Noun and adjective: Guinean
    Chief of state: President
    Head of government: Prime minister
    Other high officials:
        Ministers of *(portfolio)* in the Council of Ministers
        Secretaries General of *(portfolio)*
        Deputies of the People's National Assembly
        Judges of the Court of First Instance, Court of Appeal, and Supreme Court
        Governor of the Central Bank of the Republic of Guinea

NOTE: Address the president and prime minister by *(office)* or as *His/Her Excellency*. Also address a minister in the Council of Ministers as *His/Her Excellency*. Address deputies as *the Honorable*. Address judges as *The Judge (full name)*. Address other officials by *(honorific)* + *(name)* and identify by *(office)*.

Guinea-Bissau

Official name: Republic of Guinea-Bissau
    Embassy of Guinea-Bissau
    Noun and adjective: Guinean
    Chief of state: President
    Head of government: Prime minister
    Other high officials:
        Ministers of *(portfolio)*
        Secretaries of state for *(portfolio)*
        Members of the National People's Assembly
        Justices of the Supreme Court

Guyana

Official name: Cooperative Republic of Guyana
    Embassy of Guyana
    Noun and adjective: Guyanese
    Chief of state: President and Commander-in-Chief of the Armed Forces
    Head of government: Prime minister
    Other high officials:
        First and second vice presidents
        Head of the Presidential Secretariat
        Ministers in the office of the president for *(portfolio)*
        Ministers of *(portfolio)*
        Attorney General
        Parliamentary secretaries of *(portfolio)*
        Speaker and members of the National Assembly
        Justices of the Supreme Court of Judicature:
            High Court, Judicial Court of Appeal
        Judges of the Caribbean Court of Justice
        Governor of the Bank of Guyana
NOTE: Address the president and prime minister by *(office)* or as *His/Her Excellency.*
Address a vice president, member of the Cabinet, parliamentary secretary, or member of
the National Assembly as *the Honourable.* Address other officials by *(honorific)* + *(name)*
and identify by *(office)*.

Haiti

Official name: Republic of Haiti
    Embassy of the Republic of Haiti
    Noun and adjective: Haitian
    Chief of state: President of the Republic
    Head of government: Prime minister
    Other high officials:
        Ministers of *(portfolio)*
        Secretaries of state for *(portfolio)*
        Senators in the Senate
        Deputies in the Chamber of Deputies
        Justices of the Supreme Court
        Judges of the High Court of Justice

476

Holy See

Official name: The Holy See/State of Vatican City
Apostolic Nunciature
Noun and adjective: (none)
Chief of state: Pope
Head of government: Secretary of State
Other high officials:
Deputy secretary of State
Secretary for Relations with States
Members of the Pontifical Commission

NOTE: Address officials by their hierarchical rank (cardinal, archbishop, bishop, etc.) and identify by *(office)*. Address laypersons in the service of the church by *(honorific)* + *(name)* and identify by *(office)*.

Honduras

Official name: Republic of Honduras
Embassy of Honduras
Noun and adjective: Honduran
Chief of state and head of government: President
Other high officials:
Vice president
Ministers of *(portfolio)*
President of the National Congress
Vice presidents and secretaries of the National Congress
Deputies of the National Congress
Magistrate president and justices (magistrates) of the Supreme Court of Justice
President of the Central Bank

NOTE: Address the president and vice president by *(office)* or as *His/Her Excellency*. Also address ministers as *His/Her Excellency*. Address members of the National Congress and justices of the Supreme Court of Justice as *the Honorable*. Address other officials by *(honorific)* + *(name)* and identify by *(office)*.

Hong Kong

Official name: Hong Kong Special Administrative Region (HKSAR)
Region of the People's Republic of China
Diplomatic representation by the People's Republic of China
Noun: Chinese/Hong Konger
Adjective: Chinese/Hong Kong
Chief of state: President (President of China)
Head of government: Chief executive
Other high officials:
Chief secretary for administration
Secretaries of *(portfolio)* of the Executive Council
President and members of the Legislative Council
Judges of the Court of Final Appeal in the HKSAR
Chief executive of the Hong Kong Monetary Authority

Hungary

Official name: Republic of Hungary
Embassy of the Republic of Hungary
Noun and adjective: Hungarian
Chief of state: President
Head of government: Prime minister
Other high officials:

Ministers of *(portfolio)* in the Council of Ministers
Speaker and members of the National Assembly
President, vice president, and judges of the Constitutional Court
Governor of the National Bank of Hungary

NOTE: Address the president and prime minister by *(office)* or as *His/Her Excellency*. Also address a minister, the president or vice president of the Constitutional Court, or the governor of the Hungarian National Bank as *His/Her Excellency*. In the National Assembly only the speaker or a chairman of a committee is addressed as *His/Her Excellency*. Below that level, address officials by *(honorific)* + *(name)* and identify by *(office)*.

Iceland

Official name: Republic of Iceland
Embassy of Iceland
Noun: Icelander
Adjective: Icelandic
Chief of state: President
Head of government: Prime minister
Other high officials:

Ministers of *(portfolio)*
Speaker and members of the Althingi/Parliament
President and justices of the Supreme Court
Director of the Central Bank of Iceland

NOTE: Address the president and prime minister by *(office)* or as *His/Her Excellency*. Also address a minister as *His/Her Excellency*. Address the speaker, a member of the Althingi, a justice of a high court, or other officials by *(honorific)* + *(name)* and identify by *(office)*.

Iles Esparses

Official name: Bassas da India, Europa Island, Glorioso Islands,
Juan de Nova Island, Tromelin Island
Diplomatic representation by the French Republic
Islands administered from Paris by the Administrateur Superieur of the Territory
of the French Southern and Antarctic Lands (TAAF)

India

Official name: Republic of India
Embassy of India
Noun and adjective: Indian
Chief of state: President
Head of government: Prime minister
Other high officials:

Vice president
Deputy prime minister
Ministers of *(portfolio)*

478

Ministers of state for (*portfolio*)
Attorney General
Chairman and members of the Council of States/Rajya Sabha
Speaker and members of the People's Assembly/Lok Sabha
Chief justice and associate justices of the Supreme Court
Governor of the Reserve Bank of India

NOTE: Address the president and prime minister by (*office*). Address the chairman of the Council of States or speaker of the People's Assembly as *the Honourable*. Address the chief justice or a justice of the Supreme Court as *the Honourable Mr./Madame Justice (name)*: See *Puisne Judges of the Supreme Court of Canada* on page 305. Address other officials by (*honorific*) + (*name*) and identify by (*office*).

Indonesia

Official name: Republic of Indonesia
Embassy of the Republic of Indonesia
Noun and adjective: Indonesian
Chief of state and head of government: President
Other high officials:
Vice president
Coordinating ministers for (*portfolio*) in the Council of Ministers
Ministers of (*portfolio*)
State ministers for (*portfolio*)
Attorney General
Cabinet secretary
Minister of the State Secretary
Members of the House of Representatives
Justices of the Supreme Court and Constitutional Court

NOTE: Address the president and vice president by (*office*). Address the speaker of the House of Representatives, a member of the cabinet, or a justice of a high court as *His/Her Excellency*. Address members of the House of Representatives and other officials by (*honorific*) + (*name*) and identify by (*office*).

Iran

Official name: Islamic Republic of Iran
Diplomatic representation through an Interests Section at the Embassy of Pakistan.
Noun and adjective: Iranian
Chief of state: Supreme Leader
Head of government: President
Other high officials:
First vice president
Vice presidents for (*portfolio*)
Ministers of (*portfolio*) in the Council of Ministers
Members of the Assembly of Experts
Members of the Expedience Council
Members of the Council of Guardians
Speaker and members of the Islamic Consultative Assembly
Justices of the Supreme Court
Judges of the High Council of the Judiciary
Governor of the Central Bank of Iran

Iraq

Official name: Republic of Iraq
    Embassy of the Republic of Iraq
    Noun and adjective: Iraqi
    Chief of state: President
    Head of government: Prime minister
    Other high officials:
        Vice presidents
        Deputy prime ministers
        Ministers of *(portfolio)*
        Members of the Council of Representatives
        Members of the Federal Council
        Judges of the Federal Judicial Authority
        Governor of the Central Bank of Iraq

Ireland

Official name: Ireland
    Embassy of Ireland
    Noun: Irish, Irishman, and Irishwoman
    Adjective: Irish
    Chief of state: President
    Head of government: Prime minister
    Other high officials:
        Deputy prime minister
        Ministers for *(portfolio)*
        Attorney General
        Members of the Council of State
        Chairman and deputy chairman of the Senate *(Seanad Éireann)*
        Senators in the Senate *(Seanad Éireann)*
        Speaker and deputy speaker of the House of Representatives *(Dáil Éireann)*
        Deputies in the House of Representatives *(Dáil Éireann)*
        Chief justice and justices of the Supreme Court
        President of the High Court
        Governor of the Central Bank of Ireland

NOTE: The Irish do not use courtesy titles when addressing their national officials. Address the president and prime minister by *(office)*. Directly address the deputy prime minister, Attorney General, a minister, or other high official as Mr./Madam *(office)*. Address in writing as Mr./Mrs./etc. *(name)* and identify by *(office)*. Address members of Parliament with the honorifics *Senator* and *Deputy*. Current members of *Dáil Éireann* use the post-nominals *TD*, an abbreviation for *Teachta Dála* or *Member of the Dail Éireann*. Address the chairman of the Senate *(Cathaoirleach)* and the speaker of the House of Representatives *(Ceann Comhairle)* by the *(office)* rather than by *(name)*. Irish courts continue to follow British forms: Address the chief justice in the Supreme Court as *The Chief Justice, The Honourable Mr./Madam Justice (full name)*, and other justices as *The Honourable Mr./Madam Justice (full name)*. Address other officials by *(honorific)* + *(name)* and identify by *(office)*.

Isle of Man

Official name: Isle of Man
   A British crown dependency
   Diplomatic representation by the United Kingdom
   Noun: Manxman, Manxwoman
   Adjective: Manx
   Chief of state: The King/Queen Lord of Mann
         (hereditary monarch of the United Kingdom)
   Vice-royal representative: Lieutenant governor
   Head of government: Chief minister
   Other high officials:
         Lord bishop of Sodor and Man
         Ministers of *(portfolio)* in the Council of Ministers
         Chief secretary, Attorney General, chief financial officer,
               secretary to the council
         President and members of the Legislative Council/Tynwald
         Speaker and members of the House of Keys
         First, second and deputy deemsters of the High Court of Justice
NOTE: *Mann* with two *N*'s is the ancient spelling: *Man* with one *N* is the everyday spelling. You will see both, so follow the form presented when possible. Address the lieutenant governor as *His/Her Excellency*. The lord bishop is a bishop of the Anglican Church: See that form on page 271. Address a member of the Legislative Council as *the Honourable (name)*, MLC. Address a member of the House of Keys as *the Honourable (name)*, MHK. Address a minister as a member of the House of Keys and identify by *(office)*. Address a deemster as *the Honourable*. Address other officials by *(honorific)* + *(name)* and identify by *(office)*.

Israel

Official name: State of Israel
   Embassy of Israel
   Noun and adjective: Israeli
   Chief of state: President
   Head of government: Prime minister
   Other high officials:
         Deputy prime minister
         Vice prime minister
         Ministers of *(portfolio)*
         Attorney General
         Speaker and members of the Knesset/National Assembly
         Justices of the Supreme Court
         Governor of the Bank of Israel
NOTE: Address the president and prime minister by *(office)* or as *His/Her Excellency*. Also address the deputy prime minister, vice prime minister, Attorney General, or a minister as *His/Her Excellency*. Address all members of the Knesset, justices, and other officials by *(honorific)* + *(name)* and identify by *(office)*.

Italy

Official name: Italian Republic
    Embassy of Italy
    Noun and adjective: Italian
    Chief of state: President
    Head of government: Prime minister/president of the Council of Ministers
    Other high officials:
        Deputy prime ministers/vice presidents of the Council of Ministers
        Ministers of *(portfolio)* in the Council of Ministers
        Attorney General
        Deputy ministers
        President of the Council of State
        President of the Court of Accounts
        President and vice presidents of the Senate
        Senators in the Senate
        President and vice presidents of the Chamber of Deputies
        Deputies in the Chamber of Deputies
        President, vice president, and justices of the Constitutional Court
        First president, presidents, and justices of the Supreme Court of Cassation
        Vice president of the High Council of Courts
        Governor of the Bank of Italy
NOTE: Address the president and prime minister by *(office)* or as *His/Her Excellency*. Address a deputy prime minister, member of the Cabinet, senator, deputy, or judge of a high court as *the Honorable*. Address other officials by *(honorific)* + *(name)* and identify by *(office)*.

Ivory Coast

    See *Cote D'Ivorie*

Jamaica

Official name: Jamaica
    Embassy of Jamaica
    Noun and adjective: Jamaican
    Chief of state: The King/Queen of Jamaica
        Elizabeth the Second, by the Grace of God, Queen of Jamaica and of Her
        other Realms and Territories, Head of the Commonwealth
    Vice-royal representative: Governor-general
    Head of government: Prime minister
    Other high officials:
        Deputy prime minister
        Ministers of *(portfolio)*
        Attorney General
        President of the Senate
        Senators in the Senate
        Speaker and members of the House of Representatives
        Chief justice of Jamaica and justices of the Supreme Court of Jamaica
        President and justices of the Court of Appeal
        Governor of the Central Bank
NOTE: Address the governor-general as *His/Her Excellency*. Address the prime minister

as *the Right Honourable* and members of the Cabinet as *the Honorable*. Address the chief justice or a justice of a high court as *My Lord Chief Justice* and *My Lord Justice (name)*, respectively. Address members of Parliament and other officials by *(honorific)* + *(name)* and identify by *(office)*. Include *Sir* or *Dame* in the forms of address of knighted officials.

Japan

Official name: Japan
    Embassy of Japan
    Noun and adjective: Japanese
    Chief of state: Emperor
    Head of government: Prime minister
    Other high officials:
        Chief cabinet secretary
        Ministers of *(portfolio)*
        State ministers for *(portfolio)*
        President and members of the House of Councillors
        Speaker and members of the House of Representatives
        Chief justice and justices of the Supreme Court
        Governor of the Bank of Japan

NOTE: Address the prime minister by *(office)* or as *His/Her Excellency*. Also address the chief justice in the Supreme Court, president of the House of Councillors, speaker of the House of Representatives, a former prime minister, or minister as *His/Her Excellency*. Address other officials by *(honorific)* + *(name)* and identify by *(office)*.

Jersey

Official name: Bailiwick of Jersey
    A British crown dependency
    Diplomatic representation by the United Kingdom
    Noun and adjective: Channel Islander
    Chief of state: Queen (monarch of the United Kingdom)
    Vice-royal representative: Lieutenant governor
    Head of government: Chief minister
    Other high officials:
        Bailiff
        Deputy bailiff
        Ministers of *(portfolio)*
        Senators in the Assembly of the States of Jersey
        Connétables (or Constables) in the Assembly of the States of Jersey
        Deputies in the Assembly of the States of Jersey
        Judges of the Royal Court

NOTE: With the exception of the lieutenant governor, who is addressed as *His/Her Excellency*, address Channel Island officials without a courtesy title. Some office names are used as honorifics: Address a senator as *Senator (name)* and a deputy as *Deputy (name)*. Address a connétable as either *Connétable (name)* or *Connétable (name of the parish the represent)*. A chief minister who is also a senator would be addressed by either or both honorifics: *Senator (name)*, *Chief Minister (name)* or *Chief Minister Senator (name)* depending on the circumstance. Address other officials by *(honorific)* + *(name)* and identify by *(office)* unless the individual has a personal title in which case address by title and identified by *(office)*.

Jordan

Official name: Hashemite Kingdom of Jordan
  Embassy of the Hashemite Kingdom of Jordan
  Noun and adjective: Jordanian
  Chief of state: King
  Heir apparent: Prince
  Head of government: Prime minister
  Other high officials:
       Deputy prime minister
       Ministers of (*portfolio*)
       Speaker and senators in the House of Notables or Majlis al-Ayan
       Speaker and members in the Chamber of Deputies or Majlis al-Nuwaab
       Justices of the Court of Cassation and the Supreme Court
       Governor of the Central Bank of Jordan
NOTE: Address the king as *Your Majesty*. Address the prince as *Your Royal Highness*. Address the prime minister by (*office*). Address the speaker of either house of Parliament, governor of the Central Bank of Jordan, a minister, senator, member of Parliament, former minister, justice, judge, mayor, or president of a university as *His/Her Excellency*. Address other officials by (*honorific*) + (*name*) and identify by (*office*).

Kazakhstan

Official name: Republic of Kazakhstan
  Embassy of the Republic of Kazakhstan
  Noun and adjective: Kazakhstani
  Chief of state: President
  Head of government: Prime minister
  Other high officials:
       Head of Presidential Administration
       Deputy prime ministers
       State secretary
       Ministers of (*portfolio*)
       Chairman of (*portfolio*)
       Senators in the Senate
       Members of the Mazhilis
       Justices of the Supreme Court and Constitutional Court
       Chairman of the National Bank
NOTE: Address the president and prime minister by (*office*) or as *His/Her Excellency*. Also address a member of the Cabinet, senator, member of the Mazhilis, or justice of a high court as *His/Her Excellency*. Address lower officials by (*honorific*) + (*name*) and identify by (*office*).

Kenya

Official name: Republic of Kenya
  Embassy of the Republic of Kenya
  Noun and adjective: Kenyan
  Chief of state and head of government: President
  Other high officials:
       Vice president
       Ministers for (*portfolio*)

Ministers of state for (*portfolio*)
Attorney General
Speaker and members of the National Assembly
Chief justice and justices in the Court of Appeal and the High Court
Governor of the Central Bank of Kenya

NOTE: Address the president and vice president by (*office*) or as *His/Her Excellency*. Address the Attorney General or a minister as *the Honourable*. Address the speaker of the National Assembly as *Mr. Speaker*, and the chief justice as *Mr. Chief Justice*, without courtesy titles. Address other officials by (*honorific*) + (*name*) and identify by (*office*).

Kiribati

Official name: Republic of Kiribati
Kiribati does not have an embassy in the United States
Noun and adjective: I-Kiribati
Chief of state and head of government: President
Other high officials:
Vice president
Ministers for (*portfolio*)
Members of Parliament
Judges of the Court of Appeal and the High Court

Korea, North

Official name: Democratic People's Republic of Korea
Permanent Mission of the Democratic People's Republic of Korea
to the United Nations
Noun and adjective: Korean
Chief of state: Chairman of the National Defense Commission
Head of government: Premier
Other high officials:
Vice premiers
President of the Presidium of the Supreme People's Assembly
Vice president, and General Secretary of the Supreme People's Assembly
Chairman and vice chairmen of the Supreme People's Assembly
Honorary vice presidents and members of the Supreme People's Assembly
Ministers of (*portfolio*)
Chairmen of commissions
Judges in the Central Court
President of the Central Bank

Korea, South

Official name: Republic of Korea
Embassy of the Republic of Korea
Noun and adjective: Korean
Chief of state: President
Head of government: Prime minister
Other high officials:
Deputy prime ministers
Ministers of (*portfolio*) of the State Council (cabinet)
Chairman of (commissions)
Chief of staff, office of the president

Chief secretary to the president for (portfolio)
Members of the National Assembly or Kukhoe
Chief justice and justices of the Supreme Court
Chief justice and justices of the Constitutional Court
Governor of the Bank of Korea

NOTE: Address the president and prime minister by (office) or as His/Her Excellency. Also address all members of the Cabinet as His/Her Excellency. Address members of the National Assembly as the Honorable. Address a chief justice as the Honorable Chief Justice, and a justice as Justice (name). Address other officials by (honorific) + (name) and identify by (office).

Kuwait

Official name: State of Kuwait
Embassy of the State of Kuwait
Noun and adjective: Kuwaiti
Chief of state: Prince (constitutional emirate)
Head of government: Prime minister
Other high officials:
Crown prince
First deputy prime minister
Deputy prime ministers
Ministers of (portfolio) in the Council of Ministers
Speaker and members of the National Assembly or Majlis al-Umma
Judges of the High Court of Appeal
President of the National Security Bureau
Governor of the Central Bank

NOTE: Address the chief of state by (office) or as His Highness. Certain high office holders (such the prime minister) will also have a noble title: Address as His Highness Sheikh (name). Address the speaker, president of the National Security Bureau, or a member of the National Assembly, minister, judge of the High Court of Appeal as His Excellency. Some officials will also include an honorific such as Sheikh, Dr. or both in their name string: Follow the presentation of the name. Address other officials by (honorific) + (name) and identify by (office).

Kyrgyzstan

Official name: Kyrgyz Republic
Embassy of the Kyrgyz Republic
Noun and adjective: Kyrgyzstani
Chief of state: President
Head of government: Prime minister
Other high officials:
First vice prime minister
Vice prime minister
Ministers of (portfolio)
Chairmen of state committees of (portfolio)
Chair of the Central Election Committee
Commander of the National Guard
Chairman of the Border Service
Secretary of the National Security Council

Prosecutor General
Speaker, vice speaker and deputies of the Supreme Council/Parliament
Governors of the states
Judges of the Supreme and Constitutional Courts

NOTE: Address the president and prime minister by *(office)* or as *His/Her Excellency.* Address the speaker, vice speaker, a minister, vice minister, chairman of a state committee with the rank of minister, a high member of the president's staff, or a deputy in Parliament as *the Honorable.* Other officials, including the judges of the Supreme or Constitutional courts, receive no courtesy title: Address by *(honorific)* + *(name)* and identify by *(office).*

Laos

Official name: Lao People's Democratic Republic
Embassy of the Lao People's Democratic Republic
Noun and adjective: Lao, Laotian
Chief of state: President
Head of government: Prime minister
Other high officials:
Vice president
Deputy prime ministers
Ministers of *(portfolio)*
Ministers and chairmen of national committees
Minister and head of *(portfolio)*
Chairmen of committees and commissions
Members of the National Assembly
President, vice president and justices of the People's Supreme Court
Governor of the National Bank

Latvia

Official name: Republic of Latvia
Embassy of Latvia
Noun and adjective: Latvian
Chief of state: President
Head of government: Prime minister
Other high officials:
Ministers of *(portfolio)* in the Council of Ministers
Special task ministers for *(portfolio)*
Speaker and members of Parliament
Judges of the Supreme and Constitutional Courts
Governor of the Bank of Latvia

NOTE: Address the president by *(office)* or as *His/Her Excellency.* Also address the prime minister, minister of foreign affairs, and speaker of Parliament as *His/Her Excellency.* Address other officials by *(honorific)* + *(name)* and identify by *(office).*

Lebanon

Official name: Lebanese Republic
Embassy of Lebanon
Noun and adjective: Lebanese
Chief of state: President
Head of government: Prime minister

Other high officials:
Deputy prime minister
Ministers of *(portfolio)*
Speaker and members of National Assembly/Parliament
Chief justice and justices in the Courts of Cassation
Chief justice and justices in the Constitutional Council and Supreme Council
Governor of the Central Bank

NOTE: Address the president and prime minister by *(office)* or as *His/Her Excellency.* Also address the speaker, a member of the Cabinet, or member of the National Assembly as *His/Her Excellency.* Address other officials by *(honorific)* + *(name)* and identify by *(office).*

Lesotho

Official name: Kingdom of Lesotho
Embassy of the Kingdom of Lesotho
Singular noun: Masotho
Plural noun: Basotho
Adjective: Basotho
Chief of state: King (hereditary monarch)
Head of government: Prime minister
Other high officials:
Deputy prime minister
Members of the Council of State
Ministers of *(portfolio)*
President, vice president, and senators in the Senate
Speaker, deputy speaker, and members of the National Assembly
President and justices of the Court of Appeal
Chief justice and justices of the High Court
Governor of the Central Bank of Lesotho

NOTE: Address the king and queen as *Your Majesty,* and chiefs as *Chief (name).* Address the prime minister by *(office)* or *the Right Honourable.* Address the deputy prime minister, a minister, all senators of the Senate, and members of the National Assembly as *the Honourable.* The chief justice is addressed as *His Lordship the Chief Justice.* Address other justices and judges as *His/Her Honor Justice/Judge (name).* Address lower officials by *(honorific)* + *(name)* and identify by *(office).*

Liberia

Official name: Republic of Liberia
Embassy of the Republic of Liberia
Noun and adjective: Liberian
Chief of state and head of government: President
Other high officials:
Vice president
Ministers of *(portfolio)*
Senators in the Senate
Speaker and members of the House of Representatives
Chief justice and justices of the Supreme Court
Executive governor and governor of the Central Bank of Liberia

NOTE: Address the president and vice president by *(office)* or as *His/Her Excellency*. Address a minister, senator, member of the House of Representatives, or justice as *the Honorable*. Address other officials by *(honorific)* + *(name)* and identify by *(office)*.

Libya

Official name: Great Socialist People's Libyan Arab Jamahiriya
    Embassy of the Libyan Arab Jamahiriya
    Noun and adjective: Libyan
    Chief of state: Revolutionary Leader/
        Brotherly Leader and Guide of the Revolution
    Head of government: Secretary of the General People's Committee/prime minister
    Other high officials:
        Secretary General of the General People's Committee
        Secretaries of the General People's Committee for *(portfolio)*
        Secretary, assistant secretary, and members of the General Peoples Congress
        Justices of the Supreme Court
        Governor of the Central Bank

Liechtenstein

Official name: Principality of Liechtenstein
    Embassy of the Principality of Liechtenstein
    Noun: Liechtensteiner
    Adjective: Liechtenstein
    Chief of state: Reigning Prince
    Heir apparent: Crown Prince
    Head of government: Prime minister
    Other high officials:
        Deputy prime minister
        Ministers of *(portfolio)*
        Attorney General
        Parliamentary Secretary
        President and vice president of Parliament
        Members of Parliament
        Justices of the Supreme Court
        Justices of the Court of Appeal
        Judges of the Court of Justice
        Judges of the Administrative Court, and Constitutional Court
        Chairman of the Liechtenstein State Bank

NOTE: Address the chief of state and members of the ruling family by personal title. Address the Attorney General or a minister as *His/Her Excellency*. Address the listed high officials below cabinet level as *the Honorable*. Address other officials by *(honorific)* + *(name)* and identify by *(office)*.

Lithuania

Official name: Republic of Lithuania

> Embassy of the Republic of Lithuania
>
> *Noun and adjective:* Lithuanian
>
> *Chief of state:* President
>
> *Head of government:* Prime minister
>
> *Other high officials:*
>
> > Ministers of *(portfolio)* in the Council of Ministers
> >
> > Members of Parliament
> >
> > Judges of the Constitutional, Supreme, and Court of Appeal
> >
> > Governor of the Bank of Lithuania

NOTE: Address the president by *(office)* or as *His/Her Excellency.* Also address the minister of foreign affairs as *His/Her Excellency.* Address other officials by *(honorific)* + *(name)* and identify by *(office).*

Luxembourg

Official name: Grand-Duchy of Luxembourg

> Embassy of the Grand Duchy of Luxembourg
>
> *Noun:* Luxembourger
>
> *Adjective:* Luxembourgian
>
> *Chief of state:* Grand Duke
>
> *Head of government:* Prime minister
>
> *Other high officials:*
>
> > Deputy prime minister/vice prime minister
> >
> > Ministers of *(portfolio)* in the Council of Ministers
> >
> > Secretary of state for *(portfolio)*
> >
> > Deputy ministers of *(portfolio)*
> >
> > Deputies in the Chamber of Deputies
> >
> > Judges of the judicial courts, tribunals, and administrative courts
> >
> > Chairman of the Luxembourg Central Bank

NOTE: Address the grand duke and heir apparent as *Your Royal Highness.* Address the prime minister and vice prime minister as *His/Her Excellency.* Address a secretary, deputy minister, or another official by *(honorific)* + *(name)* and identify by *(office).*

Macau

Official name: Macau Special Administrative Region

> Special administrative region of China
>
> Diplomatic representation by the People's Republic of China
>
> *Noun and adjective:* Chinese
>
> *Chief of state:* President (president of China)
>
> *Head of government:* Chief Executive
>
> *Other high officials:*
>
> > Secretary for *(portfolio)* in the Executive Council
> >
> > President and members of the Legislative Assembly
> >
> > President and justices of the Court of Final Appeal

Macedonia

Official name: Republic of Macedonia
  Embassy of the Republic of Macedonia
  Noun and adjective: Macedonian
  Chief of state: President
  Head of government: Prime minister
  Other high officials:
      Deputy prime ministers for *(portfolio)*
      Ministers of *(portfolio)* in the Council of Ministers
      President and members of the Assembly
      Judges of the Supreme and Constitutional Courts
      Governor of the Macedonian National Bank

NOTE: Address the president and prime minister by *(office)* or as *His/Her Excellency.* Also address the deputy prime minister, president of the Assembly, or a member of the Cabinet as *His/Her Excellency.* Address a member of the Assembly or judge of a high court as *the Honorable.* Address other officials by *(honorific)* + *(name)* and identify by *(office).*

Madagascar

Official name: Republic of Madagascar
  Embassy of the Republic of Madagascar
  Noun and adjective: Malagasy
  Chief of state: President
  Head of government: Prime minister
  Other high officials:
      Ministers of *(portfolio)* in the Council of Ministers
      Vice ministers and state secretaries for *(portfolio)*
      President and senators of the Senate
      President and deputies of the National Assembly (General Assembly)
      President and justices of the Supreme Court of Madagascar
      Chief justice and judges of the Court of Appeal and High Court of Justice
      Chief justice and judges of the High Constitutional Court
      Governor of the Central Bank of Madagascar

NOTE: Address the president by *(office)* or as *His/Her Excellency.* Also address the president of the Senate or president of the National Assembly as *His/Her Excellency.* Address a minister, state secretary, senator, deputy, judge, or justice by *(honorific)* + *(name)* and identify by *(office).*

Malawi

Official name: Republic of Malawi
  Embassy of Malawi
  Noun and adjective: Malawian
  Chief of state and head of government: President
  Other high officials:
      Vice-president
      Ministers of *(portfolio)*
      Attorney General
      Speaker and members of the National Assembly
      Chief justice and justices of the Supreme Court of Appeal

Judges of the High Court

Governor of the Reserve Bank of Malawi

NOTE: Address the president by (office) or as His/Her Excellency. Address the vice president as the Right Honourable. Address members of the cabinet, members of the National Assembly, justices and judges of high courts as the Honourable. Address other officials by (honorific) + (name) and identify by (office).

Malaysia

Official name: Malaysia

Embassy of Malaysia

Noun and adjective: Malaysian

Chief of state: Paramount ruler (the Sultan)

Head of government: Prime minister

Other high officials:

Deputy paramount ruler

Deputy prime minister

Ministers of (portfolio)

The president and senators in the Senate

The speaker and members of the House of Representatives

The chief justice and judges of the Federal Court

The president and judges of the Court of Appeal

Governor of the Bank Negara Malaysia

Royalty:

Sultans and rulers of the Malaysian states

Crown princes of the Malaysian states

Members of the royal household:

Comptroller of the Royal Household

Grand Chamberlain of the Royal Household

NOTE: Malaysians use a wide variety of indigenous courtesy titles for high officials which are variously translated as the Most Honourable for a minister, the Most Learned for the chief justice or president of a high court, the Learned for other judges, and His/Her Excellency for governors. However, the Embassy of Malaysia suggests that in English-speaking countries the prime minister, deputy prime minister, a minister, judge, or member of either house of Parliament can be appropriately addressed as the Honourable.

Maldives

Official name: Republic of the Maldives

Embassy of the Republic of the Maldives

Permanent Mission of the Republic of Maldives to the United Nations

Noun and adjective: Maldivian

Chief of state and head of government: President

Other high officials:

Ministers of (portfolio)

Attorney General

Members of the People's Council/Majlis

Judges of the High Court

Governor of the Maldives Monetary Authority

NOTE: Address the president by (office) or as His/Her Excellency. Also address the minister of foreign affairs as His/Her Excellency. Address the Attorney General, a minister, member of the People's Council, or judge of a high court as *the Honourable*. Address other officials by *(honorific)* + *(name)* and identify by *(office)*.

Mali

Official name: Republic of Mali
    Embassy of the Republic of Mali
    Noun and adjective: Malian
    Chief of state: President
    Head of government: Prime minister
    Other high officials:
        Ministers of *(portfolio)* in the Council of Ministers
        President and deputies of the National Assembly
        Chief justice and justices of the Supreme Court

NOTE: Address the president by *(office)* or as *His/Her Excellency*. Also address the prime minister or a minister as *His/Her Excellency*. Address the chief justice, a justice of the Supreme Court, or deputy in the National Assembly as *the Honorable*. Address other officials by *(honorific)* + *(name)* and identify by *(office)*.

Malta

Official name: Republic of Malta
    Embassy of Malta
    Noun and adjective: Maltese
    Chief of state: President
    Head of government: Prime minister
    Other high officials:
        Deputy prime minister
        Ministers of *(portfolio)*
        Members of the House of Representatives/Parliament
        Judges of the Constitutional Court and Court of Appeal
        Governor of the Central Bank

NOTE: Address the president and prime minister by *(office)* or as *His/Her Excellency*. Address the deputy prime minister, a minister, member of Parliament, or judge of a high court as *the Honourable*. Address other officials by *(honorific)* + *(name)* and identify by *(office)*.

Marshall Islands

Official name: Republic of the Marshall Islands
    Embassy of the Republic of the Marshall Islands
    Noun and adjective: Marshallese
    Chief of state and head of government: President
    Other high officials:
        Ministers of *(portfolio)*
        Members of the Legislature/Nitijela
        Justices of the Supreme Court
        Judges of the High Court and Traditional Rights Court

NOTE: Address the president by *(office)* or as *His/Her Excellency*. Address a minister, member of the Nitijela, justice, or judge as *the Honorable*. Address other officials by *(honorific)* + *(name)* and identify by *(office)*.

Mauritania

Official name: Islamic Republic of Mauritania
    Embassy of the Islamic Republic of Mauritania
    Noun and adjective: Mauritanian
    Chief of state: President
    Head of government: Prime minister
    Other high officials:
        Ministers of *(portfolio)* in the Council of Ministers
        Secretary General of Government
        Senators in the Senate
        Members of the National Assembly/Majlis al-Watani
        Justices of the Supreme Court and the Court of Appeals

NOTE: Address the president by *(office)* or as *His/Her Excellency*. Also address the prime minister or a minister as *His/Her Excellency*. Address senators and members of the National Assembly as *the Honorable*. Address the Secretary General, or justice of a high court without a courtesy title as *Justice/Judge/Mr./Mrs. (name)*, and identify by *(office)*. Address other officials by *(honorific)* + *(name)* and identify by *(office)*.

Mauritius

Official name: Republic of Mauritius
    Embassy of the Republic of Mauritius
    Noun and adjective: Mauritian
    Chief of state: President
    Head of government: Prime minister
    Other high officials:
        Vice president
        Deputy prime ministers
        Ministers of *(portfolio)*
        Attorney General
        Members of the National Assembly
        Chief justice and justices of the Supreme Court
        Chairman of the board and directors of the Bank of Mauritius
        Governor and first deputy governor of the Bank of Mauritius

NOTE: Address the president and vice president by *(office)* or as *the Honourable*. Also address a deputy minister, member of the Cabinet, or member of the National Assembly as *the Honourable*. Address a justice, judge, or other official by *(honorific)* + *(name)* and identify by *(office)*.

Mayotte

Official name: Territorial Collectivity of Mayotte
　　An overseas collectivity of France
　　Diplomatic representation by the French Republic
　　Noun: Mahorias
　　Adjective: Mahoran
　　Chief of state: President of the French Republic
　　　　Representative of the chief of state: Prefect
　　Head of government: President of the General Council
　　Other high officials:
　　　　Members of the General Council
　　　　Senator in the French Senate from Mayotte
　　　　Member to the French National Assembly from Mayotte
　　　　Justices of the Supreme Court

Mexico

Official name: United Mexican States
　　Embassy of Mexico
　　Noun and adjective: Mexican
　　Chief of state and head of government: President
　　Other high officials:
　　　　Chief of staff
　　　　Secretaries of *(portfolio)* of the Cabinet
　　　　Attorney General
　　　　President, vice presidents, and secretaries of the Senate
　　　　Senators in the Senate
　　　　President of the Chamber of Deputies
　　　　Deputies in the Chamber of Deputies
　　　　Justices of the Supreme Court of Justice
　　　　Governor of the Bank of Mexico
Note: High elected officials from Mexico should generally be addressed in writing as
His/Excellency (name), and orally as *Mr./Madam (office)*.

OFFICE	IN WRITING	IN CONVERSATION
President	*His/Her Excellency*	Mr./Madam President
Chief of Staff	*His/Her Excellency*	Mr./Mrs./etc. (name)
Secretary of (portfolio)	*His/Her Excellency*	Mr./Madam Secretary
Attorney General	*His/Her Excellency*	Mr./Madam Attorney General
President of the Senate	*His/Her Excellency*	Mr./Madam President
Vice president of the Senate	*His/Her Excellency*	Mr./Madam Vice President
Secretary of the Senate	*His/Her Excellency*	Mr./Madam Secretary
Senator	*His/Her Excellency*	Mr./Madam Senator
President, Chamber of Deputies	*His/Her Excellency*	Mr./Madam President
Deputy, Chamber of Deputies	*His/Her Excellency*	Mr./Madam Deputy
Justices of the Supreme Court	*His/Her Excellency*	Mr./Madam Minister
Governor of the Bank of Mexico	*His/Her Excellency*	Mr./Madam Governor

Address other officials by *(honorific)* + *(name)* and identify by *(office)*.

Micronesia

Official name: Federated States of Micronesia
   Embassy of the Federated States of Micronesia
   Noun: Micronesian
   Adjectives: Micronesian, Chuukese, Kosraen, Pohnpeian, Yapese
   Chief of state and head of government: President
   Other high officials:
      Vice president
      Secretaries of *(portfolio)* in the Cabinet
      Speaker and members of Congress
      Justices of the Supreme Court
NOTE: Address the president by *(office)* or as *His/Her Excellency.* Address the vice president, a secretary in the Cabinet, or justice of the Supreme Court as *the Honorable.* Address other officials by *(honorific)* + *(name)* and identify by *(office)*.

Moldova

Official name: Republic of Moldova
   Embassy of the Republic of Moldova
   Noun and adjective: Moldovan
   Chief of state: President
   Head of government: Prime minister
   Other high officials:
      First deputy prime minister
      Deputy prime ministers
      Ministers of *(portfolio)*
      Secretary of the Supreme Security Council
      Prosecutor General
      President and members of Parliament
      Justices of the Supreme and Constitutional Courts
      President of the National Bank
NOTE: Address the president by *(office)* or as *His/Her Excellency.* Address the prime minister and all other officials in the executive, legislative, and judicial branches by *(honorific)* + *(name)* and identify by *(office)*.

Monaco

Official name: Principality of Monaco
   Embassy of Monaco (Chancery in New York for the United Nations)
   Noun and adjective: Monegasque, Monacan
   Chief of state: Prince (hereditary monarch)
   Head of government: Minister of state
   Other high officials:
      Ministers of *(portfolio)* in the Council of Government
      President and counsellors of the National Council/Conseil National
      President and justices of the Supreme Court
NOTE: Address the reigning prince in conversation initially as *Your Serene Highness,* and subsequently as *Monseigneur: Sir* is not used in conversation with the reigning prince. Monegasque citizens do not address their national officials as *His/Her Excellency* or *the Honorable.* Officials are directly addressed as *Mr./Madam (office): Mr. Minister of State (Monsieur le Ministre d'Etat), Mr. President of the National Council (Monsieur le Président*

du Conseil National), or Mr. Counsellor *(Monsieur le Conseiller)*. When the official's name is used in writing, the *(office)* is on the first line, the *(honorific)* *(full name)* is on the second line. Address other officials by *(honorific)* + *(name)* and identify by *(office)*.

Mongolia

Official name: Mongolia
>
> Embassy of Mongolia
> *Noun and adjective:* Mongolian
> *Chief of state:* President
> *Head of government:* Prime minister
> *Other high officials:*
>> Deputy prime minister
>> Chief of the Cabinet Secretariat
>> Secretary of the National Security Council
>> Ministers of *(portfolio)*
>> Members of the General Council of Courts
>> Speaker and members of the State Great Hural/Parliament
>> Justices of the Supreme Court
>> Governor of the Bank of Mongolia

NOTE: Address the president by *(office)* or as *His/Her Excellency*. Also address the prime minister, deputy prime minister, a secretary, or minister in the Cabinet as *His/Her Excellency*. Members of Parliament are addressed as *the Honorable*. Address justices and judges as *Justice (name)* and *Judge (name)*, respectively. Address other officials by *(honorific)* + *(name)* and identify by *(office)*.

Montenegro

Official name: Republic of Montenegro
>
> Embassy of the Republic of Montenegro
> *Noun and adjective:* Montenegrin
> *Chief of state:* President
> *Head of government:* Prime minister
> *Other high officials:*
>> Deputy prime ministers for *(portfolio)*
>> Ministers of *(portfolio)*
>> Members of the Assembly
>> Justices of the Constitutional and Supreme Courts

Montserrat

Official name: Montserrat
>
> An overseas territory of the United Kingdom
> Diplomatic representation by the United Kingdom
> *Noun and adjective:* Montserratian
> *Chief of state:* King/Queen (hereditary monarch of the United Kingdom)
> *Vice-royal representative:* Governor
> *Head of government:* Chief minister
> *Other high officials:*
>> Attorney General
>> Finance secretary
>> Members of the Legislative Council

Chief justice and justices of appeal of the Eastern Caribbean Supreme Court
President and judges of the Caribbean Court of Justice
Judge of the High Court

Morocco

Official name: Kingdom of Morocco
Embassy of the Kingdom of Morocco
Noun and adjective: Moroccan
Chief of state: King (hereditary monarch)
Head of government: Prime minister
Other high officials:
Ministers of *(portfolio)* in the Council of Ministers
Secretary General of the government
Secretary of state to the ministry of *(portfolio)*
Counsellors in the Chamber of Counselors
Members of the Chamber of Representatives
Justices of the Supreme Court
Governor of the Central Bank

Mozambique

Official name: Republic of Mozambique
Embassy of the Republic of Mozambique
Noun and adjective: Mozambican
Chief of state: President
Head of government: Prime minister
Other high officials:
Ministers of *(portfolio)*
Attorney General
Members of the Assembly of the Republic/Parliament
Justices of the Supreme Court
Governor of the Bank of Mozambique

NOTE: Address the president and prime minister by *(office)* or as *His/Her Excellency.*
Also address a member of the Cabinet, member of Parliament, or justice of the Supreme
Court as *His/Her Excellency.* Address other officials by *(honorific)* + *(name)* and identify
by *(office).*

Myanmar

Official name: Union of Myanmar
Consulate General of the Union of Myanmar
Chief of state: Chairman of the State Peace and Development Council
Head of government: Prime minister
Other high officials:
Vice chairman of the State Peace and Development Council
First and second secretaries of the State Peace and Development Council
Ministers of *(portfolio)*
Members of the People's Assembly
Governor of the Central Bank

Namibia

Official name: Republic of Namibia
    Embassy of the Republic of Namibia
    Noun and adjective: Namibian
    Chief of state: President
    Head of government: Prime minister
    Other high officials:
        Deputy prime minister
        Ministers of (*portfolio*)
        Directors of national commissions
        Attorney General
        Chairperson and members of the National Council
        Speaker and members of the National Assembly
        Chief justice and justices of the Supreme Court
        President and judges of the High Court
        Chairman of the board and board members of the Bank of Namibia
        Governor of the Bank of Namibia

NOTE: Address the president by (*office*) or as *His/Her Excellency*. Address the prime minister, deputy prime minister, Attorney General, speaker of the National Assembly, chief justice, president of the High Court, or a minister as *the Honourable*. Also address all members of the National Assembly and justices of the high courts as *the Honourable*. Address other officials by (*honorific*) + (*name*) and identify by (*office*).

Nauru

Official name: Republic of Nauru
    Embassy of the Republic of Nauru
    Noun and adjective: Nauruan
    Chief of state and head of government: President
    Other high officials:
        Minister assisting the president
        Ministers of (*portfolio*)
        Members of Parliament
        Justices of the Supreme Court

Nepal

Official name: Nepal
    Embassy of Nepal
    Chief of state: Girija/king (hereditary monarch)
    Noun and adjective: Nepalese
    Head of government: Prime minister
    Other high officials:
        Deputy prime ministers
        Ministers of (*portfolio*) in the Cabinet
        Ministers of state of (*portfolio*)
        Members of the Interim Parliament
        Chief justice and justices of the Supreme Court
        Chief justice and justices of the Constitutional and Judicial Councils
        Governor of the Central Bank

NOTE: Address the chief of state as *Your Majesty*. Address the prime minister, speaker of

Parliament, and the chief justices of the Supreme Court, or Constitutional and Judicial Councils as *the Right Honourable*. Address the deputy prime minister, a minister, member of Parliament, or judge of a high court as *the Honourable*. Address other officials by *(honorific)* + *(name)* and identify by *(office)*. Nepal calls its ambassador the *Nepalese Ambassador*

Netherlands

Official name: Kingdom of the Netherlands
>Embassy of the Kingdom of the Netherlands,
>*Noun:* Dutchman, Dutchwoman
>*Adjective:* Dutch
>*Chief of state:* King/Queen (hereditary monarch)
>*Heir apparent:* Crown prince/princess
>*Head of government:* Prime minister
>*Other high officials:*
>>Deputy prime ministers
>>Ministers of *(portfolio)* in the Council of Ministers
>>State secretaries for *(portfolio)*
>>President and members of the First Chamber of Parliament
>>>Eerste Kamer/Senate
>>President and members of the Second Chamber of Parliament
>>>Tweede Kamer/House of Representatives
>>Justices of the Supreme Court
>>President of the Netherlands Central Bank

NOTE: Address the chief of state as *Your Majesty* or *Her Majesty the Queen of the Netherlands*. Address the crown price as *His Royal Highness* or *His Royal Highness the Prince of Orange*. Address all members of parliament as *His/Her Excellency*. Use the honorific *Senator* for a member of the First Chamber. Use the post-nominal MP with a member of the Second Chamber. Address other officials by *(honorific)* + *(name)* and identify by *(office)*.

Netherlands Antilles

Official name: Netherlands Antilles
>An autonomous country within the Kingdom of the Netherlands
>Diplomatic representation by the Kingdom of the Netherlands
>>Minister Plenipotentiary at the Embassy of the Kingdom of the Netherlands
>*Noun and adjective:* Dutch Antillean
>*Chief of state:* Queen (monarch of the Netherlands)
>*Vice-royal representative:* Governor
>*Head of government:* Prime minister
>*Other high officials:*
>>Deputy prime minister
>>Ministers of *(portfolio)* in the Council of Ministers
>>Members of the States or Staten
>>Judges of the Joint High Court of Justice
>>Director of the Bank of the Netherlands Antilles

NOTE: Address the governor as *His/Her Excellency*.

New Caledonia

Official name: Territory of New Caledonia and Dependencies
    An overseas collectivity of France
    Diplomatic representation by the French Republic
    Noun and adjective: New Caledonian
    Chief of state: President of the French Republic
        Representative of the chief of state: High commissioner
    Head of government: President of the Government
    Other high officials:
        Members of the Cabinet
        Members of the Territorial Congress/Congres du territoire
        Senator of the French Senate from New Caledonia
        Member of the French National Assembly from New Caledonia
        Judges of the Court of Appeal

New Zealand

Official name: New Zealand
    Embassy of New Zealand
    Noun: New Zealander
    Adjective: New Zealand
    Chief of state: The King/Queen of New Zealand
        Elizabeth the Second, by the Grace of God, Queen of New Zealand
        and Her Other Realms and Territories, Head of the Commonwealth,
        Defender of the Faith)
    Vice-royal representative: Governor-general
    Head of government: Prime minister
    Other high officials:
        Deputy prime minister
        Ministers of (*portfolio*) in the Executive Council
        Attorney General
        Speaker and member of the House of Representatives/Parliament
        Chief justice and justices of the Supreme Court
        President and puisne judges of the Court of Appeal
        Chief high court judge and judges of the High Court
        Governor of the Reserve Bank
NOTE: Address the governor-general of New Zealand, prime minister, speaker of the
House of Representatives, chief justice, a member of the Executive Council, judge of
the Supreme Court, judge of the Court of Appeal, or judge of the High Court as *the
Honourable* with following caveat: If he or she is a member of the Privy Council, address
as *the Right Honourable (name)*. Typically the prime minister, senior and long serving
ministers, the chief justice, and judges of the Court of Appeal are Privy Counsellors.
Address members of Parliament as *Mr./Mrs./etc. (name)*, MP. Address the Governor and
a member of the Board of the Reserve Bank as *Dr./Mr./Mrs./etc. (name)* and identify by
(office). Address other officials by *(honorific)* + *(name)* and identify by *(office)*. Include
Sir or *Dame* in the forms of address of knighted officials. Peers who are Privy
Counsellors will use the post-nominal abbreviation, *PC*.

Nicaragua

Official name: Republic of Nicaragua
    Embassy of the Republic of Nicaragua
    Noun and adjective: Nicaraguan
    Chief of state and head of government: President
    Other high officials:
        Vice president
        Ministers of *(portfolio)* in the Council of Ministers
        Secretary General of the Ministry of Defense
        Attorney General
        President of the National Assembly
        Deputies in the National Assembly
        President, vice president and justices of the Supreme Court
        President of the Central Bank
NOTE: Address the president by *(office)* or as *His/Her Excellency.* Address the vice president, a member of the Cabinet, the president or deputy in the National Assembly, or officer or justice of the Supreme Court as *the Honorable.* Address other officials by *(honorific)* + *(name)* and identify by *(office).*

Niger

Official name: Republic of Niger
    Embassy of the Republic of Niger
    Noun and adjective: Nigerien
    Chief of state and head of government: President
    Other high officials:
        Prime minister of the Cabinet
        Ministers of *(portfolio)* of the Cabinet
        Deputy of the National Assembly
        Judges of the State Court and the Court of Appeals
NOTE: Address the president by *(office)* or as *His/Her Excellency.* Also address the prime minister or a minister as *His/Her Excellency.* Address members of the National Assembly as *The Honorable Deputy* and justices of a high court as *Mr. Justice (name).* Address other officials by *(honorific)* + *(name)* and identify by *(office).*

Nigeria

Official name: Federal Republic of Nigeria
Embassy of the Federal Republic of Nigeria
Noun and adjective: Nigerian
Chief of state and head of government: President
Other high officials:
Vice president
Ministers of *(portfolio)*
Ministers of state for *(portfolio)*
Senators in the Senate
Members of the House of Representatives
Justices of the Supreme Court and Federal Court of Appeal
Governor of the Central Bank of Nigeria

NOTE: Address the president by *(office)*. Address the vice president, a minister, senator, member of the House of Representatives, or judge of a high court as *the Honourable.* Address other officials by *(honorific)* + *(name)* and identify by *(office)*.

Niue

Official name: Niue
Diplomatic representation by New Zealand
Noun and adjective: Niuean
Chief of state: The King/Queen of New Zealand
Vice-royal representative: Governor-general of New Zealand
Head of government: Premier
Other high officials:
New Zealand High Commissioner
Ministers of *(portfolio)*
Members of the Legislative Assembly
Justices of the Supreme Court of New Zealand
Judges of the High Court of Niue

Norfolk Island

Official name: Territory of Norfolk Island
Self-governing territory of Australia
Noun and adjective: Norfolk Islander
Chief of state: King/Queen (hereditary monarch of the Australia)
Vice-royal representative: Governor-general of Australia
Head of government: Administrator
Other high officials:
Members of the Executive Council
Members of the Legislative Assembly
Justices of the Supreme Court
Judges of the Court of Petty Sessions

Northern Mariana Islands

Official name: Commonwealth of the Northern Mariana Islands
    Diplomatic representation by the United States
    Chief of state: President of the United States
    Head of government: Governor
    Other high officials:
        Lieutenant Governor
        Special assistants to the Governor
        Heads of principal departments
        Senators in the Senate
        Members of the House of Representatives
        Justices of the Commonwealth Supreme Court
        Judges of the Superior and Federal District Courts

Norway

Official name: Kingdom of Norway
    Royal Norwegian Embassy
    Noun and adjective: Norwegian
    Chief of state: King/Queen
    Heir apparent: Crown prince/crown princess
    Head of government: Prime minister
    Other high officials:
        Lord Chamberlain
        Marshal of the Court
        Ministers of *(portfolio)*
        President of the National Assembly/Storting
        Vice president of the National Assembly/Storting
        President of the National Assembly's upper division/Lagting
        Vice president of the National Assembly's upper division/Lagting
        President of the National Assembly's lower division/Odelsting
        Vice president of the National Assembly's lower division/Odelsting
        Members of Parliament
        Chief justice and justices of the Supreme Court
        Governor of the Bank of Norway

NOTE: Address the chief of state as *Your Majesty*, and the crown prince/princess as *Your Royal Highness*. Address the prime minister and chief justice by *(office)* or as *His/Her Excellency*. Also address the president of the National Assembly/Storting as *His/Her Excellency*. Address the presidents of the Lagting and the Odelsting as *the Right Honorable*. Address vice presidents of the Lagting and Odelsting as *the Honorable*. Address members of Lagting and Odelsting as *Mr./Mrs./etc. (name)* and identify as a member of Parliament. Address other officials by *(honorific)* + *(name)* and identify by *(office)*.

Oman

Official name: Sultanate of Oman
　　Embassy of the Sultanate of Oman
　　Noun and adjective: Omani
　　Chief of state and head of government: Sultan and prime minister
　　Other high officials:
　　　　Personal representative for His Majesty the Sultan
　　　　Deputy prime minister for *(portfolio)*
　　　　Ministers of *(portfolio)*
　　　　Ministers of state for *(portfolio)*
　　　　Chairman of the ministry of *(portfolio)*
　　　　Special advisor to His Majesty the Sultan for *(portfolio)*
　　　　Inspector General of police and customs
　　　　Senators in the Majlis al-Dawla
　　　　Members of the Majlis al-Shura
　　　　Justices of the Supreme Court
　　　　Governor of the Central Bank of Oman

NOTE: Address the sultan as *Your Majesty*. Certain high office holders, such the sultan's personal representative or the prime minister, will have a noble title and are addressed by *(title)* and identified by *(office)*. For example, such address would be *His Highness Sayyid (name), the (name of office) of Oman*. Address a commoner member of the Cabinet rank as *His Excellency (name)*. If an official of this rank also has a personal honorific, complete address might be *His Excellency Sayyid (name), His Excellency Sheikh (name), His Excellency General (name), His Excellency Dr. (name)*, etc. Address a senator or member of the Majlis al-Shura as *the Honorable*. Address other officials by *(honorific)* + *(name)* and identify by *(office)*.

Pakistan

Official name: Islamic Republic of Pakistan
　　Embassy of Pakistan
　　Noun and adjective: Pakistani
　　Chief of state: President
　　Head of government: Prime minister
　　Other high officials:
　　　　Ministers of *(portfolio)*
　　　　Attorney General
　　　　Senators in the Senate
　　　　Members of the National Assembly
　　　　Justices of the Supreme Court
　　　　Governor of the State Bank

Note: Pakistanis do not address their high national officials with courtesy titles. When a high official's *(name)* is used in writing, the *(name of office)* is on the first line, the *(honorific) (name of official)* is on the second line. Address as *President (name), Prime Minister (name)*, or *Senator (name)* is typical. Formally address the chief justice, or a justice of the Supreme Court in writing as *the Honourable Chief Justice* or *the Honourable Justice*. Address other officials by *(honorific)* + *(name)* and identify by *(office)*. When the president, vice president, or a minister travel abroad he or she is often addressed as *His/Her Excellency*.

Palau

Official name: Republic of Palau
 Embassy of the Republic of Palau
 Noun and adjective: Palauan
 Chief of state and head of government: President
 Other high officials:
  Vice president
  Ministers of *(portfolio)*
  Senators in the Senate
  Delegates of the House of Delegates
  Justices of the Supreme Court
  Judges of the Court of Common Pleas
  Judges of the Land Court

NOTE: The president is addressed by *(office)* or as *His/Her Excellency*. Address the vice president, a minister, senator, delegate, justice, or judge as *the Honorable*. Address other officials by *(honorific)* + *(name)* and identify by *(office)*. Palau is a former U.S. territory, so forms of address are influenced by U.S. styles.

Panama

Official name: Republic of Panama
 Embassy of the Republic of Panama
 Noun and adjective: Panamanian
 Chief of state and head of government: President
 Other high officials:
  First vice president
  Second vice president
  Ministers of *(portfolio)*
  Attorney General
  President of the National Assembly
  First and second vice presidents of the National Assembly
  Members of the National Assembly
  Justices of the Supreme Court of Justice
  Judges of the Superior Court
  Manager of the National Bank of Panama

NOTE: Address the president by *(office)* or as *His/Her Excellency*. Also address a vice president or member of the cabinet as *His/Her Excellency*. Address a leader or member of the National Assembly, or justice or judge of a high court as *the Honorable*. Address other officials by *(honorific)* + *(name)* and identify by *(office)*.

Papua New Guinea

Official name: Independent State of Papua New Guinea
 Embassy of the Papua New Guinea
 Noun and adjective: Papua New Guinean
 Chief of state: The King/Queen of Papua New Guinea
  Elizabeth the Second, Queen of Papua New Guinea and of Her Other Realms
  and Territories, Head of the Commonwealth
 Vice-royal representative: Governor-general
 Head of government: Prime minister
 Other high officials:

506

Deputy prime minister
Ministers of *(portfolio)* in the National Executive Council
Attorney General
Members of Parliament
Chief justice and justices of the Supreme Court
Governor of the Central Bank

NOTE: Address the governor-general as *His/Her Excellency*. High officials in the government are members of the Privy Council and are addressed as *the Honourable*: This includes the prime minister, speaker of Parliament, the chief justice, a minister of *(portfolio)*, or justice of the Supreme Court. Address a member of Parliament as *Mr./Mrs./etc. (name)*, MP. Include *Sir* or *Dame* in the forms of address of knighted officials.

Paraguay

Official name: Republic of Paraguay
    Embassy of Paraguay
    Noun and adjective: Paraguayan
    Chief of state and head of government: President
    Other high officials:
        Vice president
        Ministry General Secretary and Chief of Cabinet
        Ministers of *(portfolio)* advisors to the president
        Ministers of *(portfolio)*
        Secretaries of *(portfolio)*
        Senators in the Chamber of Senators
        Deputies in the Chamber of Deputies
        President and justices of the Supreme Court of Justice
        Governor of the Central Bank

NOTE: Address the president by *(office)* or as *His/Her Excellency*. Also address a minister of cabinet rank or official of equal or greater rank as *His/Her Excellency*. Address a senator, deputy, or the president or a justice of the Supreme Court of Justice as *the Honorable*. Address other officials by *(honorific)* + *(name)* and identify by *(office)*.

Peru

Official name: Republic of Peru
    Embassy of Peru
    Noun and adjective: Peruvian
    Chief of state and head of government: President
    Other high officials:
        First vice president
        Second vice president
        Prime minister and president of the Council of Ministers
        Ministers of *(portfolio)* in the Council of Ministers
        President, vice presidents, congressmen and congresswomen
            of the Congress of the Republic
        President and justices of the Supreme Court of Justice
        President of the Central Reserve Bank

NOTE: Address the president by *(office)* or as *His/Her Excellency*. Also address the prime minister, president or vice president of the Congress of the Republic, president of the Supreme Court, or a minister as *His/Her Excellency*. Address a congressman or congresswoman of Congress, or justice of the Supreme Court as *the Honorable*. Address other officials by *(honorific)* + *(name)* and identify by *(office)*.

Philippines

Official name: Republic of the Philippines
  Embassy of the Republic of the Philippines
  Noun and adjective: Filipino
  Noun and adjective: Philippine
  Chief of state and head of government: President
  Other high officials:
    Vice president
    Chief of staff
    Secretaries of *(portfolio)*
    National security advisor
    President of the Senate
    Secretary of the Senate Secretariat
    Deputy secretary of the Senate Secretariat
    Senators in the Senate
    Speaker and members of the House of Representatives
    Chief justice and associate justices of the Supreme Court
    Presiding justice and associate justices of the Sandiganbayan
    Presiding justice and associate justices of the Court of Appeals
    Presiding justices and associate justices of the Court of Tax Appeals
    Governor of the Central Bank
NOTE: Address the president by *(office)* or as *His/Her Excellency*. Address all members of the executive, legislative, and judiciary branches of government as *the Honorable*. Address other officials by *(honorific)* + *(name)* and identify by *(office)*.

Pitcairn Islands

Official name: Pitcairn Islands
  An overseas territory of the United Kingdom
  Diplomatic representation by the United Kingdom
  Noun and adjective: Pitcairn Islander
  Chief of state: King/Queen (hereditary monarch of the United Kingdom)
  Vice-royal representatives:
    Governor-general to New Zealand and the Governor of Pitcairn Islands
    Commissioner
  Head of government: Mayor and Chairman of the Island Council
  Other high officials:
    Members of the Island Council
    Justices of the Court of Appeal and the Supreme Court
    Judges of the Magistrate Court

Poland

Official name: Republic of Poland
    Embassy of the Republic of Poland
    Noun: Pole
    Adjective: Polish
    Chief of state: President
    Head of government: Prime minister
    Other high officials:
        Deputy prime minister
        Ministers of *(portfolio)* in the Council of Ministers
        Secretary of State
        Chairman of the National Bank of Poland
        Chairman of the Supreme Chamber of Control
        Chairman of the Chancellery of the President
        Marshal of the Senate
        Senators in the Senate
        Marshal of the Sejm
        Members of the Sejm
        Chief justice and justices of the Supreme Court
        President and judges of the Constitutional Tribunal
        President of the Polish National Bank

NOTE: Address the president by *(office)* or as *His/Her Excellency.* Also address the prime minister or a member of the Cabinet as *His/Her Excellency.* Address a secretary, chairman, senator, member of the *Sejm,* or judge of a high court by *(honorific)* + *(name)* and identify by *(office).*

Portugal

Official name: Portuguese Republic
    Embassy of Portugal
    Noun and adjective: Portuguese
    Chief of state: President
    Head of government: Prime minister
    Other high officials:
        Ministers of *(portfolio)* in the Council of Ministers
        Speaker and members of the Assembly of the Republic
        President, vice president, and justices of the Supreme Court of Justice
        Judges of the Constitutional and Magistrate Courts
        Governor of the Bank of Portugal

NOTE: Address the president by *(office)* or as *His/Her Excellency.* Also address a minister or member of the Assembly of the Republic as *His/Her Excellency.* Address a justice of a high court as *the Honorable.* Address other officials by *(honorific)* + *(name)* and identify by *(office).*

Puerto Rico

Official name: Commonwealth of Puerto Rico
> An unincorporated organized territory of the United States
> > with commonwealth status
> Diplomatic representation by the United States
> *Noun and adjective:* Puerto Rican
> *Chief of state:* President of the United States
> *Head of government:* Governor
> *Other high officials:*
> > Secretaries of (*portfolio*)
> > President and vice president of the Senate
> > Senators in the Senate
> > Speaker of the House of Representatives
> > Members of the House of Representatives
> > Chief justices and justices of the Supreme Court
> > Judges of Superior, District, and Municipal Courts

NOTE: Officials from Puerto Rico can be addressed exactly as their U.S. counterparts.

Qatar

Official name: State of Qatar
> Embassy of the State of Qatar
> *Noun and adjective:* Qatari
> *Chief of state:* Emir
> *Head of government:* Prime minister
> *Other high officials:*
> > Crown prince/heir apparent
> > Deputy prime minister
> > Ministers of (*portfolio*) in the Council of Ministers
> > Ministers of state for (*portfolio*)
> > Speaker and members of the Advisory Council
> > Members of the Consultative Council
> > President and justices of the Supreme Court
> > Governor of the Central Bank

NOTE: Address the chief of state as *Your Highness*. Address the prime minister, deputy prime minister, or a member of the cabinet as *His/Her Excellency*. The honorific *Sheikh* is used when addressing a member of the ruling family (Al-Thani): *Sheikh (name)*. So, address a minister who is a member of the ruling family as *His Excellency Sheikh (name)*. Otherwise, address a member of a legislature, the president or a justice of the Supreme Court, or other officials by (*honorific*) + (*name*) and identify by (*office*).

Romania

Official name: Romania
> Embassy of Romania
> *Noun and adjective:* Romanian
> *Chief of state:* President
> *Head of government:* Prime minister
> *Other high officials:*
> > Deputy prime minister
> > Ministers of (*portfolio*) in the Council of Ministers

510

President of the Senate
Senators in the Senate
Secretary General of the Chamber of Deputies
Deputies in the Chamber of Deputies
Justices of the High Court of Cassation and Justice (Supreme Court)
Judges of the Constitutional Court
Governor of the National Bank of Romania

NOTE: Address the president by (*office*) or as *His/Her Excellency*. Also address the deputy prime minister or a member of the Cabinet as *His/Her Excellency*. Address the leadership and members in both houses of the legislature, and justices and judges of the high courts as *the Honorable*. Address other officials by (*honorific*) + (*name*) and identify by (*office*).

Russia

Official name: Russian Federation
Embassy of the Russian Federation
Noun and adjective: Russian
Chief of state: President
Head of government: Premier
Other high officials:
First deputy premiers
Deputy premiers
Ministers of (*portfolio*) in the Council of Ministers
Directors of services
Secretary of the Security Council
Members of the Federation Council
Members of the State Duma
Justices of the Supreme Court
Judges of the Constitutional Court
Judges of the Supreme Arbitration Court
Chairman of the Central Bank of Russia

NOTE: Russians do not address their national officials with courtesy titles. But the embassy advises that when their high officials travel abroad it is appropriate to use courtesy titles. Address the president and premier by (*office*) or as *His/Her Excellency*. Also address deputy premiers and ministers as *His/Her Excellency*. Address a member of a legislature or judge of a high court as *the Honorable*. Address other officials by (*honorific*) + (*name*) and identify by (*office*).

Rwanda

Official name: Republic of Rwanda
Embassy of the Republic of Rwanda
Noun and adjective: Rwandan
Chief of state: President
Head of government: Prime minister
Other high officials:
Ministers of (*portfolio*) in the Council of Ministers
Minister in the office of the president of (*portfolio*)
Ministers of state of (*portfolio*)
Attorney General
President and vice presidents of the Senate

> Senators in the Senate
> Speaker and vice speaker of the Chamber of Deputies
> Deputies in the Chamber of Deputies
> Chief justice and justices of the Supreme Court
> Judges of the High Courts of the Republic
> Governor of the National Bank of Rwanda

NOTE: Address the president by (*office*) or as *His/Her Excellency*. Address the prime minister as *the Right Honourable*. Address a minister, leader of, or member of the Senate or Chamber of Deputies as *the Honourable*. Address the chief justice, justice, or judge without a courtesy title as *Chief Justice (name)*, *Justice (name)*, or *Judge (name)*, respectively. Address other officials by (*honorific*) + (*name*) and identify by (*office*).

Saint Barthelemy

Official name: Overseas Collectivity of Saint Barthelemy
> An overseas collectivity of France
> Diplomatic representation by the French Republic
> *Chief of state:* President of the French Republic
>> Representative of the chief of state: Prefect
> *Head of government:* President of the Territorial Council
> *Other high officials:*
>> Members of the Executive Council
>> Members of the Territorial Council

Saint Helena

Official name: Saint Helena
> An overseas territory of the United Kingdom
> Diplomatic representation by the United Kingdom
> *Noun and adjective:* Saint Helenian
> *Chief of state:* King/Queen (hereditary monarch of the United Kingdom)
> *Head of government:* Governor and Commander in Chief
> *Other high officials:*
>> Chief secretary
>> Financial secretary
>> Attorney General
>> Members of the Executive Ministers (Cabinet)
>> Members of the Legislative Council
>> Justices of the Supreme Court and Court of Appeal

NOTE: Address the governor as *His/Her Excellency*. Address other officials by (*honorific*) + (*name*) and identify by (*office*). Members of the Legislative Council use the post-nominal abbreviation MLC.

Saint Kitts and Nevis

Official name: Federation of Saint Kitts and Nevis
> Embassy of St. Kitts and Nevis
> *Noun and adjective:* Kittian, Nevisian
> Federation of Saint Christopher (St. Kitts) and Nevis
> *Chief of state:* The King/Queen of Saint Christopher and Nevis
>> Elizabeth the Second, by the Grace of God, Queen of Saint Christopher and Nevis and of Her Other Realms and Territories, Head of the Commonwealth
> *Vice-royal representative:* Governor-general

512

Head of government: Prime minister
Other high officials:
> Deputy prime minister
> Ministers of *(portfolio)*
> Attorney General
> Speaker, deputy speaker, senators, and representatives of
> > the National Assembly
> Leader of the Opposition in the National Assembly
> Chief justice and justices of appeal of the Eastern Caribbean Supreme Court
> President and judges of the Caribbean Court of Justice
> Judge of the High Court

NOTE: Address the governor-general as *His/Her Excellency.* Address the prime minister, a minister, senator, or member of the assembly as *the Honourable.* Address the chief justice as *His Lordship, the Honorable Chief Justice,* or as *the Honourable (name),* the justices of appeal and other judges of courts as *the Honourable (name).* Address other officials by *(honorific)* + *(name)* and identify by *(office).* Include *Sir* or *Dame* in the forms of address of knighted officials.

Saint Lucia

Official name: Saint Lucia
> Embassy of Saint Lucia
> *Noun and adjective:* Saint Lucian
> *Chief of state:* The King/Queen of Saint Lucia
> > Elizabeth the Second, by the Grace of God, Queen of Saint Lucia and of Her other Realms and Territories, Head of the Commonwealth
> *Vice-royal representative:* Governor-general
> *Head of government:* Prime minister
> *Other high officials:*
> > Minister of *(portfolio)*
> > Attorney General
> > President of the Senate
> > Senators in the Senate
> > Speaker of the House of Assembly
> > Representatives in the House of Assembly
> > Chief justice and justices of appeal of the Eastern Caribbean Supreme Court
> > President and judges of the Caribbean Court of Justice
> > Judge of the High Court

NOTE: Address the governor-general as *His/Her Excellency.* Address the prime minister, a member of the cabinet, senator, or member of the House as *the Honourable.* Address the chief justice as *His Lordship, the Honorable Chief Justice,* or as *the Honourable (name),* the justices of appeal and other judges as *the Honourable (name).* Address other officials by *(honorific)* + *(name)* and identify by *(office).* Include *Sir* or *Dame* in the forms of address of knighted officials.

Saint Martin
Official name: Territorial Collectivity of Saint Martin
    An overseas collectivity of France
    Diplomatic representation by the French Republic
    Chief of state: President of the French Republic
        Representative of the chief of state: Prefect
    Head of government: President of the Territorial Council
    Other high officials:
        Members of the Executive Council
        Members of the Territorial Council

Saint Pierre and Miquelon
Official name: Territorial Collectivity of Saint Pierre and Miquelon
    A self-governing overseas collectivity of France
    Diplomatic representation by the French Republic
    Noun: Frenchman, Frenchwoman
    Adjective: French
    Chief of state: President of the French Republic
    Representative of the chief of state: Prefect
    Head of government: President of the General Council
    Other high officials:
        Senator in the French Senate from Saint Pierre and Miquelon
        Member of the French National Assembly from Saint Pierre and Miquelon
        Members of the General Council

Saint Vincent and the Grenadines
Official name: Saint Vincent and the Grenadines
    Embassy of Saint Vincent and Grenadines
    Noun and adjective: Saint Vincentian, Vincentian
    Chief of state: The King/Queen of Saint Vincent and the Grenadines
        Elizabeth the Second, by the Grace of God, Queen of Saint Vincent
        and the Grenadines and of Her Other Realms and Territories,
        Head of the Commonwealth
    Vice-royal representative: Governor-general
    Head of government: Prime minister
    Other high officials:
        Deputy prime minister
        Ministers of (*portfolio*)
        Attorney General
        Representatives and senators in the House of Assembly
        Chief justice and justices of appeal of the Eastern Caribbean Supreme Court
NOTE: Address the governor-general as *His/Her Excellency.* Address the prime minister, a minister, or representative in the House of Assembly as *the Honourable.* Address a senator as *Senator (name)* without a courtesy title. Address the chief justice as *His Lordship, the Honorable Chief Justice,* or as *the Honourable (name),* the justices of appeal and other judges of courts as *the Honourable (name).* Include *Sir* or *Dame* in the forms of address of knighted officials.

Samoa

Official name: Independent State of Samoa
    Mission of the Independent State of Samoa to the United Nations
    Noun and adjective: Samoan
    Chief of state: Head of state
    Head of government: Prime minister
    Other high officials:
        Deputy prime minister
        Ministers of *(portfolio)*
        Attorney General
        Speaker, deputy speaker, and members of the Legislative Assembly
        Chief justice and justices of the Supreme Court
        Chief justice and justices of the Court of Appeals
        Governor of the Central Bank

NOTE: Address the elected Samoan chief of state as *His/Her Highness the Head of State*. Address the prime minister, deputy prime minister, Attorney General, speaker, deputy speaker, a minister, or member of Parliament as *the Honourable*. Address the chief justice or a justice of the Supreme Court as *His/Her Honour Chief Justice (name)* or *His/Honour Justice (name)*, respectively. Address the chief justice or a justice in the Court of Appeal as *His/Her Lordship, the Chief Justice (name), or His/Her Lordship Justice (name)*. *Mr/Madam (office)* is a frequent form of direct address, such as in *Mr./Madame Attorney General* or *Mr./Madam Governor*. Address other officials by *(honorific)* + *(name)* and identify by *(office)*.

San Marino

Official name: Republic of San Marino
    Mission of the Republic of San Marino to the United Nations
    Noun and adjective: Sammarinese
    Co-chiefs of state: Captain regent (there are two)
    Head of government: Secretary of state
    Other high officials:
        Secretaries of *(portfolio)* in the Congress of State
        Members of the Grand and General Council
        Judges in the Council of Twelve

Sao Tome and Principe

Official name: Democratic Republic of Sao Tome and Principe
    Embassy of Sao Tome & Principe
    Noun and adjective: Sao Tomean
    Chief of state: President
    Head of government: Prime minister
    Other high officials:
        Vice prime minister/deputy prime minister
        Ministers of *(portfolio)*
        Secretary of state for administration
        President and members of the National Assembly
        Justices of the Supreme Court
        Governor of the Central Bank of Sao Tome and Principe

Saudi Arabia

Official name: Kingdom of Saudi Arabia

Royal Embassy of Saudi Arabia

Noun: Saudi

Adjective: Saudi, Saudi Arabian

Chief of state and head of government:

King, prime minister, custodian of the two holy mosques

Other high officials:

Crown prince (heir apparent)

Deputy prime ministers

Ministers of *(portfolio)* in the Council of Ministers

Members in the Shura Council (Majlis al-Shura)

Judges of the Supreme Council of Justice

Governor of the Saudi Arabian Monetary Agency

NOTE: Address the king in conversation as *Your Majesty.* Address the crown prince as *Your Royal Highness.* All direct descendants of King Abdulaziz Al-Saud (1865-1953), the founder of Saudi Arabia, carry the title *prince* or *princess.* Address a descendant on the paternal side as *His/Her Royal Highness* and a descendant on the maternal side as *His/Her Highness.* Address an official without a personal title with the rank of minister or above, a judge of the Supreme Council of Justice, or governor of the Saudi Arabian Monetary Agency as *His/Her Excellency.* Also address members of the Consultative Council as *His/Her Excellency.* Many members of the Shura Council are addressed as *His/Her Excellency,* but not all: The rank is granted individually and is not granted just by membership. Address other officials by *(honorific)* + *(name)* and identify by *(office).*

When an individual has several titles, the order is:

Military rank + Dr. (medical or Ph.D.) + Engineer + Royal title + Name

Sheikh (religious title) + Dr. (medical or Ph.D. + Name

Senegal

Official name: Republic of Senegal

Embassy of the Republic of Senegal

Noun and adjective: Senegalese

Chief of state: President

Head of government: Prime minister

Other high officials:

Ministers of State for Foreign Affairs

Ministers of State of *(portfolio)*

Ministers of *(portfolio)*

President of and senators in the Senate

President of and deputies in the National Assembly

Justices of the Constitutional Court

Justices of the Supreme Court (Court of Cassation or Court of Final Appeal)

Judges of the Council of State

Governor of the Central Bank of West African States

NOTE: Address the president by *(office)* or as *His/Her Excellency.* Also address the minister of foreign affairs as *His/Her Excellency.* Address a minister directly as *Mr./Madam Minister (name)* or as *Mr./Mrs./etc. (name)* and identify by *(office).* Address a deputy of the National Assembly or justice of a high court as *the Honourable.* Address other officials by *(honorific)* + *(name)* and identify by *(office).*

Serbia

Official name: Republic of Serbia
    Embassy of the Republic of Serbia
    Noun: Serb
    Adjective: Serbian
    Chief of state: President
    Head of government: Prime minister
    Other high officials:
        Deputy prime minister
        Secretary General
        Ministers of *(portfolio)*
        Speaker and deputy speaker of the National Assembly
        Deputies of the National Assembly
        Judges of the Constitutional Court
        Justices of the Supreme Court (Court of Cassation)

NOTE: Address the president by *(office)* or as *His/Her Excellency.* Also address the prime minister, deputy prime minister, Secretary General, and a minister as *His/Her Excellency.* Address members of the National Assembly, justices, and judges as *the Honorable.* Address other officials by *(honorific)* + *(name)* and identify by *(office).*

Seychelles

Official name: Republic of Seychelles
    Embassy of the Republic of Seychelles
    Noun and adjective: Seychellois
    Chief of state and head of government: President
    Other high officials:
        Vice president
        Chief of staff
        Ministers of *(portfolio)*
        Attorney General
        Speaker, deputy speaker, and members of the National Assembly
        Chief justice and justices of the Supreme Court
        President and judges of the Court of Appeal
        Governor of the Central Bank of the Seychelles

NOTE: Address the president and vice president by *(office)* or as *His/Her Excellency.* Address a member of the Cabinet, member of the National Assembly, or judge of a high court as *the Honourable.* Address other officials by *(honorific)* + *(name)* and identify by *(office).*

Sierra Leone

Official name: Republic of Sierra Leone
    Embassy of Sierra Leone
    Noun and adjective: Sierra Leonean
    Chief of state and head of government: President
    Other high officials:
        Vice president
        Ministers of *(portfolio)*
        Members of Parliament
        Chief justices and justices of the Supreme Court

Chief justices and justices of the Appeals Court
Judges of the High Court
Governor of the Central Bank of Sierra Leone

NOTE: Address the president by (office) or as His/Her Excellency. Address the vice president, a minister, member of Parliament, or judge of a high court as the Honourable. Address other officials by (honorific) + (name) and identify by (office).

Singapore

Official name: Republic of Singapore
　　Embassy of the Republic of Singapore
　　Noun: Singaporean
　　Adjective: Singapore
　　Chief of state: President
　　Head of government: Prime minister
　　Other high officials:
　　　　Deputy prime ministers
　　　　Senior minister
　　　　Coordinating minister
　　　　Minister mentor
　　　　Ministers of (portfolio)
　　　　Secretary to the Cabinet
　　　　Speaker, deputy speakers and members of Parliament
　　　　Leader and deputy leader of the House
　　　　Chief justice and justices of the Supreme Court
　　　　President and justices of the Court of Appeal
　　　　Chairman of the Monetary Authority of Singapore

NOTE: Singaporeans do not use courtesy titles when addressing their national leaders. They directly address officials as Mr./Madam (office): Mr. Prime Minister, Madam Minister, Mr. Speaker, etc. When the official's name is used in writing, the (office) is on the first line, the (honorific) (full name) is on the second line. Address other officials by (honorific) + (name) and identify by (office). However, when the president, prime minister, or a minister travels abroad he or she is often addressed as His/Her Excellency.

Slovakia

Official name: Slovak Republic
　　Embassy of the Slovak Republic
　　Noun and adjective: Slovak
　　Chief of state: President
　　Head of government: Prime minister
　　Other high officials:
　　　　Deputy prime ministers of (portfolio)
　　　　Ministers of (portfolio)
　　　　Chairman and deputy chairman of the
　　　　　　National Council of the Slovak Republic
　　　　Deputies in the National Council of the Slovak Republic
　　　　Chairman and deputy chairman of the Supreme Control Office
　　　　Chairman, deputy chairman, and justices of the Supreme Court
　　　　Chairman, deputy chairman, and judges of the Constitutional Court
　　　　Governor of the Central Bank of Slovakia

518

NOTE: Address the president by (office) or as His/Her Excellency. Also address the prime minister, deputy minister, or a minister as His/Her Excellency. Address all other officials by (honorific) + (name) and identify by (office).

Slovenia

Official name: Republic of Slovenia
    Embassy of the Republic of Slovenia
    Noun: Slovene
    Adjective: Slovenian
    Chief of state: President
    Head of government: Prime minister
    Other high officials:
        Ministers of (portfolio)
        Members of the National Assembly
        Group leaders and secretaries of interest groups in the National Council
        Representative members of interest groups in the National Council
        President, vice presidents, and justices of the Supreme Court
        President and judges of the Constitutional Court
        Governor of the National Bank
NOTE: Address the president by (office) or as His/Her Excellency. Also address the prime minister or a minister as His/Her Excellency. Address other officials by (honorific) + (name) and identify by (office).

Solomon Islands

Official name: Solomon Islands
    Mission of the Solomon Islands to the United Nations
    Noun and adjective: Solomon Islander
    Chief of state: The King/Queen of the Solomon Islands
        Elizabeth the Second, by the Grace of God, Queen of the Solomon Islands and of Her Other Realms and Territories, Head of the Commonwealth
    Vice-royal representative: Governor-general
    Head of government: Prime minister
    Other high officials:
        Deputy prime minister
        Ministers of (portfolio) of the Cabinet
        Members of Parliament
        Justices of the Court of Appeal
        Governor of the Central Bank
NOTE: Address the governor-general as His/Her Excellency. Many high officials who are members of the Privy Council are addressed as the Right Honourable: This includes the prime minister, deputy prime minister, speaker of Parliament, chief justice of the Court of Appeal, or a minister. Address a member of Parliament as the Honourable Mr./Mrs./etc. (name), MP. Include Sir or Dame in the forms of address of knighted officials.

Somalia
Official name: Somalia
> No embassy in the United States
> *Noun and adjective:* Somali
> *Chief of state:* Transitional Federal President
> *Head of government:* Prime minister
> *Other high officials:*
>> Deputy prime ministers
>> Ministers of (*portfolio*) in the Council of Ministers
>> Speaker and members of the Transitional Federal Parliament
>> Judges of customary Somali courts
>> Governor of the Central Bank of Somali

South Africa
Official name: Republic of South Africa
> Embassy of South Africa
> *Noun and adjective:* South African
> *Chief of state and head of government:* President
> *Other high officials:*
>> Executive deputy president
>> Ministers of (*portfolio*)
>> Deputy ministers of (*portfolio*)
>> Speaker, deputy speaker and members of the National Assembly
>> Chairperson and deputy chairperson of the National Council of Provinces
>> Delegates to the National Council of Provinces
>> Chief justice and deputy chief justice of South Africa (Constitutional Court)
>> Judges of the Constitutional Court
>> President, deputy president, and justices of the Supreme Court of Appeal
>> Judge presidents, deputy judge presidents, and judges of the High Courts
>> Governor of the South African Reserve Bank

Spain
Official name: Kingdom of Spain
> Embassy of Spain
> *Noun:* Spaniard
> *Adjective:* Spanish
> *Chief of state:* King/Queen
> Heir apparent: Crown prince/crown princess
> *Head of government:* President of the Government
> *Other high officials:*
>> Consort of the monarch
>> Infante/infanta
>> The Chief of the House of H.M.
>> First vice president
>> Second vice president
>> Deputy prime minister
>> Ministers of (*portfolio*)
>> Attorney General
>> The president and vice-president of the Senate

520

Senators of the Senate
The president and vice-president of the Congress of Deputies
Deputies in the Congress of Deputies
Chairman and members of the General Council of the Judiciary
President and justices of the Constitutional Court
Presidents of the autonomous communities
Mayors of autonomous cities
Governor of the Bank of Spain

NOTE: Address the chief of state as *Your Majesty* and royal family as *Your Royal Highness*. While high officials were once addressed as *the Honorable*, the practice is now abolished and all Spanish officials are addressed without a courtesy title. Address by *(honorific)* + *(name)* and identify by *(office)*.

Sri Lanka

Official name: Democratic Socialist Republic of Sri Lanka
Embassy of the Democratic Socialist Republic of Sri Lanka
Noun and adjective: Sri Lankan
Chief of state and head of government: Executive president or president
Ceremonial official: Prime minister
Other high officials:

Ministers of *(portfolio)*
Speaker and members of Parliament
Justices in the Supreme Court and the Court of Appeals
Governor of the Central Bank

NOTE: Address the president by *(office)* or as *His/Her Excellency*. Address the prime minister, speaker of Parliament, a minister, member of Parliament, or judge of a high court as *the Honorable*. Address other officials by *(honorific)* + *(name)* and identify by *(office)*.

Sudan

Official name: Republic of the Sudan
Embassy of the Republic of the Sudan
Noun and adjective: Sudanese
Chief of state and head of government: President
Other high officials:

First vice president
Vice president
Ministers of *(portfolio)* in the Council of Ministers
Attorney General
Members of the Council of State
Speaker, deputy speaker, and members of the National Assembly
Justices of the National Supreme Court
Justices of the Constitutional Court
Justices of the National Court of Appeal
Governor of the Bank of Sudan

NOTE: Address the president by *(office)* or as *His/Her Excellency*. Also address all other high officials in the Cabinet, National Assembly, and high courts as *His/Her Excellency*.

Suriname

Official name: Republic of Suriname
    Embassy of the Republic of Suriname
    Noun: Surinamer
    Adjective: Surinamese
    Chief of state and head of government: President
    Other high officials:
        Vice president
        Ministers of *(portfolio)*
        Members of the Council of State and the National Security Council
        Members of the National Assembly
        Members of the United People's Assembly
        President, vice president and justices of the Court of Justice
        Judges of the Cantonal Courts
        President of the Central Bank

Svalbard

Official name: Svalbard
    A territory of Norway
    Diplomatic representation by Norway
    Chief of state: King/Queen (hereditary monarch of the Norway)
    Head of government: Governor
    Other high officials:
        Assistant Governor

Swaziland

Official name: Kingdom of Swaziland
    Embassy of the Kingdom of Swaziland
    Noun and adjective: Swazi
    Chief of state: King
    Head of government: Prime minister
    Other high officials:
        Deputy prime minister
        Ministers of *(portfolio)*
        Attorney General
        Deputy ministers
        Secretaries of ministries
        Speaker and deputy speaker of the House of Assembly
        Members of House of Assembly
        President and deputy president of the Senate
        Senators in the Senate
        Chief justice and justices of the Court of Appeal/Supreme Court
        Judges of the High Court
        Governor of the Central Bank of Swaziland
NOTE: Address the monarch as *Your Majesty*. Address the prime minister as *the Right Honourable*. Address members of the Cabinet as *the Honourable*, except for the Attorney General who is addressed as *the Learned Attorney General (name)*. Address a member of

the House of Assembly as *the Honourable*. Address a senator as *Senator (name)*. Address a judge of a high court as *the Honourable*. Address other officials by *(honorific)* + *(name)* and identify by *(office)*.

Sweden

Official name: Kingdom of Sweden
Embassy of Sweden
Noun: Swede
Adjective: Swedish
Chief of state: King/Queen
Head of government: Prime minister
Other high officials:
Heir apparent: prince/princess
Deputy prime minister
Ministers of *(portfolio)*
Speaker and members of the Riksdag
Justices of the Supreme Court
Governor of the Swedish Central Bank

NOTE: Address the chief of state as *Your Majesty,* and other members of the royal family as *Your Royal Highness*. Otherwise, Swedes do not address their national officials with courtesy titles. Address officials in a salutation or direct address as *Mr./Madam (office)*: *Mr. Prime Minister, Madam Minister, Mr. Justice, etc.* When the official's name is used in writing, the *(office)* is on the first line, the *(honorific) (full name)* is on the second line. Address other officials by *(honorific)* + *(name)* and identify by *(office)*.

Switzerland

Official name: Swiss Confederation
Embassy of Switzerland
Noun and adjective: Swiss
Chief of state and head of government: President
Other high officials:
Vice president
Federal councillors/chiefs of federal departments in the Federal Council
Federal chancellor of the Confederation
President of the Council of States
First and second vice-presidents of the Council of States
Members of the Council of States
President of the National Council
First and second vice-presidents of the National Council
Members of the National Council
President, vice president, and justices of the Federal Supreme Court
Presidents of the cantonal governments
Chairman of the Swiss National Bank

NOTE: The Swiss do not address their officials with courtesy titles, but typically the president, vice president, and federal councillors are addressed as *His/Her Excellency* when traveling abroad. Address other officials by *(honorific)* + *(name)* and identify by *(office)*.

Syria

Official name: Syrian Arab Republic
    Embassy of the Syrian Arab Republic
    Noun and adjective: Syrian
    Chief of state: President
    Head of government: Prime minister
    Other high officials:
        Vice presidents
        Deputy prime minister
        Ministers of *(portfolio)* in the Council of Ministers
        Members of the People's Council
        Judges of the Supreme Judicial Council
        Justices of the Supreme Constitutional Court
        Judges in the Court Cassation
        Governor of the Central Bank

NOTE: Syrians do not use courtesy titles when addressing their national leaders. Address officials in a salutation or direct address as *Mr./Madam (office)*: *Mr. Prime Minister, Madam Minister, Mr. Justice,* etc. When the official's name is used in writing, *the (office)* is on the first line, the *(honorific) (full name)* is on the second line. Address other officials by *(honorific)* + *(name)* and identify by *(office)*.

Taiwan

Official name: Taiwan
    Unofficial representation through the Taipei Economic and
        Cultural Representative Office and the American Institute in Taiwan
    Noun and adjective: Taiwan
    Chief of state: President
    Head of government: Premier/president of the Executive Yuan
    Other high officials:
        Vice president
        Vice premier/vice president of the Executive Yuan
        Secretary General of the Executive Yuan
        Ministers of *(portfolio)* in the Executive Yuan (cabinet)
        Chairmen of councils and commissions
        President and members of the Legislative Yuan
        President and justices of the Judicial Yuan
        Governor of the Central Bank of China

Tajikistan

Official name: Republic of Tajikistan
    Embassy of the Republic of Tajikistan
    Adjective: Tajikistani
    Chief of state: President
    Head of government: Prime minister
    Other high officials:
        Deputy prime ministers
        Ministers of *(portfolio)* in the Council of Ministers
        Chairmen of state committees
        Prosecutor General

524

Chairman and members of the National Assembly
Chairman and members of the Assembly of Representatives
Justices of the Supreme Court
Chairman of the National Bank

NOTE: Address the president by (office) or as His/Her Excellency. Also address the prime minister, a minister, justice of the Supreme Court, or chairman of Parliament as His/Her Excellency. Address members of Parliament, judges, justices and other officials by (honorific) + (name) and identify by (office).

Tanzania

Official name: United Republic of Tanzania
    Embassy of the United Republic of Tanzania
    Noun and adjective: Tanzanian, Zanzibari
    Chief of state and head of government: President
    Other high officials:
        Vice president
        Prime minister
        President of Zanzibar
        Ministers of (portfolio)
        Ministers of state for (portfolio)
        Attorney General
        Speaker and members of the National Assembly
        Speaker and members of the Zanzibar House of Representatives
        Chief justice and appellate justices of the Court of Appeal
        Principal judge and judges of the High Court
        Governor of the Bank of Tanzania

NOTE: Address the president by (office) or as His/Her Excellency. Also address the vice president or president of Zanzibar as His/Her Excellency. Address the prime minister as the Right Honourable. Address the Attorney General, a minister, member of the National Assembly or the Zanzibar House of Representatives, justice, or judge of a high court as the Honourable. Address other officials by (honorific) + (name) and identify by (office).

Thailand

Official name: Kingdom of Thailand
    Embassy of Thailand/Royal Thai Embassy
    Noun and adjective: Thai
    Chief of state: King
    Head of government: Prime minister
    Other high officials:
        Crown prince
        Deputy prime ministers
        Ministers of (portfolio) in the Council of Ministers
        Senators in the Senate
        Members of the House of Representatives
        Justices of the Supreme Court
        Governor of the Bank of Thailand

NOTE: Address the chief of state as Your Majesty. Address members of the immediate royal family as Your Royal Highness, but some of the crown prince's children are addressed as Your Serene Highness. Address the prime minister, a deputy prime minister, or minister as *His/Her Excellency*. Address a senator, member of the House of Representatives, or justice of the Supreme Court without a courtesy title as *Senator (name)*, *Mr./Mrs./etc. (name)*, or *Justice (name)*, respectively. Address other officials by *(honorific) + (name)* and identify by *(office)*.

Timor-Leste

Official name: Democratic Republic of Timor-Leste
    Embassy of Democratic Republic of Timor-Leste
    Noun and adjective: Timorese
    Chief of state: President
    Head of government: Prime minister
    Other high officials:
        Deputy prime minister
        Ministers of *(portfolio)* in the Council of Ministers
        Members of the National Parliament
        Justices of the Supreme Court of Justice

NOTE: Address the president by *(office)* or as *His/Her Excellency*. Also address the prime minister, deputy prime minister, or a minister as *His/Her Excellency*. Address all members of Parliament and justices of the Supreme Court as *the Honorable*. Address other officials by *(honorific) + (name)* and identify by *(office)*.

Togo

Official name: Togolese Republic
    Embassy of the Togolese Republic
    Noun and adjective: Togolese
    Chief of state: President
    Head of government: Prime minister
    Other high officials:
        Ministers of *(portfolio)* in the Council of Ministers
        Minister-delegate to the president for *(portfolio)*
        Minister-delegate to the prime minister for *(portfolio)*
        Secretary of state of *(portfolio)*
        Members of the National Assembly
        Judges of the Court of Appeal and the Supreme Court
        Director of the Central Bank

Tokelau

Official name: Tokelau
    A territory of New Zealand
    Diplomatic representation by New Zealand
    Noun and adjective: Tokelauan
    Chief of state: King/Queen (hereditary monarch of New Zealand)
    Vice-royal representative: Governor-general of New Zealand
    Head of government: Faipule (village leaders)
    Other high officials:
        Administrator (representative of New Zealand)
        Members of the General Fono (the legislature)

Tonga

Official name: Kingdom of Tonga
  Embassy of the Kingdom of Tonga: Representation by the
    Permanent Mission of the Kingdom of Tonga to the United Nations
  Noun and adjective: Tongan
  Chief of state: King/Queen
  Head of government: Prime minister
  Other high officials:
    Nobility
    Deputy prime minister
    Ministers of *(portfolio)* in the Privy Council (cabinet)
    Attorney General
    Members of the Fale Alea or Legislative Assembly
    Justices of the Supreme Court
    Chief justice and high court justices of the Court of Appeal
    Governor of the National Reserve Bank
NOTE: Address the chief of state as *His/Her Majesty,* and other members of the ruling family (consort of a queen, crown prince/princess, prince, or princess) as *His/Her Royal Highness.* Address the prime minister, deputy prime minister, Attorney General, speaker of the Legislative Assembly, chief justice, a minister, or justice as *the Honourable.* Address members of the Legislative Assembly as *Dr./Mr./Mrs./etc. (name).* Address by *(honorific)* + *(name)* and identify by *(office).*

Trinidad and Tobago

Official name: Republic of Trinidad and Tobago
  Embassy of the Republic of Trinidad and Tobago
  Noun and adjective: Trinidadian, Tobagonian
  Chief of state: President
  Head of government: Prime minister
  Other high officials:
    Ministers of *(portfolio)*
    Attorney General
    President and vice president of the Senate
    Senators in the Senate
    Speaker, deputy speaker and members of the House of Representatives
    Chief justice, justices, and Justices of the Supreme Court of Judicature
    Governor of the Central Bank
NOTE: Address the president by *(office)* or as *His/Her Excellency.* Address a minister who is the president of the Senate, vice president of the Senate, a Government Senator, or member of the Senate as *Senator the Honourable* and identify as minister of *(portfolio).* Address a minister who is the speaker, deputy speaker, or a member of the House of Representatives as *the Honorable (full name),* MP and identify as minister of *(portfolio).* Address the chief justice, a justice, or judge as *the Honourable Mr./Madam Justice.* Address a member of the House of Representatives as *the Honourable (full name),* MP. Address other officials by *(honorific)* + *(name)* and identify by *(office).*

Tunisia

Official name: Tunisian Republic
   Embassy of Tunisia
   Noun and adjective: Tunisian
   Chief of state: President
   Head of government: Prime minister
   Other high officials:
          Special adviser to the president and spokesman of the republic
          Ministers of *(portfolio)* in the Council of Ministers
          Secretary General of the presidential cabinet
          Deputies in the Chamber of Deputies
          Members of the Chamber of Advisors
          Judges of the Court of Cassation
          Governor of the Central Bank

NOTE: Tunisian citizens do not use courtesy titles when addressing their national leaders. They directly address most officials as Mr./Madam *(office)*: Mr. *President, Madam Prime Minister, Mr. Minister, Madam Deputy, etc.* When the official's name is used in writing, the *(office)* is on the first line, the *(honorific)* *(full name)* is on the second line. Address other officials by *(honorific)* + *(name)* and identify by *(office)*. However, when the president, prime minister, or a minister travels abroad he or she is often addressed as *His/Her Excellency.*

Turkey

Official name: Republic of Turkey
   Embassy of the Republic of Turkey
   Noun: Turk
   Adjective: Turkish
   Chief of state: President
   Head of government: Prime minister
   Other high officials:
          Deputy prime minister
          Chief of the Turkish General Staff
          Ministers of *(portfolio)* in the Council of Ministers
          Ministers of state in the Council of Ministers
          Speaker and deputy speakers of the Grand National Assembly/Parliament
          Members of the Grand National Assembly/Parliament
          President, vice president, and justices of the Constitutional Court
          First president and justices of the High Court of Appeals
          Chief justice and justices of the Council of State
          First president, justices of the Court of Jurisdictional Disputes
          President of the Audit Court
          Governor of the Central Bank

NOTE: Address the president by *(office)* or as *His/Her Excellency.* Address the prime minister, deputy prime minister, chief of staff, a minister, or minister of state as *His/Her Excellency.* Address a member of Parliament or judge of a high court as *the Honorable.* Address other officials by *(honorific)* + *(name)* and identify by *(office)*.

Turkmenistan

Official name: Turkmenistan
  Embassy of Turkmenistan
  Noun: Turkmen
  Adjective: Turkmenistani
  Chief of state and head of government: President
  Other high officials:
      Deputy chairmen of the cabinet of ministers for *(portfolio)*
      Ministers of *(portfolio)*
      Prosecutor General
      Members of the People's Council or Halk Maslahaty
      Members of the National Assembly or Mejlis
      Justices of the Supreme Court
      Chairman of the Central Bank
NOTE: Address the president by *(office)* or as *His/Her Excellency*. Also address a member of the Cabinet or member of either assembly as *His/Her Excellency*. Address other officials by *(honorific)* + *(name)* and identify by *(office)*.

Turks and Caicos Islands

Official name: Turks and Caicos Islands
  An overseas territory of the United Kingdom
  Diplomatic representation by the United Kingdom
  Chief of state: King/Queen (hereditary monarch of the United Kingdom)
  Vice-royal representative: Governor
  Head of government: Premier
  Other high officials:
      Deputy governor
      Deputy premier
      Ministers of *(portfolio)*
      Speaker, deputy speaker, and members of Parliament
      Justices of the Supreme Court and the Court of Appeal
NOTE: Address the governor as *His/Her Excellency*. Address the deputy governor, premier, deputy premier, a minister, or a member of Parliament as *the Honorable*. Members of Parliament use the post-nominal abbreviation, MP. Address other officials by *(honorific)* + *(name)* and identify by *(office)*.

Tuvalu

Official name: Tuvalu
  Diplomatic representation by the United Kingdom
      and by Tuvalu's permanent mission to the United Nations
  Noun and adjective: Tuvaluan
  Chief of state: The King/Queen of Tuvalu
      Elizabeth the Second, by the Grace of God, Queen of Tuvalu and of
      Her Other Realms and Territories, Head of the Commonwealth
  Vice-royal representative: Governor-general
  Head of government: Prime minister
  Other high officials:
      Deputy prime minister
      Ministers of *(portfolio)*

The Protocol of Names, Titles, and Forms of Address

Members of Parliament/Fale I Fono/House of Assembly
Chief justice of the High Court

Uganda

Official name: Republic of Uganda
 Embassy of the Republic of Uganda
 Noun and adjective: Ugandan
 Chief of state: President
 Head of government: President and prime minister
 Other high officials:
  Vice president
  First, second, and third deputy prime ministers
  Ministers for *(portfolio)*
  Ministers of state for *(portfolio)*
  Chief Whip
  Attorney General
  Speaker and members of the National Assembly/Parliament
  Chief justice and justices of the Supreme Court
  Chief justice and justices of the Court of Appeal
  Chief judge and judges of the High Court
  Governor of the Bank of Uganda
NOTE: Address the president and vice president by *(office)* or as *His/Her Excellency.* Address the prime minister as *the Right Honourable.* Address members of parliament as *the Honourable (full name),* MP. Address a minister as a member of Parliament and identify as a minister of *(portfolio).* Address a justice or judge without a courtesy title as *Chief Justice (name), Justice (name),* or *Judge (name).* Address other officials by *(honorific)* + *(name)* and identify by *(office).*

Ukraine

Official name: Ukraine
 Embassy of Ukraine
 Noun and adjective: Ukrainian
 Chief of state: President
 Head of government: Prime minister
 Other high officials:
  First vice prime minister
  Vice prime minister
  Minister of the cabinet of ministers
  Minister of *(portfolio)*
  Prosecutor General
  The chairman and first-deputy chairman of the
   Supreme Council or Rada/Parliament
  Members of the Supreme Council
  The chairman, first-deputy chairman, and justices of the Supreme Court
  The head, deputy heads, and judges of the Constitutional Court
  Chairman of the National Bank

United Arab Emirates

Official name: United Arab Emirates
  Embassy of the United Arab Emirates
  Noun and adjective: Emirati
  Chief of state: President
  Head of government: Vice president and prime minister
  Other high officials:
    Deputy prime ministers
    Ministers of *(portfolio)* in the Council of Ministers
    Ministers of state for *(portfolio)*
    President, vice president, and members in
        the Federal Supreme Council (Rulers)
    Speaker, deputy speakers, and senators in the Federal National Council
    Justices of the Union Supreme Court
    Governor of the Central Bank

NOTE: The highest officials in the UAE are members of the ruling families of the emirates. Address by noble title and identify by *(office)*. For example, address the president or a ruler as *His Highness Sheikh (name)* and identify by *(office)*. Address other officials by *(Senator/Justice/Mr./Mrs./etc.)* + *(name)* and identify by *(office)*.

United Kingdom

Official name: United Kingdom of Great Britain and Northern Ireland
  British Embassy
  Noun: Briton
  Adjective: British
  Chief of state: The King/Queen of the United Kingdom and Northern Ireland
        Elizabeth the Second, by the Grace of God, of the United Kingdom of Great
        Britain and Northern Ireland and of Her Other Realms and Territories, Queen,
        Head of the Commonwealth, Defender of the Faith
  Heir apparent: Prince of Wales
  Head of government: Prime minister
  Other high officials:
    Secretaries of state of *(portfolio)*
    Leader of the House of Lords
    Lords in the House of Lords
    Members of the House of Commons
    Lord of Appeal in the Ordinary
    Lord chief justice of England and Wales
    Master of the Rolls
    Vice-president of the Courts of Appeal
    Senior Presiding Judge for England and Wales
    Judge of the Court of Appeal of England and Wales
    Lord High Chancellor/Lord Chancellor of the High Court of Justice
    The Chancellor of the High Court
    President of the Family Division of the High Court
    President of the Queen's Bench of the High Court
    Justice of the High Court, Chancery Division
    Justice of the High Court, Family Division
    Justice of the High Court, Queen's Bench

Governor of the Bank of England

NOTE: See page 357 for forms of address. The United Kingdom of Great Britain and Northern Ireland calls its ambassador *the British Ambassador*.

United States

Official name: United States of America
Embassy of the United States of America/American Embassy
Noun and adjective: American
Chief of state and head of government: President
Other high officials:
Vice president
Secretaries of (*portfolio*)
Attorney General
President of the Senate
Senators in the Senate
Speaker of the House of Representatives
Representatives in the House of Representatives
Chief justice and associate justices of the Supreme Court
Chairman of the Federal Reserve Bank

NOTE: Address the president, vice president, secretaries in the Cabinet, speaker of the House of Representatives, and chief justice of the Supreme Court by (*office*). In the United States, all officials who are appointed by the president or elected are addressed as *the Honorable*. Address other officials by (*honorific*) + (*name*) and identify by (*office*).

Uruguay

Official name: Oriental Republic of Uruguay
Embassy of Uruguay
Noun and adjective: Uruguayan
Chief of state and head of government: President
Other high officials:
Vice president
Ministers of (*portfolio*)
President of the Chamber of Senators
Senators in the Chamber of Senators
President of the Chamber of Representatives
Deputies in the Chamber of Representatives
Justices of the Supreme Court
President of the Central Bank

NOTE: Address the president and vice president by (*office*) or as *His/Her Excellency*. Also address a minister as *His/Her Excellency*. Address a senator, deputy, or justice of the Supreme Court as *the Honorable*. Address other officials by (*honorific*) + (*name*) and identify by (*office*).

Uzbekistan

Official name: Republic of Uzbekistan
Embassy of the Republic of Uzbekistan
Noun and adjective: Uzbekistani
Chief of state: President
Head of government: Prime minister

Other high officials:
    Deputy prime ministers
    Ministers of *(portfolio)*
    Chairman of the Supreme Assembly
    Senators in the Senate of the Supreme Assembly
    Members of the Legislative Chamber of the Supreme Assembly
    Justices of the Supreme Court
    Chairman of the State Bank
    Chairman of the National Bank for Foreign Economic Activity

Vanuatu

Official name: Republic of Vanuatu
    Diplomatic representation through Vanuatu's Permanent Mission
        to the United Nations
    Noun and adjective: Ni-Vanuatu
    Chief of state: President
    Head of government: Prime minister
    Other high officials:
        Deputy prime minister
        Ministers of *(portfolio)* in the Council of Ministers
        Members of Parliament
        Chief justice and justices of the Supreme Court

Venezuela

Official name: Bolivarian Republic of Venezuela
    Embassy of the Bolivarian Republic of Venezuela
    Noun and adjective: Venezuelan
    Chief of state and head of government: President
    Other high officials:
        Vice president
        Ministers of *(portfolio)* in the Council of Ministers
        President, first- and second-vice presidents of the National Assembly
        Secretary and sub-secretary of the National Assembly
        Deputies in the National Assembly
        President, first- and second-vice presidents of the Supreme Tribunal of Justice
        President and vice president of the Supreme Tribunals of Justice
        Magistrates in the Supreme Tribunal of Justice
        President of the Central Bank
NOTE: Address the president and vice president by *(office)* or as *His/Her Excellency.*
Address a minister, leader or member of the National Assembly, or justice of a high
court as *the Honorable.* Address other officials by *(honorific)* + *(name)* and identify by
(office).

Vietnam

Official name: Socialist Republic of Vietnam
    Embassy of Vietnam
    Noun and adjective: Vietnamese
    Chief of state: President
    Head of government: Prime minister

Other high officials:
>Vice president
>Deputy prime ministers
>Ministers of (*portfolio*)
>Chairman of the Central Committee of the Vietnam Fatherland Front
>Chairman of the Vietnam Federation of Labour
>Chairman and members of the National Assembly
>Standing Committee of the National Assembly
>Members of People's Councils
>Chief justice of the Supreme People's Court
>Justices of the Supreme People's Court
>Governor of the State Bank

NOTE: The Vietnamese do not address their national officials with courtesy titles, but the Embassy advises that the use of U.S. forms for Vietnamese officials visiting the United States is appropriate: Address the president by (*office*). Address high officials as *the Honorable*. Address other officials by (*honorific*) + (*name*) and identify by (*office*).

Virgin Islands

Official name: United States Virgin Islands
>Diplomatic representation by the United States
>*Noun and adjective:* Virgin Islander
>*Chief of state:* President of the United States
>>Vice president of the United States
>*Head of government:* Governor
>>Lieutenant governor
>>Senators in the Senate
>>Judges of the U.S. District Court of the Virgin Islands
>>Judges of the Superior Court of the Virgin Islands

Wallis and Futuna

Official name: Territory of the Wallis and Futuna Islands
>An overseas territory of France
>Diplomatic representation by France
>*Noun and adjective:* Wallisian, Futunan, Wallis and Futuna Islander
>*Chief of state:* President of the French Republic
>*Head of government:* President of the Territorial Assembly
>*Other high officials:*
>>High administrator (representative of the president of France)
>>Kings and members of the Council of the Territory
>>Members of the Territorial Assembly
>>Magistrate's court

Yemen

Official name: Republic of Yemen
>Embassy of the Republic of Yemen
>*Noun and adjective:* Yemeni
>*Chief of state:* President
>*Head of government:* Prime minister
>*Other high officials:*
>>Vice president

534

Deputy prime minister
Ministers of (*portfolio*) in the Council of Ministers
Members of the Shura Council
Members of the House of Representatives
Justices of the Supreme Court
Governor of the Central Bank

NOTE: Address the president by (*office*) or as *His/Her Excellency*. Address the prime minister, vice president, deputy prime minister, or a minister as *His/Her Excellency*. Address a member of parliament, justice or judge of a high court as *the Honorable*. Address other officials by (*honorific*) + (*name*) and identify by (*office*).

Zambia

Official name: Republic of Zambia
Embassy of the Republic of Zambia
Noun and adjective: Zambian
Chief of state and head of government: President
Other high officials:
Vice president
Ministers of (*portfolio*)
Attorney General
Solicitor General
President/speaker and members of the National Assembly/Parliament
Chief justice and deputy chief justice of the Supreme Court
Judges of the High Court
Chairman and members of the board of the Bank of Zambia

NOTE: Address the president by (*office*) or as *His/Her Excellency*. Address the vice president, or a member of the cabinet as *His/Her Excellency*. Address other high officials *the Honourable*. Address other officials by (*honorific*) + (*name*) and identify by (*office*).

Zimbabwe

Official name: Republic of Zimbabwe
Embassy of the Republic of Zimbabwe
Noun and adjective: Zimbabwean
Chief of state and head of government: Executive president
Other high officials:
Vice presidents
Ministers of (*portfolio*)
President, deputy president, and chiefs in the Council of Chiefs
Speaker and senators in the Senate
Speaker and members of the House of Assembly
Chief justice and justices of the Supreme Court
Chief justice, judge president, and judges of the High Court
Traditional chiefs
Governor and deputy governors of the Reserve Bank of Zimbabwe

NOTE: Address the executive president by (*office*) or as *His/Her Excellency*. Address a vice president, minister, leader or member of the Council of Chiefs, senator, leader or member of the House of Assembly, justice, or judge as *the Honorable*. Address other officials by (*honorific*) + (*name*) and identify by (*office*).

Bibliography

About Parliament, How to Address a Lord: United Kingdom Parliament. The Information Policy Division, Office of Public Sector Information. March 2008. <http://www.parliament.uk/about/how/members.cmf>

AfDevInfo.com. African Development Information Services, Ltd., London, United Kingdom. January 2008. <http://www.afdevinfo.com>

Air Force Wives 'Til Wheels Are Up!. MilitaryWives.com Inc., Oak Harbor, WA. December 2006. <http://www.airforcewives.com>

Ali, Datuk Abdullah. *Malaysian Protocol: Correct Forms of Address.* Second Edition. Singapore: Times Books International, Times Editions Pte. Ltd., 1988.

American Legion Department of Michigan Internal Affairs Committee, ed. *Protocol and Planning Guide for American Legion Functions.* Lansing, Michigan: American Legion Department of Michigan, 2005.

Bosrock, Mary Murray. *Asian Business Custom & Manners.* New York: Meadowbrook Press, 2007.

Bosrock, Mary Murray. *European Business Custom & Manners.* New York: Meadowbrook Press, 2006.

Bosrock, Mary Murray. *Put Your Best Foot Forward: Asia.* St. Paul, Minnesota: International Educational Systems, 1997.

Bosrock, Mary Murray. *Put Your Best Foot Forward: Mexico/Canada.* St. Paul, Minnesota: International Educational Systems, 1995.

Bosrock, Mary Murray. *Put Your Best Foot Forward: South America.* St. Paul, Minnesota: International Educational Systems, 1995.

Bosrock, Mary Murray. *Put Your Best Foot Forward: United States of America.* St. Paul, Minnesota: International Educational Systems, 1999.

British Monarchy, Official Website of the. The Crown and Royal Household of the United Kingdom. April 2008.

Canadian Heritage, Ceremonial and Canadian Symbols Promotion / Styles of Address and Precedence. Minister of Public Works and Government Services, Ottawa, Ontario. March 2008. <http://www.pch.gc.ca/>

Chief of Protocol, Department of State, editor. *United States Department of State Diplomatic List;* Revised edition. Washington, DC: Office of the Chief of Protocol, Department of State, U.S. Government Printing Office, Winter 2008.

Commonwealth Department of Finance and Administration. *Style Manual for Authors, Editors and Printers;* Sixth edition revised by Snooks & Co. for the Commonwealth Department of Finance and Administration. Canberra, Australia: John Wiley & Sons, Australia, Ltd., 2002.

Commonwealth of Virginia. *A Guide to Virginia Protocol and Traditions.* Richmond, Virginia: Office of Graphic Communications, Virginia Department of General Services, December 2002.

Country Profiles, Countries and Regions, Foreign and Commonwealth Office of the United Kingdom. Foreign and Commonwealth Office, King Charles Street, London, England. March 2008. <http://www.fco.gov.uk/>

Debrett's Correct Form. London: Headline Book Publishing, a division of Hodder Headline, PLC, 1999.

DefenseLINK. U.S. Department of Defense, September 2007. <http://www.defenselink.mil>

EISA: *Promoting Credible Elections & Democratic Governance in Africa*. August 2007. Johannesburg, South Africa. <http://www.eisa.org.za>

Federal Magistrates Court of Australia. Federal Magistrates Court of Australia , National Administration Office, Melbourne, Victoria, Australia, < http://www.fmc.gov.au>

Food and Agriculture Organization, FAO Terminology. Food and Agriculture Organization of the United Nations. February 2008. <http://www.fao.org/faoterm/nocs.asp?lang=EN>

Hawley, Sir John, KCMG, MBE. *Manners and Correct Form in the Middle East, First Edition*. London: Debrett's Peerage Limited in association with the Bank of the Middle East a member of the Hong Kong Bank Group, 1984.

Holbert, Andrea, ed. *Forms of Address: A Guide for Business and Social Use*. Contributions by Sonia Garza, Kathleen D. Kelly, and Kathleen A. Moses. Houston, Texas: Rice University Press, in association with the Houston International Protocol Alliance, 1994.

Hudson, Joel B. *A Guide to Protocol and Etiquette for Official Entertainment: Department of the Army, Pamphlet 60-600*. By order of the Secretary of the Army by Eric K. Shinseki, General, United States Army, Chief of Staff; Joel B. Hudson, Administrative Assistant to the Secretary of The Army. Washington, DC: Department of the Army, Headquarters of the Army, December 2001.

Innis, Pauline; McCaffree, Mary Jane; Sand, Richard M.; and Hofer, Madeline Deheza, ed. *Protocol: The Complete Handbook of Diplomatic, Official, and Social Usage, 25th Anniversary Edition*. Dallas, Texas: Durban House Publishing Company, Inc., 2002.

Innis, Pauline; and Innis, Walter Deane. *Attention!: A Quick Guide to the Armed Services*. Washington, DC: Devon Publishing Company, Inc., Revised Edition, 1985; Second printing 1989.

Joel, Sir Asher; and Pringle, Helen. *Australian Protocol and Procedures*. Sidney, Australia: University of New South Wales Press, Ltd.., Third Edition. 2007.

Lifetips.com, LifeTips: Writing Tips, Addresses for Letters. LifeTips Inc. January 2008. <http://writing.lifetips.com/cat/7939/addresses-for-letters/index.html>

Litsas, Fotios, editor. *A Companion to the Greek Orthodox Church, Second Edition*. New York: Department of Communication, Greek Orthodox Archdiocese of North and South America, 1988.

Matlins, Stuart M.; and Magida, Authur J. *How to be a Perfect Stranger, the Essential Religious Etiquette Handbook, 3rd Edition*. Woodstock, Vermont: Skylights Paths Publishing, 2003.

MLA Style Manual. Medical Library Association, February 2008. <http://www.mlanet.org/publications/style/>

NASA Procedural Requirements, National Aeronautics and Space Administration, Washington, DC: March 24, 2006. Online Directives Information System, Correspondence Management and Communications Standards and Style. December, 2006. <http://nodis3.gsfc.nasa.gov/main_lib.html>

538

Naval Correspondence Manual, The (Secnavinst 5216.5d): Updated June 2, 2005.
John H. Dalton, Department of the Navy, Office of the Secretary, March 2008.
<http://www.navyfitrep.com/download5216_5d.html >

New Advent: The Catholic Encyclopedia. Kevin Knight, Immaculate Heart of Mary.
November 2007. <http://www.newadvent.org/>

Official website of the British Royal Navy. The Royal Navy of the United Kingdom.
January 2008. <http://www.royal-navy.mod.uk/index.php>

Orthodox Church in America. The Orthodox Church in America, Syosset, New York.
November 2007. <http://www.oca.org>

Patrick Montague-Smith, editor. *Debrett's Correct Form: An inclusive guide to everything
from drafting a wedding invitation to addressing an archbishop.* New York:
Arco Publishing Company, Inc., 1977.

Peck, Robert, Chief of Protocol. *Diplomatic, Consular & Other Representatives in Canada.*
Ottawa, Ontario: Office of Protocol, Department of Foreign Affairs and
International Trade Canada (DFAIT), 2007.

Political Database of the Americas. Edmond A. Walsh, School of Foreign Service,
Center for Latin American Studies, Georgetown University, Washington, DC:
March 2006. <http://pdba.georgetown.edu>

Post, Emily. *Emily Post's Etiquette, 16th Edition, Edited by Peggy Post.* New York:
Harper Collins Publishers, 1997.

Samirad: Saudi Arabia Market Information Resource and Directory. Saudi Arabia Market
Information Resource and Directory. December 2007. <http://www.saudinf.com>

Shah, Pravin K., ed. *Essence of World Religions: Truth is One – Paths are Many.*
Cary, North Carolina: Previn K. Shah; President, Jain Study Center of North
Carolina (Raliegh); Chairman, Jain BBS Committee, Federation of Jains. 1994.

Shanson, T. L. *International Guide to Forms of Address.* London: Macmillan Publishers,
Ltd.., 1977.

St. George Church: How to Greet Orthodox Clergy. St. George Church, Lenexa, Kansas,
December 2007. <http://www.st-george-church.org>

Swartz, Oretha D. *Service Etiquette, Fourth Edition.* Annapolis, Maryland: Naval
Institute Press, 1988.

The American Heritage® Dictionary of the English Language. New York: Houghton Mifflin
Company, 2004.

*The Official Website of the Synod of Bishops of the Russian Orthodox Church Outside Russia,
New York.* November 2007. The Russian Orthodox Church Outside Russia.
<http://www.russianorthodoxchurch.ws>

Tiller, Veronica E. Velarde, ed. *Tiller's Guide to Indian Country: Economic Profiles of
American Indian Reservations.* Albuquerque, New Mexico: BowArrow Publishing
Company, 1996.

Titles and Forms of Address, A Guide to Correct Use. London: A&C Black Publishers
Limited, 2002.

U.S. Department of State, Country Pages A-Z. April, 2008. U.S. Department of State,
Public Communication Division, Washington, DC.
<http://www.state.gov/misc/list/index.htm>

United States Conference of Catholic Bishops. December 2007. United States Conference of Catholic Bishops, Washington DC. <http://www.usccb.org/>

University of Chicago Press. *The Chicago Manual of Style, Thirteenth Edition.* Chicago and London: The University of Chicago Press, 1982.

University of Melbourne, External Relations, Faculty of Law, ed. *Salutations Guide.* Melbourne, Australia: University of Melbourne, February 2003.

Von Drachenfels, Suzanne. *The Art of the Table: A Complete Guide to Table Settings, Table Manners and Tableware.* New York: Simon & Schuster, 2000.

mayor, 38, 346, 377
military, 384
of appeal in ordinary, 371
president of the council,
362
privy seal, 358
Speaker, 358, 364
steward, 38
Lutheran: See Protestant, 280
Luxembourg, 490
Ma'am, 38, 64
Macau, 490
Macedonia, 491
Madagascar, 491
Madam, 38, 64
Madame, 38
Mademoiselle, 38
Magistrate, 38, 197, 242, 345,
376
chief federal 337
federal 337
Mahatma, 38
Maiden name, 38
Majesty, 39
Majesty, imperial, 34
Major, 208, 220, 316, 354, 388
general, 207, 220, 316, 388,
354
clergy, 291
Majority leader, 177, 181
Malawi, 491
Malaysia, 492
Maldives, 492
Mali, 493
Malta, 493
Man, business, 156
Man, social, 156
Marchioness, 39, 398
Marine Corps
British, 386
DOD abbreviations, 95
United States, 206
Marquess, 39, 364, 398
daughter, 399
eldest son, 398
wife of younger son, 399
younger son, 398
Married woman, 157
Marshall, 39, 176
Air Force, 354, 388
of the court, 39
Marshall Islands, 493
Master chief petty officer, 221,
222

of the Coast Guard, 221, 222
of the Navy, 221, 222
Master:
corporal, 317
gunnery sergeant, 221
of the Horse, 40
of the Roll, 372
queen's music, 40
seaman, 317
sergeant, 211, 213, 214, 221
warrant officer, 317
Mauritania, 494
Mauritius, 494
Mayor, 40, 79, 199, 347, 378
elect, 79, 200
former, 199
His Worship, 346
lord, 346
Mayotte, 495
Medical doctor, 159
Mekko, 40, 239
Member:
foreign assembly, 413
House of Commons, 300,
301, 359, 370
House of Lords, 359
House of Representatives,
14, 78, 328
knight, 35
Parliament, 100, 343, 413
Presidency of the Seventy,
257
Quorum Twelve Apostles,
256
Quorums of the Seventy, 258
state assembly, 79
territorial legislature, 311
Methodist bishop, 6, 280
Methodist: See Protestant, 280
Metropolitan, defination, 40
bishop, 6, 41, 249
Mexico, 495
Micco, 40, 239
Micronesia, 496
Middle initials, 94
Middle name, 41
Midshipman, 219, 353, 354,
388
Military:
abbreviations, 95
attaché, 41
joint form of address, 147
rank in introductions, 114
Minister, 41, 302, 303, 310,
330, 331, 358

clergy, 281, 292
counselor, 41, 433
diplomat, 20, 350
international/foreign, 411
plenipotentiary, 432
Minority leader, 177, 181
Miquelon and Saint Pierre, 512
Mission, 41
Missionary, 261
Moldova, 496
Molla, mollah, 43
Monaco, 496
Monarch, monarchy, 41
Mongolia, 497
Monk, 42, 252
Monsignor, 42, 287
Montenegro, 497
Montserrat, 497
Mormon: See The Church of
Jesus Christ of Latter-day
Saints, 255
Morocco, 498
Mosques, Custodian of the
Two Holy, 17
Most Reverend, 76
Mother superior, abbess,
1, 252, 289
Mother, 25, 274, 279
Mozambique, 498
MP, 42, 100
MPP, definition of, 42
Ms., 42, 156
Mufti, 42
Mulla, mullah, 43
Municipal official,
the Honorable, 79
Muslim, 264
Myanmar, 498
n.b. (notez bien), 7, 43
Name(s):
badge, 107
order in addresses, 139
order in foreign names, 90
in introductions, 112
on place cards, 108
with numbers, 87
with particles, 87
abbreviated, 93
compound, 88
difficult to pronounce, 119
joint forms of address, 139
Namibia, 499
Nation, definition of, 43

For more information about

The Protocol School of Washington®

visit

www.PSOW.com

Find the Traditional Form of Address